THE BURIED PAST

THE BURIED PAST

An Archaeological History of Philadelphia

John L. Cotter · Daniel G. Roberts · Michael Parrington

With the assistance of Sarah S. Evans

A BARRA FOUNDATION BOOK

UNIVERSITY OF PENNSYLVANIA PRESS   *Philadelphia*

Copyright © 1992 by John L. Cotter, Daniel G. Roberts, and Michael Parrington
All rights reserved
Printed in the United States of America

Excerpt from T. S. Eliot "Little Gidding" in *Four Quartets*
(copyright © 1943 by T. S. Eliot, renewed 1971 by Esme Valerie Eliot)
reprinted by permission of Harcourt Brace Jovanovich, Inc.

Library of Congress Cataloging-in-Publication Data

Cotter, John L.
   The buried past: an archaeological history of Philadelphia / John L. Cotter, Daniel G.
Roberts, Michael Parrington; with the assistance of Sarah S. Evans.
     p.   cm.
   Includes bibliographical references and index.
   ISBN 0-8122-3142-2
   1. Philadelphia (Pa.)—Antiquities.   2. Philadelphia (Pa.)—History.   3. Archaeology and
history—Pennsylvania—Philadelphia.   4. Indians of North America—Pennsylvania—Phila-
delphia—Antiquities.   I. Roberts, Daniel G.   II. Parrington, Michael.   III. Title.
   F158.39.C68   1992
   974.8′11—dc20   92-10736
                                                                         CIP

Designed by Adrianne Onderdonk Dudden

We shall not cease from exploration
And the end of all our exploring
Will be to arrive where we started
And know the place for the first time.

T. S. Eliot, "Little Gidding"
in *Four Quartets*

Contents

4 Old Philadelphia   152

5 The Delaware Waterfront   216

Preface

Philadelphia has at various times in its history been a leader not only in industry, shipping, trade, and banking, but also in medicine, science, architecture, and art. It has long been a favorite research topic of historians, sociologists, and architectural historians—and, since the 1950s, of archaeologists as well. Philadelphia has, in fact, received more archaeological attention than any other major city in North America. Given its place in history and its numerous historic sites, the amount of archaeological attention the city has received is not surprising. What is perhaps surprising is that the reports of these investigations have for the most part never been formally published, let alone brought together in a single volume. The purpose of this book is to summarize in as readable a fashion as possible the results of over thirty years of archaeological work—nearly 300 reports of some 150 site investigations—in Philadelphia and its environs.

In the 1960s the pioneer modern dancer Ted Shawn offered this advice to his trainees at Jacob's Pillow: "Too many dancers today are satisfied with technical accomplishments. . . . I will always give my accolades to those dancers, who, having mastered the language, say something." Archaeology, like dancing, involves both technique and interpretation. Its technical accomplishments should likewise enable the practitioner to say something, and that something should be worthy of note, a contribution to the body of knowledge that makes up the archaeological record. While archaeological investigations of Philadelphia sites have not always produced hoped-for results, they have invariably in some measure enhanced our knowledge of the city's cultural past.

In this review of Philadelphia archaeology, the reader should be able to perceive why an investigation was undertaken, what it accomplished, and what it means. Readers seeking extensive new light on the past may be disappointed. The presentation invokes no tablet of laws interpreting the cultural identity of Philadelphians. Rather, it presents the physical evidence of the past, which can and often does fill in gaps and illuminate the historical record. Our intent is to place the archaeological findings so far made in a major metropolitan area in the context of history and to let those findings speak for themselves. Our hope is that the book will succeed in inserting some meaningful threads of archaeological evidence into the historical tapestry, and that it will fill out the pattern and add texture and color.

J. L. C.
D. G. R.
M. P.

Philadelphia
June 21, 1992

Acknowledgments

First and foremost, we are deeply indebted to the numerous archaeologists whose work forms the basis of this book. Each of the following has contributed in some way to the story of Philadelphia's historic archaeology, and without their collective efforts, the archaeological heritage of the Philadelphia region would be much the poorer. Doubtless there are others whom we have inadvertently omitted; to them we apologize, secure in the knowledge that their contributions are no less significant than those whose names are listed below.

Leland Abel
Brenda Barrett
David Barrett
Kenneth J. Basalik
Marshall J. Becker
Brooke Blades
Belinda Blomberg
Peter Bogucki
Beth Anne Bower
Sharon Ann Burnston
Douglas Campana
Paul Chace
Betty J. Cosans-Zebooker
J. Lee Cox, Jr.
George D. Cress
Daniel G. Crozier
LuAnn DeCunzo
Richard Diehl
Brian Egloff
Lucia Esther
Richard Fidler
Vincent P. Foley
Joel T. Fry
Jacob W. Gruber

Joseph H. Hall, IV
David J. Hally
Edward F. Heite
William R. Henry, Jr.
Paul R. Huey
Charles E. Hunter
Richard H. Jordan
Susan Kardas
Barry C. Kent
Jeffrey L. Kenyon
Charles C. Kolb
Edward McM. Larrabee
M. E. Colleen Lazenby
Charles H. LeeDecker
Lynne G. Lewis
Mary Butler Lewis
Barbara Liggett
William K. Macdonald
J. Alden Mason
John P. McCarthy
William P. McHugh
Henry C. Mercer
Jackson W. Moore
Edward Morin
Elizabeth Ann Morris
David G. Orr
Vance Packard
B. Bruce Powell
Robert W. Preucel
Elizabeth C. Righter
Douglas Sanford
Helen Schenck
Paul J. F. Schumacher
Robert Schuyler
Ronald Shuster
Helen Smith
Garry Wheeler Stone
Thomas L. Struthers
Roberta Z. Taylor
Ronald A. Thomas

Evelyn M. Tidlow
Alex H. Townsend
Richard C. Waldbauer
Steven Warfel
Carmen A. Weber
C. A. Weslager
Budd Wilson
John Witthoft
Werner S. Zimmt

Other professionals whose work has touched and enhanced the archaeology of Philadelphia include numerous architects, historians, architectural historians, conservationists, museum curators, archivists, administrators, geologists, physical anthropologists, geophysicists, and other professionals. Among them are the following:

John Alviti
J. Lawrence Angel
Kathryn Ann Auerbach
Frank Barnes
Penelope Batcheler
Bruce Bevan
Frank M. Boeshore
John R. Bowie
G. Edwin Brumbaugh
J. Duncan Campbell
William M. Campbell
Richard Candee
Hobart Cawood
Ward Childs
Pam Crabtree
Robert L. DeSilets
John M. Dickey
Carl Dobley
Robert Dockhorn

Charles Dorman
Reed Engle
Anthony N. B. Garvan
Bea Garvan
Carl W. Gatter
Robert L. Giannini III
Bruce L. Gill
Angus Gillespie
Henry Glassie
Charles S. Grossman
Alice Hemenway
Bernard Herman
Theodore Hershberg
William Hershey
Edward Hinderliter
David Hollenberg
Cheryl Holt
Graham Hood
Henry A. Judd
Jennifer O. Kelley
David Kimball
Muriel Kirkpatrick
Virginia Knauer
Nancy D. Kolb
Reed Knox
Dennis Kurjack
Emma Lapsansky
Herbert W. Levy
Sandra MacKenzie Lloyd
James C. Massey
Richard Meyer
John Milley
John D. Milner
Jefferson Moak
Roger D. Moss
Hyman Myers
Susan H. Myers
Gary B. Nash
Murray Nelligan
Lee H. Nelson
Patrick W. O'Bannon
R. Brognard Okie
Stanley J. Olsen
Steven E. Patrick
Charles E. Peterson
Stephanie Pinter
John Platt
F. Neale Quenzel
Elizabeth Ralph
Jeffrey Ray

Horace G. Richards
Edward M. Riley
Martin J. Rosenblum
Allen G. Schiek
Alice Kent Schooler
Allan H. Steenhusen
Jacqueline Thibaut
George Thomas
Marianna Thomas
Harry Tinkcom
Margaret B. Tinkcom
Richard Tyler
Robert Venturi
Daniel Wagner
Anthony F. C. Wallace
David Wallace
Sam Bass Warner
William W. Weaver
Nancy Webster
Richard J. Webster
Russell F. Weigley
Edwin Wolf II
Martha Wolf
Gretchen Worden
Martin I. Yoelson

We would also like to thank the following organizations and agencies for their efforts in fostering, sponsoring, or otherwise assisting in historic archaeological research in the Philadelphia region:

The Athenaeum
Atwater Kent Museum
Barra Foundation
Bell Fuel Company
Bensalem Township Supervisors
Bishop Mills Historical Institute
Bourse Garage Associates
Bucks County Conservancy
Chadds Ford Historical Society
Chester County Historical Society
City of Philadelphia (Departments of Water and Public Property)
Department of the Army, Corps of Engineers (Philadelphia and Baltimore Districts)
Kevin F. Donohoe Co.
Fairmount Park Commission

Federal Highway Administration
Forest City Dillon
Franklin Institute
Friends of the Grange
Harriton Association
Historical Society of Pennsylvania
John Bartram Association
Library Company of Philadelphia
Montgomery County Commissioners
Museum Applied Science Center for Archaeology at the University Museum
Mütter Museum of the Philadelphia College of Physicians
National Park Service (Mid-Atlantic Region, Independence National Historical Park, and Valley Forge National Historical Park)
National Society of Colonial Dames
National Trust for Historic Preservation
Pennsbury Society
Pennsylvania Department of Transportation
Pennsylvania Historical and Museum Commission
Philadelphia City Archives
Philadelphia Historical Commission
Philadelphia Industrial Development Corporation
Philadelphia Landmarks Society
Redevelopment Authority of the City of Philadelphia
Rouse and Associates
Smithsonian Institution
University of Pennsylvania (Department of Facilities Planning, Health Care Facilities Committee, and University Museum Archives)
William Penn Foundation
Wyck Association
Yellow Springs Foundation

Many students from the University of Pennsylvania and Temple University participated in the research, fieldwork, data analysis, and reports involved in some of the investigations described in this book. For their contributions, we would particularly like to thank former students Linda Keller Brown, Donald Callender, Philip Carstairs, Richard E. Cauffiel, Brian Crane, George M. Danko, Mary Hancock, Edwin Iwanicki, Jiyul Kim, Robert King, Coryl Lassen, Sara Matthews, Ellen Miller, Mark Ohno, William G. Stead, Janet Wideman, and James R. Zakas.

For their contributions to archaeological fieldwork, we thank the students of Cheltenham High School, Lower Merion High School, Ridley High School, and Bucks County Community College, and the teachers who carefully trained them: Emmanuel Kramer, Stephen McCarter, Lyle Rosenberger, and Ronald A. Tirpak. We also acknowledge and thank the scores of archaeological students and avocational archaeologists who labored long and hard as members of field teams collecting the field data that, taken together, have enabled the story of Philadelphia's archaeology to unfold.

We would especially like to thank the Fels Foundation, the Barra Foundation, and John Milner Associates for their efforts in seeing this book to completion. The Fels Foundation provided a generous grant to assist in word processing, editing, and graphics expenses, while the Barra Foundation underwrote the production of the book. John Milner Associates provided generously of its resources throughout numerous drafts of the text and provided Daniel G. Roberts the time necessary for him to see this book through to completion. Without the assistance of each of these organizations, the completion of this book would not have been possible.

Finally, we would like to acknowledge the assistance of several individuals who made significant contributions during the editorial and graphics production processes. These include: for proofreading and editorial asistance, Virginia Cotter, John P. McCarthy, Marie E. Roberts, and Helen Schenck; for many of the line illustrations appearing in the book, Joseph McCarthy and Sarah Ruch; for photographic reproductions, Fred Schoch; and for typing and word processing assistance, Margy Schoettle.

A Note on How This Book Was Produced

The project of writing the story of Philadelphia's archaeology began in 1965, while John Cotter, as Regional Archaeologist for the National Park Service, was overseeing investigations at Independence National Historical Park and simultaneously conducting field classes in historical archaeology at the University of Pennsylvania. At that time, Cotter began work on a monograph of Philadelphia's archaeology that focused primarily on work accomplished to date at Independence National Historical Park. Publication plans lapsed, however, when writing failed to keep up with rapid field developments and to meet the standards Cotter hoped to maintain. Twenty years later, Daniel G. Roberts and Michael Parrington joined Cotter in bringing the manuscript to fruition, by developing an extensive bibliography and providing contributions on archaeological work undertaken in the Philadelphia region during the past two decades. The story of Philadelphia's archaeology as presented herein, then, is largely current through 1989.

The efforts of the three authors, however, fell short of objectives of style, continuity, and broad appeal to interested lay as well as professional readers. Accordingly, Sarah Evans, in addition to compiling the volume's comprehensive index, provided what has amounted to a general recasting of much of the text for continuity, cohesion, and interest, for which the authors are deeply grateful, knowing the readers will be, too. The authors, of course, are responsible for any errors of fact or interpretation that occur in the following pages.

Introduction

He who calls what has vanished back into being, enjoys a bliss like that of creating.

—Barthold Niebuhr

In the bicentennial year of the signing of the Constitution of the United States of America, the 1987 telephone directory for the City of Philadelphia listed in its front matter no fewer than forty-six "fabulous firsts" that transpired within the city. One pioneering "first" that the directory somehow managed to overlook was that Philadelphia was the first major city in the nation to be the focus of comprehensive archaeological attention.

Archaeological studies of Philadelphia's historic sites began almost forty years ago at a time when the specialty of historical archaeology was in its infancy. An offspring of the branch of archaeology that studies prehistoric cultures, the new subdiscipline, like the old, retrieves and analyzes the physical evidence of the past. The goal of both specialties is an understanding of past cultures; the difference between them is that while the archaeology of prehistoric sites focuses on cultures that left no written records, the archaeology of historic sites deals with literate cultures that left at least some, and in many cases ample, written documentation of their lifeways.

Although gentleman scholars of the Victorian era devoted considerable effort to investigation of prehistoric sites, investigation of historic sites was not at that time a particularly popular pursuit. It was, however, not unknown. One of the earliest investigations of a historic site took place in 1856 in the small town of Duxbury, Massachusetts, where James Hall, using surprisingly careful methods, excavated the house site of his famed ancestor, Myles Standish (Deetz 1971:209). A few other investigations of historic sites occurred later in the nineteenth century, but it was not until 1934, when Jamestown in the rural reaches of Virginia became the focus of study, that historical archaeology began emerging as a distinct subdiscipline.

After World War II, London, its streets bombed and its historic sites agape, provided a prime urban laboratory for the practice of the new subdiscipline. Shortly thereafter, in the 1950s, archaeological studies in Philadelphia began at Independence National Historical Park, and they have been pursued with vigor ever since, making Philadelphia not just the first large urban area in the nation to be archaeologically investigated, but also the most thoroughly investigated one in North America (Cotter and Orr 1975).

Historical archaeology throughout the United States received a good deal of impetus in the 1960s, when the federal government enacted two laws, the National Historic Preservation Act of 1966 and the National Environmental Policy Act of 1969, that provided for the protection of historic sites. The 1966 act created the National Register of Historic Places to designate "districts, sites, buildings, structures, and objects significant in American history, architecture, archaeology, and culture." The act also provided for the granting of funds to states "for the purpose of preparing comprehensive statewide historic surveys and plans . . . for the preservation, acquisition, and development of such properties." With its numerous historic landmarks, Philadelphia was a prime beneficiary of this legislation.

Among the nearly 150 sites that make up the subject matter of this book are some of the best-known historic public buildings in America, as well as the homes of some of the country's most historic figures. Equally as important to the archaeological record, however, are the historically anonymous places also described in the chapters that follow: the domestic and commercial sites where people who left no imprint on the written record lived and worked. As shown in

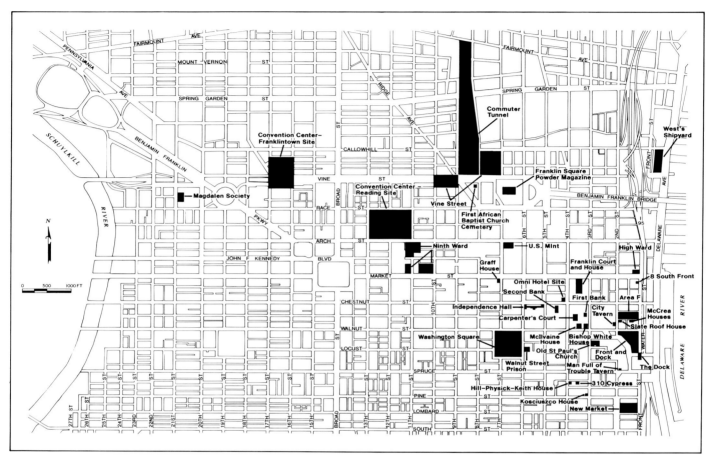

Figure 1.

Archaeological sites in downtown Philadelphia.

Archaeology: How and Why

Figures 1 and 2, some of the sites, both well-known and unknown, are in downtown Philadelphia; others are in the "Philadelphia region"—Germantown and elsewhere in Philadelphia County and the surrounding Bucks, Montgomery, Chester, and Delaware counties. Although no undisturbed prehistoric site has yet been fully excavated in the Philadelphia region, it is possible, as Chapter 1 demonstrates, to infer Philadelphia's prehistory from several important prehistoric sites in the outlying regions of Pennsylvania and New Jersey.

Whether historic or prehistoric, urban or rural, archaeology, if it is to tell us something more meaningful about the past than a random scavenger hunt would, is expensive and difficult to accomplish. It involves excavating from the earth the portable objects, or "artifacts," that earlier people made and left behind them—tools, dishes, cooking utensils, and the like—as well as pollen, seeds, garbage bones, and other natural remains. It also involves the identification of more permanent, immovable, man-made "features" of the landscape, such as

pits that people dug for wells or food storage and the foundations of the structures they built.

Artifacts and archaeological features generally appear in layers, or strata, deposited in the earth over time. To make sense of what the artifacts and features mean—to see them in relation to one another and to understand the people who made them and how they used them—the archaeologist must record their stratigraphic positions. Careful recording is essential, since excavation permanently disrupts the site and the evidence it contains. The archaeologist must therefore painstakingly create maps, grid plans, and site profiles showing the strata of the earth so that horizontal and vertical relationships can be correlated.

After the artifacts have been provenienced (that is, labeled according to where they were found), cleaned, and catalogued, the job of laboratory analysis begins.* Such analysis requires that the artifacts be described in terms of space (where they were found), time (when they were made), and form (physical appearance), and in a way that allows for comparisons with other artifact collections. When archaeological data have been integrated in this way, they generally reflect specific cultural patterns, and from them the archaeologist is able to make logical inferences about what the evidence means. The problem that arises in interpreting the data, however, is that although artifacts are concrete, physical objects, they are not necessarily hard, incontrovertible facts. Like Gertrude Stein's "rose is a rose is a rose," a ceramic sherd is, of course, a ceramic sherd. But like historical data, the archaeological artifact can often be interpreted in different ways.

Interpreting archaeological evidence within the historical context entails the double-edged risk of achieving nothing more than a documentation of the obvious or of assuming too much on the basis of the written record. James Deetz (1988:367), noting that "precise certainty is rarely achieved," has described the ideal process as "a gradual refinement of explanation, as more and more factors are incorporated into the construction of the past that one is trying to create. In historical archeology, this refinement is best accomplished by maintaining a balance between the documentary and material evidence,

* Once excavated, artifacts should be kept in carefully controlled storage. The artifacts described in this book are stored in various places, since Philadelphia presently has no central artifact repository. The Atwater Kent Museum maintains a sizable collection of artifacts, some of which are on display. The National Park Service exhibits a part of its huge artifact collection at 318 Market Street in Franklin Court. The University of Pennsylvania has a small collection that it houses in the Palestra sports arena on the Penn campus.

Figure 2.

Archaeological sites in the Philadelphia region. (Insets for downtown Philadelphia and Valley Forge refer to Figures 1 and 10.34, respectively.)

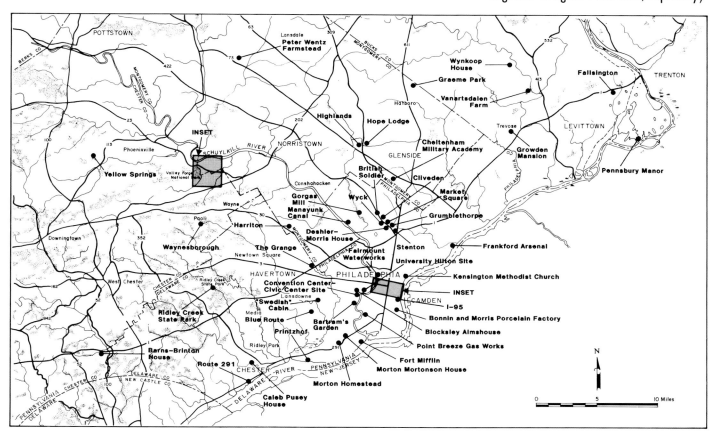

being always mindful that, to be a productive exercise, the results should provide a more satisfactory explanation than would be forthcoming from either set of data alone."

For clues to the meaning of the material evidence of the past, the archaeologist must often consult not just the historical record, but period paintings and museum pieces as well. The job requires interdisciplinary knowledge and, above all, endless patience.

For all this effort and expense, archaeology of prehistoric sites at least has the justification that without the physical evidence it produces, we would know little, if anything, of the culture of civilizations that existed before the age of record keeping. But where historical records are available to document the lifeways of the past (and such documentation is certainly more than abundant on the subject of Philadelphia), why go to the trouble of digging up material that merely confirms what we already know from written records? But then, why study history?

The answer, it seems, is securely fixed in the constitution of human beings. The present, once past, is history, and the future, completely hypothetical, never arrives; it eternally recedes before us as the past recedes behind us. To feel the comfort of perspective as we venture into the future, we seek some understanding of the past. We look for precedents, analogues, and guidelines, and for evidence to sustain them. History provides the intangible evidence, archaeology the tangible. Although historians and archaeologists ask different questions and work with different data—the former with written documents, the latter with ceramic sherds, foundation walls, and even

old garbage bones and seeds—the relationship between the two disciplines is of mutual benefit. The historical record provides archaeologists with a background against which to interpret their findings. In turn, what archaeologists find in the earth can do more than just confirm the historical record. Sometimes it disproves it; more often, and perhaps more important, it augments it. The physical evidence when combined with the written evidence can provide an insight into the past that the written word alone or the artifact in unknown context seldom, if ever, achieves.

Moreover, archaeological findings frequently shed light on facets of everyday life that never make it into the history books. Historians, like the rest of us, must be selective about what they process; to attempt to process all the available data would overwhelm and immobilize us. Inevitably, some data are omitted from the historical record in favor of those the historian considers more important. And until quite recently, what most historians thought was important generally had to do with the elite and the famous and their praiseworthy and not-so-praiseworthy deeds. Indeed, so little was written about the poor and illiterate or about slaves, servants, and children that they could be said to be "the people without a history." The annals of history also rarely, if ever, included mention of the commonplace material objects of daily life—the cuts of meat that eighteenth-century Philadelphians preferred, for example, and the size of the oysters they ate (very large, indeed), or the pencil boxes that nineteenth-century children toted to school and the kinds of toys they played with. Although archaeologists occasionally unearth sensational finds, such as evidence of eighteenth-

century pornography, very often what they find are mundane things like these.

As will be evident in the chapters that follow, archaeology, like justice, is blindfolded. It impartially uncovers physical evidence of the lifestyles and deeds of both the famous and the not-so-famous, and it has even brought to light the *corpora delecti* of deeds the long-dead perpetrators would no doubt just as soon had been left forgotten. These deeds, or misdeeds, range from nineteenth-century schoolboy pranks to eighteenth-century infanticide.

The precise reasons archaeological investigations are undertaken are varied, and the investigations described in this book cover most of them. The object may be to locate a lost site or to salvage data from one that is about to be disturbed in some way, perhaps by demolition but also (as was happily often the case in Philadelphia) by restoration. The object may also be to answer specific research questions posed by historians and architects, or even by archaeologists themselves. Or it may be to comply with the federal legislation of the 1960s that requires a determination of the significance of a federally owned site or a site on which federal money is being spent before it can be disturbed in any way.

What archaeologists do depends on the object of the study and the time and funding allotted for the work. Generally, however, archaeologists begin their investigations by surveying all historical documentation pertaining to the site and perhaps also doing some limited field testing. They then proceed to carry out test excavations to determine the significance of any physical evidence that survives. The initial historical research is commonly called a "Phase I study";

Figure 3a.

Eighteenth-century imported ceramics. *Left to right:* Delftware, three plates, English, ca. 1700–1750; stoneware, white glazed plate, English, ca. 1745–1770; creamware, tortoise-shell type, English, ca. 1745–1770; creamware, mottled-brown hexagonal plate, English, ca. 1755–1765; hexagonal plate stamped on bottom "DD & Co./Castleford," English, ca. 1765–1785; creamware, cream-colored Queens Ware pattern, English, ca. 1775–1785; creamware, cream-colored feather-edge pattern plate, English, ca. 1765–1785; pearlware, blue-painted shell-edge pattern plate, English, ca. 1790–1810; pearlware, blue shell-edge pattern plate, Leeds type, English, ca. 1790–1820. (Courtesy of Independence National Historical Park; Robert L. Giannini III)

Figure 3b.

Eighteenth-century ceramics. *Left to right:* mocha ware, custard cup with sponge decoration, English, ca. 1810–1850; banded ware, mug with black-and-white checkered decoration, English, ca. 1810–1850; ironstone wares, a variety of saucers and plates, some with sponge decorations and others with transfer-printed decorations, flow-blue, imitation Chinese export porcelain, to centennial souvenirs, English and America, ca. 1820–1876; transfer-printed wares, some with maker's marks or pattern titles: "LAWRENCE," "STONEWARE BARKER & SON," "PEARL STONEWARE VENUS PW & CO.," "Girard's Bank Philadelphia, JACKSON'S WARRANTED," "INDEPENDENCE HALL, PHILADELPH." (Courtesy of Independence National Historical Park; Robert L. Giannini III)

Figure 3c.

Eighteenth-century ceramics. *Left to right:* red earthenware, tulip slip-decorated "Moravian" dish, English or American, ca. 1730–1760; earthenware, brown-and-green glazed bowl, English (North Devonshire type) or American, ca. 1700–1730; red earthenware, yellow-band slip-decorated dish, English or American, ca. 1730–1760; salt-glazed stoneware, cobalt blue decorated small salver, Philadelphia (Anthony Duché), ca. 1730–1760; salt-glazed stoneware, cobalt blue decorated chamber pot (Anthony Duché), ca. 1730–1760; red earthenware, dark brown glazed porringer, probably Philadelphia, ca. 1730–1760; red earthenware, yellow-slip comb-decorated pie plate with serrated rim, probably Philadelphia, ca. 1750–1800. (Courtesy of Independence National Historical Park; Robert L. Giannini III)

Figure 4a.

Examples of eighteenth-century wine bottles. *Left to right:* Dark olive-green, English, ca. 1700–1725; dark olive-green, English, ca. 1725–1750; medium dark green, English, with dated seal "1773"; medium black, English, ca. 1775–1800. (Courtesy of Independence National Historical Park; Robert L. Giannini III)

Figure 4b.

Eighteenth-century American glass. *Left to right:* bottle, aqua glass demijohn, "South Jersey" type, ca. 1800; bottle, dark green glass chestnut, "South Jersey" type, ca. 1775–1800; bottle, green glass wine, "South Jersey" type (Wistar Glass Works, Salem County, New Jersey), ca. 1775–1800; bottle, green glass chestnut, "South Jersey" type, ca. 1740–1770; mug, green glass with handle, "South Jersey" type (Wistar Glass Works, Salem County, New Jersey), ca. 1740–1770; bottle, green glass chestnut, "South Jersey" type, ca. 1775–1800. (Courtesy of Independence National Historical Park; Robert L. Giannini III)

the test excavations are known as a "Phase II study." If the Phase II study indicates that significant archaeological evidence does survive, and if impending development or some other factor is threatening the site, the archaeologist carries out a "Phase III study" to excavate the site fully and to conserve a sample of the data. If, however, the site is not being threatened, it is often left as is to await future excavation, which presumably will be conducted with less destructive methods than those in use today.

The Archaeological Puzzle: Of Patterns, Sherds, and Privies

Many of the investigations described in the chapters that follow were conducted before the late 1970s, when archaeologists began paying more attention to quantified data as a means of establishing relationships among artifact collections. By quantifying data according to artifact categories, Stanley South (1977) demonstrated patterns of artifact usage so regular,

he believed, as to amount to "cultural laws." South's patterns pertain to life along the Eastern Seaboard during the eighteenth and early nineteenth centuries, and among them are the Brunswick pattern, having to do with patterns of refuse disposal; the Carolina pattern, in which kitchen-related artifacts outnumber artifacts in other categories, such as architecture (e.g., nails and hinges), furniture, arms, clothing, personal use, and activities (e.g., farm tools and military objects); and the Frontier pattern, which is the

Figure 4c.

Nineteenth-century bottles. *Left to right:* case bottle, black glass, probably English, ca. 1800–1820; chestnut bottles, two olive-green glass bottles, probably English, ca. 1800–1820; demijohn bottles, two small, olive-green bottles, probably English, ca. 1800–1830; wine bottle, tall, black glass, spirits bottle with dated seal "1818," English, ca. 1818–1860; inkwell, small, aqua, two-piece, molded glass inkwell, American, ca. 1830–1870; pickle bottle, tall, aqua, press-molded glass jar, marked "SJG," American, ca. 1840–1870; decanter, tall, clear cut glass whiskey decanter, etched "UPPER TEN, CATHERWOOD," American, ca. 1830–1870; mustard jar, small, two-piece, molded, aqua glass jar, marked "N.W./OPERMANN MUSTARD FACTORY," American, ca. 1850–1870; wine bottle, tall, amber glass bottle marked with paper label "Geisenhein," European, ca. 1860–1900; soda or beer bottle, short, dark green glass bottle with crown lip marked "P. ERTEL/THIS BOTTLE NEVER SOLD/DYOTTVILLE GLASS WORKS/PHILAD*a*," American, ca. 1840–1870; soda bottle, short, pale green, blob-top glass bottle marked "J.O. KANE, PHILAD*a*," American, ca. 1870–1900. (Courtesy of Independence National Historical Park; Robert L. Giannini III)

inverse of the Carolina. The Frontier pattern is typical of forts and other primitive outposts, while the Carolina pattern is characteristic of more established settlements.

Although most of the artifact collections from Philadelphia sites have not been subjected to the kind of analysis employed by South, they nonetheless quite clearly demonstrate the changing patterns of life over the centuries and the evolution of the city. One thing they make abundantly clear is that from the time William Penn founded Philadelphia in 1682 until well into the nineteenth century, British tastes and British imports—particularly ceramic imports—predominated over those of other countries. Even the plentiful locally made redwares closely resembled their English counterparts (Giannini 1980). Both before and after the Revolution, Philadelphia, despite a marked Germanic influence, was a very English city. The upper class favored the ceramic wares produced by the English, and the middle class and working class emulated these tastes.

Ceramic pieces are of abiding interest to archaeologists. Inorganic and nondegradable, more enduring than iron or hardwood, they are the most common things found on historic sites. They provide a means not only of dating a site but also of interpreting and assessing the lifestyle and status of the people who occupied it. The large number of British ceramics found on Philadelphia sites supports the contention that until late in the eighteenth century, local potters, who were making ceramics almost from the moment the city was founded, hardly challenged the imports that Philadelphians favored, and even then they do not seem to have made much of a dent except in utility wares. As can be seen in Figures 3a, b, and c, most of the local ceramics were humble wares (Miller 1984) intended for kitchen use; the imported wares were generally much finer (Giannini 1980). The best-documented potter in the early city was Anthony Duché, a Huguenot who immigrated to Philadelphia from England, where his family had gone to escape persecution. From the 1720s until his death in 1762, Duché operated a stoneware kiln near Fifth and Chestnut streets. There his sons Anthony, Jr., Andrew, and James also learned the trade (Hood 1968; Giannini 1981). Glassware, just as enduring as any ceramic ware and originally imported also, came to be made in Pennsylvania and New Jersey. Figures 4a, b, and c show some of the kinds of glass archaeologists have found at Philadelphia sites.

In the few instances in which ceramics, glass, and other artifacts from Philadelphia's eighteenth-century sites were analyzed according to South's categories, they did indicate an adherence to the Carolina pattern, and if enough artifacts dating from the time of the first settlement could be found to make up a statistically significant sample, they might indicate an adherence to the Frontier pattern. But in many ways, this is like a clergyman relating the sins of his parishioners to all those listed in the Holy Scriptures; if we try hard enough, we can find a category for everything.

As for South's Brunswick pattern, Philadelphians had, and still have, their own patterns of refuse disposal. They threw their trash where it was convenient—sometimes in abandoned cisterns at the front of the house or in cooling pits for food and wine beneath the cellar floor, but more often behind the kitchen in backyard trash pits, ash pits, wells, and privies (or necessaries, as the latter were sometimes also aptly called). In such places, protected from subsequent site development, archaeologists have found tens of thousands of inorganic, nondegradable ceramic and glass sherds. Most of the ceramics have been pieces of table and kitchen ware, but fragments of clay tobacco pipes have been very numerous, too. Given that most of the trash was probably organic, huge amounts of it must have long ago rotted away; nonetheless, Philadelphia sites have yielded many objects of wood and leather, since, when sealed in moist earth, these organic materials can last for hundreds of years. A good deal of trash probably went where archaeologists will never find it—up the chimney, into the Delaware River or the nearest creek, or carted off to a remote dump.

Wells, used for drinking water, and cisterns, which collected rain water that was used both for fighting fires and for laundry, were no doubt kept as clean as possible while in use. Privy pits, to stay in use, were periodically cleaned of human waste and of the household litter customarily deposited in them. What the archaeologist normally finds in these pits are therefore only those items around the edges that escaped the final cleaning and the trash that was deliberately deposited to fill them after they were abandoned. It is possible, of course, for the last cleaning to have occurred long before the pit was abandoned, and when that is the case, the archaeologist usually finds a number of items that predate the time of abandonment and filling.

Regardless of when the artifacts were deposited, the question always arises: were these items actually used on the premises where the archaeologist finds them, or did they come from farther afield? In other words, can we be certain that a broken eighteenth-century ceramic tile found in a privy pit on Benjamin Franklin's property really belonged to him? Lending some certitude to the assumption that it did is that Franklin, unlike many of his neighbors, had a private privy. Communal privies and wells were common, however, and when no longer in use, these communal facilities were no doubt filled with discards from the multiple households they had served. The huge number of sherds found in a few pits—too many to have come from just the households of the neighborhood—suggests that sometimes the fill was deposited by a carter who, hired to take away the waste products of a distant potter, butcher, or other entrepreneur, had availed himself of an abandoned pit that the property owners wanted filled. Another complicating factor is that when privy pits were cleaned, it was apparently common practice to throw in large numbers of ceramic sherds to improve drainage (Cosans 1975); such items may or may not have come from the household the privy served. All we can say with absolute certainty is that site-specific or not, the artifacts found at Philadelphia sites can tell us a great deal about the overall patterns of the city's cultural past.

Patterns, like beauty, however, are in the eye of the beholder. Each individual site has its own unique history, and each beholder a particular way of viewing the evidence. The extent to which a collection of artifacts expresses "laws" of culture is up to the common sense of the beholder. The object, of course, is to be able to see the people behind the artifacts. The trick for the archaeologist is not to see three people where only one existed or one where a dozen were involved, and not to despair when not even one lone soul looms into view. Archaeology offers no instant revelation of past culture. What it does offer is a measurable inventory of artifacts from a given time at a given place, an inventory that makes a positive contribution to the archaeological record, the general body of knowledge of investigated sites. It is the evidence from many sites and the cultural analyses of this evidence that allows us to glimpse how past generations worked and played, ate and drank, and lived and died.

A Note on the Book's Organization

Part I provides some background information for the investigations of historic sites described in the next two parts of the book. Chapter 1 briefly describes the physical environment of the Philadelphia region as it emerged from prehistoric times into historic, as well as the cultural patterns of the

Amerindians who inhabited the Delaware Valley during those many thousands of years. Chapter 2 sketches the history of the region from the early 1600s, when the first European settlers arrived, through to the early twentieth century. The intent here is not to give the full body of the history—an obviously impossible task in the space of one short chapter—but rather to highlight the historical themes that have a bearing on the sites described in subsequent chapters.

The chapters in parts II and III are organized according to geographic location, rather than by historical theme. Inevitably, however, the themes implicit in Chapter 2 are often apparent in the sections that make up the chapters in these two parts of the book. Each section provides a brief history of the site, a description of the investigation, and, where possible, an interpretation of the findings. Pertinent data from site investigations are included in chapter appendixes.

In Part IV, Chapter 11 reviews the archaeological evidence so far produced in Philadelphia, relating it to the historical framework. Chapter 12 suggests some directions and priorities for future Philadelphia archaeology.

An appendix to the book contains information on minor archaeological investigations. While these investigations produced either few data or none at all, they are valuable in that they contribute to the general body of knowledge, even if in a negative way; knowing where sites do not exist can be almost as valuable to the archaeologist as knowing where they are. Professional archaeologists will also find the bibliography of interest. The glossary defines a number of terms that may be unfamiliar to lay readers.

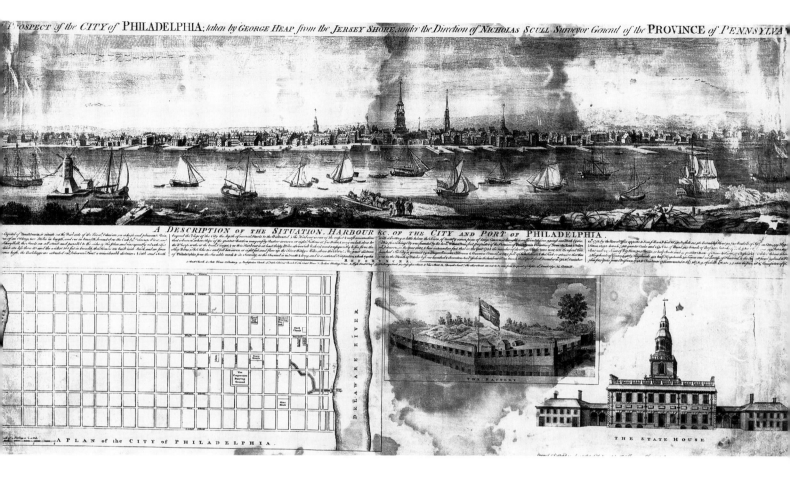

PART I

Setting the Stage

I

The Philadelphia Region from Prehistory into History

THE ENVIRONMENT

PREHISTORIC INHABITANTS

THE LENAPE OF THE HISTORIC CONTACT PERIOD

Philadelphia, like any city great or small, however recent or ancient, is a place and an interval of time in the story of man's occupation of the earth. Not surprisingly, given its particular place and time in that long story, Philadelphia has been fertile ground for historical archaeologists, whose eighteenth-century findings have added color to the already colorful story of Philadelphia's role in the founding of the nation. The very color of that interval of history has, however, tended to obscure the rest of the interval of time that is Philadelphia. In the shadow of the artifacts, archives, landmarks, and history books that speak so eloquently of America's historical beginnings, the actual beginnings of man's occupation of the landscape that would ultimately become Philadelphia have faded. The city's prehistoric past and the indigenous people who inhabited it from prehistoric times into historic have been largely forgotten or, worse, ignored.

To begin the story of Philadelphia with the advent of the European settlers in the early 1600s would be like walking into a play in the middle of the second act. To appreciate the full drama, one has to know something of what went before.

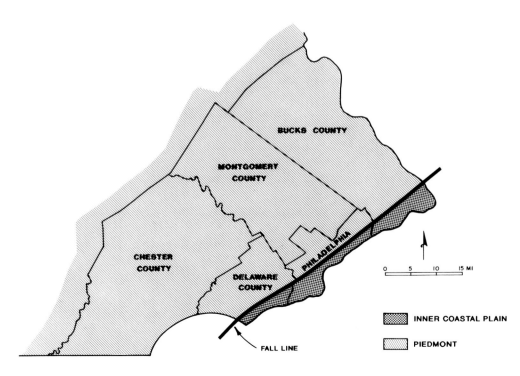

Figure 1.1.

The physiographic provinces of the Philadelphia region. (From Raber 1985)

THE ENVIRONMENT

In rivers, the water that you touch is the last of what has past and the first of that which comes: so with time present.

> —Leonardo da Vinci, *Notebooks*

In the metaphor of time and rivers, Philadelphia's place in time is fixed upon two great rivers. Their flow to the present reaches back and controls the continuity of all generations through history into prehistory. The flow of these rivers, together with an abundance of other natural resources, ensured that the region would be as much a magnet for European colonists as it had been for prehistoric people. It was not by happenstance that in the seventeenth century, Dutch and Swedes chose to settle in the Delaware Valley, nor was it by happenstance that the town William Penn founded there grew into one of the great metropolitan areas of the world. Philadelphia owes much of its good fortune to its physical environment, and it is there that its story must begin.

The Modern Environment

Although some aspects of Philadelphia's environment have changed over the past 450 years, today's environment is in many respects identical to that which greeted the first Europeans to set foot in the Delaware Valley— itinerant traders and trappers who probably began wandering through the area some time around 1550 and who were followed some seventy years later by waves of more permanent settlers. This same environment has prevailed in the Philadelphia region for some 2,800 years, offering its bounty

and challenges both to the prehistoric inhabitants of the area, who first arrived in this part of the world over 10,000 years ago, and to their historic descendants, the Lenape Amerindians, who were on hand to welcome the first Europeans.

Situated between the Delaware and Schuylkill rivers, the Philadelphia region—which comprises parts of Bucks, Montgomery, Delaware, and Chester counties as well as Philadelphia County—straddles two major physiographic provinces, the Inner Coastal Plain to the southeast and the Piedmont to the northwest (Figure 1.1). The two provinces offer considerable contrast. The Inner Coastal Plain is characterized by very low relief, most of it less than 100 feet in elevation, while the Piedmont, in which most of the Philadelphia region lies, consists of interspersed lowlands, gently rolling uplands, and some low hills and ridges.

To the southeast, the hills of the Piedmont merge with the lowlands of the Inner Coastal Plain to form the so-called Fall Line. The Fall Line, which runs roughly from Trenton southwest through Philadelphia and Wilmington at the interface of the two provinces, marks the limit of tidewater and of upriver navigation on both the Schuylkill and the Delaware. A relatively abrupt ridge, it borders a gently rolling plateau, which in some places is as much as 300 feet above sea level. The Fall Line is well marked at the Falls of the Schuylkill, near the Philadelphia Museum of Art, and at

the Falls of the Delaware, just below Trenton.

While the beauty and navigability of Philadelphia's two rivers must have been obvious attractions to the Lenape Amerindians and their ancestors, as well as to European colonists, the many streams that swiftly descend the Piedmont to the Fall Line were of utility, too. They provided the aboriginals with ideal sites for fish traps and the Europeans with equally excellent sites for water-powered mills. Many streams that once emptied into the Delaware—Pegg's Run, Dock Creek, Gunners Run, and Hay Creek among them—are no longer to be seen, most of them having succumbed in the nineteenth century to a welter of urban development (Cee Jay Frederick Associates and John Milner Associates 1981:Figure A5). Typical of the demise of most is the story of Pegg's Run, which archaeological investigations have shown was bricked in and channeled into an underground culvert in an effort to create more usable land at the northern edge of the city (Cosans-Zebooker and Barrett 1985). Dock Creek went underground a bit earlier than Pegg's Run, and for reasons of health rather than urban expansion; by the late 1700s, its two branches, which flowed from west and northwest to empty into a tiny tidal basin south of Walnut Street, were polluted and malodorous sewers (Liggett 1971a).

The Delaware River, which empties into Delaware Bay and meets the sea beyond Rehoboth Beach, and the Susquehanna River, which empties into Chesapeake Bay just above Baltimore, provide drainage for southeastern Pennsylvania. As it is part of the Delaware River watershed, the Schuylkill River is not in itself the region's major drainage system; it is, however, the Delaware's largest tributary. Other principal waterways that provide local drainage include Brandywine, Perkiomen, Skippack, French, Neshaminy, Poquessing, Darby, Crum, and Ridley creeks. Figure 1.2 shows

Figure 1.2.

The waterways of the Philadelphia region as they appear today. (From Higbee 1965)

the waterways of the Philadelphia region as they appear today.

Like the rivers and streams of the Philadelphia region, its geologic foundations, shown in Figure 1.3, have been important factors in development. The Wissahickon Formation, an extensive metamorphic rock formation that underlies all of Philadelphia County, produced the "Wissahickon schist" of which so many of the region's eighteenth- and nineteenth-century houses were built. The schist in the central portion of the Wissahickon Formation long ago turned to granite; that part of the

formation is known locally as the "Swarthmore granodiorite" (Goodwin 1964:32–33). Just north and west of the Wissahickon Formation, one of the earliest rock formations in the area appears, an underground deposit of so-called Baltimore gneiss that runs through south-central Chester County.

As can be seen in Figure 1.3, gabbro, limestone, and dolomite predominate in the region surrounding the Wissahickon Formation, and some serpentine—a dull-green, mottled rock—appears there as well. The limestone and dolomite were

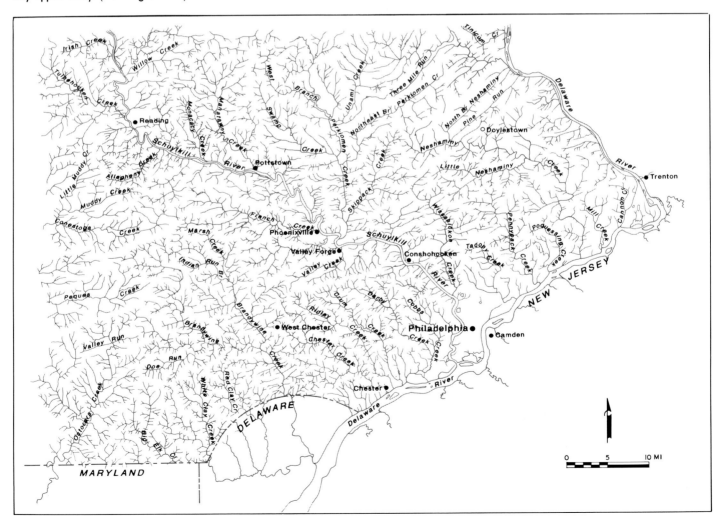

once extensively quarried, and the serpentine was occasionally (and somewhat unwisely, given its susceptibility to erosion) used in the construction of buildings, particularly in Chester County. Much earlier, this same area provided prehistoric people with high-quality chert and jasper, fine-grained cryptocrystalline rocks that they flaked and chipped into tools. To the far north, quartzite and red sandstone and shale make their appearance. The quartzite is known as "Chickies quartzite," and, like the chert and jasper, it provided the aboriginal inhabitants of the area with a high grade of stone for their tools.

The aboriginals also made use of the argillite—a soft, compact clay stone cemented by silica—found in the Lockatong Formation, which stretches from northwest of Doylestown, Pennsylvania, into central New Jersey (Bascom et al. 1931:29–30; Struthers and Roberts 1982). Argillite from the same formation has been extensively quarried in historic and modern times for building material and crushed stone (Smith 1967:185). Numerous secondary deposits, such as pebbles and cobbles from streambeds, provided the region's prehistoric inhabitants with yet another source of fracturable, siliceous rock that could be flaked and chipped into tools.

The soils of the Philadelphia region have also been hospitable. Despite continued agricultural use for over 300 years, they continue to produce excellent yields, as evidenced by numerous farms still operating at a profit in the counties surrounding Philadelphia. In places, however, the intensity of agricultural processes has almost completely eroded the original land surfaces (Jehle and Carr 1983:10). Urbanization, suburban sprawl, and various kinds of land engineering have also taken their toll on the land, substantially altering the natural soil profiles in many parts of the area.

Philadelphia and its environs have a "continental climate"; that is, summer and winter temperatures vary significantly, and fluctuations in day-to-day temperatures are relatively large (Robichaud and Buell 1973:55). In January, the average temperature is 32°F; in July, it is 77°F. The average temperature over the year is 57°F. The relatively large fluctuations in daily temperatures are due to warm and cold weather systems moving into the region from north and south, but since these systems move rapidly through the region, long periods of extreme heat or cold are rare (Smith 1967:181–82). High humidity is, however, a prevalent characteristic of the summer months.

Yearly average precipitation is about 42 inches, with ranges between 32 and 58 inches. The wettest month is normally August, while the driest is October. Approximately thirty thun-

Figure 1.3.

The geologic foundations of the Philadelphia region. (From Goodwin 1964)

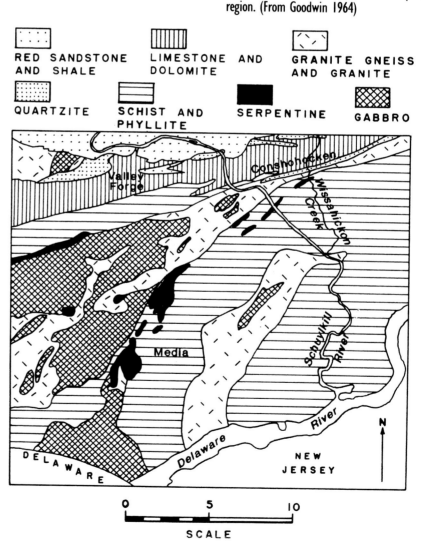

derstorms occur each year, resulting in severe flooding in low-lying areas. In winter, large storm systems moving north along the Atlantic coast frequently bring snowstorms. Although these storms occasionally reach blizzard proportions, snow usually covers the ground for only a short time. The yearly average snowfall for the Philadelphia region is between 20 and 30 inches (Smith 1967:182–83).

The growing season, or the time between the last frost in spring and the first frost in autumn, is relatively long—usually between April 9 and October 29, a period of 203 days. While the growing season does vary, it has never been less than 190 days or more than 223 days (Smith 1967:182).

The mighty chestnut that once graced the forests of the Philadelphia region has long since fallen to blight, as has many a graceful elm, but a multitude of other trees abound. They include oak, hickory, white pine, beech, walnut, ash, tulip poplar, maple, wild cherry, cedar, and sycamore. Although timbering and agricultural practices have dramatically altered the ecology of the forest, its actual composition seems to be much as it was before the European colonists arrived. Beech and sugar maple, which were apparently not of great economic importance to early settlers, were probably found in much the same numbers as they are today. Hickory, which was important in the early colonial economy, may have been sparser, and such species as white pine, which tend to regenerate and spread rapidly after a forest fire, may be more prevalent today (Russell 1981:10).

The undergrowth of the forest, though it varies from place to place, generally consists of dogwood, chest-nut sprouts, ironwood, maple leaf, viburnum, sumac, poison ivy, spicebush, greenbrier, witch hazel, and honeysuckle (Kunkle 1963:103–4; Jehle and Carr 1983:11). Contributing to the diversity of the undergrowth are various kinds of fruits, berries, mushrooms, and herbs. The Lenape Amerindians used most of the fruits and berries as food and the herbs for cooking or medicinal purposes (Tantaquidgeon 1977); the European colonists used some of them, too.

The wildlife that presented itself to the Lenape and the early settlers was doubtless as plentiful and varied as the vegetation of the forest. Although greatly reduced in numbers, the white-tailed deer, wild turkey, beaver, otter, muskrat, raccoon, rabbit, woodchuck, fox, squirrel, porcupine, opposum, and skunk that the Lenape and the colonists hunted and trapped still inhabit the region (Newcomb 1956:14; Russell 1981:6; Jehle and Carr 1983:12). The black bear and wolf do not, nor do the mountain lion, panther, and elk that in earlier times roamed the forest. Another former resident, the mastodon, has long since become extinct.

Ducks, geese, wild pigeons, pheasant, grouse, and partridge added to the variety of the early inhabitants' diet. The rivers and streams, too, offered their bounty: eels, turtles, crayfish, mussels, trout, perch, catfish, pike, bass, sturgeon, shad, and herring (Newcomb 1956:15–16; Jehle and Carr 1983:12). Most of these species are still to be found in the Philadelphia region today, but in reduced numbers. Since they were most abundant in the Inner Coastal Plain, along the Delaware where it meets the Schuylkill, it is not surprising that that is where the first European colonists chose to settle.

The Holocene and Pleistocene Environments

The environment that so hospitably greeted the first European colonists did not smile so brightly on earlier inhabitants of the region. When man first made his appearance in the Delaware Valley some 10,000 to 12,000 years ago, the climate was considerably colder than it is today. Although green savannas and burgeoning evergreen forests were quite abundant, much of the land was harsh and barren taiga. The last of three (or possibly four) glaciers, which reached as far south as Stroudsburg, Pennsylvania, had only recently begun its retreat north, leaving a scoured and striated landscape in its wake. The ice moving over the Canadian Shield was a mile thick on Hudson's Bay and north of the newly forming Great Lakes, and, with so much water locked up on land, the ocean was at least a hundred feet lower. Thus the Delaware emptied much farther out to sea in a now-drowned mouth, and inland tidewater was well below where it is now. The sites that the earliest inhabitants of the region occupied along the river's edge are today well under water or buried in coastal or riverine marshes. Some, in fact, are believed to be many miles out in the Atlantic Ocean, on the Outer Continental Shelf, where the nets of modern trawlers periodically scoop up evidence in the form of a wooly mastodon's tooth or an occasional stone tool.

Inland in those distant days, wooded hills and swamps stretched between the Delaware and the Schuylkill, and the region was locked north and south by the wilderness fastness of the Wissahickon and the Brandywine Valley. Here and in the woodlands beyond, the first people in the region hunted large mammals such as the mastodon, and in savannas of tall grass and streams, they pursued the caribou, elk, giant beaver, and perhaps the musk-ox. By about 7000 B.C., or close to 9,000 years ago, environmental conditions had changed radically enough to cause the extinction of all these animals. Most likely, the aboriginals did not bemoan the change. With the gradual retreat of the ice sheets, the warming of the atmosphere, and the higher levels of rivers and ocean, floral and faunal resources grew more diverse, and the inhabitants of the Philadelphia region now had at their disposal a variety of small game, as well as fish, shellfish, nuts, seeds, and other foodstuffs. As the warming and drying trend that began at this time continued, flora and fauna became ever more plentiful and varied. About 2,800 years ago, climatic conditions stabilized, and the climate as it was then is essentially the same as today's.

As Table 1.1 shows, geologic time is divided into eras, periods, and epochs, and the time during which all these environmental changes were taking place—from about 10,000 years ago to the near present—is known as the Holocene epoch. The Holocene marked not only the advent of man in the New World but also the retreat of glaciation. During the preceding Pleistocene epoch, which began about 1,000,000 years ago, glacial activity had surged out of the north at least three times (Richards 1956:20–21). The last glacial stage, known as the Wisconsin, began at least 65,000 years ago, and it started its final retreat some 18,000 years ago. It extended irregularly, with pulsating advances and retreats, from northern Pennsylvania into the Appalachians, along

Table 1.1. Geologic time scale.

ERA	PERIOD	EPOCH	MILLIONS OF YEARS AGO
CENOZOIC	QUATERNARY	HOLOCENE	
		PLEISTOCENE	
	TERTIARY	PLIOCENE	1
		MIOCENE	
		OLIGOCENE	
		EOCENE	
		PALEOCENE	70
MESOZOIC	CRETACEOUS		
	JURASSIC		
	TRIASSIC		225
PALEOZOIC	PERMIAN		
	PENNSYLVANIAN		
	MISSISSIPPIAN		
	DEVONIAN		
	SILURIAN		
	ORDOVICIAN		
	CAMBRIAN		
PRECAMBRIAN			600

From Goodwin 1964.

the Ohio River and northwest to the valley glaciers of the Rockies, and beyond that to the Pacific Northwest. Although the ice of the Wisconsin never reached as far south as the Philadelphia region, both the Delaware and the Schuylkill rivers served as channels for the runoff that followed its retreat. The lower Delaware Valley today shows ample evidence of the gravel and sand that the thawing glacier left in its wake. Such glacial "outwash" has also been identified in the Schuylkill Valley as far south as Norristown (Leverett 1957:86).

A detailed fossil pollen study of two marshes in Chester County, the only such study ever undertaken in the Philadelphia region, gives us a documented glimpse of climatic conditions during the Pleistocene-Holocene interface, when man was

first making his appearance known in this area. With the help of radiocarbon dating,* Martin (1958:470, 494) was able to demonstrate that a tundra-like environment existed in unglaciated areas near the border of the Wisconsin ice sheet some 13,500 years ago. He was also able to define the vegetation that had sprung up in southeastern Pennsylvania after the glacial retreat began: here, about fifty miles south of the Wisconsin glacial border, was a forest consisting principally of jack pine, spruce, fir, birch, and willow, listed in their order of dominance. Table 1.2 provides a sum-

* Radiocarbon dating, introduced in 1949 by physicist Willard F. Libby, measures the amount of lingering radioactivity manifested in carbon 14, which is present in all organic substances, to establish a time scale indicating years since life ceased.

Table 1.2. Environmental characteristics of the Middle Atlantic region during the late Pleistocene and Holocene epochs.

Years before Present	Epoch	Episode	Climate	Forest Composition	Environmental Conditions	Fauna
1,000	HOLOCENE	Sub-Atlantic	Warm	Oak, chestnut, pine, cedar	Oak-chestnut forests	Modern fauna
			Cool and moist	Oak, chestnut, pine		
2,800		Sub-Boreal	Warm	Oak, hickory, hemlock, pine	Oak-hickory forests; open, grassy areas	Modern fauna—e.g., beaver, muskrat, black bear, squirrel, rabbit, white-tailed deer
5,550		Atlantic	Warming and drying	Oak, hemlock, pine	Oak-hemlock forests; boggy conditions	Many Pleistocene mammals by now extinct; elk and caribou moving north; introduction of modern fauna
9,000		Pre-Boreal/boreal	Cool	Pine, oak, birch, hemlock, northern shrubs	Last, brief glacial advance, pine-hemlock forests; boggy conditions	Start of gradual extinction of most Pleistocene mammals
11,000	PLEISTOCENE	Late Glacial	Cool and moist	Spruce, pine, oak, birch, alder	Retreat of glaciers; grasslands and extensive swamps, similar to today's Canadian taiga	Mastodon, caribou
			Cold			
18,000		Late Wisconsin	Very cold and dry	Spruce, pine, northern shrubs and herbs	To the north, glaciers; south of glacial border, tundra and open parkland	Caribou, giant beaver, mastodon, and other Pleistocene mammals
23,000						

Sources: Martin 1958; Carbone 1976:184–92; Sirkin 1977:214; Bernabo and Webb 1977; Hartzog 1979:16; Custer and Wallace 1982:146; Custer 1984:32.

mary of the overall environmental picture that emerged from these pollen profiles, as well as others in the middle Atlantic region.

The late Pleistocene epoch produced one of the most interesting pieces of environmental evidence ever found in the Philadelphia region. In 1931, while digging a new subway line near Eighth and Locust streets in Philadelphia, workmen uncovered several tree stumps of bald cypress in upright positions 38 feet below street level and some 10 feet below sea level. With no means then available to date the stumps precisely, some suggested that they might be remnants of a colonial or precolonial swamp. Because of their stratigraphic position, however, Richards (1931) argued that the stumps were of Pleistocene age, perhaps dating to the last interglacial stage over 65,000 years ago, when the bald cypress, now at home in the southern United States, thrived in a warm, moist coastal environment. There the debate on the age of the "subway tree" rested until some twenty-five years later, when a laboratory at the University of Pennsylvania, using the new method of radiocarbon dating, analyzed a sample of the stumps. Although the wood was too old for precise dating, the report stated that the sample "is definitely older than 36,600 years and probably older than 42,200 years" (Richards 1960:107). Clearly, Richards' suggestion of late Pleistocene age was correct, and the earliest piece of evidence of Philadelphia's prehistoric environment had been corroborated.

PREHISTORIC INHABITANTS

Human beings were relatively late in making their appearance in the New World, and later still in arriving in that part of it known as the Delaware Valley. Ecologically, the New World was always as habitable for them as the Old. Fossil primates that predate the Pleistocene have been found in western North America, but not in the human line: no hominids before *Homo sapiens* finally made the journey. Before tackling the New World, *Homo sapiens* had first to devise effective clothing to combat its subarctic cold, as well as tools for hunting big game to ensure a steady food supply. In the eastern hemisphere, human beings had made their presence known much earlier. By 600,000 years ago, during relatively mild weather, *Sinanthropus pekinensis* was in Northern China, and by some 60,000 to 25,000 years ago, eastern Asiatic and Japanese-Ainu peoples had reached the approaches to Beringia—the Bering land bridge of dry tundra that once connected Asia and Alaska (Shutler 1983; Fladmark 1983). Although evidence is rapidly accumulating that human beings may have crossed Beringia into Alaska as early as 20,000 years ago, or possibly much earlier, conservative archaeologists who question all evidence not tightly carbon 14–dated hold that before 12,000 years ago, the landscape of the New World cannot yet be proved to have included human inhabitants.

The earliest inhabitants of the New World, long known as Paleo Indians and more recently called Paleo Amerindians, were first studied and are still best known in the American Southwest. There is no doubt, however, that these people wandered beyond the Mississippi Valley eastward and that, by at least 10,000 years ago, they were fixing fluted chert blades to their spears and hunting the length of the Delaware River. They, or perhaps their ancestors, were the first people to sojourn in the Delaware Valley.

Table 1.3. Prehistoric cultural-chronological traditions in the Middle Atlantic region

Tradition	Approximate Dates	Projectile Points and Other Distinctive Implements	Primary Habitats	Dwellings	Primary Subsistence Modes
Late Woodland	A.D. 1000–A.D. 1550	Small, triangular arrowheads for bows; more refined ceramic vessels; hoes and other horticultural tools	Floodplains of major rivers	Oval houses in villages or hamlets	Agriculture plus some hunting, fishing, and foraging
Early–Middle Woodland	800 B.C.–A.D. 1000	Stemmed, lanceolate bifaces; same tools as Transitional, but ceramics replace soapstone	Floodplains of major rivers	Circular to oval houses in small settlements	More reliance on a sedentary hunting and fishing economy
Transitional or Terminal Archaic	1800 B.C.–800 B.C.	Broad, leaf-shaped points; same tools as Archaic, but more soapstone bowls	Floodplains of major rivers	Probably much like the Archaic	Fishing and some migratory hunting and foraging
Archaic	7500 B.C.–1000 B.C.	Notched and stemmed points; drills, axes, mortars and pestles, soapstone vessels	Along small streams in uplands and on floodplains	Circular, bark-covered wood frameworks	Migratory hunting and seasonal food gathering
Paleo Amerindian	12,000 B.C.–7500 B.C.	Fluted points; knives, scrapers	River valleys	Caves and rock outcrops	Big-game hunting in migratory bands

Research into the prehistoric inhabitants of the Delaware Valley owes a good deal to a heated debate that raged among noted scientists and scholars of the late 1800s. The debate began in 1872 with C. C. Abbott's [*] contention that "Paleo lithic" implements were to be found in the "Trenton gravels," a coarse cobble layer of glacial outwash occurring in the terraces of the Delaware River. Although we now know that Abbott was wrong and that the "Trenton gravel implements" date no earlier than about 800 B.C., the debate he engendered sparked considerable interest in the prehistory of the Middle Atlantic region.

The archaeological research that followed Abbott's lead resulted in the discovery of a number of prehistoric sites throughout the Delaware Valley; however, no undisturbed prehistoric site has yet been excavated in Philadelphia or its immediate environs.[†] And, given the amount of development that has occurred there over the years, it seems somewhat unlikely that one ever will be. Thus, the prehistory of the Philadelphia region must be largely inferred from the results of excavations in the surrounding areas of Pennsylvania, New Jersey, and Delaware. These investigations have contributed to an impressive,

* Charles Conrad Abbott, M. D. (1843–1919), gained archaeological experience as field assistant to Harvard's Frederick Putnam. From 1889 to 1893, Abbott was curator of American prehistoric archaeology at the University of Pennsylvania Museum of Archaeology and Palaeontology (now Archaeology and Anthropology) and an ardent investigator of early human evidence in the Delaware Valley.
† The largest assemblage of prehistoric artifacts found to date in Philadelphia proper surfaced during excavations near Front and Dock streets in 1984 (see chapter 5, "Front and Dock Streets"). The evidence suggested that the earth containing the artifacts had been dug up from a prehistoric camp in the vicinity—probably one devoted to food procurement—and redeposited to fill a swamp in the 1700s.

and still growing, body of knowledge, including the delineation of five cultural-chronological traditions for the prehistoric inhabitants of the Middle Atlantic region. Table 1.3 summarizes some of the characteristics of these traditions.

The Paleo Amerindian Tradition (ca. 12,000 B.C.–7500 B.C.)

The Paleo Amerindian tradition is the earliest widespread cultural tradition for which there is abundant evidence all over North, Middle, and South America. Artifacts of this tradition are, however, uncommon in the Delaware Valley, primarily because the Paleo Amerindian groups in this area were small. Another reason for the scarcity of these artifacts is that thousands of years ago, melting ice from the receding Wisconsin glacier left many Paleo Amerindian river sites in the region well under water or buried in coastal or riverine marshes. In those sites that still exist on land, later depositional and erosional processes have tended either to wash away the evidence or to bury it, often deep beneath the surface. The best evidence is in cave deposits, but these are rare.

The Paleo Amerindian's hallmark, shown in Figure 1.4, is the fluted spear point, a lance-shaped projectile point that characteristically has a lengthwise groove, or flute, extending from the base on each of its faces. This artifact, as well as others of the Paleo Amerindian tradition, has often been found with the bones of large mammals, particularly with the bones of bison and mammoth in the West. For this reason, archaeologists have concluded that Paleo Amerindians were big-game hunters who lived in

tightly knit, highly mobile groups, geared to the seasonal pursuit of herds of large mammals. Although site investigations have shown that the Paleo Amerindians also exploited other biotic resources, such as grapes, berries, and fish (Kauffman and Dent 1982; McNett 1985), big game was their prime source of food. In the postglacial climate of the Philadelphia region some 10,000 to 12,000 years ago, where luxuriant bosks coexisted with waning taiga, the Paleo Amerindians would have done their best big-game hunting and foraging in the tall grass of the green savannas and in the burgeoning evergreen forests of the Wissahickon and the Brandywine.

For making their fluted spear points and other stone tools, the Paleo Amerindians of the Middle Atlantic region favored jasper and chert, which can be shaped by chipping. They either quarried these materials at outcrops or gathered them in pebble form from streams and rivers. By far the most heavily utilized outcrops of jasper in the area were the Macungie and Vera Cruz quarries near Allentown, Pennsylvania. Here the jasper was underground, and the aboriginals were forced to dig for it (Deisher 1933; Schrabisch 1937; Roberts, Hoffman, Meyer, and Cosans 1982; Anthony and Roberts 1987).

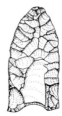

Figure 1.4.

Fluted spear points of the Paleo Amerindian tradition. (From Witthoft 1952)

And dig they did: great pits, some as deep as 20 feet, dot the landscape at Vera Cruz and other quarries in the area. After mining the jasper, the aboriginals reduced it to smaller pieces and transported the pieces to their campsites throughout the Middle Atlantic region. There they fashioned the jasper into projectile points, knives, and other tools. As recently as four or five centuries ago, the descendants of the Paleo Amerindians who first discovered and quarried these outcrops were still making heavy use of them.

While Paleo Amerindian sites in the Delaware Valley are not numerous, many a fluted point has turned up here at sites where only a scatter of other lithic evidence—if any at all—remains. These numerous isolated finds have led at least one authority (Mason 1959) to speculate that Paleo Amerindians preferred to live in the major river valleys, roaming the uplands mainly to hunt. Most of what we know about the earliest inhabitants of the Middle Atlantic does not, however, come from such isolated finds, but from the few known and excavated sites in the region, among them the Shawnee Minisink site near Stroudsburg, Pennsylvania.*

Located on the first floodplain terrace at the confluence of the Delaware River and Brodhead Creek, the Shawnee Minisink site is just at the edge of the last Wisconsin glacial advance. Radiocarbon dates derived from the site and from nearby bogs indicate that the glacier probably began to melt and retreat by about 13,000 B.C. and that it was not until about 8600 B.C. that Paleo Amerindi-

* Another significant Paleo Amerindian site in the Middle Atlantic is the Shoop site near Harrisburg, Pennsylvania. Excavated by John Witthoft (1952), it was the focus of a study by Kurt Carr (1989) some 35 years later.

ans set up their camp at the site. The camp, now buried 8 to 10 feet deep, was situated on fine alluvial sand deposited as overbank sediment during flooding. The sand itself sat directly on top of coarser gravel laid down as a direct result of deglaciation (Crowl and Stuckenrath 1977:219–21; McNett 1985).

The Shawnee Minisink site yielded over seventy-five stone tools, including knives, scrapers, hammer stones, and an anvil stone; surprisingly, only one fluted spear point appeared (McNett, McMillan, and Marshall 1977:293–96; McNett 1985:88). Most of the tools were made of a black flint quarried from local outcrops or gathered from the beds of nearby streams. While the black flint is of good quality, it is odd that the inhabitants of the Shawnee Minisink site did not make any great use of the exceptionally good jasper available at the quarries of Macungie and Vera Cruz, less than twenty miles away.

The most significant finds at the Shawnee Minisink site were floral and faunal data that give us a glimpse of the lifeways and diet of the Paleo Amerindian. Much of this evidence came from a hearth radiocarbon dated to 8460 B.C. Although 1,427 seeds were recovered, only 76 could be definitely dated to the Paleo Amerindian period; among them were grape, hawthorn plum, smartweed, blackberry, and hackberry seeds (McNett 1985:67; Kauffman and Dent 1982:10). The growing requirements of these plants and the time of year they are available suggest that the Paleo Amerindians occupied the site between May and November and that the site was quite damp. The site also yielded a few small fishbones. Together, these data not only give us an insight into how Paleo Amerindians east of the Mississippi lived, they

also provide one of the first glimpses of what they ate other than the meat of big game.

The Archaic Tradition (ca. 7500 B.C.–1000 B.C.)

As the ice sheets continued retreating and the climate grew warmer, the big game the Paleo Amerindians had hunted grew scarcer. In the new climate, smaller, modern fauna such as white-tailed deer, bear, and turkey began moving north into the Middle Atlantic, and nuts, berries, herbs, and other foodstuffs became more plentiful. The changed lifeway that came about as human beings adapted to these altered conditions is known as the Archaic tradition.

The Archaic tradition has no uniform culture type, for as groups in different habitats adjusted to different conditions, they developed different cultural traits. Groups who lived along the coast adapted to maritime resources; those in upland environments adapted to resources and conditions at high altitudes and in dense forest. The evidence from southeastern Pennsylvania indicates that a favored habitat of the Archaic people in this region was the Piedmont, where they seem to have gravitated more toward small tributary streams than to the major rivers. Here, they clustered on upland slopes adjacent to springheads, as well as at the base of slopes next to swampy floodplains (Custer and Wallace 1982:154).

In the Philadelphia region, as elsewhere, most Archaic groups probably lived in widely scattered, migratory bands, similar to those of the Paleo Amerindians. Although in this respect their lifestyle resembled that of the Paleo Amerindians, it was somewhat

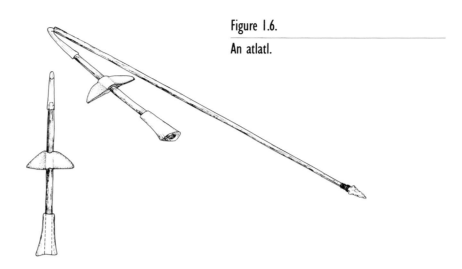

Figure 1.6.

An atlatl.

Figure 1.5.

Diorama of an autumn camp of Archaic hunters and gatherers. (Courtesy of the State Museum of Pennsylvania)

more sedentary. With more floral and faunal resources available, they depended less on unrestricted wandering in pursuit of big game and more on seasonally timed food-gathering activities. Large base camps were generally occupied year-round, but the number of people present at the base camp varied with the season. During the late spring, some of the group left the base camp for fishing camps located near spawning areas, and in the early autumn they traveled to nut-gathering and hunting camps, no doubt much like the one shown in Figure 1.5. As the bow and arrow were not yet known, Archaic man probably hunted with a spear and a spear-thrower, known as an atlatl. The atlatl (Figure 1.6) was made of wood or bone and gave the weapon more thrust and killing power. Evidence of Archaic house structures is quite rare, but the few traces that have been found suggest the houses were circular and consisted of sapling frameworks covered with bark or other vegetal matter (Kent 1980:25).

Most of what we know about the Archaic people derives from analyses of the artifacts they chipped and occasionally ground out of stone, for, except for rock hearths, very little else of their culture has survived. The chipped-stone tools include notched and stemmed spear points (Figure 1.7), drills, knives, and scrapers; the ground-stone implements include axes, soapstone cooking vessels, and mortars and pestles. At one Archaic site in the Delaware Valley—Raccoon Point, two miles southwest of Bridgeport, New Jersey—numerous small blades were found in association with soapstone vessels. The occupants of the site might have used these "micro-blades" to inscribe their soapstone vessels with stylized decorations (Kier and Calverly 1957:97).

This evidence, together with a number of storage pits found at the site, suggests that toward the end of the Archaic period, the aboriginals' lifestyle was becoming more sedentary.*

The Transitional or Terminal Archaic Tradition (ca. 1800 B.C.–800 B.C.)

Chronologically overlapping with the Archaic Tradition is another cultural tradition, usually referred to as the Transitional but increasingly as the Terminal Archaic. The cultural changes evident in this tradition came about, at least in part, because of changed environmental conditions. By about 1000 B.C., an essentially modern climate had been established, and floral and faunal resources were more abundant and diverse than ever before. Transitional people thus had a wider choice of subsistence strategies than their Archaic ancestors had, and they appear to have been more specialized. Their strategies varied somewhat from region to region, depending on landscape and ecological conditions.

The distinctive artifacts of the Transitional people include broad, leaf-shaped spear points, some quite asymmetrical (Figure 1.8). The pur-

* Two other places in the Delaware Valley that have yielded evidence of Archaic people are the Byram site near Stockton, New Jersey (reported by Kinsey 1975), where the evidence indicated considerable variation in tool-making style and technology, and the Bachman site, located about two miles south of the confluence of the Delaware and Lehigh rivers. The latter site, investigated by Anthony and Roberts (1987), was noteworthy for its stratigraphic integrity. Whereas most prehistoric sites in the Delaware Valley were occupied again and again by different generations of prehistoric people, the Bachman site was apparently occupied only about 1800 B.C., and it may then have been occupied for only a few days (Anthony and Roberts 1987:95, 159–60).

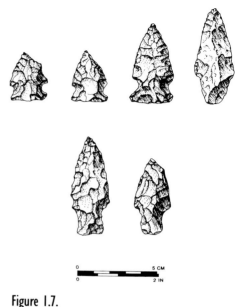

Figure 1.7.

Notched and stemmed spear points of the Archaic tradition. (Courtesy of John Milner Associates)

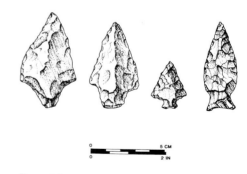

Figure 1.8.

Transitional projectile points. (Courtesy of John Milner Associates)

pose of the large size and flat shape of the spear points may have been to facilitate resharpening, which would have prolonged the life of the tool. On the other hand, the spear points may have been made that way because they were specialized tools used to hook or spear fish. Whatever the purpose of the size and shape of the spear points, the Transitional people almost always made them and other kinds of lithic tools from rhyolite—the volcanic, chippable equivalent of granite—or from yellow jasper, much of the latter quarried at Vera Cruz and Macungie.

Another of the Transitional people's specialties was the manufacture of soapstone bowls. The Transitional people of the Middle Atlantic quarried most of their soapstone near Christiana in Lancaster County, Pennsylvania. They may, however, also have availed themselves of a fine soapstone outcrop on the western bluffs of the Schuylkill River, north of Mill Creek just outside Philadelphia.

Although Transitional people had some small camps in upland areas where they went to hunt and gather food (Custer and Wallace 1982:158–59), most of their camps were, like the one shown in Figure 1.9, located along major rivers, and as they traveled by canoe or dugout, it seems likely that they were more mobile than their Archaic predecessors. But aside from this riverine adaptation and their distinctive spear points, the Transitional people seem generally to have continued the way of life the Archaic people had begun nearly 6,000 years earlier. A truly sedentary lifestyle had not yet been adopted.

The best-known Transitional site in the Delaware Valley is Miller Field in Warren County, New Jersey. Among the archaeological finds here were numerous hearths, pits, soap-

stone cooking vessels, projectile points, and other tools (Kraft 1970). The Byram site near Stockton, New Jersey, has also yielded a number of artifacts from this period (Kinsey 1975), as well as some from the Archaic period.

The Early-Middle Woodland Tradition (ca. 800 B.C.–A.D. 1000)

About 1000 B.C., the inhabitants of the vast, heavily wooded lands east of the Mississippi began experiencing some profound changes in their lifeways. Three important new themes became evident: the development of horticulture, village life, and ceramics. The cultural expressions of these themes by the people of the Allegheny Plateau and the Ohio Valley are quite well known and chronologically well defined, but their expression by the people of the Middle Atlantic is less well known, and their chronology is uncertain. For these reasons, rather than being known as Early and Middle Woodland people, as their contemporaries to the west are, the people of the Middle Atlantic are usually lumped together in an Early-Middle Woodland continuum.

Whereas horticulture and village life were apparently quite slow to develop in the Middle Atlantic, the manufacture of ceramics was quick to materialize, and it no doubt represents one of the first truly significant technological revolutions in North America. Some of the first ceramics to appear in the region—called Marcey Creek wares because of the creek where they were first found—were relatively crude, thick-walled, flat-bottomed vessels, quite similar in shape and size to the soapstone bowls carved by the Transitional people. In-

terestingly, the clay used in these early ceramic wares was tempered with crushed soapstone, which probably came from soapstone bowls that had been accidentally broken. The potters may have hoped that the soapstone, which did not fracture in fire and which distributed heat so well and so evenly, would impart its useful qualities to their experimental products. The crude Marcey Creek wares gave way in the later years of the Early-Middle Woodland period to more refined, conical-shaped vessels with much thinner walls and surface decorations (Figure 1.10). The decorations were made by pressing cord- or net-wrapped paddles into the clay while it was still wet, and their purpose may have been more than ornamental—the decorations made the surface of the vessel virtually skid-proof.

Few Early-Middle Woodland groups lived far from major bodies of water, and the Early-Middle Woodland folk in the Delaware Valley were no exception. Here, like their Transitional predecessors, they tended to cluster near the major river bottoms and in the adjacent uplands, but sites near swampy floodplains, sinkholes, and springheads were also common (Custer and Wallace 1982:158–59). They apparently lived in small family groups in compact settlements that consisted of only a few houses. The limited nature of these settlements indicates they were not truly villages, as were sites of the same period in the Ohio Valley. The Early-Middle Woodland people of the Delaware Valley also do not seem to have been as horticulturally advanced as their contemporaries in western Pennsylvania and Ohio; very few deep storage pits of the Early-Middle Woodland era have been found in this region. The few pits or subsurface basins that

Figure 1.9.

Diorama of a Transitional riverine camp, with soapstone bowl in the foreground. (Courtesy of the State Museum of Pennsylvania)

Figure 1.10.

Ceramic vessels from the later years of the Early-Middle Woodland period: *a*, cord-impressed; *b*, net-impressed. (From Cross 1956)

a

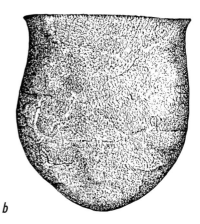

b

have been found here have been small, shallow, and saucer-shaped.

Not surprisingly, since Early-Middle Woodland people relied on major waterways for their subsistence, sites of this period are fairly plentiful in the Delaware Valley. Like sites of other prehistoric periods in this region, however, these sites are plagued with the stratigraphic intermixing of artifacts from different periods. Among the best-defined contexts of the Early-Middle Woodland period in the Delaware Valley are those from the Faucett site near Bushkill, Pennsylvania (Kinsey 1975), and those from the Abbott Farm site near Trenton, New Jersey (Cross 1956; Cavallo 1983–84; Stewart 1982). The picture of the Early-Middle Woodland period that has emerged from investigations of these sites is of a people who were gradually shifting from a semimigratory existence that relied on foraging to a more sedentary lifestyle that relied on a riverine-based hunting and fishing economy.

The Late Woodland Tradition (ca. A.D. 1000–A.D. 1550)

The Late Woodland period that began toward the end of the first millenium A.D. was to be the culmination of at least ten millenia of prehistoric Amerindian adaptations to environmental changes. The period probably came to an end in the Delaware Valley some time around 1550, when, in the wake of Giovanni da Verrazano's exploration of the Middle Atlantic seacoast in 1524, European traders and trappers began making their appearance in the region. At this time, the prehistoric inhabitants of the region emerged into the historical record as the Lenape.

The remains of the Late Woodland

Figure 1.11.

Munsee longhouses of the Late Woodland period. (From Kraft 1975)

people of the Delaware Valley far outnumber those of earlier inhabitants, and they indicate that by the time this era began, foraging bands were well established throughout the Philadelphia region. Well before the European settlers arrived in the early 1600s and began clearing the forest for agriculture, the Amerindians themselves had already cleared scattered tracts of land around their summer fishing stations along the Delaware (Barnes 1968; Becker 1988). The forest that greeted the first Europeans was nonetheless very dense, though essentially of the same composition as today's.

The Late Woodland people of the Delaware Valley hunted in the uplands of the interior during the winter, but during the warm months they gathered at sites at the mouths of rivers, where their ancestors had lived

before them (Custer and Wallace 1982:159). Usually, these sites were small hamlets, and since they show no signs of stockades, ditches, earth embankments, or other defensive works we can assume the people who occupied them, unlike their Iroquois neighbors to the north, engaged in little warfare. The dwellings in which they lived—wickiups consisting of bark-covered frameworks made of arched saplings—were generally not tightly clustered, but distributed about the hamlet in such a way as to suggest individual plots or properties. These shelters were relatively small and probably housed single families. None were as large as the Munsee houses depicted in Figure 1.11, which were similar in many ways to Iroquois longhouses.

The stone hoes, mortars, pestles, and milling stones that appear in abundance at Late Woodland sites suggest that plants gathered or gardened were an important part of the diet of the prehistoric inhabitants of the Delaware Valley. In the spring, they planted maize, as well as beans, pumpkins, squash, and perhaps sunflowers. Although they apparently raised dogs for food, they do not seem to have engaged in animal husbandry.

The Late Woodland people continued to hunt and fish and to gather wild foodstuffs. Shellfish—particularly the freshwater mussel—was an important part of their diet. For hunting, they used the bow and arrow, a significant technological improvement over the spear and atlatl. The projectile points on their arrows were small and triangular, rather than stemmed or notched. They also apparently sometimes hunted with bola stones— small, heavy balls in pouches secured to the ends of strong cords. They may have used these devices when they hunted marsh birds or some species of small game. For fishing, they usually used nets (see Kingsley et al. [in preparation]).

The pottery of the Late Woodland people was generally much more refined and sophisticated than that of their ancestors. Most vessels had simple, everted lips or high, decorative collars. All pieces were round-bottomed, so they would have had to be supported by rocks or set in sand when in use. Although many pottery vessels and other goods have been found in Late Woodland burials at sites in Ohio, only an occasional piece of pottery or clay tobacco pipe has been found in graves of this period in the Delaware Valley. The funeral practices of the Late Woodland people in this area appear to have been fairly simple. They built no elaborate mortuary structures, as their Hopewellian predecessors did in Ohio, but instead buried their dead in tightly flexed positions, similar to the fetal position, in shallow graves just large enough to hold the body.

Two Delaware Valley sites have contributed significantly to our understanding of the late Woodland people.* At the Abbott Farm site, floral and faunal remains and different types of camps of the Late Woodland period suggested diversified subsistence modes and a complex social organization (Stewart, Hummer, and Custer 1986; Stewart 1986a, 1986b, 1987). Goods found buried in one of the graves at the Abbott Farm suggested that the person buried there had been of high status, thus supporting the notion of a ranked society (Cross 1956).

At the Harry's Farm site in Warren County, New Jersey, evidence dating from the thirteenth and fourteenth centuries indicates that a diversified subsistence pattern had developed among the ancestors of the Munsee, the northern neighbors of the Lenape. They relied not only on the wild game of the forest but also on riverine resources and agriculture. The site yielded over 270 food-storage pits, postholes delineating the shapes of five houses, and a host of tools, among them projectile points, knives, scrapers, netsinkers, pestles, milling stones, and hoes (Kraft 1975). Clearly, by the 1300s, the Late Woodland inhabitants of Harry's Farm had settled into a fairly comfortable, sedentary lifestyle very different from that of the people in the Philadelphia area. Seven human burials of the Late Woodland period were also found at Harry's Farm. All the bodies were in a flexed position, and most were facing southwest (Kraft 1975:89), an orientation slightly different from that used by the historically documented Lenape, who believed that the west is the direction in which both the sun and the dead ultimately go.

* Two other important Late Woodland sites in the Delaware Valley are the Overpeck site near Kintnersville, Pennsylvania (Forks of the Delaware Chapter 1980), and the Lambertville site in Lambertville, New Jersey (Struthers and Roberts 1982).

THE LENAPE OF THE HISTORIC CONTACT PERIOD *

The Historic Contact period, the interval during which the Amerindians of the Eastern Woodlands first came into contact with Europeans, was a time of turmoil. The Lenape of the

* This section edited by Marshall J. Becker.

Delaware Valley, all too willing to coexist peacefully with the Europeans, found themselves between European traders and Susquehannock merchants to the west. Thus, materialism, greed, and power marked the prevailing trade system that confronted the

Lenape, a system in which they apparently opted not to participate to any great extent.

The Historic Contact period began sometime after 1524, when Verrazano, exploring the American coast in the caravel *Dauphine*, saw and

Figure 1.12.

Cultural boundaries of the Lenape, "Jerseys," and Munsee. (From Becker 1990b)

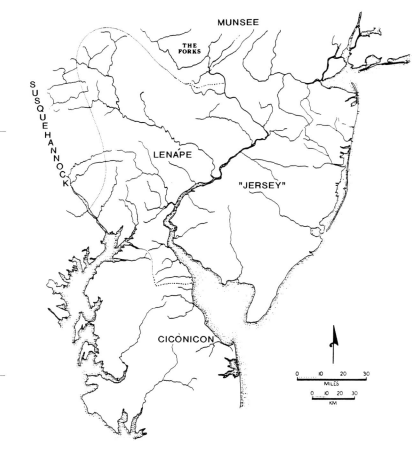

Figure 1.13.

Presumed sites of Lenape settlements in the Philadelphia region. (From Mercer 1923; Donehoo 1928; Cacchione and Mion 1934; Weslager 1956; Shoemaker n.d.; Becker 1976; Bucks County Conservancy 1979; Wolf and Snyder 1982; Kent, Rice, and Ota 1981; Auerbach and Marshall 1983)

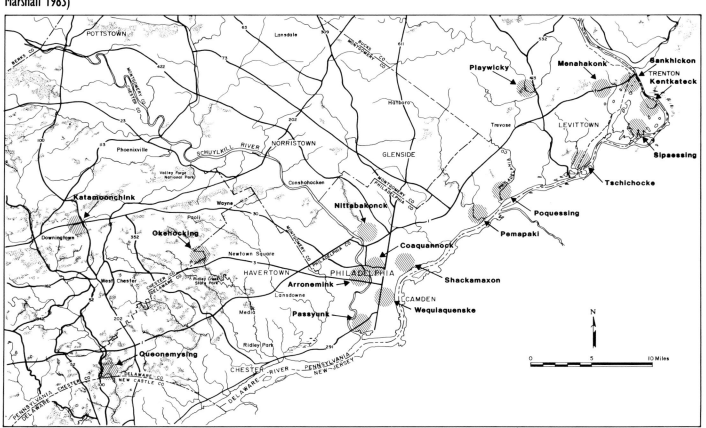

described the Amerindians of the Middle Atlantic region (Kraft 1974: 1). His discovery signaled the beginning of vast changes in the lifeways of the Lenape that had begun over 10,000 years before in the Eastern Woodlands, not the least of which resulted from the introduction of decimating European diseases. By 1750, after more than 200 years of accommodation to the Europeans, the Lenape bands had relocated to the west, where they continued to maintain their traditional lifestyle.

Lenape Lifeways

At the start of the Historic Contact period, the dozen or so Lenape bands in the Philadelphia region occupied the west banks of the Delaware River, from Old Duck Creek in northern Delaware up to Tohickon Creek. They called themselves the Lenape or Renappi, meaning "the people." Because of their ties to the river named after Lord De La Warr, the first British colonial governor of Virginia, the Europeans called them (as well as the Munsee and various peoples of New Jersey) the *Delaware*—a term scholars now rarely use in reference to the Lenape, particularly when referring to these groups before their migrations in the 1700s. William Penn, who had his first glimpse of the Lenape in 1682, described them as:

. . . generally tall, straight, well built . . . ; they tread strong and clever, and mostly walk with a lofty chin. . . . Of complexion . . . swarthy. Their eye is little and black . . . and the noses of several of them have . . . much of the Roman. . . . Boys . . . go a-fishing till ripe for the woods, which is about fifteen; then they hunt; and after having given some proofs of their manhood by a good return of skins, they may marry, else it is a shame to think of a wife. The girls . . . hoe the ground, plant corn, and carry burdens. . . . The wives are the true servants of their husbands. Otherwise the men are very affectionate to them. . . . If a European comes to see them, or calls for lodging . . . they give him the best place and first cut. If they come to visit us [and] you give them anything to eat or drink, [that is] well, for they will not ask; and, be it little or much, if it be with kindness, they are well pleased. . . . In liberality they excel; nothing is too good for their friend. . . . Light of heart, strong affections, but soon spent, the most merry creatures that live, [they] feast and dance perpetually; they never have much, nor want much. . . . In *sickness*, impatient to be cured, and for it give anything, especially for their children, to whom they are extremely natural. (Soderlund et al. 1983:312–15)

Penn was also much impressed with the language of the Lenape, which he thought "lofty, yet narrow, . . . like shorthand in writing; one word serves in the place of three. . . . Not a language spoken in Europe . . . has words of more sweetness or greatness" (Soderlund et al. 1983:312–13). The Lenape, in fact, spoke the "Unami" dialect, closely related to the language spoken by the "Jerseys" in southern New Jersey. Today the terms "Munsee" and "Unami" refer not just to languages, but also to the peoples who spoke them.* Munsee speakers lived north of the Raritan River in New Jersey; only the Lenape spoke Unami (Figure 1.12). The area around the Forks of the Delaware, near Easton, Pennsylvania, was a "buffer zone," where both Munsee and Lenape bands exploited the natural resources (Becker 1983b).

Each Lenape band comprised an extended family consisting of, at most, thirty or forty people (Becker 1989). Each band inhabited a specific territory along a creek or river; the band collectively inherited its rights to

* Since it was apparently the Unami-speaking bands who referred to themselves as the Lenape or Renappi, those terms should technically be used only in reference to them (Kraft 1984:1).

this land from the previous generation (Becker 1984a). Among the many Lenape groups was the Brandywine band which moved its summer station from Wilmington to White Clay Creek in Chester County about 1660. Later they moved to Queonemysing at the Great Bend of Brandywine Creek in Delaware County. The Okehocking had their summer stations along Ridley Creek (Goddard 1978:215; Becker 1986). Other bands lived along Neshaminy Creek, just north of the future city, as well as at Passyunk, Shackamaxon, and other settlements, within or near the present city limits (Dunn and Dunn 1982:3). Figure 1.13 shows the presumed locations of Lenape sites in the Philadelphia region during the Historic Contact period. Appendix 1.A provides a description of these, as well as a listing of other Lenape place names.

Leadership and Livelihood

The political organization of the Lenape was not strongly defined. Each band had several leaders, known as sachems, but their roles seem to have been largely advisory. They apparently had little power other than the personal power of persuasion. After 1750 these sachems designated successors through matrilineal reckoning, thereby ensuring an unbroken succession of titular heads. All important decisions were made by a council, a nonelected, loosely defined body consisting of all the old and wise men in the group (Goddard 1978:216; Weslager 1985:21). With no strong, centralized leadership, the Lenape bands tended to function quite independently of each other. Some of their endeavors, however, such as hunting drives and diplomatic relations with the neighboring Iroquois or

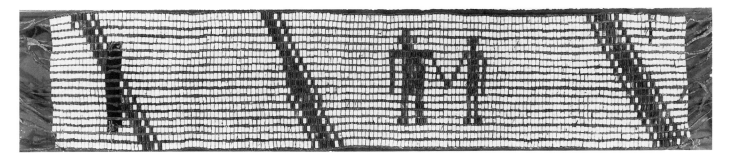

Figure 1.14.

Wampum belt made of clam-shell beads and leather, ca. 1682. According to legend, William Penn negotiated a treaty with the Lenape at Shackamaxon, north of what were then the limits of Philadelphia, where Kensington now stands, in November 1682, and this belt was the Lenape's gift to Penn on that occasion. (Courtesy of the Historical Society of Pennsylvania)

the Europeans, did require considerable cooperation among bands.

For their subsistence, the Lenape exploited a wide variety of natural resources (Barnes 1968). From ca. 1640 to 1660 the Lenape grew corn for sale to the colonists, thereby creating a cash crop within their foraging economy (Becker 1985). The Lenape also grew tobacco, beans, squash, and watermelon to supplement their diet of nuts, berries, fruits, and other wild foodstuffs that they gathered in the forests. During the fall, the men turned from fishing to hunting, while each spring and summer they again turned their attention to fishing. Although they hunted primarily with bows and arrows, they also often had large-scale hunting drives and fire surrounds in which they bagged different kinds of game; these undertakings sometimes required the cooperative efforts of many people. For fishing, they used bows and arrows, hooks, weirs, small nets, and large seines (Goddard 1978:216–17).

The Lenape's technological pursuits involved a wide array of tools, ranging from large axes and knives to small drills and needles. Although they chipped or carved their tools mainly from stone and bone, the Lenape made good use of many other materials as well. From clay, they made pots with round or conical bottoms, as well as pipes for tobacco; from gourds, they carved bowls and ladles; out of grasses and rushes, they wove baskets; and from hemp, nettles, and tree bark, they created cordage (Becker 1990b).

The Lenape used "wampum" as a type of currency (Becker 1980c), threading shell beads together to form belts for use as gifts (Figure 1.14). In addition to being given as a gift, wampum was also used as restitution; a Lenape who had offended someone routinely presented the injured party with an offering of wampum (Weslager 1985:23). According to William Penn, the restitution was "proportioned to the quality of the offense or person injured, or of the sex they are of. For in case they kill a woman, they pay double; . . . the reason [being] that she breeds children, which men can not do." Penn added that "it is rare that they fall out, if sober; and if drunk they forgive it, saying, it was the drink, and not the man, that abused them" (Soderlund et al. 1983:316).

While artifacts of stone, bone, clay, and shell are found in abundance at Lenape sites, so too are artifacts that bespeak the European presence—as well as changes in the Lenape way of life. When the Europeans arrived, they created a ready and lucrative market for the furs of the animals the Lenape hunted and trapped in the woods; beaver pelts were particularly highly prized. In exchange for the furs, the Europeans provided the Lenape with guns, powder, bullets, liquor, brass and iron tools, clothing, and other items of European manufacture (Goddard 1978:220–21). Evidence of this bartering still turns up on Lenape sites today.

Shelters

The structures in which the Lenape lived closely resembled those of their Late Woodland forebears. These were small versions of Munsee houses, which were frameworks of upright poles covered with sheets of bark tied or hung over the framework so that they overlapped like shingles or clapboards (Figure 1.15). For added insulation, they sometimes hung more bark sheeting inside the structure. The houses were often oval in shape, and their roofs were probably pitched or arched. The typical house was low, no more than 20 feet wide, and less than 100 feet long, with a door at either end. It was often occupied by as many as seven or eight related families. Inside, it was dark for lack of windows and probably smoky as well, for the smoke from the fires of several families found its way uncertainly to a small opening in the center of the roof; this opening ran the length of the structure. Each family apparently occupied a separate compartment with its own cooking hearth. The compartments, furnished with woven reed or bark mats—some of which were elaborately decorated—were relatively comfortable (Goddard 1978:218–19; Weslager 1985:11–12). Nearby their houses, usually next to a stream, they had "sweathouses" for bathing. Ultimately, under the influence of the Europeans, the simple structures, like their builders, changed, and by the end of the eighteenth century many Lenape were living in log houses modeled after those that Swedish settlers had by then built up and down the Delaware Valley.

The precise nature of Lenape settlements is somewhat unclear, and archaeological evidence is meager. Those areas attractive to the Lenape because of their natural features were equally attractive to the early settlers and to later inhabitants as well, and for precisely the same reasons. Making the Lenape sites even more attractive to the early settlers was the fact that the Lenape or their forebears had already cleared them, no small task in the Eastern Woodlands (Russell 1981).

What we do know about Amerindian settlements indicates that the Munsee, north of the Raritan River, fortified theirs with stockades like those shown in Figure 1.15, but there is little evidence to suggest that the Lenape bands to the south did the same (Weslager 1985:12). While the Lenape probably spent much of the year in semi-permanent settlements where they fished and gathered food, they spent the winter months dispersed in the forests and engaged in hunting (Becker 1988). Figure 1.16 shows the re-creation of a typical Lenape summer station. These settlements have traditionally been called villages, but since they were quite small, with populations of no more than a few dozen people (Becker 1989), they were probably more like hamlets (Goddard 1978:218–19).

Figure 1.15.

Diorama of Munsee houses. The stockade in the background was typical of Munsee settlements but not of Lenape. (Courtesy of the State Museum of Pennsylvania)

Figure 1.16.

Diorama of a Lenape summer station along the banks of a major river. Cornstalks appear at the river's edge. (Courtesy of the State Museum of Pennsylvania)

The Advent of the Europeans

As suggested by the lack of stockades around their hamlets, the Lenape seem to have been a relatively peaceful lot. In this they differed from the Munsee, who had fortified their settlements against their northern neighbors, the Iroquois, even before the early 1600s brought the first waves of European colonists. A good deal of the friction and bloodshed that occurred after the Historic Contact period began was occasioned by the fur trade, and most of it took place in Munsee and Iroquois territory.

The majority of the first European settlers in the Delaware Valley were

Dutch and Swedes. By the mid-1600s they had purchased from the Lenape several tracts along the western shore of the Delaware. In the late 1600s, after the Dutch had overpowered the Swedes and the English had in turn overpowered the Dutch, the Lenape began feeling the pressure of colonization even more intensely, as William Penn, surveying his new city for the first time and finding it wanting, began negotiations to expand his holdings (Dunn and Dunn 1982:3, 5).

Penn acquired land from the Lenape by perfectly legal means, paying each Lenape band generous quantities of goods for their territories (Kent 1979; Becker 1984c). The Lenape's customs regarding land rights aided Penn in his quest. Not only did each band, or extended family, collectively inherit its rights to a specific drainage

along the Delaware or the Schuylkill from the previous generation, it also had the right to sell this land independently of other bands (Becker 1984c). It was this indigenous mechanism that allowed Penn to systematically purchase each Lenape tract.

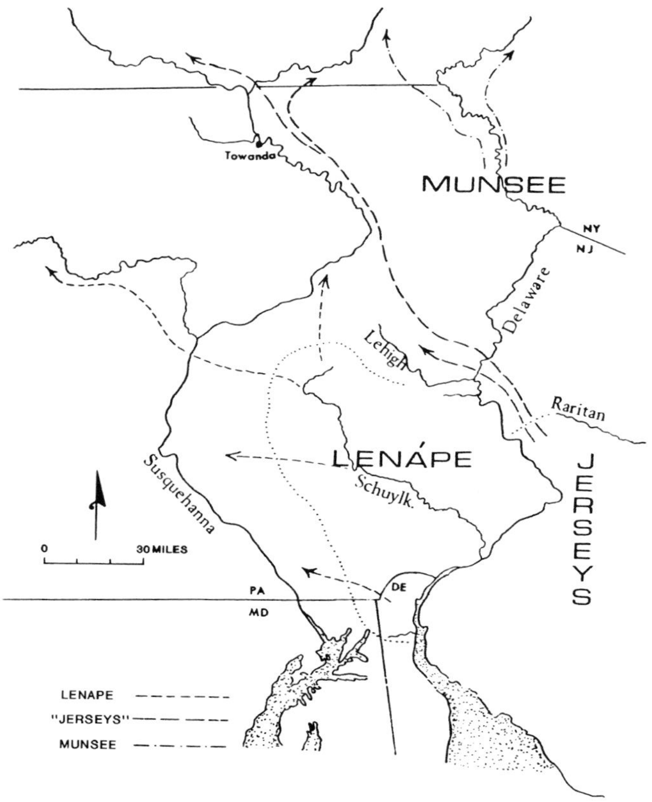

The Lenape Migration Westward: The Historical Documentation

What happened to the Lenape after they left their homeland, and just exactly what paths they took as they left it, has yet to be recovered from a mist of demographic confusion. We know that in the late 1600s and early 1700s the Lenape bands relocated their summer stations further up the streams along which they hunted. In the 1730s the traditional bands left the Delaware Valley and began a long westward trek, moving on to Paxtang on the Susquehanna River; some may even have settled as far west as the Allegheny and Ohio valleys (Goddard 1978:222). Figure 1.17 indicates the probable paths of the early phase of these westward migrations.

Through an exhaustive search of early deeds and indentures, Marshall Becker (1983a, 1983b, 1984b 1986, 1987a, 1987b) has been able to shed more light on the migrations of the Lenape and some of their neighbors. His research identified the movements of the Okehocking and the Brandywine, two bands that occupied the Philadelphia region before 1700 and who, like all the Lenape bands, ultimately succumbed to the pressures of colonization and began their westward migration in the 1730s.

The earliest traces of the Okehocking band indicate that before 1640 these people summered in the vicinity of Tinicum Island, near the conflu-

Figure 1.17.

Probable migration routes of the Lenape, "Jerseys," and Munsee. (From Becker 1990a)

ence of the Delaware and the Schuylkill. Between 1680 and 1700 they
were living well upstream along Ridley Creek, and in 1701 they were
deeded a parcel of land near the
source of Ridley Creek (Figure 1.18).
By 1737 members of the Okehocking
band were summering at Tulpehocken, and soon after they left the
Philadelphia region (Becker 1986).

The Brandywine band followed a
similar pattern. Before the 1600s they
summered at Hopokahocking, just
south of present-day Wilmington. By
1680 they were summering at the
Great Bend of Brandywine Creek,
northwest of Wilmington. Between
1700 and 1730 they were living at
various places even farther to the
northwest in Chester County, including areas near the present towns of
Northbrook and Embreeville (Becker
1984a:25). By the mid-1700s the
Brandywine, like the Okehocking,
were gone from the Philadelphia
region, leaving few traces behind. It is
believed that at this time both they
and the Okehocking, like other bands
of Pennsylvania Lenape, relocated
west to the Susquehanna Valley and
perhaps even beyond that into the
Monongahela River Valley.

While the Pennsylvania Lenape
were moving west into the Susquehanna drainage and beyond in the
mid-1700s, groups of New Jersey na-
tives were moving northwest into the
area around the Forks of the Delaware near Bethlehem, Pennsylvania.
On the basis of these differing movements, Becker (1983a:7–8, 1983b:
27) has questioned the traditional
view that the boundary between the
Munsee and Unami dialects ran east-
west at the Raritan River. His hypothesis is that the different paths the
migrating New Jersey and Pennsylvania Lenape took signifies a linguistic
boundary that ran north and south
along the Delaware.

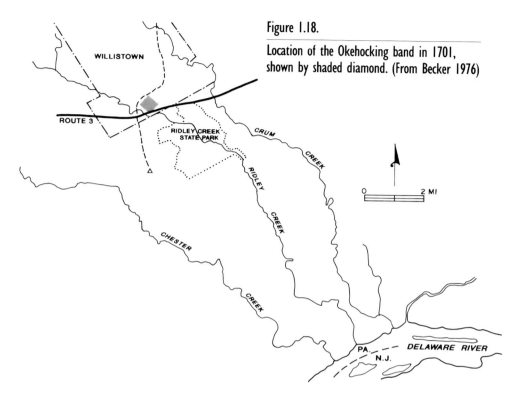

Figure 1.18.

Location of the Okehocking band in 1701,
shown by shaded diamond. (From Becker 1976)

The Material Culture of the Lenape: The Archaeological View

Although most Lenape hamlets in the
Philadelphia region may lie buried
beneath urban and suburban development, we have had occasional archaeological glimpses of Lenape
lifeways. Two sites that have produced
some remarkable data are the Broomall rockshelters, located about six
miles west of Philadelphia's city limits
in Delaware County, and the Montgomery site, located in the rolling
Piedmont uplands of Chester County.

The Broomall Rockshelters

In 1941, three avocational archaeologists working in an upland setting
near Broomall discovered two small
rockshelters that appeared to contain

Lenape remains (Mason 1947; Smith
1956). Fortunately, they enlisted the
aid of a trained investigator, Mary
Butler, who recorded (1947) the
burial of a woman about thirty-seven
years of age lying flexed on her right
side, her face to the rock wall of one
of the shelters. The woman's head
faced northwest, possibly reflecting
the Lenape belief that the dead, like
the sun, go west. Her bones rested on
bedrock, which was about 10 centimeters below the surface. She had
been about 5 feet 3 inches tall, and
indicative of her short and strenuous
life was the fact that she had not only
lost twenty-five teeth before her death
but had also suffered from arthritis of
the cervical and lumbar vertebrae—a
disease archaeologists have documented as common in hard-working
people of both the Lenape period and
prehistoric times.

Figure 1.19.

Objects from the Broomall rockshelter: *a* and *b,* knives; *c* and *d,* flake scrapers; *e,* grooved bannerstone fragment; *f,* pottery vessel with open mouth, conoidal base; *g,* pottery vessel with open mouth, flattened base; *h,* pottery vessel with constricted neck. (From Butler 1947)

No grave offerings surrounded the body, but it had been covered with a thin layer of white clay from a nearby streambed, apparently as a ceremonial gesture. Also suggestive of ceremony was a posthole about 30 centimeters in diameter. Situated about 50 centimeters beyond the skull, this hole had probably once held the Lenape equivalent of a tombstone, for, according to one historic account (Loskiel 1794), "at the head of the [Lenape] corpse . . . a tall post is erected, pointing out who is buried there. If the deceased was the Chief of a tribe or nation, this post is only neatly carved, but not painted. But if he were a captain, it is painted red and his head and glorious deeds are portrayed upon it." Further documentation of the Lenape "tombstone" is found in a description of the ceremonies that followed the 1762 burial of "a woman of highest rank and respectability, the wife of the valiant Delaware chief Schingask":

A painted post, on which were drawn various figures emblematic of the deceased's situation in life and of her having been the wife of a valiant warrior, was brought by two men and delivered to a third, a man of note . . . then while he held the post erect and properly situated, some women filled up the grave with hoes, and having placed dry leaves and pieces of bark over it, so that none of the fresh ground was visible, they retired. (Heckewelder 1819)

On the basis of these ethnohistoric accounts, Butler (1947:247) concluded that the body in the Broomall rockshelter was that of "an important [Lenape] woman, possibly a chieftain's wife, who had done plenty of hard work during her lifetime, but was laid away in the style befitting her rank." Although the rockshelter contained no grave offerings, it did contain a number of other artifacts that offered more proof of the woman's culture and its period. The earth fill around the grave yielded numerous items that had been chipped out of chert: 25 knives and blades, 10 drills, 5 scrapers, and 66 arrow points, most of them triangularly shaped. Other stone implements included a sandstone pestle, possibly used to pound corn in a stone mortar or one carved out of a tree trunk, as well as a number of hammer stones suitable for breaking animal bones for marrow, cracking nuts, or chipping other stone tools. The ceramic items included approximately 1,000 sherds from the same vessel; reconstruction of these pieces produced a deep, wide-mouthed bowl with a slightly constricted neck. The surface of the bowl had been roughened with a cord-wrapped stick. Other ceramic pieces, also obviously native-made, included five fragments of simple, undecorated clay tobacco pipes. Figure 1.19 shows some of the various objects found in the rockshelter.

Had these objects been all that the rockshelter produced, we could not be so certain that the woman had lived in historic times. However, it also yielded fragments of white-clay tobacco pipes that had clearly been made in England. The shapes of the pipes were characteristic of those made during the reign of William III, from 1689 to 1702, and the maker's marks "WE" and "LE"—the first incised on a pipe bowl and the latter on a stem fragment—indicated that the pipes had been made by the Evans family of Bristol, whose business prospered during this same period. Luellin Evans is first heard of in 1661, and William Evans in 1667; both would presumably still have been making pipes after 1689 (Butler 1947:250). The pipes were therefore strong evidence that the rockshelter was still in use sometime after 1661, providing a *terminus post quem* for the site, and they indicated that in all probability the woman had been buried after 1689.

The location of the Broomall rockshelters is somewhat puzzling, as it is far removed from the floodplain of a major river, where most Lenape made their homes. Butler (1947:247) hypothesized that the Lenape used the site as a temporary camp where they hunted or gathered food, and that the woman might have died in winter, when the rockshelter provided the only unfrozen piece of ground in

which she could be buried. As an alternate explanation of the rockshelter burial, Butler suggested that the survivors might have thought it afforded the body more protection from wild animals.

The Montgomery Site

Although the Montgomery site is not mentioned in any historical documents, its location in Chester County suggests that it may have been the last summer station of the Brandywine band before they moved west some time after 1730 (Becker 1984a:28). The site was first tested in 1952, when C. A. Weslager (1956:112–14) dug a pit near the trunk of a massive tree, which, according to an oral tradition, had marked a Lenape site. The only evidence Weslager uncovered was a single grave. The head of the deceased, which rested on two stones, pointed to the east so that it faced west. Encircling the neck were beads dating from about 1720 to 1740, which established a *terminus post quem* for the burial. The grave also contained 3 clay pipes, 2 gun flints, 61 glass beads, a brass button, and numerous pieces of rusted iron (Becker 1982).

In 1978, Becker (1980b, 1982) tested this site for the Pennsylvania State Museum. His excavations of several test units, as well as an extensive trench that passed directly over the burial that Weslager had discovered, produced evidence of twenty-two burials. Quite clearly, this had been a significant Lenape burial ground. Consultations with the late Nora Thompson Dean and other Lenape living in Oklahoma demonstrated the interest of these descendants in knowing more about this period of their history.

All of the graves were found to be regularly spaced and aligned east-west, with the head of the deceased pointing east. But though the grave-diggers had been orderly, they had not dug very deep, and the earth where the shadow graves lay had been plowed under many times over the years. Adding to the difficulty of obtaining information about the deceased was the highly acidic nature of the soil; preservation of the bones and other organic material was at best poor and at worst nonexistent (Becker 1982). Nonetheless, as shown in Table 1.4, Becker was able to identify the age and sex of some of the deceased.

Although the damaged and poorly preserved state of most of the remains precluded the possibility of determining the general health of the deceased, their teeth were in a fair state of preservation, and Becker was therefore able to make some observations about their dental health and diet. Only three or four individuals had dental caries, and only one showed signs of periodontal disease. Tooth wear in most was remarkably unpronounced, suggesting they had not eaten many "raw, slightly cooked, or gritty products" (Becker 1982).

The deepest grave found at the site, identified in Table 1.4, extended to about 75 centimeters from the surface. The additional labor needed to dig it could suggest that the individual buried there had been of high status. This grave was also the only one of the twenty-two to have been looted shortly after interment, perhaps suggesting that there had been something there worth looting, which would again indicate high status. On this basis, Becker (1982) speculated that the remains might be those of Checochnikon, an elder of the Brandywine Lenape. Whether that is so or not, whoever was buried there was

Table 1.4. Burials and associated artifacts from the Montgomery site.

Burial	Sex	Age	Artifacts/Inclusions
1	Male	23–25 years	61 glass beads encircling neck 3 clay pipes 2 gun flints 1 embossed brass button 2 rusted iron lumps, possibly a pocket knife and container 2 stone "pillows"
2	?	Infant	1 possible buckle or toy fragment
3	?	5 years	2 iron belt buckles at the waist 5 pewter shirt buttons 48 doughnut-shaped, "root-beer–colored" beads above head, as if on a hat 8 white, oval, ceramic beads, found above head
4	Male	19–25 years	30 spherical, root-beer–colored glass beads, encircling the neck 1 pewter pipe, at right shoulder 1 iron buckle, at the waist
5	Female (?)	Mature adult	None reported

6	?	9–10 years	8 objects found in a "pouch," long since disintegrated:
			    1 unidentified bronze object
			    2 bronze buckles
			    1 pewter or silver buckle
			    1 brass thimble
			    1 iron buckle
			    1 brass buckle
			    1 brass loop
			18 objects found in another "pouch," long since disintegrated:
			    2 brass thimbles
			    1 brass hawk bell
			    1 brass or copper button
			    1 buckle with zinc or silver coating
			    2 brass buckles
			    1 possible needle case
			    1 possible iron knife blade
			    8 small iron rings
			    Several pieces of cloth, possibly cotton
			403 beads found in a "pouch," long since disintegrated
			    Possible cordage
			103 red beads
			246 white beads
			44 black beads
			9 blue beads
			1 black wampum bead
			3 independent finds:
			    1 small glass bottle
			    2 large clusters of blue glass beads

7	?	7 years	1 possible shell bead or pendant 12 root-beer–colored beads, at neck 1 oval, blue glass bead (*Note:* This child was buried in a wooden coffin of yellow poplar and had a large stone placed at its head.)
8	Male (?)	Adult (possibly Checochnikon)	1 garment buckle 3 brass fasteners 1 pewter button 1 possible piece of leather (*Note:* This grave had been substantially looted shortly after its interment.)
9	?	Infant	None reported
10	?	4–5 years	16 magenta beads, encircling the neck 2 opaque, green, oval beads, encircling the neck
11	?	11–13 years	22 coffin nail fragments 1 iron blade with tang, possibly a knife 42 root-beer–colored beads, probably a necklace 8 blue, faceted, five-sided beads

continued next page

Burial	Sex	Age	Artifacts/Inclusions
12	?	Adolescent or young adult	56 small, circular, red beads, at waist, probably decoration on a disintegrated pouch (*Note:* This child was buried in a wooden coffin of yellow poplar.)
13	?	9–10 years	None reported (*Note:* Individual appeared to be resting on a large, flat rock. The burial also appeared to have been covered with sticks, bark, or logs.)
14	?	6 years	1 brass buckle, at waist (*Note:* A layer of organic material, probably a covering of blankets or robes, was overlying the interment.) 39 clear glass beads, encircling the neck 1 opaque black bead, tied with twine 22 clustered brass thimbles, pierced with cord 2 brass thimbles, one on either side of head (ear pendants?)
15	?	Adolescent	26 blue, faceted glass beads 1 jacknife with wooden handle

From Becker 1982.

most likely an important member of a Lenape band.

The contents of fifteen of the twenty-two graves are listed in Table 1.4. The numerous beads and other artifacts found in the eleven children's graves substantiate William Penn's observation that the Lenape were "extremely natural" to their children. Also of interest is the fact that only adolescents seem to have been buried in coffins (Becker 1984a:29). The artifacts also attest to a rather utilitarian outlook. Rather than being ceremonial offerings, they are for the most part objects that the deceased would doubtless have worn or used. Practically all the artifacts were of European origin, which established that these were burials of the Historic Contact period. However, the rich material culture of the Lenape, in wood, fiber, skin, fur, and quills, which continued into the twentieth century (Becker 1990b), unfortunately did not survive in these archaeological contexts.

One particularly interesting artifact—a silver brooch with a crowned-heart design—appeared in one of the graves. It bore the mark of Cesar Ghiselin, the first known American goldsmith, who plied his trade in the growing gold and silver market of early eighteenth-century Philadelphia until his death in 1733 (Becker 1984a: 29). How the brooch got from his hands into the Lenape grave we shall probably never know, but it is the earliest known piece of trade silver ever documented.

APPENDIX 1.A:

Lenape Settlements and Place Names

Documented Lenape Settlements

Historical documents (Lindestrom [1656] 1925; Heckewelder 1819) and secondary sources (Mercer 1923; Donehoo 1928; Cacchione and Mion 1934; Weslager 1956; Shoemaker n.d.; Rivinus 1965; Becker 1976; Bucks County Conservancy 1979; Kent, Rice, and Ota 1981; Wolf and Snyder 1982; Auerbach and Marshall 1983) indicate that during the Historic Contact period we can identify no fewer than seventeen different Lenape hamlets in the Philadelphia region. Although the precise locations of these hamlets remain elusive, Figure 1.13 shows their presumed sites. Listed by present-day counties, the hamlets are as follows:

Philadelphia County

Arronemink: Once located near the mouth of Mill Creek where it empties into the Schuylkill, Arronemink is variously referred to in historical documents as Oronnmink and Aroenemeck (Donehoo 1928:8).

Coaquannock: Coaquannock, meaning "Grove of Tall Pines," was apparently near Laurel Hill Cemetery, on the east bank of the Schuylkill a few miles upriver from the Philadelphia Museum of Art (Cacchione and Mion 1934).

Nittabakonck: Variously referred to as Nittabonck and Mittabakonck, this campsite or hamlet was on the southeast side of Wissahickon Creek at its juncture with the Schuylkill (Donehoo 1928:130; Cacchione and Mion 1934; Weslager 1956:179). The name means "Place of the Warrior."

Passyunk: Passyunk was an unusually large Lenape summer station on the eastern shore of the Schuylkill where it empties into the Delaware (Donehoo 1928:144; Weslager 1956:179). The name has at least a dozen spellings, but it is probably most accurately spelled Pachsegink or Pachsegonk, which means "In the Valley." Present-day Passyunk Avenue traverses a portion of the original site.

Pemapaki: This was the word the Lenape used to denote what is now Pennypack Creek. While it is uncertain whether a Lenape hamlet or campsite was located here (Donehoo 1928:151–52; Weslager 1956:179), it seems likely that there was something located at the juncture of Pennypack Creek with the Delaware, in Holmesburg. The word Pemapacki loosely translates as "Lake Land" (Donehoo 1928:152).

Poquessing: This was a small hamlet or campsite located at the mouth of Poquessing Creek, probably on the northeast side, where it empties into the Delaware at the extreme northeast boundary of present-day Philadelphia. It is probably a derivative of Poquesink, which means "Place of the Mice" (Donehoo 1928:160).

Shackamaxon: Once situated where modern Kensington is now, this town was one of the Lenape's best "known" locations. The derivation of the name is elusive; it may be a derivative of Schachamesink, which means "Place of Eels" (Cacchione and Mion 1934). Given its presumed role among the Lenape, however, it is more likely that it derives from Sakimaucheen, or "The Place Where Chiefs Are Made." Penn's legendary treaty with the Lenape in 1682 is supposed to have taken place at Shackamaxon (Donehoo 1928:185).

Wequiaquenske: Wequiaquenske, also called Wicaco, may have been a Lenape hamlet located just south of present-day Philadelphia, on the north side of Hollander Creek at its juncture with the Delaware River. While there are countless variations of the word, it probably derives from Wiquek, or "Head of Creek," and Kuwe, or "Pine Tree," and means "Place of Pine Trees at the Head of a Creek" (Donehoo 1928:252–53).

Bucks County

Kentkateck: This area was located on the northern end of Moon Island in Falls Township. Presumably there was a small Lenape hamlet located there, although this is not certain. According to Shoemaker (n.d.) and Rivinus (1965), the word means "Place of the Dance."

Menahakonk: The Bucks County Conservancy (1979) places this Lenape fishing station near the present village of Fallsington. Unfortunately, little more is known about the site.

Playwicky: This large Lenape hamlet was the home of "King" Tammany, who sold large tracts of land to William Penn on June 23, 1683 (Donehoo 1928:157). The site is located approximately two and a half miles west of Langhorne, near Neshaminy Creek (Kent, Rice, and Ota 1981; Auerbach and Marshall 1983:39; Mercer 1923:5a) on or near a historic farm known as the Snodgrass or Vanartsdalen Farm.

Sankhickon: Shoemaker (n.d.), based on earlier accounts, places this Lenape hamlet in the vicinity of present-day Morrisville. The name refers to "Flint Rock at the End of the Tide" (Rivinus 1965:23).

Sipaessing: The Bucks County Conservancy (1979) and Shoemaker (n.d.) place this Lenape hamlet at Pennsbury, the site of William Penn's manor house, in Falls Township. The word is probably a derivative of Kschipehellen, which means "Place Where the Waters Flow Rapidly" (Donehoo 1928:183).

Tschichocke: This Lenape site is reported to be in the vicinity of Bristol (Bucks County Conservancy 1979), but little further is known about it.

Delaware County

Queonemysing: This large Lenape summer station was located at the Great Bend in the Brandywine River in present Birmingham Township, adjacent to the Delaware state border (Kent, Rice, and Ota 1981; Weslager 1956:8). William Penn purchased the land on which the site was located on December 19, 1683 (Donehoo 1928:166).

Chester County

Katamoonchink: According to Wolf and Snyder (1982:10), this Lenape site was located along Valley Creek, near the present village of Exton. The name apparently meant "Hazlenut Grove" (Wolf and Snyder 1982:10). Although the presence of Amerindian sites in this area has been archaeologically documented (Roberts, Hoffman, and Meyer 1983), no Lenape artifacts have been verified.

Okehocking: This site, located in present Willistown Township, is the name given to a 500-acre parcel of land deeded to the Lenape at the turn of the eighteenth century (Donehoo 1928:134; Becker 1976:24, 30; 1986). The site is an important one because it reflects an unusual Lenape response to land stress generated by the European colonists.

Lenape Place Names

Many place names still in use in the Philadelphia region derive from the terms the Lenape used to describe various features of the landscape. While none of these seem to have been the name of a Lenape settlement, they no doubt had some significance in the Lenape way of life. Some of these place names, listed by county, are as follows:

Philadelphia County

Aramingo: Aramingo was the Lenape name for a creek that entered the Delaware near present-day North Philadelphia, where there is now an Aramingo Street. Known as Gunner's Run during colonial days, the creek long ago disappeared from the landscape. The word Aramingo is apparently a corruption of Tumanaraming, meaning "Wolf Walk" (Donehoo 1928:7).

Kingsessing: Kingsessing was the Lenape name for a tract of land between the Schuylkill River and Cobbs Creek, at the southwest border of Philadelphia. Soon after the Swedes arrived in the Delaware Valley, they established a town of the same name on the tract (Donehoo 1928:80).

Manayunk: The Lenape name for the Schuylkill River, it is probably a variation of Meneiunk, which translates as "Place Where We Go to Drink" (Donehoo 1928:104). Other variations include Manaiunk and Manaiunck.

Tacony: Tacony is the name of a small stream that rises in lower Montgomery County and flows into Frankford Creek. The Lenape derivation of the word is not clear, but it may be a variation of Tachan, which means "At the Woods" (Donehoo 1928:221). Present-day Tookany Creek Parkway reflects an additional, modern corruption of the word.

Tioga: Tioga is the name presently given to a section of Philadelphia, as well as to a street. It originally referred to a large Amerindian settlement near Athens, in Bradford County, Pennsylvania. Because large numbers of Lenape from the Philadelphia region were known to have lived there in the mid-eighteenth century (Donehoo 1928:226–27), the name subsequently came to refer to an undocumented place back in the Philadelphia vicinity.

Tulpehocken: The name of a creek in Berks County, Pennsylvania, it also is the name of a street in the Mount Airy–Germantown section of Philadelphia. The name is a corruption of Tulpewi-hacki, meaning "Turtle Land" (Donehoo 1928:232). How the name came to be applied in Philadelphia is not known.

Wingohocking: Wingohocking is the name given by the Lenape to the south branch of Frankford Creek (Donehoo 1928:256). The branch is no longer a feature of the landscape. Wingohocking is today the name of a street in the Olney section of Philadelphia.

Wissahickon: This is the name given to a creek that rises in Montgomery County and empties into the Schuylkill River. It is probably a corruption of Wisameckhan, which translates as "Catfish Stream" (Donehoo 1928:257).

Wissinoming: Wissinoming is the name of a small creek that once flowed into the Delaware River north of Frankford Creek. The creek no longer is a feature of the contemporary landscape. The name is probably a corruption of Quessinawomink or Wischanemunk, which means "Where We Are Frightened" (Donehoo 1928:257). Currently, it is the name of a neighborhood near where Wissinoming Creek once flowed.

Bucks County

Neshaminy: A corruption of Nischam-hanne, the name applies to a creek that enters the Delaware River near Croyden in Bucks County. This creek is noted in the first deed from the Lenape to William Penn on July 15, 1682 (Donehoo 1928:8).

Tinicum: This name formerly applied to Burlington Island, situated in the Delaware River adjacent to Bucks County, but now a part of New Jersey. The name also applied to an island in the Delaware River near the mouth of the Schuylkill. The name apparently is a corruption of Menatey, which translates as "Island" (Donehoo 1928:223). (See Delaware County, Tinicum.)

Montgomery County

Conshohocken: This name originally applied to a hill in Montgomery County; a modern-day town now bears the name. The derivation of the word is uncertain, but it may relate to *guneu,* meaning "long," *schigi,* meaning "fine," and *hacki,* meaning "land." Taken together, these words translate as "At the Long, Fine Land" (Donehoo 928:47).

Mingo: This is the name of two creeks entering the Schuylkill River, one near Royersford, Pennsylvania, the other upstream from the Schuylkill's confluence with the Delaware. The name is a variation of Minquas, the name the Lenape used for the Susquehannock.

Ogontz: This name refers to a neighborhood in lower Montgomery County, at the Philadelphia border. The derivation of the word is unclear, but it may have been the name of a Lenape sachem (Donehoo 1928:132).

Perkiomen: The name of a creek that flows into the Schuylkill River near Valley Forge, the word apparently is a derivative of Pakihmomink, meaning "Where There Are Cranberries" (Donehoo 1928:153).

Skippack: Originally, this name applied to a small creek that feeds Perkiomen Creek from the east; it is now also the name of a small village in central Montgomery County. The name probably derives from Skappenhacki, meaning "Wet Land," or from Schkipeek, meaning "Pool of Stagnant, Offensive Water" (Donehoo 1928:207).

Delaware County

Lenni Mills: This now is the name of a small village in Delaware County (Donehoo 1928:91). Its origins are unknown.

Muckinipattus: This is the name applied to a branch of Darby Creek that traverses portions of Glenolden and Folcroft (Donehoo 1928:121). The Lenape derivation or meaning of the word is unclear.

Secane: Secane now is the name of a small town in Delaware County. It derives from the name of a Lenape sachem, who was instrumental in deeding lands between the Delaware and Schuylkill rivers to William Penn (Donehoo 1928:177).

Tinicum: Tinicum is the name of an island in the Delaware River below the mouth of the Schuylkill. The name also formerly referred to present-day Burlington Island, located in the Delaware opposite Burlington, New Jersey, and Bristol, Pennsylvania. The word evidently is a derivative of the word Menatey, meaning "Island" (Donehoo 1928:223). (See Bucks County, Tinicum.)

Wawa: Now the name of a small town in Delaware County, the word is doubtless a corruption of a Lenape word, although its derivation and meaning are unknown (Donehoo 1928:250). (See Chester County, Wawaset.)

Chester County

Lenape: Lenape is now the name of a small town in Chester County.

Pocopson: Pocopson is the name applied to a village, township, and a small creek in Chester County. The word is believed to be derived from a Lenape word meaning "Roaring Creek" (Donehoo 1928:159).

Toughkenamon: The name of a village in southern Chester County, as well as the name of a nearby hill, the word may derive from Pethakwon, meaning "Thunder." The name is also said to translate as "Fire-Brand Hill" (Donehoo 1928:231).

Wawaset: This is the name of a small town in Chester County, with its origins unknown (Donehoo 1928:250). (See Delaware County, Wawa.)

2

Philadelphia in Historic Times

PERIOD OF INITIAL SETTLEMENT: 1624–1682

FOUNDING OF THE TOWN: 1682–1701

THE COLONIAL CITY: 1701–1775

THE CITY AT WAR: 1775–1783

THE CITY IN THE FEDERAL ERA: 1783–1830

THE EARLY INDUSTRIAL CITY: 1830–1860

THE INDUSTRIAL CITY IN ITS PRIME: 1860–1901

THE CITY IN THE EARLY
TWENTIETH CENTURY: 1901–1930

Figure 2.1. (opposite page)

Philadelphia Region ... as First Seen by the White Men, conceptualized by Edward Cacchione and Bernard Mion (1934). Hamlet locations are based on various historical sources. (Courtesy of the Philadelphia City Planning Commission)

When contrasted with the many thousands of years that Amerindians inhabited the Philadelphia region, the 450 years that have passed since Europeans first ventured into the Delaware Valley seems a very short time span indeed. Yet it would take an entire, lengthy book to do justice to all the history Philadelphia has witnessed in that time. The purpose of this chapter is not even to attempt such an exposition, but rather to sketch a picture of the cultural backdrop against which Philadelphia and the nation grew. Such a backdrop, gleaned from the written record, is an essential part of the archaeologist's approach; without it, the sites investigated would exist in a social, economic, and political vacuum. In this regard, the historical archaeologist is usually more fortunate than the archaeologist of prehistoric sites, for while both must go—to use William Graham Sumner's phrase—"upstream in history" from what is known to what can only be surmised from the archaeological findings, the prehistorian has farther upstream to go. In the absence of historical records, the prehistorian must depend on ethnological analogues and ecological analyses for a plausible reconstruction of the setting. Historical archaeologists, on the other hand, sometimes have available to them a dazzling amount of documentation. Such is certainly the case for the archaeologist working in Philadelphia and its environs, but, as will be evident in the chapters that follow, it is by no means a one-sided relationship. While the historical record has contributed much to the archaeology of Philadelphia's historic sites, the archaeological record has also contributed to the historical picture.

Here dwelt the Leni-Lenape "Real Men" of the Algonquian Group. They were divided into three great Tribes: the Unami "Turtle", the Unalachtigo "Turkey", and the Munsee "Wolf"... Their Government which they called Sachema, was by Kings "Sachamakers", and these came into power by succession, but always on the Mother's side.

PHILADELPHIA
REGION
WHEN KNOWN AS
COAQUANNOCK
"Grove of Tall Pines"
AND AS FIRST SEEN
BY THE WHITE MEN

WITH INDIAN VILLAGES · ABORIGINAL
NAMES OF LOCALITIES · STREAMS AND
ISLANDS AND THEIR INTERPRETATION

PERIOD OF INITIAL SETTLEMENT: 1624–1682

In comparison with the vast amount written about Philadelphia since its founding in 1682, the earlier history of the region has gotten rather short shrift. Lacking documentation, we cannot even be certain which European explorer first happened upon the Delaware River. Verrazano's explorations in 1524 may have taken him there; Henry Hudson's search in 1609 for an all-water route to the East Indies certainly did. Like many a mariner after him, Hudson ran aground in the shoals of the lower Delaware Bay, and there the *Half Moon*, flying the banner of the United East India Company of Holland, anchored for a brief late-August stay. Although some itinerant European traders and trappers doubtless traversed the Delaware Valley between 1550 and 1609, the first settlers apparently did not arrive until the mid-1620s, some fifteen years after Hudson's tangle with the shoals (Weslager 1961:25–27). Europeans in the Delaware Valley were very few in number, however, until the 1640s, and even then it would be almost another half century before they set about developing the region in earnest. Until that time, the Philadelphia region probably looked much like the idealized scene shown in Figure 2.1.

William Penn, describing the state of his new colony in 1683, sums up much of what we do know about the settlers who preceded him:

. . . The first *planters* in these parts were the Dutch, and soon after them the Swedes and Finns. The Dutch applied themselves to traffic, the Swedes and Finns to husbandry. There were some disputes between them [for] some years; the Dutch looking upon them as intruders upon their purchase and possession, which was finally ended in the surrender made by John Rising, the Swedes' governor, to Peter Stuyvesant, governor for the States of Holland, anno 1655. (Soderland et al. 1983:317)

The Dutch "traffic" was the result of the presence and industry of the Dutch West India Company, which in 1624 established a small colony of Dutch settlers on Burlington Island, north of the future site of Philadelphia. Two years later, the company built its first trading post, Fort Nassau, on the east side of the Delaware River just south of Camden, where Gloucester, New Jersey, now stands. Among the other Dutch settlements that followed were Fort Casimir, built in 1651 on the present site of New Castle, Delaware, and Fort Beversreede, a trading post that in 1648 occupied a site on the east bank of the Schuylkill, little more than a mile above its confluence with the Delaware (Weslager 1961:80, 125, 146, 156).

The area near the confluence of the Delaware and the Schuylkill, popular with the Lenape because of its abundance of natural resources and with the Dutch because of its strategic location for trade, also attracted the Swedes and Finns, who established small, scattered farms along the creeks that flow into the two rivers. Johan Printz, the third Swedish colonial governor, chose nearby Tinicum Island—then in the Delaware River and now inland just below Philadelphia International Airport—as his seat of government. There in 1643 he built the "Printzhof," a fortified log house where he lived for ten years. Since the Dutch efforts at colonization ultimately failed, the settlement that Printz established on Tinicum Island was the first permanent one in what is now Pennsylvania. The colony that he ruled, known as New Sweden, was founded five years before his arrival, when in March 1638 a band of Swedish soldiers, weary after a winter at sea, disembarked at present-day Wilmington, Delaware, and there erected an outpost called Fort Christina. Another early Swedish settlement in the lower Delaware Valley was founded about 1644 by a young immigrant named Jören Kyn. Kyn's town was called Upland until 1682, when William Penn renamed it Chester (Soderlund et al. 1983:85).

The supremacy of the Dutch in the Delaware Valley was, as Penn noted, established in 1655, when soldiers from New Netherland under the command of Peter Stuyvesant swept through the Swedish territory. This supremacy was short-lived, however, for in the late summer of 1664 English forces began conquering New Netherland in the name of James, Duke of York, brother of King Charles II. Earlier that year, Charles had granted James proprietorship of all the land south of New England to and including the eastern shore of the Delaware. By October the English troops had not only established James's claim to what would become the colonies of New York and New Jersey, they had also enforced English rule on the western shore of the Delaware, on lands that were not part of his claim (Weslager 1961:237).

As it turned out, James had little interest in his New World domains. By 1674 the title for West New Jersey had passed from him to John Fenwick and Edward Byllynge, both members of the Society of Friends. The two Friends fell out over their land holdings, and a third—a thirty-year-old Quaker gentleman named William Penn—was called in to settle their differences. Although Byllynge won the dispute and emerged as owner of nine-tenths of the province, he was deeply in debt; Penn was one of three trustees appointed to manage his New Jersey estate for the benefit of his creditors. Penn immediately launched a plan to sell shares of Byllynge's land to fellow Quakers who wanted refuge from the persecution they suffered in Europe (Reps 1965:158).

This experience in colonial enterprise was to stand Penn in good stead, for a few years later, in March 1681, a charter from Charles II made him Lord Proprietor of 45,000 square miles of American land. The terms of Penn's grant were rather open-ended and placed few restrictions on him. Like all colonial proprietors, he had not only powers of government, subject though they were to English review (Garvan 1963:180), but also hereditary ownership of the land. In return, Penn was obliged to pay a rent of two beaver skins a year and one-fifth of all the gold and silver found in the province (1680 Charter of Pennsylvania, quoted in Du Ponceau and Tysan 1852:18). His colony, named Pennsylvania in honor of his father, was the twelfth of the thirteen English colonies to be established.

At the time Penn received his charter, the total population along both shores of the Delaware consisted of fewer than two thousand Europeans and not too many more Lenape. About fifty farmers—mostly Swedes and Finns, with a smattering of Dutch and English—inhabited the area that would become Philadelphia. Although each farm occupied about 200 acres, most of these acres were still uncleared and uncultivated, and the farmers' log houses, modeled after those of Scandinavian peasants, lay nestled amid dense woods on the banks of the Delaware, the Schuylkill, and their tributaries (Dunn and Dunn 1982:3). The people who inhabited these lands were apparently an easy-going, unambitious group, although at the same time hardworking and God-fearing. Penn, arriving in his colony in 1682, found them

a plain, strong, industrious people, yet [they] have made no great progress in culture, or propagation of fruit trees, as if they desired rather to have [just] enough rather than plenty. . . . As they are people proper and strong of body, so they have fine children, and almost every house full; rare to find one of them without three or four boys, and as many girls; some, six, seven, and eight sons. And I must do them that right, I see few young men more sober and laborious. . . . The Dutch have a meeting place for religious worship at New Castle, and the Swedes, three: one at Christiana, one at Tinicum, and one at Wicaco, within half a mile of this town. (Soderlund et al. 1983:317)

Wicaco (also known as Wequia-quenske), situated on the banks of the Delaware three-quarters of a mile below Dock Creek, was evidently so-called because a Lenape hamlet of the same name had formerly stood on the site; after Penn's settlers arrived, the area became known as South-wark. Located just below what is now South Street, Wicaco was in 1682 the only clustered European settlement within the present bounds of Philadelphia, and the Swedish church there was a relatively new phenomenon. In 1669 the Swedes had built a log blockhouse on the site, fashioning it in the Scandinavian style out of sections of tree trunks notched at the ends and cross-laid (Wolf 1975:22). The land on which the blockhouse stood had been patented in 1653 by Queen Christina to a Sven Shute, whose heirs—three brothers named Swanson—owned the land at the time the blockhouse was built. In 1677 Swan, Oele, and Andries Swanson and the other Swedes of Wicaco converted their log fort into a place of Lutheran worship (Figure 2.2). Their first minister was the Reverend Jacob Fabritius, a "turbulent character" who had come to America in 1669 to preach to Dutch Lutherans in the Hudson Valley.* Various scrapes with the law, including "committing assault and battery on a woman in her own house," earned him his dismissal from that post, and so, having wandered south, the fractious Fabritius came to be the first ordained minister within the present bounds of the "city of brotherly love" (Scharf and Westcott 1884:1230–31).

Although they no longer had so far to travel of a Sabbath day, the residents of Wicaco and the surrounding areas had a bit farther to go when they had to pursue legal business. Court sessions were held at Upland and at Kingsessing, a small town several miles from Wicaco on the west bank of the Schuylkill. The court re-

* Francis Daniel Pastorius, Germantown's first leader, was evidently not one to mince words. In 1684 he wrote of Fabritius, "The Lutheran preacher, who . . . ought to show the Swedes the way to heaven, is, to say it in one word, a drunkard" (Soderlund et al. 1983:356).

Figure 2.2.

The first Swedish church and the house of Swan Swanson. (From John Fanning Watson, manuscript draft of *Annals of Philadelphia*, v. 2:369, ca. 1820–1850; courtesy of the Historical Society of Pennsylvania)

cords, like the Swedes' conversion of a blockhouse into a church, indicate that the lives of the early settlers were relatively secure and peaceful, though certainly not without event. Fines, when paid at all, were often paid in tobacco, and, in addition to endless disputes over unpaid debts, the common legal issues of the day included suits against neighbors who owned "cruell" and marauding boars, accusations that unwed persons kept "unlawfull Company," and complaints of being libeled as a "hogh thief" by an inebriated neighbor (Armstrong 1860:50, 52, 175, 180). This insular style of life was soon to end, and when it did, it left little enduring physical evidence behind. Most of the ephemeral wooden structures that the early settlers built have vanished without trace.

FOUNDING OF THE TOWN: 1682 – 1701

From the start, the profit motive played an important role in the Quaker colony of Pennsylvania. Its founder needed money to bail himself out of debt, and the settlers who followed him, as ambitious as the earlier settlers had been easygoing, also had high hopes of achieving material gain. Many of them did profit; the founder, however, did not. But profit was not Penn's sole motivation. In an age of religious intolerance and persecution, he wished to establish a colony where all people would be free to worship as they pleased. In this respect, Penn's colony was most "un-English," as was his original plan for the great town that would grace his colony.

The Philadelphia of Penn's dreams offered a sharp contrast to the typical, crowded English city. It was to occupy 10,000 acres "in the most convenient place upon the river for health and navigation" (Soderlund et al. 1983:72), and large house lots, some with 800 feet of river frontage and 100 acres of land, were to be strung out for fifteen miles along the Delaware. With the houses sitting in the middle of their generous plots surrounded on all sides by gardens and orchards, it would be a "green country town, which [would] never be burnt, and always be wholesome." What Penn apparently had in mind was a town that would reflect the lifestyle of the landed English gentry—his own lifestyle, in fact—for he assumed that the owners of these grand urban properties would also own large country estates beyond the town limits (Dunn and Dunn 1982:6–7; Garvan 1963:189–90, 192). What Penn wound up with, however, was a somewhat different matter.

The first snag was that when Penn's commissioners arrived late in 1681 to arrange for the 10,000 acres of the town, they, of course, found Scandinavian, Dutch, and English settlers already in possession of most of the land along the Delaware. Having to abandon Penn's notion that Upland would be a promising site, they moved farther up the Delaware, where the brothers Swanson of Wicaco were willing to sell 300 acres with a mile of river frontage between the area now bounded by Vine and South streets. When Penn arrived in the autumn of 1682, he was dissatisfied with this cramped site, and he bought from two other Swedish farmers a mile of river frontage on the Schuylkill opposite his frontage on the Delaware. The rectangle of 1,200 acres that resulted from this purchase measured one mile from north to south and stretched east and west for two miles across the narrowest point between the two rivers. Within this rectangle, Thomas Holme, Penn's surveyor general, laid out a grid of spacious blocks with an eight-acre public square in each quadrant of the town and a ten-acre central square for civic buildings at the intersection of two main thoroughfares (Figure 2.3.). These thoroughfares—Broad Street and High (now Market) Street—were, and still are, 100 feet wide, much wider than any street in seventeenth-century London (Garvan 1963:193–94; Reps 1965:161). Reflecting the pacifist views of the Quaker founder was the total absence of city walls or other fortifications.

Although Penn's town was larger in size than any other in the colo-

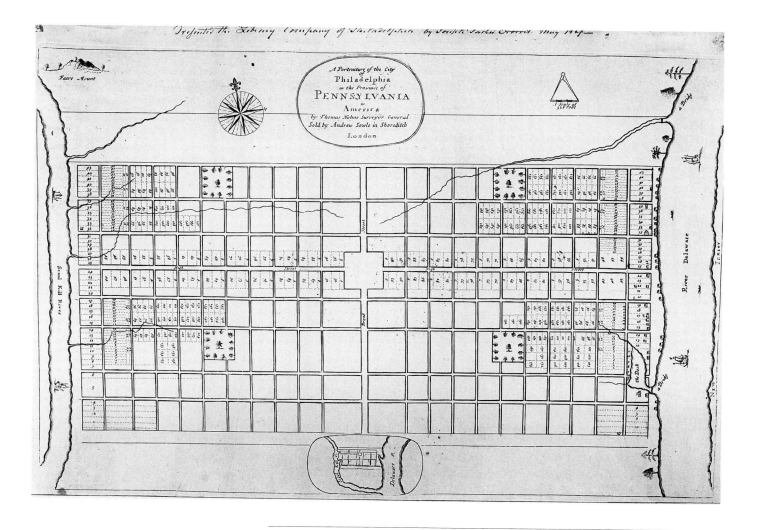

nies at the time, it was much smaller than he had intended, and he was thus forced to reduce the size of the city lots. To encourage land sales, he had originally promised the first buyers a bonus of 10 acres in the town for every 500 acres purchased in the countryside; thus someone who bought 5,000 country acres was to have received a 100-acre city lot. Since Penn could not make good on this promise and had instead to apportion lots of only one-half or one acre, he attempted to make amends to the "First Purchasers" by reserving for them some 8,000 to 10,000 acres of "liberty lands" in the area now occupied by North and West Philadelphia. Each First Purchaser of 5,000 country acres received 80 suburban acres in the "greenbelt" of the Northern or Western Liberties and a one-acre lot in town (Soderlund et al. 1983:204–5; Dunn and Dunn 1982:7; Garvan 1963:191–93). Not all the First Purchasers were pleased with this arrangement, and it was to cause Penn a good deal of political discomfort.

Penn was no doubt as unhappy about the greatly reduced size of the city house lots as were the First Purchasers. Very early in the life of his town, with the profit motive clearly at work, Holme's spacious blocks were cut by alleys, and lots were divided and subdivided. Thus, the narrow workmen's houses that were built on these lots gave the town an aspect reminiscent of cramped and crowded London. Penn's vision of a public esplanade along the high banks of the Delaware vanished, too, as merchants soon covered the area east of Front Street with warehouses, shops, and dwellings, and wharves began sprouting out into the river (Reps 1965:167–68). Along the riverfront, to link the buildings they had erected there, merchants created a street not shown

on Holme's plan of the city, a narrow artery known as Water Street.

South of Dock Creek, marshy land that could be drained and filled offered more opportunity for profit. The area right around the tiny, navigable tidal basin into which the two branches of Dock Creek flowed took on a particularly commercial aspect and reflected, as did the appearance of the town in general, the make-up of the people attracted to Penn's colony because of his liberal religious philosophy and his offer of land at affordable prices. While Penn might have envisioned a town inhabited mainly by landed gentry, most of them Quakers, what he ended with was a town made up chiefly of merchants, shopkeepers, and artisans of a heterogeneous mix. No doubt he did not regret this development, for these people provided the energy and skills that very quickly turned the raw frontier town into a flourishing city, whose prosperity, like that of other cities of the pre-industrial era, depended on trade.

Philadelphia's first merchants, who formed the backbone of the economy, were in the main shrewd, experienced British Quaker entrepreneurs with knowledge of colonial, West Indian, and European markets. Most of the first artisans and shopkeepers in Philadelphia were British Quakers, too. By 1700, however, by which time the city had about two thousand inhabitants, the population was more diverse. Quakers of English, Welsh, Dutch, and German backgrounds probably made up about 40 percent of the population; Swedish Lutherans, Scots-Irish Presbyterians, and Anglicans and Baptists of other backgrounds accounted for most of the rest (Dunn and Dunn 1982:28).

Despite the considerable heterogeneity of the early city's population, the Quaker influence was very evident. The political, economic, and social

leaders of both the city and the province were Quakers, and the legal codes reflected their moral beliefs. The Friends did as much as any mortals could to legislate the concepts of brotherly love and the Ten Commandments. Reflective of a concern about upright business dealings were two laws enacted in 1683 that ensured the reliability of the barrel staves manufactured in the province and the weight and quality of the bread and butter sold in the markets. Other laws prohibited everything from scolding, swearing, and sodomy to sedition, "prophane speaking," drunkenness, incest, polygamy, and "rude sports, plays, and games" (George, Nead, and McCamant 1879:133, 135, 190).

All these laws were enacted by the Pennsylvania Assembly, which until 1701 was responsible for the city's legislation while a council saw to its administration. Penn, mindful that English municipal charters usually resulted in power struggles between lords and commoners, resisted those Philadelphians who wanted a more distinct form of city government, one that would give them more power over their own affairs. A long absence from the colony seriously undermined Penn's position; he left for England in 1684 to settle a dispute with Lord Baltimore, proprietor of Maryland, over the Pennsylvania-Maryland border and did not return until 1699. By then the political situation was such that before leaving Pennsylvania for the last time in 1701, Penn was forced to grant the city a corporate charter (Dunn and Dunn 1982:25–27).

The new city government, consisting of a mayor, a recorder, aldermen, and a common council, was a self-perpetuating, nonelected, "closed" corporation, immune to public opinion. Modeled after the medieval municipal governments of England, it had the judicial and legislative powers of the city and the responsibility of supervising the markets and fairs, the wharves, and city-owned property. Until 1712, however, the corporation lacked all taxing power. In that year the assembly granted it a small measure of taxing authority to enable it to pay for repairs of streets, markets, wharves, and so on, but—suspicious of the elitist nature of the closed corporation and its indifference to public needs—the assembly saw to it that an elected board of assessors worked with the corporation in establishing the sums to be collected. The as-

sembly's suspicions were apparently fully justified. The corporation was by all accounts a totally inept body, too weak or uninterested even to collect rents or fines issued for violations of its own ordinances. Petitions to the mayor's court frequently resulted in the reduction of fines, and when people who flatly refused to pay any fine at all were jailed and thus became an expense to the city, the council did not hesitate to vote for their release (Bridenbaugh 1938:145, 305; Bridenbaugh 1955:8; Diamondstone 1966:186, 190–91).

In spite of the ineptitude of the city

corporation, the town grew, and like the laws that governed it and the corporation itself, it showed both a Quaker influence and an English one. Even the appearance of the Swedish church of Gloria Dei, built between 1698 and 1700 and still standing on the site of the old log blockhouse in Southwark, reflected these influences. The Swedes, breaking with their tradition of building with wood, chose brick for their new church, and they hired English masons and carpenters to build it. The result was the simple, solid, tidy-looking building shown in Figure 2.4. The same look characterized the brick houses that were going

Figure 2.4.

Gloria Dei, also called Old Swedes' Church, photographed in 1854. (Courtesy of the Free Library of Philadelphia)

Figure 2.5.

Early houses. These houses, photographed in 1868, were probably located in Southwark. (Courtesy of the Free Library of Philadelphia)

up in increasing numbers along the streets and alleys of Philadelphia. With the memory of the Great Fire of London in 1666 still fresh in the minds of many of the builders, their choice of nonflammable brick over flammable wood is not surprising. In other ways, too, these houses revealed the English origins of their builders. The earliest ones, modeled after the country houses of English yeomen, had steeply pitched roofs, large chimneys, small windows, and usually one modest-sized room per floor. Built individually or in pairs without side windows, they could be, and eventu-

ally were, joined as rowhouses. Most of them had pent eaves—small roofs projecting between the first and second floors to protect the facades from rain—and their bricks were usually laid in the checkerboard pattern known as Flemish bond (Figure 2.5). The Flemish bond, a Dutch method of alternating glazed headers with stretchers, probably came into the repertoire of English masons in the 1650s, when many Englishmen fled to Holland during the reign of Oliver Cromwell.

Although in the late 1600s most of Philadelphia's population lived in

Figure 2.6.

Mapp of Yᵉ Improved Part of Pensilvania in America, Divided into Countyes, Townships and Lotts, surveyed by Thomas Holme and published about 1700 by John Harris. Pennsbury Manor is in the lower right-hand corner. (Courtesy of the Library Company of Philadelphia)

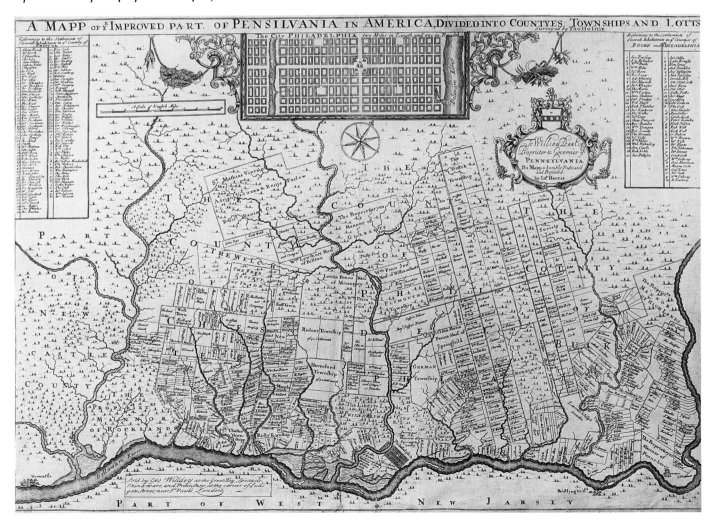

modest brick townhouses and the country estates of gentlemen farmers were very few, William Penn set a trend that would continue when he built a country estate at Pennsbury Manor in 1683. To such havens, later generations of affluent Philadelphians would repair in the heat of the summer months to escape the smells, dust, and bustle of the increasingly crowded city. As can be seen in Figure 2.6, Pennsbury Manor was located about twenty-five miles north of Philadelphia along the Delaware River in Bucks County. It was but one of several tracts of manorial lands that Penn set aside for himself and members of his family. Among the others were the Manor of Springettsbury just north of the city limit in Philadelphia County and Letitia Penn's Manor of Mountjoy in Chester County.

The three counties into which Penn divided Pennsylvania—Philadelphia, Bucks, and Chester—were blessed with rich agricultural land, and, in addition to the occasional country estate around Philadelphia, they had a number of working farms. Within these various counties were some independent townships with their own mayors and councils. Penn fostered the creation of these townships by offering to sell 5,000 acres to individuals of similar backgrounds or interests who purchased the land as a group (Garvan 1963:187–88). Welsh Quakers founded the townships of Merion, Haverford, and Radnor; German Township, today called Germantown, was established by Dutch Quakers, Dutch Mennonites, and German pietists, who soon became famous for their fine weaving of linen.

By the time Penn took his final leave of Pennsylvania in 1701, his "great town" had undergone a considerable transformation. In its earliest days, it was a primitive outpost where pigs and goats ran freely through muddy, garbage-laden lanes (George, Nead, and McCamant 1879:187) and people lived in caves dug into the riverbanks, engaging in activities that scandalized Penn (1909:303) with their "clandestine looseness." By 1701 the town, though still dirty, had a somewhat more civilized appearance, and with open spaces still existing around many of the houses, it also probably had something of the "green country" look that Penn had hoped for. It was, however, a far more congested place than he had imagined. Not only were the lots a good deal smaller, but practically all two thousand of the town's inhabitants insisted on living as close to the Delaware as they could get. There was little Penn could do to entice them to move across the wooded interior to the lots on the Schuylkill; almost no one lived west of Fourth Street. Within its narrow confines, the town had about four hundred houses, a brickyard, three breweries, at least six churches and as many taverns, a market of open stalls at Second and High streets, a ropewalk, four shipyards, and numerous riverfront wharves (Dunn and Dunn 1982:10–14).

Such was the town William Penn left behind him. While it might not have been quite the bucolic and lordly paradise he had imagined it, it was—thanks to his policies and the people they attracted, as well as to the bounty of nature—well on its way to becoming a major city fit to be the birthplace of a nation.

THE COLONIAL CITY: 1701–1775

From a small provincial settlement of 2,000 people in 1701, Philadelphia had by 1775 grown into a cosmopolitan city with a population of over 23,000.* Founded more than fifty years later than Boston and New York, it had in the space of little more than seventy years outdistanced both of them, becoming the largest city in the British colonies. Much of this growth was due to the immigrants who streamed through the port of Philadelphia throughout the eighteenth century, most of them fleeing poverty, war, famine, and religious persecution in Europe. Germans from the Rhine Palatinate, Scots, and northern Irish accounted for the bulk of the newcomers, with Germans in the overwhelming majority. In 1749 alone, more than 7,000 Germans landed in Philadelphia (Wolf 1975: 39; Bridenbaugh 1955:134–35).

Many of these eighteenth-century immigrants, attracted by Pennsylvania's liberal religious and political philosophies, chose to stay on in Penn's colony. Some remained in Philadelphia, adding their talents to the city's pool of skills and crafts. Others, among them the forebears of

* There is considerable disagreement over population figures for Philadelphia before 1790, when the first federal census took place. Based on his study of tax records and other data, Warner (1987:245) estimates that in 1775 the city, together with Southwark and the Northern Liberties, had a population of no more than 23,739. Nash and Smith (1975:366) set the urban population for the same year at 31,410, while Bridenbaugh (1955:216) estimates it at 40,000.

the Amish and Mennonites who inhabit the "Pennsylvania Dutch" country today, settled on farms in the rich agricultural countryside (Baltzell 1979:117). This combination of productive urban and rural populations, coupled with the region's natural resources and favorable location for trade, was to be the stuff of which Philadelphia's growth was made and the reason why it so quickly outdistanced all the other settlements in the colonies, both to the north and to the south.

Of Colonial Prosperity and Disparity, "Wet Quakers" and Tolerance

Philadelphia's immigrants not only created a market for the imported goods of merchants; they also produced commodities that the merchants could profitably export—wheat, flour, bread, meat, flaxseed, furs, lumber, barrel staves, and iron among them. In return, the rest of the world sent shiploads of goods. By the 1750s the city's import-export trade was booming, and its warehouses along the Delaware were bulging with Irish linens, Portugese wines and Madeira, West Indian rum and molasses, and fine English woolens, cutlery, and ceramics (Bronner 1982:37–38). At the same time, the needs of the growing population created business for the city's shopkeepers and kept its community of artisans busily and profitably engaged in making cloth, ale, shoes, ceramics, glass, metal tools and utensils, and a variety of other objects. The availability of these goods meant that Philadelphia was less reliant than other colonial cities on imported manufactures, and it was therefore less troubled with finding the hard

cash to pay for them. Also contributing to the city's prosperity was its intercolonial trade. The value of the agricultural goods it exported to other American ports was greater than the value of the goods it imported, and the difference was made up in cash payments (Bridenbaugh 1955:44).

The merchants of the city, who controlled the import-export business, also owned most of the ships on which the trading economy depended. While they undoubtedly profited most from the boom, others profited as well. In 1754 at least twelve shipyards were in operation for a mile along the Delaware—all the way from Gloria Dei Church to Pegg's Run at the northern limit of the city. As shipyards prospered, so did all the many artisans whose skills and products were necessary to the building of Philadelphia's merchant fleet—shipwrights, ship carpenters, ship chandlers, blacksmiths, riggers, ropemakers, and sailmakers, to name but a few.

In fact, all Philadelphians shared in the prosperity, but in disparate proportions. At the very bottom of the colonial social ladder, if they could be said to have had any place on that ladder at all, were the slaves. First imported to the Delaware Valley by the Dutch in the 1630s, they numbered about one thousand in 1750; by 1775, with Quaker sentiment against slavery growing ever more militant, their numbers had decreased to about six hundred. A cut above the slaves were the dock laborers, stablehands, carters, seamen, and indentured servants who made up the working class. Indentured servants were fairly numerous in the early city, numbering about nine hundred in 1775 (Warner 1987:6); many immigrants, lacking passage money, signed on in this capacity. Seamen, known as "jack tars," were,

however, the largest occupational group. They were also among the most poorly paid. Often unemployed and facing the hazards of life at sea when they were not, the jack tars while ashore clustered in boarding houses along the docks and, in the company of dock laborers and prostitutes, sought solace in the numerous tippling houses of the area.

Artisans, who were very often shopkeepers as well, comprised the bulk of the middle class. Known also as "mechanics," these craftsmen had a strong influence on the politics of both city and nation. They thought of themselves as a group apart, distinct from the wealthy merchants and professionals in the upper class above them, as well as from the common laborers below. Benjamin Franklin—archetypical artisan himself—reflected the self-image of this group of Philadelphians when he wrote, "The Husbandman is in honor there, and even the Mechanic, because their Employments are useful. The People have a saying, that God Almighty is himself a Mechanic, the greatest in the Universe, and he is respected and admired more for the Variety, Ingenuity, and Utility of his Handiworks, than from the Antiquity of his Family." Proof of the validity of Franklin's observation is that many artisans of humble origin, through the "variety, ingenuity, and utility of their handiworks," rose into the ranks of the upper-middle class. Among this group were the cabinetmakers, silversmiths, goldsmiths, clockmakers, and printers who, by the mid-1700s, had established a reputation for Philadelphia craftsmanship throughout the colonies. Members of the Carpenters' Company, an organization founded by ten master builders in 1724, also often attained upper-middle-class status; in a city so quickly building, the skilled Carpenters were highly valued citizens.

Like the merchants and professionals of the upper class, members of the upper-middle class often owned land and property. What separated them from the upper class of the 1750s was that by then upper-class status was limited to those who had inherited their wealth and position (Thayer 1982:97–98). Another change in the social fabric at mid-century was that the Quakers, although still a very influential group, no longer dominated the upper social echelon or the city's economic and political scene. By 1760 they accounted for little more than a fifth of the population (Tolles 1948:232), and as they became less visible in the seats of power, Anglicans and Presbyterians became more so.

Immigration of large numbers of non-Quakers contributed, of course, to the diminishing proportion and power of the Quakers. But at the same time, as the "counting house" took precedence over the "meeting house," many newly prosperous Friends were falling from the fold. No doubt wearied by the conscientious struggle between opulence and plainness, an increasing number of "wet Quakers," as those Friends who succumbed to the worldly temptations of prosperity were called, converted to Anglicanism. One wet Quaker who contributed to the depletion of the Friends' ranks and the swelling of the Anglicans' was Samuel Powel, last mayor of Philadelphia before the Revolution and the first person to hold that office afterward. Grandson and namesake of a wealthy Quaker carpenter, Powel traveled throughout Europe in the 1760s, reveling in the sensuous delights of European culture. Returning to Philadelphia in 1767, he not only soon became an Anglican, he also threw every vestige

of Quaker restraint to the wind when he decorated his elegant new home, still standing at 244 South Third Street (Tolles 1948:123–32, 140–42, 232; Bridenbaugh 1955:139, 154).

Powel's house was but one of many built after 1760 that reflected the prosperity of Philadelphia's merchant class. Before then, most merchants were content to live in modest townhouses, biding their time until they could afford the ultimate symbol of having arrived: a lavish country estate where one could entertain guests in high style. By the 1750s, approximately 150 of these country showplaces existed within a twelve-mile radius of the city, and Quakers had led the way in their building (Bridenbaugh 1955:143, 145; Tolles 1948:132). One of the first was Stenton, built in Germantown in 1728 for James Logan, a shrewd Scottish Quaker who had served as Penn's provincial secretary. Still standing at Eighteenth Street and Windrim Avenue, Stenton is a fine example of Georgian architecture, somewhat restrained by the Quaker influence of its owner. Among the other surviving Georgian buildings within the city that attest to the prosperity of the colonial era are Christ Church, built in 1727 for a prestigious Anglican congregation; Independence Hall, originally the Pennsylvania State House, whose construction began in 1732 at the behest of the provincial assembly; and Carpenters' Hall, completed by the Carpenters' Company just in time to serve as the meeting place for the First Continental Congress in 1774.

By the 1770s Christ Church, with its graceful balustrade, fine Palladian east window, and soaring steeple (Figure 2.7), was but one of eighteen churches that graced the city. These handsome churches reflected not only the city's wealth but also the religious

Figure 2.7.

Christ Church on Second Street between High and Mulberry (now Market and Arch) streets. Begun in 1727 under the direction of John Kearsley, a physician and "gentleman-architect," construction was completed in 1744. The steeple, designed by Scotsman Robert Smith, a member of the Carpenters' Company, was added ten years later. Soaring 196 feet high, it was a prominent landmark in the colonial city. (Courtesy of the Historical Society of Pennsylvania)

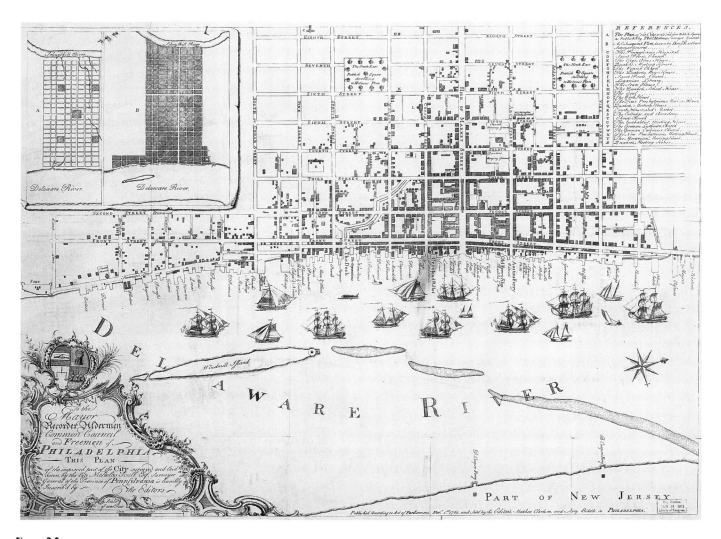

Figure 2.8.

Plan of Philadelphia, 1762. (Courtesy of the Library of Congress, Map Division)

freedom its citizens enjoyed. In addition to Anglican churches and Quaker meeting houses, there were Presbyterian, German Reformed, Lutheran, Moravian, Baptist, Methodist, and Roman Catholic churches. St. Joseph's, the first Catholic parish in the city, began holding services in 1732 in a chapel on Willing's Alley, just south

of Walnut Street; by 1750 the city had ten other Catholic congregations. Puritan Boston, by contrast, had few Catholics and no Catholic church throughout the 1700s; its first Catholic church was not built until 1803 (Thayer 1982:101). Although early Philadelphia's Jewish population was small, informal Jewish services are reputed to have been held in a house near Race Street as early as the 1740s, and the first synagogue in the city was built in 1782 (Baltzell 1979:117, 419–20; Wolf and Whiteman 1975:32).

The Ingredients of a Stratified but Open Society

Despite its obvious social stratification, colonial Philadelphia was a unified and open society where people of all classes intermingled, if not on an equal footing, at least on an intimate one, and a sense of freedom and social mobility prevailed. Several factors conspired to make this apparently paradoxical situation so. Not the least of these factors was that the city, though large for its time, was small by modern standards, and people from all walks of life lived in densely populated blocks in a narrow strip of land along the Delaware (Figure 2.8). Under such circumstances, it would have been impossible not to be on intimate terms with one's neighbors. But perhaps the most basic factor in the unity of colonial Philadelphia was that all classes shared the same ambition—the desire for profit that had guided the colony from the beginning—and, in the prosperity that reigned, hopes of achieving this ambition were not unrealistic. Although the upper social echelon was a closed circle, even an unskilled laborer, if clever and hardworking enough, could make his way into the ranks of the upper-middle class. Labor was in demand, and with employers willing to pay board and wages, a laborer could save enough to buy tools that would give him entrée to the community of artisans. Moreover, no trade guilds existed, as they did in Europe, to bar his way (Warner 1987:5, 7–8, 16).

Workplaces and businesses in colonial Philadelphia were small; even the shipyards, ropewalks, and breweries had no more than five to ten people working as a group. The one-man shop was the basic unit of the economy, and it was an entrepreneurial experience shared by middle-class artisan and upper-class merchant alike. Artisans either hired themselves out by the job or worked alone in small shops in their homes, where they made and sold their goods (Warner 1987:6). Merchants, too, worked relatively unaided, usually with the help of no more than one partner and a single clerk, and even some of the wealthiest of them lived above their countinghouses. In addition, merchants and artisans very often lived side by side. The colonial town had no "wrong side of the tracks," and the

idea of residential and commercial zoning seems never to have crossed anyone's mind. Tanneries and breweries coexisted in the same block with mansions and modest dwellings, most with a shop on the ground floor.

Many such blocks characterized Society Hill, as the neighborhood between Walnut and Cedar (now South) streets was called. Society Hill derived its name not from its fashionable nature or its topographical features (for certainly not all of it was fashionable, nor was it generally hilly), but from the Free Society of Traders, a joint stock company that had been a First Purchaser of Pennsylvania land; until the company's dissolution in 1723, its offices had been on a rise overlooking Dock Creek and the Delaware River. In the 1740s Society Hill was one of the fastest growing areas in the city, and in 1745, to accommodate the people moving there, a second city market, called New Market, was built at Second Street and Lombard. The modest dwellings and substantial houses that sprang up around the market reflected the comfortable, if thrifty, lifestyle enjoyed by the middle class and the prosperity of Philadelphia's merchants.

Because the entrepreneurial pace of colonial Philadelphia was relaxed and houses and shops were generally small, warm weather often found artisans, shopkeepers, merchants, and customers out in the sun or under the shade of a tree engaged in conversation. In all weather, however, the tavern beckoned as a welcoming place to discuss business, gossip, get the news, or just pass the time of day. The city's taverns—and they were legion—were a microcosm of the colonial society: stratified but open. Each had its clientele of regulars, with the tippling houses along the docks catering to the lowest elements,

while such establishments as the London Coffee House at Front and Market streets served as clearinghouses for the city's merchants. Unlike the business exchanges and boardrooms of later centuries, the London Coffee House and its counterparts were not bastions that insulated the leaders of commerce from the rest of the world around them; rather, they opened directly out onto the life of the streets (Warner 1987:7, 19–21; Bridenbaugh 1955:156–62).

While taverns abounded, other opportunities for social exchange were plentiful, too. Clubs, if not quite as numerous as taverns, were just as diverse. Two of the most famous clubs—the Junto and the American Philosophical Society, both founded by Benjamin Franklin—were devoted to self-improvement and "the pursuit of useful knowledge." The artisans who formed the Junto in 1727 met regularly to present papers on scientific, social, and moral issues, and their club in turn spawned the first subscription library in the country, the Library Company, founded in 1731 with forty members (Bronner 1982:55).

Not all social endeavors were so cerebral. Bachelor clubs, billiard clubs, and bowling clubs flourished, and other sports were popular, too. In summer there was fishing, swimming, or boating; in winter there was ice skating or, for those who could afford the horses, sleigh riding. Despite Quaker disapproval, Philadelphians also danced and "gamed." Cock fighting, bear baiting, and bull baiting were popular, but horse racing took first place in spectator sports. Theater, anathema to the Quakers, had a difficult time getting established, but by 1767 Philadelphians were able to attend regularly performances at a theater in Southwark, just across the street from the city line. Music, too, frowned on by Quakers, resounded from church organs, as well as in the salons of the upper class, whose lavish balls and banquets became famous throughout the colonies (Thayer 1982:96).

The Colonial Commonweal: Of Commissioners and Community

As Philadelphia grew in the first half of the eighteenth century, so did the need for a municipal government that could effectively administer public services. That such a government was woefully lacking must have been all too evident to visitors. Until mid-century, the city's streets were not only unpaved and thick with mud or dust, depending on the season, but also rank with the smell of animal excrement and the garbage the citizenry habitually dumped there. What garbage was removed was usually removed by dogs, which had replaced the pigs and goats that once roamed freely through the streets. Bridges over the city's many creeks were more often than not out of repair and unusable. A drawbridge built over Dock Creek on Front Street in 1700 was so hazardous that in 1718 it was re-

placed by a causeway (Figure 2.9). Washed out as it often was, the causeway turned out to be not much of an improvement.

Absorbed in circumnavigating the many obstacles at his feet, the unwary visitor might have found himself rudely jostled by one of the drunks who habitually tumbled out of the city's less reputable taverns, or relieved of his purse by one of the many pickpockets on the streets. Assaults, robberies, and burglaries were commonplace occurrences in the colonial city, and the constabulary was not much of a deterrent. At night, the watch consisted of two paid constables and twelve unpaid, and usually very reluctant, citizens. A forbidding stone jail enclosed by a high wall, erected at High and Third streets in 1722 to replace the "cages" and wooden jail of earlier years, was also apparently not a very effective deterrent. Between 1729 and 1732, at least fifteen inmates managed to scale the wall to freedom (Bridenbaugh 1938:162, 216–17, 377; Bronner 1982:59–60).

So feckless was the city corporation that, to get things done, the provincial assembly continued the tradition it had begun in 1712 of creating elected commissions to oversee municipal functions. Between the efforts of the

commissioners and the initiative of private citizens, conditions in the city slowly began to improve. By the mid-1700s most householders had laid their own brick or flagstone sidewalks, and some of the city's merchants had paved the streets in front of their businesses with cobblestones. Merchants had also taken to hanging lamps outside their buildings to light the streets at night. Perhaps galvanized by the approach of the fiftieth anniversary of Philadelphia's corporate charter, Philadelphians in 1749 began urging the assembly to enact a law that would make street lighting the city's responsibility and that would at the same time create a paid night watch. When the assembly did pass such an act in 1750, it circumvented any shilly-shallying on the part of the corporation by making the City Wardens, an elected commission, responsible for the administration of both services, as well as for the supervision of public wells. Thus, in 1751, lamplighters began making their nightly rounds of Philadelphia's newly installed whale-oil lamps (Bridenbaugh 1955:33–34, 109).

It may well be that the determination of Philadelphians to have their streets lighted had something to do not just with street crime but also with

Figure 2.9.

The causeway over Dock Creek, looking north to the Blue Anchor Tavern. The oldest tavern in Philadelphia, the Blue Anchor was standing when William Penn first arrived in the town in 1682. (Painted by Frank H. Taylor in the early twentieth century; courtesy of the Library Company of Philadelphia)

the condition of the streets. It was not until 1762 that the city finally assumed responsibility for paving and cleaning them, and, again, it was a board of elected commissioners that supervised these services. The newly appointed Street Commissioners were apparently an efficient bunch. By 1769 they had paved more than 120,000 square yards and had hired laborers on a weekly basis to remove the garbage and dirt from the streets and to collect tradesmen's rubbish. Visitors were soon marveling at the cleanliness of the Quaker city (Figure 2.10; Bridenbaugh 1955:218, 239–41).

Chimney blazes that spread into major conflagrations were a threat to all colonial towns, and an important part of the night watch's duty was to be on the lookout for them. That Philadelphia suffered fewer such disasters than other cities may have been a tribute to the alertness of its night watch; certainly, though, the city corporation could lay only small claim to any part in this achievement. Although Philadelphia as early as 1694 had an ordinance requiring all households to have chimney-cleaning swabs and water buckets (George, Nead, and McCamant 1879:260), the corporation was typically either powerless or too lethargic to enforce this regulation. What preventive measures were taken were taken by the individual citizen, and they owed much to the sense of community that prevailed. In 1736, six years after the city's first major fire destroyed a wharf, warehouses, and adjacent dwellings, Benjamin Franklin's efforts at fire-prevention education resulted in the establishment of the city's first volunteer fire company, an institution that was part social club and part self-supporting fire-fighting unit. Members of these units, who equipped themselves with buckets and pumping

Figure 2.10.

Arch Street in the late eighteenth century. The City Wardens were responsible for the whale-oil street lamps and for the public water pumps. In 1762 the Street Commissioners assumed responsibility for paving and cleaning the streets. The posts along the sidewalks were to protect pedestrians from vehicular traffic. (Engraving by W. Birch & Son; courtesy of the Free Library of Philadelphia)

engines, met regularly for business, inspections, and pleasure. By the early 1750s about eight such brigades were in existence, and at about the same time, also in response to Franklin's urgings, the Philadelphia Contributionship for the Insurance of Houses from Loss by Fire was formed (Bridenbaugh 1938:368–69; 1955:102–3). The Philadelphia Contributionship was the country's first successful fire insurance company, and is still in business today.

Throughout the seventeenth and eighteenth centuries, the water that Philadelphians used in fighting fires, like the water that they drank, came from wells, from cisterns that collected rainwater, or from the Delaware River. Because the rainwater in the cistern was typically used for laundry as well as for fighting fires, this pit was often located in front of the house and extended part way into the cellar. Here the water was kept

from freezing in winter, when the wooden pumps in the outdoor wells were sometimes frozen solid. Cisterns were usually made water-tight with mortared brick sides and floors and were generally about 8 feet in diameter and less than 10 feet deep. Wells, ranging from 3 to 5 feet or more in diameter, were usually lined with dry-laid bricks and were left open at the bottom. Initially rather shallow, since the water table was in Philadelphia's early days only about 15 feet from the surface, wells became deeper as street paving and cisterns channeled off more and more rainwater. Archaeological investigations have shown that by the end of the 1700s, to ensure a flow of water, they were on average 23 feet deep (Cosans 1975, 1; McCarthy, Cosans-Zebooker, and Henry 1985). In 1756, after a surprise inspection by a volunteer fire company revealed that the pumps of thirty-nine public wells were in need of repair, the assembly enlarged the duties of the City Wardens. In addition to supervising the care of public wells, the City Wardens were now to inspect the pumps, to order new wells dug when necessary, and to buy up privately owned pumps situated on the city's streets (Bridenbaugh 1955:106, 109).

Although the City Wardens did acquire most of the privately owned street pumps, the majority of wells were located in the cellars or backyards of private dwellings, where there was typically also a convenient privy. The privy pit was usually constructed in the same fashion as the well—lined with dry-laid bricks and unpaved at the bottom—but as of 1769 it was by law supposed to be shallower. By then the seepage between privies and wells had become so widespread and the contamination of drinking water so obvious that a city ordinance forbade the digging of a privy pit to the level of the water table (Cosans 1975; McCarthy, Cosans-Zebooker, and Henry 1985). It was also illegal to place a privy above an abandoned well.

The proximity of wells to privy pits no doubt explains the bacterial intestinal ailments that afflicted so many eighteenth-century Philadelphians. The connection seems even more evident when, as so often happened, a privy was illegally placed on top of a well that had gone dry, as so many wells did in the wake of street paving and the use of cisterns to collect rain water. As the population grew, so did the problem of water pollution; underground streams were soon tainted. Exacerbating the problem were a number of tanneries that spewed offal into Dock Creek, which by the 1760s was an open, foul-smelling sewer.

Fortuitously, the medical care available to Philadelphians was among the best to be had in the colonies, but judging from the number of eighteenth-century patent-medicine bottles archaeologists have found in the city, it would seem that quite a few people preferred not to avail themselves of it or could not afford to do so. Rather than submitting to what the physicians of the day prescribed—bleedings, purgings, and the like, which were often more unpleasant and debilitating than the complaints they were supposed to cure—many Philadelphians evidently turned to the more pleasant, if equally ineffective, cures of patent medicines, usually heavily laced with alcohol, stimulants, or narcotics. Heeded or not, Philadelphia's physicians counted among their ranks some distinguished figures, including Dr. Thomas Bond, who, with the support of Benjamin Franklin, founded the Pennsylvania Hospital. The first institution of its kind in the colonies, the Pennsylvania Hospital was second to none anywhere in its accommodations, design, and care. Modeled after the charity hospitals of London and Paris, it admitted both paying and charity cases and the mentally as well as the physically ill; only those suffering from incurable illnesses or contagious diseases were barred (Bridenbaugh 1955:132). Construction of the hospital began in 1755, when the east wing of the complex was built at Eighth and Pine streets, then at the fringe of the city (Figure 2.11).

In 1713 the Society of Friends established the city's first almshouse; true to the Quaker tradition, it was open to the poor of all creeds. With the private sector taking up the slack in this area of public welfare, the city fathers managed to drag their heels for thirteen years before finally implementing the assembly's 1717 order to build a structure to accommodate the poor. Erected in 1730–1733, the City Almshouse was in the block of land bordered by Spruce, Pine, Third, and Fourth streets. As the century progressed and an increasing number of destitute immigrants landed in Philadelphia, both the Friends' Almshouse and the City Almshouse became overcrowded. By 1729 the Friends' Almshouse had already moved to larger quarters (Tolles 1948:67, 71). But even though the City Almshouse was at times housing four to six men in rooms 10 or 11 feet square, it stayed as it was until 1767. By that time, the land on which it stood had become so valuable that it was razed and a new public almshouse for the "poor and helpless" and a "House of Employment" for the poor capable of work were built on Spruce Street between Tenth and Eleventh (Figure 2.12). Later, another building known as the "Bettering House" was added to the complex (Scharf and Westcott 1884:1450–51).

Until 1751, when Benjamin Franklin's efforts resulted in the founding of a nonsectarian academy, church schools and private schoolmasters provided all the formal education that was to be had in Philadelphia; it was not until 1818 that the city had anything approaching a public school system (Richardson 1982:226). Reflecting the Quaker view that classical curriculum was an aristocratic frip-

Figure 2.11.

The Pennsylvania Hospital. The east wing (at the right) was designed by Robert Smith and promoted and managed by Samuel Rhoads. It was built in 1755. The west wing and the center pavilion, though specified in Rhoads' plans, were not built until after 1794. Designed together with the west wing by David Evans, Jr., the center pavilion reflects the Federal style that came into vogue after the Revolution. (Engraving by W. Birch & Son; courtesy of the Free Library of Philadelphia)

Figure 2.12.

The Almshouse (at left) and the House of Employment, erected in 1767 on Spruce Street between Tenth and Eleventh. The pattern of moving the almshouse and workhouse west onto less valuable land was to continue; these buildings were demolished in the 1830s when the Blockley Almshouse was built in West Philadelphia. (Engraving by W. Birch & Son; courtesy of Independence National Historical Park)

pery and higher education unnecessary, the first Friends' schools concentrated on practical, useful subjects. By the 1740s, however, the city's growing prosperity and the social ambitions that accompanied it had led even the Quakers to establish a Latin school for more affluent students. Nonetheless, when the academy that Franklin had helped found was chartered as the College of Philadelphia in 1755, the Quakers reacted hostilely. Since the college's curriculum included both practical and classical subjects, their hostility probably had at least as much to do with their realization that the college would increase the power of the Anglicans as with their views on education. In 1790, thirty-five years after it received its charter, the College of Philadelphia emerged, in the wake of much political discord and wrangling, as the University of Pennsylvania (Bridenbaugh and Bridenbaugh 1942:29–32, 41; Tolles 1948:149–51; Miller 1982:167–68).

The City on the Eve of the Revolution

By 1770 Philadelphia's citizens and elected commissions had accomplished a great deal, and the lessons they had learned in self-government would serve them well in the coming years.* Thanks to their efforts, Philadelphia's streets were paved, illumi-

* Philadelphia committees would, in fact, play a major role in the American Revolution. Although outnumbered by Pennsylvanians who opposed separation from England, committees of Philadelphia Whigs managed in May 1776 to bring about the downfall of the Pennsylvania Assembly and to establish a new state government squarely in line with the revolutionary cause.

nated, and lined with handsome buildings. With their diverse backgrounds and penchant for profit and sociability, they had created a cosmopolitan community where ideas flowed freely. Although their city was by no means completely built-up and vast spaces still lay undeveloped west of Seventh Street, it was a far cry from the frontier town of the 1690s. Situated at the geographical center of the colonies, it was also a center of trade, finance, and printing. Moreover, thanks once again to its foremost citizen, Benjamin Franklin, it had a fairly efficient postal service, and improved stagecoach/stageboat service made it as accessible a place as any in the colonies. It was therefore a most logical meeting place for the gentlemen of the First Continental Congress, who gathered in Carpenters' Hall in September of 1774 to decide the fate of the colonies.

THE CITY AT WAR: 1775 – 1783

While Philadelphia might have been a logical meeting place for political conventions, it was not a particularly well-equipped place for waging war. Quaker sentiment had long resisted the expenditure of public money for military defense, and the city's location—shielded from the Atlantic by New Jersey and situated about a hundred miles up a river full of shoals and shallows—had given its citizens a false sense of security (Thayer 1982:103). When the Revolutionary War began in 1775, Philadelphia was virtually defenseless. The Association Battery (Figure 2.13), a riverfront fortification of cannons in Southwark that was erected as a defense against French and Spanish privateers in 1748, had apparently been abandoned for some time. The most promising means of protecting the city from attack by the British fleet was an unfinished fort on Mud Island, just south of the city and separated from the mainland by a narrow channel. Begun under the direction of British engineers in 1772 to defend the city against raiding ships, the fort was left unfinished the following year when the funds appropriated for its construction ran out. The British had been apprehensive throughout the Seven Years' War (1756–1763), an extension of the French and Indian War (1754–1763) that involved all of Europe, including Great Britain and Spain. In 1777 the Americans hastily completed it, christening it Fort Mifflin. It was very soon to play a memorable role in the unfolding military drama.

On September 26, 1777, fifteen days after the Battle of the Brandywine, Maj. Gen. Charles Lord Cornwallis marched the vanguard of Gen. Sir William Howe's victorious army into Philadelphia. And there, despite the best efforts of the patriots at Fort Mifflin, 20,000 British and Hessian soldiers remained for the better part

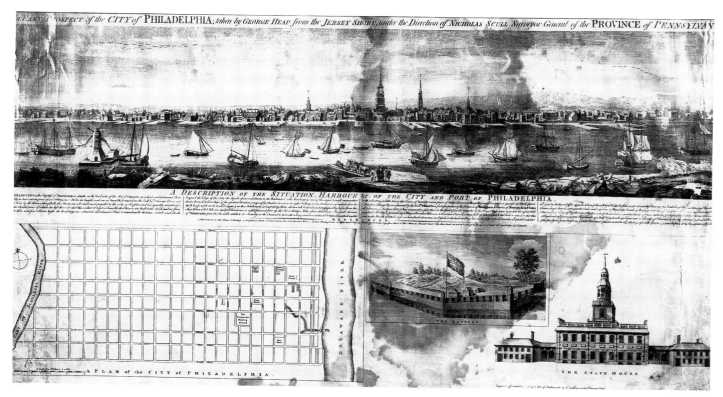

Figure 2.13.

The Association Battery, an inset from George Heap's *East Prospect of the City of Philadelphia,* done under the direction of Nicholas Scull, surveyor general of Pennsylvania, 1754. (Courtesy of the Historical Society of Pennsylvania)

of a year. Although a large crowd turned out to greet Cornwallis and his regiment, most of the crowd were women and children; also much in evidence were Quakers, whose meetings had forbidden them to help the war effort in any way. Many citizens loyal to the revolutionary cause had already fled, and of those who remained, males over the age of eighteen were noticeably scarce. What war supplies could be removed from the city had been; the state government and the Congress had fled to Lancaster, the former settling there for the duration of the occupation while the latter went on to York; and the city's bells, including the one from atop the State House, had been carted off for safekeeping to Allentown (Siebert 1972:22, 29, 48; Tinkcom 1982:133).

Relatively empty though the city may have been, the presence of so many soldiers and the rapid appearance of numerous refugees created a great strain. Food, usually abundant and cheap, was often extremely scarce, as were shoes and clothing. Prices became exorbitant, with tea selling for $50 and $60 a pound and silk for $100 a yard, and wood was sometimes unobtainable. Until the British left on June 18, 1778, people such as Mayor Samuel Powel and his family, who had chosen to remain in the city, were relegated to the rear of their houses, while British officers enjoyed the luxurious furnishings of the front (Siebert 1972:46–47; Morton 1877:35; Warner 1987:35; Watson 1909, v. 2:285; Tinkcom 1982:140).

While people such as the Powels suffered inconveniences during the

British occupation, the Continental soldiers in the new Walnut Street Prison suffered far worse. The prison, built in 1775 and intended to serve as a model of Quaker penal reform, served instead as a military prison, and the Americans confined there during the nine months the British occupied the city apparently suffered tortures as bad as any experienced by military prisoners in the twentieth century (Watson 1909, v. 2:300–2). Others in the occupied city did not have such a bad time of it; some, in fact, seem to have had quite a good time of it, and to have seen that their British visitors did as well. No doubt relieved at the departure of the Congress, which had prohibited gaming, theater, and other amusements for the duration of the war, wealthy Philadelphians of a Tory persuasion went on with their usual style of entertaining—lavish balls and dinners that had shocked the recently departed puritanical congressmen from New England and pleased the more relaxed ones from the South. The social season was a gala one (Tinkcom 1982: 152–53; Watson 1909, v. 2:290–93; Siebert 1972:51), and the hospitality the British received was such that it prompted Benjamin Franklin to remark, with considerable accuracy, that rather than Howe's having taken Philadelphia, Philadelphia had taken Howe (Van Doren 1956:585). After the ratification of the French alliance in May 1778, the British, anticipating an attack by the French fleet at New York, at long last decamped for the north, and some three thousand of their former Tory hosts decamped with them (Warner 1987:25, 29). By the end of June, there was but one minister of the Anglican faith left in the city, a young member of the city's elite by the name of William White.

White, like other Philadelphians, suffered the ruinous inflation that beset the city in 1779. Beginning with a poor wheat crop even before the British departed, food prices began rising, and they rose ever higher as repeated issues of Continental paper money caused the currency to depreciate to the point that vendors refused to accept it. Prices jumped 45 percent in one month alone, and money was worth seven times less than it had been in 1777. While all suffered, the working class suffered the most, and, with the economy in such dire straits and the populace in turmoil, the fate of the war hung in the balance (Warner 1987:29–30; Watson 1909, v. 2:299). Help appeared in the form of Robert Morris, known today as the financier of the American Revolution. Shortly after his appointment by Congress in 1781 as Superintendent of Finance—the equivalent of today's Secretary of the Treasury—Morris created the Bank of North America, which helped muster the resources necessary to carry the army through to end of the war. Another important figure in revitalizing the economy was Haym Salomon, an exiled Polish Jew who served as broker in Morris's Office of Finance and as agent for the French in America (Tinkcom 1982:147; Wolf and Whiteman 1975:101, 105).

Before the last major battle of the Revolutionary War was fought at Yorktown in 1781, many Philadelphia properties had been put to uses for which they were not originally intended. The British colonial State House had housed the rebel American government, and State House Yard behind it, now known as Independence Square, had served as an artillery park for the rebels and, while the British occupied the city, for them as well. Carpenters' Hall had become the Continental Army's Commissary of Military Stores, and, as the need arose, it had also served as a military hospital. In 1776 and 1777, when camp disease and smallpox took a terrible toll, the Pennsylvania Hospital and the new "Bettering House" for the poor on Spruce Street had overflowed with dying soldiers, and the pauper's burial ground in nearby Washington Square had become a military cemetery. The Bonnin and Morris Porcelain Factory in Southwark, defunct since 1772, had been hastily converted to a cannon foundry, and pastoral Franklin Square in the northeast quadrant of the city had become the site of a powder magazine. Private homes intended for genteel entertaining had served as officers' quarters, and as wood grew scarce, fine flooring and paneling had been ripped up and fed to warming fires. For all these "adaptive uses," there is abundant archaeological evidence.

When the war officially ended in 1783, Philadelphia, looking quite bedraggled, clearly showed the effects of long years of neglect. House shutters sagged, trim was unpainted, and broken window panes abounded. Pavements were in disrepair, public buildings that had lately quartered soldiers and horses still bore the scent of their former occupants, and State House Yard looked as if an army had tramped through it, which it had. All this was reparable, however, and, overall, Philadelphia had emerged from the war relatively unscathed. Estimated damages from the vandalism and theft that occurred during the British occupation of the city amounted to £187,280 5s. (Siebert 1972:55). It would not be long before Philadelphians once again set their city to rights.

THE CITY IN THE FEDERAL ERA: 1783–1830

In 1783 Philadelphia, together with Southwark and the Northern Liberties, had a population estimated at close to 39,000 people, a significant increase over the population of pre-war days (Nash and Smith 1975:366). Many of these people had been profitably engaged in making munitions, uniforms, and blankets for the Continental Army. The businesses of printers, tavern keepers, and other tradesmen had also flourished as the result of the presence of Congress and the small bureaucracy it engendered. When the war ended, some economic displacement was inevitable. Congress's abrupt and acrimonious departure from the city in June 1783, occasioned by the refusal of the state government to use force against mutinous soldiers who were demanding back pay from Congress, did not help the city's foundering economy (Watson 1909, v. 2:331–32). Nor did the rapid resumption of trade with Britain, which glutted the market with cheap imported goods. Local manufacturers were unable to compete, unemployment rose, and commerce and industry stagnated (Miller 1982:157).

Philadelphia was not alone in its economic difficulties. Many of the states were also feeling the postwar economic pinch and were appealing to the national government for assistance. Interstate commerce was in a particular shambles, for under the Articles of Confederation that Congress had adopted in November of 1777, each of the thirteen states regulated its own commerce and currency. The upshot of all this was that Philadelphia once again became the scene of a historic meeting, the Constitutional Convention of 1787. With the Constitution's creation of a strong, centralized government and a Congress empowered "to regulate commerce with foreign nations, and among the several states," the economy of the new republic, and particularly that of Philadelphia, began to prosper. By 1789 the city's volume of shipping had increased some 50 percent over the volume of the best prewar years (Miller 1982:199). Commerce expanded even more dramatically in the next decade, as Philadelphia merchants set their sights not just on the markets of Europe and the Caribbean, but also on those of the Orient (Figure 2.14).

While the changes in federal government were of great benefit to Philadelphia, reorganization in city government was also a boon. In 1789 the state legislature granted the city a new charter, which in effect modernized the municipal government. For the first time, the city was to be governed by elected officials: a board of aldermen and a Common Council elected by the voters and a mayor

Figure 2.14.

The Philadelphia ship *Globe,* anchored in the Pearl River, Canton, China, ca. 1831. After the 1790s, more and more such ships plied the waterways of the Orient. (Courtesy of the Atwater Kent Museum)

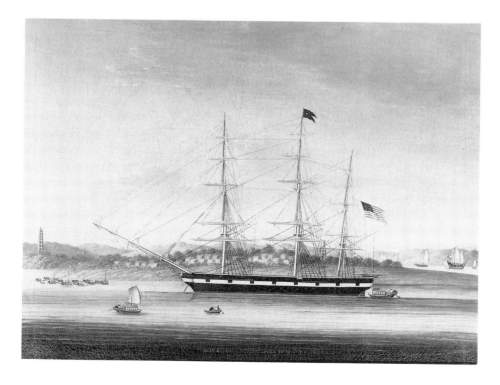

elected by the aldermen from among their own number. In marked contrast to the old corporation, the new one had effective taxing power, invested in 1790 in the Common Council. In 1796 the state again amended the charter by splitting the Common Council into a Select Council and a Common Council, which together had the legislative power of the city (Miller 1982:166, 203). As a result of these changes, municipal services expanded, as befitted a city again about to play host to the nation's government.

The 1790s: Philadelphia as the Nation's Capital

With the federal government temporarily ensconced in New York in the late 1780s, the subject of a permanent site for the capital of the new nation was a matter of great interest to Philadelphians, and the object of much political wrangling and bargaining as well. The city's councilmen offered some incentives to congressional representatives, promising that Philadelphia would be a fitting setting, with new buildings and houses ready to accommodate the federal government and its officials (Figure 2.15). Although the best that Philadelphia got

out of the bargain was a ten-year reign as the nation's capital, the councilmen were as good as their word. By the time the House of Representatives and the Senate arrived in 1790, a new county courthouse at the northwest corner of State House Yard was ready for their use, and Robert Morris's mansion on Market Street near Sixth was being remodeled at city expense for President Washington and his family (Miller 1982:170). By the end of the following year, a new city hall at the northeast corner of State House Yard was ready to house the U.S. Supreme Court.

The Philadelphia that greeted federal officials in 1790 was a far sprightlier-looking city than the one those gentlemen had left behind seven years before. Householders had been busy refurbishing their properties, and the city itself had been busily paving streets and trying to improve sewers. One of the Street Commis-

sioners' notable endeavors in 1784 was to pave over part of evil-smelling Dock Creek between Second and Front Streets south of Walnut (Liggett 1971a). Although that eliminated one source of offensive odors, those returning to the city would have found it by no means completely rid of its familiar stench. Open sewers still ran through the streets, cow hides still putrified in the yards of tanneries, and the heavy smell of fermenting hops in the breweries still mingled with the odors emanating from stables and privies. The residents of the city must have been inured to the stench, for in Philadelphia's heterogeneous neighborhoods, they often lived right next door to the source of the fumes. In 1788, for example, the Reverend William White, now a bishop, moved into his elegant new home on Walnut Street, built within a stone's throw of a tannery and a soap-boiler and tallow chandler.

Figure 2.15.

Mansion on Ninth Street, ca. 1797, looking west across open land toward the public almshouse complex. The Commonwealth of Pennsylvania began building this house for President Washington in 1792. By the time it was finished in 1797, John Adams was president, and he declined to live in it. In 1800 the University of Pennsylvania took it over. (Engraving by W. Birch & Son; courtesy of the Free Library of Philadelphia)

Even though the wooded land west to the Schuylkill had been cleared during the war, federal officials returning to Philadelphia would have found most of the population still living east of Seventh Street. People were, however, continuing to push north and south along the Delaware beyond the city limits, and as those areas grew, they were incorporated as separate political entities. Although Southwark had by the 1760s become large enough to warrant its incorporation as a separate district, it was not until the 1790s that the area north of the city experienced similar development. The boom there began when the Commonwealth of Pennsylvania, owner of all Penn's holdings at the end of the war, sold off sizable portions of the Northern Liberties to pay off war debts (Garvan 1963:197–98). Those lands had soon become house lots, and by 1803 the process of subdividing the Northern Liberties into districts, townships, and boroughs had begun (Warner 1987:51).

Had the members of Congress been able to foresee the yellow fever epidemics that would plague the city throughout the 1790s, they might have thought twice about making Philadelphia the nation's temporary capital. The first, and the worst, epidemic occurred in 1793, and it was followed almost annually by other outbreaks of varying degrees of severity until the early 1800s. In the first epidemic, over 4,000 people—or about a tenth of the population—died between August and November. Some 23,000 others fled the city (Warner 1987:103). Among those absent from Philadelphia was George Washington, who spent November of 1793 in the cooler and healthier air of Germantown in what became known as the first "summer White House." Washington liked the Deshler-Morris

House well enough to return the following summer with his family, setting a precedent for seasonal escape from the White House increasingly honored by American presidents ever since.

As panic grew in the summer of 1793 and more and more people fled the city in terror, the mayor asked for volunteers who would remain behind to help the sick and dying. Only two people came forth: Absalom Jones and Richard Allen, both black clergymen. Jones and Allen had once been members of St. George's Methodist Episcopal Church, but both had withdrawn from that predominantly white and segregated congregation. Jones had gone on to establish St. Thomas's, the first Episcopal church for blacks in the country, while Allen had formed the African Methodist church of Mother Bethel at Lombard Street and Sixth. In 1787 Jones and Allen had together founded the Free African Society, whose members were among the unsung heroes of the plague years of the 1790s. In 1793, when an unknown but rapidly rising financier by the name of Stephen Girard organized an asylum for the unwanted plague victims at a remote suburban estate, it was mainly blacks who carted the sick there and who carted the dead away. Throughout the 1790s and on into the 1800s, blacks did more nursing of the "yellow jack" victims than their share of the population or their status would have warranted; in 1808 they accounted for only about 11 percent of the population, and only thirty of them were slaves (Wolf 1975:141).

When the first yellow fever epidemic struck in 1793, Dr. Benjamin Rush, the city's most eminent physician, declared that in his opinion the disease was caused by noxious vapors. Very soon thereafter, Philadelphians

were carrying scent bottles about with them and covering their faces with handkerchiefs doused in camphor. As the plague-ridden decade progressed, they also paid more attention to their privies, cleaning them and giving them generous applications of lime. In her diary for March 5–7, 1799, Elizabeth Drinker records these practices:

Five men with two Carts &c. are about a dirty Jobb in our yard to night, they are removing the offerings from ye temple of Cloacine, which have been 44 years depositing—Jacob, Sarah, Peter and Sally are burning incense in the kitchen . . . 'tho . . . we have not been offended by any bad smell—as yet—clear and cold tonight—we have desired the watchman to attend to our alley, as those Goldfinders may leave the gate open. . . .
. . . The men are at work again to night in our Yard. . . . [They] say that they never emptied a necessary that was so little disagreeable [smelling]—whether it is oweing to the cold weather, or to the lime that we have put in three times, when the fever raged, I know not. . . .
. . . The job in our yard is finish'd. . . . They were at work two nights, from . . . nine . . . till . . . 4 & 5 in the morn'g and were very industrious. I believe it is now sunk near 16 feet from the seat; upwards of 13 from the top of the well, a dreadful gulph it looks like—they would have dug [if permitted] nearer to the Antipodes, . . . for the sake of 3 dollars pr foot, and good living during the night, for they not only eat at their business, but it appears, have a good appetite! (Manuscript of *Diary of Elizabeth Drinker*, Historical Society of Pennsylvania)

The industriousness of the hearty privy cleaners notwithstanding, such efforts had little or no effect on the *Aedes aegypti* mosquito that actually spreads yellow fever. By the end of the decade there was a growing public suspicion that polluted drinking water was the cause of the disease. This was

Figure 2.16.

The Bank of Pennsylvania, designed in the Greek Revival style by Benjamin Latrobe in 1798. The City Tavern (at left), built in 1773, was just south of the bank on Second Street between Walnut and Chestnut. (Engraving by W. Birch & Son; courtesy of the Free Library of Philadelphia)

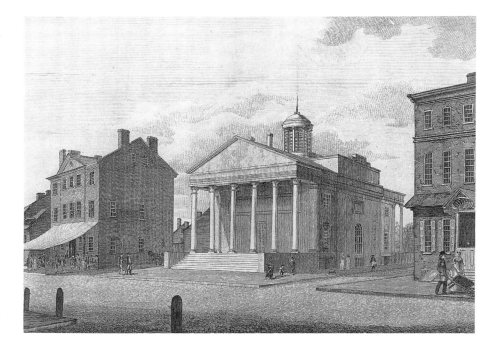

somewhat more to the point, for no doubt the mosquitos found the city's numerous creeks, stagnant puddles, open sewers, and marshy areas hospitable breeding places.

Despite the epidemics of the 1790s, Philadelphia grew and prospered. It began the decade with just over 44,000 citizens, including those living in Southwark and the Northern Liberties; by 1800, the urban population numbered almost 68,000 (Warner 1987:51, 245). By that time, too, the city's architecture had begun to change. When the federal government arrived in 1790, the prevailing style was the sturdy, robust Georgian. Ten years later, the city had a number of new mansions and public buildings designed in the lighter and more graceful Federal style, derived from classical Roman design. One of the finest examples of Federal architecture still standing in America is the center pavilion of the Pennsylvania Hospital designed, with its west wing, in 1794 by David Evans, Jr. In 1800 the city also had at least one example of the Greek Revival style: the Bank of Pennsylvania, designed by architect-engineer Benjamin Latrobe in 1798 (Figure 2.16). The Greek Revival style did not, however, really catch on until after 1820. Among its most famous proponents were William Strickland, designer of the Second Bank of the United States, and John Haviland,

who published the first design book in America to include the Greek orders. At the root of the popularity of both the Federal and Greek Revival styles was the new republic's wish to identify itself with the ideals of the ancient republics of Rome and Greece.

When the federal government departed for Washington in 1800, it left behind at 35–43 North Seventh Street the first U.S. Mint, established in 1792 to produce a decimal currency. It also chose to make Philadelphia the home of two other important national institutions: the Navy Yard, built in Southwark shortly after the turn of the century to produce men-of-war, and the Schuylkill Arsenal, a storage depot for munitions constructed near Gray's Ferry Road in 1802–1806. By 1816 the storage capacity of the Schuylkill Arsenal had become inadequate, and the Frankford Arsenal, which not only stored matériel but also repaired and manufactured munitions, was built on the northern outskirts of the city. One

compelling reason for locating these institutions in Philadelphia was that the city had the good fortune of having many talented inventors and engineers capable of developing new technology and machinery, as well as a skilled labor force capable of using the new tools (Richardson 1982:240–41).

Inventors in the Federal City

By 1799 public outrage over the presumed link between polluted water and the yellow fever epidemics had reached such proportions that the city had hired Benjamin Latrobe to design Philadelphia's first waterworks. Located at Center Square and designed by Latrobe in the guise of a small Greek temple (Figure 2.17), the pumphouse in 1801 began delivering water from the Schuylkill to the most densely populated parts of the city. A steam-engine pump lifted the water from a basin dug to 3 feet below the water table at the river's edge and forced it along a tunnel to the central pumphouse, where another steam engine pushed it up into a reservoir 30 feet above ground. From there the water flowed by gravity through a network of wooden conduits (Richardson 1982:226–27).

Latrobe's waterworks soon proved inadequate to the task of supplying the growing city with water, and in 1815 the Fairmount Waterworks, designed by Frederick Graff, began pumping water up into a reservoir on the hill where the Philadelphia Museum of Art now stands. The Fairmount Waterworks initially used a high-pressure steam engine for pumping. But when the city councils got the bill for the wood needed to fuel the pump, engineer Graff was soon per-

suaded to find another means of power. By 1822 he had not only installed an economical hydraulic system that operated with large waterwheels but had also replaced the wooden water conduits with cast-iron pipes. The Fairmount Waterworks, a harmonious collection of classical buildings in a

picturesque setting, were a favorite tourist attraction and the inspiration of many a nineteenth-century artist (Figure 2.18). They continued to serve the city until 1909.

The high-pressure steam engine that first powered the Fairmount Waterworks was the creation of Oliver

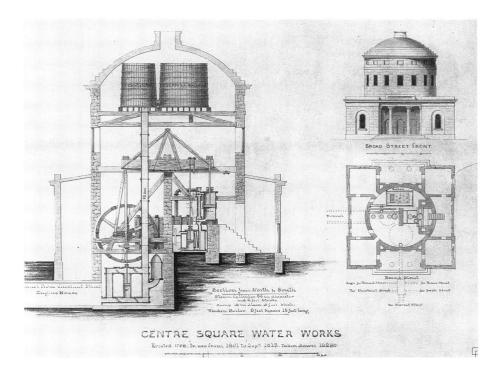

Figure 2.17.

Benjamin Latrobe's design for the waterworks at Center Square, drawn by Frederick Graff about 1828. (Courtesy of the Historical Society of Pennsylvania)

Figure 2.18.

View of the Fairmount Waterworks, 1829. (Engraving published by Cephas Grier Childs after Thomas Doughty; courtesy of the Free Library of Philadelphia)

Figure 2.19.

The *Orukter Amphibolis.* (Courtesy of the Historical Society of Pennsylvania)

Evans, perhaps the most outstanding of the many inventive talents in the early nineteenth-century city. After moving to Philadelphia from his native state of Delaware, Evans opened the Mars Iron Works at Ninth and Race streets, where in 1800 he began manufacturing steam engines. There he also proceeded to build the world's first self-propelled amphibious vehicle, which he named, for reasons known only to him, the *Orukter Amphibolis* (Figure 2.19). In June 1805, this remarkable vehicle powered its way by means of one of Evans' own high-pressure steam engines all the way from Eighth and Market streets up around Latrobe's pumphouse in Center Square and thence to the Schuylkill River, into which it waddled on wheels, only to sail triumphantly away by means of a stern paddlewheel. Although the *Orukter* returned safely to its Philadelphia home, it engendered no revolution in vehicular or nautical transportation. Of more enduring value and utility were Evans' high-pressure steam engines, which would play an important role in the industrial evolution of the city, and the automated flour mill that he had earlier developed in Delaware. The latter became the prototype for the gravity flow of grain from the top floor of a mill through a milling process to a barreling operation on the ground floor, where the flour was ready to be carted away.

Charles Willson Peale, known today primarily for his portrait painting, also contributed to the mania of inventiveness that gripped the city in

the early 1800s. In 1816 Peale installed gas lights—one of the first such uses of gas in the city—to illuminate his paintings and natural science exhibits, which were housed in a rather unlikely spot: Independence Hall. A wood-fired retort placed in the tower room of that august building produced the gas from wood chips. Providentially, the retort was removed before it could send the hallowed hall up in flames.

Philadelphia on the Eve of the Industrial Revolution

The presence of so many gifted inventors was an important factor in setting the stage for the industrial city that Philadelphia would soon become. But there were other factors as well. In 1800 Philadelphia was already one of the world's largest manufacturing

centers, with numerous small textile and paper mills, printing plants, foundries, brickyards, breweries, and factories devoted to making everything from shoes, carpets, and wire to pottery, snuff, and nails. It also had in place the beginnings of a wage-labor system, inaugurated during the boom years of the 1790s when entrepreneurial artisans, reorganizing their workplaces to meet the demand for goods, began abandoning the time-honored contractual agreement between master and apprentice.

Philadelphia was in addition a banking center, with investment capital available to fund new technology, and its government was controlled by businessmen willing to accept innovation and already intent upon improving transportation (Warner 1963:65). When New York, with its ice-free and more accessible harbor, began usurping Philadelphia's place as the major port in America, Philadelphia's merchants were quick to realize that the way to the wealth of the future lay not in oceanic shipping lanes but in the path to the interior. As early as 1795 a paved turnpike—the first one in America—connected Philadelphia with Lancaster, sixty-six miles to the west (Smith 1862:405). By 1828 the private and public sectors had spent some twenty million dollars on creating a network of turnpikes, bridges, and canals to connect Philadelphia with the interior (Watson 1909, v. 2:465).

The natural resources of the region also favored industrial development. The many streams that descend the Piedmont to the Fall Line had always provided abundant water power and, since the earliest days of the city, had been dotted with water-powered mills. The water power generated by the fall to the Delaware and the Schuylkill would not, however, be great enough to supply the demands of the industrial age; the transformation of the city into an industrial metropolis needed yet another component.

Anthracite coal, capable of producing tremendous heat at low cost, was the missing link, and it was to be found in plenty in northeastern Pennsylvania. Although it was discovered there sometime before 1768, when blacksmiths in Wyoming, Pennsylvania, began using it, it was generally considered to be of little value. Unlike bituminous coal, which responds to poking, anthracite coal ignites best when left alone. Not realizing that, most people could not get it to burn, and it was in any case very difficult and expensive to transport from the wild country where it was found down to Philadelphia. As so often happens, the first real breakthrough came about by accident. One day in 1815, Josiah White, Erskine Hazard, and their colleagues became totally exasperated after repeated attempts to get the "black stones" to burn in the furnace of White and Hazard's rolling mill and wire factory at the Falls of the Schuylkill. They slammed the door on the furnace and walked off. One of them, however, had left his jacket in the factory and when he returned to get it, he found the doors of the furnace red from the intense heat within. That one fire provided enough heat to process three separate runs of iron (Hagner 1869:42–42).

Having seen the industrial usefulness of hard coal, White immediately turned his attention to its domestic possibilities, creating grates in which it could be burned to heat homes. He also lost no time in devising a plan for bringing the anthracite down from the mines above Reading. Before 1815 was out, he had formed the Schuylkill Navigation Company, which over the next ten years constructed the Schuylkill Canal, a complex of canals, locks, and dams running from north of Reading to Fairmount in Philadelphia. Disgusted with that company's management and slow progress, White in 1818 formed the Lehigh Coal and Navigation Company, which built a system of canals along the Lehigh River to transport the coal from the mines above Mauch Chunk (Hagner 1869:42–51). Down the canals to Philadelphia came the coal, first in trickles, soon in tens of thousands of tons. So began the saga of Pennsylvania's anthracite industry, which would soon fuel the fires of the Industrial Revolution.

THE EARLY INDUSTRIAL CITY: 1830–1860

Some fifty years after the American Revolution ended, Philadelphia found itself in the vanguard of yet another revolution—one that would irreversibly alter the patterns of urban life. In 1830 the city was, as it had been for many years, a pleasant but booming place; both a port and a manufacturing center, it had a trans-Atlantic orientation and a somewhat sleepy southern air overlying its commercial bustle. By 1860 much of that would change. The city would look increasingly to the interior for its wealth, and it would begin taking on many of the earmarks of the modern metropolis, among them mechanized industries with large workforces, a sizable number of commuters, inner-city slums, and expensive residential and shopping districts. As Philadelphia's one-man shops and heterogeneous neighborhoods began fading into oblivion, the gap between the haves and have-nots, accepted with equanimity by so many generations of Philadelphians, would widen. Strikes and violent riots would mark the early years of industrial Philadelphia.

Signs of Industrial Progress and Prosperity

A myriad of factors contributed to the city's transformation. Each year after

1825, the canals brought an increasing tonnage of anthracite coal to Philadelphia, where it was used to fire industrial steam engines and, more and more, to heat homes and buildings; what coal was not used in the area was shipping out to other ports. In addition to transporting coal, the canals transported goods to and from the water-powered mills situated along them, and in doing so they fostered the growth of mill towns (Warner 1963:65). Between 1820 and 1830, Manayunk, situated along the Schuylkill Canal, was transformed from a lonely backwater into a thriving textile center (Hagner 1869:55, 79:80). The use of coal, however, meant that mills no longer had to be located along waterways, and they soon began springing up at random throughout the city and its environs.

Early on in the industrial age, lo-

comotives were competing with the canal barges for the coal-transport business. Among the competing railroad companies were the Philadelphia, Germantown & Norristown Railroad, which began operations in 1832, and the Philadelphia and Reading Railroad. Chartered in 1833, the Reading began service between Philadelphia and Reading in 1839, and in 1842 it opened another branch to connect with its coal wharves at Port Richmond on the Delaware (Figure 2.20). Two years later the Reading had clearly won the battle with the canals; it was by then transporting almost 450,000 more tons of coal per year than the Schuylkill Canal (Fisher 1962:162, 166, 168). At the insistence of the citizens of Pittsburgh that there be an unbroken line between their city and the East, the Pennsylvania Railroad came into being in 1846. It

took eight years to complete the connection, but in 1854 the Pennsylvania inaugurated service along its main line from Philadelphia to the future steel capital of the world (Scharf and Westcott 1884:2189–90).

Carrying passengers as well as freight, the Pennsylvania, like all the other railroads, made stops at suburban places a convenient distance from the city. The railroad companies thus spawned the first generation of commuters. Unlike later commuters, the ones who rode the early trains had to disembark at the outskirts of the city, where horse power replaced steam. Philadelphians, ever-cautious about fire, feared that sparks from the locomotives' steam engines, which until the late 1850s were fired by wood, would set shingled roofs ablaze. Although public apprehension about accidents also delayed the introduction of horse-drawn railway streetcars until 1858, the city by 1840 had numerous horse-drawn omnibuses and cabs that enabled people to get about the city (Wainwright 1982:285; Geffen 1982:316). As coal-powered steam engines became ubiquitous and an increasing number of manufacturing plants were scattered throughout the city, more and more people used these conveyances to get to their jobs. By 1860 perhaps a third of Philadelphians were no longer living in the neighborhoods in which they worked (Warner 1987:61).

Figure 2.20.

Port Richmond from the air ca. 1925, showing the fan of railroads serving the coal export elevators. (Courtesy of the City of Philadelphia Archives)

Figure 2.21.

View of Philadelphia, ca. 1855, looking east toward the Delaware. Plumes of smoke rise above new factories. The Fairmount Reservoir is visible at lower left and the gasworks at lower center. (Drawn by Asselineau from a watercolor by John Bachman, published by John Caspar Wild, Paris, ca. 1855; courtesy of the Historical Society of Pennsylvania)

The caution with which Philadelphians initially approached innovations in transportation also characterized their attitude toward other technological developments. Compared with New Yorkers and Bostonians, they were slow to accept the use of gas. It was not until 1836 that the Philadelphia Gas Company, a semiprivate enterprise located at Market Street and Twenty-Third, began producing gas from soft coal. But when the first gas street lamps illuminated Second Street from Vine to South in 1837, they were a huge success. They dazzled Philadelphians with their brilliance and evoked much favorable comment. Four years later the city bought out the gasworks, and by 1863, 450 miles of pipes were carrying gas to half a million lamps all over the city.

A strange mixture of caution and daring characterized Philadelphia's industries in 1860. Some seemed to be still clinging to the ways of the eighteenth century, while others were anticipating those of the twentieth. Among the latter was the Baldwin Locomotive Works, which in 1832 produced the first locomotive for the Philadelphia-Norristown railway line.

Figure 2.22.

"Portico Row," built in 1831–32 at 700–730 Spruce Street. Designed by Thomas U. Walter for a real estate speculator, the houses were sold to affluent, upper-middle-class merchants and professionals. Projecting over their entrances are porticoes supported by marble Ionic columns. (Photo by J. L. Cotter)

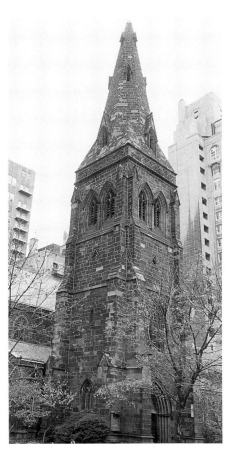

Figure 2.23.

St. Mark's Church. (Photo by J. L. Cotter)

Six years later Baldwin was producing almost half the nation's locomotives (Wainwright 1982:276). Like its hold on the market, Baldwin's large work-force was an omen of things to come; in 1860 Baldwin employed over six hundred people. The cotton-goods industry was also in the avant-garde. Fully mechanized outside the city proper, it had an average of ninety-four employees per factory. In 1860, however, such sizable workforces were exceptional. Many people still worked in small shops, making shoes or furniture, sewing garments, spinning wool, or rolling cigars by hand (Warner 1987:71, 77). But in time they, too, would be caught up in the web of industrialization.

A series of economic setbacks during the first half of the nineteenth century—among them the Panic of 1837—resulted in Philadelphia's losing its place as financial leader to New York. Nonetheless, the city's population grew dramatically and, as shown in Figure 2.21, its appearance changed, too. Between 1800 and 1850 the population of the city proper almost tripled, increasing from 41,220 to 121,376. But as fast as the city grew, Philadelphia County, with its numerous new smoke-belching factories, grew even faster. By 1860 the combined population of city and county was 565,529. Foreign-born immigrants accounted for about 30 percent of the population, with Irish Catholics making up an ever-larger proportion of the population after 1830. Germans, too, contributed substantially to the influx (Warner 1987: 51, 56, 138).

Many of the newcomers settled in manufacturing centers in the county—such places as Manayunk, Kensington, and Frankford. The rest were scattered throughout the city, which was in effect a large melting pot. It was not until later in the nineteenth century that the city began to be characterized by a distinct "core of poverty" surrounded by a "ring of affluence." Well before 1860, however, the city's first slums had sprung up in parts of Society Hill and Southwark, where by mid-century impoverished immigrants were laboring in garment sweatshops (Warner 1987:56, 59). With immigrants flooding into the city, new housing was in great demand, and as early as 1825 those who could afford it had begun moving west beyond Seventh Street, where entrepreneurs were building rows of spacious houses on a speculative basis (Figure 2.22). Heated by coal furnaces and having the luxury of indoor plumbing, many of these houses had granite fronts or marble trim and pillars—an imitative tribute to the marble temples that Greek Revival architects were by then building all over the city.

By 1850 the tree-lined streets west of Broad had begun to witness some expensive development, including the "High" Episcopal church of St. Mark's in the 1600 block of Locust Street (Figure 2.23). Founded by members of six Episcopalian congregations to "restore Catholic worship" to the Episcopalian rite, the church was designed by John Notman and built in 1849–50. It still stands as one of the finest examples of Gothic Revival architecture in America. The tone was thus set for what would become the prestigious neighborhood of Rittenhouse Square. After Joseph Harrison, Jr., fresh from making a fortune build-

ing Russian railroads for Czar Nicholas I, erected his regal mansion on the east side of Rittenhouse Square in 1855, the press of wealthy gentility to establish addresses in the area was on—and continues to this day (Vaux 1985:14–15).

With four railroad lines serving the suburban areas and horse-drawn streetcars soon to come, Germantown, Chestnut Hill, and Mount Airy northwest of the city and picturesque villages in West Philadelphia also experienced a building boom, one that anticipated the development of the bedroom suburbs. Like the villa shown in Figure 2.24, many of the suburban houses of this period were designed in the Italianate style, with elaborate detailing, as were a fair number of the commercial buildings that were being erected on the sites of older structures in the downtown area.

Some of the new commercial structures were made from prefabricated

cast-iron units. Cast-iron construction made it possible not only to mass-produce richly ornamented facades at a low cost, but to create large windows that provided ample light for the interior of commercial buildings. One of the most noteworthy commercial structures of this period was the Jayne Building, the city's first "skyscraper." Erected in 1849–50 on Chestnut Street near Third for David Jayne, M.D., a manufacturer of patent medicines and one of the nation's new class of millionaires, the eight-story building, shown in Figure 2.25, had a Venetian Gothic granite facade. The observation tower and sculptured mortars and pestles on its roof were the creation of Thomas U. Walter, one of the period's most eminent architects.

In 1853 the old High Street market sheds were demolished, and soon thereafter a new farmers' market, forerunner of today's Reading Termi-

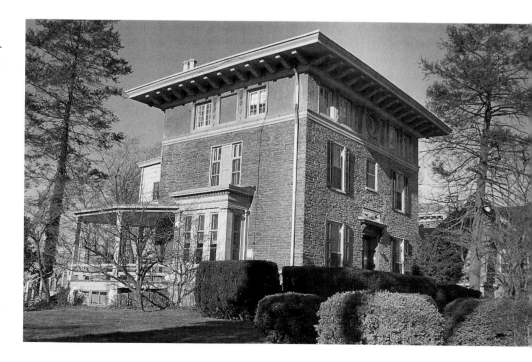

Figure 2.24.

Villa in Chestnut Hill, ca. 1854, typical of the Italianate-style house. (Photo by J. L. Cotter)

Figure 2.25.

The Jayne Building. (Courtesy of the Library Company of Philadelphia)

as Lemon Hill, was dedicated as a public park, and on South Broad Street, construction of a lavish opera house—the Academy of Music—began under the direction of architects Napoleon LeBrun and Gustave Runge.

The Other Side of Industrial Progress

Juxtaposed with the conspicuous evidence of Philadelphia's affluence was the somewhat less obvious evidence of a great deal of human misery. As industry became increasingly mechanized and the unending flood of immigrants provided a superabundance of cheap labor, the poorly paid and unemployed crowded into mean tenements. Some lived in the chopped-up spaces of large houses that the affluent had abandoned as they fled west. Others lived in narrow, three-story dwellings, each with one small room to a floor; known as "Father, Son, and Holy Ghost" houses, these miniature tenements often faced on narrow alleys or were hidden away like rabbit warrens in courtyards behind larger buildings that fronted on the main streets. Some of these buildings dated from the 1700s; similar ones went up in the Northern Liberties and Southwark in the 1840s and 1850s. In these crowded environments, the poor succumbed by the hundreds to typhus, dysentery, smallpox, scarlet fever, and tuberculosis. Malaria was a particularly prevalent killer in the swampy areas south of the city limits, but cholera epidemics took the quickest and most dramatic tolls of all. Between July and October 1832, 985 Philadelphians died of the disease, and in 1849 another cholera epidemic claimed 1,012 lives (Wainwright 1982:299; Geffen 1982:315, 318).

nal Market, opened at Market Street and Twelfth. By this time, most of the rest of Market Street was given over to business firms and manufacturers, and Chestnut Street, shown in Figure 2.26, had been for quite some years a fashionable shopping district, interspersed with grand hotels (Smith 1852:417, 419, 421). Two events in 1855 offered further testimony to the affluence of the industrial city at mid-century. Fairmount Park, known then

Figure 2.26.

The north side of Chestnut Street between Sixth and Seventh streets, painted by Benjamin Ridgway Evans in 1851. The Philadelphia Arcade, an indoor gallery of shops designed by John Haviland and built in 1827, stood between the Bolivar House and Columbia House hotels. On the other side of the Bolivar House was the Chestnut Street Theatre. By the early 1860s, hotels, like the city, would be larger; the Continental Hotel at Ninth and Chestnut streets had six floors, 476 rooms, and an elevator, one of the first in the city. (Courtesy of the Library Company of Philadelphia)

Figure 2.27.

The Dyottville Glass Works near Kensington, ca. 1831. Dr. Thomas W. Dyott, proprietor, built a chapel for his three hundred adult and child employees, hired a clergyman to preach to them three times on Sunday, had prayer meetings held on weeknights, established a temperance society on the premises, and promised "extra rewards and compensation to such as were faithful and did over-work" (Scharf and Westcott 1884:2299). This curious institution closed its doors in 1839, when its proprietor, convicted of fraudulent insolvency, was sent to prison. It reopened, under new management, in 1842. (Courtesy of the Library Company of Philadelphia)

Epidemics like these are not difficult to comprehend in view of the conditions under which the poor lived. In the late 1840s the Sanitary Committee of the Board of Health described the city's slums as

degraded or illy-ventilated purlieus, where extremes of filth and misery and loathsome disease met the eye; where horrid heaps of manure from hog and cow pens; putrifying garbage and refuse of every kind; carcases in disgusting decomposition; filthy rooms and damp, dirty and mouldy cellars, full and foul privies in close and illy-ventilated locations gave off their noxious gases. Many of these localities were in close proximity to contracted and badly contrived houses, crowded by occupants, filthy and poor, without ventilation or drainage, or receptacles for refuse, or supply of water, or the common comforts of life. (Cited in Geffen 1982:318)

Thus were future archaeologists provided opportunities to glimpse evidence of "the people without a history."

Bad as the living conditions of the poor were, their working conditions were little better. In 1833 most mill workers were putting in fourteen hours a day, six days a week, with no vacations and one holiday: ironically enough, Independence Day. For their labors, they received an average of $4.33 a week. When about three hundred Irish coal heavers walked off the Schuylkill wharves in 1835 and prevented others from working as well, they inaugurated a general strike, for house painters, bricklayers, carpenters, masons, and members of practically every other trade in the city soon followed suit. The sole concessions of the 1835 strike were a ten-hour working day and a small increase in wages. Child labor was common; of the three hundred employees at the Dyottville Glass Works just north of Kensington (Figure 2.27), more than two hundred were "apprentices"—which is to say, children. The poor who could not work at all often begged or stole and spent their "earnings" on the rum that taverns sold at a penny a glass, leading some of the more affluent to conclude that "rum is at the root of the trouble" (Sullivan 1950:23–29, 33–34; Bernstein 1950:337–39; Scharf and Westcott 1884:2299; Geffen 1982:335).

With so many immigrants and a fair number of African-American Philadelphians competing for jobs, employers were little moved by voices raised in objection to labor conditions. As the old order of apprentice and master disappeared and the factory of the industrial age took over, workers had to adjust to the new reality of job insecurity and to the fact that downward mobility was the direction of the day for Philadelphia's artisans. That a fortunate few did rise as businessmen and managers into the ranks of the affluent new middle class merely added salt to the wounds of the others. Powerless, anonymous, and per-

manently consigned to the working class, they looked on as new comforts and luxuries bloomed around them (Warner 1987:65–67).

With the gap between the haves and have-nots widening, social tensions grew and periodically exploded. During the 1830s, as the abolitionist movement gathered strength in Philadelphia, African-Americans became the focus of bitter resentment (Figure 2.28). The violence and riots that characterized this decade became even more pronounced during the 1840s, as resentment focused in turn on Irish Catholics. The violence reached a crescendo in May 1844 with riots that left several Catholic schools, churches, and private residences burned to the ground. As if all this violence was not enough, the volunteer fire companies added to the persistent turmoil, engaging in violent street fights and sometimes setting fires themselves for the honor of putting them out (Warner 1987:125–55).

Consolidation

The political division between the city and Philadelphia County's townships, boroughs, and districts made it difficult, if not impossible, for the police on either side of the city line to enforce the law and maintain the peace in these turbulent years. The political division resulted not only in inefficient law enforcement, but in a lack of uniformity in other public services—fire protection, water, gas, sewerage, and street lighting, cleaning, and paving. In 1854, in an effort to solve or at least to ameliorate some of these problems, the state legislature passed the Act of Consolidation. As a result, the county and city, which originally consisted of 2.3 square miles between Vine and South streets and the two rivers, were merged into one political entity covering 129 square miles, all governed by the same municipal body.

Figure 2.28.

On May 17, 1838, after the Anti-Slavery Convention of American Women met at Pennsylvania Hall, recently built by Philadelphia abolitionists, a mob burned the building to the ground. (Courtesy of the Library Company of Philadelphia)

Figure 2.29.

The Centennial Exposition of 1876. The dome of Memorial Hall is visible near the center of the picture. (Courtesy of the Athenaeum of Philadelphia)

THE INDUSTRIAL CITY IN ITS PRIME: 1860 – 1901

With the passage of the Act of Consolidation, Philadelphia entered the Civil War years more effectively organized to handle prosperity as it came its way. And come it did. As a result of the federal government's spending, Philadelphia emerged from the war more prosperous than ever before. Even the working class benefited. Piecework seamstresses throughout the city made uniforms for the Union troops, and the Frankford Arsenal and the Navy Yard took on additional workers to meet the demand for munitions and ships (Weigley 1982: 396, 398).

In the early postwar years, in fitting tribute to its status as the nation's industrial leader and to its role in the nation's history, Philadelphia was the hands-down choice in a contest among major American cities over which would be the site of the Centennial Exposition of 1876. The exposition, a world's fair that celebrated modern technology, was held west of the Schuylkill in Fairmount Park, which by then totaled almost 3,000 acres on both sides of the river. The guiding light behind the design of 34 of the exposition's 249 buildings (Figure 2.29) was a young Austrian immigrant and former artillery officer named Hermann Joseph Schwarzmann. Although as engineer for the Fairmount Park Commission Schwarzmann had pre-

Figure 2.30.

Houses in the 2000 block of Spruce Street, built in the 1870s and designed in the Second Empire style. (Photo by J. L. Cotter)

viously laid out the park's zoo, he had no formal training either in landscape design or architecture; at the time the exposition opened, he was thirty years old. Still standing in testimony to Schwarzmann's remarkable gifts is Memorial Hall, its imposing glass-and-iron dome rising above the bluffs of the Schuylkill (Maass 1973:40).

While Schwarzmann was busy at the exposition grounds, other builders throughout the city were also hard at work. The population had continued to grow, from 674,000 in 1870 to about 817,000 in 1876, and toward the end of the century, as poverty-stricken Italians and pogrom-driven Jews from eastern Europe and Russia began arriving in ever-increasing numbers, it approached 1,294,000. With cheap land available for expansion, Philadelphia was better equipped than geographically restricted cities such as Boston and New York to meet the demand for housing, and it soon would achieve a repu-

tation as a "city of homes." As early as 1867, about 4,500 inexpensive, single-family rowhouses were being built each year (Beers 1982:419–21; Burt and Davies 1982:488–89). This trend would continue, as would a trend toward segregation of neighborhoods along the lines of ethnicity, race, and income. Many working-class families would buy and occupy their own homes in South Philadelphia, while middle-class homeowners would gravitate toward the north and west. Meanwhile, many of the well-to-do continued their migration to the area around Rittenhouse Square, erecting large rowhouses capable of accommodating live-in servants (Figure 2.30).

Houses were not, however, the only things going up in the optimistic days of the last half of the nineteenth century. In 1864–65 there arose at Broad Street and Sansom a building designed with a mansard roof in the Second Empire style. The work of ar-

chitect John Fraser, it was the headquarters of the Union League, bastion of Republicanism and symbol of the financial achievements of the Civil War years. Probably the supreme expression of the self-confidence of the era was another Second Empire building: City Hall, the largest municipal building in the nation. Built at Center Square between 1871 and 1901 to replace the modest structure at the corner of Chestnut Street and Fifth, the new City Hall, with its scores of sculptured symbols and its 548-foot tower, gave full vent to the grandiosity of the times (Figure 2.31). Gazing upward from Logan Square to Alexander Milne Calder's mammoth statue of William Penn topping the tower is said to have sent delicate ladies of the day into swoons, but the cost of City Hall might just as well have, too. Originally estimated at $10 million, City Hall cost two and a half times that—a monument to municipal boodle and the corruption into which the city government had sunk in the years since its reorganization in 1854.

The construction of City Hall prompted a variety of organizations in need of larger quarters to build in Center City. By the centennial year of 1876, the southwest corner of Broad and Cherry streets was resplendent with the Pennsylvania Academy of the Fine Arts (Figure 2.32), the creation of Frank Furness, who was to become the most renowned Philadelphia architect of the eclectic Victorian tradition. In the same year Logan

Square, which since 1864 had been home to the Roman Catholic Cathedral of Saints Peter and Paul, witnessed the completion of the Academy of Natural Sciences. The railroad companies also followed City Hall's trail; the Pennsylvania Railroad established a central depot west of City Hall, and the Reading Railroad built its grand terminal at Market Street and Twelfth between 1891 and 1893. Toward the end of the century, banks and office buildings also began sprouting up in the vicinity of Center Square.

Other buildings at the turn of the century bore witness to the rise of a new kind of store and a new kind of magnate. In 1895, as a result of successful advertising, Lit Brothers began expanding their small specialty shop into a department store at Market and Eighth streets. Empty and rundown for many years, the building was restored to its original Victorian

Figure 2.31.

City Hall in 1899. (Courtesy of the Free Library of Philadelphia)

Figure 2.32.

The Pennsylvania Academy of the Fine Arts. (Photo by J. L. Cotter)

grandeur in 1987. In 1901 John Wanamaker began moving his emporium into impressive new quarters at Market Street and Thirteenth. Wanamaker was but one of several of the new Philadelphia merchant-princes whose names became famous throughout the country. The names of others—Stetson the hatmaker, for example—became synonymous with the products they manufactured. Other old and famous-name Philadelphia products include Hires root beer, Burpee seeds, Breyers ice cream, and Whitman's chocolates.

THE CITY IN THE EARLY TWENTIETH CENTURY: 1901 – 1930

No longer the nation's financial or cultural center, but secure in the knowledge that it led the way in industry and technological know-how, Philadelphia, though sooty-faced, surged into the twentieth century on a wave of confidence and optimism. The population continued to grow, approaching the two million mark in 1930, where it hovered for the next forty years. Until 1915, when World War I began choking it off, immigration went on unabated, with Italians, Russians, and eastern Europeans still making up the bulk of the newcomers. As foreign immigration declined during the war and the demand for labor grew, the migration of African-Americans from the South increased dramatically. Between 1900 and 1920, the city's African-American population grew from 63,000 to 134,000 (Abernethy 1982:531).

The first two decades of the twentieth century witnessed some fundamental changes in industry. As companies merged in an effort to avoid competition, businesses and their workforces became larger; retail chain stores, having received the stamp of public approval, spread throughout the countryside; and advertising, which formerly served an ancillary business function, emerged as a distinct and powerful business in its own right. Ominously, however, Philadelphia's industrial growth rate took a dip at this time; particularly prophetic of things to come was the shift of the cotton-goods industry to the South (Abernethy 1982:532–33). But in the boom of World War I, it was easy to overlook such aberrations. In 1917 and 1918, Philadelphia yards were turning out ships at an unprecedented rate, and the Frankford Arsenal, the Baldwin Locomotive Works, and many other factories were working overtime producing munitions and other war supplies.

As of 1912 the city had more owner-occupied houses than any other large city in the country, if

Figure 2.33.

Eighteenth-century buildings at Spruce and Second streets as they appeared before Society Hill experienced a renaissance in the 1950s and 1960s. The Man Full of Trouble Tavern (center) is on Spruce, and the house in the rear left is on Second. (Courtesy of the Historical Society of Pennsylvania)

Figure 2.34.

The Philadelphia Museum of Art. (Photo by J. L. Cotter)

not the world, and nine thousand new houses were going up each year (Taylor and Schoff 1912:77). Very few of these were built within the original city limits, however, which by the 1920s was most aptly described as "downtown." The northwest was now the fastest-growing sector of the city, the northeast had the heaviest concentration of manufacturing plants, West Philadelphia was a bedroom community of downtown commuters, and Center City was predominantly commercial, with banks and offices clustering around Center Square and retail shops strung along Market Street from Wanamaker's all the way to Lit Brothers. The only residential neighborhood within the old city limits that appeared to be prosperous was the area around Rittenhouse Square. Society Hill was given over largely to wholesale food markets and small manufacturers. What was not commercial in that area was an unsightly slum or fast on its way to becoming

one (Figure 2.33). Although working-class Italians hung on in South Philadelphia, where they had first clustered, many other people left the old neighborhoods. Some moved to new houses in the northwest; others went to Germantown, Chestnut Hill, and West Philadelphia; and still others beat a trail right out of the city to the northern and western suburbs. With its neighborhoods segregated according to income, ethnicity, and race, and its business and industry clustered in clearly defined areas, Philadelphia had by 1930 lost all traces of the heterogeneity that had characterized it for so many years. It had become a "core city of poverty . . . surrounded by a ring of working-class and middle-class homes" (Warner 1987:171 177 ff.).

What made the exodus out of the downtown area possible were the suburban railroads, some of them in service since the 1830s and 1840s; the electric trolleys, which began sup-

planting horse-drawn streetcars in 1892; and the Market Street elevated-subway line that in 1907 connected Sixty-Ninth Street in West Philadelphia with Center City. By 1912 more than a quarter of the city's population was living west of the Schuylkill (Taylor and Schoff 1912:67). After the Frankford elevated line and the northern branch of the Broad Street subway opened in the 1920s, the city's north and northeast sectors also experienced considerable growth. Although the main line of the Pennsylvania Railroad to Pittsburgh had run through the western suburbs of Philadelphia since before 1854, the "Main Line" remained the exclusive enclave of families with inherited wealth until the 1920s, when the middle class began moving there in droves. Not even

Figure 2.35.

The Free Library of Philadelphia. (Architect's rendering, ca. 1923; courtesy of the Free Library of Philadelphia)

Figure 2.36.

Aerial view of Philadelphia in 1924. The ferries can be seen plying between Philadelphia and Camden before the opening (in 1926) of the Benjamin Franklin Bridge, here under construction. (Courtesy of the City Archives of Philadelphia)

the new millionaires at the turn of the century had crossed the barrier; such self-made merchant-princes as Wanamaker and Stetson had built their great mansions in the reaches of Old York Road north of the city in Cheltenham Township.

As the downtown area became increasingly commercial and more and more people commuted to work there, it also became increasingly congested with clanging trolleys and honking cars and trucks. Between 1905 and 1918 the number of motor vehicles in the city grew from about 500 to more than 100,000 (Abernethey 1982:524). The obvious need for new roads and traffic patterns coincided with a nationwide "City Beautiful" movement. One of Philadelphia's responses was to create the Benjamin Franklin Parkway, a grand boulevard leading diagonally from Center Square through Logan Square out to the Schuylkill. Designed in 1917 by Jacques Gréber and modeled after the Champs Élysées, the Benjamin Franklin Parkway was completed in 1925.

While the parkway was under construction, the architectural firm of Horace Trumbauer was overseeing the construction of two imposing neoclassical public buildings that would grace it. At the Schuylkill end of the parkway, construction of the Philadelphia Museum of Art, consisting of three connected Greek temples, got underway in 1916 but was not completed until 1928 (Figure 2.34). On the shrewd assumption that the city might happily scrimp on a wing or two but would not leave the center unfinished, Trumbauer built the two wings first. In 1917 construction of the Free Library at Logan Square began. Completed in 1927, it was modeled after the palaces of the Place de la Concorde in Paris (Figure 2.35).

Julian Abele, Trumbauer's chief designer and the first black graduate of the University of Pennsylvania's school of architecture, seems to have had a hand in the creation of both buildings; each reflects the ideas that Abele gathered in his European travels.

The early years of the twentieth century also saw the first high-rise construction in Center City. By the 1920s numerous new hotels, office buildings, and apartment houses were ten to twenty stories tall (Figure 2.36). The brakes applied by the Great Depression of the 1930s brought all the building in Center City—and everywhere else, for that matter—to a rather abrupt halt. It took War World II to revitalize the economy, but the war years, during which Philadelphia's shipyards, arsenal, and factories worked at full tilt, were to be the last hurrah for Philadelphia's industrial economy. In the aftermath of the war, manufacturing declined, with most heavy industries going out of business and textile companies moving South, where labor was cheaper. Service industries would soon be the staple of the city's economy.

Probably Philadelphia's greatest achievement in the first third of the twentieth century was what it did not do. The age of Art Deco and the mania for destroying what was "out of date" passed over Philadelphia, leaving some memorabilia but little wreckage. With the mass of high-rise buildings concentrated around Center Square, a good deal of the original cityscape east of Eighth Street survived intact, if sadly dilapidated. In the ensuing decades the seeds of civic and cultural concern would sprout, and the inner city would undergo a remarkable revitalization (Figure 2.37).

Figure 2.37.

City Tavern, reconstructed. (Photo by J. L. Cotter)

PART II

Archaeological Sites in Downtown Philadelphia and Philadelphia County

3

Independence National Historical Park

Independence National Historical Park holds the greatest concentration of historic and archaeological sites in Philadelphia. The idea for such a park, germinated in the 1920s and 1930s, acquired roots and supporters during World War II as concern about possible fire-bombings mounted. To reduce the risk of fire to some of the nation's most historic buildings, Philadelphia Court Judge Edwin O. Lewis, in concert with several other influential Philadelphians, proposed the razing of various deteriorating structures just north of Independence Square and the creation of a small, open park in the cleared space. Other prominent participants in the genesis of the park were Dr. William E. Lingelbach, a distinguished professor of history at the University of Pennsylvania and librarian of the American Philosophical Society, and Charles E. Peterson, F.A.I.A., chief representative of the National Park Service in the negotiations for the park and a strong advocate of preserving all buildings of merit.*

From an initial plan for a modest park adjacent to Independence Square, the scope of the project steadily grew. The result was a full-scale federal park, authorized by an act of Congress on June 28, 1948. Today Independence National Historical Park, as the site was named, has at its center the tract of land between Chestnut and Walnut streets and Second Street and Independence Square (Figure 3.1). The park also encompasses Franklin Court, which juts north above the main tract at Chestnut Street, as well as some relatively more distant sites, including the Graff House at Seventh and Market streets,

* This section reflects Charles Peterson's personal recollections of the development of Independence National Historical Park.

the Kosciuszko House at Pine and Third, and the Deshler-Morris House in Germantown. In the area above Independence Square where Judge Lewis first proposed a small clearing is Independence Mall, an open area that extends three blocks north to Race Street.

The National Park Service, established in 1916 to preserve for posterity natural resources and cultural values of national significance, was charged with developing the park and maintaining it. Empowered by the Historic Sites Act of 1935 to "contract and make cooperative agreements . . . to protect, preserve, maintain, or operate any historic building [or] site," the Park Service moved to take over the necessary land and buildings. The "cooperative agreements" that it worked out with individual owners are interesting and varied. The city of Philadelphia, for example, owns Independence Hall, but the National Park Service is responsible for its care, while Carpenters' Hall, in the center of the park, is both maintained and owned by the Carpenters' Company of Philadelphia, which cooperates with the Park Service in preserving the building. A cooperative arrangement for preservation similar to that with the Carpenters' Company applies to four privately owned and administered religious sites within the park: Christ Church; St. Joseph's Church;

Figure 3.1.

Map of Independence National Park. (Adapted from map supplied courtesy of Independence National Historical Park)

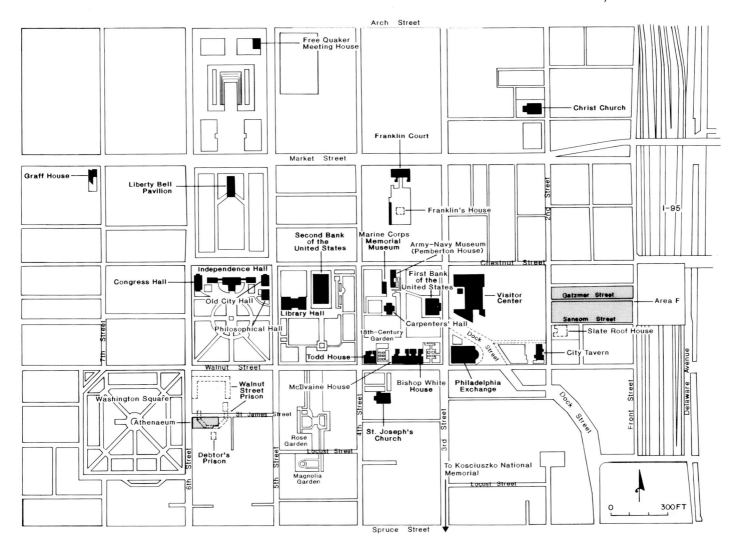

Figure 3.2.

The "cradle of the nation" as it appeared in September 1950. The pediment of the First Bank of the United States is visible in the foreground, and the cupola of Carpenters' Hall is just behind it. Between them and to the right is the Guarantee Trust Bank, a nineteenth-century edifice designed by Frank Furness. (Photo by Fawcett; courtesy of Independence National Historical Park)

St. George's Methodist Church, on Fourth Street between Race and Vine; and Mikveh Israel Cemetery, on Spruce Street between Eighth and Ninth. Under its agreement with the Park Service, the American Philosophical Society retained control of the part of Independence Square it has owned since 1785, and in reciprocation for its commitment to restore its hall on the square to its original 1789 appearance, it was allowed to construct a library—a replica of the original Library Company building—on park-owned land just across the street. Under other cooperative agreements, the Park Service leased properties that it had bought outright to various tenants, including the Pennsylvania Horticultural Society, which occupies a park-owned building on Walnut Street.

As another critical step in develop-

Figure 3.3.

The area shown in Figure 3.2. as it appeared in the mid-1960s. Just to the right of Carpenters' Hall is New Hall, and directly above it are the Second Bank of the United States and Independence Hall. (Courtesy of Independence National Historical Park)

ing the park, the Park Service, using the authority given it by the 1935 act to engage in preservation-oriented research, sponsored numerous archaeological investigations, as well as a great deal of historical and architectural research. As is characteristic of most archaeological work done under the auspices of the National Park Service, the investigations conducted in Independence National Historical Park focused generally on providing proof of location and on recording the character of the artifacts and architectural remains encountered. A chief goal was to produce evidence that would enhance the authenticity of the restoration, and the archaeological reports issued were for the most part descriptive rather than analytical. Most of the park's archaeological collections were analyzed before today's relatively more sophisticated systems of data quantification were developed, and establishing relationships between individual collections was not a specific focus. Some collections, including those from Franklin Court and the McIlvaine House privy, were subjected to comparative analysis, but, in the main, the reports of the investigations, summarized in this chapter, were descriptive and site-specific. Even without elaborate statistical demonstration, however, the related aspects of the sites are obvious.

Immediately upon the establishment of the park, a staff of archaeologists, historians, architects, planners, and administrators set to work to research and conserve what existed, to restore what was no longer intact, to construct various structures for interpreting the past, and ultimately to create a landscape that would accurately reflect the nation's earliest days in Philadelphia. As Figure 3.2 clearly demonstrates, the staff indeed had their work cut out for them. Given the planned emphasis on the period

of the revolutionary war and the presence within the park of several notable nineteenth- and twentieth-century buildings, dilemmas inevitably arose as to what to conserve and how to conserve it. After prolonged and often heated debate, the proponents of a strictly Colonial-Federal ambiance won out, and a number of fine buildings of a later date were removed, together with many structures of less, or no, distinction. Among the noteworthy casualties were the Guarantee Trust Bank, a building designed by Frank Furness that stood on the edges of Carpenters' Court; the tall, granite-fronted Jayne Building, which stood approximately where the Visitor Center at Chestnut Street stands today; and the twentieth-century Irwin Building, which occupied the northwest corner of Fourth and Walnut streets. Such demolition created a good deal of open space (Figure 3.3), as well as the opportunity for rewarding archaeological investigation (Powell 1957, 1958b; Moore 1959 a, 1959b, 1960).

The findings of archaeologists came to influence planning and interpretive decisions within the park, especially at Franklin Court. Here archaeology contributed to the proof of exactly where Franklin's house had stood, revealed the scanty traces of walls and flooring and pits, and suggested the metal framework above the site that now delineates the outlines of the house. Archaeological investigations of a less spectacular nature, but which contributed to the authenticity of interpretation, took place in Independence Square, where remnants of historic foundations were recorded and traces of old wells and privies provided a glimpse of water-supply and sanitation problems solved or left unsolved at the nation's most historic site.

Following the familiar pattern of

Figure 3.4.

Historic Philadelphia in September 1984. The building in the immediate foreground is the visitor's center of the park. (Photo by Thomas Davies; courtesy of Independence National Historical Park)

artifact deposition at other historic urban sites, privy pits within the park contained thousands of items of domestic and commercial use. Artifacts recovered from privy pits at New Hall in Carpenters' Court, the Kosciuszko House, the McIlvaine House, and the vanished Slate Roof House illuminated the historical record of these sites. Particularly productive was a privy-sewer channel at the Bishop White House. Exploration of these and other areas revealed not only artifacts, but also structural evidence of historic interest. Two exceptions to this rewarding pattern were the City Tavern and the Second Bank of the United States. Unfortunately, while the fascinating history of either of these sites could fill a book, neither site yielded much to archaeological investigation.

The massive amount of investigation and research done by historians, architects, and archaeologists at Independence National Historical Park not only created an authentic restoration and interpretation of scenes of the American Revolution, it also had a salutary effect on the city of Philadelphia itself (Figure 3.4). The development of the park sparked a revitalization movement that quickly enveloped Society Hill and soon spread to other parts of the historic downtown area and to outlying areas as well. The effort that began in the 1950s has resulted in an urban renaissance, one of the most extensive and successful movements of this kind in any American city to date.

THE HOUSES OF WILLIAM PENN

William Penn (1644–1718) was a unique combination of privileged, patrician cavalier and zealous, nonconformist Quaker. Successful as a promoter of real estate, he was notably unsuccessful as a businessman. To many of his contemporaries, however—and most especially to his father—he was above all else a painfully outspoken embarrassment to the established social order. Sole male heir of a titled naval career man who became Vice Admiral of England at the age of thirty-one, Penn was not yet twelve when he became convinced that "the seal of divinity" had been set upon him. What the admiral might have had to say about this revelation we can only guess, but it is certain that at seventeen, Penn managed to incur his father's full wrath. Expelled from Oxford University in 1662 because of his nonconformist religious views and behavior, Penn returned home to face his irate parent, who greeted him, so Penn wrote, with "bitter usage . . . whipping, beating and turning out of doors" (Jennings 1852:23).

The admiral's subsequent strategy in sending his son to France in the hope that he would come to his social senses may, in fact, have overshot its mark, for Samuel Pepys reported in his diary that Penn returned to London in 1664 adorned in French clothing and displaying "an affected manner of speech and gait." Two years later, he was painted clad in a suit of armor (Figure 3.5). This state of conformity or overconformity did not last long, however. In 1667, two years after witnessing the great plague that swept London, Penn became a Quaker, and in the ensuing four years, as he persisted in preaching religious tolerance

in an age of intolerance, he was jailed no less than three times (Soderlund et al. 1983:4).

Penn's motives in petitioning King Charles II in 1680 for a colony in America seem to have been a mixture of "for God, for King and Country, and for Profit," with the first and last predominating. The royal authorities' motives in granting the petition may have been equally mixed: an expedient way of ridding the Establishment of this bothersome social anomaly and at the same time a cheap way of repaying an old debt to Admiral Penn and honoring his memory (Soderlund et al. 1983:5, 19–20).

Penn's need to turn a profit is documented by his financial records from the 1670s, which show that he lived well beyond his means and was by the end of the decade over £10,000 in debt; his devotion to the tenets of Quakerism apparently did not extend to forgoing the worldly trappings of an upper-class life. One of his hopes in seeking an American colony was that proprietorship would bring him new sources of rental income. The other side of his motivation in founding a colony is revealed in a letter he wrote to James Harrison, a Quaker minister in the north of England, on August 25, 1681: "For my country, [I eyed] the Lord in the obtaining of it; . . . and desire [to] do that which may . . . serve His truth and people; that an example may be set up to the nations. There may be room there, though not here, for such a holy experiment" (Soderlund et al. 1983:77). Penn put his religious beliefs into governmental practice in 1682 when he drafted the laws that would govern the province of Pennsylvania. Law 35 guaranteed religious freedom to all

Figure 3.5.

William Penn in armor. The date on the painting, October 14, 1666, was Penn's twenty-second birthday. A year later he became a Quaker. (Courtesy of the Historical Society of Pennsylvania)

the inhabitants of the province who believed in one God (Soderlund et al. 1983:5, 19, 132).

While Penn may have been pleased with the outcome of the "holy" part of his experiment, he was surely disappointed in its "for-profit" aspects. Through glowing descriptions of the environment and the inhabitants, he was able to draw Quakers and non-Quakers alike to his new colony; his ability as a promoter of real estate does not, however, seem to have been matched by his acumen as a businessman. Additionally burdened by the doings of his profligate son William,

Figure 3.6.

The Letitia House. (Courtesy of the Historical
Society of Pennsylvania)

Jr., whose high living caused Penn
more than financial distress, Penn
himself was sued for nonpayment of
loans. In 1704 he lamented his losses
in a letter to his provincial secretary,
James Logan: "O Pennsylvania, what
hast thou not cost me! Above £30,000
more than I ever got from it, two hazardous and most fatiguing voyages,
my straits and slavery here, and my
son's soul almost!" Four years after
writing this letter, Penn was jailed
again, this time in a debtors' prison
(Soderlund et al. 1983:66, 170–73).

If part of the reason the royal authorities gave Penn a land grant was
to be rid of him, then they too must
have been disappointed. In all, Penn
spent less than four years away from
England in his new colony. He arrived for the first time, without his
family, on October 28, 1682. In
August 1684 he returned to England to counter the claims of Lord
Baltimore in the dispute over the
Pennsylvania-Maryland boundary.
When he returned in 1699, his second wife, Hannah Callowhill Penn,
and his twenty-one-year-old daughter
Letitia accompanied him. In October
1701, after two unrewarding years of
trying to quiet the "noisy disaffections" of the politically squabbling
colonists and to launch an era of
maturation and growth, he left America, never to return (Robbins 1986:71–
72; Nash 1986:339). In 1712, as his
own disaffections and financial mis-
fortunes were forcing him to negotiate
the sale of Pennsylvania, Penn suffered a stroke that left him partially
paralyzed, and on July 30, 1718, he
died in England without having seen
again the land of his "holy experiment."

During his four interrupted years in
America, Penn occupied three residences. One, Pennsbury Manor, was located in Bucks County (see Chapter 8).
The other two houses were in Philadelphia, one of them within the present
confines of Independence National
Historical Park.

The Site of Penn's
First Philadelphia House

All that is known of the house that
Penn occupied during his first sojourn
in Pennsylvania is that it was a modest frame and clapboard structure
situated on the south side of High
Street between Front and Second. On
January 29, 1701, Penn deeded part
of this site with all the structures on it
to his daughter Letitia. Letitia's lot
extended 172 feet south from High
Street and 402 feet east and west between Front and Second streets (Watson 1909:162).

Just when Letitia Penn built a

house on this lot is not certain, granting she did so. The house that survives, shown in Figure 3.6, has been
the subject of much speculation, having been romantically referred to as
the first brick house in Philadelphia
and, even more absurdly, as the first
State House of Pennsylvania. Architectural historian Thomas Tileston
Waterman (1950:28), who drew a
more accurate bead on it, dated it
as "c. 1714," more than a decade
after Penn took his final leave of
Pennsylvania.

The architecture of the Letitia
House demonstrates the cultural borrowing and blending of ideas from
abroad through which Philadelphia,
like other seaboard cities, created a
distinctive architectural style of its
own. Waterman found the Letitia
House worthy of note as the earliest
surviving example of the Swedish influence in urban construction in the
Delaware Valley. That influence is
evident in the first-floor plan of two
rooms, each with a corner fireplace

joined to the same chimney. English influence is evident in the long, rather narrow shape of the house; in the absence of windows along its side walls, which would allow it to stand in a row of adjoining houses; in its pitched roof; in the dormer windows in the attic above the second floor; and in its pent eaves. Such characteristics derive from the brick rowhouses built in London after the Great Fire of 1666. This kind of cultural borrowing and blending is also evident in archaeological finds that demonstrate how local artisans created their own distinctive wares by adapting features of eighteenth-century European products.

Unfortunately, it has been the fate of the Letitia House to have all its archaeology above ground and in plain view. In 1888 a burst of historical solicitude, then rare in Philadelphia, carried the little house bodily away from its increasingly grimy environs to be restored on a pleasant promontory in Fairmount Park, overlooking the Schuylkill River. There it still sits, opposite the Philadelphia Zoo, forlornly isolated by motor roads on all sides. The original site was usurped by a large warehouse on the southwest corner of a small alley, and the chances of the trowel's reclaiming any trace of the Letitia House foundation or related artifacts are dim, and dimmer still for recovering any trace of Penn's original clapboard house. However, as Philadelphia continues following its historical (and not unprofitable) conscience, it is not inconceivable that the Letitia House may one day be returned to its original site.

The Slate Roof House

Penn's last Philadelphia residence was a large and distinctive mansion on the east side of Second Street be-

Figure 3.7.

Top, painting of the Slate Roof House by William L. Breton, ca. 1830; *right,* plan, with archaeological features indicated (annotations by Barbara Liggett). The Slate Roof House was the birthplace of Penn's son John. (Courtesy of the Historical Society of Pennsylvania)

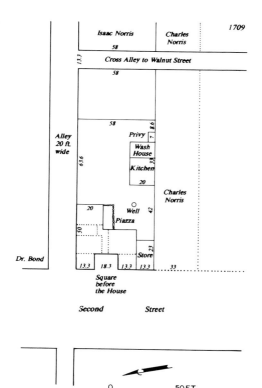

tween Walnut and Sansom. Known as the Slate Roof House, the mansion was built in 1687 for Samuel Carpenter, a Quaker merchant from Barbados. The most notable of the two or three hundred houses then standing in Philadelphia, the Slate Roof House was architecturally unique. Its front was distinguished by two large, bastion-like corner rooms extending toward Second Street and separated by an indented space before the main entrance. As shown in Figure 3.7, a colonnaded "piazza" or portico ran along the south side of a room at the rear. Separate from the house and east of it, along the southern property line, was the kitchen, which was joined at the rear by the wash house, and behind that was the privy.

Although Penn had paid a handsome rent of £80 for two years of occupancy and intended to return to Philadelphia with his family, he did not attempt to retain the Slate Roof House when he left for England in 1701. Instead he advised his secretary, James Logan, "Thou may continue in the house I lived in till the year is up." Logan, however, who was soon a political force in the city and the province, serving as mayor in 1723 and as acting governor from 1736 to 1738, remained in the house until 1704, when William Trent, then the owner, sold it to Quaker merchant Isaac Norris. The house had some distinguished occupants thereafter, including Governor James Hamilton, who lived there about 1735; British General John Forbes, who died in the house in 1759; and American Revolutionary War General Charles Lee,

who was buried from the house in 1782 following his death at a Market Street inn. Later a Mrs. Burdeau kept a ladies' boarding school in the old house. In its final incarnation, before it was razed in 1867 to make way for the Commercial Exchange Building, it was a boarding house or inn run by "the Widow Graydon" (Watson 1909:165–66).

The sad fact about the Slate Roof House is that it managed to survive the vicissitudes of neglect and decay nearly intact until its razing (Figure 3.8). As late as 1857, Philadelphia historian John Fanning Watson (1909:163–66) wrote, "The 'Slate House' as it was called, . . . still standing in humble guise at the southeast corner of Second and Norris' Alley [as Sansom Street was then known], was once an edifice with 'bastions and salient angles,' like a fortress, having behind it a great garden enclosure adorned with a lofty grove of trees." Watson

concluded, "Such a house should be rescued from its present forlorn neglect; it ought to be bought and consecrated to some lasting memorial of its former character, by restoring [it]" to its original appearance.

Another early champion of restoration of the Slate Roof House was William J. Clark, Jr., editor of the *Daily Evening Telegraph* and an able draftsman. Clark described the history of the old house in the November 24, 1866, issue of the paper and recorded its demolition on August 5, 1867, after his urging and that of the City Council that the house be preserved had failed. Clark also made some remarkable pencil drawings of each room in the structure, showing how the rooms appeared in May 1867 (Figure 3.9), as well as a pen-wash view of the rear of the house from the north and pencil drawings of three broken delft tiles from a fireplace (Gatter 1981).

The Commercial Exchange Building that was erected on the site burned the year after it was completed. Redesigned by James H. Windrim, architect of the Masonic Temple at Center Square, it was rebuilt in 1870 (Webster 1976:42). In 1903 the Keystone Telephone Company, one of the more enduring and successful competitors of the Bell Telephone System, took over the building. Keystone ultimately gave way to Bell, which installed the country's first automatic telephone ex-

Figure 3.8.

The Slate Roof House shortly before its demolition in 1867. The portion between the two front wings was added when the house was altered for commercial use. (Courtesy of the Library Company of Philadelphia)

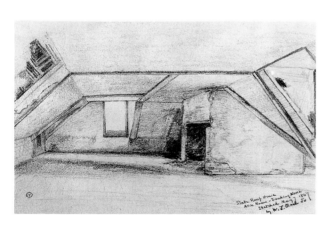

Figure 3.9.

Sketches of rooms in the Slate Roof House by William J. Clark, Jr., 1867. (Courtesy of the Historical Society of Pennsylvania)

change on the premises. Bell sold the property in 1944. In 1976, after a mild motion to preserve the structure as a historic site in its own right had evaporated, the Philadelphia Redevelopment Authority razed the 1870 building. The land was later acquired for the National Park Service through privately raised funds.

That the site of the Slate Roof House was not snapped up for further commercial exploitation in 1976 was due in large measure to the efforts of Carl W. Gatter, historical conservation advocate and activist. Before the site was cleared, Gatter was busy researching every archival reference in Philadelphia that related to the Slate Roof House, concentrating on the drawings William Clark had made of the structure before its demolition in 1867. The documentation that Gatter collected from the archives of the Historical Society of

Pennsylvania, where Clark's sketches are housed, and from other Philadelphia repositories filled nine large binders. This information was supplemented by the preliminary studies for reconstruction that Penelope Batcheler, National Park Service architect, had done in 1972. By November 1979, John Milner Associates had completed reconstruction plans.

Although it was clear that the available documentation would allow for accurate reconstruction of the Slate Roof House (a fact already demonstrated by a detailed but temporary reconstruction during the Sesquicentennial Exposition in 1926) the decision of the early 1980s was not to reconstruct but rather to memorialize the house with a landscape plot on the site. Today, in a small, paved enclosure of the site, not even the wall locations of the Slate Roof House are delineated—hardly the memorial

John Fanning Watson had in mind when he surveyed the house with a rueful eye in the mid-nineteenth century.

Archaeology at the Site of the Slate Roof House

Because the deep basement of the 1870 Commercial Exchange Building had obliterated all traces of the foundations of the Slate Roof House, Carl Gatter began archaeological investigations in the spring of 1980 by checking a backhoe ditch adjacent to where the north wall of the house had stood. The ditch, which had been dug for a

Figure 3.10.

Left, the well; *right,* the privy pit at the Slate Roof House. The well was southeast of the house, about halfway between the house and the kitchen. The privy was at the rear of the washhouse behind the kitchen. (Courtesy of Carl Gatter)

drainage system, was 2 feet wide and 3 feet deep and extended along the entire east-west length of the house site. Unfortunately, it revealed no building material attributable to the historic house. The only artifacts uncovered—a salt-glazed stoneware sherd, a queensware transfer-printed sherd, a pearlware sherd, and a fragment of a green bottle—were all from the eighteenth or nineteenth century. Measurements indicated that the level of adjacent Sansom Street had been lowered approximately 12 inches, explaining the almost complete absence of artifacts.

Investigations of a well and a privy pit on the site (Figure 3.10) proved somewhat more rewarding, despite some weighty setbacks and rigorous time constraints. Two days after Gatter and archaeologist Barbara Liggett began excavating these pits in July 1982, truck after truck bearing tons of clean fill had arrived, striving diligently to fill both areas. Happily, Liggett's protests were availing, and a backhoe was provided to remove the fill, with a two-day grace period allowed for exploration of both pits.

As indicated in Figure 3.7, the well was located about halfway between the house and the kitchen. Uncovered beneath several feet of sand and gravel, it appeared to have been capped earlier than 1840 * and then reopened for fill in the mid-nineteenth century, possibly about the time the Slate Roof House was razed in 1867. Artifacts from the top of the well dated from about 1840 to 1860 (Gatter 1982).

After 8 feet of brick well casing had been removed, additional digging soon revealed that during the demolition of the telephone building, an oil

* As early as 1803, Benjamin Latrobe's waterworks at Center Square were pumping water to this part of Philadelphia.

tank adjacent to the well had ruptured. Heating oil had permeated the rest of the well fill, making digging difficult and permanently coloring the artifacts. Artifacts from the last half of the nineteenth century were found as deep as the well could be probed (about 20 feet below street level), which Liggett regarded as nearly the bottom. That the bottom had been almost reached was indicated by the termination of the brick casing and, below that point, a 6-inch increase in the diameter of the well, which might have provided a wider area for water accumulation. However, the termination of the brick casing might also indicate that at that point the investigators had already reached bottom. They found no wooden well-pump parts, suggesting that if a pump had been installed, it was removed before the well was filled (Barbara Liggett, personal correspondence, 1985). Five bricks recovered from the bottom of the well casing were hand-molded and had a mean measurement of 8¾ by 4 by 2½ inches.

When the collection of artifacts from the well had been cleaned, the ones that most impressed Gatter were several tiny crucibles of fired clay. These might have been used by Thomas Lee, refiner of gold, who occupied a shop on the first floor of the north wing of the Slate Roof House just before its demolition, or they might have been used by Joseph Marshall and Robert Tempest, jewelers, who rented the same shop earlier in the nineteenth century (Gatter 1982). Had time and circumstances permitted a complete retrieval of the well fill, artifacts of an earlier date might have been recovered; however, it is also probable that the well was cleaned of earlier deposits a number of times before its final filling.

While Gatter and his team investigated the well, Liggett and her two assistants located and excavated the privy pit. It yielded a small but choice collection of late seventeenth- and early eighteenth-century artifacts. Gatter was particularly impressed by a broken delft tile with a "bug" or "spider's-head" corner design. The design was identical to that on two of the three delft tiles from the Slate Roof House that William J. Clark, Jr., had drawn in 1867. Clark did not record the color of the tiles, but the excavated sample has violet decoration (Barbara Liggett, personal correspondence, 1985).

The privy pit also contained the debris of roofing slates, some with the wooden pegs used to affix them still in position. The triangular shape of some of the slates suggested to Liggett that most, if not all, of the slates had come from a dormer window. The bricks lining the privy were, like those in the well casing, hand-molded. A sample of four from 15 feet below street level were uniformly 2½ inches thick and ranged in length from 8½ to 8⅞ inches and in width from 4 to 4¼ inches—typical sizes of common red brick at the end of the seventeenth century. Other hand-molded bricks, which may have been used in the Slate Roof House, were found in a pile near the south wall of the north wing (Gatter 1982).

Although the archaeological traces of Penn's presence in Philadelphia are slight, they have, though sorely compromised, endured—an interesting parallel to the endurance of his supreme achievements: the city and the province that he founded and the legacy of religious freedom that he bestowed on the inhabitants of his lands. Penn's "holy experiment," if more secular than he hoped, goes on.

BENJAMIN FRANKLIN'S LOST HOUSE

In the words of Richard H. Shryock, late librarian of the American Philosophical Society, Benjamin Franklin is "a man we can't leave to the imagination." Indeed we can't. Ben Franklin's own imagination and prodigious energy have succeeded in making him one of the best-recorded personalities in American history. So fascinating were his qualities to his contemporaries that even before his death he was the subject of voluminous writings. Later commentators, as diverse in character as Mark Twain, D. H. Lawrence, and Mayor John F. ("Honey Fitz") Fitzgerald of Boston, added their daubs to Franklin's portrait, not all of it in a complimentary hue. For another view of Franklin, we owe thanks to his habit of meticulously retaining his correspondence and, of course, to his autobiographical writings. Franklin, however, like many another autobiographer, was not immune to presenting himself to the reader in the kindest light possible.

Perhaps the clearest view we have of the man is in the house he began building at the age of fifty-seven and in which he closed his life in 1790 at the age of eighty-four. Here the clichés that have clung to him like barnacles fall away, and we see Franklin plain, as he was, full of zest, energy, and ambition. Always working to promote comfort and ease—with more effect than most people achieve purchasing them—Franklin found a suitable focus for his inventive talents in the building of his house. Although obliterated to a remnant of its foundations in 1812, the house has been the subject of exhaustive archaeological investigation and research and, as such, has been as fully and carefully recorded as other aspects of Franklin's life. In fact, few other Philadelphia sites have been as meticulously studied as Franklin's property, referred to today as his "court."

Franklin Court Today ...

During his sojourn in France, Benjamin Franklin (who never ceased to exercise his speculative imagination) once pondered the apparent revival of two of a trio of flies that had been poured out of a bottle of wine. Assuming the flies had been bottled with the wine and preserved alive by the alcohol (we suspect Franklin may have been the unwitting butt of a practical joke), he commented wistfully that he could entertain the dream of being preserved in wine for a hundred years, to awaken in a new age in his beloved country and witness its state of progress with his own eyes (Van Doren 1945:431). Had he succeeded in awakening in 1966, he would no doubt have been fascinated to find the site of his obliterated house the subject of lively interest and debate as archaeologists and architects attempted a hypothetical reconstruction.

Had Franklin returned ten years later, during the Bicentennial of the Nation in 1976, he would have found the foundations of his house visible below ground and the exact dimensions of the house outlined by a steel frame rising above the site (Figure 3.11). On slate flagstones around the house site, which occupies the middle of a rectangular court, he would have seen excerpts from letters that he and his wife Deborah exchanged while the house was being built, in which she described to him in labored characters and originally spelled words the progress of the construction.

Just to the north of the house site, another steel frame marks the site of a print shop that Franklin built for his grandson, Benjamin Franklin Bache. Beyond that stand Franklin's three Market Street houses, rental properties he erected in his old age after his final return to Philadelphia in 1785. Though the front and rear of the houses have been reconstructed, they are still reached by the original brick archway between them (Figure 3.12). Within the house at 318 Market Street, nothing has been restored, so that the visitor can discern in the stripped walls of all three and a half floors and basement the original joist holes, flue scars, and remnants of old plaster. An open staircase connects the various levels of the house, and on display at each landing are artifacts from the site that tell the story of domestic activities in eighteenth- and early nineteenth-century households. In the basement, some artifacts have been left on view, undisturbed at the bottom of a partially excavated pit.

Just west of Franklin's house site, an underground museum portrays his multifaceted career as printer, publisher, statesman, scientist, diplomat, and inventor. No doubt that inveterate tinkerer and gadgeteer would have been intrigued by the electronic devices of late twentieth-century ingenuity that the museum uses to portray him. Still, the essence of the man is perhaps best evoked by the many clues unearthed by archaeologists and other historical researchers, working above as well as below ground around his house site.

... And Yesterday

"Three removes are equal to a fire," Franklin once observed. He knew from experience whereof he spoke.

Franklin had lived, all told, at thirteen previous rented locations in Philadelphia when he decided enough "removing" was enough. At the time he began building a house of his own in 1763, he had only recently returned from London, where he had served as colonial agent. He was fifty-seven years old and had been a resident of Philadelphia for over thirty-five years. He had been married to Deborah Read for thirty-three years, had an illegitimate son thirty-four years old and a daughter nineteen, and was a prosperous businessman, as well as a highly successful leader of the Popular party in Pennsylvania (Cotter 1980:17).

The property on which Franklin decided to build was in the middle of the block bounded by Market and Chestnut streets and Third and Fourth streets, just behind the house that had belonged to John Read, carpenter.

Figure 3.11.

Franklin Court in 1976. The steel frame in the foreground marks the dimensions of Franklin's house; the one in the center delineates his grandson's print shop. In the background are his Market Street houses. The concrete shelters in the foreground cover windows that look down onto excavated areas. The idea of using the steel frames was suggested by archaeologist James Deetz's drawing of the dimensions of a "ghost house" in Wellfleet, Mass., which he based on the dimensions of its excavated foundations. (Photo by Dick Freer; courtesy of Independence National Historical Park)

Figure 3.12.

Franklin's Market Street houses restored, north elevation. Number 318 Market Street, which houses an archaeological and architectural exhibit, is to the right of the original brick archway. (Photo by Thomas Davies; courtesy of Independence National Historical Park)

From the doorway of that dwelling, Deborah Read one day in 1723 had her first glimpse of her future husband Ben: a seventeen-year-old runaway apprentice just arrived from Boston, walking by with two puffy loaves of white bread under his arm, eating a third, and cutting no dashing figure, as Franklin later recalled in his *Autobiography*.

"If you are going to build a house, build it modern" is another of Franklin's many aphorisms (Lopez 1981: 23). He was not one to ignore his own advice. Designed by Robert Smith, master carpenter and builder from Scotland who worked in the fashionable Georgian mode, Franklin's house was indeed modern in its day. It was 34 feet square, boasted three rooms on each of its three floors, and was topped by a garret. At the foundation, its brick-and-mortar walls were a solid 14 inches thick, tapering to 9 inches at the second floor. Open to the light on all four sides in the middle of a court, it fronted north toward Market Street. Long mindful of the hazard of house fires, Franklin took several precautions in his own house: no wood trim communicated from room to room, and, for ready access in case of a roof fire, each side of his pitched and shingled roof had three dormer windows. The roof also boasted lightning rods of Franklin's original design (Van Doren 1945:168–70).

The building of the house had scarcely begun when Franklin was appointed Agent of the Province of Pennsylvania to the English Government, and on November 7, 1764, he departed for London again, leaving his friend Samuel Rhoads, master carpenter, to assist Robert Smith in overseeing the construction and to disburse funds for the work (Platt 1969:26–42). Though Franklin was doubtless somewhat torn about leaving his house plans in the care of any-

one other than himself, it was perhaps a fortunate event for posterity, for it is in the letters that shuttled back and forth across the Atlantic between Ben and Deborah that we learn the details of the house building—and are reminded that the trials and tribulations associated with that particular endeavor have not been so very different over the ages.

Between weary intervals of waiting, Franklin pieced together from his wife's labored reports the progress of the construction. By April 1765 the interior walls had been plastered, the fireplaces installed, and the cellar floor bricked with the same bricks that are visible in the court today. With the interior painting and decorating well advanced, Mrs. Franklin moved in, a little furniture and personal effects at a time. A month later she was settled, but it was another year before the final touches were made.

It would be interesting to know Deborah Franklin's reaction to the advice and direction her husband offered from London, a safe 3,000 miles away:

I could have wished to have been present at the finishing of the kitchen, as it is a mere machine and, being new to you, I think you will scarce know how to work it; the several contrivances to carry off steam and smell and smoke not being fully explained to you. The oven I suppose was put up by the directions in my former letter. You mention nothing of the furnace. If that iron one is not set, let it alone until my return, when I shall bring a more convenient copper one. . . . I cannot but complain in my mind of Mr. Smith that the house is so long unfit for you to get into, the fences not put up, nor the other necessary articles got ready. The well I expected would have been dug in the winter, but I hear nothing of it. You should have gardened long before the date of your last, but it seems the rubbish was not removed. I am much obliged to my good old friends who did me the honor to remember me in the unfinished kitchen. I hope soon to drink with them in the parlour. (Platt 1969:47–48)

As colonial representative, Franklin was absent from Philadelphia for over ten years, and he might have stayed away longer, had Deborah consented to move to London with their daughter Sarah. He did not return until 1775, some months after Deborah's death in December 1774. The house Franklin came home to was far from empty, however, either of people or of possessions. Occupying it were his daughter Sarah; Richard Bache, the son-in-law he had acquired during his absence; three lively grandchildren; and a multitude of belongings. The rich embellishment of the house as early as 1766 is attested to by a fire insurance survey made on August 5 of that year for the Philadelphia Contributionship.

Preeminent among Franklin's possessions were his books. Thanks to the labors of Edwin Wolf, former director of the Library Company of Philadelphia, we know the titles of 3,480 of the 4,726 volumes that lined Franklin's shelves. Not surprisingly, two of Franklin's best-known inventions are closely related to his passion for books: bifocal glasses, which he never patented but simply offered to humanity as a convenient means of reading without sacrificing distance vision, and the "long arm," a long pole topped by a pair of slats cinched by a cord that Franklin devised to retrieve books from high shelves.

Other articles about his house would have borne further witness that Franklin was all his life a gadgeteer. Somewhere in an attic storeroom, one might have had a glimpse of Franklin's earliest invention: a pair of wooden palettes for his hands that he devised at the age of fourteen to increase his purchase on the water as he swam. No doubt he would have devised something like the frogman's rubber flippers for his feet had he found a suitably flexible material from which

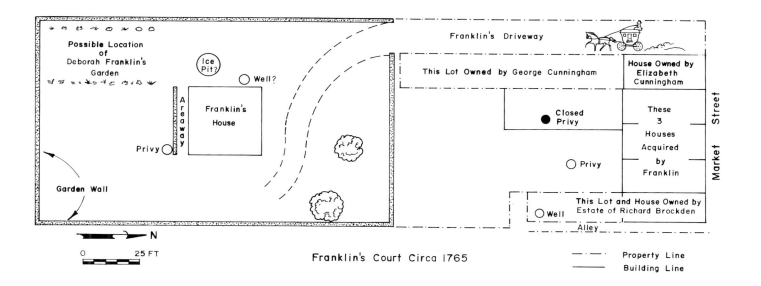

Possible Location
of
Deborah Franklin's
Garden

Ice Pit?

Well?

Areaway

Franklin's House

Privy

Garden Wall

N

0   25 FT

Franklin's Court Circa 1765

Franklin's Driveway

This Lot Owned by George Cunningham

House Owned by Elizabeth Cunningham

Closed Privy

Privy

Well

These 3 Houses Acquired by Franklin

This Lot and House Owned by Estate of Richard Brockden

Alley

Market Street

— · — · — Property Line
—————— Building Line

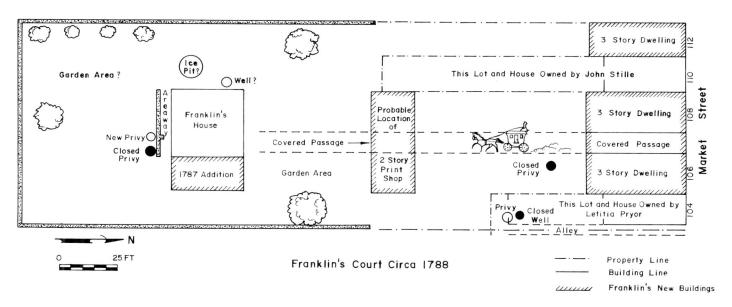

Garden Area?

Ice Pit?

Well?

Areaway

Franklin's House

New Privy

Closed Privy

1787 Addition

Covered Passage

Garden Area

Probable Location of

2 Story Print Shop

3 Story Dwelling   112

This Lot and House Owned by John Stille   110

3 Story Dwelling   108

Covered Passage

Closed Privy

3 Story Dwelling   106

Privy   Closed Well

This Lot and House Owned by Letitia Pryor   104

Alley

Market Street

N

0   25 FT

Franklin's Court Circa 1788

— · — · — Property Line
—————— Building Line
/////// Franklin's New Buildings

Figure 3.13.

Franklin Court ca. 1765 and 1788. (From Liggett 1971b, 1973; courtesy of Independence National Historical Park)

to fashion them. A visitor to the first floor of the house might have found gracing one of the drawing rooms Franklin's glass "armonica," the musical instrument he devised from bottomless glass tumblers. Ranged in a graduated series on a spindle turned by a crank and a foot-operated treadle, the tumblers were played with a moistened finger. The armonica's quietly haunting, bell-like tones captivated

early composers, Mozart and Beethoven among them, and inspired them to write pieces employing its plaintive sounds.

Elsewhere in the house, the visitor would have found a glass heart filled with red fluid to show the circulation of the blood, as well as all kinds of electrical paraphernalia. Using the electricity he stored in Leyden-type jars, Franklin once nearly killed himself in the middle of a picnic while demonstrating for the edification of his friends, and for their subsequent dining pleasure, how to electrocute a turkey. That and his famous kite-flying experiment were not the only close calls he had while fiddling with electricity. On an earlier occasion, while living in a rented house, he had led the ground wire from the lightning rod on the roof down a banister, leaving a gap in the wire—across which he was pleased to observe sparks popping during a thunderstorm.

The "modern conveniences" that were to be found at Franklin Court offer yet more testimony to the tinkerer in the man. Not only did he plan "the several contrivances to carry off steam and smell and smoke"* from the kitchen; he also had a large refrigerating pit dug at a convenient distance from the kitchen. Among Franklin's other home improvements was a rigging device that enabled him to close the door to his bedroom while lying on his bed and to pull the bolt from the door to admit a visitor while in the same supine position. He also invented a system of dampers and ducts that connected fireplaces and ranges, and, of course, the Franklin stove. The latter consisted of cast iron panels enclosing a firebox surrounded by flue ducts which extended out from the fireplace and radiated warmth into the room. This stove, which was vented through the closed hearth front, was a distinct improvement over the open fireplace, which sent most of the heat directly up the chimney.

With the outbreak of the Revolution, Franklin was not destined to remain in his house for very long. In

1776, after having been home only eighteen months, he was off again, this time as the new republic's minister to France, where he would remain for over eight years. During the war, the house contributed 313 pounds of its lead spouting to ammunition; it also lost a number of books and musical instruments during the British occupation of Philadelphia. But otherwise the Revolution left it largely untouched.

In 1785, as his eightieth year approached, Franklin returned to Philadelphia for the last time. By now he had six grandchildren, and his house was fairly bursting with people and possessions (Faÿ 1933:68–72; Platt 1969:103). Straightaway, hardly pausing for breath, he began building an additional third to the east side of the house; that he was able to supervise this project in person no doubt gave him great pleasure. He also erected three substantial buildings as rental properties on Market Street and a print shop behind them for his grandson, as well as a privy and a bathhouse. Figure 3.13 shows a plan of the court about 1765 and another as it would have appeared about 1788, after the additions. Although the privy Franklin added has been verified archaeologically, the bathhouse has never been found; nor, for that matter, has the slipper tub in which he took warm baths to ease his kidney stones while he received callers, or the sedan chair that he brought back with him from France. We do know that the sedan chair was stored for many years at Pennsylvania Hospital before it was finally discarded.

The only contemporary drawings we have of Franklin's house are a plan of the first floor, sketched in his own hand on the back of a memorandum (Figure 3.14), and another plan that he sketched of the second floor on the back of a receipt dated May

17, 1764. No trace of a southeast perspective of the house said to have been made by artist James Thackara has ever been found. From a letter Franklin wrote to his sister Jane Mecom, we do know that the addition to the east side of the house, which was 16½ feet wide and 33 feet long, provided the family with a large cellar for wood, a drawing room/dining room on the first floor in which a company of twenty-four persons could dine, a library on the second floor where Franklin could escape the noise of his grandchildren, two new bedrooms on the third floor, and two garret rooms. The drawing room/dining room, as Franklin described it, had "two windows at each end, the north and the south, [to] make it an airy summer room; and for winter there is a good chimney in the middle, made handsome with marble slabs" (Platt 1969: 57–67, 103). Figure 3.15 is an architect's conceptualization of what the house would have looked like after the addition.

To his sister Jane, Franklin also wrote, "Considering our well-furnished, plentiful market as the best of gardens, I am turning mine, in the midst of which my house stands, into grass plots and gravel walks, with trees and flowering shrubs." Such was his pleasure, as after 1787 Franklin slowly retired from public life while the world came to pay him homage at his court. Among those who regularly gathered at Franklin's house in his last years were the fellows of the American Philosophical Society and members of the Society for Abolishing Negro Slavery. At about eleven o'clock on the evening of April 17, 1790, Benjamin Franklin died in his bedroom, in the house he had built and that was so inimitably his.

Ironically, both Franklin's posthumous reputation and his house underwent strange eclipse. Only two

* This and other quotations from Franklin's and his wife's letters regarding the house appear on the flagstones above the house foundations. They are from the Deborah Franklin Correspondence, *Proceedings of the American Philosophical Society*, vol. 95, No. 3, pp. 239–45, Philadelphia, 1951.

years after his death, his daughter and her husband moved to their Delaware River farm, becoming Philadelphia suburbanites, as was then the fashion. A series of short-term tenants followed as the house went into decline, until it became a boardinghouse and finally a "Ladies' Academy." But the Baches did return at last. Sarah Franklin Bache died in her father's house in 1808, and Richard Bache died there in 1811. The following year the penurious grandchildren of "Poor Richard," whose frugality and genius had raised him to the status of America's first citizen, tore down his unique house to sell the land it stood on. By then the memory of Franklin was so dim in Philadelphia that English manufacturers of earthenware figurines, in an attempt to revive sales of the Franklin figurine, relabeled it "George Washington."

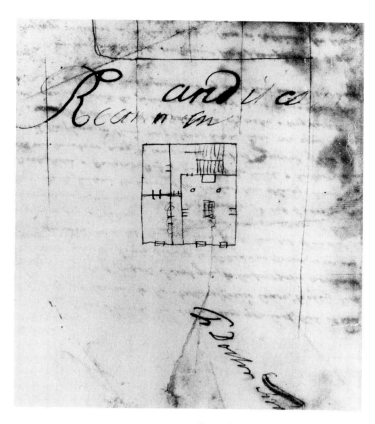

Figure 3.14.

First-floor plan of Franklin's house, thought to have been sketched by Franklin himself. (National Park Service photo; courtesy of the American Philosophical Society)

Figure 3.15.

Franklin's house as it might have appeared after the addition on the east side. This conceptualization by architect William B. Campbell is based on archival references and archaeological data. (Courtesy of Independence National Historical Park)

Figure 3.16.

Orianna Street looking north to the archway of Franklin Court, March 1950. (Photo by E. M. Riley; courtesy of Independence National Historical Park)

Figure 3.17.

Plan and profile of Franklin Court excavations. (From Liggett 1971b; courtesy of Independence National Historical Park)

Archaeology at Franklin Court

When the National Park Service began developing Independence National Historical Park in 1949, one of the prime objectives was to identify the exact spot on which Benjamin Franklin had built his house. This was not an altogether simple task. The site had been covered for more than a century by parts of three buildings with basements of varying depths and by narrow Orianna Street, which had been driven straight through the middle of the house site to connect

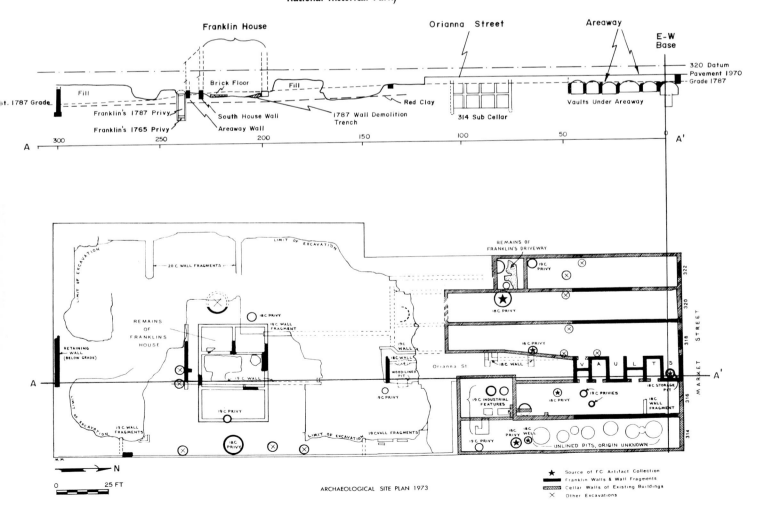

Chestnut and Market streets. The extension of Orianna Street was part of the Bache children's scheme to open up Grandfather's urban snuggery for real estate development. Figure 3.16 shows the court as it appeared in 1950, before it was cleared of nineteenth-century buildings.

The first archaeological exploration, supported by the American Philosophical Society, was made by National Park Service archaeologist Paul J. F. Schumacher in 1953. Schumacher, working in and around the wreckage of buildings being removed from the site, found the first traces of the foundations of the Franklin home in patches of eighteenth-century fill. From the same fill, he retrieved quantities of artifacts dating from the time the Franklins lived on the site. In addition, Schumacher was able to locate one of the Franklins' "necessaries"—a freestanding privy situated, as shown in Figure 3.17, near the northwest corner of the house. This privy probably served the residence from 1765 until 1786 (Schumacher 1956e).

One eighteenth-century artifact that came to light in 1955 was the cause of some excitement (Powell 1962a:33). It was a fragment of a delft fireplace tile showing a man holding the end of what might have been a kite string, but whether that was so or not was impossible to tell, as the other part of the tile was missing (Figure 3.18). The intriguing question was, could Franklin have acquired a tile commemorating his kite-flying quest for electricity in a storm? Alas, research inexorably identified a theme in contemporary Dutch delft tile-painting, whereby our kite-flier became a shepherd and the string over his shoulder a staff. So much for an exciting find.

In 1959, almost 200 years after Mrs. Franklin moved into her new house to try her mysterious new kitchen, National Park Service archaeologists Bruce Powell and Jackson Moore located a circular cold cellar or ice pit just west of where the kitchen had been and convenient to it. As indicated in Figure 3.17, they also found traces of foundation walls, as well as remnants of an areaway outside the south foundation (Powell 1962a:20). Although later builders had salvaged stones from all foundations, the construction trenches for walls could still be traced as shadows in the undisturbed earth—in archaeological parlance, "robbed trenches." The location of the fence that ran across the north end of Franklin's property on Market Street before he built his rental houses there is also reasonably certain. No traces of his carriage house and stables have ever appeared, but they were probably somewhere in the rear of his Market Street houses.

Just outside the areaway they uncovered in 1959, Powell and Moore found a cylindrical, brick-lined privy pit with a very unusual feature (Powell 1962a:21–22). In contrast to the freestanding privy Schumacher had discovered, this one, probably dug when Franklin expanded the house in 1786–87, was adjacent to the house and connected to it by a pipe that had once sloped down from the house to drain into the pit (Figure 3.19). Powell was tempted to speculate that Franklin had introduced the first mechanical flush toilet into the Western hemisphere. Unfortunately, neither archaeological nor documentary evidence confirms this. A simple bucket of water poured into a closet drain was probably the flushing mechanism.

In 1960 Powell and Moore made another curious and intriguing discovery. Under the granite blocks that had paved Orianna Street between

Figure 3.18.

Delft tile decorated in purple and blue found near Franklin's house. (Courtesy of Independence National Historical Park)

Figure 3.19.

Privy pit on the south side of Franklin's house. The inclined, brick-sided drain led from the house underneath a passageway and wall to empty into the brick-lined pit. (Courtesy of Independence National Historical Park)

Figure 3.20.

Utility earthenware from Franklin Court: a two-handed glazed jug with crudely painted vertical stripes; two brown, lead-glazed pitchers; and two slip-decorated bowls. (Courtesy of Independence National Historical Park)

Figure 3.21.

Franklin Court looking south toward Chestnut Street, October 1960. The bricks of the basement floor are visible in the foreground. In the center is the privy pit that connected with the house, and to the right, partially revealed, is the circular ice pit. (Courtesy of Independence National Historical Park)

Franklin's house and the archway on Market Street lay scores of red-clay pottery kiln props, called trivets, as well as kiln bricks still bearing the drippings of brown lead glaze (Powell 1962a:26–27). Also much in evidence were fragments of "wasters"—unsuccessful ceramic pieces spoiled in the kiln and discarded; some five thousand of them were recorded (Cosans 1975, v. 6:57–59). Evidently, somewhere in the rear of the brick-and-frame building that Deborah Read's father had built around 1711, there had been a pottery kiln.

In his *Autobiography*, Franklin offers us an interesting clue as to the genesis of the mysterious kiln. Describing his return to Philadelphia from London, where he had worked for a time as a printer's helper earning money to set up shop at home (and had all the while kept Deborah waiting), Franklin wrote, "I should have been . . . much asham'd at seeing Miss Read, had not her friends . . . persuaded her to marry another, one Rogers, a potter, which was done in my absence. With him, however, she was never happy, and soon parted from him, refusing to cohabit with him or bear his name, it being now said that he had another wife. He was a worthless fellow, tho' an excellent workman. . . . He got into debt, ran away in 1727 or 1728, went to the West Indies, and died there" (Van Doren 1945:253).

Historians at Independence National Historical Park picked up the story from there. On August 5, 1725, John Rogers did indeed marry Deborah Read in Christ Church, a block away and just around the corner from her father's house. According to a notice in the *American Weekly Mercury* of May 9, 1728, Rogers left Philadelphia in December 1727, taking along with him a "likely young negro lad about eighteen years of age"—who, it should be noted, belonged to someone else.

If the ceramic pieces found in Franklin Court were evidence of John Rogers' potting, he was, sure enough, a skilled potter. He had fashioned quantities of earthenware bowls, dishes, pitchers, and the like, glazed on the inside with brown lead, and now and then some more aesthetically pleasing pieces in brown-and-yellow—decorated redware (Figure 3.20).

Among the sherds and kiln props were some curious cones of burnt clay. Twisted, about 1½ to 2 inches high, they bore a resemblance to "Seger cones," a temperature-testing device attributed to a nineteenth-century German ceramist. The question arose, had that tricky, able, and worthless fellow Rogers anticipated this technological innovation? Probably not. Like other craftsmen whose art has historical roots measured in milennia, potters have tricks and wiles that are passed down from master to apprentice—now lost, now rediscovered. In fact, the German ceramist after whom the Seger cone is named may well not have been the first potter to use such a temperature-testing device.

An Interpretation of the Findings

From the evidence archaeologists unearthed at Franklin Court, we are able to deduce a few things about the architecture of Franklin's house and about the daily life of its occupants. The house, we know, was of brick, and the bricks—red to rust-brown, with an occasional glazed header end—were about the same size as modern building bricks. Although no trace of a house wall remained standing, the bricks of the basement floor (Figure 3.21) and the brick debris found on the site indicate that all the house bricks were hand-molded and that many were warped in the making and firing. The sturdy footing on which the walls of the house rested consisted of roughly shaped fieldstones of Pennsylvania mica schist. The mortar of the stone and the brick masonry was made of slaked lime, coarsely ground and mixed with sand and sometimes with a quantity of earth that gave it a brown cast. The pointing had been done with a rounded tool. Other kinds of stone found on the site included slate from some kind of trim (not from the roof, as it was wood-shingled) and part of a marble mantle.

If the samples of eighteenth-century plaster found on the site tell a true tale, the interior of Franklin's house must have been sunny, warm, and cheerful. The surfaces of the plaster retained several coats of paint, among which yellow, white, and red predominated; samples of black, blue-gray, and cream paint were also found, but in smaller quantities. As the house was being painted for the first time, Deborah wrote to Ben in some exasperation that "we had a great number of flies. . . . It is observed they are very fond of new paint," a fact substantiated almost two centuries later when archaeologists determined that the paint had a sourmilk base. Although plaster from the nineteenth century was also found, the eighteenth-century samples were distinguishable by their thickness and coarseness, as well as by their stratigraphic position. The plaster had been applied to stone, brick, and splitlath backing.

Most of the eighteenth-century artifacts found near the foundations of Franklin's house came from privy pits, and most were ceramic items. Of these, locally made kitchen items of undecorated, lead-glazed redware were most common and included parts of deep pots, wide-mouthed jugs, mugs, jars, pitchers, pie plates, and heavy platters (Figure 3.22).

Creamware and porcelain were the next most common types of pottery, with the porcelain representing 12.4 percent of the total 3,189 ceramic sherds reported by Powell (1962a).* Judging from the amount of creamware and porcelain recovered, it would seem that the Franklins had a fondness for good-quality ceramic tableware and did not stint in indulging it. Included in the creamware was some queensware, as decorated cream-

---

* Appendix 3.A contains a list of the artifacts Powell (1962a) found near the foundations of Franklin's house, as well as tables of data from six of the twenty-two pits excavated in the basements of Franklin's three Market Street houses. The data from the Market Street houses were reported by Liggett (1970a, 1970b, 1971b, 1971c, 1973) Cosans (1975), and Huseman (1975) and analyzed by Basalik and McCarthy (1982) according to South's (1977) artifact categories.

Figure 3.22.

Lead-glazed American redware found near Franklin's house. (Courtesy of Independence National Historical Park)

Figure 3.23.

Porcelain sherds found near Franklin's house. (Courtesy of Independence National Historical Park)

ware was called after Wedgwood scored a thumping success with it in the second half of the eighteenth century. We can surmise its presence on the site may have had something to do with Sarah Bache's letter to her father on October 30, 1773: "We have no plates or dishes fit to eat before your friends. The Queen's ware is thought very elegant here, perhaps you could bring them when you return."

Of the porcelain, ten pieces were Japanese and one was French, but most were Chinese, decorated in the blue-and-white Canton style (Figure 3.23). Chinese porcelain and English cream-ware virtually drove the French out of the pottery export market in the eighteenth century, but Franklin, who esteemed things French, once sent

Sarah a porcelain tea set from Paris. A sample of that set can be seen today at the Franklin Institute in Philadelphia.

Of the nearly 1,000 glass fragments recovered, almost a third came from bottles; wine bottles accounted for 278 of the fragments and medicine bottles for 15. Also found were pieces of 4 decanters, 3 lamps, 5 glass tubes, and 53 hand-blown, stemmed drinking vessels. Of the very few tumbler fragments found, one can only hope that one of them may have come from Franklin's glass "armonica."

From the fragments of animal bones and shellfish unearthed at the site, it seems a fairly safe bet that the residents of Franklin Court were much fonder of beef than of pork and preferred oysters to clams. Of the 2,600 bone fragments recovered, 84 percent were beef, 15 percent were sheep or goat, and 1 percent was pig.

Either the residents must not have liked venison, or it was a rare treat; deer bones accounted for only 0.5 per cent of the total. Shellfish remains were abundant, but for every clam shell found, there were three oyster shells.

The remaining artifacts are few and speak for themselves: two three-tined forks, a knife blade of iron, a bone handle, and a couple of spoons of iron and pewter, much deteriorated. There were also bits of hardware from furniture, iron stove parts, a hand sickle, and a piece of a horseshoe. Three stone marbles, a fragment of a child's shoe, a clasp knife, six copper buttons, and an English penny dated 1720 complete the account, on which we may observe that the penny saved by the archaeologist was a penny hard-earned, and at considerable cost (Cotter 1980:20).

CARPENTERS' COURT: A SURPRISING FIND

For a small alley, only 14 feet wide and not much more than 125 feet long, Carpenters' Court has witnessed an unusually large share of history, as well as a rather unusual archaeological find. Situated just to the south and west across Chestnut Street from Franklin Court, the alley has for over two centuries led to a modestly sized but elegantly proportioned building known as Carpenters' Hall. The hall, built from 1770 to 1774, was constructed to serve as a meeting place for the Carpenters' Company of Philadelphia, an association of master builders formed in 1724. Modeled after medieval craft guilds, the Carpenters' Company provided instruction in building design to craftsmen and apprentices and assistance to members who, because of work-related accidents, were in need of support.

The hall that the Carpenters' Company erected, and which they still own and maintain, is of red brick, Georgian in style, and topped with a handsome cupola. Roughly 50 feet square, it indents 10 feet at each corner so that it has the shape of a cross. Fronting toward Chestnut Street with doors both north and south, it is open to the light on all sides. In this, Carpenters' Hall is reminiscent of Franklin's house, long vanished from across the street. The resemblance is not surprising; plans for both buildings were drawn by the same member of the Carpenters' Company, master builder and carpenter Robert Smith.

North of the hall on the east side of Carpenters' Court stands a reconstruction of the exterior of Pemberton House, an eighteenth-century merchant's mansion (Figure 3.24); today the interior houses an Army and Navy museum. On the west side of the court is a replica of New Hall, a building erected by the Carpenters' Company in 1791 to meet the need for more office space in the new nation's temporary, bustling, and crowded capital. Since its reconstruction in the early 1960s (see Figure 3.3), New Hall has served as a museum commemorating the early history of the U.S. Marine Corps.

History in Carpenters' Court

The Carpenters' Company had scarcely put the finishing touches to its elegant Georgian structure when in September 1774 Philadelphia found itself host to an august body of

Figure 3.24.

The Pemberton House (left), and New Hall, reconstructed. (Photo by J. L. Cotter)

gentlemen. Representing every colony in the land except Georgia, the gentlemen, if august, were anything but of one mind. As delegates to the First Continental Congress, they represented those who vowed to resist British tyranny at all costs and those who were eager to mend the quarrel. Among the latter group was Joseph Galloway, Speaker of the Pennsylvania Assembly, who offered the delegates the State House Assembly Room for use as a meeting place. The decision of the delegates to accept in-

stead the invitation of the Carpenters' Company to use their hall was indicative of the strength of the radicals—and prophetic of the Revolution that was to follow.

For the eight weeks the delegates were in town, Carpenters' Hall was the nerve center of Philadelphia. Rumors flying around Carpenters' Court were as thick as the late-summer flies and caused, even in the soberest of Philadelphians, ripples of apprehension, alarm, and elation. Then, as suddenly as the delegates had come, they were gone, and Philadelphians returned to the industrious ways that had served them and their city so well for over seven decades. Stolidly, the members of the Carpenters' Company took up where they had left off their long-standing deliberations on developing the land around Carpenters' Hall.

The development of the land had been a concern to the Carpenters ever

since they acquired it in 1768. On February 15, 1770, having determined to build a hall for themselves, they placed a notice in the *Pennsylvania Gazette* describing a "commodious lot of ground" to be sold "for ground rent" (Platt et al. 1966:9). Their entire lot had a frontage of 66 feet on Chestnut Street and a depth of 255 feet, and access was, as it still is, through the center alley. On the east side of the alley, fronting on Chestnut Street, was a house occupied by two shops. Thirty feet beyond that were an office and a garden. On the west side, a series of contiguous buildings ran along the alley to a depth of 73 feet. Benjamin Loxley, the member of the Carpenters' Company who had arranged the purchase of the lot for the Carpenters, identified these buildings as the Front House, which had five tenants, and the North and South kitchens, each of which had one tenant. Just beyond the South Kitchen was a garden, and near the end of the alley, a possible privy or woodshed. Until the Carpenters built their hall, the back half of the entire lot was given over to a vegetable garden. The only recorded change in the court between the time the Carpenters bought the land in 1768 and their construction of the hall in 1770 was the fitting of a 32-foot pump in an old well. Sometime around 1770, they put paving down around the well and erected a fence along the alley (Powell 1958b).

Three months after Philadelphia lapsed back into its workaday world in the wake of the delegates' departure, Joseph Pemberton, a Quaker merchant, offered to buy the 26-by-140-foot lot on the east side of the alley. The Carpenters must have been overjoyed. From their perspective, it would have been hard to imagine a more ideal buyer—a wealthy merchant desirous of erecting a fine resi-

Figure 3.25.

Carpenters' Court after demolition of New Hall in the spring of 1958. At the rear of the excavated area are the pits identified in Figure 3.26 as features 1 and 2. (Courtesy of Independence National Historical Park)

dence that would reflect his status and ambitions. The brick mansion that went up on the east side of the lot in 1775 was three stories high. It occupied the entire 26-foot width of the lot and was about 42 feet deep. Outbuildings behind it included a two-story kitchen and a one-story privy (Platt et al. 1966:1–2, 10). When Pemberton bought the lot, the alley was still unpaved; one of the stipulations of the purchase was that he pave the east half of its 14-foot width. Later, in 1811, wooden water pipes were laid down in the alley, and in 1838 gas pipes were installed.

If Pemberton had been looking for a tranquil setting for his house, he must have been disappointed. The Carpenters, pleased with their experiment in letting out their hall, continued to rent it to various groups, including the Library Company of Philadelphia and the American Philosophical Society, and on occasion members of these groups must have caused the court to ring with animated conversation. Shortly after the house was erected, with the war in full swing, Carpenters' Hall was functioning as a military hospital and the court was the noisy hub of the army's supply operations.

The Commissary General of Military Stores occupied Carpenters' Hall continuously from 1778 through the 1780s. In 1790 the new republic's War Department moved in, followed shortly thereafter by the First Bank of the United States. Crowded out of their own premises by their esteemed tenants, the Carpenters voted in 1791 to quickly construct a building on the west side of the alley. "New Hall," as it was called, was two stories high and about 20 feet wide and 61 feet long. It had three offices on the ground level and a "long room" for meetings on the floor above. The Carpenters were not to have New Hall to themselves

for very long. No sooner had it been completed than Secretary of War Henry Knox moved himself and his staff from Carpenters' Hall across the court to the new building.

After the removal of the federal government to Washington in 1800, the Carpenters' Company took over the second floor of New Hall, but they continued to rent space on the first floor to various community groups. In 1833 a third story was added to the building to accommodate an architectural school, and sometime after 1850 the structure underwent other extensive alterations. By that time its neighbor across the court was no longer standing. Sold by its original owner, who went bankrupt shortly after its construction, Pemberton House passed into the hands of a merchant named William Sykes. Later, from 1816 until 1823, it served as a post office run by Richard Bache, Benjamin Franklin's grandson. Finally, in the 1840s, Pemberton House was demolished (Platt et al. 1966:16–17).

Carpenters' Hall met a somewhat kinder fate. After the turn of the nineteenth century, it was occupied first by the U.S. Customs House and then by the Second Bank of the United States. A series of other tenants followed, and by 1828, its halls reverberating to the clang of the auctioneer's gavel, it had become the Philadelphia Auction Market. Fortunately, in 1857 the Carpenters' Company decided to rescue the building and to restore and preserve it as a historic landmark.

Archaeology in Carpenters' Court

By 1955, when Independence National Historical Park was in the planning stages, New Hall bore practically no semblance of its original appearance, and the area surrounding Carpenters' Court was, one might venture to say, somewhat lacking in eighteenth-century ambiance. A decision was made to clear the land on both sides of the court (Figure 3.25) and to re-

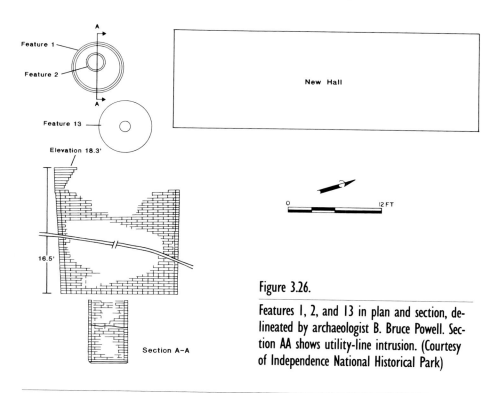

Figure 3.26.

Features 1, 2, and 13 in plan and section, delineated by archaeologist B. Bruce Powell. Section AA shows utility-line intrusion. (Courtesy of Independence National Historical Park)

Figure 3.27.

Brass finial from an eighteenth- or early nineteenth-century pipe tamper found in a privy pit just south of New Hall. (Courtesy of Independence National Historical Park)

construct Pemberton House on the east and New Hall on the west. The clearing of the land, though to the benefit of eighteenth-century ambiance, was to the detriment of Philadelphia's architectural heritage, for it resulted in the razing of Frank Furness's Guarantee Trust Bank, which had stood just east of the court.

With the yard and alley from Carpenters' Hall to Chestnut Street cleared for the reconstruction, Paul J. F. Schumacher (1956d) began archaeological investigations in 1956, and B. Bruce Powell took up the work in 1958. The principal discovery was made 10 feet south of New Hall (Figure 3.26). It consisted of a brick-lined pit 9.2 feet wide and 16.5 feet deep, which Powell (1958b) called feature 1. Inside that pit, feature 2—a smaller

brick-lined pit 3.9 feet in diameter—had been sunk to extend another 5.7 feet into the earth. Close to this pit within a pit, Powell also found a complete brick cistern (feature 13). The cistern had a diameter of 10.3 feet and was 12.8 feet deep. Covered by an arched brick roof in which there was a pump hole 2-feet wide, the cistern was filled with 2 feet of mud and 8.5 feet of water and was devoid of artifacts.

Powell (1958b) concluded that feature 1 was the remains of a privy the Carpenters' Company had built in 1770–71. Records describe that privy pit as being 9 feet 2 inches wide and 15 feet deep. Later records show that a privy, perhaps this one, was cleaned in 1794 and again in 1840. Powell believed feature 2 was the "well" described as sunk into the Carpenters' privy in 1840 "to correct the foul smell arising from the same."

The top 15 feet of the privy pit was filled with construction debris—bricks, mortar, plaster, and wood. It contained few artifacts, and all dated from the late nineteenth century. From a depth of 15 feet to the very bottom of the privy extension at 22.2 feet, the fill consisted of blackish-green, compacted, feculent soil. This fill yielded artifacts ranging in date from the mid-eighteenth century to the late nineteenth century. The earlier artifacts came from the fill at the edges of the pit that the 1794 and 1840 privy cleanings had failed to remove.

Artifacts dating from the last half of the nineteenth century included an earthenware shaving dish inscribed with the name of X. Bazin, a perfumer who occupied a store at 114 Chestnut Street from 1850 to 1895; a U.S. nickel, date illegible but of a type minted only from 1867 to 1895; a seal from an olive oil bottle bearing the la-

bel of Jauretche and Carstairs, importers from 1850 to 1861; and a molded glass bottle made for "E. Roussels' Superior Mineral Waters" by the Dyottville Glass Works. Although Roussel operated from the 1840s until 1854 and again from 1862 until 1867, this type of bottle was not made until after 1855 (Powell 1958b).

The most unusual artifact from the eighteenth century was a finial broken off from a brass pipe tamper. Pipe tampers were a fairly common eighteenth-century smoking accessory, as the number of them dug up at Williamsburg and other eighteenth-century sites attests. This particular pipe tamper, however, was anything but usual, distinguished as it was by the explicitly pornographic character of its finial. The finial, shown in Figure 3.27, was evidently a popular item in Philadelphia in the late 1700s and on into the 1800s, for it is exactly the same as that attached to an intact pewter pipe tamper found in the nineteenth-century fill of a Society Hill privy. (The excavation of that pit, located at 310 Cypress Street, is described in Chapter 4.) To date, the only other pornographic item discovered at the historic sites of Philadelphia has been the carved phallic end of a wooden shaft; speculation about it has ranged from its possible use as a barrel stopper to the more obvious. As described in the next section, this item was retrieved from the mixed nineteenth-century fill of a privy pit situated near the East Wing of Independence Hall.

Philadelphia does not have an exclusive claim to archaeological pornography in America. A pornographic tile is rumored to have been found at a historic site in Boston, but no published report has ever confirmed it. Similar artifacts have doubtless been found in other American cities, but such items have rarely been preserved or publicized. In London, however, an archaeological find of a pornographic nature has been fully described, documented, and illustrated (Henig and Munby 1976:156–59). Discovered behind the chimney breast of a room on the second floor of the Cheshire Cheese tavern were eight mid-eighteenth-century tiles depicting explicit episodes of aberrational sexual dalliance. The tiles may have furnished a bawdy room of the old inn at a time when Dr. Samuel Johnson preferred the Cheshire Cheese to more dangerous haunts on the other side of Fleet Street. So far in Philadelphia, all eighteenth- and nineteenth-century pornography has been found in the choicest parts of the old city, beneath grounds well trod by the Founding Fathers and the elite denizens of Society Hill.

ARCHAEOLOGY IN THE CRADLE OF THE NATION: INDEPENDENCE HALL AND ITS SURROUNDINGS

The nation that was born in Independence Hall and the hall itself offer several interesting parallels. Both have been venerated, both have withstood hard usage and the threat of destruction, and both have required constant care and reinforcement to endure the hazards and demands that time has imposed on them. The historian, economist, and anthropologist have devoted much effort to the conservation of the United States. The archaeologist and architect, joined by the historian, have devoted much effort to the conservation of Independence Hall.

Historically, the parallel between nation and hall is further enhanced by the observation that both prevailed despite a far from unanimous public sentiment in favor of the creation and preservation of either. Both also prevailed against challenges that threatened to extinguish them in their infancies. And both have lived through some subsequent and distinct ages.

At various stages in its life cycle, Independence Hall has suffered everything from benign neglect to misuse and inaccurate restoration. Fairly early in its life, it narrowly escaped demolition; somewhat later, its basement served as the city's dog pound. Having survived all that, it lived on into the Victorian era to become the object of a corporeal resurrection in which enthusiastic restorationists undertook the job of reissuing it—as Benjamin Franklin once proposed the Creator reissue him, like a book—"in a new and more elegant Edition." Franklin would have had his new edition "revised and corrected *By the Author*"; buildings, on the other hand, must be restored by fallible mortals.

In the twentieth century the work of restoration has continued, but in a somewhat different vein. By the end of the 1950s, a small army of historians, architects, and archaeologists was engaged in the task of reissuing Independence Hall in a facsimile edition. The task is an ongoing one and continues to this day.

The Age of Construction: 1732–1777

From its very beginning in 1732 as the Pennsylvania State House, Independence Hall was a symbol of the nation to come. Conceived forty-four years before the Declaration of Independence, it was the most ambitious public building undertaken to that date in the thirteen colonies. It cost far more than the amount appropriated for it, and it was almost beyond the means of the struggling province that built it. For lack of funds, it was finished piecemeal. It was not until twenty-one years after its groundbreaking in 1732 that the State House finally emerged with full appointments in 1753.

It took a Philadelphia lawyer to initiate the project and to keep it alive amid acrimony, delay, and expense—the original "Philadelphia lawyer" to whom the term was applied in token of shrewdness and ability. His name was Andrew Hamilton. A member and speaker of the assemblies in both Pennsylvania and Delaware, Hamilton won fame by his successful defense of Peter Zenger in a 1735 New York trial that was to become a freedom-of-the-press landmark. Having earned his accolades, Hamilton returned to his home, Bush Hill, just west of Seventeenth and Spring Garden streets.* There he resumed his duties as a member of the committee that the Pennsylvania Assembly had appointed in 1729 to oversee the construction of a state house. Together with fellow committeemen Thomas Lawrence and Dr. John Kearsley, Hamilton began once again poring over architectural plans for the building.

The plans were not of a piece, nor were the members of the committee architects; in fact, architecture did not emerge as a profession until the nineteenth century. No less than a dozen sets of plans are known to have contributed to the final design, but the basic concept was probably taken from the most popular British architectural guide of the time: James Gibbs' *Book of Architecture*, published in London in 1727. Among the Gibbs drawings is one of the Right Honorable Earl of Litchfield's house at Ditchley, Oxfordshire, which is strikingly like Independence Hall, even to its keystoned windows. Connecting arcades and wing buildings identical to those of Independence Hall appear in the same book in "A Draught made for a Gentleman in Wiltshire." Thus the inspiration for the hall was apparently not a public building, but a private mansion in the Palladian mode, highly fashionable in Georgian England (Platt et al. 1962:14). Charles Peterson (personal communication, 1991) limits Gibbs's influence to the Entrance Hall paneled walls.

Hamilton no doubt wondered from time to time in his declining years, until death took him in 1741, how he had ever become involved in such a quagmire of contention, shortages of

funds, and interminable construction. In 1738 the first audit of the expenditures on the State House showed that a total of £5,003.16.2½ in labor, services, and materials had found their way into the structure and grounds. Of this the province of Pennsylvania had paid £3,616.12.7, and Hamilton himself had paid the balance, no less than £1,387.3.7½, out of his own pocket. For his trouble and expense, Hamilton received a 5 percent commission and allowances, worth an aggregate £402.3.9½ (Platt et al. 1962: 23). The future Shrine of Liberty was not to be erected without patriotic sacrifice.

The Main Hall and Its Wings

For all the grief of monetary and material shortages and frequently replaced workmen and artisans, the central part of the building—the main hall—somehow became a masterpiece. What documentation exists points to Hamilton and his fellow committeemen as the arbiters of the design (Figure 3.28). Edmund Woolley, one of the founders of the Carpenters' Company, and Ebenezer Tomlinson were the master carpenters who, in keeping with the accepted practice of the day, devised and carried out the actual building plans; craftsmen such as these were at once engineers, architects, draftsmen, and builders. Of all the original collaborators, Woolley alone was still on the job in 1753, overseeing the final touches. Hamilton, who until his death in 1741 worked closely with Woolley on the project, lived long enough to see only the exterior of the main hall and the wings completed. The Park has a photocopy of Woolley's bill for five pounds, payment due, for drawings of the plans for the State House submitted to Governor

John Penn. The bill records payment July 22, 1736 (Peterson, personal communication, 1991).

Whether owing to Hamilton's skill or Woolley's or to the collaboration between them, the result was that the main hall, first and best built, lasted longest and changed least. It has remained a conscious expression of the times in which it was built and of the people who built it. Essentially a two-story colonial mansion, it has a gabled roof, balustraded roof walk, and wings balanced in the Palladian manner (Figure 3.29). When the small bell cupola shown in Figure 3.28 was removed in the early 1750s, clock faces were installed in the east and west ends of the main building. The clocks reflected not only a concern about telling time but also a certain thrifty logic on the part of the builders. The clock on the west end looked like a giant "grandfather's clock"; it was perched above a stone casing that reached to the ground. The east clock had no case. The two clocks shared a common mechanism in the attic, to which the dials were connected by rods, and the casing in the west wall contained the clock weights. The canny logic of the builders was that with the clock weights in the west casing, why build another casing for the east wall?

The exterior of the main hall is brick, laid in Flemish bond and trimmed with soapstone and marble; its window frames and doors are made of wood. So well planned was the brickwork that hardly a cut brick is to be found in the building—a mark of superior craftsmanship. The masonry has survived to the present day in a remarkably well-preserved state. Inevitable deterioration of the exterior woodwork, despite regular (if not always judicious) painting, has resulted in its being replaced from time to time. With few exceptions, how-

---

* Bush Hill served as the asylum that Stephen Girard organized for yellow fever victims in 1793. By the 1830s it had been replaced by a carpet factory (Miller 1982:186; Wainwright 1982:277).

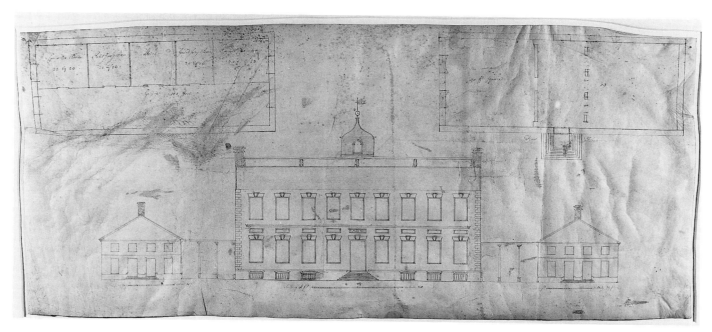

Figure 3.28.

Design for the Pennsylvania State House, 1732. This unsigned ink drawing may have been one of a set that Andrew Hamilton submitted to the Pennsylvania Assembly in August 1732. It is uncertain whether Hamilton himself drew it or it was the work of Edmund Woolley. (Courtesy of the Historical Society of Pennsylvania)

Figure 3.29.

Independence Hall in 1989. (Photo by J. L. Cotter)

ever, the exterior is still as it was in the late 1730s, and no section of the walls has ever been altered or replaced because of a structural fault.

Work on the interior of the hall apparently dragged on for some time. It was not until ten years after the groundbreaking that the two main rooms of the first floor emerged decently, if modestly, finished with wood paneling. The west room housed the Supreme Court of the Province of Pennsylvania. On the east was the Assembly Room, in which the Declaration of Independence was later signed. The second floor was not finished until 1747. On the south side, it contained the governor's office, a committee room, and a council room; on the north side, a long gallery running the width of the building served both as a waiting room and a banquet hall.

The East and West wings were started almost at the same time as the main hall, but just when the arcades between the wings and the main hall were built is in doubt. The wings, each 22 feet deep and with a frontage of 50 feet along Chestnut Street, provided office space for clerical workers. Each wing had two floors, a hipped roof, plain cornices, and one center chimney.

Additions and Embellishments

The Pennsylvania Assembly must have been pleased with what it saw taking place on Chestnut Street in 1732. Twenty years after the construction of the main hall and the wings had begun, the assembly ordered the erection of a small structure adjacent to the southeast corner of the main building "for the accommodation of the Committee of this House"—a convenient encroachment on the scene,

but a conspicuous one, marring, as it did, the back aspect of it (Sullivan 1959:1). The following year the assembly installed its library in the little addition. Another small addition once connected the West Wing with Congress Hall (Charles Peterson, personal communication, 1991).

Six years later, in 1759, with the State House standing though still lacking interior appointments, the Province of Pennsylvania obtained title to little more than half the block that is today Independence Square. To make sure that the setting for its new home would be tidy, the assembly resolved "that Materials be prepared for encompassing the Ground with a Wall in the ensuing Spring." The wall was built around State House Yard, and in 1770, after the province had purchased the whole square, it was partially rebuilt to extend to the new, southernmost property line at Walnut Street (Sullivan 1959:2). Made of brick, the wall stood 7 feet high and enclosed the square on three sides.

The assembly's concern for tidiness reflects the ethos of Philadelphia in the 1740s. A Quaker town, staid and substantial, it was also relatively unrelieved by ornament, and—the steeple of Christ Church not yet having been erected—there was not a single notable spire anywhere to be seen. As the fiftieth anniversary of the city's corporate charter approached, Philadelphians, casting critical eyes over their city's skyline, found the small bell cupola over the State House wanting. Public sentiment was soon ripe for yet another addition to the building. Interestingly, the Friends of the Quaker Party spearheaded the drive for the new embellishment to the State House. Led by Isaac Norris, Jr., Speaker of the Assembly, and motivated by their disapproval of military expenditure, even for defense, the Friends moved to put funds out of the

reach of the advocates of armament in such a way as to confound their criticism (Platt et al. 1962:14). Thus in January 1750 the assembly voted the following action: "*Ordered*, That the Superintendent of the State-house proceed, as soon as conveniently they may, to carry up a Building on the South-side of the said House to contain the Staircase, with a suitable place thereon for hanging a bell."

By 1753 the original bell cupola had been removed, the brick base of the new bell tower was finished, and two clock faces were adorning the end walls of the main building. The bell tower's stone walls veneered with brick were—and still are—as solid as the hall itself, being "three feet in thickness at the base and 18 inches at the top." The brick base was joined to and centered on the main hall's south wall. It extended 30 feet out from the hall, enclosing a new staircase, and rose to a height of 69 feet. Centered in the tower's 34-foot south wall was a door adorned with columns and topped by a Palladian window. A grand stair hall now opened onto both floors of the main hall and steps continued to the steeple above, eliminating the clutter and inconvenience of the original stairs, which had been within the main building.

On March 29, 1753, the raising of the tower's wooden steeple began (Figure 3.30). The first level of the steeple had a pilaster at each corner and a window surmounted by a pediment on each of its four sides; a balustrade graced by eight urns ran along its roof line. Rising above this level was an octagonal cupola, and above that was a smaller cupola, also octagonal, topped by a spire and vane (Nelson 1976:287–89). Protecting the new structure was a lightning rod, installed to Benjamin Franklin's specifications.

By the first week of June 1753, the

Figure 3.30.

The State House as it appeared after the tower, steeple, and clock faces were added in 1753, from a detail in a painting by Charles Willson Peale. The low sheds next to the wings may have housed visiting Amerindian delegations. Congress Hall now occupies the site of the shed on the right, and Old City Hall is at the opposite end of the block. (Courtesy of the American Philosophical Society)

steeple was ready for its bell. An English casting that cracked upon its first testing, the bell was recast by the local founders Pass and Stow. It was inscribed with a quotation from Leviticus, "Proclaim liberty throughout all the land and unto all the Inhabitants thereof"—a truly prophetic sentiment, as it turned out: the bell was to become the familiar symbol known to later generations as the "Liberty Bell." In 1835, long after it triumphantly proclaimed liberty on July 4, 1776, the bell cracked again, and by 1846 it had become a permanently silent symbol. In 1955 it was the number-one artifact to be catalogued in the inventory of Independence National Historical Park.

For more than two decades after the bell tower was finished in 1753, the State House was spared any major alterations. By 1777, however, both the nation and the building had entered a new era, a fact made quite evident to Philadelphians by the British

fighting forces who were then camping in State House Yard.

The Age of Alteration: 1777–1828

Alteration of the bell tower signaled a new age in the life of Independence Hall. For some twenty years after its construction, the tower had stood neglected and unrepaired. By 1774 its wooden steeple was so weakened the assembly ordered it taken down. The Revolutionary War intervened to give it a stay of execution, but by September 8, 1781, a carpenter had completed "pulling down the woodwork of the . . . Steeple, putting a new Floor and Roof on the brickwork." To this modest roof was added a small spire with a ball and vane (Figure 3.31). The tower was to remain in this truncated state, with the Liberty Bell safely stored away, until 1828, when Independence Hall entered yet an-

other phase. Before that, however, Independence Hall was to experience a variety of other alterations; it was also to witness some changes in its immediate surroundings.

If the walled yard behind the State House was a rather uninviting place while American and British artillerymen camped in it during the Revolutionary War, it must have been even more dismal when they packed up their gear and left. In 1784 Samuel Vaughan was commissioned to landscape the area. He had much to do. Over the years, the ground, which had once sloped markedly toward the center and then risen slightly before dipping again toward Walnut Street, had been filled, leveled, and refilled. Vaughan did not level the square but hauled in large quantities of sand, gravel, earth, and loam to create a wide central walk with a gravel surface and gravel serpentine walks along the sides of the yard. In December 1784 and January 1785, James

Pearson, the carpenter who assisted Vaughan, recorded spending £1.9.6 on spirits for the men who were digging holes for shrubs in State House Yard. Clearly, eighteenth-century labor relations dictated that if laborers were to work under adverse conditions, such as a Philadelphia winter spent outdoors, management had to provide more than money as inducement to brave the cold (Powell 1959a).

By the spring, Vaughan was ready for his plantings. They included one hundred elm trees, ninety-two hollies, and numerous other types of trees purchased from the celebrated horticultural firm of John Bartram & Son. The ground around the trees was planted in clover, and Windsor benches and garden seats of red cedar were installed along the walks. The scene was thus set for the growth of a sylvan snuggery enclosed on three sides by a 7-foot brick wall. Some twenty years after Vaughan completed his landscaping, the sides of the wall on Fifth and Sixth streets were lowered to 3 feet and topped by an iron fence, but the Walnut Street side remained high and imposing, with a 20-foot ornamental gate (Figure 3.32) in its center, until 1812, when the walls were brought to a uniform height (Sullivan 1959:8–11).

While Vaughan was busy planting his trees in the spring of 1785, other

workmen on the northeast side of the yard were getting ready to lay the foundations for Philosophical Hall, headquarters of the American Philosophical Society. This symmetrical, red-brick structure, built on a part of the square that the society had just bought from the state, was completed in 1789. In 1787 a county courthouse was begun just west of Independence Hall, on the corner of Chestnut Street and Sixth. Here, upon the building's completion in 1790, the Congress of the new nation met, the representatives occupying the first floor, while the senators convened in the chamber above. By the end of 1791 the city had erected a matching building at the east end of the block, just north of Philosophical Hall; built as a City Hall, it would also house the U.S. Supreme Court.

Not too many years after this spate of building activity, both the state government and the federal government left Philadelphia, in each case because a political fulcrum for the population was sought. In 1799 the state government, following the westward movement of the population, decamped for Lancaster (from which it departed in 1812 for the new state capital at Harrisburg), and in 1800 the federal government left for Washington. The buildings of Independence Square were not to go unoccupied, however. The municipal government

took over City Hall; Congress Hall, as the building at the other end of the block was called, reverted to use as the Philadelphia County Courthouse; and state courts continued to use the courtroom on the first floor of Independence Hall.

During the first quarter of the nineteenth century, the second floor of Independence Hall and the Assembly Room on the first floor housed two rather unusual tenants. In 1802 Charles Willson Peale, Philadelphia's prolific and enterprising painter, persuaded the legislature to grant him the use of the upper floor for his natural history museum and portrait gallery and to allow his son Rembrandt to use the Assembly Room as a portrait studio. Soon thereafter, Peale's portraits of the signers of the Declaration of Independence were looking down from the walls of Independence Hall on the skeleton of a mastodon from New York and on shelf after shelf of stuffed birds and animals

(Figure 3.33). Peale's exhibit of scientifically classified natural history collections was a unique contribution to American history and culture. The first such display in America, it was also one of the first efforts to combine recreation with popular education (Platt et al. 1962:74–79).

Although the city of Philadelphia bought Independence Hall from the state in March 1818, Peale's museum remained until 1828, and not until then did the city acquire full use of the structure. After 1828 the museum moved up the street to the top floor of America's first indoor shopping gallery: the Philadelphia Arcade, designed by John Haviland and situated on the north side of Chestnut between Sixth and Seventh streets (see Figure 2.26). There the mastodon, its many-specied companions, and the portraits of the Founding Fathers found fleeting sanctuary. The indoor gallery was an avant-garde and visionary venture, anticipating the shopping malls of the

Figure 3.33.

The second floor of Independence Hall as it appeared when it housed the Peale Museum. By 1816 Peale had installed gaslights in the gallery, but this painting, which Peale began in 1822, shows the oil chandeliers that replaced the gaslights. (Courtesy of the Detroit Institute of Arts, Founders Society Purchase, Director's Fund)

Figure 3.34.

Alexander Lawson's unfinished engraving of *An Election Day at the State House,* painted by John Lewis Krimmel in 1815. The Mills Buildings have replaced the arcades and wings. Congress Hall appears at the right and Old City Hall at the left. The truncated tower came after the original tower was removed and prior to the present Strickland Tower. (Courtesy of the Library Company of Philadelphia)

twentieth century, but an unsuccessful one. The Peale Museum eventually moved to Baltimore.

Peale and his eclectic interpretation of the nation's heritage—patriotic and intensely inquisitive into the science of nature—were part of a gathering popular movement. Americans, reflecting on their country's recent, proud past, were beginning to show concern about conserving the cultural and natural symbols of their heritage. By 1812 an embryonic historic preservation movement was in evidence in Philadelphia and other urban centers.

Ironically, the year 1812 also witnessed the razing of the arcades and East and West wings of Independence Hall, demonstrating that when "big-

ger and better" is possible, sentiment in favor of preservation may take a back seat. These structures, as well as the small addition on the southeast corner of the hall that the assembly had used as a library, were torn down to make way for the spacious and utilitarian Mills Buildings (Figure 3.34). The latter were named after architect Robert Mills, a pupil both of Thomas Jefferson, with whom as a young man Mills studied drawing and architecture, and of Benjamin Latrobe. Mills's fireproof buildings were erected to accommodate the expanding business of the municipal government, which was finding its quarters in City Hall increasingly cramped (Platt et al. 1962:82–83).

Just how near total destruction all the buildings of Independence Square came during this period is evidenced by the state legislature's Act of March 11, 1816. In need of funds to pay for the new capital at Harrisburg, the government proposed to sell its holdings on Independence Square; the act authorized the removal of all state-owned structures on the square so that building lots could be laid out. Fortunately, the act also allowed the city of Philadelphia to purchase the property. This it did for $70,000, thus saving the site from obliteration, and since March 14, 1818, the city has owned all of Independence Square except that portion of it still owned by the American Philosophical Society.

Clearly, the proponents of the budding preservation movement had their hands full. One of their first concerns was to preserve what was wearing out not only by keeping it whole and sound but also by redoing it in the current style. By 1816 the preservationists had apparently won over to their ranks the Philadelphia County Commissioners, who were serving as temporary custodians of Independence Square while the city negotiated its purchase of the property. In that year the commissioners, in an early manifestation of the bureaucratic approach to restoration, were proposing a rehabilitation of the "old-fashioned" Assembly Room that would bring it up to date in the late Federal style. The minutes of the meeting record hot discussion over the matter, however. Voices raised in objection to this treatment of the Assembly Room were heard, and one man—John Thompson—even ran for public office on the issue. As it turned out, the commissioners won the battle, but they exceeded their authority and had to pay up out of their own pockets for the extras.

In 1819, when John Trumbull exhibited his painting of the signing of the Declaration of Independence, he had to defend his portrayal of the Assembly Room against critics who thought it too plain and modest in appearance for such an august occasion. Trumbull's painting was based on his observations of the Assembly Room in 1790, before "the spirit of innovation," as Trumbull later put it, "had laid . . . hallowed hands upon it, and violated its venerable walls by modern improvement, as it is called." Dourly, Trumbull concluded, "The alterations which have been made in the Room where Congress actually sat on the famous 4th July are such that the picture cannot be hung in it" (Mulcahy 1956:79). A late echo of these unhappy innovations was contained in the 1854 memoirs of John Binns, editor of the *Democratic Press*, who recalled that "the floor and the heavy old-fashioned cornice of that sacred hall, to give a job to one of our commissioner's relatives, were torn up and torn down, and cut and sawed and broken to pieces, many of which were sold at high prices as relics."

In the 1820s, as a patriotic nostalgia swept the nation, antiquarians with a well-nurtured passion for the past appeared. Historian/annalist John Fanning Watson (1779–1860) was busy calling for recollections from those old enough to have lived through the days of the founding of the nation, and *Hazard's Register*, a "newspaper" of the 1820s uniquely devoted to "the old days" and their memorabilia, was adding to the fervor. Nonetheless, it did not fully dawn upon the City Fathers that they had a shrine on their hands until 1824, when the Marquis de Lafayette returned to Philadelphia for a visit. This event quickly fanned public interest into a flame of patriotism. The re-

vered French ally and Revolutionary War veteran was received with near idolatry on what was suddenly hallowed ground. Fortunately for the occasion, the ground was by then handsomely ornamented with mature plantings, those Samuel Vaughan had installed in the yard in 1785. The triumphal arch under which Lafayette was to pass was, of course, erected in front of Independence Hall, sym-

Figure 3.35.

Strickland's Steeple. (Photo by J. L. Cotter)

bol of the freedom he had helped the new nation achieve (Platt et al. 1962:92–97). The year after the marquis's visit, State House Yard was officially renamed "Independence Square" (Sullivan 1959:8–11).

The Age of Restoration: 1828 to the Present

Having survived the age of construction and endured the age of alteration, Independence Hall faced the next challenge: the age of restoration. The first restoration was, in fact, not a restoration of an original feature, but rather a new creation. Interestingly, it involved the same structure that had been the first focus of alteration: the bell tower, which had lacked both bell and steeple since 1781. In 1828 the Philadelphia Common and Select Councils selected William Strickland, student of Benjamin Latrobe and noted architect of the Second Bank of the United States, to design a new steeple for the tower. In some ways, the new steeple resembled the old one, except that it was slightly higher and the first tier had a clock face on each of its four sides, with a carved wreath under each (Figure 3.35). Despite its early–nineteenth-century neoclassical adornment, the councilmen who had ordered the work were pleased to regard the new steeple as a restoration. For the next 130 years, neither the steeple nor the bell tower underwent major structural work, an indication that Strickland's men had done their work well (Platt et al. 1962:50–53).

After Strickland's steeple was installed in 1830, the Liberty Bell was reinstalled, and, with four clock faces on the new steeple, the clocks that adorned the east and west ends of the main hall were removed. The city sold the clocks to the Roman Catholic Church of St. Augustine, located on Fourth Street near Vine Street. The sale included the bell from the original cupola, which had been removed from Independence Hall when the bell tower was added in 1753. When the Church of St. Augustine was gutted by fire during the anti-Catholic riots of May 1844, both the clocks and the bell perished, the latter to be recast and subsequently presented to Villanova University (Kimball 1989:70).

The next restoration of Independence Hall involved repair and renovation of the second floor and, once again, the Assembly Room. The object of this restoration of the Assembly Room was "to render the appearance similar to that which it bore when our ancestors there assembled on the 4th of July, 1774" (Platt et al. 1962:106). John Haviland, the well-known Greek Revival architect who was selected in 1830 to direct the work, is supposed to have refitted the room with old paneling that had been stored in the attic. Little can be surmised, however, except that Haviland, like Strickland, was not prepared to ensure historical accuracy; Haviland's "restoration" of the Assembly Room was in Doric style.

A flurry of repairing and repainting went on in the mid-1840s, still without much regard for original appearances, and in 1852 the 2,081-pound Liberty Bell, now cracked and mute, was brought down from the tower and reverently placed on a pedestal in the Assembly Room. Another bell, weighing four-and-a-half tons, was then installed in the tower. In the centennial year of 1876, this bell was replaced by yet another. The last, weighing 13,000 pounds, still graces the tower and reflects a trend toward the bigger, if not the better—a trend that was to continue in America long after the close of the nineteenth century (Platt et al. 1962:103–5).

Despite the growing public reverence for Independence Hall, it was a city office facility, and as such it was not immune to the usual pragmatic and unsentimental usages of municipal property. On July 3, 1851, the city councils passed a resolution that gives a hint of the possible olfactory and auditory realities of the hall in the mid-nineteenth century. It read: "Resolved that the cellar of Independence Hall shall not, from this time forth, be used as a receptacle for dogs taken up under the Ordinances." Since then, visitation to the hall has been restricted to human beings only. As late as June 4, 1868, the Committee on City Property granted to Mrs. Mary Gould a permit to operate a refreshment stand "in the passage-way of Independence Hall." The committee granted the permit despite protests it had been receiving ever since 1861 from "sundry citizens against the vending of coffee and refreshments in the vestibule of the State House." Indeed, in the 1860s, when the proposed and imposing new City Hall was in need of a site, consideration was once more given to removing the historic structures of Independence Square. Happily, and in accordance with William's Penn's original plan for his great town, the site chosen for the new City Hall was at Center Square.

Another possibly fortunate occurrence for Independence Hall was the painting its exterior masonry received in the middle years of the nineteenth century. Undertaken in 1842, 1860, and again in 1868 as protection against the blight of soot afflicting soft bricks, stone, and mortar in the increasingly industrialized city, the painting may in part account for the well-preserved state of the brickwork and stonework today.*

Independence Hall managed to emerge nearly unscathed from the centennial celebrations of 1876. In honor of the occasion, the tower was graced with its present six-and-a-half-ton bell, and the Assembly Room was "disencumbered of its anachronisms" (Platt et al. 1962:119). Fortunately, the "disencumbering" consisted chiefly of moving the Liberty Bell out of the room and moving the Signers' ink-stand in.

The real trouble began with the "restorations" of 1895–97, when the Philadelphia Common and Select Councils vacated the second floor of the hall and the Daughters of the American Revolution (DAR) took up the task of restoration. The ladies began their mission by accepting the generous offer of T. Mellon Rogers, an architect of Philadelphia and Devon, who proposed to donate his services free of charge. Although not a member of the American Institute of Architects, Rogers had proved his skill to the ladies' satisfaction by restoring St. David's Church in Radnor. The members of the DAR compared Rogers's plans "with the original drawings . . . in the possession of the Historical Society," and approved them (Platt et al. 1962:114–16).

The hall was then to experience a most thoroughgoing face-lift. Interior woodwork, masonry, and plastering were redone; old paint was burned off; fireplaces were banished and a steam-heating system installed; the

* When the paint was removed and the walls cleaned and repainted in 1893–94, it was apparent that the raw brick surfaces needed protection. Three years later the brick was doctored with a paraffin solution. In the early 1960s the walls were water-cleaned of soot and treated with Hydrozo, a non-discoloring, patented product intended to retard the inevitable deterioration of the masonry. Two more coats were added in 1976. The effectiveness of the latest treatment awaits the test of time.

1812 Mills Buildings came down; and the arcades and wing buildings were rebuilt on their original sites (approximately). On July 4, 1898, amid much fanfare, the remodeling was dedicated and opened to the public. The architect, however, following a mixed reception of his work by his professional peers, had already sought seclusion. Soon afterward he was dismissed from all connection with the project. Nevertheless, his work would persist into the first quarter of the twentieth century—time enough for the full wrath of the American Institute of Architects (AIA) to gather.

At the request of the city, an AIA committee under the chairmanship of Horace Wells Sellers examined Rogers' work. Surveying the "restor-

Figure 3.36.

The Assembly Room before restoration by the National Park Service. Most of the details shown, including cornices and mantels, were the work of T. Mellon Rogers in the 1890s. The tabernacle frame within the niche and the flanking pilasters were done by John Haviland in the 1830s. The intricately carved cockleshell frieze above the tabernacle frame is one of the few original pieces of woodwork remaining. (Courtesy of Independence National Historical Park)

WEST WALL · KEY TO ILLUSTRATION NUMBERS

Figure 3.37.

Top, west wall of the Assembly Room during restoration; *bottom*, east wall after restoration. The white rectangles in the top photo are key areas in which architectural historians located evidence verifying elements of wall trim. (Courtesy of Independence National Historical Park)

ation" with mounting distaste, the committee concluded that Rogers' "details were largely determined by individual fancy unrestrained—it would seem—by an intimate knowledge of the architecture of the period to which the building belongs" (Platt et al. 1962:132). Members of the institute then prepared measured drawings of the whole structure and a new set of plans and, with the blessing and financing of the city, set about redressing, insofar as was possible, the sins of the past. Before the job was done, both Congress Hall and Old City Hall had also been restored, and a great deal of woodwork, especially on the second floor of Independence Hall, had been ripped out.

As 1924 drew to a close, the members of the AIA concluded that "during the past 10 years the buildings of Independence Square have been brought nearer their original appearance than at any time since the close of the 18th century," which was undoubtedly true (Platt et al. 1962:131). Over the preceding 125 years, only the tower room and the entry hall of Independence Hall had escaped substantial alteration. The Assembly Room had been gutted, refinished, gutted again, restored, and re-restored (Figure 3.36). The paneling of the first-floor courtroom, which had managed to remain intact for more than a century and a half, had ultimately suffered Rogers' "improvements."

The second floor had been altered at least four times, and then restored and re-restored. The arcades and wing buildings had been swept away entirely, together with the small structure that had housed the assembly's library at the southeast corner of the hall. Even the brick floors of the main hall and tower had been relaid at least twice. The Chestnut Street walk had been repeatedly altered, and the square south of the hall had undergone various landscapings. All these changes have been documented; none was adequately described.

By 1951, when the National Park Service took over from the city the care of Independence Square and its buildings, time, deterioration, and the devastation of pragmatic good intentions had conspired to make this historic site a challenging and fitting subject for archaeological investigation and architectural analysis. The restoration that followed was the first total one ever undertaken. It encompassed the main hall, Congress Hall, and Old City Hall (Powell 1962b; Abel 1964). The approach was a new one, too: an unhurried, comprehensive historical, architectural, and archaeological program that would provide analysis for every part of each structure from foundation to roof and steeple. Every clue that could possibly enhance authenticity was pursued.

Since the time the restoration began, a team of historians has scouted out and carefully combed every possible documentary source—written, graphic, and photographic. Among the findings have been some that escaped the notice not only of the Daughters of the American Revolution but also of the architects of the previous restorations: Strickland, Haviland, Rogers, and the gentlemen of the AIA. Perhaps the most valuable new find of all was a pencil sketch

from the private collection of George Vaux of Bryn Mawr, now at the Athenaeum of Philadelphia. The work of Joseph Sansom, it was a faithful rendition of the west wall of the Assembly Room as it appeared in 1776. Other such references were a painting of the Assembly Room begun by Robert Edge Pine in 1784 and completed after his death by Edward Savage and the one John Trumbull based on his observations of the room in 1790. Trumbull used Sansom's sketch to correct his final view, showing one door.

Architects uncovered other kinds of valuable evidence. They found, for instance, that when previous "restorationists" had removed the old woodwork, they had sometimes thriftily reversed and reused it, thus preserving the original evidence. Another very useful architectural discovery was that the eighteenth-century builders had painted their wood trim before plastering the adjoining walls; thus the shape of the original woodwork could be traced in the paint left on the masonry beneath the plaster. Similarly, the width of butt-joint floorings was marked by ridges of dirt and water stains between the boards, the donation of long-vanished charwomen to the restoration. To their amusement, the architects also found, hidden intentionally away in the woodwork, the graffiti of past generations of carpenters and their helpers. One such find was made in the paneling of the central hall, where penciled notations described one of the original workmen in pungent four-letter words (Batcheler 1976:309–11).

In 1961 restoration began somewhat ahead of schedule when the tremors of heavy traffic on Chestnut Street finally shook down the ceiling of the gallery above the Assembly Room. The entire interior of the main

hall was then stripped of all wall trim, and steel girders were installed to support the original framing and new flooring. This time when the interior walls were laid bare, historical architects went over every scar and shadow of the original framing and paneling, meticulously comparing all existing pictorial and written records. Not only did the architectural historians contribute to a painstaking restoration, they also recorded every bit of the restoration accomplished (Figure 3.37). As the restoration progressed, the cracked walls of Congress Hall were mended, and the structural framing of the bell tower of Independence Hall was strengthened beneath its renewed weather vane. Roofing was replaced, and over one hundred layers of exterior paint were thin-sectioned, time-identified, classified, and recorded for future reference.

Thus the restorationists of the future—and there will be a steady procession of them as long as the historic buildings stand—should have no trouble identifying what was done, why, where, and by whom. Conceivably, a thousand years from now, five billion people could have walked through Independence Hall. That would necessitate structural renewal half a dozen times, plus constant conservation and, when required, restoration.

Archaeology in Independence Square

In 1955 archaeologists set to work in the earth of Independence Square to uncover any evidence that would supplement surviving historical documentation. Their quest was complicated in several ways, beginning with the presence of a sacrosanct statue of Commodore John Barry, father of the U.S. Navy, which has stood since 1907 in the center of the square, defying all suggestion of removal. The archaeologists left the central area, the statue, and the walks about it to future research. Reluctantly, they also had to leave to future research the discovery of the little pavilion overlooking the square, near the hall, from which John Nixon first read the Declaration of Independence to the public on July 8, 1776. Though it is known that the American Philosophical Society built the little structure in 1768 as an observatory for viewing Venus's transit across the sun, no trace of it has yet been found.

What the archaeologists did find in the various grass plots of the square was, however, enough to tell quite a story—a long one that starts well before Andrew Hamilton initiated the building of the Pennsylvania State House (Schumacher 1955, 1956b). That Independence Square began as

a wooded, uneven patch of ground on which prehistoric Amerindians moved and their historic descendants occasionally camped was recalled by the discovery of a complete projectile point of chipped stone, one of the 30,577 artifacts recovered from the square. The large number of artifacts found is not so surprising; where people gather and walk about, they lose things or purposefully dispose of them, and Independence Hall, as the hub of public affairs, was from its very beginning a busy gathering place. More than 3,600 lineal feet of test trenches were dug to undisturbed earth to reveal the places where these artifacts had long been hidden (Figure 3.38); the test trenches also revealed the foundations of some vanished buildings (Powell 1959a: 1–12).*

* Among the foundations revealed by the test trenches were those of the Mills Buildings, erected in 1812; those of a "Judges' Retiring Room," erected at the rear of Congress Hall in 1862; and those of the New District Court Building, erected just south of Congress Hall on Sixth Street in 1866.

A house foundation—one of three uncovered within the square—and an old well yielded more physical evidence of the early history of the site. Toward the close of the 1600s, soon after William Penn deeded to Welsh Quakers a number of lots in what is now Independence Square, houses began to spring up on the south and east borders of the site. The house foundation, situated on a lot near Fifth and Walnut streets, had apparently belonged to one of these structures. Historical records showed that a house had been built on this lot sometime between 1695 and 1716 for a carpenter named John Bird. It must have been a modest little structure, for the foundation, which was uncovered 6 feet below present ground level, was just over 20 feet long and 12 feet wide. Its east wall was right on the property line, indicating that it followed the typical Philadelphia pattern of small houses adjoining each other or separated by narrow alleys. At the rear of a neighboring lot, which had belonged to a Charles Townsend, archaeologists found a brick- and stone-lined well dating from between 1743 and 1769. The bottom of the well, 22 feet below the old soil line, yielded the remains of several earthenware pots, a pewter spoon, and the iron hoops of a well bucket. The houses on Townsend's and Bird's lots, together with their neighbors, were torn down in 1770, after the Province of Pennsylvania acquired the entire square and extended the brick wall around it to the new property line at Walnut Street.

The archaeologist's trowel also un-

Figure 3.38.

Test trenches in Independence Square, 1959. (Courtesy of Independence National Historical Park)

covered what later generations might have viewed with alarm as evidence of governmental encroachment upon the private domain. In 1739, when the provincial government voted to build a wall around the part of Independence Square that it then owned, which was at the time little more than half the block, the task was clear enough. But how was the province to handle the southern portion of the wall, when the property line ran from Sixth Street 99 feet eastward, made a right-angle turn and ran north for 80 feet, turned east again for 198 feet, turned south for 80 feet, and finally turned and ran east 99 feet to Fifth Street (Sullivan 1959:2)? Since such an irregular wall line was impractical, historians had assumed that the wall was built straight across the northern portion of the property line. When archaeologists located the wall, however, it actually ran straight across the square in line with the southernmost property boundary. Thus, the wall enclosed some 15,480 square feet of land that did not yet belong to the province, which did not finish purchasing the whole square until 1769 (Powell 1959a:6).

The rebels and redcoats who camped in the square and used it as an artillery park during the Revolutionary War left ample evidence of their presence. Scattered beneath the grass plots of the square, archaeologists found iron cannonballs and lead musket balls, gunflints, military buttons, and a sword. Wherever soldiers are, they eat—as much and as often as fortune allows. Among the finds in Grass Plot 4, just south of the main hall, were a vast quantity of bones from fowl, mostly chicken, and even several whole carcasses that had escaped a final picking.

Archaeological test trenches also revealed a few elements of the landscaping done by Samuel Vaughan in

Figure 3.39.

Stoneware sherd bearing the monogram "AD," found underneath a sidewalk near Philosophical Hall. (Photo by J. L. Cotter; courtesy of Independence National Historical Park)

1784–85. A related discovery was that before Vaughan arrived on the scene, the ground inside the square had been filled and ballast laid for the walkways around it. Whoever did this work had apparently taken the fill from a nearby, handy deposit. The fill included wasters from stoneware pottery production, suggesting that it came from the stoneware kiln Anthony Duché operated near the northeast corner of Fifth and Chestnut streets from the 1720s until his death in 1762 (Cotter 1964a:1–6).* In the ballast of the walk near Philosophical Hall—and in front of the Second Bank half a block east of Independence Square (Cotter 1965)—archaeologists found other evidence of

---

* For more on Duché, see the discussion of industrial sites in Chapter 12.

Duché's work: scores of fragments of "sagger pots," large vessels in which stoneware objects were fired within the kiln to control the heat and prevent uneven firing, as well as the monogrammed stoneware sherd shown in Figure 3.39.

That old paintings, prints, and informal sketches can be a useful part of the archaeologist's tool kit was illustrated one day in 1965, when a puzzling feature came to light a foot beneath the sidewalk in front of the East Wing of Independence Hall. The feature consisted of a low brick arch some 10 feet wide. It had been made by laying the bricks on their long edge, side by side, over a closed form, which was removed after the mortar set. The arch did not support anything but the sidewalk, and it rested on nothing but an earth footing. Inside, beneath a shallow space, was clean sand, very much like the undisturbed earth around the arch. A bit of careful troweling revealed a clue; an eighteenth-century painting by Charles Willson Peale provided another (Cotter 1966a).

What the trowel revealed was a circular shadow in the sand, which, when traced completely, outlined the top of a pit 6 feet in diameter. What Peale's painting showed was a detailed front view of Independence Hall and the buildings adjacent to it as they appeared in the eighteenth century before Congress Hall and Old City Hall were built (see Figure 3.30). There, between the East Wing and cobbled Chestnut Street, was a well; another just like it appeared west of the main hall. A similar arch found in front of the West Wing confirmed the existence of the second well, but that pit was left unexcavated for future investigation (Hershey 1974; Cotter and Nelson 1964).

The brickwork lining the pit in front of the East Wing had been removed above the bottom section, making ex-

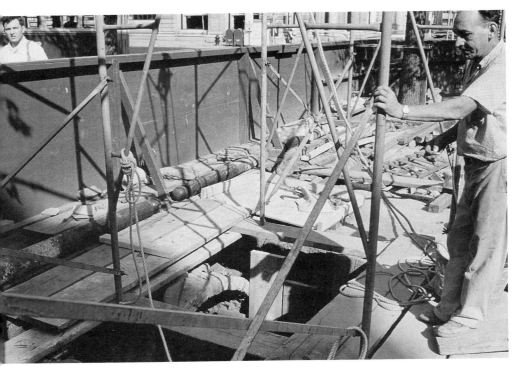

Figure 3.40.

Brick arch of west wing sidewalk well shored for excavating, September 1965. (Photo by J. L. Cotter; courtesy of Independence National Historical Park)

Figure 3.41.

Wooden pump parts found at the bottom of the well in front of the East Wing of Independence Hall. (Photo by J. L. Cotter; courtesy of Independence National Historical Park)

ploration of the interior risky. After a shaft had been built and stout frame shoring erected (Figure 3.40), the pit was finally and painstakingly traced to its full depth of 23 feet. There it yielded, still preserved in moist sand, parts of a wooden well pump (Figure 3.41). The pump, an octagonal log drilled to form a pipe, had a wooden valve at the bottom that retained the water as the pump at the top sucked each successive charge to the surface (Nelson and Cotter 1964: notes and diagram).

The pump parts and other artifacts found in the well, plus some circumstantial historical evidence, indicated that the well might have been in use before the Revolution and had continued in use into the first quarter of the nineteenth century. It and its companion well in front of the West Wing probably went dry, as most city wells did during the nineteenth century,

when the paving of streets and the drainage of roofs, yards, and gutters into sewers reduced groundwater to a minimum. Here, then, were two more wells for the archaeological record, which had doubtless, among other duties, filled the fire buckets that guarded the buildings of Independence Square.*

Old Philadelphia had hundreds of wells and hundreds of privies, but at no other place in the city have archaeologists noted so many privies replaced, renovated, obliterated, and displaced as in Independence Square. To life, liberty, and the pursuit of happiness was added comfort. Only a representation of these pits was explored archaeologically. From them and from the ground around Independence Square nearly one hundred coins were recovered. The coins ranged in date from 1723 to the 1900s and were from England, Ireland, Spain, France, the Netherlands, and the United States; also found were several coins minted by New England states when those territories were known as republics in the days just before the Revolution. In addition to yielding the inevitable clay pipes, pottery and glass sherds, and metal tools, hardware, and trinkets, the privy pits yielded objects of wood and leather, including shoes, and enough bones to give a fair statistical estimate of the dietary preferences of those who frequented the square. It seems they were very fond of beef and fowl, liked pork, and enjoyed deer when they could get some (Powell 1959a).

A 1968 investigation of a privy pit under an alley that had run between the East Wing of Independence Hall, Old City Hall, and Philosophical Hall

---

* In 1967 an enigmatic, dry and empty, brick-lined well was discovered beneath the floor of the north entrance foyer. No reference to the well could be found before or after 1732 (Wilson 1967).

yielded some other interesting finds. It also proved to be the most hazardous archaeological investigation ever undertaken in Independence National Historical Park. It was owing only to the stamina and agility of the principal investigator, Elizabeth Gell of Temple University, and of the twenty students who assisted her that the investigation was possible at all, let alone successful.

The pit, 7 feet in diameter and lined with dry-laid bricks, was discovered by workmen who were digging a utility trench under the restored East Wing. Beneath the point of exposure, Gell's team determined that the pit was 11 feet 6 inches deep. Near the bottom, a brick-and-mortar arch surmounted a second pit, also lined with dry-laid brick. The lower pit extended another 7 feet 2 inches into the earth, and more than half its 4-foot diameter was set off to the south of the pit above it (Figure 3.42). Since two other pits had already been found in the adjoining basement of Old City Hall and labeled as cisterns 1 and 2 (Cotter 1964b), Gell (1968) called the top pit cistern 3 and the bottom one cistern 3A. Cistern 3A's diameter of only 4 feet indicated that it was originally constructed as a well; it had, however, subsequently served as a privy pit.

The factor that called for acrobatic skill on the part of the investigators, and that made determination of the historical relationship between the two pits particularly difficult, was a deep trench that had been dug earlier in the twentieth century to lay a horizontal pipe 6 inches in diameter. The pipe bisected cistern 3 and exited by a hole punched through the west side of the pit (Figure 3.43). A branch of the pipe rose at a 45° angle and exited near the top of the pit on the south side. Such disturbance not only made a shambles of the stratigraphic depo-

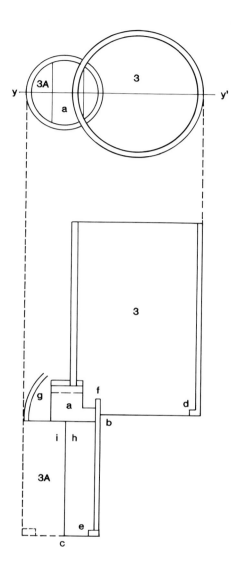

sition of the privy material; together with the offset location of cistern 3A, it also made the exploration very hazardous.

The upper 8 feet of cistern 3 consisted of light-brown, sandy earth, fragments of wall plaster, various-size boards, and numerous molded bricks, both whole and in parts. The debris found here suggested that the pit was closed in the late nineteenth century. The fill of the lower 4 feet of cistern 3

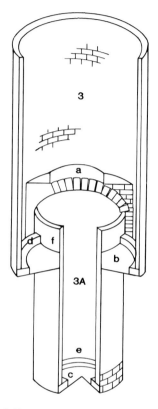

Figure 3.42.

Plan, sections, and cutaway view of cisterns 3 and 3A, excavated east of Independence Hall. (Courtesy of Independence National Historical Park)

was quite different; it consisted of partly decomposed organic matter, moist and black. An analysis of the black organic matter by Dr. Andrew McClary, a parasitologist at Michigan State University, showed the presence of the parasite *Trichuris*, a species of small nematode worm that infests the voluntary muscles of humans and swine. When the deep trench for the 6-inch pipe was laid and the arch separating the two cisterns broke, the brown, sandy fill from above, together with a few artifacts, cascaded down into the upper portion of cistern 3A. The middle portion of cistern 3A appeared to be a redeposited part of the black layer of cistern 3; the lowest portion yielded the oldest artifacts.

Appendix 3.B contains an inventory of the artifacts recovered from both cisterns. The artifacts were quite diverse but included relatively few domestic objects; ceramics, cutlery, and buttons were at a minimum. Cistern 3 did, however, yield numerous medicine bottles of various shapes and sizes, many of which were whole and had molded on them the name and address of Frederick Brown, Druggist and Chemist. Brown operated a pharmacy on the northeast corner of Fifth and Chestnut streets from 1824 to 1864. The sawed-off human skull cap, human armbones, and chemical glassware and bottles without identi-

fying inscriptions found in the bottom of cistern 3 may also have come from Brown's pharmacy. Resting at the very bottom of cistern 3 was a five-thaler gold coin minted in a North German duchy in 1815 (Figure 3.44). The top portion of this cistern yielded one of Philadelphia archaeology's three pornographic finds: a wooden phallus, life-size and realistically carved with screw threads spiraling around the shaft below the head, the end squared off. Gell's report (1968:1–10) somewhat favors the use of the phallus as a bottle stopper or a bung for a barrel, unless a more obvious employment was intended.

Cistern 3A appears to have been empty or nearly so when the arch was built over it. Among the few artifacts found in the middle portion of cistern 3A was a half-eagle five-dollar gold piece minted in the United States in 1834 (Figure 3.44).

Although cistern 3A yielded few artifacts, its presence below cistern 3 does speak fairly eloquently about a situation on which the historical record is generally silent: sanitation—or lack thereof—in Philadelphia during the first half of the nineteenth century. That the dangerous practice of using old wells to dispose of human waste was common practice is illustrated by this example in the very shadow of Old City Hall and the American Philosophical Society's headquarters.

Figure 3.43.

Cistern 3 lay partially over a deep privy pit. Access was obstructed by a cast-iron pipe. (Photo by J. L. Cotter; courtesy of Independence National Historical Park)

Figure 3.44.

Left, half-eagle five-dollar gold piece minted in the United States in 1834; *right,* five-thaler gold piece minted in a North German duchy in 1815. The U.S. coin was recovered from the middle portion of cistern 3A; the German one came from the bottom of cistern 3. (Photo by J. L. Cotter; courtesy of Independence National Historical Park)

BISHOP WHITE'S HOUSE: HOW A GOOD MAN LIVED ABOVE THE EVILS OF INSANITATION

On November 19, 1798, a year and a half before the federal government moved to the raw, new capital on the Potomac, George Washington enjoyed the hospitality of the Reverend Dr. William White, Bishop of Pennsylvania and one of the two chaplains of Congress. The bishop's home at No. 309 Walnut Street was a commodious, three-story townhouse in the Federal style, designed and equipped in the best manner of the period, and furnished with an ample, well-stocked wine cellar. Here the bishop and his family had lived since the house was completed in early 1788, and here they would remain until the bishop's death in 1836 (Wallace 1958:1–7).

No Boswell was present to record whatever weighty, witty, or commonplace conversation took place over the dinner table, but we may assume the table was set with the best Chinese export porcelain, probably some Lowestoft, and good imported English glassware. The silver was no doubt choice, and the kitchen from which the food emerged, well equipped. In short, the hospitality Bishop White afforded his distinguished guest was among the best to be had in Philadelphia. The bishop was of service to his guest in other ways as well, for President Washington was also his parishioner at Christ Church, three blocks away, where today Washington's pew is marked and open to anyone (Kimball 1961:A8).

Bishop White's house is preserved not as a monument to architecture, but rather as a memorial to Bishop White himself (Figure 3.45). As a dwelling that belonged to an affluent, prominent citizen who risked everything he owned (to say nothing of his life and the future of his family) in the cause of the Revolution, the house is a highly appropriate feature of Independence National Historical Park.

Bishop White: The Man, His House, and His Family

When the American Revolution loomed, by no means a majority of the "best people" were ready to forsake the Establishment for the Rebellion. The young Reverend William White was. In 1773 he returned from England, where he had received Holy Orders on the recommendation of several of the most influential political figures in Pennsylvania, and at the age of twenty-six he took up his duties as assistant rector of Christ Church and St. Peter's parish. The scion of a distinguished family of English clergymen, he was comfortably wealthy by inheritance and very well connected socially. His sister Mary was married to a rising young entrepreneur, Robert Morris, who would soon achieve fame as the financier of the Revolution, and White himself had just married Mary Harrison, daughter of a former mayor of the city. Between them, the Whites' friends aggregated a "Who's Who" of Philadelphia. It was therefore of considerable significance in 1778, when Rev. Jacob Duché of Christ Church departed with the retreating British and took his other assistant rector with him, that William White, the only minister

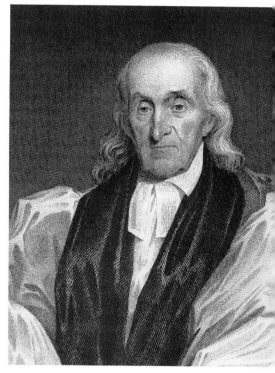

Figure 3.45.

Portrait of Bishop White. (Courtesy of the Library Company of Philadelphia)

of his faith left in Philadelphia, remained loyal to the American cause (Kimball 1961:B5).

Although White had displayed his willingness to risk his neck for his beliefs, the Revolution seems to have caused him far more trouble in estate than in body or mind. Besides earning no income from his ministerial posts from 1776 until the Protestant Episcopal Church was established in the United States in 1787, he felt the ef-

Figure 3.46.

Bishop White's house, restored. (Courtesy of Independence National Historical Park)

fects of the devastating inflation that afflicted practically everyone else in the city. Some individuals of an entrepreneurial bent who had something they could gainfully sell or property they could gainfully manipulate did profit from the economics of the Revolutionary War, but they were the exception. Years later, in his autobiography, White was to estimate that the loss he suffered "by the said Disaster" was not less than "ten thousand Pounds, as Money was then called" (Kimball 1961:B3).

With the war over, White's fortunes began taking a turn for the better. In 1787 he was appointed Bishop of the Diocese of Pennsylvania, and in that role he gained a place for himself in history as the creator and elder statesman of the Protestant Episcopal Church in the United States. His diplomacy, bolstered by the influence of John Adams, resulted in the establishment of an American Episcopal Church that was at once independent of England and the Church of England, but authorized by an act of Parliament to have its bishops consecrated by the Church of England. Seldom has the English capacity for compromise been so successfully or narrowly tested.

The bishop's financial fortunes prospered, too. By the close of 1790, three years after a considerable outlay of money for the construction of his new house, he had inherited from his mother and an aunt the then considerable sum of $20,000. When he died in 1836, he left an estate valued at $36,000 (Kimball 1961:B5). In purchasing power today, that sum would be not less than $1,000,000.

Although we do not know the exact amount Bishop White spent on his house, its assessment in 1788 at £1,900 indicates that it was one of the more substantial properties in the city.

Made of red brick, it stood—and still stands—three stories high beneath a wood-shingled roof (Figure 3.46). A cornice and symmetrically placed windows adorn its front, where glazed headers give a Flemish-bond pattern to the brickwork. Above the front door, a pediment repeats the motifs of the cornice and the two dormer windows in the garret. Constructed as a rowhouse, in that its plain, blank side walls could stand alone or be joined to the next house, it was, as Philadelphia houses had been since 1682, patterned after houses built in England during the Restoration, when Charles II reigned (Gowans 1964). Today the house is joined to another only on its west side. The building that once adjoined it on the east is long gone, and that lot has been turned into a garden, creating a pleasant, open prospect for Bishop White's house.

The plot on which the bishop's house stands is 26 feet wide and 120 feet deep. The house itself is 25½ feet across the front, and the main part of it is 44 feet deep. Extending the house deeper into the rear of the lot are three attached buildings. The first is three stories high and has a vestibule with a side door on the ground level; the door opens onto a courtyard at the east side of the house. Across the vestibule from the door is an open staircase with turned balusters and quarter landings leading to the third floor. Behind this extension is a kitchen, and behind that an attached privy. The kitchen has two rooms above it that served as bedrooms. A winding stairway off the kitchen leads from cellar to loft. The privy at the very rear of the house has two closets, each with two seats; it also has one floor above it.

On the first floor of the main house, a hallway leads from the front door

Figure 3.47.

on the west side of the house past a parlor and dining room to the rear building containing a vestibule and staircase. The second floor of the main house also has two rooms, a large, bright bedroom in the front and the bishop's book-lined study in the rear, as well as a short hallway along the west wall. Happily for the restorationists at work on Bishop White's house well over a hundred years after he departed it, John Sartain made a painting of the bishop's study sometime about 1836; the painting, shown in Figure 3.47, meticulously details the furnishings of the study and also offers a glimpse of the front bedroom beyond. Overhead, the third floor is divided into three bedrooms and two hallways; the garret has three rooms and one hallway. The servants were quartered in the garret rooms or in the back buildings.

Commodious though it may sound, 309 Walnut Street was at times all but overflowing with two generations of the bishop's progeny. When the Whites moved into their new house in early 1788, the household consisted of ten people: the bishop, his wife Mary Harrison White, their five children—two daughters and three sons ranging in age from eleven to two—and three servants. No doubt the scene of great excitement and joy on the day the Whites first occupied it and on many other occasions, the house was also to witness much sorrow, for death came often to the White family. Indeed, the bishop was to outlive them all. Before 1788 was out, Henry, the

youngest of the family, had died at the age of three. In 1797 the bishop's wife died, and in the same year William, his second youngest child, died at the age of thirteen. Nonetheless, the bishop's family grew. All three of his surviving children married and had children of their own. On February 11, 1826, Bishop White wrote to his friend, the Bishop of Nova Scotia, "It consists, under my Roof, of my Daughter Mcpherson, known to you as Elizabeth White, now a Widow, and her two Daughters, young Ladies; and of my Son, with his two Daughters, young Ladies also, and his two Sons, 15 and 13 years of age. My daughter, Mary Bronson, a Widow also, has four Daughters and a Son" (Kimball 1961:B1–2). Mary died before 1826 had ended, and her five children joined the White household, so it then consisted of the bishop, his son, his daughter, eleven grandchildren, and the servants. Ten

years later, when the bishop died and the household dispersed, seven grandchildren were still there.

When the house was sold on November 22, 1836, for the benefit of the estate, Charles Chaucey, a leading lawyer and family friend who lived next door at 307 Walnut Street, bought it for $25,000. The house remained in the Chaucey family until 1870, when it passed into the hands of Edward S. Whelen, a broker who had been renting part of the house as offices. In 1920 the executors of Whelen's estate sold it to William C. O'Neill and Sons for $37,500. Its sale price of $13,500 in 1946 marked the nadir of property values in the neighborhood, reflecting the tawdry commercialism that characterized Society Hill before the development of Independence National Historical Park sparked its revitalization.

By the time the National Park Service acquired the old house in 1948,

Bishop White would scarcely have recognized it (Figure 3.48). The years and a series of short-term rentals had altered the facade and the downstairs interior almost completely. By 1877 at least nineteen tenants had come and gone. There had been five brokers, two railroad companies, seven coal mining and shipping firms, a white-lead manufacturer, a commission agency, a liquor dealer, a maritime merchants' association, and a brick manufacturing company. It cost the National Park Service over half a million dollars to research, restore, and furnish Bishop White's house.

The Restoration of Bishop White's House

What the National Park Service purchased in 1948 was a ghost of the Philadelphia housewright's craft. The goal in restoring it was to re-create as faithfully and vividly as possible the fabric of the house's past—to evoke the essence of the patriot and clergyman who built it and the spirit of the stirring times in which he lived. The maimed relic of the past that presented itself to the historians, architects, and archaeologists charged with this task constituted no mean challenge.

First on the scene were the historians, who furnished a documentary study of the original house and its inhabitants. Next came the architects, who, after all post-1836 alterations had been removed, investigated and recorded all remaining features of the original building. Then came the archaeologists, who fleshed out the body of historical data with physical evidence. At that point, to fill in the gaps, comparative research of similar buildings of the period was undertaken. Finally, all the evidence was

evaluated, and restoration drawings and plans for refurnishing the house were prepared. In all, it took twelve years to carry out these steps.

The Archaeological Investigations

The first excavations, carried out under the direction of archaeologist Paul J. F. Schumacher, took place below the complex of buildings at the rear of the house. Beneath a welter of late nineteenth- and early twentieth-century alterations, Schumacher (1956a, 1956c) uncovered some original foundation walls and a cold cellar (Figure 3.49), as well as a cistern, a well, and an unusual privy-sewer complex. The privy-sewer complex consisted of a marble trough that drained from the privy behind the kitchen into a vaulted, brick-lined channel (Figure 3.50). The channel, 45 feet long, ran north to Harmony Street (as the 12-foot-wide alley running across the rear of the house was called), where it connected to Dock Creek. The well and cistern (Figure 3.51) were just east of the sewer channel, while the cold cellar was 10 feet away (Schumacher 1956a).

By the end of 1956, archaeologists had recovered from the sewer channel an amazingly extensive and telling collection of artifacts: sherds of ceramic and glass, and bits and whole pieces of personal items such as buttons and toothbrushes. Supplemented by what had been located as heirlooms in the hands of Bishop White's descendants and in the archives of historical societies and museums, these artifacts began to paint an interesting picture (Figure 3.52). The White family was reappearing through the medium of casually lost household objects, including some

Figure 3.48.

Bishop White's house in the spring of 1950 before restoration began. (Photo by Leonard Oveturf; courtesy of Independence National Historical Park)

that had been surreptitiously and purposefully disposed of in the privy—an age-old habit of children, servants, and others who would rather the *corpora delecti* of objects accidentally broken not be discovered.

A smaller cache of artifacts was found in a trash-filled pit near the rear of the house. Although Philadelphia's Street Commissioners had by the 1770s instituted weekly street cleanings and a weekly collection of

Figure 3.49.

The basement of Bishop White's house. The original foundation of the east wall of the kitchen is visible at right. The stairwell leads to the cold cellar. (Courtesy of Independence National Historical Park)

Figure 3.50.

The privy-sewer complex in Bishop White's basement, looking north toward Harmony Street. (Courtesy of Independence National Historical Park)

Figure 3.51.

The well and cistern just east of the sewer channel in Bishop White's basement. (Courtesy of Independence National Historical Park)

Figure 3.52.

Artifacts excavated during investigations of Bishop White's house. (Courtesy of Independence National Historical Park)

tradesmen's rubbish, servants in private houses in Bishop White's era were still carrying and disposing of household trash as short a distance as possible from the back door. The trash pit that archaeologists unearthed near Bishop White's back door had a prepared hard-clay floor whose purpose remains a mystery, but its fill yielded many enlightening artifacts dating from the late eighteenth century, among them pieces of earthenware from the kitchen and porcelain from the dining room. Such items were also found in abundance in remnants of a long-submerged dark soil zone, which in the bishop's day had sprouted grass on the ground that sloped away toward Dock Street.

Given the goal of the investigation, the cistern was a disappointment. Built of brick sometime between 1836 and 1880, it was cement-lined, 6.3 feet deep, and 8.3 feet wide at its inside diameter. The artifacts recovered here were mostly objects that had accidentally fallen into the collecting pipe from the roof of the rear building (erected in 1880 and removed during restoration) or items from fill dumped into the cistern when it was closed before the turn of the twentieth century. Since it was clear the cistern had not been on the property during Bishop White's occupancy of the house, it was removed in the interest of accurate restoration.

Another aspect of the archaeological investigations—an essential one in any investigation where the goal is the restoration of an old house—was to determine the level of the ground at given historical periods so that the site could be restored to its original appearance with maximum accuracy. Test trenches showed that the courtyard east of the rear buildings had several successive soil zones. Near the house, the original topsoil appeared at a depth of 7 inches; to the north, where the ground sloped toward Dock Creek, the original soil lay 3½ feet below the surface. Plainly, the original builders had done their work well; the earth was carefully contoured to drain water away from the foundations of the house, thus eliminating an all-too-common grievance of twentieth-century homeowners. For this the Whites no doubt owed a debt of thanks to their friend Mayor Samuel Powel, perhaps the most refined Philadelphian of the time and certainly one of the wealthiest, who kept a careful watch over the young clergyman and his family. In White's absence, Powel "rode herd" on the builders as the house was being constructed and was, as Mary White wrote to her husband on November 27, 1786, "indefatigable in hurrying the Workmen about" (Powell 1958a: Sec. 1, 4).

B. Bruce Powell, who completed the archaeological investigations behind and beneath Bishop White's house, had this to say about the fruits of the archaeologists' labors:

It is rare to recover such a large and fine collection [of artifacts] which can be definitely attributed to an historic personage. The relics, from a toothbrush and razor to porcelain pitcher and earthenware flower pot, can impart an authenticity to the restoration which just cannot be obtained in any other way. Whether used themselves (although few pieces are complete), carefully copied, or replaced by the purchase of exact duplicates, the Bishop's belongings will enable the visitor to identify himself with the era of 150 years ago and to see people of the distant past as persons very much like himself. The Bishop's social position and his obvious good taste combined to leave posterity a picture, in this case an exceptionally complete one, of the articles of daily living among the leaders of the period from the age of the Confederation to the age of Jackson. (Powell 1958a: Sec. 2, 2)

Setting the Stage to Interpret the Past

The reward at the end of all the historical, architectural, and archaeological research lay in furnishing the restored house—setting the stage on which, although the actors will never appear, their character and actions are implied, and the imagination is left to re-create them amid the scenes where they walked, talked, and pursued their daily lives. Creating such a stage setting is a vastly elaborate puzzle, and the mental exercise it involves is impressive. The museum curator, who is responsible for the setting and whose speciality is a knowledge of the customs of the period, must complete by analogy any gaps in the physical and written evidence produced by the other specialists.

With the aid of the historian and the archaeologist, Charles Dorman, curator of the Bishop White House, was able to develop a detailed plan for furnishing every space in the house, from wine cellar to garret. The furnishings were to include not just period pieces but also older items the bishop might have inherited from his family. Dorman's elaborate plan has never been fully implemented; only the first two floors of the main house and the first floor of the kitchen and privy have been furnished and opened to the public.

A narrative suggesting what the bishop's busy household might have looked like accompanied Dorman's plan. Here is the way the kitchen scene was interpreted:

From the late 18th century kitchens in Philadelphia houses the impression survives that the mistress paid close attention to the kitchen as an important part of her domain. More often than not it was light and airy, and—in contrast to those of the present—commodious as well as well-planned for in its function.

It is the custom in households where servants are employed for the care of the house and children, for the servants and young children to eat apart from the family. Thus a table and suitable chairs for this purpose have been placed in the kitchen. The bulk of the cooking for the household would have been done at the fireplace in this kitchen, but additional foods could have been prepared in the basement scullery and laundry. In general, there is an eating area in the northeast corner of the room; a cooking area in the northwest corner; and a food preparation and cleaning area in the southeast corner.

. . . In the northeast corner . . . is a gate-leg dining table surrounded by three out-of-date Delaware Valley rush seat side chairs, a child's chair of the type that might have been saved from [Bishop White's father's] house, and a more recent comb-back Windsor armchair. . . .

A stretcher-base worktable has been placed between the east windows. It contains a breadboard and rolling pin, and a brass mortar and pestle. Above it hangs a cupboard for the storage of spices and other condiments. Beneath the window to the right of the worktable is the tentative solution to the Bishop's city water supply,* a large stone water basin cantilevered through the wall. This is supplied with water by a copper pipe and brass spigot, connected to a pipe which runs from the water main in the middle of Walnut Street to the kitchen. . . .

The large closet in the southeast corner serves as a china storage area and pantry. . . . An eighteenth century pewter dresser and a well-equipped fireplace occupy the west wall. The pewter dresser is furnished with Canton dinner plates, pewter chargers, Pennsylvania pottery, and other eating accessories. The fireplace is fitted with spit andirons and a clock jack. (Clockwork devices for turning spits over the fire were operated by chain weights and gears.) . . .

On the hearth we find various spider pots and frying pans, a bellows, fire tools and a reflecting oven. . . . Near the fireplace is an eighteenth century pine worktable containing a [wooden] bowl partially filled with prepared vegetables, while on the table are a paring knife

* City water was available only after 1801. Until that time the Whites would have drawn their water from the well.

and other vegetables. Alongside the table, facing the large cooking area, is a rush seat armchair where Mrs. Boggs, the cook, could observe the food being cooked as she prepared other items at the worktable. (Kimball 1961:D, sec. 12, 2–4)

On the basis of the sherds archaeologists recovered from the site, Dorman was able to estimate the contents of Bishop White's china, glassware, and pottery cupboards (Kimball 1961:B). His list gives us a rare, documented picture of what a historic American family actually used at their table. Dorman concluded that the Whites would have owned at a minimum:

12 Nanking dinner plates

12 Nanking soup plates

12 Nanking dessert plates

12 Canton dinner plates

12 molded-rim creamware dinner plates

6 Nanking platters

12 Nanking covered custard cups

12 stemmed wine glasses

12 etched-glass punch cups

4 blue-and-white export porcelain plates

1 Nanking butter dish

12 Lowestoft tea cups and saucers

1 Lowestoft cider jug

1 Lowestoft spoon tray

1 Whieldon redware teapot

1 decorated Whieldon sugar bowl

4 large slip-decorated redware bowls

6 Pennsylvania slipware pie plates

2 mochaware handled mugs

6 redware bean pots

6 assorted creamware bowls

12 plain creamware dinner plates

12 plain creamware soup plates

4 slipware meat dishes

Another feature of the restoration that found archaeologist, historian, and curator in collaboration was the wine cellar in the southwest corner of the basement. Historians provided incontrovertible evidence that the wine cellar was well and amply stocked: not only did the bishop drink wine with his meals and with his guests, he also shared his house with his sole surviving son Thomas, who became a prominent wine merchant. The archaeologist's trowel uncovered evidence that the wine cellar had had a convivial opening in its own right: the stone masons had placed some whole wine bottles, whose contents they had emptied, into the masonry they were constructing, where the evidence survives today. Hence reasonable caution prompted the bishop to equip the cellar with a stout door secured with a large lock and to bar the cellar's windows and air vent, thereby discouraging any servant or outside intruder who might want to slake a thirst.

With the value of the wine to its owner historically established and with the archaeological reminder that it could be purloined, Dorman drew up a plan for furnishing the wine cellar. As visualized in the plan, a large rack on the north wall of the room, out of range of any rays of sun from a window, holds bottled champagnes and white wines. The bottles are stored at an angle to keep their corks wet and expanded. Projecting from a nearby wooden shelf is a wrought iron bracket supporting a wood-and-glass lantern. The lantern gives just enough light for a leisurely perusal of the vintages. Against the east wall is a pine table with a bench before it. On the table are sampling glasses, a candlestick, wine ledger, pen, labels, and a pastepot. Against the south wall and in the center of the wine cellar are wicker-jacketed demijohns holding

Figure 3.53.

The shallow well in Bishop White's cold cellar. The iron rods for a swinging crane are at upper left. (Courtesy of Independence National Historical Park)

anywhere from one to ten gallons. Arranged along the west wall is the "artillery" of the collection: large casks holding about two hogsheads, or 126 gallons, fitted with spigots and installed in racks adorned with drip pans and funnels (Kimball 1961:D, sec. 2, 2). In such a setting, we can assume Bishop White would have felt reasonably at home.

An unusual feature of Bishop White's cold cellar provoked some de-bate among the restorationists. The cold cellar, a vaulted, 13½-by-5-foot subcellar with a 4-foot, L-shaped projection, maintained a relatively constant temperature of 40°F. Its purpose was self-evident: cold storage for root vegetables (turnips, potatoes, beets, carrots, and so on) and possibly also for eggs and preserved fruits. There was little cause here for argument. However, in the center of the cold cellar was a shallow, brick-lined, circular well, just deeper than arm's length, and on the south wall next to it, in line with the well, were iron rods for a swinging crane (Figure 3.53). And here the debate began.

The feature could hearken back to a medieval English practice: a cooling pit for wine, such as that found in the Outward Cellar Court of Henry VIII's palace "Nonsuch" in the suburbs of London (Dent 1962:84, plate 9). Supporting this hypothesis was a comparable cellar-pit arrangement found in two seventeenth-century domiciles in Jamestown, Virginia, the first permanent English settlement in America (Cotter 1958:143). On the other hand, the pit could have been used solely to store blocks of ice. There was virtue to both sides of the argument. The sophisticated crane arrangement found in the center of Bishop White's cold cellar could, in fact, have been used to lower either heavy ice or a large bucket filled with wine bottles, or both, into the hole. What its actual use was will probably always be uncertain, but since the pit had no bottom drain for melting ice, the probability is that its primary purpose was not ice storage.

The most difficult and intriguing problem for the restorers of Bishop White's house was the necessary, or privy. Although such a well-named device was to be found in some form in every Philadelphia house or outside it, no documentation of its furnishings could be found; historians of the time and the later Victorian period were notoriously queasy about recording anything so topically indelicate. The restorationists therefore turned their attention to archaeological evidence from privies at other historic locales. Jamestown was no help, since there no privy pits had been found. Presumably, as was the practice of later centuries in rural tidewater Virginia, the inhabitants of Jamestown disposed of human waste by emptying hoppers or other receptacles from outdoor privies or bedrooms. The interpreters of the past at Williamsburg had had a somewhat easier time with the puzzle of the privy; in privy pits there, archaeologists had discovered numerous corn-cobs, and so the obvious solution was to furnish the restored privies with lidded bins of corn husks and cobs. This, too, was of little help to the restorers of Bishop White's privy; such usage, although familiar in rural environments, as living memory attests, was unknown in cities even in the eighteenth century. At least, no corn cobs had appeared in the multitudinous privies in Independence National Historical Park. At the Bishop White House, the solution for the restorationist was some scrap paper near at hand, within the privy closet.

Of greater cogency is that the privy was adjacent to the kitchen, and the channel from the privy to the sewer was next to the water well and 10 feet away from the cold cellar. Thus did a good man live above the evils of insanitation, and his hardy constitution survived placing godliness above cleanliness. The early deaths of the bishop's wife and two boys suggest that others in the household may not have been so fortunate. The complaint of diarrhea was almost universal in eighteenth-century Philadelphia, and the dehydration it caused was often quickly fatal, particularly to babies. Not until the early nineteenth century did Benjamin Latrobe's pumphouse at Center Square begin delivering water from the Schuylkill to the city, and adequate sewers were not installed until the 1850s. Until then contaminated wells and water lines—and bacterial intestinal infections—abounded (Powell 1949: 71–72).

That the bishop remained in Philadelphia to organize the assistance for those stricken in the cholera epidemic of 1832—and survived to tell the tale—is further evidence of the hardiness of his constitution. He had done the same during the yellow fever epidemics of the 1790s, and for all these good acts the bishop is well remembered (Kimball 1961: B7).

A Final Glimpse

Except for the formal historical canvas upon which his considerable good works are delineated, little is known of Bishop White as he was in real life. What we have detailed here are only those aspects of his life that can be inferred from the painstaking archaeological and historical research that went into restoring and furnishing his house. The rest has to be left to speculation and imagination. A nineteenth-century marble recovered from the sewer channel could have belonged to any of the many children in the house, but of their days the record is silent, and unless the bishop had a liking for marbles left over from his childhood, it tells us nothing about him. The recollection of one of his childhood playmates, Hannah Paschall, does, however, give us a glimpse of the young William White: "Billy White was born a Bishop. I never could persuade him to play anything but church. He would tie his own or my apron around his neck, for a gown, and stand behind a low chair, which he called his pulpit; I, seated before him in a little bench, was the congregation; and he always preached to me about being good" (cited in Stowe 1937: 10). But whether the child who was born a bishop was any good at marbles we will, alas, probably never know.

THE GRAFF HOUSE AND THE KOSCIUSZKO HOUSE: FLEETING VISITS AND LASTING FAME

Both the Graff House and the Kosciuszko House have as their sole claim to memorialization within Independence National Historical Park a brief stay by a distinguished public figure. The Graff House, which has been partially reconstructed on its original site at the corner of Seventh and Market streets, was Thomas Jefferson's temporary resting place while he wrote the Declaration of Independence in the spring of 1776. The Kosciuszko House, so called in honor of the Polish patriot and American Revolutionary War hero who lived there for a scant six months in 1797–98, was actually owned by Mrs. Grace Allison, who rented it to a widow named Ann Relf, who ran the little dwelling at 301 Pine Street as a rooming house for students and apprentices of modest means. Interestingly, the two famous men whose brief visits were to bestow lasting fame on each of these houses were close friends. Jefferson, in fact, was to play a central role in Kosciuszko's final, clandestine exit from Mrs. Relf's rooming house.

It is unlikely that either the Graff House or the Kosciuszko House would have been included in the park had it not been for private donations to the National Park Service, and the Kosciuszko House almost certainly would not have been included—the donation notwithstanding—had it not been for the force of Polish patriotism in Philadelphia in the 1970s. The Park Service resisted the offer of the Kosciuszko House by Edward J. Piszek, a prominent Philadelphia industrialist and second-generation Pole who purchased the property in 1970, as long as it politically could; in 1972, in the face of mounting pressure by various prominent Polish scholars, military men, and educators,

it capitulated. Fortunately, the house, shown in Figure 3.54, had only to be restored, since most of it was intact, and, happily and surprisingly, it turned out to be an excellent stimulus for historical research. The Graff House, on the other hand, required reconstruction; a double structure in the style of Philadelphia twin houses, it had been razed in the 1880s. In 1975 the National Park Service, using privately raised funds, built a half-replica of the Graff house on the east side of the original site, the rationale being that Jefferson's rooms had been in that half of the house. Where the other half had stood, a cast-concrete addition was built, for reasons best known to the National Park Service. Figure 3.55 shows the reconstruction and addition as they appeared in 1976.

Figure 3.54.

The Kosciuszko House at Pine and Third streets. (Photo by J. L. Cotter)

Figure 3.55.

Reconstruction of the Graff House and addition to the site at Market and Seventh streets, 1976. (Photo by J. L. Cotter)

The Graff House

Jacob Graff, Jr., bricklayer, American-born son of a German immigrant, and father of Frederick Graff who in the early 1800s would design the Fairmount Waterworks, had barely put the finishing touches on his red-brick, three-story double house on the southwest corner of Seventh and Market streets when, in the third week of May 1776, he rented out the two second-floor rooms on the east side of the house to a tall, thirty-three-year-old, redheaded Virginian. Thus Graff—unwittingly, no doubt—assured himself a place in the annals of history . . . and got 35 shillings a week out of the bargain to boot (Yoelson 1975).

When Thomas Jefferson first visited Philadelphia in 1775 as one of Virginia's delegates to the First Continental Congress, he lodged for three months at the house of Benjamin

Randolph, a cabinetmaker who resided on the north side of Chestnut Street between Third and Fourth, not far from Benjamin Franklin's house. When he arrived in Philadelphia for the second time on May 14, 1776, as a delegate to the Second Continental Congress, Jefferson again obtained lodgings in Randolph's house, but a week later moved to Jacob Graff's new house. Although on the "skirts of town," Graff's house was just a short walk from the State House, where the Second Continental Congress convened each day from about nine in the morning until two in the afternoon.

The Graff House, a typical Philadelphia residence of the time—16 feet 8 inches across each of its twin fronts and 50 feet deep along Seventh Street, with two rooms per floor in each half of the house—became destined for fame on June 11, 1776, when the Second Continental Congress appointed Jefferson to a five-member committee charged with drafting a Declaration of Independence. The committee, as committes are wont to do, in turn charged one of its junior members with doing the actual work of preparing the draft.* Seated in the north-facing, second-floor parlor of the Graff House with a writing desk of his own devising on his lap, Jefferson labored over the document. In between his labors, he read, soaked his feet in a pan of cold water each morning to ward off colds, carefully checked the temperature and barometer, shopped, and visited with friends at the City Tavern, where he often had meals charged to his account. After some private editing of the document by Benjamin Franklin

* The only member of the committee younger than Jefferson was Robert R. Livingston, who was then thirty. The other members of the committee were Benjamin Franklin, John Adams, and Roger Sherman.

and John Adams, and considerable public haggling in the Congress itself, the Second Continental Congress adopted Jefferson's Declaration of Independence on July 4, 1776 (Yoelson 1967, 1975).

Having thus been brushed by history, the Graff House entered the nineteenth century under somewhat more prosaic circumstances. In 1802 two prosperous merchants, Hyman and Simon Gratz, acquired the property and ran it as a business for thirty years. Hyman Gratz did the reconstructionists of the twentieth century a considerable service by making a sketch of Jefferson's two second-floor rooms as they appeared on July 6, 1855 (Yoelson 1967); in 1856 the exterior of the house appeared as shown in Figure 3.56. The house continued in commercial use until the 1880s, when it was razed to make way for the Penn National Bank, an imposing stone structure built in 1884 and demolished in the mid-twentieth century. For a number of years after the bank was torn down, a curb-side historical marker identified the site of the Graff House, while a parking lot took up the rear of the site and a hamburger stand occupied the corner (Figure 3.57).

The last owner of the Graff House was a newspaper man by the name of Thomas Donaldson. Like William J. Clark, Jr., who salvaged artifacts from the Slate Roof House, Donaldson took pains to save fixtures and pieces of trim from the Graff House. His hope was that the city of Philadelphia would build a replica of the house on another site. After storing the material for some years, Donaldson finally despaired of ever seeing a reconstruction of the house where his artifacts could be used, and he gave the collection away piecemeal. One of the items in Donaldson's collection was a stone

Figure 3.56.

The Graff House in 1856. Here flat stepping stones for pedestrians intersect the cobbled street. (From a color print made by Warren McCullough; courtesy of Independence National Historical Park)

Figure 3.57.

Site of the Graff House as it appeared before the house was reconstructed in 1975. (Photo by J. L. Cotter)

lintel, which he presented to Francis Newton Thorpe, a University of Pennsylvania law professor. Donaldson would no doubt have been pleased to know that many years later, through a serendipitous series of events, his lintel did indeed find its way into a reconstruction of the Graff House. In the 1960s Thorpe's granddaughter, while touring Independence National Historical Park with her family, casually mentioned to the tour guide, who happened to be Carl Gatter, then one of the park's summer employees, that a lintel from the house where Jefferson wrote the Declaration of Independence was stored at her home in upstate New York. Gatter introduced the family to James Sullivan, a park historian, who remembered that the park had an authenticated Graff House lintel in its collection—one that Donaldson had given the city of Philadelphia in 1911. When the two lintels were compared, the New York lintel proved authentic. Subsequently, when the Graff House was reconstructed in 1975, Professor Thorpe's descendants presented the lintel to the park, and today the two original lintels frame the parlor windows on the second floor of the reconstructed house (Carl Gatter, personal correspondence to J. L. Cotter 1985).

Gatter's contributions to the reconstruction of the Graff House did not end there, for he also assisted in the archaeological investigation that took place in 1975, when the site was cleared in preparation for the reconstruction. Because the cellar of the Penn National Bank had intruded upon the entire site and because no funds were available for the excavation, archaeological efforts were limited to looking for structural evidence of the old house and for pits that might have existed below the cellar floor.

On the Market Street side of the site, an original bulkhead, which had probably once led to a storage cellar, had managed to survive the construction of the bank building. In this wood-framed entryway, Gatter found early nineteenth-century ceramic sherds, bones, oyster shells, paving bricks, and a fragment of interior plaster (Independence Park Collection GR2952). Here Gatter also uncovered a piece of Pennsylvania blue marble from a fireplace facing. Since an eighteenth-century insurance survey of the Graff House indicated that the fireplaces in the front parlors on the first and second floors were faced with marble, it seemed likely that this fragment came from one of those rooms. Gatter had previously rescued three sections of similar blue marble fireplace facing from a demolished eighteenth-century house on Front Street, and when the Park Service learned that the quarries from which the marble was obtained no longer existed, it readily accepted Gatter's finds for installation at the Graff House.

At the Graff House site, Gatter also found a section of blue marble capping identical to that shown supporting an outside stair railing in the 1856 photograph that appears in Figure 3.56. In addition, he found a piece of a mantle and two molded bricks layered with paint. The bricks corresponded to authenticated Graff House bricks in the Carpenters' Hall collection of artifacts related to early Philadelphia construction.

A somewhat enigmatic artifact appeared in a deep pit some 30 feet south of the Market Street sidewalk on the west side of the site. At the bottom of the pit, far beneath the original cellar floor of the double house, dark, humic soil yielded a three-pound iron cannonball, as well as fragments of a

Figure 3.58.

Artifacts found at the bottom of the pit on the west side of the Graff House site. (Photo by J. L. Cotter)

lead-glazed, slip-decorated redware platter (Figure 3.58). The pit may have been dug as a well or privy pit before the Graff House was fully constructed (John Cotter, notes in Graff House Research File, Independence National Historical Park). The most likely explanation of how the cannonball got there is that a heavy shot fallen from one of the many munitions wagons that traveled through Philadelphia before the Revolution, as well as during and after it, could easily have found its way as a weighty nuisance to the bottom of a convenient pit.

The Kosciuszko House

Gen. Thaddeus Kosciuszko (1746–1817), a Pole who fought valiantly and effectively for liberty in the American Revolutionary War, fought just as bravely but futilely for the same cause a few years later during the Polish insurrection against Russia. He arrived in the United States for a second time in the summer of 1797. Twenty-one years earlier, at the age of thirty, he had offered his military services to Congress, been accepted, and served in the Continental Army continuously until the war ended seven years later. Trained in Poland and France as a military engineer, Kosciuszko was a specialist in fortification. He distinguished himself during the Revolutionary War by fortifying West Point to keep the British from the upper Hudson Valley and by planning the fortification of Bemis Heights at Saratoga. The fortification of Bemis Heights resulted in the victory of General Gates' army over the forces of General Burgoyne in the battle that turned the American fortunes. Later, Kosciuszko reconnoitered the defense of the rivers of North and South Carolina to thwart the British in the south (Wilson 1976:5–12).

The Polish insurrection against Russia ended with the Battle of Maciejawice in 1794. Painfully wounded, Kosciuszko was imprisoned for two years before being released by the new czar, Paul I. In return for promising Paul that he would leave Poland forever and oppose the czar no more, Kosciuszko was awarded 12,000 rubles and some superb furs. Paul also later commissioned a team of ten distinguished British physicians, including the personal physician of the King of England, to diagnose and recommend treatment for his respected enemy. On

Kosciuszko's arrival in Philadelphia, Dr. Benjamin Rush, the city's most celebrated man of medicine, received a five-page letter from the team detailing the condition of the patient and prescribing treatment for his incapacitating hip wound, which had sundered his sciatic nerve, and for the sabre cut in the back of his head (Budka 1965:xxiii–xxiv).

When Kosciuszko, his young aide Julian Ursyn Niemcewicz, and his servant Stanislaus Dombrowski arrived in Philadelphia on the *Adriana* on August 18, 1797, they were warmly greeted by distinguished citizens, as they had been in Sweden and England during their previous six months of travel. An enthusiastic crowd drew their carriage from the ship to Mrs. Sarah Lawson's boarding house at 7 South Fourth Street. Reflecting the social heterogeneity of eighteenth- and early nineteenth-century Philadelphia, Mrs. Lawson's, a fashionable and respectable establishment, was located in an area frequented by certain young women of style but few morals—in short, a "red-light" district. The fifty-one-year-old Kosciuszko, though a lifelong bachelor, was not averse to the company of the opposite sex; however, before the month of August was out, he and his party had taken their final leave of Mrs. Lawson, who charged them a handsome $50 for their brief stay. On the advice of Dr. Rush, the three men left Philadelphia, where a yellow fever epidemic was spreading, for the healthier clime of New Brunswick, New Jersey. There they stayed at the farm of General Anthony White until cold weather ended the menace (Roberts and Roberts 1947:313).

As the trio prepared to return to Philadelphia, Kosciuszko, having had a taste of life at Mrs. Lawson's, instructed Niemcewicz to find them

quarters "as remote, and as cheap" as possible (Wilson 1976:3). Through the services of Dr. Rush, the party wound up at the rooming house of Mrs. Ann Relf. Situated at the corner of Pine and Third streets across from St. Peter's Church, the house was the last in a block of middle-class rowhouses that master builder Joseph Few had erected in 1776 (Wilson 1976:23). There, on the second floor, the general occupied a small rear room with fireplace and access to a small parlor. Niemcewicz and the servant probably had rooms in the garret, for, as Niemcewicz (Budka 1965:32) described the accommodation in his diary, "no fire was made there."

At Mrs. Relf's, Kosciuszko set about realizing the three objectives that had brought him to America again: improving his health, gaining American support for the Polish struggle for freedom, and collecting back pay due him for his services in the Continental Army. He intended to use the funds to pursue his patriotic aims, as he was loath to use the czar's money for the purpose. On January 23, 1797, Congress passed a bill giving the Polish patriot $18,912.03. It had already conferred on him American citizenship, a large annual pension, an estate in Franklin County, Ohio, and the rank of brigadier general. Further evidence of Kosciuszko's success in America was that the Society of Cincinnati, which had honored George Washington with membership in its ranks, similarly honored Kosciuszko (Bogucki and Cauffiel 1975:1–5).

Having learned that General Dembrowski was forming Polish legions in northern Italy in the hope of liberating Poland, Kosciuszko, with the aid of Thomas Jefferson, abruptly and secretly departed for Europe on May 5,

Figure 3.59.

The second-floor room occupied by Kosciuszko, furnished according to historical data. (Photo by George Eisenman; courtesy of Independence National Historical Park)

1798. Before leaving, Kosciuszko informed the servant Dombrowski of his plan but swore him to secrecy and, giving him $300, instructed him to give $200 of it to Niemcewicz after his departure. Dombrowski, however, prematurely revealed the plan, and Niemcewicz thus was able to witness his mentor being helped into a carriage, departing from him without so much as a farewell. Embittered, Niemcewicz gave the abandoned servant the entire $300 and prepared to set off on a journey that would make it appear, as Kosciuszko had requested, that Niemcewicz was still conducting the general's affairs. Thus on May 7 Neimcewicz noted in his diary, "I had the effects of Kosciuszko carried to Mr. Jefferson. The books to Sutcliffe, my things to Dr. Bache." *

Two years after Kosciuszko departed for Europe, where he died in 1817 without having achieved his goal of liberating Poland, Mrs. Relf left the Allison house that was to be memorialized because of his six-month stay. After 1811, the house

passed through a series of short-term owners, among them merchants, millers, and a surgeon. From 1841 until 1942, however, the house was continuously occupied by the family of John Tack. In 1967, after another series of short-term owners, Edward Pinkowski, a noted Polish-American historian, acquired it, and he in turn sold it to Edward Piszek, who delivered it to the National Park Service in 1972 (Wilson 1976:33). Since then the exterior of the house and the room that Kosciuszko occupied have been meticulously restored. The room, shown in Figure 3.59, contains an authentic duplication of every artifact known to have been in Kosciuszko's quarters (Giannini 1988). The rest of the house and its neighbor next door at 340 South Third Street have not been restored; they accommodate the Park Service's "interpretive facilities" and in no way reflect the original decor of either dwelling.

Historical Investigation

It took an impressive amount of historical research and sleuthing to achieve the accuracy of restoration evident at the Kosciuszko House. One very valuable source of information, which made it possible to furnish the back room at 301 Pine Street almost exactly as its distinguished occupant left it, was an inventory of Kosciuszko's "Sundry Kitchen furniture and personal items," which Thomas Jefferson commissioned John Barnes to make in May 1798.* Barnes' listing of the possessions the general had about him in his temporary quarters gives us a vivid glimpse of his stay there. They included two "very large leather port-

* Niemcewicz's diary, which he continued to keep as he traveled throughout America, provides a remarkable view of the new nation as seen through foreign, and very keen, eyes. Unpublished in his lifetime, it was discovered in the Polish Archives in 1956 by Metchie J. E. Budka, who edited the volume. It reveals Niemcewicz as a cultivated, witty, perceptive observer and records his American experiences—his visit with Washington at Mount Vernon in May 1798, his election to the American Philosophical Society on the motion of Thomas Jefferson, and his marriage in 1800 to Susan Livingston Kean, niece of William Livingston, first governor of the state of New Jersey. In all, Niemcewicz spent a decade in the new nation; in 1807 he returned to his native land.

* The inventory is in the archives of the Massachusetts Historical Society, as are letters between Jefferson and Kosciuszko regarding money, belongings, and the latter's American estate. Similar letters are in the Archive and Museum of the Polish Roman Catholic Union (No. 10A) and in the Jefferson papers at the Library of Congress.

mantua [portmanteaus]" for his personal papers; one "very small Chafing dish/to light pipes by"; a carpet valued at $41; four fine candlesticks; a pair of wrought iron snuffers and their stand; a small backgammon table and counters, with box and dice; a set of chess figures; a small iron axe; an elaborate tomahawk mounted with silver;* and a surprisingly large assortment of equipment for preparing and serving meals. Included in the latter were two large square damask tablecloths, sixteen napkins, four bottle stands, two "large oval waiter(s)," a large bread basket, three silver plates engraved with "The Friends of Liberty in Bristol to The Gallant Kosciuszko, 1797," other silver items "in an Elegant, Mahogany Case," and numerous plates, bowls, pots, pans, griddles, kettles, and cutlery made of iron, tin, and pewter. The considerable cooking equipment, which no doubt had been part of the general's field gear, leaves little doubt that the servant Dombrowski had his work cut out for him in providing for the general and his guests.

The only clothes noted in the inventory were "1 pr. Nanken breeches" and, valued at $6, "a waist & short plain coat," indicating that Kosciuszko must have taken most of what he wore with him on his departure. He had, however, already given Jefferson a valuable sable fur, a magnificent fur-trimmed greatcoat, and a bearskin, all presumably gifts of Czar Paul I.

* The tomahawk was the gift of Chief Little Turtle, who, while visiting Philadelphia to negotiate Miami tribal boundaries with the federal government, had been one of Kosciuszko's many callers. In return, Kosciuszko gave the chief a bourka—a loose-fitting, sleeveless cloak of felt or wool introduced to Poland by the Tartars—and a pair of spectacles the chief had noticed in the room and greatly admired. According to Niemcewicz (Budka 1965:45), the Miami chief was indefatigable in examining objects thus magnified, exclaiming all the while, "You have given me new eyes."

Barnes' account of the general's possessions also lists "1 wooden crutch covered in red-Morocco leather & brass nails," "1 wooden rest or stay—for the foot," and "1 broad hoop/a foot in diameter covered with green baize," the last possibly for raising the general's knee to a bent position to ease the pain from his damaged sciatic nerve. A "Diagnosis of Kosciuszko's Physical Condition," signed on June 3, 1797, by the ten British physicians who had examined him, rounds out the picture of the general's physical sufferings.* This document includes an impressively detailed and perceptive account of the famous patient's wounds, as well as a treatment plan and prognosis. The physicians regarded the head wound as non-threatening and with a favorable prospect of healing. For the hip wound, they foresaw a degree of regeneration of the sciatic nerve, albeit nerve damage was known to be very slow to mend. They recommended the promotion of sense and motion in the leg by warm bathing "not to exceed 92 degrees of Farenheit's Thermometer," rubbing three times a day for twenty to thirty minutes, and manipulation of hip, knee, and toe joints "to give them their natural motion and to preserve the pliability of the Limb." The patient should also "try to move his Toes, his foot, his Leg and Thigh as much as possible, be it ever so little and should continue some time to repeat his efforts in this way." The doctors "further recommended the use of Electricity to promote the restoration of the action of the Muscles," which was to be accomplished "by gentle sparks, through the Muscles of the Legs and Thigh, so as moderately

* Robert Giannini, associate museum curator at Independence National Historical Park, discovered this document in the papers of Dr. Benjamin Rush at the Library Company of Philadelphia (7246 F.39).

to excite their contractions."* This therapy was not to be pursued to painfulness.

Archaeological Investigation

Eighteenth-century insurance surveys describe the property at 301 Pine Street as 31 feet wide and 15 feet deep, and the property next door at 340 South Third Street as the same width but 26 feet deep. A sketch accompanying the surveys shows two outhouses along the back property line of 340 South Third Street. These privies served both properties, with an alleyway at the rear of 301 Pine Street providing access to them. The privies were placed over a single pit, identified in Figure 3.60 as feature B. In 1975 Peter I. Bogucki and Richard E. Cauffiel, then anthropology students at the University of Pennsylvania, investigated this privy pit, as well as another one, identified as feature A.

Feature A was curiously located under the entryway to the cellar at the front of 340 South Third Street, indicating that the privy may have been a convenient, indoor, cellar facility. The pit itself was brick-lined and had an external diameter of 3.1 feet. The brick casing was laid up in a spiral, topped by level courses. This unusual construction had already been noted in three eighteenth-century privy pits excavated at Franklin Court. The pit had been closed with clay and rubble, and at 7.15 feet below the casing top, its fill became black.

The artifacts in the privy spoil of feature A were typical of the mid-nineteenth century in type and date.

* The potential use of electricity for physical therapy had not escaped the notice of Benjamin Franklin, many years earlier.

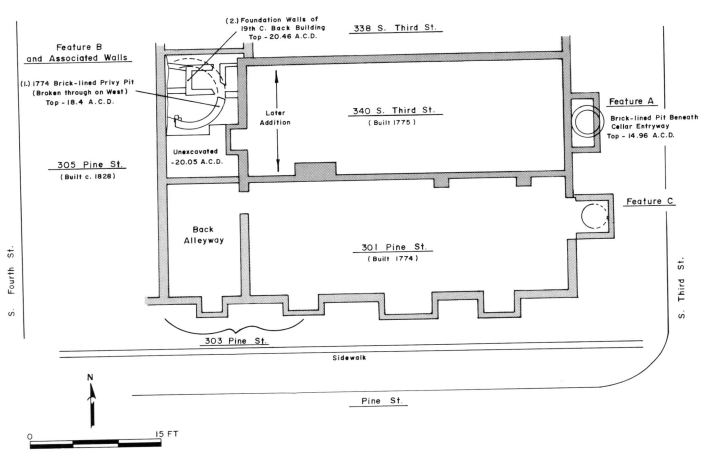

Figure 3.60.

Plan of the Kosciuszko House at 301 Pine Street and of the house next door at 340 South Third Street. (From Bogucki and Cauffiel 1975)

The ceramics were mostly ironstone, with some representation of redware, creamware, porcelain, and stoneware. It was possible to reconstruct several whole vessels from the ceramic sherds; the reconstructions included two saucers, one pitcher of Victorian design, and ceramic ale bottles of a type imported from Germany in the mid-nineteenth century. The glass items found were also characteristic of the mid-nineteenth century; they included spirit, medicine, and pressed-glass bottles dating from about 1860 to 1870. Bogucki and Cauffiel (1975) concluded that feature A was a late eighteenth-century pit that had been last cleaned sometime around 1840 to 1850, repaired with machine-made brick at about the same time, and closed about 1870.

The masonry of feature B, the single pit serving the two outhouses at the rear of the properties, began at 20.45 feet A.C.D. (meaning "above the city datum," a consistent Philadelphia surveying reference to mean high tide at the foot of Chestnut Street). The pit had a diameter of 7 feet, and its walls consisted of a double thickness of partially mortared, hand-made brick stretchers tied by headers. When it was closed, a dome of two thicknesses of brick had been built over it. At 17.63 feet A.C.D., an ash seal had been thrown in. The fill of ash, cinders, and light-colored clay extended to a depth of 14.5 feet

A.C.D., where the excavation ended. Above the ash seal, at 18.4 feet A.C.D., the bricks on the west side of the pit had been cut to lay a drain pipe, one of two drains from different periods found within the pit (Figure 3.61). Above the drain pipe, at 18.05 feet A.C.D., a trap and soil pipe had been installed (Bogucki and Cauffiel 1975: 1–5). Feature B was thus an example of how privies were converted by installing pipes to link the pits in order to make toilet facilities available inside the house.

Artifacts recovered from the top fill of feature B reflected the use of the houses at 301 Pine and 340 South Third streets as bakeries during the second quarter of the twentieth century. The lower fill yielded ceramics dating from 1869 to 1900. Obviously,

the pit had long since been cleaned of its original, eighteenth-century deposits. In fact, the earliest artifact found on the site—a dark-green spirit bottle dating from 1760 to 1780—did not come from either of the privy pits Bogucki and Cauffiel investigated, but from a construction trench revealed when the walls of 301 Pine Street were being underpinned in the course of restoration. A similar bottle, this one dating from 1775 to 1800, was found beneath the brick floor of the cellar where the original kitchen had been. Although it may never have been in the service of the general and his companions, the bottle is representative of the period during which Kosciuszko lived at 301 Pine Street, and it was therefore spruced up and placed in the general's restored room.

Figure 3.61.

Nineteenth-century privy pit at rear of the Kosciuszko House. (Courtesy of Independence National Historical Park)

THE McILVAINE HOUSE PRIVY AND AREA F: HISTORICAL ARCHAEOLOGY IN PRACTICE

The McIlvaine House at 315 Walnut Street and Area F, the National Park Service's designation for the block of land bounded by Front and Second streets and Ionic and Sansom streets, are, like all the other sites described in this chapter, part of Independence National Historical Park. Unlike the other sites, however, neither the McIlvaine House nor Area F is associated with a particularly famous figure or historic event, nor are they distinguished by any particularly noteworthy architectural feature. Although both sites were investigated archaeologically, neither yielded any find of earthshaking, immediate importance. What these investigations

did yield was bits and pieces of evidence pertaining to the daily lives of ordinary people—bits and pieces that, when put together, produce a sum of knowledge that is greater than its parts. In this and other respects, the investigations of the McIlvaine House privy and Area F typify the actual practice of historical archaeology—its frustrations, disappointments, and rewards.

The McIlvaine House Privy

The McIlvaine House, built just up the street from Bishop White's house from 1791 to 1793 (Figure 3.62),

was originally owned by Dr. William McIlvaine and later by William B. Fling. Fling owned the property from 1826 to 1878 and lived there until 1855. A sometime cabinetmaker and glazier, he ultimately turned to real estate development, a career change that may indicate some upward social strivings on his part (Basalik 1980:6). If that was indeed Fling's motivation for making the jump from artisan to business entrepreneur, he would not have been the only Philadelphia cabinetmaker to act out such aspirations. In less than two hundred years, the Bouvier family advanced from producing Philadelphia furniture of fine quality to producing the wife of

Figure 3.62.

The 300 block of Walnut Street, a row of restored and reconstructed eighteenth- and early nineteenth-century buildings. Bishop White's house is at the far right. The McIlvaine House is the third from the left. (Photo by J. L. Cotter)

Figure 3.63.

Excavation of the McIlvaine House privy. (Photo by J. L. Cotter)

President John F. Kennedy; further evidence of the Bouviers' social success is the small Philadelphia street named after them.

The McIlvaine House, which Fling occupied for over a quarter of a century, today serves as part of the headquarters of Independence National Historical Park. The building came into the archaeological limelight in 1961, when site preparation revealed a privy pit at the rear of the house. In May 1962, working under contract to the National Park Service, Prof. Jacob Gruber of Temple University and some of his anthropology students began excavating the pit (Figure 3.63). Cylindrical and brick-lined, it proved to be 14 feet 2 inches deep. A sewer pipe had been run through it at the 8-foot level sometime after 1850, and the fill above that consisted of relatively clean sand. Below that, however, in the bottom 4 feet of the pit beneath a seal of nonartifact-bearing fill, Gruber and his students discovered a wealth of material. It was not until 1980 that a report analyzing these artifacts was issued. The report was produced as a master's thesis by Kenneth J. Basalik, who sought to analyze the data using current methodologies and theory. Basalik's tabular analyses are shown in Appendix 3.C, and the account that follows is based on his 1980 thesis.

Basalik concluded that most of the artifacts from the privy had been deposited there while William Fling occupied the house between 1826 and 1855. In reaching this conclusion, Basalik analyzed the mean date of manufacture of 2,481 of the 2,779 ceramic sherds recovered from the pit. The mean date proved to be 1837.8, to which one would add approximately twenty years to allow for usage of the ceramic item before it was disposed of in the privy. This date coincided fairly well with the 1840–1850 date of window-glass fragments found in the pit. In determining the age of the window glass, Basalik used a scheme developed by Roenke (1978:116–18) based on the fact that window glass of later-nineteenth-century manufacture tends to be thicker than that produced earlier in the century.

Basalik categorized all 2,779 ceramic sherds recovered from the pit according to type of ceramic and type of vessel. Stoneware was the least common ceramic type; Basalik identified only 6 stoneware sherds, all from the same undecorated brown bottle. Undecorated whiteware was the most common ceramic, accounting for 1,037 of the sherds. It was used in both tableware and kitchenware. Most of the kitchenware, however, was made of unglazed redware (252 sherds), while blue, transfer-printed pearlware (687 sherds) predominated in the tableware category. That green-edged pearlware and green-edged whiteware accounted for 384 sherds, while blue-edged pearlware accounted for only 35, indicates a non-conforming preference in taste at the Fling establishment. At most other early nineteenth-century sites, archaeologists have recovered far more sherds of blue-edged ware than of green-edged. Basalik also identified 155 porcelain fragments from 8 teacups and 10 saucers; with the exception of one plain teacup, all the porcelain was in the willow pattern.

Glass objects were, after ceramics, the next most plentiful artifact. They were as revealing in what they did not represent as in what they did represent. The Fling household was, if not teetotal, at least moderate in its consumption of alcoholic drinks, unless medicinal intake contributed significantly, as it may have. Basalik

identified 7 ale bottles, 3 wine bottles, 1 spirit decanter, and 23 medicine/alcohol bottles. Also included in the inventory were 54 tumblers and 9 wine glasses.

Using the model developed by South (1977:95–96), Basalik classified the artifacts into the following "functional groups": clothing (mostly fragments of shoes and slippers); personal items (4 toothbrushes, 5 combs, 1 key, and 1 Elgin National watch); tobacco pipes (2 white clay bowls and 1 stem); kitchen items (3 lead seals and 2 spoons); and arms (1 cartridge, 3 lead shot, 1 iron shot). Basalik also had two catchall groups: miscellaneous and "activity." Included in the latter were 4 clasp knives, 1 tool handle, 5 pencils, 3 scrub-brush fragments, 1 ceramic marble, and 1 lead weight. The inventory of metal objects included 23 cut nails, 2 spikes, 1 door hinge, 1 knocker, 7 bucket fragments, and many other pieces of hardware.

Of the 293 animal bones Gruber and his assistants took out of the pit, Basalik was able to identify all but 30. Cattle, sheep, swine, and chicken bones were, in that order, the four most common, followed by turkey, rabbit, and deer. Basalik's analysis of the numerous seeds removed from the pit gives us a further glimpse of the Fling household's diet. Among the many kinds of fruits identified were sour cherry (154), grape (53), blackberry (37), and peach (33). Strangely enough, only one apple seed appeared. Though less abundant than the fruit seeds, peanuts, chestnuts, walnuts, and hickory nuts were also represented.

After devoting many pages to his analyses of the artifacts and food traces retrieved from 4 feet of fill at the bottom of the McIlvaine House privy pit, Basalik (1980:70–71) came to this regretful conclusion:

What the relationship of the people represented in the McIlvaine assemblage [was] to other groups and the world at large can only be guessed. Future studies combining the data throughout the city may answer this and other such questions for Philadelphia as well as other areas. McIlvaine will not.

Had the contents of all the other privy pits at historic sites in Philadelphia been as exhaustively analyzed as the McIlvaine deposit, Basalik—and many another archaeological researcher—might have been spared disappointment. Such analyses would produce a truly unique base of material evidence from an American city in the eighteenth and nineteenth centuries, one that would allow for comparisons among individual collections, and possibly also for fresh insights into urban lifeways of the past. Unfortunately, few such comparisons are possible, since most collections are, to date, only partially or incompletely analyzed.

Taken alone, the contents of the McIlvaine privy document the familiar practice of using the privy pit as a place to dispose of much of the household litter of broken glass and ceramic objects, worn-out pieces of metal and leather, and bone and vegetal refuse. The presence of 2,779 ceramic sherds and some 1,500 glass sherds in 4 feet of privy fill might also suggest that at least some of those items were deliberately put there to facilitate drainage, in which case they may have come from somewhere other than the Fling household. With hundreds of pieces of leather, metal, bone, and seed included in the deposit, however, it seems safe to assume that a fair number of artifacts originated on the site and are representative of life as it was lived there.

Presuming the evidence from the McIlvaine privy is site-specific, it at-

Figure 3.64.

The McCrae Houses as they appeared in the summer of 1983. (James L. Dillon & Co., Photographers; courtesy of Ellen Miller)

tests to the Fling household's modest taste in tableware, kitchenware, and glassware, and to its moderate but constant use of common objects, easily and cheaply procured during the first half of the nineteenth century. The liberal variety of seeds, nuts, and animal bones indicates a varied, healthy diet, adequately supplied with vitamins and minerals. The fragments of footwear attest to the thrift of the household; the shoes of adults and children alike were well used and re-used before the unusable remainders

were finally discarded in the privy. Little of value was lost there—no coins, and only one watch. The children seem to have been unusually careful; only one lost marble appeared.

Abstemiousness seems to have been another of the household's distinctive features. Out of the remarkable variety of domestic objects concentrated in the fill of the McIlvaine privy, only three items had to do with tobacco use. Of the ninety-nine glass vessels indentified, only twenty were directly related to alcoholic beverages. Apparently, tobacco and alcohol were far less popular in Mr. Fling's household than in others of the period.

Area F

The block of land bordered by Front and Second streets on the east and west and by Ionic and Sansom streets on the north and south, which the National Park Service calls Area F (see Figure 1), was developed very early in the life of the colony. It started out as part of the block that Thomas Holme, William Penn's surveyor general, had laid out. The block was bounded north and south by Chestnut Street and Walnut, and east and west by Front and Second. Holme laid out the first lot in this block on November 29, 1682, just a month and a day after Penn arrived in Pennsylvania for his first visit (Cosans 1977:13). The lot belonged to a Christopher Taylor, and, like the other Front Street lots that followed, it was large and deep. Taylor's lot, for example, measured 102 feet north-south along Front Street and 396 feet east-west. By the middle of the eighteenth century, this pattern of land use had changed. To accommodate more houses, the block had been divided by three east-

west alleys, all of which had houses fronting on them (Cosans 1977:43). The northernmost alley was Ionic Street; the southernmost was Sansom Street, known then as Norris's Alley. Between them was Gatzmer Street, known until 1860 as Gray's Alley.

Intensive land use continued to characterize the neighborhood until the mid-nineteenth century, when its numerous small buildings were gradually cleared to make way for large commercial structures. A century or so later, the large commercial structures were in turn demolished, many of them victims of the twentieth century's need for parking space. The site of William Penn's Slate Roof House just south of Area F narrowly missed being turned into a permanent parking lot when the Commercial Exchange Building, which had occupied the site since 1870, was torn down in 1976 (Webster 1976:67–68). The latest casualties in this saga were a pair of unusually elegant, late eighteenth-century residences known as the McCrae Houses. Built in 1798 at 108–110 Sansom Street, the twin houses were unspoiled examples of late-Georgian, middle-class dwellings (Figure 3.64). Occupying the basement of one of the houses was a large, early, commercial bake oven, used in producing hardtack for ships' stores (Figure 3.65).* The McCrae Houses were razed in 1984 when the restaurant that then owned them decided to add ten spaces to its parking lot.

The need for more parking space was also the National Park Service's motive in acquiring Area F. In anticipation of the construction of a multistory parking garage between Gatzmer

---

* The bake oven and the cellar floor plan of the McCrae Houses were drawn for the Historic American Buildings Survey before the houses were razed.

and Sansom streets, the Park Service authorized a number of archaeological excavations. In 1976 Temple University carried out some preliminary work, which included a thorough historical survey by Betty Cosans (1977), and in 1977 the same group located and excavated a number of eighteenth- and nineteenth-century privy pits (Crozier 1977a, 1977b). A detailed report on that work is still in progress, but an unpublished master's thesis (Taylor 1981) describes one aspect of it: the analysis of 138 botanical samples recovered from privy pits by flotation. In April and November 1979, the Museum Institute for Conservation Archaeology (MICA) of the University Museum of the University of Pennsylvania carried out further excavations (Parrington 1979a, 1980a, 1980c; Parrington and Schenck 1979).

A Botanical Analysis

The preserved state of botanical remains recovered from prehistoric archeological sites generally results from their having been carbonized before being deposited at the site. At Area F, however, the seeds recovered were apparently preserved because they were in an alkaline, partially waterlogged environment, which tended to mineralize them and thus prevent decomposition. The problem of contamination by modern vegetation, which often plagues the specialist engaged in analyzing seed samples, was minimized at Area F, since the pits were excavated under cover of a building.

Figure 3.65.

Top, cellar floor plan, McCrae Houses; *bottom,* bake oven elevation. (From James S. Collins for the Historic American Buildings Survey)

Of the 138 seed samples Taylor (1981) tested, 76 contained preserved botanical material. Some seeds appeared to be directly related to human diet: three samples were associated with preserved fecal matter, and the seeds from these samples represented 67 percent of the total edible species found at the site.

An interesting observation in Taylor's thesis was that wetland species seemed to be associated with the eighteenth-century samples retrieved from the privy pits but not with any of the nineteenth-century material. Taylor speculated that the presence of wetland species was due to the proximity of Dock Creek, which

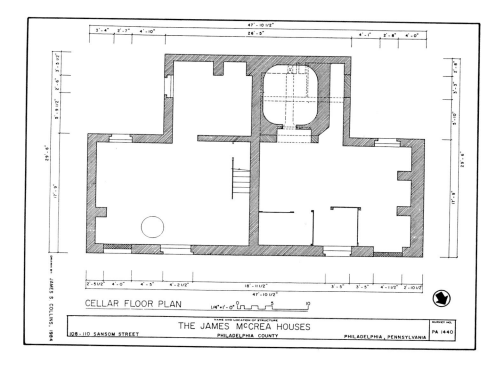

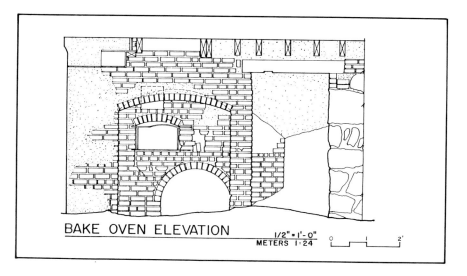

ran just south of Area F until it was paved over during the last half of the eighteenth century. The paving of the creek would have reduced the number of wetland species and would account for their absence in the nineteenth-century contents of the privy pits.

Taylor also suggested that seed analysis can document periods of economic stress. A high percentage of seeds from wild species might indicate that domestic plants were temporarily unavailable and that people had been forced to collect food from other sources. Another of Taylor's hypotheses was that in late eighteenth-century archaeological contexts, seeds from imported plants would be missing because of trade embargoes and the general dislocation of trade caused by the Revolution.

Pit 100

When MICA began its excavations at Area F in April 1979, archaeological conditions were less than ideal. Construction of the parking garage was going on at the same time, and the construction dictated the methods of excavation. The archaeological team recorded all pertinent features that appeared in trenches mechanically dug for the parking garage's foundations (Parrington 1980a, 1980c); they excavated only those the parking garage would disrupt. One of the trenches ran north of Sansom Street; another ran along Gatzmer. Among the features recorded here were masonry remnants of the side and rear walls of eighteenth- and nineteenth-century structures.

Of the four pits the team recorded, two were left unexcavated. One of the

unexcavated pits was empty; the other was located where it would be unaffected by the piles being driven for the garage and so was left intact for future investigation. One of the two excavated pits was shallow and unlined and contained a small assortment of late eighteenth-century pottery. The other, however, proved to be a much more substantial affair. Situated on Gatzmer Street, it was identified as pit 100.

Brick-lined, 7 feet wide, and 9 feet 6 inches deep, pit 100 contained nine separate layers of fill, with varying quantities of artifacts in each layer. The artifacts included a diverse assortment of ceramics and glass. Of the 2,200 ceramic sherds recovered, 69 percent were imported; 60 percent of these were English pearlware and creamware, and 6 percent were Chinese porcelain. There were also a few sherds of imported, white, salt-glazed stoneware and delft. The domestic ceramics were predominantly redware, with some representation of stoneware and earthenware. About a third of the more than 1,300 sherds of glass found in pit 100 had come from beer or wine bottles; medicine bottles accounted for only 3.5 percent of the total. Most of the rest of the glass sherds had come from table tumblers, wine glasses, and window glass.

A number of the imported ceramic sherds bore the imprint of manufacturers' stamps. The earliest of these stamps was that of J. Heath, which dates ca. 1780–1800; the latest was that of Enoch Wood and Sons of Burslem, which dates from 1818 to 1846. A nearly intact blue and white, transfer-printed, pearlware bowl that bore the mark "WR" and the pattern name "Persian Opaque China" was instrumental in determining the date pit 100 was filled. Godden (1964) attrib-

utes the mark "WR" to William Ridgway and dates it to 1830–1834. If the bowl had not been made before 1830, it could not have been deposited before 1830. Moreover, since it was almost whole and was found at a depth of more than 2 feet 6 inches, it is unlikely that it had somehow intruded on an earlier layer of fill. Thus the conclusion was that the pit was filled after 1830.

The presence of a relatively large number of sherds from press-molded tumblers in deeper layers of the pit was another useful indicator of date. The press-mold machine was patented in 1827 (Lorrain 1968:43), and although press molding was known before that date, the presence in the pit of numerous sherds made by this process suggests that the pit was filled after the machine was in general use.

At the other end of the dating spectrum, the fact that none of the fragments of the 436 beer or wine bottles recovered were from two-piece molded bottles suggests that the pit was filled before ca. 1840, when the two-piece bottle mold was invented (Lorrain 1968:43). Thus the archaeological evidence indicated that the pit was filled between 1830 and 1840. It also seems likely that the pit was filled within a short period during this decade, as pieces from the same vessels were found in all layers of the pit and were assembled by cross-mending.

In addition to ceramics and glass, pit 100 contained a variety of other objects: bone toothbrushes, clay marbles, brass and bone buttons, a glass bead, a slate pencil, faunal remains, and a considerable amount of building rubble. The faunal remains included large numbers of oyster shells and, in addition to the usual range of domestic animal bones, a number of turtle bones. The turtles may well have been eaten, but this evidence does bring to mind the nineteenth-century custom of keeping turtles in the cellar to rid the place of slugs. The building rubble, which consisted of large quantities of bricks, wall plaster, window glass, iron nails, and iron masonry braces, was found in most of the pit's nine layers, and much of it was coated with charcoal-stained soil (Parrington 1980c).

Although the condition in which pit 100 was found reflects its final use as a trash pit, it was originally used as a privy pit. When excavated, it was in extremely good condition; its brickwork was in good order, and the construction seemed stable. No doubt, like other privy pits in the area, it was cleaned periodically, a practice documented by the will of James Cox, who lived in the Thomas Bond House, which still stands at the corner of Second Street and Sansom. The will records payments from Cox's estate for emptying the privy pit on his premises in 1821 and 1824 and for making it 7 feet deeper, presumably to increase its capacity (Greene 1974:43).

The need to increase the capacity of the pit on Cox's property may be related to communal use of the privy. Documentary evidence suggests that such communal usage was common. A deed of 1750 related to an Area F property specifically grants access to a privy on an adjoining property (Cosans 1977:32). That the archaeological team from Temple University (Crozier 1977a, 1977b) uncovered only nine privies in their extensive excavations at Area F is further indication that privies were shared; nine privies would not have been enough to allow one to a family. Indeed, in some parts of the city, families lived without the use of any facilities. In the 1830s, according to Mathew Carey (1837),

thirty Philadelphia tenements, which housed 253 people, had no privy on their premises. Area F, located in the Fifth Ward, which in 1820 had the third highest tax assessment in Philadelphia (Blumin 1973:42), probably enjoyed better sanitation in the 1830s than the slums described by Carey.

The movement to the suburbs that began in the 1830s and 1840s may have helped to ease overcrowding and to improve social conditions in some areas of the city (Jackson 1975:123), but in other areas overcrowding persisted. By 1853 the situation in the Fifth Ward had worsened to the extent that slums there were described as "not fit to be the abiding places of swine" (Sutherland 1973:179).

If privies were used communally, then it seems likely that when they were to be closed, they would have been communally filled. The large volume of material found in pit 100 suggests that the pit was filled with trash from a number of households. The large number of cross-mends noted throughout the layers of the pit may indicate that before dumping the trash in the privy, the people of Area F stored it in middens, or refuse heaps, where whole or nearly whole vessels broke into sherds, which were then scattered throughout the heap. The eighteenth-century material found in the pit also suggests midden storage; these artifacts may have been scooped up from backyard trash deposits together with the contemporary material as the pit was filled during the 1830s.

In 1840 (the date suggested for the final filling of the pit) a disastrous fire destroyed 23 houses and damaged 20 others on South Front Street close to Area F (Scharf and Westcott 1884:654). The charcoal-stained soil adhering to the building rubble recov-

ered from the pit strongly suggests that the rubble came from those burned buildings. The fire may also account for a layer of charcoal-stained soil found near the Front Street end of the site.

The Sansom Street Cartway

In November 1979, when MICA carried out further work at Area F, the construction of the parking garage was well under way. Archaeological attention therefore shifted to Sansom Street, just south of the area that had been investigated in the spring. A scatter of twenty 18-by-18-inch test units dug into the bed of Sansom Street revealed the remains of a stone cartway and, beneath that, the re-

Figure 3.66.

The Sansom Street cartway. (Courtesy of the Archives, the University Museum, University of Pennsylvania)

mains of a wooden telephone conduit (Parrington 1980a, 1983). The Keystone Telephone Company had laid the "pump log conduit," as it was called, beneath each side of the cartway in 1900, the year it began competing with the Bell Telephone Company in Philadelphia (Bureau of Water 1902:37, 730). The conduit was made of sections of creosoted timber, $4\frac{1}{2}$ inches square and bored longitudinally with a 3-inch hole (Fagen 1975:225–26). Six larger test units dug along the north side of Sansom Street revealed the front walls of the eighteenth- and nineteenth-century structures that had been noted in April. They also revealed a sealed privy pit, which was left intact.

The cartway found in the bed of Sansom Street consisted of two parallel rows of massive granite slabs laid end to end (Figure 3.66). The one complete slab that was uncovered was 5 feet 8 inches long, 1 foot 4 inches wide, and 7 inches thick. Measured

from the outside edges of the slabs, the cartway was 6 feet 6 inches wide. Longitudinal grooves cut into both rows of slabs were a little less than 5 feet apart, indicating that this was the axle width of the vehicles that had used the cartway. To conform to an 1834 city ordinance that "in all streets under twenty-five feet in width, the gutters shall be placed in the center," the cartway, which the minutes of the Common Council of Philadelphia indicate was built in 1852 at a total cost of $459.91, would have had a gutter running down its center.

Cartways were widely used in the nineteenth century, as their smooth surfaces were greatly superior to the surfaces of conventional roads, which were usually paved with cobblestones or with the small granite blocks known as Belgian block. A nineteenth-century road expert (Gillespie 1873: 248) calculated that it would take 294 pounds of tractive force to draw one ton over a conventional road sur-

face, whereas on a cartway it would require only 132 pounds. Cartways also lasted longer than conventional roadways. Several examples of Belgian block roads still exist in the area around Sansom Street, and their rutted appearance contrasts sharply with the virtually unworn condition of the granite cartway.

A Final Note

The archaeological work done at Area F has added to our knowledge of how eighteenth- and nineteenth-century Philadelphians lived in this part of the city. The picture is incomplete, as archaeological data always are, but what was learned is now preserved in the form of notes, drawings, photographs, and artifacts, and as such forms a small but significant segment of the archaeological history of Philadelphia.

APPENDIX 3.A:
ARTIFACTS FROM FRANKLIN'S HOUSE AND
MARKET STREET RENTAL PROPERTIES

Artifacts from Franklin's House.

Artifact group	Description
CERAMICS (3,189 sherds)	
Earthenware	50.7% locally made, with the rest European (mostly English), plus stonewares, oriental porcelains, and a few far eastern earthenwares.
Undecorated lead-glazed redware (1,337 sherds)	
Pots	Ranged in size from small (base diameter of 3 to 4 inches) to massive (base diameter of 7 inches, mouth diameter of 11 inches, height of 12 inches); glazed on interior only, with lug handles and folded rims 1½ inches deep. One rim was flat for receiving a cover. One pot was three-legged, with a base diameter of 3¾ inches, glazed on the interior only.
Jars, jugs, pitchers	Glazed both interior and exterior, with everted rims and strap handles.

continued next page

Artifact group	Description
Mugs	Straight-sided, glazed inside and out, with strap handles.
Slip-decorated redware (188 sherds)	Platters or pie plates, glazed on the interior only, trailed, combed, or sgraffito. Trail-slipped sherds were most numerous; these were probably locally made.
Unglazed redware (93 sherds)	Probably from glazed vessels; a few were from flower pots.
Slip-decorated, buff-paste (187 sherds)	Represented wares from England, with yellow to clear glaze decorated with trailed lines or dots of dark-brown slip. Forms were small cups with flaring rims, mugs glazed inside and out, pie plates glazed on interior only. The small cups may have been spotted or combed and spotted.
Delft wall or fireplace tile (24 sherds)	14 undecorated, 2 from one blue-and-purple decorated tile, 2 from 1 purple decorated tile, 2 blue decorated. The blue-and-purple fragments showed the head and shoulders of a shepherd with a staff. The purple fragments also depicted a shepherd. These tiles were eighteenth-century Dutch.
Delft-type earthenware (117 sherds)	English, tin-enamelled, with underglazed blue painting.
Creamware (653 sherds)	20.5% of all ceramic sherds. Queensware (creamware) included some early transfer-printed ware: 1 "Wedgwood" base of a gravy boat; 1 sherd had the "I H" mark of Joshua Heath of Shelton, Staffordshire, 1740–1780.
Pearlware	48 feather-edge blue or green; the preference was 5 to 3 for green over blue pearlware. The forms were plates, saucers, and cups.
Stoneware (217 sherds)	All but 6 were salt-glazed; these 6 were from an "Egyptian black" stoneware representing the mid-1760s in Staffordshire. English white salt-glazed sherds represented 65% of the stoneware, in the forms of mugs, cups, pitchers, plates, and saucers. There were a total of 9 scratch-blue sherds.
Porcelain (397 sherds)	12.4% of the total sherd count. Chinese porcelains were represented by 370 sherds, of which 284 were "Canton." Ten sherds were of Japanese manufacture, and 1 was French. Unidentified porcelain sherds of European character totaled 16. Thirteen sherds were blue-and-white Canton with overglazed enamel in red. Of the Chinese sherds, 71 were overglazed enamel decorated in blue, red, gold, silver, and green, singly or polychromatically, over a grayer glaze.
GLASS (1,000 fragments)	
Window-pane fragments (600)	Slight green tint with small bubbles; thickness 1 mm to 2 mm, with 80% between the two extremes; probably cast plate glass, not crown.
Bottles (278)	43 base, 205 body, 28 neck. Heavy green blown wine bottles of a mid- to late-eighteenth-century form: 13 square-sided, flat-bottomed case bottles; 15 medicine bottles, white to faintly green.
Drinking vessels	53 stemmed, all hand-blown; 3 tumbler fragments.
Decanters (4)	
Lamps (3)	
Tube glass (5)	
Salt (1)	
Unidentified (28)	
METAL TABLEWARE	One bone knife or fork handle and iron stem; 1 iron knife blade; 1 iron fork shaft; 2 three-tine forks; 2 spoon fragments (1 pewter handle, 1 iron handle).
MISCELLANEOUS METAL	One iron-shafted wooden pully 1½ inches in diameter; 1 clasp knife; 1 English penny dated 1720; 6 copper buttons.
LEATHER	Six pieces representing children's or women's shoes.
HORN	17 fragments of flattened horn, for lanterns.
STONE	3 marbles
CLAY	114 tobacco pipe stems: diameters indicated probable late-eighteenth- to early nineteenth-century dating, but are nondiagnostic; 23 bowl fragments of a late eighteenth-century type.
BONE (2,600 fragments)	Beef (84%), sheep or goat (15%), pig (1%), and deer (present, but very few—less than 0.5%).
SHELLFISH	Abundant—3 oysters for every 1 clam.
MISCELLANEOUS	Coconut shell (1), peach stone (1), pecan shell (1), butternut shell (5).

From Powell 1962a.

Artifacts from Franklin's Market Street Rental Houses

Basalik and McCarthy (1982) grouped artifacts from six of the twenty-two pits excavated at Franklin's Market Street rental houses into South's (1977) artifact categories for the Carolina pattern; the artifacts were reported by Liggett (1971b, 1971c, 1973) and Cosans (1975). The dates in Basalik and McCarthy's tables, which follow, are modal, and the percentages, particularly for the kitchen and architecture groups, correspond closely to South's means for the Carolina pattern.

Artifact classifications for analysis.

Artifact Group	Pit Feature No. (Context)					
	9 (1790)	9 (1750)	22 (1800)	22 (1750)	25 (1750)	26 (1800)
KITCHEN GROUP	681	1,791	1,268	2,385	2,170	1,426
1. Ceramics	292	1,106	1,070	1,926	2,094	954
2. Wine bottles	209	326	179	270	54	348
3. Case bottles						2
4. Tumbler				11		
5. Pharmaceutical	85	136				3
6. Glassware	94	223	19	178	21	118
7. Tableware	1				1	1
8. Kitchenware						
BONES	106	438	907	967	911	422
ARCHITECTURE GROUP	446	451	286	200	122	654
10. Window glass	417	447	158	143	72	553
11. Nails	28	4	127	57	50	100
12. Spikes	1					
13. Const. hardware						1
14. Door lock parts				1		
FURNITURE GROUP						
15. Furniture hardware						1
ARMS GROUP	1					
16. Musket ball, shot	1					
17. Gunflints						
18. Gun parts						
CLOTHING GROUP	3	8	10	5		5
19. Buckles			2	1		
20. Thimbles				1		
21. Buttons	3	8	6	1		5
22. Scissors						
23. Straight pins			2	1		
24. Hook/eye fasteners						
25. Bale seals						
26. Glass beads				1		
PERSONAL GROUP				1		3
27. Coins				1		2
28. Keys						
29. Personal items						1
30. Tobacco pipes	33	93	96	30	61	17
ACTIVITIES GROUP	8	37	5	5	12	
31. Const. tools					1	
32. Farm tools						
33. Toys			1			
34. Fishing gear						
35. Stub-stemmed pipes						
36. Colono-Indian pot.						
37. Storage items						
38. Ethnobotanical	1	5				
39. Stable and barn						
40. Misc. hardware					2	
41. Other	7	31	5	5	9	
42. Military objects						

From Basalik and McCarthy (1982), after South (1977:162–63).

Franklin's Market Street Houses.

	Pit Feature No. (Context)					
Group	9 (1790)	9 (1750)	22 (1800)	22 (1750)	25 (1750)	26 (1800)
Kitchen	681 (53.29)	1,791 (63.56)	1,268 (49.30)	2,385 (66.38)	2,170 (66.24)	1,426 (55.75)
Architecture	446 (34.90)	451 (16.00)	286 (11.12)	200 (5.57)	122 (3.98)	654 (25.81)
Bones	106 (8.30)	438 (15.54)	907 (35.26)	967 (26.91)	911 (27.81)	422 (16.69)
Furniture	0 (0.00)	0 (0.00)	0 (0.00)	0 (0.00)	0 (0.00)	1 (0.04)
Arms	1 (0.08)	0 (0.03)	0 (0.00)	0 (0.00)	0 (0.00)	0 (0.00)
Clothing	3 (0.23)	8 (0.28)	10 (0.40)	5 (0.14)	0 (0.00)	5 (0.20)
Personal	0 (0.00)	0 (0.00)	0 (0.00)	1 (0.03)	0 (0.00)	3 (0.12)
Tobacco pipes	33 (2.58)	93 (3.30)	96 (3.73)	30 (0.83)	61 (1.86)	17 (0.67)
Activities	8 (0.62)	37 (1.31)	5 (0.20)	5 (0.14)	12 (0.37)	0 (0.00)
Total	1,278	2,818	2,572	3,593	3,276	2,528

From Basalik and McCarthy (1982). Numbers in parentheses indicate percentages of the total number of artifacts from each pit.

APPENDIX 3.B:
ARTIFACTS FROM CISTERNS 3 AND 3A,
INDEPENDENCE HALL EAST WING BASEMENT

Artifacts found in the light-brown, sandy fill of the upper portion of cistern 3.

Whole and fragmentary bricks
Paving cobblestones
Board fragments
Plaster fragments
Slate fragments
Coal fragments
Mica fragments
Sewer tile fragments
Sewer tile grate fragment

Oyster shells
Bones from domestic animals
Grape seeds
Peach seed

Scraps of cloth
Scraps of leather
Scraps of tar paper

Rusty lumps of iron (mostly nails and screws)
Corroded copper fragment
Corroded brass fragment

Fragments of ceramic dishes
Bone knife handle
Clay pipe bowl and stem fragments, one marked "Davidson, Glasgow"
Brass ring
Wooden phallus
Cork bottle stopper
Fragments of glass tumblers
Fragments of milky-white glass lamp bowls
Fragments of window glass

Soda bottles labeled:
    C. W. Otto & Co. Philadelphia
    R. Riddle, Philadelphia

Unlabeled medicine and chemical bottles
    5 whole and numerous fragments

Unlabeled beer, wine, and spirit bottles
    4 whole and numerous fragments

Medicine bottles labeled:
    Frederick Brown, Druggist & Chemist, Northeast corner, 5th & Chestnut, Philadelphia
    Mathay Caylus a Paris
    Vogelbach's Pharmacy, 1716 Frankford Rd., Philadelphia
    Dr. Grove's Anodyne for Infants
        . . . syrup of . . wild cher. . compound
        . . al., Philad. . , . . nt, m. . . , 186.

From Gell 1968.

Artifacts found in the black organic layer filling the bottom portion of cistern 3.

Whole and fragmentary bricks
Paving cobblestones
Board fragments
Plaster fragments
Coal fragments
Sewer tile grate fragment
Sewer tile fragment labeled:
    . . . racotta works, 7th & German-
    town Ave.

Oyster shells
Domestic animal bones
Grape seeds
Watermelon seed
Lobster claw
Hard-boiled egg
Sawed-off human skull cap
Human humerus distal end fragment
Human radius proximal end fragment

Scraps of cloth
Scraps of leather

Rusty lumps of iron (mostly nails and screws)
Plumbing fixture handles
Corroded copper fragments
Corroded lead or zinc fragments

Cosmetic crock and lid labeled:
    J. B. Thorn, Chemist, London
    John A. Tarrant, sole agent for the United
    States
White chamber pot fragments
Heavy gray vessel fragments

Heavy brown vessel fragments
Blue-and-white whiteware plates labeled:
    Opaque Granite China
    W. R. and Co.

Dressmaker's pin
Gold locket fragments
1815 five-thaler German gold coin
U.S. nickel, shield, date?
Pocket watch
Bone utensil handle
Lead pencil fragment
Bottle cork
Clay pipe bowl and stem fragments
Key

Fragments of glass tumblers
Fragments of milky white glass lamp bowls
Fragments of window glass
Fragments of heavy plate glass
Glass bottle stopper
Chemical glass tubes and stirring rods
Lamp chimney fragments
Cut-glass lamp base
Glass jar lid and jar neck
Glass jar lid labeled:
    A. Stone & Co. Philada.
    Patented Oct. 19, 1858

Soda bottles labeled:
    C. A. Dubois & Bro. Phila.
    R. Riddle, Philadelphia.
    Wm. Hoffius, Phila.
    Thos. Scott, Phila.

Twitchell, Phila.
    Lewis & Scott, Phila.
    Watson Mineral water, Phila.

1-quart ink bottle fragment labeled:
    Carters Ink

Unlabeled medicine bottles
    13 whole and numerous fragments

Unlabeled beer, wine, and spirits bottles
    5 whole and numerous fragments
    molded seal: wheat whiskey 1825

Medicine bottles labeled:
    Frederick Brown, Druggist Chemist
        Northeast corner 5th & Chestnut
    Frederick Brown, Druggist & Chemist
        Northeast corner 5th & Chestnut
    Mutter's Cough Syrup
    Hegeman & Co. Chemists, New York
    J. Hauel & Co. Phila.
    Wild Cherry Compound
    London Hair Restorer
    H. C. Blair, Druggist
        8th & Walnut, Phila.
    Dr. D. Jayne, Indian Expectorant
    J. B. Thorn
    H. C. Helmbold, Genuine Fluid Extracts,
        Phila.
    D. Thompson, Dye Water, New London,
        Conn.
    U.S.A. Hosp. Dept.

From Gell 1968.

Artifacts from light-brown, sandy earth filling the upper portion of cistern 3A.
This is probably a redeposited part of the upper deposit in cistern 3.

Whole and fragmentary bricks
Paving cobblestones
Coal fragments
Slate fragments
Sewer tile fragments
Sewer tile grate fragment

Oyster shells
Domestic animal bones

Scraps of tar paper
Scraps of leather
Leather shoe buckle strap

Rusty lumps of iron (nails and screws)
Corroded lead (?) emblem

Carved horn cylinder (possibly pen shaft)

Cosmetic whiteware jar lid fragment
Fragments of dishes
Blue-and-white whiteware plates labeled:
    Opaque Granite China
    W. R. & Co.

Fragments of glass tumblers
Fragments of milky-white lamp bowls
Window glass fragments
Thick plate glass fragments
Lamp chimney fragments

Soda bottles labeled:
    C. W. Otto & Co., Phila.
    J. J. Solomon, 631 Front St.
    Cream soda, S , Phila.

Unlabeled medicine bottles
    4 whole and numerous fragments

Unlabeled beer, wine, and spirits bottles
    1 whole and numerous fragments
    2 bottoms labeled:
        Whitney Glass Works
        Glassboro, N.J.

From Gell 1968.

Artifacts from the black, organic stratum filling the central portion of cistern 3A.
This is probably a redeposited part of the black layer of cistern 3.

Brick fragments
Plaster fragments
Sewer tile fragments

Oyster shells
Domestic animal bones

Leather shoelace fragment (?)

Iron hatchet head and handle fragment
Corroded copper wire
Rusty iron lumps (nails and screws)

1834 U.S. $5.00 gold piece
Cork bottle stopper

China demitasse cup
Heavy ceramic crock fragments

Fragments of window glass
Fragments of milky-white lamp bowls
Cut-glass vase (?) bottom

Whole 1-quart bottle labeled:
  Carter's Ink

Unlabeled medicine bottles
  1 whole and numerous fragments

Unlabeled beer, wine, and spirits bottles
  numerous fragments

From Gell 1968.

Artifacts from the lowest portions of cistern 3A.
These specimens represent the earliest deposits excavated.

Board fragments
Sewer tile fragments

Oyster shells

Scraps of leather

Lead nail (?) with double head

Ceramic crock fragments
Ceramic dish fragments

Fragments of window glass
Fragments of milky-white lamp bowls

Unlabeled medicine bottles
  Few fragments

Unlabeled beer, wine, and spirit bottles
  Few fragments

From Gell 1968.

APPENDIX 3.C:
ARTIFACTS FROM THE MCILVAINE HOUSE PRIVY

McIlvaine ceramic type by sherd and vessel.

Ceramic Type	No. of Sherds	Percentage of Sherds	No. of Vessels	Percentage of Vessels
Porcelain	155	5.6	18	8.7
Stoneware	6	0.2	1	0.5
Earthenware				
Blue-transfer-printed	687	24.7	55	26.7
Green-edged	384	13.8	36	17.4
Blue-edged	35	1.3	3	1.4
Annularware (banded)	98	3.5	7	3.4
Undecorated whitewares	1,037	37.3	55	26.7
Redware	252	9.1	23	11.2
Miscellaneous	125	4.4	8	3.9

From Basalik 1980: app. 4a.

McIlvaine vessel by ceramic type.

Ceramic type	Plates	Bowls	Cups	Saucers	Mugs	Pitchers	Teapots	Pots	Chamber Pots	Other
Porcelain			8	10						
Stoneware										1
Earthenware										
Blue-transfer-printed	20	8	13	3		2	3		1	1
Green-edged wares	27	6		2						1
Annularwares (banded)		5				2				
Undecorated whitewares	9	8		3		1	1	4	7	1
Redwares			1		2	1		11		5
Miscellaneous	3		3			1	1		1	
Total	59	27	25	18	2	7	5	15	9	9

From Basalik 1980.

McIlvaine tableware by percentage.

	McIlvaine Privy	Planter's Kitchen*	Overseer's House*	Slave Cabin*	Black Lucy's Garden†
Serving bowl	29	8	24	44	41
Flatware	63	84	72	49	51
Other	8	8	4	7	8

Note: The researchers took the cultural import of the above comparisons in usage to be that black southern slaves and the free blacks in Massachusetts (Lucy) used serving bowls more than did the planter's family. The Fling family usage at McIlvaine House was somewhere in between. If "social status" is implied here, it presumably involves more use of plates and saucers in "polite society," ignoring the possible recourse to unpreserved wooden plates or pewter plates—in all, a dubious set of criteria.
*Otto, John S. 1977. "Artifacts and Status Differences: A Comparison of Ceramics from Planter, Overseer and Slave Sites in an Antebellum Plantation." In *Research Strategies in Historical Archaeology,* edited by Stanley South. New York: Academic Press.
†Baker, Vernon. 1978. "Historical Archaeology at Black Lucy's Garden, Andover, Massachusetts: Ceramics from the Site of a Nineteenth Century Afro-American." In *Papers of the Robert S. Peabody Foundation for Archaeology.* Vol. 8. Boston: Harvard University Press.
From Basalik 1980.

Inventory of ceramic objects.

Type	Number	Description
Porcelain	10	Saucers, willow pattern, painted blue underglaze (oriental).
	7	Teacups, willow pattern, oriental.
Stoneware	1	Brown bottle fragment, undecorated.
Earthenware		
Blue transfer-printed whiteware	3	Plates
	1	Cup
	4	Bowls
	1	Ewer (?)
Blue transfer-printed pearlware	2	Serving dishes
	2	Saucers
	9	Plates
	3	Soup plates
	1	Sugar bowl
	1	Serving dish
	8	Cups

continued next page

Type	Number	Description
	1	Cream pitcher
	2	Bowls
	6	Butters
	1	Chamber pot
	1	Teapot
	1	Coffee pot
Green-edged whiteware	2	Soup plates
	1	Bowl lid
	1	Platter
	1	Egg cup
Lead-glazed redwares	1	Pitcher
	2	Porringers
	2	Mugs
	1	Ink bottle
	2	Jugs
	2	Pie plates (?)
	3	Bowls
	1	Cup
	4	Pans
	1	Flower pot (unglazed)
	1	Jar (?)
	1	Spittoon
Green-edged pearlware	2	Platters
	17	Plates
	4	Serving bowls
	4	Soup plates
	2	Saucers
	1	Gravy boat

From Basalik 1980.

Inventory of glass objects.

Item	Contents	No. of vessels
GLASS VESSEL FORMS		
Bottle	Ale (?)	7
Bottle	Wine	3
Decanter	Spirits	1
Bottle	Medicine/alcohol	23
Tumbler		54
Glass (receptacle)		2
Wine glass		9
Total		99
OTHER FORMS OF GLASS		
Jar		3
Cup plates		2
Knobs		7
Inkwells		3
Lamps		3
Vases		3
Handles (cup?)		2
Total		23

Note: Of the medicinal propietary bottles, 2 were round and embossed with "(..E)R's (COR)dial (PHILAD)A," and 3 of hexagonal shape were embossed with "(..).R. Rowand (P)hilad?." From Basalik 1980.

Window glass by thickness and quantity.

Thickness (inches)	Quantity	Percentage
0.035	55	5.2
0.045	379	35.5
0.055	306	28.7
0.065	256	24.0
0.075	26	2.4
0.085	5	0.5
0.095	18	1.7
0.105	4	0.3
0.112	18	1.7

From Basalik 1980.

Inventory of bones.

Animal	Species	Number	Percentage
Cattle	Bos taurus	97	33.1
Sheep	Ovis aries	64	21.8
Swine	Sus scrofa	33	11.3
Deer	Odocoileus sp.	9	3.1
Chicken	Gallus domesticus	30	10.2
Turkey	Melagris gallopavo	11	3.7
Fowl	Indeterminate	1	0.3
Rabbit	Sylvilagus sp.	11	3.7
Rat	Rattus sp.	2	0.7
Groundhog	Marmota monay	2	0.7
Fish	Indeterminate	3	1.0
Unidentifiable		30	10.2
		293	

From Basalik 1980.

Inventory of seeds.

Seed	Species	Number	Percentage
Sour cherry	Prunus cerasus	154	39.8
Grape	Vinifera sp.	53	13.7
Blackberry	Rubus fruticosus	37	9.6
Peach	Prunus persica	33	8.5
Watermelon	Citrullus vulgaris	30	7.8
Coffee	Coffea sp.	17	4.4
Acorn	Quercus sp.	12	3.1
Tomato	Lycopersicon esculentum	9	2.3
Peanut	Arachis hypogaea	9	2.3
Chestnut	Castanea dentata	8	2.1
Walnut	Juglans sp.	7	1.8
Hickory	Carya cordiformus	6	1.6
Cucumber	Cucumis sativus	5	1.3
Plum	Prunus domestica	3	0.8
Coconut	Cocos nucifera	3	0.8
Apple	Malus domestica	1	0.3
		387	

Adapted from Basalik 1980.

Artifacts by functional group.

Functional group	Number	Item
Clothing	2	Pointed-toe, pegged flat heel shoes
	16 pairs, 8 soles	Square or blunt-toed shoes
	2½ pairs	Slippers, round-toed
	2	Children's shoes, round-toed
	1	Complete shoe, laced, sewn, and pegged
	24	Upper shoe fragments
	22	Sole welts
	5	Heel welts
	19	Heel reinforcements
	11	Heels
	4	Laces
	4	Pins
	10	Buttons
Personal	4	Toothbrushes
	5	Combs
	1	Key
	1	Watch (an Elgin National). Note: Elgin came into existence in 1864, thus providing a latest terminal date for the privy deposition. Basalik chose to exclude the watch from further analysis.
Activity (a manifest catch-all)	4	Knives, clasp
	1	Tool handle
	5	Pencils
	3	Scrub-brush fragments
	1	Marble, ceramic
	1	Weight, lead
Tobacco pipes, white clay	2	Bowls
	1	Stem
Kitchen	3	Seals, lead
	2	Spoons
Arms	1	Cartridge
	3	Shot, lead
	1	Shot, iron
Miscellaneous	1	Wood, polished, undefined
	1	Quarter-section bone
	1	Slag piece
Metal	23	Nails, cut
	2	Spikes
	1	Hinge, door
	1	Knocker
	1	Door hardware, unspecified
	1	Sprocket
	2	Washers
	2	Valves (?)
	2	Vessel rim fragments
	11	Metal lid fragments
	1	Lid, jar
	7	Bucket fragments
	1	Pulley, small
	21	Bands, flat
	2	Cylinders, solid
	2	Spacers
	2	Pots, tin plant

From Basalik 1980, adapted from South 1977:95–96.

4

Old Philadelphia

NEW MARKET: OF ENTERPRISE AND INFANTICIDE

MAN FULL OF TROUBLE TAVERN: NOT SO GENTEEL

THE WALNUT STREET PRISON WORKSHOP:
HOW TO REDUCE RECIDIVISM

310 CYPRESS STREET: ANOTHER SURPRISING FIND

THE HILL-PHYSICK-KEITH HOUSE:
DOWN ALMSHOUSE, UP MANSION

THE U.S. MINT: FROM COINAGE TO COIN BANK

OLD ST. PAUL'S CHURCH: PHILADELPHIA'S
ELITE BURIAL CUSTOMS

WASHINGTON SQUARE: THE SAGA OF THE UNKNOWN
SOLDIER AND THE ANONYMOUS ARCHAEOLOGIST

The Colonial and early Federal sites of Independence National Historical Park did not, of course, exist in isolation. They sat in the very heart of old Philadelphia, surrounded by numerous churches and more numerous taverns, a prison, a hospital, docks, shops, markets, an almshouse, a paupers' burial ground, and the homes of the wealthy, the middle class, the poor, and the very poor. It was a teeming, bustling, heterogeneous mix. Sitting cheek to jowl with the freestanding Federal mansion of Col. Henry Hill on Fourth Street were the older and far less pretentious middle-class rowhouses of narrow Cypress Street. There, in small shops on the ground floors of their homes, tradesmen and artisans plied their crafts.

Looking south from Independence Square in 1775, those tempted by the taverns of Second Street and the bawdy houses of the area had a clear and sobering view of the new Walnut Street Prison, where felons worked off their crimes and debtors languished. Southwest, the view was of Potter's Field, now known as Washington Square. Soon to be invaded by the mass graves of soldiers of the Revolutionary War, Washington Square was the final resting place not only of the impoverished but also of those who succumbed to the epidemics that all too often devastated the city. Disease was rampant throughout the eighteenth century, as malodorous tanneries polluted creeks with their offal and waste from privies contaminated underground streams and wells.

All was not peaceful even in the world of churches. In 1760 a group of disgruntled parishioners split off from the Christ Church congregation to go their somewhat dissident Anglican way at the then new St. Paul's. A few years later, as the Revolutionary War approached, many a Quaker was torn between a conscientious objection to the fighting and attachment to the American cause. Quakers who supported the war effort in any way did so at the risk of being disowned by their meetings. Many reacted to the crisis by abandoning the worldly trappings and views they had adopted in recent years and reverting to a simpler, more spiritual way of life. A few openly sided with the British. For two such Quakers, the consequence was a death sentence for treason imposed after the American forces retook Philadelphia in June 1778 (Figure 4.1).

Quakers were not the only Philadelphians of the 1770s to feel themselves impaled on the horns of a dilemma. Divided loyalties rent some families asunder. Franklin's son William, royal governor of New Jersey at the start of the war, remained loyal to the crown; the ensuing animosity between father and son was such that they never reconciled. Indeed, the war was not easy on any of the householders of old Philadelphia, who long remembered that during the British occupation of the city, tea sold for $50 and $60 a pound, wood on occasion was not to be had at any price, and markets sometimes had no flour, butter, or eggs.

After the war, having first witnessed enraged protests against the Stamp Act of 1765 and then experienced the suffering and privation that the war years created, Philadelphia burgeoned again. Reflecting the prosperity of the Federal era were a number of new public buildings—among

them the U.S. Mint—and the city's flourishing taverns, which counted among their patrons numerous commercial visitors to the city, as well as congressmen, senators, and other members of the tiny bureaucracy the federal government engendered. Also reflecting the postwar prosperity were the city's bustling marketplaces. New Market, built in 1745 at Second Street and Lombard, expanded all the way from Pine Street to South Street, and it was thronged by the tradesmen, artisans, and gentry who inhabited Society Hill.

As the nineteenth century progressed, Society Hill went into decline, taking on an increasingly commercial

aspect. By the end of the century, it had fallen into a state of unsightly, if lucrative, decay. The fashionable population had moved west across the city, and their former residences had grown ever more dilapidated as wholesale food merchants and small manufacturers took over the blocks between Walnut and South, Front and Sixth. Until the 1950s, when the development of Independence National Historical Park sparked the revitalization of the neighborhood, the colonial name "Society Hill" must have struck visitors to the area as the height of incongruity.

Since the time the revitalization movement began in the 1950s, resto-

Figure 4.1.

Judgment Day of Tories. This engraving by E. Tisdale depicts the harsh punishment meted out to many Loyalists. Some were beaten and hung; others were exiled and deprived of their property. (Courtesy of Library of Congress)

rations of properties in Society Hill and its environs have created the opportunity for archaeological investigations. Unlike the archaeological studies carried out in Independence National Historical Park, these investigations, described in the pages that follow, were not part of an overall plan for restoration. Nonetheless, the sites studied are among the earliest, most significant, and most representative properties of old Philadelphia, and the physical evidence they yielded has put flesh on the bones of the old city's history.

NEW MARKET: OF ENTERPRISE AND INFANTICIDE

Second Street between Pine and South was one of the busiest places in eighteenth-century Philadelphia. There, today, in the center of Second Street, one can see the reason for all the activity: a long shed of market stalls extending south from Pine Street (Figure 4.2). The stalls, together with their "head house," were restored in the early 1960s, but, with no private business then willing to undertake the enterprise, not to their original use. Today the empty market shed houses an occasional flea mar-

ket. In 1973, perhaps perceiving the wisdom of the eighteenth-century Philadelphians who built a market in this thriving area (now thriving again), a private developer began constructing a shopping mall along Second Street in the block directly east of the old market shed and running through to Front Street. The mall was called "New Market," after the old market across the street, which from the time it was founded in 1745 was known by that name. The new New Market, which for clarity's sake we shall refer

to as New Market East, is a melange of shops and restaurants housed in modern and eighteenth-century structures (Figure 4.3).*

The most notable of the old buildings still standing in the block occupied by New Market East is a large house on the southeast corner of Second Street and Pine. It was built as a freestanding residence in 1791 for John Ross on the site of an earlier structure and renovated in the early nineteenth century by architect John Haviland. In the middle of the block, at 419 and 421 South Second Street, are the Harper Houses, visible in Figure 4.3. Built in 1788 by Thomas Harper, the twin houses have a cov-

* The new New Market has obviously not been a complete success, as vacant spaces have often attested. It therefore seems rather ironic that the old New Market, which flourished for over a century, stands empty, particularly as the open-air Italian Market on Ninth Street, which is about as close an approximation of the scene in eighteenth-century Philadelphia as one is likely to get, continues to thrive, as it has for several decades.

Figure 4.2.

Market shed and head house at Second Street and Pine after restoration in the early 1960s. The head house once served as a firehouse. (Photo by J. L. Cotter)

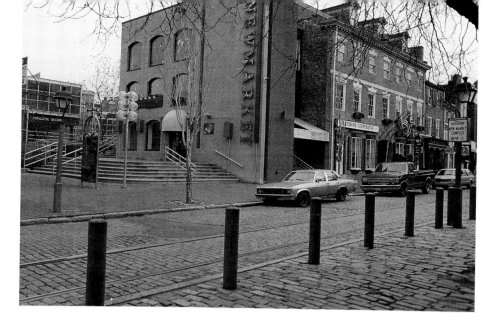

Figure 4.3.

New Market East, viewed from Second Street in 1989. A contemporary structure appears in the background at left; out of view on the other side of it is Front Street. To the right are some of the complex's eighteenth-century buildings, including the Harper Houses, with a covered passageway between them. (Photo by J. L. Cotter)

Figure 4.4.

Second Street looking north from Market Street in the late eighteenth century. The building at left was built from 1707 to 1710. Its arcaded ground floor was the town's first permanent market. The rest of the building served as a town hall or courthouse. Beyond is the steeple of Christ Church. (Engraving by W. Birch & Son; courtesy of the Free Library of Philadelphia)

ered passageway between them that once connected to various commercial structures at their rear. Among the other eighteenth-century buildings in the block is the Stocker House on Front Street, erected in 1791 by John Stocker on the site of Francis Trumble's earlier house and cabinet-making shop, built about 1745.

The Philadelphia Redevelopment Authority, owner of the land on which New Market East was to be built, specified in its contract with the de-

veloper that archaeological investigations be carried out while the construction of new buildings and restoration of old ones was proceeding. Barbara Liggett, as consulting archaeologist to the Philadelphia Historical Commission, contracted with the developer to direct this archaeological work. The majority of what follows is based on her excavation reports (Liggett 1978a, 1981) and on an exhibit catalog of the artifacts found on the site (Liggett 1978c).

New Market and Early Neighborhood Development: A Need Fulfilled

Philadelphia's first markets were open stalls in the middle of High Street, as Market Street was first known. Originally clustered near Front Street, the stalls had by 1692 extended to Second Street, and by 1710 a permanent marketplace had been established there (Figure 4.4). By 1736 the High Street

Figure 4.5.

Plan of the New Market East block, ca. 1978.
(from Liggett 1981; courtesy of the Athenaeum
of Philadelphia)

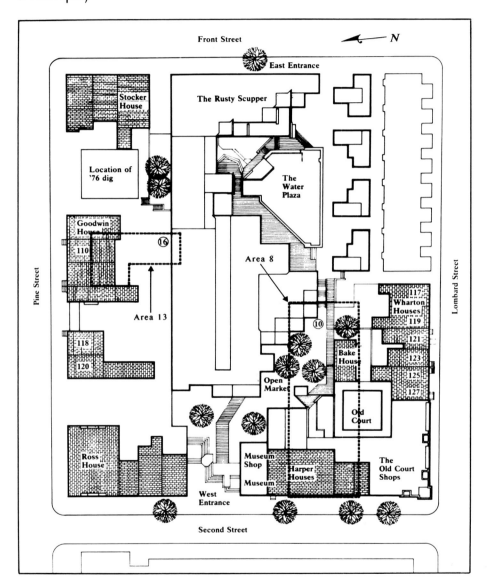

stalls were running as far west as Third Street (Jackson 1932:874; Bronner 1982:62). Anyone living south of Walnut Street in the Society Hill area had a rather long walk to get to the High Street Market, and as Society Hill grew during the 1740s, so did the need for a "new market."

In 1745, recognizing this need in one of the fastest-growing areas of the city, Edward Shippen and Joseph Wharton, both wealthy merchants, built a long, covered market shed at Lombard Street and Second. The shed of New Market consisted of two rows of brick pillars that supported a gable roof, under which was a vaulted plaster ceiling. The original shed had sixteen stalls, which Shippen and Wharton rented out to vendors. To get the land they needed to build New Market, Shippen and Wharton had prevailed upon the owners of the land directly east of the market site to donate some of their frontage to the project. Wharton himself had been one of the property owners to do so; others included Anthony Morris, Gov. Thomas Penn, and Samuel Powel, Jr., whose son and namesake later became mayor of the city. Each of these gentlemen donated 40 feet of their Second Street frontage, secure in the knowledge that their charitable action would repay them by increasing the value of the rest of their property. And so it did.

When New Market opened for business, the land across the street from it soared in value, and dramatic development ensued. Between 1745 and 1791, buildings in this block went up and came down in rapid succession, with new structures often being built over the foundations of earlier ones. By 1791 the block was almost completely developed. Around its perimeter were stately homes such as that of John Ross, as well as the more mod-

Figure 4.6.

New Market at the end of the eighteenth century, shortly before the head house at Pine Street was built. The firehouse at South Street appears here in the background. (Engraving by W. Birch & Son; courtesy of the Free Library of Philadelphia)

est dwellings of artisans, who worked in small shops at the rear of their houses. Alleyways and brick paths, together with the passageway between the Harper Houses, provided access to the interior of the block, where the artisans' shops were interspersed among gardens, paved courtyards, stables, storehouses, and other utility structures. Prominent among the commercial structures were two bake houses that made bread for local householders and other kinds of baked goods for ships' stores. Only one of these structures survives. Another demolished building worthy of note is the Pine Street Quaker Meeting House. It was erected in the 1750s on a sizable piece of land midway between Front and Second streets, the posthumous gift of Samuel Powel, Jr., to the Quaker meeting. The building, 60 feet long and 43 feet deep, was torn down in the 1860s and replaced by a row of Victorian houses—the only

significant addition to the block after the eighteenth century. Figure 4.5 shows the properties that stood on the site in the late 1970s.

As the neighborhood that had benefited by the construction of New Market grew, New Market itself benefited and burgeoned. It was not a steady burgeoning, for the market experienced lean times during the Revolution; however, business was booming shortly thereafter. By 1797 the market stalls ran from just south of Pine Street all the way to Cedar Street, as South Street was then known, where a firehouse marked the southern terminus of the market (Figure 4.6). The head house at Pine Street, shown in Figure 4.2, was built in 1804, and it, too, functioned as a firehouse. On the ground floor, at either side of the arched passageway that connects with the market shed, members of volunteer fire companies stored their equipment; on the floor above, they

regularly gathered for business and pleasure; and from the cupola on top of the building, alarms of fire once pealed.

The scenes of teeming life around New Market during the late 1700s and early 1800s reflected the vitality and prosperity of the growing city and the heterogeneous mix of the people who inhabited it. In the cold, crisp air of an early winter day, the smoke from warming fires mingled with the steamy breath of hundreds of people from all walks of life, bathing New Market in a suffused glow. Farmers' carts clogged the streets, housewives haggled over weights and prices, and fishwives loudly proclaimed their wares. Vendors came from near and far, by boat and by horse-drawn wagon, to hawk their goods, swap stories, trade political gossip, and rub shoulders with the prospering artisans, tradesmen, and gentry who lived and shopped in the neighborhood.

Archaeology at New Market East

The construction schedule for New Market East dictated the field methods used at the site. In the interior of the block bounded by Pine, Lombard, Second, and Front streets, where the construction workers excavated ap-

Figure 4.7.

Excavation at New Market East, April 1973. *Top,* southeast view; *bottom,* southwest view. (Photos by J. L. Cotter)

proximately 10 feet of fill (Figure 4.7), the archaeologists monitored and recorded the earth moving. When the excavations revealed a pit or well, they examined it, and if it appeared to date from before the early 1800s, they excavated it as formally as the construction schedule would allow. In the southwest corner of the block, the schedule was more flexible, and there it was possible to carry out a more controlled archaeological excavation.

Among the structural remains that the archaeologists discovered were a bake oven and the remnants of a blacksmith's forge. The major finds, however, accounting for almost 80 percent of all the features recorded, were pits of various kinds. Of the total of fifty-three pits uncovered, forty-three were brick-lined; the rest were lined with wood. Most of the pits contained eighteenth- and nineteenth-century artifacts. Ongoing backhoe disruption of the area did not allow a thorough excavation of each pit, but in the twenty-one that were exposed to their full depth, there was considerable disparity in the number of artifacts found. For instance, a barrel-lined privy pit on the Harper property (shown in Figure 4.5 as feature 10, area 8) yielded 893 artifacts, while a brick-lined privy pit (feature 16) at the southeast corner of the Quaker Meeting House lot (area 13) yielded over 30,000 artifacts and more than 11,000 bones. At the time of Liggett's excavation report (1981), the artifacts from twelve of the pits had been fully analyzed.

Feature 16, the privy pit at the Quaker Meeting House, was made of a single thickness of dry-laid brick set in consecutive stretcher courses. It was just over 4 feet in diameter and approximately 12½ feet deep. The top 6 feet of fill were removed by backhoe. At this point, a highly concentrated trash deposit appeared, and the archaeologists excavated the rest of the pit by hand. Except for thin bands of red and gray sand just a few inches apart and running through the pit in the upper part of the trash deposit, the stratigraphy of the soil was uniform throughout, consisting of dark-brown, sandy clay. In the absence of any interpretable soil stratigraphy, the archaeologists had to rely solely on laboratory analysis of the 9,722 ceramic sherds found in the pit to obtain dates for the deposit. For purposes of the analysis, the artifacts were divided into three "contexts," each representing a specific position in the pit. The ceramics retrieved from context I, near the top of the trash deposit, dated from about 1780 to 1785. Those in context II, the middle part of the deposit, had a modal date of 1760. Dates for the sherds in context III, near the bottom of the pit, clustered between 1755 and 1760.

Appendix 4.A provides a breakdown of the ceramics and faunal remains found in feature 16. As noted there, creamware, popularized by Wedgwood in the second half of the eighteenth century, was the most common kind of ceramic ware. It accounted for 33.7 percent of all ceramic sherds and 26 percent of the 747 vessel types represented. There were 30 examples of creamware in the Feather Rim pattern and 24 in Royal Rim. There were also a number of sherds from plain-rimmed octagonal plates. Such a large number of sherds of the same type indicated that they came from matching table services. A matching service is usually interpreted as a symbol of wealth and high status, as poorer folk could not afford the outlay required to buy a complete, matching set of dishes. The creamware sherds found in feature 16

did, however, bear the marks of different makers—Leeds, Melbourne, Wedgwood, and W. B. Fenton—so it is possible they were not all bought at the same time. Rather, perhaps a thrifty housewife, saving her pennies, bought herself matching items a piece at a time from the local china shop. On the other hand, various glass objects found in this pit supported the notion that whoever had owned these artifacts had been of substantial means. Included in the assemblage were Silesian stem wine glasses, a number of wine bottles, and some rare cruciform decanters dating from 1720 to 1740 (Figure 4.8).

Of the more than 11,000 bones recovered from feature 16, chicken bones were the most numerous. As indicated in Appendix 4.A, they accounted for almost 20 percent of the total. Analysis by weight, however, showed that the most significant food was beef, followed by the meat of sheep and pigs. Also found were the bones of ducks, geese, turkeys, and three species of turtles. Game was represented by deer and rabbit. Fish species included cod, sturgeon, shad, herring or smelt, and bluefish or bass. Other evidence of diet included egg shells, peach pits, cherry stones, grape and berry seeds, and oyster and clam shells. Even dregs of wine appeared. Like the ceramic sherds and glass objects found in the pit, the age of the bones found here indicated that the households from which they had come had been prosperous ones. The proportion of young bones was large— certainly larger than that found in the pits of Franklin's Market Street houses. The animals and fowl had been slaughtered while still young and tender, before they could live out useful lives as producers of milk and eggs, and whoever had dined on them

Figure 4.8.

Cruciform decanter dating from 1720 to 1740 found at New Market East. (Courtesy of the Atwater Kent Museum)

had dined very well indeed, on veal, spring lamb, and suckling pig, as well as on a goodly number of young, juicy chickens. Compared with the evidence from Franklin's rental properties, thought to reflect the dietary habits of middle-class artisans and merchants, the evidence from feature 16 indicated a better and more varied diet.

At the time of Liggett's 1981 report, the other objects recovered from feature 16 had not yet been subjected to the same kind of analysis and quantification as the bones and ceramic sherds. Nonetheless, these artifacts are quite revealing. Representative of household furnishings and equipment were a brass Chippendale-style drawer pull, a brass clock key, fragments of a wood-and-bristle scrub brush, and some small finishing nails or pins made of iron. The bone handles of the several pieces of cutlery that were found terminated in indistinct lumps of rust; it seems likely that their blades or fork ends had been iron, for most of the other iron objects had deteriorated beyond recognition. Other items, some of which are shown in Figure 4.9, provide interesting vignettes of personal habits, activities, and dress. They included a brass thimble and numerous brass straight pins; a slate pencil; a false tooth; a man's straight razor in a bone case; a brass-wire garment hook; fragments of a shoe; pieces of a dark, woven cloth and of a fabric knitted in garter stitch; a bone bodice stay; and bone, brass, and pewter buttons. The only coin found was a halfpenny, its copper so deteriorated it could not be dated. Among the items that may have been kept purely for their curiosity value were two pieces of coral and two small pearls with no holes for stringing or any evidence of a setting. An Amerindian grinding stone also invited conjecture about why it was in the pit, as did a few potter's implements and some unfired lumps of white pipe clay. A lead seal for a champagne bottle, bottle corks, some lengths of brass wire for securing corks, and fragments of red wax, which were probably used as bottle seals, attested to some conviviality. Evidence of a different sort was offered by bird shot, musket balls, cannonballs, and a small gunflint from a handgun or sporting piece.

The problem in interpreting what any of the material recovered from the Quaker Meeting House pit means

Figure 4.9a. (above)

Artifacts of a personal nature found at New Market East. (Courtesy of the Athenaeum of Philadelphia)

Figure 4.9b. (left)

Earthenware, probably the work of eighteenth-century Philadelphia potters. (Courtesy of the Athenaeum of Philadelphia)

for the history of the New Market East block is complicated by the sheer quantity of material found there. The bones recovered from context I represented some 300 to 500 pounds of meat; those in context II, some 2,300 pounds; and those in context III, roughly 1,300 to 1,500 pounds. The amount of meat found in any of these contexts would have been far too much for one household to have eaten except over a long period, and the bones showed no evidence of weathering or gnawing by rodents, which would have been the case had they been stored for a long time in a trash heap before being deposited in the pit. Thus the evidence suggested that the trash found in each context was a single deposit made all at once or within a short time (Burnston 1975, 1976).

The huge volume of the faunal remains in feature 16, together with that of the ceramic objects and other artifacts, raises the question of where all this trash originated. Obviously not from just one household, it may have been the accumulation of several households in the block, or it may have come from farther afield—from another site entirely—or it may have come from both. Wherever it came from, however, the excellent condition of the bone indicates that it was not stored for long, which would seem to eliminate its having come from a town dump. This suggests that at least some of the artifacts came from houses on the block, especially the small personal or domestic items such as the straight pins, buttons, false tooth, and garment hook. The faunal analysis concluded that while some waste or garbage bones had probably come from an off-site source, at least some of the bones of the food animals and the food debris had also come from the site.

Working against the likelihood of all the artifacts having come from local households were a large number of single, unmatched sherds; the most plausible explanation for these is that they were picked up in a load of trash from elsewhere, were carted in to be dumped in the privy as fill, and in the process got separated from their mates.

The large number of ceramic sherds in the pits may be further evidence of an off-site source. The workman hired to clean the privy may have acquired the sherds elsewhere in the city—from a potter or shipper, perhaps—and deposited them in the privy pit to aid in percolation. Given the uncertainty of the source of the artifacts found in feature 16, it cannot be assumed that they reflect the lifestyles of the people who lived in the New Market East block, nor can they serve as an unequivocal basis for answering other site-specific questions.

In another privy pit within the block, however, there did appear to be a clear association between the contents of the pit and the occupant of the house. This pit was on the Stocker property, where cabinetmaker Francis Trumble occupied a house and shop from about 1745 until his death in 1791. The rectangular privy pit excavated on this property appeared to have been closed after Trumble's death, and it yielded woodworking tools—iron gouges, chisels, gravers, and an iron rasp—as well as iron spikes and nails and wooden and bone tool handles. These artifacts, it seems safe to say, undoubtedly passed through the hands of Francis Trumble.

Perhaps the most interesting finds of the entire New Market East investigation were the remains of two human infants, one a seven-month fetus, the other full-term. Both were found in the prolific Quaker Meeting House pit. The discovery prompted Sharon Ann Burnston, who analyzed all the faunal remains of the pit, to prepare a thesis and write a separate article devoted to this aspect of the inves-

tigation (Burnston 1978, 1982). In it, she examined historical practices of disposing of stillborn infants and of infants who died shortly after birth. She concluded that in the eighteenth century, infants such as these were customarily buried in churchyards. It seems likely that the reason the two little bodies found in the Quaker Meeting House privy pit were disposed of in this clandestine way was that they were bastards; mothers of illegitimate children faced a social stigma, and if they were servants, they could also very well lose their jobs. Burnston also concluded that despite the hanging sentence the law could invoke for the crime of infanticide, murder might very well have been how the two infants concealed in the Quaker Meeting House privy had met their ends. As Burnston (1982:186) points out, "Successfully concealed abnormal behavior is historically invisible," and only archaeological research can bring to light the physical evidence of its having taken place.

Here, then, were two examples of deviant human behavior from the archaeological record, together with considerable evidence of the lifestyle, culture, and diet of a wealthy segment of Philadelphia's late eighteenth-century population. Whether or not the artifacts found here actually belonged to the people who lived in the New Market East block, they do document the prosperity of the early city, the tastes of its well-to-do, and the wide range of imported and domestic goods available to those who could pay for them.

MAN FULL OF TROUBLE TAVERN:
NOT SO GENTEEL

. . . at a tavern there is general freedom from anxiety. You are sure you are welcome, and the more noise you make, the more trouble you give, the more good things you call for, the welcomer you are. No servant will attend you with alacrity which waiters do, who are incited by the prospect of an immediate reward in proportion as they please. No, sir, there is nothing which has yet been contrived by man by which so much happiness is produced as by a good tavern or inn.

—Samuel Johnson, in Boswell's *Life of Dr. Johnson*

Philadelphia has from its very beginnings been a town of taverns. In 1683, a year after William Penn first arrived in his new colony, there were 7 of them; in 1758, 117; and in 1828, at the climax of this hospitable enterprise, there were no fewer than 1,239 (DeSilver 1828). In 1773 a visitor disembarking from a boat at the Philadelphia docks along the Delaware River would have had 21 such establishments to choose from on Second Street alone. Had he chosen the elegant City Tavern,* just opened on Second Street near Walnut, the visitor might have found himself in agreement with Samuel Johnson. As described in the *Transylvania Journal and Weekly Advertiser* in March 1773, the City Tavern was a "large commodious new House . . . intended to be kept as a genteel" establishment. In

* The site of City Tavern (see Figure 2.37) was nearly obliterated by subsequent building, and limited archaeological observations yielded little (Crozier 1978b).

addition to spacious lodging rooms and entertainment rooms, it had two kitchens and a license to sell wine and spirits (Batcheler 1973). Its very name would have told a knowledgeable colonial traveler something, for every sizable American city of the time had its City Tavern, which was invariably its best. Among the earliest patrons of Philadelphia's City Tavern were those elite but argumentative gentlemen who attended the First Continental Congress. In 1774, travel-weary and just arrived from Boston for the occasion, John Adams observed that "dirty, dusty and fatigued as we were, we could not resist the importunity to go to the tavern, the most genteel one in America" (Burnett 1921–36, v. 1:1). Repairing to the new hostel from Carpenters' Hall, Adams and his fellow delegates continued deliberations in a more informal and convivial atmosphere, as they made more noise, called for good things, and felt themselves welcome.

A less elegant choice for the less elite visitor might have been Man Full of Trouble Tavern, or, as it was probably originally known, Man with

Figure 4.10.

Man Full of Trouble Tavern in 1967, after complete restoration by the Knauer Fund for Historic Preservation. (Photo by J. L. Cotter)

Figure 4.11.

Artifacts from beneath the cellar floor of Man Full of Trouble Tavern and from the cistern in front of the Paschall House. The ceramics were surprisingly eclectic for such a modest establishment. (Courtesy of Virginia Knauer)

probably not closed until the 1850s. After examining these artifacts, the class began five months of intensive archival research and excavation of a small, untouched cul-de-sac in the cellar of the tavern. The following historical and archaeological accounts are based on their reports (Cotter 1966b).*

The Story Told by Historical Documentation

Man Full of Trouble was one of a numerous and typically urban institution, the tavern, where food, drink, and some type of lodging might be had. The tavern's rural counterpart was the inn. Rural or urban, this type of establishment was licensed by the local government, and the local clientele was interested chiefly in the beverages that it sold. Larger and better taverns, such as Philadelphia's City Tavern and the Indian Queen on Front Street between Market and Chestnut, were licensed to sell wine and spirits; more modest taverns were licensed to dispense beer and cider only. In contrast to the inn or tavern, which always sold some type of alcoholic beverage, an ordinary served mainly as a place to eat, comparable to a restaurant that

a Load of Mischief, proclaimed by a sign depicting a man bearing a woman piggyback on his shoulders—a scene too indecorous for later Victorian sensibilities. Today the sign shows a man with a woman on his arm and a monkey on his shoulder. Built about 1760 at Second and Spruce streets, a block south of the future City Tavern, Man Full of Trouble was neither the best nor quite the worst of taverns. Nonetheless, it is the only tavern in downtown Philadelphia to have survived from pre-Revolutionary days to the present era. It is also the only one to have yielded its secrets to archaeological investigation.

In the spring of 1966, Virginia and Wilhelm Knauer invited the graduate class in historical sites archaeology at the University of Pennsylvania to explore a small area of the tavern's basement. The Knauers had already

restored both the tiny tavern and the abutting and matching Paschall House (Figure 4.10)—which, at the time the restoration began, had leaned together reciprocally for support— and created a foundation for preserving and interpreting them. Virginia Knauer, then a Philadelphia councilwoman, had saved various artifacts recovered during the restoration and used them as reference in furnishing the restored tavern and as objects in a wall display (Figure 4.11). These objects had been found in a brick drain beneath the tavern's cellar floor and in the fill of a cistern under the sidewalk in front of the Paschall House. Although not identified by strata or area where they were found, the artifacts were no doubt representative of life on the premises from the earliest days of the tavern until well into the nineteenth century, for the cistern was

* The members of the class whose reports were compiled by Cotter (1966b) and whose research is summarized here were Linda Keller, Charles I. Wilson, Richard Candee, Edwin Iwanicki, and Paul R. Huey. All became researchers, teachers, or archaeologists.

might also function as a boarding-house. The coffeehouse, which catered to merchants, was a somewhat elevated kind of tavern, where patrons could enjoy not only coffee but liquors as well. At the bottom of the social scale was the tippling house, an unlicensed tavern providing strong drink and entertainment for the least choosy of the urban population, especially the sailors of a bustling port. The character of tippling houses is best perceived in the docket books of the Court of Quarter Sessions, which heard complaints brought against the proprietors of these unlicensed establishments and often shut them down.

Taverns in colonial Philadelphia were more than just places to eat, drink, or lodge. They were busy social clearinghouses where people gathered to conduct business, to get the news, to argue politics, to attend concerts or auctions, or even just to gossip and pass the time of day. At their worst, taverns were a public nuisance. At their best, they were places where conversation flowed, ideas took root, and the cultural patterns of the new republic were forged. The tavern continued to flourish until the middle years of the nineteenth century, when the more efficient (if more impersonal) hotel of the industrial era displaced it.

Despite its less-than-best status, Man Full of Trouble Tavern somehow managed to live on into the industrial era. No doubt contributing to its inferior ranking was its less-than-choice location just west of the small tidal basin into which the two branches of Dock Creek flowed and just north of a marshy, mosquito-infested area that was gradually being filled. Before the days of William Penn, the Amerindians had called the tidal basin Cooconocon, or Place of Pines, and they had frequented it to gather whortleberries

from the fine stand that grew near the water. By 1685, however, a couple of hundred houses were scattered north of the basin along the river all the way to Market Street. The earliest of these "houses" were caves dug into the banks above the river; before the authorities decreed their destruction, the goings-on within them had shocked William Penn with their "clandestine looseness" and earned them the dubious distinction of being the first recorded houses of ill-repute in Philadelphia. South of the basin, across the marsh, were the riverfront warehouses of the Free Society of Traders. The Delaware was deep enough here to permit large ships to sail close to shore, and smaller ones could enter Dock Creek. Shallops and poled boats delivered cargoes to larger vessels to ferry to New Jersey or to transport to England, and lighters entered Dock Creek with goods for Philadelphia.* Amid all this bustle, men and small boys fished for perch and netted herring.

By 1699 two tanneries were in operation along the banks of Dock Creek, and the offal from them polluted the creek and the river, setting an unsavory precedent for the next three centuries. The game fish died. Yellow fever carried off one Lambert, owner of a tannery,† and in 1730 smallpox swept the area. The tanners were asked to remove themselves in 1739, but in the 1770s several tanneries

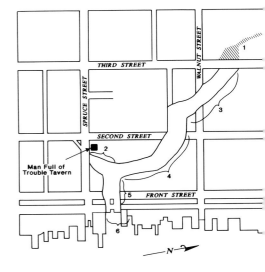

1) Head of the Swamp or Dock. Never Improved. Presumably filled during Block Development by 1740.

2) Closed by 1757 during Second Reconstruction of the Dock.

3) Closed 1763–1769.

4) Closed 1784.

5) Closed 1818–1821.

6) Closed to Water Street and Eastward with Construction of Delaware Avenue after 1821.

Figure 4.12.

Sequential closing of Dock Creek. After being paved, the creek east of Second Street became known as Dock Street. (From Liggett 1971a)

* Liggett (1971a), who conducted an archaeological investigation of the area around Front and Dock streets in 1968, has questioned the traditional view of historians that the branches of Dock Creek were natural streambeds. Her interpretation of historical documents is that Dock Creek was originally a swampy area, never used extensively for shipping, and that as its branches became increasingly offensive open sewers during the 1700s, it was sequentially filled in.
† The cause of Lambert's death, and of many other deaths in eighteenth-century Philadelphia, may well have been infectious hepatitis, caused by polluted water, rather than yellow fever, which is spread by the *Aedes aegypti* mosquito in warm climates.

were still operating. After Palatine fever and diphtheria had taken an additional toll in the 1740s, a petition was placed before the Common Council to fill in the marsh south of the basin. Although parts of the marsh were filled and used as grazing land, Dock Creek remained largely malodorous for most of the eighteenth century. While the western branch of the creek was apparently filled as early as 1757 and renamed Dock Street, it was not until 1784, when the reasonably named Man Full of Trouble Tavern had already been in existence for at least fifteen years, that the Street Commissioners finally finished paving over the northwestern branch (Figure 4.12). The atmosphere was then more agreeably charged with the activities of ship chandlers, sparmakers, sailmakers, and assorted port merchants and their warehouses.

The building that was to house the Man Full of Trouble Tavern was probably built in 1760, when Michael Sisk, a plasterer, bought the eastern half of the lot now known as 127–129 Spruce Street (once known as 2–4 Dock Street) and Benjamin Paschall bought the western half to "erect a Brick Tenement and [make] other improvements thereon" (Cotter 1966b:15). Because of the shallowness of the lot, the kitchens were located in the cellars of the houses. The pent eave overhanging the first floor of the adjoining two-story houses was an older style by then, as was the "broken-pitch" gambrel roof, which gave more head room in the garret than the more usual pitched roof.

In 1769 John Wood, a clockmaker who lived and worked near Fourth and Chestnut streets, bought Sisk's house and had it insured by the Philadelphia Contributionship. The insurance survey recorded its "2 Rooms on a floor . . . Garet plaster" and also noted that a Joseph Beeks was now keeping "a tavern there." Beeks thus apparently initiated the building's commercial use. His tavern seems to have been one of the many tippling houses in the area, for the list of tavern licenses for 1769 does not include his name or the location of the tavern. When Beeks died in 1772, he owed John Wood £40, some of it presumably for rent, and his estate—consisting of the tavern's furnishings, notes of

credit he held on others, shoe buckles, knee buckles for his breeches, coat buttons, a "Greate Coate," and a silver watch—totaled £74.5.9, which in today's terms would be a couple of thousand dollars.

Beeks died before the Revolution could cause him the problems it caused the other tavern keepers of Philadelphia. His successor at the Man Full of Trouble Tavern seems to have been James Alexander, who was licensed as a "Public House Keeper" in 1773. It was Alexander and others like him who had to deal with Congress's attempts to limit profits made at the expense of soldiers, as well as with Gen. Sir William Howe's order during the British occupation of Philadelphia that "Public Houses, taverns, etc. [be prohibited] to curb and suppress vice and immorality." In 1788, by which time the tavern had surely won its name, Alexander was still hanging on. The following year, when he was licensed to set up a tavern closer to Front Street, Thomas Wilkins took over the operation of Man Full of Trouble. Wilkins continued to rent the tavern after the owner, John Wood, died in 1793.

In 1796 the widow Martha Smallwood acquired the Man Full of Trouble. One of the women—most of them widows—who managed 20 percent of the taverns, coffee shops, and tippling houses that abounded in the city, she had taken over her husband's tavern at 9 North Front Street after his death. In 1826 the widow herself died, and the city records for that year provide a meticulous inventory of her belongings.* From it, we can assume that the widow would have greeted customers wearing her silver-rimmed spectacles and a selection from her

* City of Philadelphia: 1826 Administration for Estates No. 200, "Inventory of Goods and Chattels of the Property of the Late Martha Smallwood."

wardrobe of 6 short gowns (all worth $1.00), 9 frocks, 7 petticoats, 6 chemises, 10 pairs of stockings, 20 handkerchiefs, 4 pairs of pockets, and 2 underjackets. On a holiday, she might have emerged adorned in her silk bonnet, silk shawl, 2 gold rings, and earrings.

The barroom during the tenure of the widow Smallwood must have been somewhat crowded, for within its 18-by-22-foot area, it contained 6 Windsor chairs, 2 arm chairs, 3 "old" chairs, 14 rush-bottom chairs (all worth $5.50), and, on the north wall, an 8-by-5-foot bar. It also held a mahogany card table, a stand, 3 painted pine tables, and 1 large and 1 small serving table. Warmed in winter by the 10-plate iron stove, guests could have inspected the map, gilt-framed picture, and 2 prints on the walls and checked their appearance in one of the 2 looking glasses. They might have been served on any of the inventoried dishes: 6 china coffee cups and saucers; 11 saucers, 9 cups, and 1 teapot of queensware (all valued at 37½¢); 9 china plates; 3 bowls; 2 large tumblers; and "1 lot of crockery in the closet of the parlour." The table at which the guests ate might have been covered with any of the 14 "dining and breakfast clothes" (together with 42 napkins, these "clothes" were valued at $15.00).

Cutlery was curiously scant in the inventory, some of it perhaps having departed with the last of the widow's guests. Those remaining might have been hard-pressed to deal with her standards of etiquette while trying to feed themselves from an array of 7 tablespoons, 10 teaspoons, 1 soup spoon, 1 punch spoon, and 1 pair of sugar tongs. Guests would not have seen the equipment of the cellar kitchen. In addition to pots, pans, crockery, laundry utensils, and wood

Figure 4.13.

Man Full of Trouble Tavern at the corner of Spruce and Dock streets, painted by William L. Breton in 1835. (Courtesy of the Historical Society of Pennsylvania)

and fire equipment, it included 2 tables, 3 pieces of old carpeting, and (for the cook's repose?) 1 old, low-post bedstead.

The total value of the inventory was $207.58½. Cash in the house amounted to $332.85. The widow Smallwood apparently did not do too badly.

As a result of a sheriff's sale to settle the widow's estate, another tavernkeeper, Nicholas Stafford, acquired the property for $1,250—half its valued amount. When Stafford died in 1833, his widow became proprietress, and she in turn passed the property on to her son Emmit in 1837. By then the tavern had had at least one addition. Figure 4.13, a watercolor painted in 1835 by William L. Breton, a delineator of Philadelphia street scenes, shows a wooden lean-to attached to the northeast corner of the tavern; next door, a rack for drying laundry (a familiar part of the cityscape where space for clotheslines was lacking) adorns the roof of the little Paschall House.

Breton's watercolor suggests that both the tavern and its little neighbor were by 1835 already in rickety condition. No doubt the tavern, together with others like it, was beginning to feel the pinch of the changing eco-

Figure 4.14.

Merchant's Exchange at Third and Walnut streets in 1990. (Photo by J. L. Cotter)

Figure 4.15.

Man Full of Trouble Tavern in 1864. Then known as B. Naylor's Hotel, it apparently prided itself on its cuisine of oysters. (Courtesy of the Historic American Buildings Survey)

Figure 4.16.

Man Full of Trouble Tavern at its nadir in 1955. (Courtesy of the Historic American Buildings Survey)

nomic times. By 1832 Philadelphia's businesses had grown so numerous that the city's taverns and coffee houses could no longer accommodate their meetings. In that year, to create the needed space, the Philadelphia Exchange Company, newly formed by the merchants of the city, began erecting the handsome Merchant's Exchange at Third and Walnut streets (Figure 4.14); designed by William Strickland, the building was completed the following year. The year 1832 also saw the opening of Philadelphia's first railroad, which spelled doom for the stagecoach's tavern stop; by the late 1860s eleven railroads were serving the city. Meanwhile, multistoried hotels with spacious lobbies and opulent furnishings were appearing, drawing to them the city's more affluent businessmen and visitors. In the early 1860s the six-story Continental Hotel opened at Ninth and Chestnut streets. Built at a cost of $1 million, it was able to house 700 guests in its 476 rooms and boasted a "vertical railway"—the first hotel elevator of note in Philadelphia. Not even the elegant City Tavern was able to withstand these onslaughts; in 1855 it was demolished to make way for the large, commercial Lennig Building.

Somehow or other, the Man Full of Trouble Tavern endured. It remained in the hands of the Stafford family, who rented it out to a series of short-term tenants. About 1851 Benjamin Naylor took over its operation. Its somewhat ominous name long since abandoned, the tavern was now known as "B. Naylor's Hotel," as witnessed in the first photograph of the property, taken in 1864 (Figure 4.15). The tavern and the Paschall House were by this time in a state of mutual decrepitude, roof racks now serving the drying laundry for both premises,

and the wooden lean-to, its roof askew, huddling in the shadows at the northeast corner of the hotel. By 1900 the erstwhile tavern had become a provision store, and by 1955 it was a wholesale chicken market, gloomy beneath a sheet-iron awning, still defying gravity and masonry cracks and leaning on its equally raffish neighbor for support (Figure 4.16).

The Paschall House, like the tavern, had sheltered a series of occupants. In 1785 it was a boardinghouse kept by the widow Robinson (whose husband had left her the property on

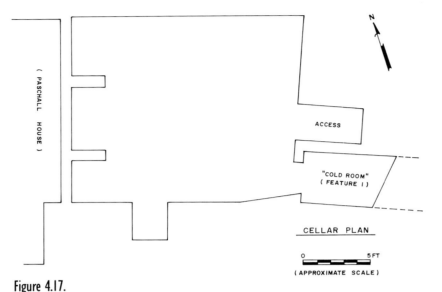

Figure 4.17.

Cellar plan of Man Full of Trouble Tavern. (From Cotter 1966b)

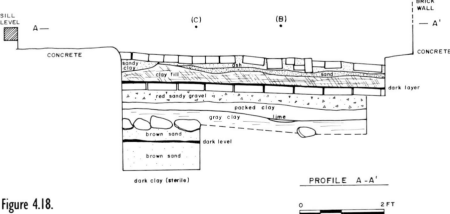

Figure 4.18.

Stratigraphy of the "cold room" in the cellar of Man Full of Trouble Tavern. (From Cotter 1966b)

delphia Redevelopment Authority. Shortly thereafter, restoration and archaeological work began.

The Story Told by Archaeological Evidence

The class started the archaeological part of its investigation by determining that the floor of the tavern's cellar kitchen was only 2.62 feet above the high-tide level of the Delaware River, two short blocks to the east. The cellar's east wall had two doors. One opened to an outside ladder, down which produce for the kitchen was lowered and up which buckets of ashes from the fireplace were hoisted. The other door, in the southeast corner, opened to a passageway that had once led underground to the notorious Dock Creek (Figure 4.17). Presumably, the passageway, which was a few bucket-spilling steps from the kitchen, had originally served as a rather unsanitary sewer drain from the kitchen to the creek. After being blocked off by a brick wall to form a small cul-de-sac, it may have been used as a cold storage room. Some 4½ to 5½ feet high, the cul-de-sac was 4 feet wide and, because the blocking wall ran at a diagonal, 7 feet long at one end and 8 feet 11 inches at the other.

Another feature of the cellar was the brick drain beneath the floor, which had yielded some of the artifacts shown in Figure 4.11. The drain led from the fireplace to an old barrel sunk 2½ feet deep; the barrel had served as a sump and possibly also as a cooling well.

Excavation

The class excavated the small cul-de-sac with meticulous care and exact

the condition she would not remarry). Thereafter it housed a confectioner, a purveyor of toys, various hairdressers and perfumers, and a glazier. It was long occupied by a sign and ship painter, Robert O'Keefe. After O'Keefe's death in 1899, his brother Moses took over the property and held it until 1907 (Cotter 1966b:15–31).

In 1962 the Knauers purchased both the Paschall House and the Man Full of Trouble Tavern from the Phila-

control, making detailed plans of each significant level of the excavated area on a grid system. The grid had six squares, each 2 feet by 2 feet, as well as an irregular triangle at the blocking wall. Stratigraphy was recorded by one longitudinal profile (Figure 4.18) and two transverse ones, and artifacts were bagged by lots, each representing a stratigraphic layer.

Just below the first few inches of loose soil covering the surface was a brick pavement. The bricks were molded and not of a modern cut. After sketching and photographing them, the class removed the bricks and, to facilitate their later replacement, reassembled them in their original pattern on the cellar floor. Below the bricks, the fill became interesting.

A layer of ashes under the bricks yielded brass pins, oyster shells, window glass, a slate pencil, fragments of Staffordshire earthenware, and many clay pipestems, one of them red and with a distinctively Victorian decorative motif. Also found were two coins: a worn, bronze U.S. two-cent piece and a corroded, Liberty-seated half-dime. Although their dates were illegible, the coins made it possible to ascertain the date of the brick floor. Half-dimes of this type were minted from 1838 to 1873, and two-cent pieces were minted only after 1864. The brick floor therefore could not have been laid before 1864, and it was probably laid sometime within the next decade.

A dense layer of sandy clay and gravel appeared next, then a surprise: an older floor of hand-molded bricks (Figure 4.19). More neatly laid out than the floor above, it extended under the stone walls of the passageway, proving that the walls were built after this floor was laid and that the area was once wider; the original walls may, in fact, still be standing behind

Figure 4.19.

The lower of two brick floors found in the "cold room" of the cellar of Man Full of Trouble Tavern. (Photo by J. L. Cotter)

the walls that are visible today. The bricks on the left, or north, side of the floor had been removed when a trench was dug for a lead gas pipe, probably in the early 1870s. The lead pipe was still in place, but twisted and broken as if it had at some time been dismantled. The fill of the trench, which extended for several layers beneath the old brick floor, yielded objects of varying age: a bowl from a late eighteenth-century clay pipe, marked "TD" on the back; fragments of white, salt-glazed stoneware, transfer-printed earthenware, black-glazed redware, creamware, and "ironstone china"; bits of leather and coal; a small glass button; and pieces of window glass.

The old brick floor had been laid on the customary bed of sandy gravel, which was clean and devoid of artifacts. Below the sandy gravel, however, embedded in a layer of packed clay that had once served as the kit-

chen floor were bits of creamware and brown-glazed redware, as well as a hand-wrought nail. Still lower, beneath the water line, a layer of gray clay yielded a small amount of blue-green window glass, many small bits of brick, pieces of leather, bones and turtle shells, and a piece of wood. Sealed in moist earth, all these items were perfectly preserved.

The deepest layer of the excavated area consisted of heavy, round cobblestones; they could have been part of some feature that predated the tavern's construction. One of the cobblestones was an Amerindian pecked and hollowed grinding stone, which may have lain by the shore of Dock Creek for centuries after last being used as a device for grinding seeds or nuts before it somehow found its way into this area. The cobbles had been placed in smooth, clean, brown sand a foot deep, and in this last stratum above the undisturbed gravelly earth lay bits of broken brick and chips of wood showing the marks of an axe—evidence dating from the tavern's construction about 1760. Also found in this bottom layer were two pieces of blue and white delft, a good marker for the period. Delftware, first produced by the Dutch as an imitation Chinese porcelain, became popular in the seventeenth century, and early in the eighteenth century the English began making it in quantity.

Interpretation

What did the physical evidence mean? Too few in number to quantify statistically, the artifacts were nonetheless the last tiny, tangible glimpses left of the everyday lives of all who had frequented the premises—the guests, families, friends, and personages of Benjamin Naylor, the widows Smallwood and Stafford, Thomas Wilkins, James Alexander, Joseph Beeks, and Michael Sisk. Such scraps of the past can remind the present of a reality as intimate as an old shoe.

The numerous fragments of white-clay tobacco pipes, dating from the last half of the eighteenth century into the Victorian era, conjure up an image of the barroom as it must have appeared over the years: customers huddled over their beer or spirits, wreathed in clouds of blue smoke. The surprisingly few fragments of drinking glasses found lead one to suspect that the libations of these wraiths were poured from the keg or spirit bottle, hand-blown and greenish in color, into leather cups, pewter mugs, or wooden vessels. Such a practice would have been in keeping with the nature of the establishment, as glass drinking vessels were a rarity in humbler taverns.

In fragments of queensware found in the lower part of the fill, one can see the undoubtedly proper widow Smallwood, silver-rimmed spectacles glinting in the candlelight as she bends over her teapot. When listed in the 1826 inventory of her possessions, the teapot may already have been an heirloom, queensware having come into vogue in the late eighteenth century—a fact that had not escaped the notice of Sarah Franklin Bache when, as noted in Chapter 3, she wrote to her father in 1773 asking him to bring some with him on his return from London.

A single stoneware marble, early nineteenth-century in type and appearing in the upper fill, might have been bought by a cajoling parent at the shop in the Paschall House next door and dropped by a wandering, fidgety child in this alcove of the cellar kitchen while the parent caroused above. The presence of salt-glazed stoneware in the lower fill is a reminder that after 1800, a suspected link between lead glazing and lead poisoning increased the popularity of salt-glazed wares.

So, the passageway to Dock Creek—probably an unsanitary sewer outlet until walled off from access by rats to become a small cul-de-sac in the basement wall, first carelessly filled with cobblestones and later twice paved with brick, littered with ashes and trash, trenched for gas lines, and at last abandoned altogether and filled with earth debris—remained to tell an archaeological story: a modest, unwritten, but meaningful link between past and present.

THE WALNUT STREET PRISON WORKSHOP: HOW TO REDUCE RECIDIVISM

The Walnut Street Prison (Figure 4.20), erected in 1775 just south of Independence Square, was remarkable for several reasons. It was the scene of the earliest and most successful experiment in rehabilitation of criminals in the United States. It was also graced by the presence of George Washington, who, although he may not have slept there, did indeed dine there, as the guest of an inmate in the debtors' part of the prison. The incarcerated debtor was, ironically and interestingly enough, Robert Morris, financier of the American Revolution and brother-in-law of Bishop White, whose very comfortable home was just down the street from the prison. Morris, his fortunes dwindled and having been brought to court by a small creditor, spent three and a half years in jail. He was finally released on August 26, 1801.

The debtors' quarters in which

Figure 4.20.

The main building of the Walnut Street Prison at the corner of Sixth Street. Across the street from the prison is the wall enclosing State House Yard. Some of the men in the foreground are engaged in moving a frame building. Others are acting as "sidewalk superintendents." The building being moved became the first church of the African-American congregation that founded the African Methodist Church of Mother Bethel at Lombard and Sixth streets. (Engraving by W. Birch & Son; courtesy of the Library Company of Philadelphia)

Figure 4.21.

The Athenaeum at 219 South Sixth Street. The first Renaissance Revival building in the city and one of the first constructed of brownstone, the Athenaeum was built in 1845 on the former site of the Walnut Street Prison workshops. The garden behind it is the only part of the original prison site not presently covered by buildings, sidewalks, or an alley known as St. James Street. (Photo by J. L. Cotter)

Morris lived were located near Prune Street, as Locust Street was then known, behind the prison's main building. Between these two buildings were the workshops in which prisoners other than debtors labored to rehabilitate themselves. Ten years after the complex of prison buildings was razed in 1835, the land on which most of the workshops had stood became the site of Philadelphia's Athenaeum. The Athenaeum, a handsome brownstone building on Sixth Street facing Washington Square (Figure 4.21), was designed in 1845 by architect John Notman as a library for a social and literary club. The garden behind it, which still blooms, saved this part of the prison site from subsequent commercial building. Today the building of the Penn Mutual Life Insurance Company occupies the main part of the prison site on Walnut Street.

In 1973 the Athenaeum's plan to extend its archival vaults underground beneath its garden presented the opportunity for an archaeological investigation. It was undertaken by the 1973 spring and summer classes in historical archaeology at the University of Pennsylvania. Amplified in subsequent years by further historical research and data analysis, the findings of the investigation brought into sharp focus Pennsylvania's seminal experiment in penal rehabilitation. The report incorporating this research (Cotter et al. 1988) provided the data for the account that follows.

Quaker Reform in Old Philadelphia

There never has been a time in the history of Philadelphia when crime, drunkenness, disease, or some other social ill has not been part of the daily news. Street vagrancy, for example, so common a problem in the 1980s, was hardly any less common in old Philadelphia. Between 1794 and 1798, when the population of the city was about 50,000, a total of 3,698 vagrants were incarcerated in Philadelphia (Skidmore 1948:172). It should be noted, however, that not all these vagrants came from the city's streets; an average of seventeen counties contributed to the city's prison population, which during the same period included 490 felons.

Prisons were not originally meant to serve as places for long-term incarceration, still less as places for reform. They were temporary holding pens, where the convict remained until sentenced. The sentences, especially for

previous offenders, were grim: ear cropping, branding, whipping, stigmatization, banishment, or death by hanging. The scenes within the prison walls were grim, too. At Old Stone Prison at Third and High streets, men, women, and juveniles, whether first-time offenders or hardened felons with long records of convictions, were thrown into the holding pen together. By 1770 Old Stone Prison had become notorious for its conditions, and Quaker consciences had begun to stir. On February 26, 1773, responding to the Quakers' push for reform, the Pennsylvania Assembly approved an act, sponsored by Gov. Richard Penn, providing for the Walnut Street Prison.

To design and build the prison, the assembly chose Robert Smith, the busy Scotsman who counted among his many other accomplishments the plans for the Christ Church steeple, Benjamin Franklin's house, and Carpenters' Hall. The jail that Smith erected across the street from State House Yard had a frontage of 184 feet on Walnut Street. The lot itself measured 200 feet east-west and 400 feet north-south. Two stories high and made of cut stone, the building had fireproof stone vaults supporting its tile floors—an architectural innovation that attracted some attention, and one that no doubt also dismayed any inmates hopeful of tunneling their way to freedom. The assembly raised the £5,000 needed to build the prison with a special issue of paper currency bearing a picture of the jail.

Very soon after it was completed in 1775, the Walnut Street Prison became a military prison, and it experienced the iniquities of military prisons as practiced both by the British during their occupation of the city in 1777–78 and by the Continental Army. In

1790, however, after the Commonwealth of Pennsylvania passed the "Act to Reform the Penal Laws of This State," the prison became an experiment in rehabilitation. Among other improvements, the act ordered separation of the sexes, separation of juveniles from adults, separation of debtors from felons, and workshops in which inmates other than debtors were obliged to labor. It also ordered solitary confinement, a Quaker innovation intended to reform the worst offenders by isolating them from bad influences and by providing them with an opportunity for quiet contemplation.

In the workshops, the prisoners worked off the costs of their incarceration by producing saleable items. As incentive to rehabilitate themselves, they were given at the end of their prison terms one-half of whatever was left over from the sale of their products after the costs of their keep (fifteen cents per day) had been deducted. Also deducted, if not previously paid, were the costs of their court and attorney fees. In some of the workshops, prisoners may have earned as much as a dollar a day, probably more than their illicit enterprises had ever garnered.

After witnessing the Walnut Street Prison in operation in the 1790s, the French observer Francois La Rochefoucauld-Liancourt noted that of seventy-three prisoners convicted before the 1790 act was passed, all were reconvicted, some as often as six times. Between 1790 and 1794 only five former prisoners were reapprehended, and their crimes were petty (La Rochefoucauld-Liancourt 1796: 10). Evidently, the new policies of the prison system—separating prisoners, hiring artisans to train them in rewarding crafts, reimbursing them for

Figure 4.22.

Plan of the Walnut Street Prison. The structure at bottom is the main building, where those who labored in the workshops ate and slept. The main building also contained administrative offices and an infirmary. Just behind the main building's east wing is the penitentiary of solitary cells (*D*), which is joined to the partial octagon of the workshops for nailmakers, stone sawyers, stone polishers, and carpenters. Not shown is the debtors' prison, which was in the southern part of the site near Locust Street. (From Joseph Bowes, "Plan and Elevation of the Jail at Philadelphia," *Philadelphia Monthly Magazine* [1798]; courtesy of the Historical Society of Pennsylvania)

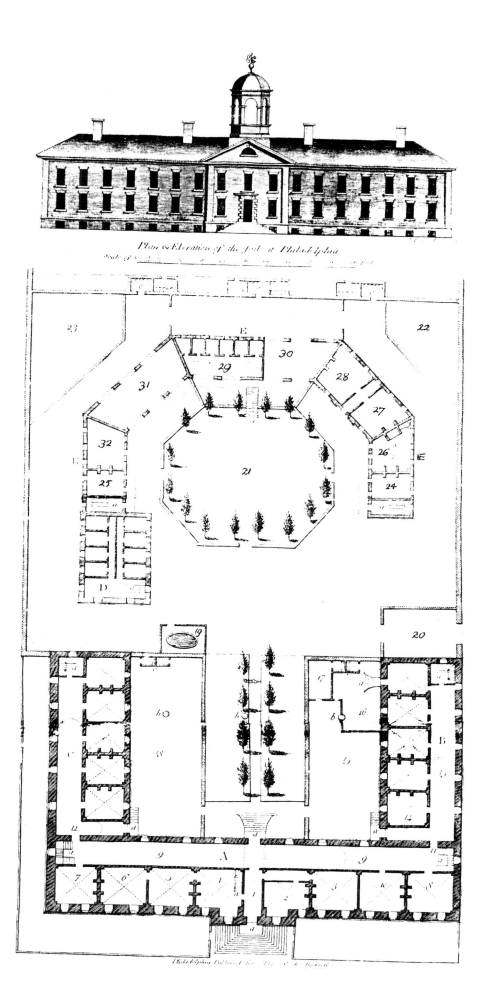

Figure 4.23.

The debtors' prison. From a sketch made in 1858, 23 years after the removal of the Walnut Street Prison and its workshops behind "the old debtors' prison." (Courtesy of the Athenaeum of Philadelphia)

Figure 4.24.

Eastern State Penitentiary at Fairmount Avenue and Twenty-first Street, 1990. (Photo by J. L. Cotter)

their work, enforcing a regular routine or "unremitted solitude," and providing uncrowded quarters—were having favorable results.

For seven years after the 1790 act was passed, the workshops operated out of makeshift quarters. The reform they produced was remarkable; recidivism was practically nil. Inspired by the success, the government in 1797 authorized the construction of a permanent building for the workshops at the rear of the main prison. The new building, two stories high, was a five-sided structure, resembling an unfinished octagon (Figure 4.22). It was made of red brick and set on a stone foundation. A second-floor balcony extended around the front of the five-sided building, providing access to the upper-floor shops of the stone polishers, whitesmiths (nonferrous metal workers), weavers, shoemakers, tailors, metal turners, and carpenters. On the ground floor were clerks' offices, storage rooms, single cells for prisoners working alone, a smith's shop, and shops for nail-making and stone-sawing.

Adjoining the workshops on the east was a "penitentiary" of solitary cells for the worst offenders. The penitentiary had eight 8-by-6-foot cells on each of its three floors. Each cell was 9 feet high and unfurnished except for a corner privy consisting of a lead pipe that flushed into a sewer duct. The prisoners in solitary confinement here survived on one meal of molasses and cornmeal a day and in winter had the dubious comfort of a stove in the passageway between the cells.

Occupying the southern portion of the prison lot near Prune, or Locust, Street was a building that served as the debtors' prison (Figure 4.23). A high stone wall separated it from the main prison and its solitary unit and workshops. The debtors who occupied these premises lived in whatever comfort they could afford, for they were entitled to bring with them any personal possessions they still owned. Comfortable or not, between Walnut and Prune streets they languished for an indeterminate time, hostages to their own debt; release came only when someone on the outside chose to bail them out or their own finances somehow took a turn for the better.

The drop in recidivism engendered by the new prison policies did not mean that prison problems ceased. The new workshops were not much more than a year old when on June 11, 1798, they were destroyed by fire, presumably at the hands of an unreformed felon or felons. The prison's Board of Inspectors moved immediately to rebuild the workshops, and the legislature voted funds for the reconstruction, which was accomplished largely by the prisoners themselves. By 1800 the shops were again in operation; in that year twenty-seven men were employed in nail-cutting, which made a profit of £742.3.6.

Before it was torn down in 1835, the Walnut Street Prison had succumbed to the syndrome of overcrowding. In 1791, the main part of the prison was housing 143 prisoners; by 1799, it was housing 600; by 1822, 804 inmates—the maximum number ever confined there—were swarming within its walls. To alleviate the problem, the Pennsylvania legislature authorized the construction of new state prisons. Among these new facilities were Western State Penitentiary near Pittsburgh, whose construction was authorized in 1818, and a new debtors' prison built in 1834 at Moyamensing Prison in what is now South Philadelphia.

Another noteworthy penal institution built to relieve overcrowding was Eastern State Penitentiary, which opened in Philadelphia County, north of the old city limits, in 1829. The instructions given to the architects who competed for the design of Eastern State testify that Pennsylvania prison administrators were interested not just in reform but in deterrence as well: "The exterior of a solitary prison should exhibit . . . great strength and convey to the mind a cheerless blank indicative of the misery that awaits the unhappy being who enters within its walls" (Teeters 1957:59). John Haviland won the competition, and the cheerless result of his work still stands today at Fairmount Avenue and Twenty-First Street (Figure 4.24). Despite its forbidding facade, the new penitentiary was apparently a considerable improvement over the soon-to-be-closed Walnut Street Prison. In 1831, when the young French nobleman Alexis de Tocqueville interviewed prisoners at both institutions, he noted that the inmates at Walnut Street agreed that conditions there injured "their morals"; the responses of prisoners at the new penitentiary were more positive (Pierson 1959:302).

The new prisons that the Commonwealth of Pennsylvania created in the 1820s and 1830s were to continue the experiment that began on Walnut Street after the passage of the 1790 act, and with similar success. Between 1830 and 1872 Pennsylvania's rate of recidivism was 6.25 percent, a small fraction of the rate for U.S. penal institutions in the 1980s, long after rehabilitation through useful and rewarded work virtually vanished from prison policy. In the 1930s the demands of U.S. labor unions stifled this answer to recidivism, and to date it has not been revived.

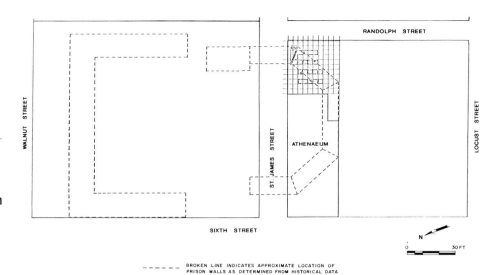

Figure 4.25.

Site plan of the Walnut Street Prison. Broken lines indicate the approximate locations of the walls of the buildings, as determined from historical data. The walls of the debtors' prison on the southern portion of the lot are not delineated. The gridded area on the east is the Athenaeum's garden, where excavations took place in 1973. (From Cotter et al. 1988)

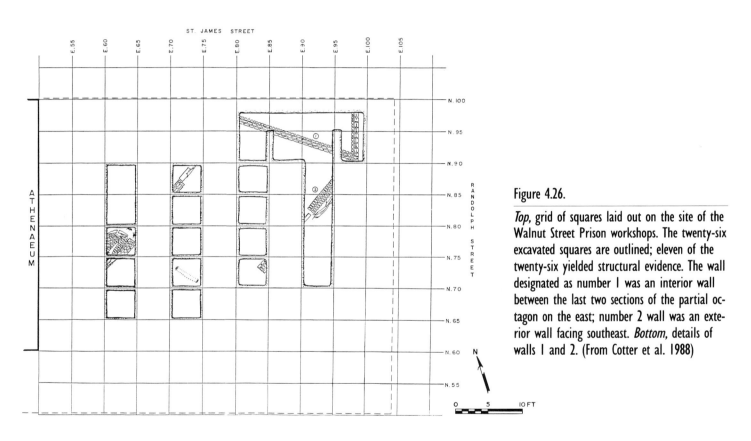

Figure 4.26.

Top, grid of squares laid out on the site of the Walnut Street Prison workshops. The twenty-six excavated squares are outlined; eleven of the twenty-six yielded structural evidence. The wall designated as number 1 was an interior wall between the last two sections of the partial octagon on the east; number 2 wall was an exterior wall facing southeast. *Bottom,* details of walls 1 and 2. (From Cotter et al. 1988)

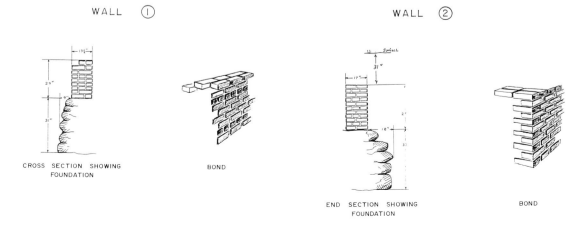

An Archaeological Portrait of a Prison and Its Inmates

The spring class of 1973 began the investigation of the Athenaeum's 50-by-54-foot garden by laying out the grid of squares depicted in Figures 4.25 and 4.26. In the six weeks during which the summer class of 1973 met, students were able to excavate twenty-six of these squares, process the artifacts, and produce a preliminary report. As shown in Figure 4.27, each square was separated from the next by a 1-foot balk, or earth partition; when wall foundations or other features that extended beyond one square were encountered, the balks were removed and the squares joined. Historical documentation, together with the physical evidence that was uncovered, indicated that the nail-making and stone-sawing shops on the ground floor of the workshops had occupied this part of the prison site.

The digging revealed a definite stratigraphy. The first foot or less of soil proved to be a layer of earth put down after the workshops were demolished to level the area and to provide a growing bed for the Athenaeum's garden; this layer yielded numerous late nineteenth-century artifacts. At roughly a foot from the surface, the first sign of the demolition debris from 1835 appeared, and it ended at about 4½ feet from the surface. The demolition debris, as well as the layers of earth beneath it, yielded artifacts representative of what had accumulated within the workshops from the time they were built in 1797 until they were demolished in 1835. Since the debtors' prison lay just to the south of the workshops, it is quite possible that some of its artifacts were mingled and scattered with the workshop debris when the whole prison complex was razed.

At 17 inches from the surface, the red brick walls of the workshops, first built in 1797 and rebuilt in 1800, came into view. The interior walls were 13½ inches thick, and their bricks were laid in English bond—that is, in alternate rows of stretchers and headers; no glazed headers were noted. The exterior walls, of a similar bond, were 17 inches thick. The bricks were well-fired and hand-molded and had a modal dimension of 8¼ by 4 by 2⅛ inches. The undressed schist footing on which the walls rested appeared at 64 inches beneath the surface. For the interior walls, the footing extended to a depth of 90 inches; for the exterior walls, to a depth of 104 inches. Figure 4.28 shows the angle of the octagon formed by the joining of interior wall no. 1 and exterior wall no. 2. This angle—sure structural evidence of the workshops—was uncovered in square N. 95 E. 95 (see Figure 4.26).

The excavations yielded very few whole or almost whole ceramic vessels. Of the 2,335 earthenware sherds

Figure 4.28.

The angle formed by interior and exterior octagon walls in square N. 95 E. 95, Walnut Street Prison workshop. (Photo by J. L. Cotter)

Figure 4.27.

The excavated squares and the balks between them. (Photo by J. L. Cotter)

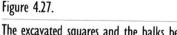

found, 988 were redware, mostly of local make. Of these, 49 were plain and unglazed, 577 were plain and lead-glazed, and 362 were slip-decorated. The ratio of humble, local redware sherds to sherds of good-quality English creamware is interesting; 449 of the latter were found. A heavy concentration of the creamware sherds, all but 79 of which were plain, was found outside exterior wall no. 2 just north of the debtors' quarters. Pearlware accounted for 822 sherds. Of these, 181 were transfer-printed, 451 were plain, 50 were green-edged and 98 blue-edged, and 42 were banded. Delft sherds, 76 in all and 2 of them possibly majolica, were mainly of English manufacture. Both the delftware and creamware characteristically came from the lower fill of the demolition debris, while the redware and pearlware were scattered throughout. In view of the general mixing of the demolition debris, however, position may mean little.

A few of the 139 oriental porcelain sherds recovered came from the upper, nineteenth-century fill of the garden bed, but most were found in the lower fill of the mixed debris, as were 27 sherds of English soft-paste porcelain. The porcelain, like the creamware and pearlware, suggests a fairly high standard of living. Of good quality, the oriental porcelain was blue and white, hand-painted under a glaze; 12 of the sherds had enameling over the glaze, a characteristic of the export porcelain of the early nineteenth century.

Of the 206 stoneware sherds identified, 140 were gray-paste utility wares, most of them decorated with cobalt blue. Also included in the stoneware count were 26 sherds of fine, white stoneware dishes; 22 of these were molded and plain, and 4 were basket-edged, salt-glazed, and decorated. These dishes were made before the main prison was built in 1775 and, in fact, would have been quite out of fashion by that time. Among the other stoneware sherds were 3 molded ones of scratch blue, 5 of unglazed black basalt, and 6 machine-turned ones of unglazed red. A few others were rare types from England.

The presence of so much good-quality ceramic ware on a site not designed or intended for genteel living is puzzling, but several explanations are plausible. First, before the prison was built, the site was an open field, and it could have been used as a town dump. Second, when good objects became outmoded, they were not discarded but were instead put to humbler uses. Third, the working prisoners' living conditions were relatively good, and they may well have had use of some decent domestic utensils. Fourth, the finer ceramics may have come from the quarters of the prison staff. Fifth, and most likely, most of the finer wares came from the nearby debtors' prison, where, if Robert Morris's entertainment of George Washington is any indication, some of the inmates lived in relatively high style. Morris undoubtedly would not have fed his distinguished dinner guests from humble kitchen redware.

Given the nature of the establishment, the small number of glass sherds found is neither puzzling nor surprising. Spirit bottles and tumblers were unwelcome in a prison, and, in any case, the inmates were unlikely to be able to afford a vice that might have brought them there; only the prison administrators and the luckiest of the debtors were in a position to indulge a thirst. The main prison did, however, have an infirmary, which presumably would have had a number of bottles for elixirs and other medicinal substances. As it turned out, pieces of small, light-green elixir bottles did come to light, and they were among the earliest types of glass recovered. Hand-blown, thin-walled, and dating from the eighteenth century, they were found at depths of 4 to 7 feet in the northwest quadrant of the excavated area. At depths of 6 to 6½ feet, the fill outside exterior wall no. 2 yielded 10 pieces of hand-blown spirit bottles with cylindrical bodies of green glass. This same fill also yielded 41 pieces of thin-walled, light-green, squared case bottles and 32 pieces of window glass. Glass fragments dating from after 1850 were found in relatively large quantities nearer the rear of the Athenaeum in the top 23 inches of fill; most of these were pieces of dark-green wine bottles.

Fragments of white clay tobacco pipes—10 pieces from bowls and 140 from pipe stems—were found in the sod zone to a depth of 100 inches. The diameter of the holes in the pipe stems was predominantly 5/64 of an inch; this diameter indicated that the pipes were made some time after 1750.* The shapes of the bowls were characteristic of those of the late eighteenth and early nineteenth centuries. The modest number of pipe fragments found suggests that the prisoners, no doubt by necessity, smoked less than the general population (see Appendix 4.B).

Metal objects included some miscellaneous scraps of iron and fragments of hand-wrought nails. Some of the nails may have been the product of the nail-making shop; others may have been used in the building itself. More evidence of the nail-making shop was found in a pair of iron pliers (shown in Figure 4.29, together with an assortment of other artifacts) and a portion of a rat-tail file. A bronze thimble and 21 straight

---

* Between 1600 and 1750 the diameters in the holes of pipe stems gradually diminished from 8/64 to 6/64 to 5/64 of an inch. By 1800 they were generally 4/64 of an inch.

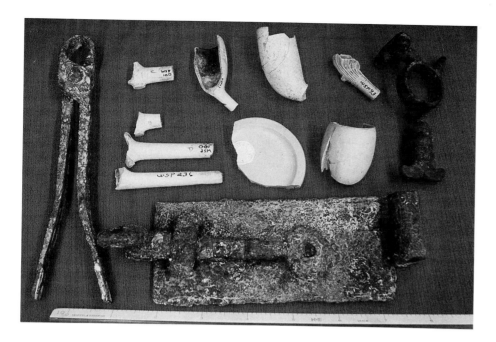

Figure 4.29.

Artifacts from the Walnut Street prison workshops: iron pliers and bolt, brass handle from a candle dish, fragments of clay pipes, and the bottom of a ceramic vessel marked "Etruria Stoneware: Wedgwood." (Photo by J. L. Cotter)

Figure 4.30.

The 10-plate, cast-iron box stove found at the site of the Walnut Street Prison workshops. Roughly assembled, the stove is shown here with its side facing the camera. (Photo by J. L. Cotter)

pins—11 of bronze, 10 of iron, and all with crimped-on heads—may have been used in the tailoring shop on the second floor of the building or by the women prisoners who sewed in some of the workshops. Other metal objects included 5 pewter spoons; 1 two-tined fork; 4 table knives with bone handles; 7 metal buttons, each with a loop on the back for sewing it to the material; and the two halves and broken link of a silver cufflink. The broken parts of the cufflink were found outside exterior wall no. 2 at 7 feet below the surface; this object might have been lost while the foundations of the workshops were being dug. Figure 4.30 shows the largest metal object found: a 10-plate, cast-iron box stove, whose various parts rested in demolition debris at about 3 feet from the surface. Apparently, the iron stove had not been considered worth saving.

The miscellaneous artifacts collected give us a further glimpse of the activities of the prison population. At least one of these activities was clandestine and forbidden. Some long-ago

Figure 4.31.

Artifacts pertaining to the activities of the inmates who labored in the Walnut Street Prison workshops. The illicit dice appear at lower left. (Photo by J. L. Cotter)

inmate, intent on circumventing the prison's ban on gambling, had fashioned five dice, each less than ½ inch square, from square strips of beef shank bone. Into one of the dice, the inmate had drilled numbers; the rest were blank, perhaps unfinished when they had to be hastily discarded. Other miscellaneous artifacts bore witness to the more orthodox labors of the inmates. A few fragments of cut and polished marble found resting in the demolition debris attested to the industry of the workers in the stone-sawing shop on the first floor of the building. Also found were a number of complete buttons with varying numbers of holes, as well as fragments of thin beef scapula and large conch shells that had provided the material for the buttons. Figure 4.31

shows evidence of the inmates' activities, both orthodox and otherwise.

Four years after students completed the field work in the summer of 1973, another student, Jiyul Kim, analyzed the more than 7,000 artifacts that had been assembled (Kim 1978). The goal of Kim's study, also described by Cotter et al. (1988), was to determine whether the pattern of artifact usage at this involuntary domestic habitation and work site of the late eighteenth and early nineteenth centuries bore any relation to the "Carolina" pattern of usage described by Stanley South (1977). South's contention is that the regularities of usage in American domestic sites of these years amount to "cultural laws." Kim's data analysis is shown in Appendix 4.B; its import is that the debtors who were incarcerated on the site lived mainly within the pattern of the average well-clad, well-fed British colonial or early Federal citizen on the Eastern Seaboard and that the inmates who labored in the workshops' left tangible, if minor, evidence of

their official and unofficial enterprises as they experienced their remarkable rehabilitation.

Kim also determined that the mean date of manufacture for the ceramic items was 1795.21. Adding 15 to 20 years to this date for use of the items before they were discarded would indicate that the ceramics were in major use between 1810 and 1815, which is entirely reasonable. A few years later, as the prison grew increasingly crowded, inmates were moved to other jails.

Although historical records confirm that the personal possessions of the debtors who inhabited the Walnut Street Prison could be as fine in quality and as numerous as the debtor could muster, no inventory describes the specifics of these possessions. An inventory of the prison taken on January 1, 1800, shortly before the rebuilt workshops opened after the fire of 1798, does, however, list the machinery and equipment used in the workshops. It also gives us a general idea of how those who labored in the workshops dined:

183 spoons
108 knives and forks
2 flesh forks and ladle
5 pitchers
121 tin and earthen cups
150 dishes and plates
250 small dishes
35 large dishes

When we add to this brief inventory the extensive historical data pertaining to the prison and all the physical evidence that was uncovered and analyzed, we gain a considerable insight into the material culture and daily life of those who were confined behind the walls of the Walnut Street Prison during the first three decades of the nineteenth century.

310 CYPRESS STREET: ANOTHER SURPRISING FIND

Like many other houses in Society Hill, the house at 310 Cypress Street has a long story to tell. Built sometime between 1785 and 1793, the middle-class dwelling—neither mansion nor "Father, Son, Holy Ghost"—was situated in the block of land formerly occupied by the City Almshouse. Here, between Spruce and Pine and Third and Fourth streets, the almshouse had loomed from 1733 until 1767, when rapid development of Society Hill and an accompanying increase in the value of the land prompted its removal to new quarters west of Tenth Street. Soon thereafter two narrow streets, Cypress and Union (now Delancey), were driven east-west through the block, and the old almshouse site was divided into house lots (Waldbauer 1976:8). By the time 310 Cypress Street was built, some two decades after the almshouse was moved, the neighborhood was quite densely populated, and diversely populated as well; adjacent to freestanding mansions on its main streets were rows of modest brick houses.

The census of 1790 listed seventy-six persons residing in the 300 block of Cypress Street. In 1793, after the first yellow fever epidemic had struck, the managers of the Pennsylvania Hospital reported that twenty deaths had occurred there, twenty-three whites and one black remained in their homes, while forty-three had fled, leaving three houses open and

seven shut. The fate of the occupants of 310 Cypress is unknown.

It is certain, however, that the modest but substantial house, like many others in the neighborhood, sheltered generations of tradesmen, craftsmen, and their families, many of them struggling immigrants in the New World. One of the immigrants to occupy the dwelling was John Foley, an Irishman who resided there in 1840 with his wife Mary and son John, Jr., who was born in England sometime before the Foleys set sail for the Land of Opportunity. Foley, Sr., a shoemaker, left the archaeologists of

the twentieth century ample evidence of his profession. In 1850 the census listed as resident of 310 Cypress Street one L. L. Dooley, age twenty-five, a printer and an Irish immigrant. Like Foley, Dooley left behind him traces of his craft.

The house, late Georgian in style, is typical of others in the neighborhood, including the one next door at 312 Cypress Street and others in nearby blocks of Spruce Street. Three stories high and 20 feet wide, with a door on the east side of its front, it is made of red brick laid in Flemish bond (Figure 4.32). Its undersills and

Figure 4.32.

310 Cypress Street (left). (Photo by J. L. Cotter)

Figure 4.33.

Brick arch over cistern in basement of 310 Cypress Street. (Photo by J. L. Cotter)

Figure 4.34.

Silver cuff link and U.S. penny, dated 1801, found in the cistern at 310 Cypress Street. (Courtesy of Ellen Miller)

cellar window lintels are of grooved blue marble. Grooved blue marble also caps its "water table" (the bricks at the base of the house that project a little beyond the facade to deflect rain) and "belt course" (the projecting bricks on the upper story). Of two original two-story backbuildings, only one remains. The missing one was a kitchen without a cellar; it had also housed a privy, whose pit is still in evidence.

Like the Paschall House on Spruce Street, the house at 310 Cypress has a large cistern under the sidewalk in front of it. The cistern, which extends partway into the cellar, is surmounted by a brick arch that provides access to the pit as well as support for the house facade above (Figure 4.33). Before water mains and fire hydrants were installed in the middle years of the nineteenth century, cisterns like this one, kept partially filled by rain, were valuable and handy sources of water for combating fires; the water they provided was also used for laundry.

The cistern and the privy pit became the object of an archaeological study in 1976 when the owners of 310 Cypress Street, Ellen and David Miller, invited a University of Pennsylvania class in historical archaeology, of which Ellen Miller was a member, to continue the investigation they had initiated.[*] The description of the class's findings (Walbauer 1976; Lassen 1976) is synthesized in the following account.

The Cistern

The pit that extends from beneath the sidewalk in front of 310 Cypress Street partway into the cellar has a dry-laid brick lining. It is quite large;

[*] David Orr, then teaching at the University of Pennsylvania, joined John Cotter in directing the class's work.

its diameter varies from 8 feet 1 inch to 8 feet 8 inches. Such a large pit would traditionally have been used as a water-storage cistern, and despite its dry-laid lining—unusual for a cistern—this pit was probably used for that purpose; the clay soil surrounding the pit may have kept the water from draining away quickly.

To keep the brick arch over the pit from collapsing, the Millers had sunk a heavy steel framework of four upright beams into the pit's formidable quantity of fill. Investigation was therefore limited to a test area that would not affect the framework. The class excavated the test area to a depth of 6 feet and probed it to the pit's probable full depth of 8 feet 2 inches. No brick bottom appeared, so if the pit was used as a water cistern, a water-holding layer of clay beneath the pit must have acted as a seal. Odors emanating from the pit during the probe suggested there may have been privy material beneath the fill.

The pit had four poorly defined layers of fill. The bottom layer, a deposit of earth above the unpaved floor of the pit, contained no artifacts. The three layers above it yielded artifacts whose dates ranged from the late eighteenth century to the second quarter of the nineteenth century. Although the artifacts found in the top layer were few in number, they were particularly interesting. Among these objects were two whole wine bottles, both cylindrically shaped and dating from the early nineteenth century; one was marked "Wisterburg." Also found in the top layer were six sherds from a yellow earthenware Spanish oil jar. The jar, 14 inches high and 9 inches at its widest point, had been lightly glazed on the inside to retain liquid. Fashioned in two pieces and joined while wet, it had a pointed bottom. It closely resembled three Spanish olive jars found in the Market

Figure 4.35.

Pewter pipe tamper found in the early nine-teenth-century fill of the privy pit at 310 Cypress Street. (Courtesy of Ellen Miller)

transfer-printed creamware, 12 sherds of pearlware, and a few fragments of early nineteenth-century clay pipes.

Glass fragments were almost as numerous as the ceramic sherds. They included 1 whole, hand-blown elixir bottle; 3 pieces of window glass; 25 pieces of thin, light-green bottle glass, most of it from case bottles; and 57 fragments from dark-green bottles. Also found were 1 copper thimble; 8 unidentifiable objects of iron; 2 metal buttons; 1 iron sash weight; 21 pieces of shells, mostly oyster; and 128 bits of garbage bones. The silver cufflink and U.S. penny shown in Figure 4.34 completed the inventory. The penny was found in the bottom layer of artifact-bearing fill, and the date on it, 1801, established a *terminus post quem* for that layer of the pit; that is, had the fill in that layer been deposited before 1801, the penny could not have been there. Cumulatively, the evidence suggested that the pit was in use until about 1825, when it became the repository of humic earth, fireplace ashes, clinkers, and kitchen refuse and sweepings.

The Privy Pit

The Millers, who had already excavated the privy pit when the class began its investigation, had retained the 370 artifacts they retrieved for analysis in stratigraphic context. The evidence indicated that by 1810 the privy was no longer in use and that after that date the pit had been used for depositing ashes and trash. No artifacts were found in stratum 5, as the bottom foot of the 12½ feet of fill was called, probably because it represented undisturbed earth beneath the clean-out level. The next two layers of fill above this, each a foot deep and designated as stratum 4 and stratum 3, yielded 95 percent of the total

370 artifacts. The artifacts included cross-matching sherds of various vessels, which made some reconstructions possible, and their dates of manufacture ranged from about 1840 to 1865. Supporting the conclusion that the pit was still being used as a repository for trash in the 1860s was a bit of vulcanized rubber comb, which had to have been made after 1860.

The ceramic sherds found in strata 3 and 4 had come from 23 vessels of plain, glazed pearlware; 5 of these were shell-edged plates. J. Clementson, who was in operation from 1839 until 1871, and Barker and Son, in business from 1843 until 1860, were the manufacturers of 10 of the 26 transfer-printed vessels from stratum 4. Two of the transfer-printed vessels, both made by Adams, a manufacturer from 1798 until 1865, had registry marks showing dates of September 3, 1853, and May 31, 1855.

Strata 3 and 4 also yielded fragments of 67 glass vessels, 28 of which had been medicine bottles made of soda glass. One of the latter was embossed with "C. Ellis and Son," who operated in Philadelphia between 1828 and 1875. Lead glass was noted in 13 vessels; 8 of these seem to have passed through the hands of the Irish printer L. L. Dooley, who lived in the house in 1850, as they were stained with black printer's ink both inside and out. The earliest glass vessel identified, possibly made about 1800, was a green case bottle, 7 inches high with delicate walls.

Over 100 fragments of shoe leather were found in a fair state of preservation in strata 3 and 4, no doubt reflecting the industry of John Foley, Sr., occupant of 310 Cypress Street in 1840, Irish immigrant, and maker of shoes. Of the 15 items of metal, shell, ivory, cork, and other materials found in this fill, a pewter pipe tamper (Figure 4.35) stands out as an unusual ex-

Street houses of Franklin Court. Goggin (1964) identifies this type of jar as having been made between 1780 and 1850, which coincides nicely with the dates of the other artifacts found in the pit.

Included among the ceramic finds in the middle two layers of the pit were a sherd of Chinese export porcelain, a small English delft cup, a piece of hand-painted blue delft, and three sherds of salt-glazed stoneware. One of the stoneware sherds was scratch blue; two were white. Most of the ceramics, however, consisted of lead-glazed, slip-decorated, red or yellow paste earthenware (80 pieces in all). Also included in the ceramic count were 30 sherds of undecorated or

ample of historical pornography in Philadelphia. It is an exact replica in pewter of the brass pipe tamper of earlier date found in the privy pit in Carpenters' Court (see Figure 3.27). That it was found in the nineteenth-century fill of the pit at 310 Cypress Street indicates the continuing popularity of this tamper model.

No doubt Messrs. Foley and Dooley and the other occupants of 310 Cypress Street before them would have been astonished—one of them perhaps even a little chagrined—to find their castoff and discarded possessions the subject of so much interest and speculation in the last quarter of the twentieth century.

THE HILL-PHYSICK-KEITH HOUSE: DOWN ALMSHOUSE, UP MANSION

The garden of the Hill-Physick-Keith House at 321 South Fourth Street became the scene of an archaeological investigation in the summer of 1967, when a class in historical archaeology at the University of Pennsylvania began searching for traces of the City Almshouse, which occupied part of the site from 1733 until 1767. Despite intensive efforts by the seven members of the class, no trace of the almshouse appeared. What did result from these efforts was, however, impressive. Archaeological evidence of various other features of the property and a thorough search of the historical records, together with some artifacts encountered in the course of the investigation, created a portrait of the material culture of the occupants of the house and of their Society Hill neighbors. The report describing both the fieldwork and the historical research (Cotter and students 1967) provided the data for what follows.

A Society Hill Vignette

The Hill-Physick-Keith House, a graceful, freestanding Federal mansion on South Fourth Street at the corner of Cypress, began life as a modest, two-story brick building.

Richard Armitt, a house carpenter and a member of the Carpenters' Company, erected the first structure on the site sometime around 1767. The house stood on one of the lots recently subdivided from the old almshouse tract, shown in Figure 4.36. Armitt's house had one 16-by-18-foot room on each of its two floors and a 22-by-10-foot, two-story backbuilding; the walls of the house were 9 inches thick. In 1768 John Nixon, who eight years later would have the distinction of being the first to proclaim the Declaration of Independence to the public, bought the house from Armitt. This not inconsequential structure became a kitchen after Col. Henry Hill, a well-to-do wine merchant, purchased the property in 1782 and there, in 1786, erected a mansion befitting his status.

The transformation of the modest house into a mogul's mansion and the proximity of the mansion to the middle-class dwelling at 310 Cypress Street form an interesting and enduring monument to what went on in Society Hill between the late 1760s and 1800. As middle-class entrepreneurs profitably speculated in the house lots subdivided from the almshouse tract, they themselves achieved an elevated social status, and the character of the neighborhood likewise changed. Between 1769 and 1780, the occupations of owners of seventeen of the subdivided properties indicated a predominantly middle-class population:

15 associated with building trades

6 associated with other crafts

7 merchants

1 schoolmaster

1 government clerk

1 gentleman (i.e., one with sufficient resources not to need an occupation)

Between 1780 and 1800, the occupations took a decidedly upward social swing:

9 merchants

7 gentlemen

2 clergymen

2 professional men

6 engaged in building trades

9 engaged in other crafts

Among the upper class who owned the subdivided properties at this time were Robert Morris; Samuel Rhoads, a master carpenter who played a role in the construction of the Pennsylvania Hospital and the Franklin homestead; Thomas Willing, one of the city's wealthiest merchants; and, of course, Henry Hill (Files of the Philadelphia Historical Commission: Physick House documents).

In addition to being a wine merchant, Hill was a dealer in transportation and goods, a politician, and a noted horse breeder. The bulk of his estate was in land, which included many acres of working farms and plantations in Philadelphia County. Carlton, Hill's country estate on the heights overlooking the Schuylkill, is said to have had a private racecourse.* On several occasions during the Revolution when the Continental Army campaigned near Philadelphia, Carlton served as Washington's headquarters. Hill himself was active during the war in procuring supplies for Washington's army. Later, from 1780 to 1788, he served as a representative to the Pennsylvania Assembly and as a member of the state's Supreme Executive Council.

The house that Hill built at 321 South Fourth Street was entirely appropriate to his social standing. In the center of its elegantly simple, red brick front is a handsome double door surmounted by a large, graceful fanlight (Figure 4.37). The interior boasts thirty-two rooms, including a ballroom with intricate woodwork on the first floor. According to an 1815 insurance survey, the house then had on its east side a plain, open, two-story piazza and a two-story brick stable. Today the house is the only example left of the freestanding mansions that once interrupted the rowhouse pattern of Society Hill. The architect is unknown, but the design of the house and particularly of the stable bears a close resemblance to plans for other properties drawn by Samuel Rhoads. Hill undoubtedly knew Rhoads, for at the time of his death in 1785, Rhoads lived at 328 Spruce Street.

After Hill died of yellow fever in 1798, the house passed to his heirs. It

* Now covered by the Queen Lane Reservoir, Carlton was in Roxborough, northwest of the city in Philadelphia County.

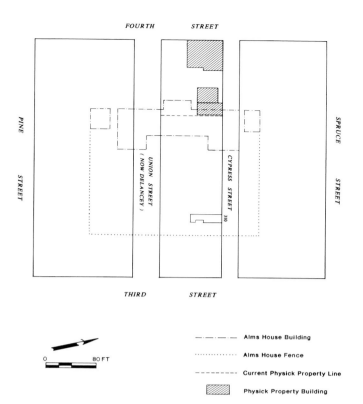

Figure 4.36.

The tract occupied by the City Almshouse from ca. 1730 to 1767. The dotted lines indicate the boundaries of the almshouse tract; the broken dashes outline the buildings of the almshouse complex. The cross-hatching shows the buildings of the Hill-Physick-Keith property, whose eastern boundary, indicated by dashes, overlaps the former site of the almshouse. (From Cotter and students 1967)

Figure 4.37.

The Hill-Physick-Keith House after restoration in the late 1960s. (Photo by J. L. Cotter)

Figure 4.38.

Portrait of Dr. Philip Syng Physick (1768–1837). (Courtesy of the Historical Society of Pennsylvania)

then passed in quick succession from James Vaux, gentleman, who bought it in 1815, to Abigail Physick, spinster, who bought it from Vaux and deeded it to her brother, Dr. Philip Syng Physick, in the same year. When Dr. Physick, who is credited as being the father of American surgery, moved into the house with his four children, he had just legally separated from his wife, Elizabeth—a rare thing in those days. Elizabeth Physick was the daughter of Samuel Emlen, a wealthy Quaker, and she bore Physick seven children, only four of whom lived. Historians have speculated that she might have suffered from depression or been addicted to laudanum, or

both. Although, by his marriage to her, Physick had improved his financial fortunes, his treatment of her at the end was apparently somewhat less than generous.*

It is unlikely that Elizabeth Emlen Physick ever lived in the house at 321 South Fourth Street. Philip Syng Physick (Figure 4.38), however, lived there until his death in 1837, and his tenure of the property was entirely in keeping with the upward social movement of the neighborhood. An inventory taken of his belongings at the time of his death gives us a very solid glimpse of the furnishings of an upper-class, early nineteenth-century Philadelphia household:

Drawingroom. 1 looking glass, 4 large landscapes, 1 small landscape, 14 chairs and cushions, 2 settees, mantle clock, 1 pier table, 1 pair of brackets, 2 lamp shades, carpeting, rug, 1 pair brass andirons, . . . 2 Venetian blinds, 1 centre lamp, 2 China vases, window curtains.

Front Room South Wing. Mantle glass, 3 mantle lamps, mahogany sideboard and knife cases, fire screen, 1 centre table, . . . shovel, . . . tongs, child's bureau, 1 print, 3 Venetian blinds, 1 secretary.

Entry. 1 dining table, 1 screen, 1 stove, 10 chairs, 1 clock in stairway.

Front Room Rear Second Floor. 10 mahogany chairs, washstand, pier glass, mahogany table, looking glass (side room).

Back Room Second Story. 2 blinds, 3 looking glasses, pair of pistols, 1 blunderbuss, . . . 1 watch, 1 mahogany table, arm chair and portable desk, carpet, sofa cushions, bed, mattress, table, 1 bedstead, 1 arm chair, mahogany pier table, clock, 2 prints.

Second Story North Wing. 2 bureaus, 2 prints, 2 tables, 1 sofa, glass, carpet, stove.

Back Room on Cypress Alley. 1 pair

of tables, 2 washstands, lot of chamberware, tongs, bellows, brush, large pair of andirons, small pair of andirons, stove, bedstead, 1 bed bolster and pillow, 2 hair mattresses, Ingram carpet, Brussels carpet (belonging to front room), night stools, 14 Windsor chairs, 1 looking glass, 1 bedstead.

Lumber Room. 2 grates, 1 box. . . .

Third Story Front Room. Carpet, sofa, 12 chairs, . . . 1 high post bedstead, 1 large mattress, 1 bed, bedding, looking glass, 3 prints, dressing table.

Back Room Third Story. Bedstead, mattress, bed and bedding, bureau, looking glass, washstand, 4 chairs.

Front Room Cypress Alley. High chest of drawers, table, looking glass, carpet.

Storeroom. Single bedstead, wardrobe, pine wardrobe, easy chair, bathtub, pine desk, 2 tables, lot of carpeting, lot of tin and tin boxes, 4 pair of blankets, lot of bed and window curtains.

Garret. 8 chairs, compass, lot of prints, easy chair, bathtub, lot of beds, . . . andiron and tongs, . . . lot of old curtains, old table, mahogany bedstead, 1 mahogany bedstead [*sic*], 13 old chairs.

Room over Kitchen. 1 mangle, bedstead, table and bureau, looking glass, Chinaware, lot of white and gold china (dinner set), knives and forks.

Front Room. Sofa, carpet, table, glass, 1 painting, shovel tongs, Canton dinner set.

Kitchen. Kitchen furniture, carpeting, looking glass, dresser, stove.

Office. 3 book cases, carpet, table and drawers, chair (old).

Stable. 1 old mare, carriage, double set Hackney's (silver mountings), 1 carriage, half interest in pr. carriage horses, 1 cow, grindstone.

Cellar. Lot of bottles, lot of coal in Cypress Alley, lot of wood, lot of wood (back cellar), lot of tubs, step ladder, lot of potatoes, fire proof, wines, lot of claret, 310 bottles of old wine ($930), lot of sherry.

Other (no room). Books, 1 lot of medical books, watch, lot of platen [*sic*] ware, silver including: tankard, gravy boats, surag [*sic*] dish, teapot, . . . snuffer and tray, soup ladles, gravy ladle, porringer, strainer, . . . wine syphon, fish knife, tea strainer, pitcher, silverware (table), salts, sugar tongs, 2 urns, 1 vase, 2 pitchers, punch bowl.

---

* In an article entitled "Dr. Physick and His House," George B. Roberts (1968) has brought to light the usually elided facts of Dr. Physick's personal life.

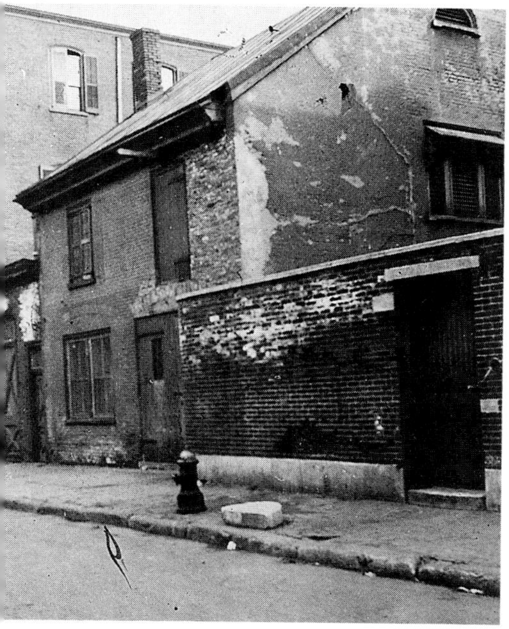

Figure 4.39.

The stable behind the Hill-Physick-Keith House before the shed that stood east of it was removed during restoration. The stable was also razed, and a service area was installed at the rear of the house. (Photographer unknown, ca. 1960)

Although this inventory clearly reflects Dr. Physick's wealth, it does not necessarily reflect all that might have been in the house at the height of his health and prosperity, when relatives, guests, and servants flocked about the premises. The estate, with debts owed, loans, land, and investments, amounted to $336,688.17 (Files of the Philadelphia Historical Commission: Physick House documents).

Dr. Physick's house escaped the worst of the abuses that were inflicted on other properties in the neighborhood between the 1850s and the 1940s. After his death the property passed down through succeeding generations of his descendants. Through the marriage of Physick's daughter, it passed first into the Randolph family and then into the Wister family. Elsie Wister Keith was the last Physick descendant to live there. During her tenure, the house underwent some rather strange renovations; she had an abhorrence of dust, and, to get rid of the dustcatchers, she had a great deal of woodwork ripped out. The baseboards were replaced by ceramic tiles, and the original banister gave way to an oak railing, which looked something like a baseball bat (Roberts 1968:85–86).

When Elsie Wister Keith died in 1940, the property was deeded to the Pennsylvania Hospital. Unused by the hospital, it deteriorated until the Philadelphia Redevelopment Authority took it over in 1965 and presented it for restoration to the Philadelphia Society for the Preservation of Landmarks. The restoration included the razing of the stable—an integral feature of the property—and of a one-story shed that had stood east of it (Figure 4.39). Also removed at this time was a greenhouse, originally 9 by 22 feet, that had been erected at the southeast end of the house in 1838. The greenhouse, which in 1921 was enlarged to 12 feet 6 inches by 25 feet 9 inches, had had a brick floor and brick furnace, a hipped slate roof, and wire-glass sides.

Figure 4.40.

Test trenches and features in the garden of the Hill-Physick-Keith House. (From Cotter and students 1967)

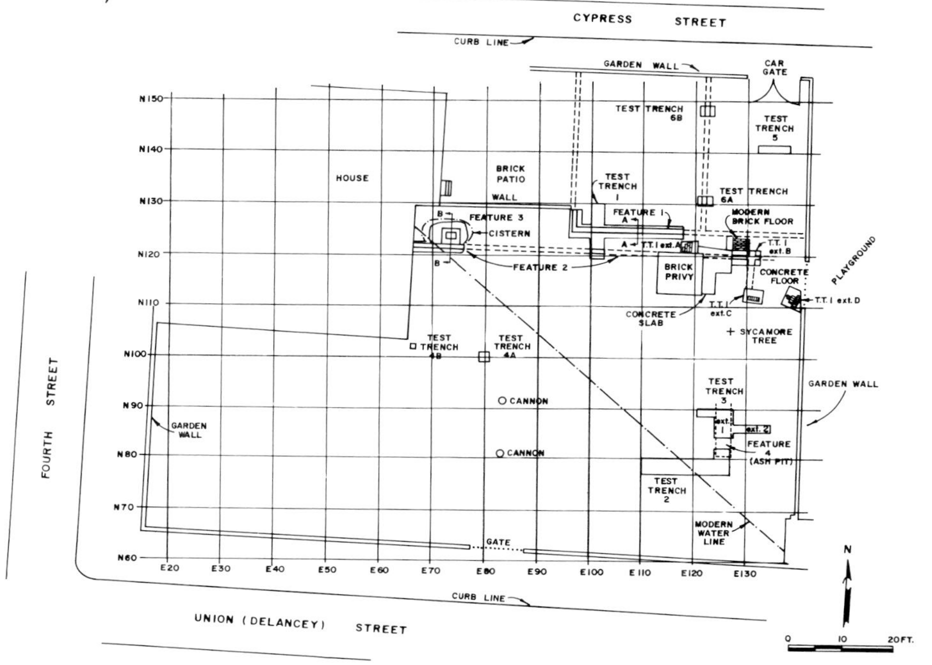

Archaeological Findings

Although a comprehensive investigation of the garden of the Hill-Physick-Keith House might yet reveal traces of the old City Almshouse, the investigation that University of Penn-

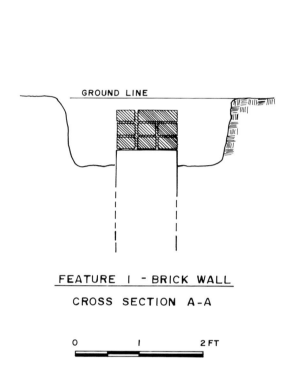

FEATURE 1 - BRICK WALL

CROSS SECTION A-A

0   1   2 FT

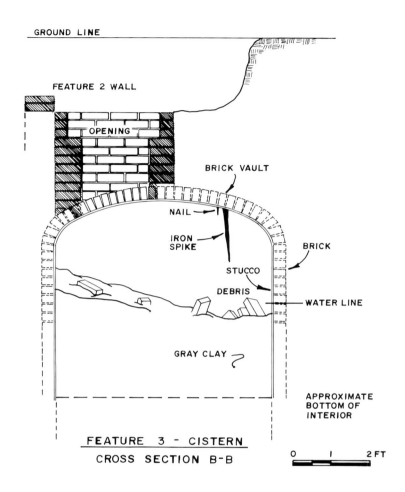

GROUND LINE

FEATURE 2 WALL

OPENING

BRICK VAULT

NAIL

IRON
SPIKE

STUCCO

DEBRIS

BRICK

WATER LINE

GRAY CLAY

APPROXIMATE
BOTTOM OF
INTERIOR

FEATURE 3 - CISTERN

CROSS SECTION B-B

0   1   2 FT

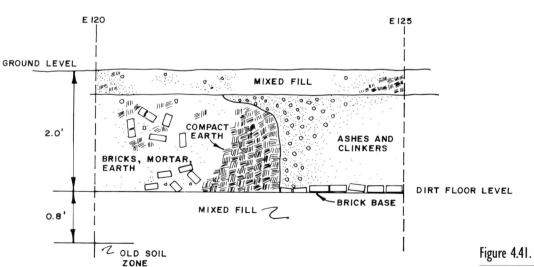

E 120

E 125

GROUND LEVEL

MIXED FILL

2.0'

COMPACT
EARTH

ASHES AND
CLINKERS

BRICKS, MORTAR
EARTH

DIRT FLOOR LEVEL

0.8'

MIXED FILL

BRICK BASE

OLD SOIL
ZONE

FEATURE 4 - ASH PIT

(NOT TO SCALE)

Figure 4.41.

Cross-sections of features found in the Hill-Physick-Keith garden. (From Cotter and students 1967)

Figure 4.42.

The brick privy (at upper right) in the Hill-Physick-Keith garden. The student is at work on test trench 1, which, to the right, intersects feature 1 (wall foundations of the stable) and, farther to the right, feature 2 (the brick walk). (Photo by J. L. Cotter)

Figure 4.43.

Opening of the cistern (feature 3) in the Hill-Physick-Keith garden. The brick walk (feature 2) appears on the left; the wall of the house is visible at upper right. (Photo by J. L. Cotter)

sylvania students carried out in the summer of 1967 did not. A comprehensive search, involving complete removal of the topsoil and total excavation of the area, was beyond the time and resources available to the class. The extensive tests that were made did, however, succeed in identifying four features mentioned in an 1815 Mutual Assurance survey of the property. Figure 4.40 shows the location of these features; Figure 4.41 shows them in cross-section.

Feature 1 consisted of the wall foundations of the recently demolished stable, located on Cypress Street 25 feet east of the mansion. The archaeological evidence, together with photographs of the structure, indicated a 32-by-16-foot brick structure on a fieldstone footing. Feature 2 was the base of a brick wall that had once run east and west 4 feet south of the stable and parallel to it. The wall had begun at the middle rear of the mansion, where, paired with another brick wall 8 feet away, it had formed a protective areaway around a brick walk. The walk had led toward the privy (Figure 4.42), which was some 40 feet east of the house and opposite the southeast corner of the stable, and had continued on past the privy toward the east garden wall. Feature 3 was a brick-lined, arched cistern (Figure 4.43) with an interior diameter of more than 5 feet. Located on the east side of the house near the walled walk, it extended partway into the cellar. Feature 4, an ash pit, was found in the southeast part of the garden, about 40 feet south of the stable.

The brick walls that enclose the garden on the south, east, and west are still intact. From Cypress Street, the east wall extends 95 feet south, where it joins the south wall, which runs 120 feet west to Fourth Street. The south wall is 40 feet from the

Figure 4.44.

Iron cannon barrels in the Hill-Physick-Keith garden, July 1967. The view beyond the garden walls is south. (Photo by J. L. Cotter)

Test trench 1 also produced 3 fragments of clay pipe stems with hole diameters of 5/64 of an inch and 2 fragments of pipe bowls suggestive of late eighteenth-century or early nineteenth-century dates; these fragments were found in two unusually deep deposits. Other artifacts found in this trench included 8 sherds of lead-glazed redware from kitchen vessels, 4 sherds of unglazed redware flowerpots, 5 sherds of salt-glazed utility stoneware, 1 mocha sherd, 1 sherd of slip-decorated earthenware, 1 of creamware, and 1 of blue-and-white-edged pearlware.

Near the ash pit, at 24 to 26 inches below the surface, test trench 3 yielded 2 clay pipe stems whose respective hole diameters were 5/64 of an an inch and 6/64 of an inch, 3 earthenware sherds with a tortoise-shell decoration, 1 sherd of creamware, 1 of blue-and-white oriental porcelain, and 1 of slip-decorated earthenware. All these artifacts appeared to date from the late eighteenth or early nineteenth centuries.

These artifacts, together with the features that were identified, give us some idea of the material culture of the Hill-Physick-Keith establishment. Augmented by the inventory of Dr. Physick's belongings and other gleanings from the written record, they paint a realistic picture of how the upper class of Society Hill lived during the late eighteenth and early nineteenth centuries.

mansion and 65 feet from the stable. Planted inside the brick walls of the garden, over 20 feet beyond the southeast corner of the mansion, were two iron cannon barrels, muzzles pointing skyward (Figure 4.44). Dating from the time of the Revolutionary War or several decades later, the barrels may have been placed there to support a garden arbor.

Since the goal of the investigation was to locate structural evidence of the almshouse, neither the privy pit nor features 3 and 4 were excavated. The artifacts retrieved in the course of the investigation came from the earth around the four identified features.

Test trench 1, dug in the vicinity of the well-traveled walkway between the house, the stable, and the privy, yielded 40 fragments of glass. Of these, 5 were from wine bottles, one of which had embossed on its bottom "S. Julien, Medoc," and 35 were from elixir or medicine bottles. Of the latter, 7 were mold-made and flat-sided; one had impressed on its side "Leidy's Chemical Laboratory, Philadelphia." The deposits in which these fragments were found began at 8 inches below the surface and extended to undisturbed earth, which generally lay between 14 and 31 inches from the surface.

THE U.S. MINT:
FROM COINAGE TO COIN BANK

The block of land bordered by Market, Arch, Sixth, and Seventh streets, where a federal office building and a multistory U.S. Court House now loom, was from 1792 until 1833 the home of the first U.S. Mint. In addition to that singular distinction, the block is historically interesting because of the changes that occurred on it between the eighteenth and twentieth centuries; these small-scale transformations were a particularly accurate reflection of the changes taking place in the city at large. The last change, which occurred in 1968–69 when the block was cleared of nineteenth-century structures and excavated for the construction of the new federal buildings, mirrored the rejuvenation of the inner city. It also gave the 1969 summer class in historical archaeology at the University of Pennsylvania the opportunity to record various features of the excavated site and to salvage a number of artifacts. The class report (Cotter and students 1969) provided the data for most of the following account.

The History of the Site

When the Pennsylvania State House was built between Fifth and Sixth streets in 1732, the land west of Sixth Street was largely wooded and uninhabited, and so it remained for many decades, with Philadelphians choosing instead to spread out north and south along the Delaware. By the 1790s, however, the city had expanded as far west as Ninth Street between Walnut and Race. In 1758 the Pennsylvania Land Company had

helped the westward expansion along by selling off several of its lots in the northern half of the block between Market, Arch, Sixth, and Seventh streets. Indicative of early attempts at developing the block is that sometime before 1762, a narrow east-west alley had been run through it; the alley came to be known as Filbert Street.

By the time the federal government took up its temporary quarters in Philadelphia in 1790, the block both north and south of Filbert Street was fairly well developed, and its heterogeneity was typical of neighborhoods throughout the city. Among the distinguished residents on the Market Street side of the block were George Clymer, a banker and one of the signers of the Declaration of Independence; Daniel Broadhead, one of Surveyor General Thomas Holme's notable successors; James Biddle, prothonotary of the Pennsylvania Supreme Court; and James Biddle's brother Charles, vice-president of the Supreme Executive Council of Pennsylvania and father of Nicholas Biddle, banker, writer, scholar, orator, and probably the most prominent Philadelphian of the 1820s and 1830s. Another famous resident of the block, although a temporary one, was the English scientist Joseph Priestley, who in 1796 lived in Susanna Stanley's boardinghouse at 607 Market Street. Among the less well known residents of the block who lent it its hybrid flavor were eight carpenters, three joiners, four blacksmiths, a wheelwright, a saddler, two coachmakers, a baker, a butcher, a grocer, some widows, and several shopkeepers and merchants. Until 1792, when the U.S. Mint took

over the premises at 35–43 North Seventh Street just north of Filbert Street, a Michael Schubert operated a distillery there.

Before the mint came into being, transacting business in America must often have been confusing, particularly in places such as Philadelphia, which drew large numbers of visitors. The most numerous coins in use were foreign ones: Spanish, French, Portuguese, and English. Adding to the confusion was that each of the states created its own currency and valued its coins at its own rates. Small wonder, then, that on April 2, 1792, less than two years after it arrived in Philadelphia, Congress passed an act to establish a mint that would produce a standard national currency. Due to the efforts of Robert Morris, Thomas Jefferson, and Alexander Hamilton, the new currency was based on a decimal system. Given that it was necessary to publish conversion books for those used to computing in British pounds and shillings, it seems safe to assume that enthusiasm for the new system was not completely unanimous. The coinage eventually produced at the mint included gold eagles (worth ten dollars), half eagles, and quarter eagles; silver dollars, half dollars, quarters (first known as "double dismes"), dismes (later "dimes"), and half dismes; and copper pennies and halfpennies.

It was not until November 1, 1800, that American merchants officially abandoned the British monetary system and adopted the new U.S. currency. In the meantime, the new mint was a busy place, with numerous obstacles to overcome. Its first director was David Rittenhouse, a talented Philadelphia clockmaker who had risen to become a noted scientist and an inventor and maker of scientific instruments. Rittenhouse's first order of business at the mint was to see to the construction of a complex of buildings—one for offices, another for smelting metal, and another for stamping coins. As shown in Figure 4.45, the office building was a double house with three entrances fronting on Seventh Street. It occupied the lots of 37–39 North Seventh; the lot next to it, at 35 North Seventh Street on the corner of Filbert, was empty, as were the two lots on its northern side. Behind the office building and separated from it by a small yard was the coinage building, and behind that was another small yard and a one-and-a-half-story smelting building. The rear of the smelting building had three windows looking out on a narrow lane called Bone Alley that connected with Filbert Street. Bone Alley prob-

ably got its name from the bones carted into the mint to be calcined and ground up into a clay paste for making crucibles. A small wooden shack with a 17-foot frontage on Filbert Street abutted the smelting building on the south.

The builders must have made quick work of it, for before 1792 was out, the mint was in operation, albeit on a largely experimental basis. It now had to deal with a number of metallurgical and technological problems. That it managed to solve them and to emerge fully mechanized by 1833 is a tribute to the talent and inventivness that abounded in the Federal city. When the mint first went into operation, its only means of power was that provided by men and horses. The solution to rolling the smelted metal was a team of horses that drove a rolling mill; for stamping the coins, a gang of men swung weighted screw presses (Richardson 1982:240–41). Very soon after the

mint struck its first issue of the penny coin, the yellow fever epidemic of 1793 ravaged the city, and Rittenhouse was forced to shut down the operation temporarily. One of the victims of the epidemic was the mint's first die designer and engraver, a portrait painter named Joseph Wright. Although Rittenhouse survived the 1793 epidemic, his tenure at the mint was short, for he died only three years later.

Other troubles were to beset the mint, including a fire that in 1816 destroyed the smelting building where the rolling mill had been housed. For the mint's workforce—both human and equine—that might not have seemed such a bad thing, for thereafter one of Oliver Evans' steam engines powered the mint's machines (Richardson 1982:241). By 1833, as the city entered the industrial age, the mint was fully mechanized and ready for larger quarters. In that year it moved to the northwest corner of Chestnut and Juniper streets, where William Strickland had designed for it a shining marble temple. Before it moved, the mint had the distinction of being the first government agency to implement a daylight-saving work schedule. From March 10 to September 10, work began at 5 A.M. and ended at 7 P.M., with an hour off for breakfast at 8 and two hours for din-

Figure 4.45.

The first U.S. Mint, painted by Edwin Lamasure in the early twentieth century. The rear building was used for smelting metal, the middle one was the coinage building, and the one fronting on Seventh Street was the office building. With the exception of the facade of the office building, the painting is conjectural, though based on historical evidence. (Courtesy of Independence National Historical Park)

Figure 4.46.

Photograph of the office building of the first U.S. Mint in July 1854. (Photo by F. D. Richards; courtesy of the Library Company of Philadelphia)

ner at 1. During the rest of the year, the workday was from 7 A.M. until 7 P.M., with an hour off for breakfast at 9 and an hour for dinner at 2 (Stewart [1924] 1974).

In 1836 the government sold the property at Seventh and Filbert streets to the Apprentices' Library for $10,000. After the library vacated the premises, the buildings were at various times occupied by a bricklayer, a carpenter, an umbrella maker, a silver plater, a restaurant, a cigar store, an electrical warehouse, a paperhanger, a shoemaker, a brass founder, a ragman, a locksmith, an expressman, and a machinist—in all, a fair sampling of the industries of the nineteenth-century city. Figure 4.46 shows the office building of the mint as it appeared in July 1854.

In 1907 the property came into hands of Frank H. Stewart, owner of an electrical supply business who wanted to clear the lot and erect a six-story steel-and-concrete building there. Stewart attempted to give the historic buildings to the city of Philadelphia with the proviso that the city move them to another site. The city, however, was dilatory about accepting the offer, and the chance to preserve the buildings was lost. On August 15, 1911, Stewart, mindful of Thomas

Donaldson's unsuccessful efforts some years before to save the Graff House, just half a block south of the mint, decided not to delay his plans any longer, and the final clearing of the lot began. The demolition resulted in the eradication of almost all structural evidence; thanks to Stewart's efforts, however, a good deal of the material evidence of the site does remain on record.

Stewart's Contributions to Historical Archaeology

As his concern for preserving the buildings might indicate, Frank Stewart was a bit of a history buff, and, as it turned out, he was also a capable researcher of historical and archaeological data. Before he was through with the first U.S. Mint, he had conducted a thorough investigation of the site and carefully recorded his findings. His final tributes to the mint were to write a book on its history, first published in 1924 and reprinted in 1974,* and to commission Edwin Lamasure to paint a picture of the site incorporating all available historical data and all the archaeological data Stewart himself had recorded. The painting is the one reproduced in Figure 4.45.

Figure 4.47 shows the measurements Stewart took of the buildings'

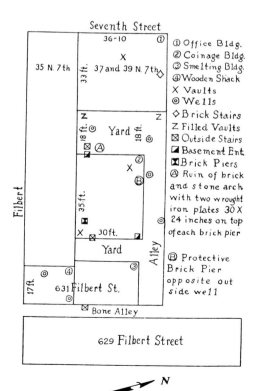

Figure 4.47.

Frank H. Stewart's diagram of the site of the first U.S. Mint. (Reproduced with permission of Quarterman Publications)

* Stewart's *History of the First United States Mint* contains not only a description of all the physical evidence he found on the site but also reproductions of photographs he took of the buildings before they were demolished. Unfortunately, the original negatives or plates of these photographs long ago disappeared, so that all that remains of the photographic record is what appears in the first edition of the book (1924) and, with some loss of clarity, in the reprint (1974), from which the data in the present account are taken. Stewart donated many of the "relics" that he found on the site, as well as some pertinent documents, to the U.S. Treasury; some are today housed in the Philadelphia Mint on North Fifth Street.

foundations and the features he recorded after the buildings were demolished. The first of the buildings to come down were the smelting building and the wooden shack next to it, which were razed in late 1907. Stewart noted that as the smelting building was demolished, a number of copper coins and planchets (metal blanks for stamping coins) fell from the overhead joists. Among the several penny and halfpenny planchets that appeared were two used for an experimental penny with a silver center, struck in 1792. Neither the smelting building nor the wooden shack had a basement, and of the two pits found beneath the shack, Stewart concluded that one had been a privy pit and the other had been a well used by the distillery that occupied the site before the mint was built.

The demolition of the coinage and office buildings in 1911, all done by hand, took four weeks to accomplish. During that time, Stewart made a number of interesting discoveries. He found, for instance, that the floors on both sides of the double building were on different levels, suggesting that the two sides of the house had been built at different times; walled-up windows in the basement wall between the two sides offered further proof of different building dates. Stewart also found a charred support from the roof of the coinage building, perhaps evidence of a fire known to have occurred in 1868 long after the mint had moved; the fire damaged both the office and the coinage buildings. Of the three vaults indicated in Figure 4.47, one was a new discovery, never before recorded. Its entrance steps were 4 feet below the basement floor, and the distance from the top step to the brick floor of the landing below was 14 feet. The landing was recessed to permit the door of the vault to swing open; the door was

missing, and the vault itself, 7 feet 8 inches deep, was empty. Because it lay where the elevator shaft for Stewart's building was to go, the vault was destroyed. Not shown in Figure 4.47 is a well that Stewart found near the south wall of 41 North Seventh Street; he had been told of its existence by an old man who remembered it from his youth.

Among the artifacts that Stewart saved in 1911 were a number of planchets and coins, including an 1816 penny, a damaged 1795 half dime, and an 1804 five-dollar gold piece. He also saved two large locks, one from the coinage building and one from the front door of 39 North Seventh Street, as well as some iron bars from basement windows and some hand-made split laths and hand-wrought nails. One item in which the Secret Service Department was particularly interested was the die of the eagle side of a half dollar, which Stewart dutifully turned over to them. Stewart also recorded finding mixed with rubbish "in one of the wells" a large number of small, white clay test cups and many large and small broken crucibles; this observation would be—for reasons that will shortly become clear—of special interest to the University of Pennsylvania class that investigated the site in 1969.

Although Stewart noted that the Philadelphia newspapers gave the demolition of the old mint buildings considerable publicity, there was obviously no effective public outcry for preservation. There was, however, as there would be more than half a century later, considerable public interest in artifact salvage. Small boys combed the dirt for "relics," and the workers who razed the buildings collected "metal scrap," which they sold to junkmen; included in the scrap were pieces of sheet lead that had been

used to level the floors of the coinage building. Unfortunately, although the coinage building's marble steps and doorsills could have been saved, they were broken up. But taken away intact by a dentist from Woodbury, New Jersey, to be used as a lawn adornment, was the sill of the middle door to 37–39 North Seventh Street.

The 1969 Investigations

In preparation for the construction of the federal buildings, the entire block between Market, Arch, Sixth, and Seventh streets was cleared of buildings in 1968, and in February 1969 a construction crew began excavating it to a depth of 15 to 20 feet. The excavation revealed some deep pits that extended below the excavation floor, and as work progressed, the site drew a number of artifact collectors (Figure 4.48). By June, when the class from the University of Pennsylvania began its investigation, the collectors had amassed quantities of bottles and ceramic items from the thirteen pits that had been uncovered. Although uncontrolled artifact collection is quite problematic to the professional archaeologist, three collectors, Albert Bauer and Dr. and Mrs. Peter Haimes, made their artifact finds available to the class for recording. Without such cooperation, important data would have been lost. In addition to examining these private collections, the class made a plane-table survey to record the locations of the thirteen pits (Figure 4.49). They also explored the pits to record natural stratigraphy and to salvage whatever artifacts remained (Figure 4.50).

As it happened, a good deal did remain. The earlier artifact collectors had selectively removed items of interest to them, generally choosing

Figure 4.48.

An artifact collector taking a contemplative moment in the bottom of a brick-lined pit south of the site of the first U.S. Mint. (Photo by J. L. Cotter)

Figure 4.49.

Student using an alidade in the plane-table survey of the block bounded by Market, Arch, Sixth, and Seventh streets. The survey recorded the locations of thirteen pits. (Photo by J. L. Cotter)

Figure 4.50.

Students uncovering the bottom of a well to record natural stratigraphy and to salvage artifacts in the vicinity of the first U.S. Mint. (Photo by J. L. Cotter)

whole or nearly whole ceramic and glass objects or those with some unique characteristic. Vast numbers of sherds were still present, but the integrity of the collection in each pit had been compromised. The class therefore had to decide which collections could be analyzed most profitably. Those chosen were the ones from the pits identified in Figure 4.51 as 2, 4, and 5. The class in due time carefully washed, labeled, sorted, identified, and inventoried each collection. Appendix 4.C contains a summary of their findings.

All three pits had evidently been dug as wells, for they were much deeper than privy pits would have been. They extended to about 15 to 25 feet below the original surface. Curiously, although the waterworks at Center Square began piping water to residences in this block between 1801 and 1807, the artifacts found in the pits indicated that the wells had not been filled until the mid-1800s. One likely explanation for the delayed

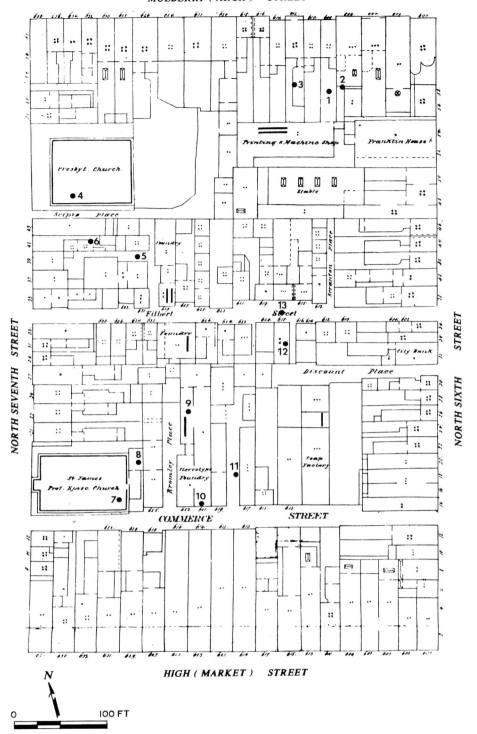

MULBERRY (ARCH) STREET

Printing & Machine Shop

Franklin House

Presbyt. Church

Stable

● 4

Scripta Place

● 6

Foundry

● 5

Filbert *Street*

13

NORTH SEVENTH STREET

Foundry

City Bank

12

Discount *Place*

NORTH SIXTH STREET

9

Soap Factory

8

11

St James Prot. Episc. Church

Bromley Place

Stereotype Foundry

7●

10

COMMERCE STREET

HIGH (MARKET) STREET

N

0   100 FT

Figure 4.51.

The locations of the thirteen pits superimposed on an 1860 insurance map of the block bounded by Market, Arch, Sixth, and Seventh streets. The site of the first U.S. Mint extended east to the alley bordering 629 Filbert Street. The Presbyterian church north of the mint was built in 1837 and razed in 1881. (From Cotter and students 1969)

closing is that the public water supply was unreliable or inadequate, or both.

The reason Stewart's mention of having found many test cups and crucibles "in one of the wells" was of such interest to the class is that three similar items appeared in the bottom fill of pit 5, which was located east of 39 North Seventh Street. It seems almost certain that this pit was the same one Stewart found near the northeast corner of the coinage building (see Figures 4.47 and 4.51) and that Stewart's cups and crucibles came from the fill at the top of it. Figure 4.52 shows the three small, fire-resistant earthenware dishes retrieved from the bottom of pit 5; all were undoubtedly used in the experimentation and testing that went on in the early years of the mint.

An equally interesting artifact from pit 5, unearthed by the Haimeses, was the turnip-shaped coin bank of unglazed redware shown in Figure 4.53. Such items were familiar to nineteenth-century Pennsylvanians of German extraction, and, indeed, as Figure 4.54 shows, they have an even longer association with the Germanic tradition, dating back to the days of Pieter Bruegel the Elder.*

Although Stewart made no mention of having found other artifacts in the same well as the test cups and crucibles, it seems likely that that was the case. In any event, it was certainly the case at the bottom of pit 5, where the earthenware dishes and coin bank were found amid a wealth

* Kittredge (1974:136) reported that a knob-topped coin bank with a slit opening on the top was found amid evidence of Norse occupation excavated in Dublin. It is tempting to speculate that such items may have been in use even as early as ca. 800 B.C. in Homeric Greece; artifacts from this period include small, globe-shaped redware models of granaries with a circular hole, rather than a slit, sitting high on the shoulder of the vessel. Such models can be seen in the University Museum of the University of Pennsylvania and in various other museums that have collections of Hellenic artifacts (also Stokes 1978:67).

Figure 4.52.

Fire-tolerant earthenware dishes found in pit 5 on the site of the first U.S. Mint. Four-and-a-half inches wide at the rims, these dishes were used to fire-test metals for minting. (Photo by J. L. Cotter)

Figure 4.53.

Left, unglazed redware coin bank from pit 5 on the site of the first U.S. Mint. (Photo by J. L. Cotter; courtesy of Dr. and Mrs. Peter Haimes) *Below left,* thirteenth-century unglazed pottery coin bank from a medieval site on High Street, Dublin. (Courtesy of O'Brien Educational, Dublin) *Below right,* eighth-century B.C. miniature graineries from Greece. (Courtesy of the University Museum, University of Pennsylvania)

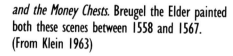

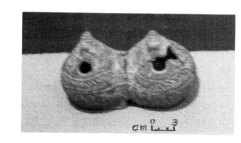

Figure 4.54.

Below, detail from Breugel's *Avarice; below right,* detail from his *Battle of the Piggy Banks and the Money Chests.* Breugel the Elder painted both these scenes between 1558 and 1567. (From Klein 1963)

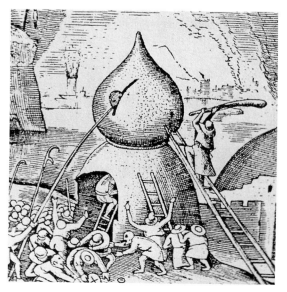

of ceramic wares of all kinds. The dates of the ceramics, which ranged from the first days of the U.S. Mint to about 1848 or slightly later, indicated quite clearly that the deposit had no relation to the distillery that occupied the site before the mint. The inference was that pit 5 was filled within a relatively short time with material that had accumulated on the site between 1792 and the mid-1800s.

Pit 2 was in the back of the lot of 606 Arch Street. Here, in 1798, William Montgomery had built a three-story tenement; the lot may, however, have been occupied by an earlier structure. In 1831 a physician by the name of Charles D. Meigs bought the property, which he in turn sold to George Burgin, who owned it for twenty-five years. In 1860 William Knight acquired it and rebuilt the house as a four-story building. The 51 ceramic vessels and 27 glass objects found in pit 2 dated from the period of Knight's ownership of the property or late in Burgin's. Among the bone objects found were 2 toothbrush handles and 2 curved brush handles, each 4 inches long.

Pit 4 was on the lot of 45 North Seventh Street, which was apparently developed as early as the 1760s. In 1807, by which time the residences in this block had piped water, John Wagner built a three-story house on the site. In 1837 Wagner's house gave way to a Presbyterian church, which was demolished in 1881. Most of the artifacts found in pit 4 dated from before 1807, and they indicated that the pit was probably filled soon after Wagner built his house on the lot and that it was in any case certainly filled before 1837. The earthenware recovered from pit 4 ranged in date from the first half of the eighteenth century into the nineteenth century. The median manufacturing date of the six scratch-blue stoneware vessels recovered was 1760. Plain creamware, with a mean manufacturing date of 1791 (South 1977: Table 31), was strongly represented, as was oriental porcelain, with a median manufacturing date of 1808. The oriental porcelain suggested an association with the merchants of the China trade who inhabited this block.

Figure 4.55 shows a few of the interesting glass objects from the Haimes and Bauer collections. Evidently, some medical-supply business had been transacted within the block in the course of the late nineteenth century. The hypodermic syringe suggests a post-1865 date; morphine, used in the treatment of casualties during the Civil War, became more widely prescribed in the postwar period.

Appendix 4.C gives some idea of the remarkable number of items recovered from what could only have been the lower fill of the wells in the block bounded by Market, Arch, Sixth, and Seventh streets. The artifacts attest not only to the experimental bent of the workers at the first U.S. Mint but also to the tastes and habits of Philadelphians from most walks of life. Whether the ceramics found in the pits were used by the diverse population that inhabited the block or whether they were the cast-off broken wares of the merchants in the block actually amounts to the same thing, for merchants, after all, usually try to deal in what sells.

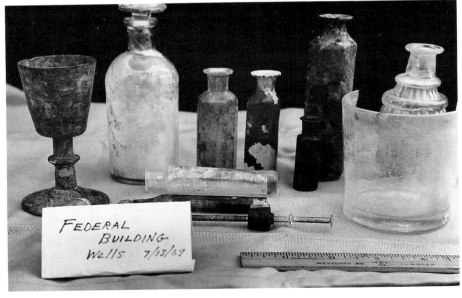

Figure 4.55.

Glass objects found in pits in the vicinity of the first U.S. Mint: a goblet, a tumbler, medicine bottles, and a hypodermic syringe. (Photo by J. L. Cotter)

OLD ST. PAUL'S CHURCH: PHILADELPHIA'S ELITE BURIAL CUSTOMS

Although a great deal of archaeological research has focused on Amerindian burial grounds, very little has focused on other American burial grounds. Most historical archaeologists in the United States have apparently been content to heed the words of Williamsburg archaeologist Ivor Nöel Hume, who in 1968 had this to say on the subject of excavating human remains: "Unless the circumstances are very special, I would advise quickly covering them over and forgetting that you ever saw them" (Nöel Hume 1970:160). Nöel Hume's advice is at odds with the viewpoint of an early English antiquarian, Sir Thomas Browne, who in the seventeenth century wrote on the subject in a more positive light, noting that in excavating human remains "we mercifully preserve their bones and piss not upon their ashes" (Wilkin 1889: 5). Sir Thomas's view reflects a long-established tradition in the Old World of interest in, and excavation of, the burial grounds of earlier periods.

Whatever the ethical rights and wrongs of excavating burial grounds, there is little doubt that a great deal of valuable anthropological information can be gained by studying the burial customs of earlier times and the physical remains of human beings, as evidenced by numerous studies of the burial customs of past civilizations. Archaeological work carried out at old St. Paul's Church, located on Third Street near Walnut, illustrates that even without osteological examination of the remains, such research can provide a wealth of cultural information. Conducted by John Milner Associates, and reported by Parrington (1984a), the archaeological study involved both extensive historical research and the examination of five burial vaults in the churchyard.

Burial Customs in Old Philadelphia

Before cemeteries came into vogue in the mid-nineteenth century, most Philadelphians were buried in churchyards, and most were buried in earth graves. Earth graves continued in popularity even after the introduction of the cemetery, for the alternative, vault burial, although it was thought more prestigious than an earth grave, was also more expensive. Vaults provided some protection against grave robbing, a common occurrence after a new earth grave was dug, but no doubt a more important factor in their popularity was the prestige associated with them. The prestige was such that it seems to have triumphed over a common belief of the eighteenth and nineteenth centuries that odors from decaying corpses were responsible for the spread of yellow fever and other contagious diseases. Vault burial received the endorsement of doctors, who declared that it was "not unwholesome to the community" (Atticus 1838:20), but it is not altogether unlikely that the doctors were influenced by wealthy patients who wished to "enjoy" the prestige of being buried in the family vault. A recommended practice for dealing with the odors in vaults was to cover the floors with lime and whitewash the walls (Atticus 1838:20); another was the use of sealed, metal coffin liners.

The most distinguished members of the community were buried not in churchyard vaults, but in crypts within the church itself—in walls or beneath floors, chancel, transept, or nave. The least distinguished— the poor and the destitute—were buried neither in the church nor in the churchyard. For them, there was the "potter's field," a public burial ground where bodies were summarily deposited at minimal expense, often in multiple, unmarked graves. Potter's field was not the exclusive domain of the poor and destitute, however. When mass contagion resulted in mass deaths, as happened in Philadelphia when the all-too-familiar plagues of typhus, yellow fever, and smallpox struck, time and sanitation did not allow delayed or ceremonious burial. Unless the family of the deceased had the power to arrange a discreet churchyard burial, the epidemic victim was interred in a mass grave, hastily dug on public ground.

In the early 1700s funerals in Philadelphia were often quite elaborate, attended by much "pomp and circumstance." By 1765 they had become more restrained; dignitaries such as Alderman W. Plumstead were buried in "the plainest manner," as was a gentleman named B. Price, who went into the ground in "an oak coffin [with] iron handles" (Watson 1909, v. 2:489–90). Funeral fashions are not static, however, and the early nineteenth century saw a return to more grandiose and costly burial rituals.

The change in funeral fashions coincides with a transition from the Quaker and Puritan view that death is the end of an earthly journey, upon which the body should be unceremoniously abandoned, to the idea that the body is a precious entity, whose remains should be treated accordingly. While the Puritans believed in a transition, the Quakers held to their view that as lack of ostentation ruled the living, so too it should grace the dead. Accordingly, the Quakers continued to bury their dead in plain boxes or in the conventional hexagonal, "pinch-toed" coffin, in graves marked, if at all, by low, unadorned headstones, without epitaphs and sometimes even without identification. Frequently, for economy's sake, graves were superimposed, with one coffin interred over another. Indicative of the Quaker attitude toward death is that when the Arch Street Meeting House was built on the site of an old burial ground on Arch Street between Third and Fourth streets in 1803–4 (Figure 4.56), the members of the meeting were neither disturbed

by the prospect of invading the graveyard nor dismayed by the skeletal remains that the excavations produced.*

For those who went along with the transition, the corollary to holding the body in high esteem after death was that it should be handsomely displayed for viewing in an elaborate and expensive container. As the concept changed, so did the container and even the terminology. By the mid-nineteenth century, the hexagonal coffin had become a rectangular "casket," denoting, of course, a con-

* In 1968 the graves beneath the Arch Street Meeting House were again disturbed when the basement of the building was enlarged. At the invitation of the Meeting, John Cotter and fellow archaeologist George Demmy inspected the evidence that the excavations had unearthed. They found and photographed clear evidence of a superimposed grave, the coffin of an infant having been buried over that of an adult. They also found traces of other burials extending as far as 8 feet 8 inches below ground level. Although a search of the records of the old burial ground might have identified the bones, the Meeting—true to tradition—took no further action; the renovations were completed without delay.

tainer for a rare and costly jewel. This period also saw the onset of attempts to preserve the corpse by placing a sealed, metal liner inside the coffin (Morley 1971:73). After the Civil War, embalming techniques replaced the sealed liner as a means of preserving remains.

As the concept of the corpse changed in the nineteenth century, it was accompanied by a growing realization that burial grounds were in appalling condition. Writing about burial grounds in rural areas, one nineteenth-century observer noted that "the state into which they have fallen shows little reverence or regard for those who sleep beneath their sods" (Brazer 1841:146). In urban burial grounds for the poor and indi-

Figure 4.56.

The Arch Street Meeting house in 1989. (Photo by J. L. Cotter)

Mausoleums in Laurel Hill Cemetery. Some of Philadelphia's most prominent nineteenth-century architects—among them John Notman, William Strickland, and Thomas U. Walter—designed mausoleums for Laurel Hill Cemetery, which in its early years was an important tourist attraction, drawing up to 30,000 visitors a year. (Photo by J. L. Cotter)

gent, the situation was equally bad, if not worse (Jackson 1980:48). Public graves were sometimes as deep as 30 feet, with coffins heaped one on top of another to within a few feet of the surface. In West Philadelphia, at the site of a mid-nineteenth-century potter's field, now occupied by Franklin Field on the Penn campus, bodies have been accidentally disinterred at a depth of over 20 feet. Burial conditions of the poor at Philadelphia's First African Baptist Church cemetery, in use from about 1823 to 1842, may have been more typical. Archaeological excavations there, described in Chapter 6, showed that as many as five bodies were interred in the same grave.

The need for more burial space in the rapidly growing city of Philadelphia was evident even before the end of the eighteenth century. By 1794 the small graveyards of the city's churches were clearly inadequate, and the municipal government had begun buying land for burials outside the city's built-up area (Brown 1905:548H). Gradually, a number of privately owned cemeteries appeared. Ronaldson's at Ninth and Bainbridge streets opened in 1828, followed in 1836 by Laurel Hill Cemetery on the east bank of the Schuylkill and in 1849 by Woodlands Cemetery in West Philadelphia at Woodland Avenue and Thirty-ninth

Street. By the 1850s the "cemetery beautiful" movement was flourishing.

Laurel Hill Cemetery, situated three miles upstream from the Fairmount Waterworks, was to become a highly elaborate resting place for the "most responsible families in every walk of life," as *Godey's Lady Book* expressed it in 1844 (McDannell 1987:276). It and West Laurel Hill Cemetery, established some years after Laurel Hill farther up the Schuylkill on the west bank of the river, were the supreme achievements of Philadelphia's "cemetery beautiful" movement. They displayed every mode of monument, from simple cross to towering obelisk and stately mausoleum (Figure 4.57), and every variation in between—all provided at substantial cost amid a landscape of well-tended lawns and carefully selected and nurtured trees.

Interestingly, the driving force behind the creation of Laurel Hill Ceme-

tery was a Quaker. After John Jay Smith, director of the Library Company and a prominent member of the Arch Street Meeting, lost his five-year-old daughter to scarlet fever, he returned to the burial ground in which she had been interred, only to find he could not be sure which unmarked grave was hers (McDannell 1987: 275–76). He recalled the disturbance of graves that the construction of the Arch Street Meeting House had incurred; he remembered how some of the graves held water like the clay basins they were; and he experienced a most un-Quakerly concern for the dead, which led him to join the majority of non-Quaker Philadelphians who favored more ostentatious and enduring memorials. In 1835 Smith, together with five other men, founded the "Laurel Hill Cemetery Company." The company soon purchased thirty-two acres of land that had been part of a large country estate on the east-

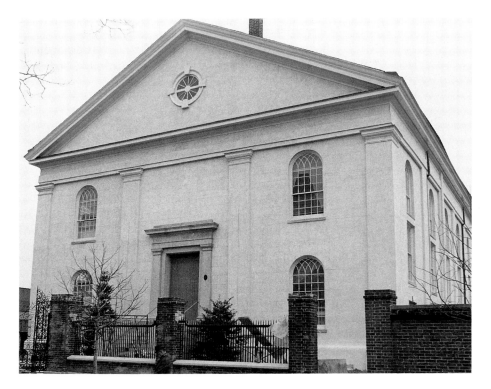

Figure 4.58.

St. Paul's Church on Third Street near Walnut. (Photo by J. L. Cotter)

ern heights overlooking the Schuyl-kill, and it hired John Notman, one of the most distinguished architects of the day, to design the grounds.

After the 1850s, an increasing number of bodies were interred in park-like suburban settings similar to that of Laurel Hill. Urban church-yards, however, remained in use throughout the nineteenth century, with vaults preferred by those who could afford them.

The Vaults of St. Paul's

The burials that took place in St. Paul's churchyard during the eighteenth and nineteenth centuries reflected the fu-neral rituals of the non-Quaker seg-ment of Philadelphia's upper class. Founded in 1760 by a dissenting group from Christ Church, St. Paul's (Figure 4.58) was located in Society Hill on Third Street near Walnut, not far from the site of the City Alms-house (soon to give way to house lots) and conveniently close to the homes of the city's elite. The church's first minister was the Reverend William McClenachan, former assistant min-ister of Christ Church and a follower of the English Methodist evangelist George Whitefield. McClenachan's "Railing and Revilings in the Pulpit" of Christ Church had led to his being relieved of his duties there, which in turn had led his outraged supporters to split from that congregation and to establish the Anglican—if somewhat dissidently Anglican—church of St. Paul's (Barratt 1917:45).

As minister of the new church, McClenachan found himself preach-ing to a congregation that was, by worldly standards anyway, impressive. The continuing prestige of the con-gregation is reflected by the church-yard's large number of burial vaults, most of them constructed during the nineteenth century to hold the remains of the deceased in a style befitting, and denoting, his or her erstwhile status on this earth. The vaults hold the remains of many once-prosperous individuals, including Edwin Forrest, a well-known actor of the mid-nineteenth century.

In 1984 five of the vaults in St. Paul's churchyard, disturbed in the course of restoration, became the focus of archaeological study. According to an exhaustive history of the church (Barratt 1917), sixty-eight individuals had been buried in these five vaults between 1788 and 1871. The history gives details of the individuals and as-signs numbers to each vault. The vaults examined were numbered as 35 through 39 (Figure 4.59).

All five vaults were constructed of brick and butted onto the south wall of the church. About 8 feet square and 10 to 11 feet deep, each was also floored with brick. In some vaults, drainage systems had been installed beneath the floors to prevent flooding. Access was provided by 5-by-2½-foot openings in the roofs of the vaults; the openings were sealed with large slabs of stone.

The remains in each vault were in variable states of preservation. Some of the coffins were intact; others had completely disintegrated, with the bones also in very poor con-dition. The contents of each vault were photographed and drawn to scale (Figure 4.60), but no osteologi-cal examination of the skeletal re-mains was carried out.

Vault 35 contained three intact cof-fins, one on top of the other, and be-neath them considerable debris from coffins that had disintegrated. One of

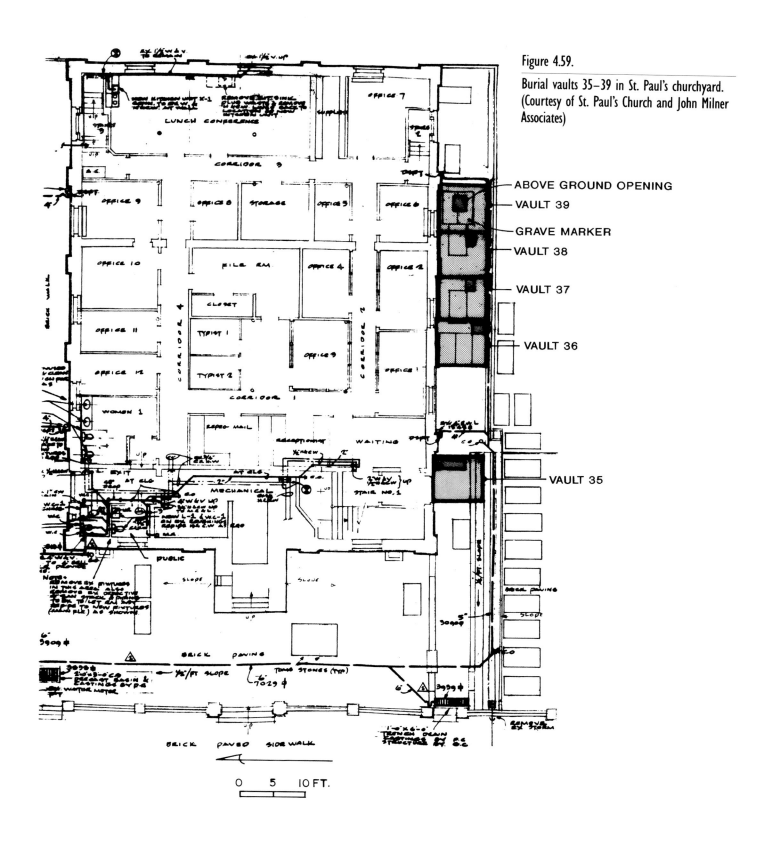

Figure 4.59.

Burial vaults 35–39 in St. Paul's churchyard. (Courtesy of St. Paul's Church and John Milner Associates)

ABOVE GROUND OPENING

VAULT 39

GRAVE MARKER

VAULT 38

VAULT 37

VAULT 36

VAULT 35

0   5   10 FT.

the two top coffins bore a plate with the individual's name and date of death; the date given, 1898, is at variance with the church history, which states that the last interment in vault 35 was in 1867 (Barratt 1917:225).

In keeping with the Christian tradition of burying the deceased with the head to the west and the feet pointing east, the bottom coffin in vault 35 was aligned east-west. The two that rested on top of it, however, were aligned north-south. In other vaults, two more coffins were found in a north-south alignment. The unorthodox alignments apparently occurred as the vaults filled up; to stabilize the top coffins and keep them from tipping over, they were placed at right angles to the ones below.

The coffins were either hexagonal or rectangular in shape. Two metal coffin liners were noted, each with a glass window at the head end. The function of these was presumably to allow the mourners to view the deceased, for, as Nöel Hume (1970:158) has pointed out, "the view from the inside must have been monotonous." The wooden cases surrounding these liners had long since rotted away, but their elaborate brass handles remained. The decoration on the handles— winged escutcheons on one pair, winged cherubs on the other—were reminiscent of the motifs on New England gravestones.

According to the church history, three bodies were interred in vault 38. All are still there. One of these was the body of a woman who died in Alabama in 1831; her remains were reburied in the family vault in 1852 in a wooden coffin 3 feet long. The church history listed relatively larger numbers of bodies buried in vaults 35, 36, 37, and 39, and with the exception of those in vault 39, all still appear to be there. Of the sixteen bodies reported

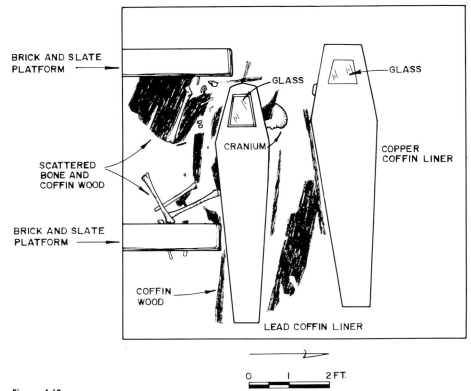

Figure 4.60.

Contents of one of the vaults in St. Paul's churchyard. (Courtesy of John Milner Associates)

to have been interred in vault 39, only four seem to remain. Although lime on the floor would hasten the deterioration of the bones and could account for the absence of the bodies, vault 39 had no lime. The reason for the conflict between the written documentation and the archaeological evidence remains a mystery, as does the discrepancy between the date of death on the coffin plate in vault 35 and the date that the church history gives for the last interment in that vault.

Despite these discrepancies, the archaeological evidence by and large bears out the written record of the burial customs of wealthy, non-Quaker Philadelphians during the nineteenth century. It substantiates

the change in the way they regarded death, as plain wooden hexagonal coffins with simple iron handles gave way to elaborate rectangular caskets with ornate handles, and sealed, metal coffin liners became rarer as embalming became more popular. The archaeological evidence also provides a few insights not forthcoming from the historical record: while some church sextons carried out their duties in orthodox fashion, sprinkling lime on the floors of the vault and whitewashing the walls, others apparently did not, and in yet other cases, the sextons disregarded the burial tradition of the Christian church, as well as the wishes of some of those interred, by placing the coffin in a north-south alignment. Although the study provided no information on the health and nutrition of the deceased, as no osteological examinations of the remains were made, it did throw considerable light on the cultural activities of the living who arranged and participated in the burial of the dead—an aspect of nineteenth-century culture that most historians and archaeologists have chosen to ignore.

WASHINGTON SQUARE: THE SAGA OF THE UNKNOWN SOLDIER AND THE ANONYMOUS ARCHAEOLOGIST

Some of the most intriguing bits of archaeological adventure and discovery are little known and not officially recorded. The saga of the search for the Unknown Soldier of the American Revolution is one such story. Other than contemporary newspaper accounts, nothing has ever been published about how the unknown soldier, whose remains today rest below an eternal flame in Washington Square (Figure 4.61), came to be identified.[*] The eternal flame flickers in front of a wall bearing a bronze replica of Jean Antoine Houdon's standing figure of Washington, which Thomas Jefferson commissioned Houdon to create in 1785. Graven on the wall are the words, "Freedom is a light for which many men have died in darkness." The words, interestingly enough, are not those of Washington, who might have wished he had said them, but of John J. Pullen, a copywriter in the 1950s for one of the several publishers on the square. The design of the memorial and of the low brick wall surrounding the square was the work of architect G. Edwin Brumbaugh; the idea for the memorial, however, was conceived by members of the Washington Square Planning Committee.

[*] Data for this account are from J. Duncan Campbell (1956) and from personal correspondence with both Campbell and John Witthoft.

The Historical Facts

The memorial and the quest for the soldier to whom to dedicate it came about because of the unsightly state of Washington Square at mid-twentieth century. Inside a dilapidated wooden fence was a scene of total neglect; below ground, a public lavatory seemed to be a particularly attractive magnet for social deviants of all kinds. To improve the setting, executives from business houses on the square combined to form the Washington Square

Figure 4.61.

Washington Square: The Memorial to the Unknown Soldier of the American Revolution. (Photo by J. L. Cotter)

Planning Committee. In 1954, as Independence Square just across the way was beginning to hum with the sounds of restoration, the committee came up with the idea of a memorial that would focus on a replica of Houdon's statue of Washington. The memorial was also to include the ca. 1714 Letitia House, which was to be moved from Fairmount Park, where, as described in Chapter 3, it had gone amid a flurry of historical solicitude in 1888. Ultimately, the committee, perceiving a certain *non sequitur,* dropped the idea of including the Letitia House, and it was left where it sat and still sits, isolated by the Schuylkill Expressway, as the committee turned its attention to the forgotten soldiers of the Revolutionary War.

Over the next two years the committee developed the idea of a Revolutionary War memorial that would include the actual remains of a Continental soldier already buried beneath the sod of Washington Square. Given the large number of bodies known to have been buried there, it would be a formidable undertaking to identify one that fit this bill. During the 1700s the square had served as a burial ground for paupers, many of whom were summarily deposited without coffins. It had also been the final place of repose for many of Philadelphia's epidemic victims, including an unknown number who fell to the notorious "yellow jack" epidemic of 1793 and to numerous epidemics of various kinds before and after that. These civilians—paupers dead of malnutrition, others of dread disease—share their final resting places, and some of their causes of death, with the thousands of soldiers who died in Philadelphia during the Revolutionary War.

Between 1776 and 1778 the earth of Washington Square was virtually crammed with mass graves containing the bodies of Continental soldiers. Some died in the Pennsylvania Hospital at Eighth and Pine streets, others in the Bettering House for the poor on Spruce Street between Tenth and Eleventh, and still others in the Walnut Street Prison, just across Sixth Street from Washington Square. After heavy fighting in New Jersey in the latter part of 1776, the Pennsylvania Hospital and the Bettering House teemed with American men dying of wounds and disease. In a letter to his wife, Abigail, on April 13, 1777, John Adams described the scene in Washington Square:

I have spent an Hour, this Morning, in the Congregation of the dead. I took a Walk into the Potters Field, a burying Ground between the new stone Prison, and the Hospital, and I never in my whole Life was affected so with so much Melancholly. The Graves of the soldiers, who have been buried, in this Ground, from the Hospital and bettering House, during the Course of the Last Summer, Fall, and Winter, dead of the small Pox, and Camp Diseases, are enough to make the Heart of stone to melt away. The Sexton told me, that upwards of two Thousand soldiers had been buried there, and by the Appearance, of the Graves, and Trenches, it is most probable to me that he speaks within Bounds. (Butterfield, Garrett, and Sprague 1963, v. 2:209)

On September 11, 1777, five months after Adams wrote this letter, the Battle of the Brandywine was waged, and fifteen days after that, on September 26, the British took Philadelphia. Shortly thereafter the Walnut Street Prison became a hellhole of pain and suffering as American prisoners of war confined within its walls perished of disease and malnutrition. In July 1983, for the benefit of the congressional subcommittee involved in granting landmark status to Washington Square, Dr. Roger Moss, executive director of the Athenaeum of Philadelphia, described the fate of the Continentals who landed in the Walnut Street Prison (Roger Moss, personal communication, 1988):

While Hollywood would have us believe that eighteenth-century wars were gentlemanly affairs, I can assure you that eighteenth-century military prisons were as bad as anything in the twentieth century. The testimony of one citizen soldier who survived the winter of 1777–1778 as a prisoner in the Walnut Street Jail should be sufficient. Jacob Ritter had been in the battle of Brandywine and was captured by Hessian troops, taken to Philadelphia, and thrown into Walnut Street Jail. According to John Fanning Watson who interviewed him later,[*] Ritter and his fellow prisoners were fed nothing for three days and were regularly beaten by their keepers. Watson reports, "As the winter advanced, the prisoners became excessively cold. They had no extra covering for sleeping, and the window panes being much broken, . . . the snow and cold entered therein freely. They huddled together for warmth; but with that they also became common companions of their lice and vermin. . . . Ritter had seen several [of the captives] pick and eat grass-roots, scraps of leather, chips, pieces of the rotten pump, &c., to assuage and abate their hunger. . . . It was common to see several [prisoners] watching for the chance of rats from the rat-holes, which, when captured, were eaten." According to Ritter, eight to twelve American captives died every day in this charnel house of pain and misery. Their bodies, dragged by the heels from the unheated cells and flung into carts, joined the 2,000 already in unmarked graves in what is now the peaceful, green space of Washington Square. We probably will never know exactly how many American prisoners of war were executed or died of starvation and illness during the winter of 1777 and 1778.

As for the fate of the British prisoners of war who occupied the Walnut Street Prison after the Americans retook Philadelphia in June 1778, historical

---

* Ritter was seventy-six years old when Watson (1909:300–1) interviewed him in May 1833.

records on this side of the Atlantic are less explicit. Certainly, however, many of them also rest in the earth beneath the green grass of Washington Square, and it is not inconceivable that as archaeological analysis of human remains continues to improve, more of the whole "melancholly" story may be revealed than Philadelphia would care to remember.

The problem before the Washington Square Planning Committee was how to distinguish among this huge number of burials and to select from them one that was undoubtedly the body of a Continental soldier of the American Revolutionary War. For this awesome task, the committee sought out the services of Lt. Col. J. Duncan Campbell (U.S.A., ret.). Then a consultant to the William Penn Memorial Museum in Harrisburg and later its director, Campbell had already made a reputation for himself as a resourceful historical and archaeological investigator at Fort Ticonderoga and elsewhere. Having accepted the assignment, Campbell soon realized that he needed assistance, especially the help of an energetic, resourceful, and able professional archaeologist. State Archaeologist John Witthoft was the perfect choice. Witthoft, whose reputation was already established, was later to become known as an authority on the archaeology of historic and prehistoric sites, as well as one of the most popular professors ever to lecture in the Department of Anthropology at the University of Pennsylvania. There was one immediate difficulty, however.

The state administration at the time was rock-bound Republican, and Witthoft worked for the state's Historical and Museum Commission in Harrisburg. Philadelphia, on the other hand, was solidly in the hands of reform Democrats, headed by Mayor Richardson Dilworth. Witthoft said

he would accept the assignment only if leave from his job at Harrisburg could be arranged, if he could work completely unidentified, and if all necessary legal and political safeguards were taken to protect the work from disruption. Above all, there was to be no publicity whatever.

The Curtis Publishing Company, then still resplendent in its building on the north side of the square and a considerable power in Philadelphia as well as a moving force behind the Washington Square Planning Committee, was, through the good offices of its vice-president, Harry A. Batten, able to assist Campbell and Witthoft in their efforts. Specifically, a court order and legal papers authorizing the removal and reburial of a body needed to be obtained; in addition, the Washington Square Planning Committee was to furnish four fit laborers to assist in the digging and all necessary tools, as well as a coffin for the reburial, and secrecy was to be the object at all times. Batten's secretary meticulously incorporated all of the necessary requirements into an agreement satisfactory to both the archaeologists and the sponsoring agency. And so the quest began.

The Dig

On a Monday morning in November 1956, four able-bodied and well-briefed laborers duly appeared, armed with tools, and the archaeologists, armed with what archival data they had been able to muster on the uses of the square as a cemetery, went to work, answering the inquiries of passersby with two words: "Soil testing." The digging started with authority and all available energy in the southwest quadrant of the square. The immediate objective was to locate a mass

grave or trench, such as those noted by John Adams, in which the soldiers who died at the Pennsylvania Hospital and the Bettering House were buried. A series of test pits 3 feet in diameter, identified in Figure 4.62 as tests 1–4, were dug to the level of the original topsoil, where Colonial and early Federal artifacts appeared. The artifacts were buried beneath a layer of fire debris, attributable to an 1810 conflagration that destroyed many buildings in old Philadelphia. The massive cleanup that followed the fire had resulted in the deposit of as much as 2 feet of rubble here and probably elsewhere in the square. By the end of the morning, the archaeologists had discovered the graves of three paupers, identifiable by their having been wrapped in canvas and interred without coffins. They were not disturbed.

At just about the moment the three paupers came to light, a contingent of Philadelphia police appeared to inquire who was disturbing the square and why. They were presently joined by the Fairmount Park Police, then in charge of all parks in the city. Campbell informed them he was not free to say any more than that they were working for the Washington Square Planning Committee and were engaged in looking for geological samples. The puzzled police had no notice from their superiors that any such work had been authorized. With considerable confidence, the archaeologists suggested that they check with police headquarters and with the mayor's office. Having checked, the police returned with the news that no one knew anything about the digging and no authorization was on record.

With this, Witthoft persuaded the police to wait while he rushed over to the Curtis Building to ask Batten what had happened to the previously assured permits. As luck would have it, Batten was in New York for the day, but his secretary was able to convince Witthoft, who was by now ready to take his final leave of Washington Square, to return and deal with the police while she attempted to get to the bottom of the problem. Meanwhile a small crowd had gathered in anticipation that the presence of the police and the disturbance of the earth could have some interesting results, especially since no explanations were forthcoming.

After a brief interval of general confusion, the secretary's call to the administrators of urban law and order to remind them of the agreements took effect. The city police at the site got a call from their chief and with a shrug of their shoulders departed. Their ranking officer resignedly explained to the archaeologists, "We're not supposed to know what you're doing. Just do it."

After this incident, the work progressed with unprecedented facility. The police set up a watch to protect against vandalism. In five days of concentrated industry, a remarkable amount of ground had been tested, but the soil beneath the late eighteenth-century sod zone had revealed only traces of single graves, with no other burials beneath them. Some were ostensibly the graves of paupers.

On the fifth day, a large dark area 6 feet wide appeared in the subsoil in the northwest corner of the square (test 9). It indicated the outline of a trench. Cautiously, and with bated breath, the archaeologists exposed an economical 2 feet of soil. This was the right area; Witthoft and Campbell recognized that they had found the end of a mass grave (areas D and C, Figure 4.62, Sketch B).

At 4½ feet below the old topsoil, the trench yielded the remnants of a pinch-toed walnut coffin; part of the coffin had been sectioned when a utility line was run through it (area B,

1. No fill: distinct undisturbed soil zones at 7' depth.

2. No fill: distinct undisturbed soil zones at 6'6" depth.

3. 13" topsoil; 24" fill rubble of brick, mortar, glass, china, animal bone. Pit dug to 5' depth.

4. No variation from #3.

5. Indeterminate fill; sand, gravel in undisturbed zone at 7'6" depth.

6. Topsoil and fill to 3' depth. Undisturbed zone at 4' depth.

7. Topsoil and fill to 2'6" depth. Undisturbed zone at 4' depth.

8. Topsoil and fill to 2'6" depth. Undisturbed zone at 4' depth.

9. Grave area. See enlarged sketch.

Washington Square

Sketch A

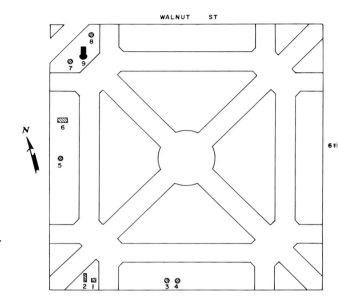

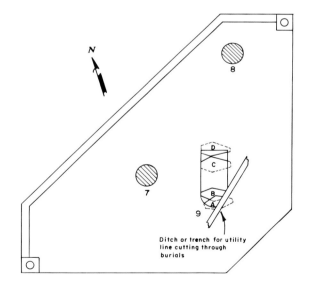

Northwest Corner
Washington Square

Sketch B

Ditch or trench for utility line cutting through burials

Figure 4.62.

Excavations in Washington Square. (From Campbell 1956)

Figure 4.62). After carefully exposing what was left of the remains, the archaeologists determined that the body had been that of a male adolescent, fifteen years of age or a little older. The lad could have been one of the many fifteen- and sixteen-year-olds who fought in the Continental Army.* To confirm that this was indeed a mass grave, Campbell and Witthoft carefully explored the earth beneath the burial. There they found the bones of a male in his late twenties. This burial, too, had been disturbed by the utility line.

Setting the evidence carefully aside once more, the archaeologists continued taking out more subsoil from beneath these two burials, working now at a depth often over their heads and in alluvial silts whose easily collapsible sides were adding anxiety to sweat. The laborers kept onlookers well back from the dig so that the archaeologists would not become burials themselves.

Presently a third burial appeared at a depth of 6 feet below the sod zone (area A, Figure 4.62). This time the undisturbed remains of a male twenty to twenty-two years old lay within the traces of an oak coffin. The epiphysial development in each tibia attested to his youth, as did his fine, full set of teeth. His crossed arms lay at a good distance from his lower rib cage, and the distance between ulnae was considerable as well, indicating muscular arms and a thick chest. The young man would have been about 5 feet 8 inches tall. Here indeed might

* One adolescent soldier of the Continental Army was Joseph Plumb Martin, who enlisted at fifteen and at the age of seventy achieved literary fame by writing his war memoirs, published anonymously by his son in 1830 in Hallowell, Maine, as *A Narrative of Some of the Adventures, Dangers and Sufferings of a Revolutionary Soldier, Interspersed with Anecdotes of Incidents That Occurred within His Own Observation.* In 1979 Acorn Press reissued the book under the title *Private Yankee Doodle.* It describes Martin's experiences during the war, in which he fought from 1776 through to the last major battle at Yorktown in 1781.

be the remains of a stocky farmboy soldier. The front of the well-preserved skull had evidence of a "plow wound," possibly caused by a musket ball that had grooved the skull without penetrating. This was as probable a soldier as the archaeological evidence permitted; no buttons from a uniform were found, but if he had had a uniform, it would probably have been too valuable to bury with him. That he had been placed in a winding sheet was indicated by the presence of two brass, round-headed straight pins. Dr. J. Lawrence Angel, physical anthropologist and forensic specialist, then at the University of Pennsylvania Medical School, later verified the sex, approximate age, and head wound of the deceased.

Just as Campbell and Witthoft were beginning to savor the sweet smell of success, some interesting, if rather disruptive, developments were taking place among the group of spectators. Not all were casual passersby. One elderly lady, still glowering among the group, had already informed Colonel Campbell that he would "not escape the fires of Hell" because he disturbed "the sacred dead." Others of the onlookers were members of a fundamentalist religious sect who were taking the occasion of a small crowd to proclaim the Word to those who would listen and not excluding those who would not listen. Among those who were letting it be known that they did not care to listen was a group recently deprived of access to one of

their favorite meeting spots, the underground public lavatory within the square. By this time, the archaeologists were in a towering hurry to collect their evidence as unobtrusively as possible and depart.

When Campbell and Witthoft presented their evidence to the vice-president of Curtis, yet one more surprise awaited them. Batten, delighted with the results of the exploration, readily complied with their request for enough lumber to erect a fence around the site of the discovery; his secretary's phone call to the right city office resulted in the timely appearance of the fencing as well as a crew to put it up. Batten then disclosed his surprise. Now that success was at hand, he had decided that secrecy for the enterprise had been a mistake, and to ensure full press and television coverage, he had called the mayor's office asking that the media be notified.

At this point, Witthoft, his cover suddenly blown by fiat, took flight, departing through the rear door of the Curtis Publishing Company with a

Figure 4.63.

J. Duncan Campbell (in the trench) fielding questions from city officials as the excavations in Washington Square drew to a well-publicized end. (Courtesy of Penn Mutual Life Insurance Company)

brief word to Campbell to carry on. And carry on the colonel did (Figure 4.63). After having found shelter and anonymity for three hours in the backroom of his friend, stamp dealer Earl Apfelbaum, whose little nook was opposite Wanamaker's, Witthoft returned to the site. There he found the fence down, the pits hurriedly filled, the entire scene trampled by hundreds of feet, and the last of the television crews and press departing. Fortunately, the bones, which he and Campbell had carefully placed in an empty carton, were safely stowed away in the Curtis Building.

The bones, encased in a handsome coffin, were in due time reinterred with appropriate ceremony at the Memorial to the Unknown Soldier of the American Revolution. The story of the quest for the unknown soldier, discreetly edited for the press, let it be known that the evidence had been "archaeologically verified." Indeed it had—with one unpublicized exception. Whether our stocky farmboy soldier hailed from the hills of New Hampshire or the downs of Devonshire we shall probably never know.

APPENDIX 4.A:
ARTIFACTS AND FAUNAL REMAINS FROM
FEATURE 16, NEW MARKET EAST

Analyses of Artifacts

Ceramic vessel types: 747 vessels from 9,722 sherds.

	Vessels (%)	Sherds (%)
Plain-glazed earthenware	15.0	15.9
Slip-decorated earthenware	10.5	8.7
Tin-glazed earthenware	6.7	8.1
Creamware	26.6	33.7
White salt-glazed stoneware	17.4	18.2
Porcelain	17.8	13.5
Miscellaneous types, less than 1% each	5.0	1.1

Tablewares accounted for 53.7 percent of creamware vessels. Rim types were:

Queen's rim	1
Scalloped rim	3
Plain rim	8
Royal rim	24 (all undecorated)
Feather rim	30

Creamware vessels:

Sugar bowls	3
Bowls of various sizes	17
Chamber pots	10
Tankards	7
Jugs	2
Miscellaneous vessels	2

Tablewares accounted for 74.1% of the white salt-glazed stoneware vessels. Rim types represented were:

Plain	5
Panel	11
Queen's	10 (molded barley decoration)
Scalloped	14
Royal	19

Other salt-glazed stonewares:

Bowls (all undecorated)	7
Chamber pots (all undecorated)	5
Tankards	4
Tea bowls	1
Jugs	1
Miscellaneous vessels	4

Porcelains:

Plates	43
Saucers	25
Tea bowls	21
Bowls	14
Coffee cups	14
Dessert dishes	7
Bleeding bowls	4
Teapot lids	1
Handles	2
Indeterminate	2

Marked porcelain pieces were:

Worcester	36
Bow	24
Oriental	16
Liverpool	11
Bristol	4
Bonnin and Morris (Philadelphia, 1769–1772)	4

From Liggett 1981:156–64.

Analysis of Faunal Remains

Faunal remains: 11,009 bones

Cattle (*Bos taurus*)	9.13%
Sheep (*Ovis aries*)	8.20%
Pig (*Sus scrofa*)	2.29%
Deer (*Odocoileus virginianus*)	0.17%
Chickens (*Gallus gallus*)	19.52%
Other domestic fowl (Ducks: *Anas platyrhyncha*; geese: *Anser anser*; turkeys: *Meleagris gallopavo*)	3.51%
Wild duck (*Anatidae* spp.)	1.17%
Wild birds (6 unknown species)	10.91%

Large migratory waterfowl (sp.?)	0.04%
Frog? (unidentified vertebrate)	2.15%
Turtle: Softshell (*Trionyx* spp.); Snapping (*Chelydra serpentina*); Diamondback terrapin (*Malaclemys terrapin*)	0.84%
Rabbit, domestic European (*Oryctolagus cuniculus*)	0.46%
Cat (*Felis familiaris*)	5.66%
Dog (*Canis familiaris*)	0.30%
Sturgeon (*Acipenser* spp.)	4.80%
Bass or bluefish (*Morone/Pomatomus*)	1.14%
Shad (*Alosa* spp.)	2.70%

Cod (*Gadidae* spp.)	0.66%
Herring or Smelt (*Culupeidae/Osmeridae* spp.)	3.32%
Human (infant)	0.47%
Unidentified or unidentifiable	19.75%

Oyster and clam shells, crayfish, crab, and whelk shell present but not counted.

From Liggett 1981:156–64.

APPENDIX 4.B:
ARTIFACTS FROM THE WALNUT STREET PRISON

Comparison of data from the Walnut Street Prison with the Carolina pattern.

Group	Walnut Street		Carolina Pattern	
	Count	Percentage	Mean	Range
Kitchen	5,033	68.84	63.1	47.5–78.0
Architectural	1,900	25.99	25.5	12.9–35.1
Furniture	3	0.04	0.2	0 – 0.7
Arms	4	0.05	0.5	0 – 1.5
Clothing	43	0.59	3.0	0 – 8.5
Personal	76	1.04	0.2	0 – 0.6
Tobacco pipes	162	2.22	5.8	0 –20.8
Activities	90	1.23	1.7	0.1– 3.7
	7,311	100.00	100.00	

Analysis by Jiyul Kim, in Cotter et al. 1988, using data from South 1977:95–96.

Artifacts from the Walnut Street Prison by group and class.

Artifact Classes and Groups	Walnut Street Prison Artifact Class Frequencies	
	Count	Percentage
KITCHEN ARTIFACT GROUP		
Ceramics	3,409	
Wine bottle	979	
Case bottle	36	
Tumbler	253	

continued next page

Artifact Classes and Groups	Walnut Street Prison Artifact Class Frequencies	
	Count	Percentage
Pharmaceutical-type bottle	64	
Glassware	274	
Tableware	16	
Kitchenware	2	
Total	5,033	68.84
BONE GROUP		
Bone fragments	(286)	
ARCHITECTURAL GROUP		
Window glass	518	
Nails	1,354	
Spikes	24	
Construction hardware	2	
Door lock parts	2	
Total	1,900	25.99
FURNITURE GROUP		
Furniture hardware	3	0.04
ARMS GROUP		
Musket balls, shot, sprue	2	
Gunflints, gunspalls	2	
Total	4	0.05
CLOTHING GROUP		
Buckles	2	
Thimbles	1	
Buttons	19	
Scissors		
Straight pins	21	
Hook-and-eye fastener		
Bale seals		
Glass beads		
Total	43	0.59
PERSONAL GROUP		
Coins		
Keys		
Personal items	76	1.04
TOBACCO PIPE GROUP		
Tobacco pipes	162	2.22
ACTIVITIES GROUP		
Construction tools	2	
Farm tools		
Toys	16	
Fishing gear		
Stub-stemmed pipes		
Colono-Indian pottery		
Storage items		
Ethnobotanical items		
Stable and barn items		
Miscellaneous hardware	1	
Other	71	
Military objects		
Total	90	1.23
TOTAL (NO BONE)	7,311	100.00

Analyses by Jiyul Kim in Cotter et al. 1988, using data from South 1977:95–96.

APPENDIX 4.C:
ARTIFACTS FROM THE VICINITY OF
THE FIRST U.S. MINT

Since collections from pits 2, 4, and 5 were made by collectors who sought mainly restorable vessels, quanta here are not fully representative of all artifacts found in the pits. However, sufficient material was saved to indicate proportions in ware vessels. The collections were made to secure as many sherds as possible so as to restore vessels. Nonceramic objects were also saved.

Artifacts from the U.S. Mint vicinity.

Artifact group	Type	Description
Collection from Pit 2		
Ceramic	Red earthenware	1 unglazed vessel; 5 lead-glazed vessels
	Yellow earthenware	2 banded bowls
	White earthenware (characteristically pearlware)	1 shell-edge blue plate; 1 plate, 9 vessels of transfer-printed blue; 2 plates of polychrome enamel—green, pink, and blue; 1 blue, hand-painted bowl; 3 undecorated plates; 24 vessels (indeterminate)
	Porcelain (oriental)	1 cup
Glass	Clear glass bottles	3 medicine-type; 2 molded scent bottles
	Green and brown bottles	2 case bottles; 8 miscellaneous shapes
	Stemmed wine glass	1
	Tumblers	3
	Plate glass	7 plain; 1 undecorated
Bone	Fowl	2
	Fish	1
	Mammal (indeterminate)	2
Stone	Slate	2 fragments
Collection from Pit 4		
Ceramic	Yellow earthenware	1 bowl
	Red earthenware	Unglazed: 4 tiles, 1 modelled finial; glazed: 1 clear-glazed vessel; lead-glazed, dark-brown: 5 chamber pots, 6 miscellaneous vessels; slip-decorated: 2 open bowls, 8 miscellaneous vessels
	Kaolin tobacco pipes	3 stem fragments
	Delft (tin-glazed enamel earthenware)	1 blue-on-white dish; 1 dish; 3 vessels
	Creamware	Plain, edge-molded decoration: 4 plates, 1 sugar bowl; plain, undecorated: 4 dishes, 5 bowls, 1 cup, 2 miniature cups, 1 miniature saucer, 1 teapot
	White earthenware (pearlware variants)	Luster-decorated, with copper band: 1 vessel; transfer-printed, dark blue: 2 pitchers, one with inscription ". . . (H)e Arrived in Am(erica) . . . sane with his purse . . . (chan)nel to France & is now . . . acclamations of a grate(ful). . . ."; mottle-decorated: 1 pitcher, 1 plate, 1 bowl; polychrome enamel: 2 bowls, 1 dish, 1 pot and lid; 1 sprig-applique decorated basket bowl (probably Leeds)
	Stoneware	Unglazed, red paste: 1 crock; white, salt-glazed: undecorated—4 vessels, 1 miniature vessel, 3 plates, 1 dish; enamel painted—1 dish; sgrafitto blue-on-white—1 pitcher, 1 bowl, 1 bowl cover, 1 condiment pot lid, 1 cup
	Porcelain (oriental)	Blue, hand-painted: 4 bowls, 10 dishes, 4 saucers, 15 cups, 10 assorted vessels; blue, hand-painted, with red-and-gold overglaze: 2 bowls, 1 cup; polychrome enamel overglaze: 1 hexagonal sauce dish, 2 bowls, 1 dish, 1 plate, 7 sauce dishes, 5 cups, 3 demitasse cups, 4 assorted vessels

continued next page

Artifact group	Type	Description
Collection from Pit 4, Continued		
Glass	Bottles	Green and brown: 1 case bottle, 2 globular, with pontil mark, 2 straight-sided without pontil marks, 2 assorted sizes; 1 clear glass with pontil mark
	Glass tumblers	2 with pontil mark on bases
	Glass goblet	1 plain
	Window glass	13 clear fragments
Metal	Iron	1 building staple; 1 3-inch nail
	Copper	1 1-inch-diameter button
Stone		1 flat slate
Faunal remains		1 oyster shell; 7 cattle bones and teeth, 1 leather fragment
Collection from Pit 5		
Ceramic	Specialty ceramics	3 4½-inch-diameter scorifying dishes
	Kaolin tobacco pipes	1 plain, 2 with Masonic symbol decoration
	Yellow earthenware	1 green-glazed tobacco pipe; mocha, banded: 3 chamber pots, 2 pitchers, 5 bowls, 1 teapot with tortoise-shell decoration, 1 condiment pot lid, 4 assorted vessels
	Red earthenware	Unglazed: 1 coin bank, 3 flower pots, 1 vessel with impressed decoration, 5 assorted vessels; clear-glazed (lead), undecorated: 2 bowls; slip-decorated, lead-glazed interior: 12 bowls, 2 crocks, 14 dishes, 1½-inch tile; clear-glazed, interior only, rope applique decoration: 3 bowls; interior-glazed, dark brown to black: 4 bowls, 4 pitchers, 1 crock, 8 pots, 1 chamber pot, 14 vessels; exterior glazed only: 1 cruet, 2 pitchers, 1 crock, 5 other vessels; glazed both sides: 2 cruets, 3 chamber pots, 4 porringers, 7 pitchers, 7 pots, 2 cups, 1 bowl, 5 other vessels; brown-glazed exterior, blue tin-glazed interior: 1 mixing bowl
	White earthenware (pearlware)	3 human figurines, glazed and painted
	Mocha-type decoration	16 bowls, 5 pitchers, 1 mug, 57 assorted vessels
	Sponge-decorated	6 saucers, 5 cups, 2 dishes
	Luster-decorated	2 saucers, 1 teapot
	Sprig-decorated	1 saucer, 5 cups, 1 tureen
	Edge-decorated	Green: 54 plates, 2 serving platters; blue: 65 plates, 3 rectangular platters, 1 round serving vessel, 1 oval platter
	Hand-painted polychrome, floral-decorated	3 sugar bowls (one with lid), 1 creamer, 1 pitcher, 1 teapot lid, 1 bowl lid, 13 teacups, 12 saucers, 3 dishes, 3 bowls, 32 assorted vessels
	Delft-style, blue-decorated	4 bowls, 1 plate, 1 cup, 3 teapots, 1 lid, 57 assorted vessels
	Transfer-printed	1 bowl with red, blue, and yellow added, marked "Tropick/J. Wedgwood" and "Peter Wright & Sons/Importers/Philadelphia"; 3 bowls with brown decoration; 6 plates with brown decoration; 2 plates, 3 bowls, 2 cups, 1 vessel with maroon decoration; 2 bowls, 1 plate, 1 vessel with green decoration; 2 cups, 1 pitcher, 1 vase, 1 bowl with lavendar decoration
	Transfer-printed, with flow-blue decoration	7 saucers marked "1846" and "38291/TF & Co." (for Thomas Fells) and impressed with "Real Ironstone"; 5 cups dated 1846, same pattern as saucers; 2 saucers marked with "JAPAN" and "TF & Co."; 3 plain saucers; 1 saucer with gold luster; 1 cup with gold luster; 4 cups; 1 teapot; 4 plates, one marked "CHINESE," 1 "WEDGWOOD"; 1 punch bowl
	Transfer-printed, with dark-blue decoration	9 plates marked "DAGGER/BORDER/J. WEDGWOOD," and 3 cups and 2 saucers marked the same; 7 plates with willow pattern; 2 willow-pattern plates marked "STONEWARE/B&T"; 1 fancy tureen, with willow pattern; 2 small tureens, 1 soup plate; 1 pitcher; 3 bowls; 1 teapot; 1 serving dish

continued next page

Artifact group	Type	Description
Collection from Pit 5, Continued		
	Transfer-printed, with light-blue decoration	2 salt cups, 4 mugs, 9 cups, 3 saucers marked "PASTORAL/J&TF"; 1 plate marked "SPANIARD/PW&Co." 1 plate marked "ORIENTAL/WR Co."; 1 teapot marked "TRELLIS/ Ra Stevenson Semi China"; 2 bowls, 1 plate marked "CAN . . ."; 2 saucers marked "W. ADAMS & SONS"; 1 plate marked "COL . . ./W. ADAMS & Sons"; 1 bowl marked with same "PASTORAL" design as above but marked "PETER WRIGHT & SONS/IMPORTERS/ PHILADELPHIA"; 2 saucers, 2 plates, 1 large round serving dish, 1 rectangular serving dish, 1 creamer, 2 tureen lids, 2 bowls marked "ABBEVILLE/Florentine China"; 1 bowl marked "BLANTYRE/I.&C. ALCOCK/COBRIDGE"; 1 soup plate marked "FLOWER . . ./JWR . . ." (for Job Ridgeway); 1 saucer marked "GARDEN SCENERY/T.J. & J. MAYER/Longport"; 31 vessel fragments
	White earthenware without decoration	Estimated 300 vessel fragments
	Delft	4 plates, probably English, blue-on-white decoration, hand-painted
	Stoneware	2 gray, salt-glazed, undecorated bottles; 2 jars; 1 vessel, sgrafitto blue-on-white; 1 black basalt, mold-decorated, unglazed vessel; 4 red-bodied with brown slip, machine-inscribed teapots; 1 red-bodied, unglazed teapot lid
	Porcelain	
	Blue oriental, hand-painted	4 cups, 1 bowl, 1 bowl with polychrome enamel overglaze, 6 plates, 1 serving dish, 1 pot lid, 1 saucer, 6 assorted vessels, fragments
	Brown-glazed, with polychrome enamel overglaze (oriental)	3 cups
	Gold-luster decorated (English)	1 dish, 1 vessel
	Silver-luster decorated (English)	2 dishes, 1 cup, 1 vessel
	Polychrome enamel overglaze (probably Japanese)	9 cups, 3 bowls, 6 dishes, 12 assorted vessel fragments
	Plain, undecorated	1 cup, 1 miniature or toy cup
Glass	Stemmed goblets	3 spiral-decorated, 1 hexagonal, 3 plain, 1 fretted, 2 clear-glass footed vessels
	Tumblers	2 plain, 1 rib-molded, 1 clear-glass
	Bottles	3 case bottles, 6 straight-sided, 3 panel-sided, 1 glass vanity bottle
	Bowls	1 mold-decorated, 1 enamel-painted
	Miscellaneous vessels	1 mold-decorated fragment, 1 enamel-painted clear-glass fragment, 1 blue glass fragment, 1 glass knob, 1 vial
	Window glass	1 green bull's-eye fragment, 6 miscellaneous fragments
	Optical	1 lens
Metal	Brass	1 name plate, 2 machined brass fragments with screw holes, 1 brass disc 1 inch in diameter
Organic	Bone	2 fighting-cock leg bones with spurs, 1 chicken wishbone, 2 turtle-shell fragments, miscellaneous indeterminate bone fragments

From Cotter and students 1969.

5

The Delaware Waterfront

Of all the forces that shaped the early history of Philadelphia, none was more important than the Delaware River. From the time the first settlers arrived in William Penn's "green country town" until well into the nineteenth century, the majority of Philadelphians lived in houses clustered near the riverfront. The river was for many of them the source of a livelihood. By 1700, less than twenty years after Thomas Holme laid out Penn's great town, many of Philadelphia's 2,000 residents were working on the wharves that lined the river, and there was enough business to keep the employees of four small shipyards busy. Seventy-five years later, the erstwhile village had grown into the largest city in the British colonies. Shipbuilding, importing, and exporting were mainstays of the economy, and a great many of the more than 23,000 people who then lived in Philadelphia were engaged in these occupations or in some other form of maritime commerce. It was not until about 1810 that New York began usurping Philadelphia's place as the major port of entry to America, and even then the Delaware would continue to play a central role in the economy of Philadelphia and in the lives of Philadelphians for well over a century.

In 1777 English-born Robert Morris described his adopted city with these words: "You will consider Philadelphia from its centrical situation, the extent of its commerce, the number of its artificers, manufacturers and other circumstances, to be to the United States what the heart is to the human body in circulating the blood" (Weigley 1982:134). But if Philadelphia was the heart of the young nation, then the Delaware was surely its aorta. It was the source both of the city's commercial growth and prosperity and of its intellectual and cultural development. It brought to Philadelphia not just rare and exotic goods but also immigrants like Robert Morris, who brought with them the greater gift of ideas. As the port of Philadelphia welcomed people of diverse backgrounds and traditions to the New World throughout the 1700s and 1800s, the city along the Delaware became a lively, cosmopolitan place—a place where taverns rang with argument and debate, and ideas cross-pollinated and flourished.

While the Delaware brought riches, both material and intellectual, it also brought the threat of invasion, and almost from the moment the first European settlers arrived in the Delaware Valley, the riverfront had some type of defensive fortification. By 1642, the early Swedish settlers had fortified Printzhof, the Swedish colonial governor's residence on Tinicum Island, and a few decades later, other Swedes built a log blockhouse on the present site of Gloria Dei Church in Southwark. By the 1740s, even the peaceable Quakers had a defensive battery situated below Gloria Dei on the banks of their city's chief river. The Quaker government was able for a while after the 1750s to choke defense spending. One day in 1772, however, British engineers began

erecting a fort on Mud Island in the Delaware, and from that day to the present, the riverfront has never been without some type of military installation.

Although the Delaware had an important influence on the daily life of the city until well into the twentieth century, that importance has not been reflected in the archaeological attention the riverfront has received. The part of riverfront that had the greatest potential for illuminating the commercial development of Philadelphia was largely compromised during the late 1960s by the construction of Interstate-95. What archaeologists were able to salvage out of the I-95 strip in the 1960s and the results of their efforts there in later years are reported in the pages that follow, as are excavations that throw some light on the lives of Philadelphians who lived near Market Street and the river during the eighteenth and nineteenth centuries. Another study described in this chapter produced evidence of prehistoric habitation near Dock Creek; it also shed light on the quality of life of the first European settlers in this area. Yet another waterfront study has added to our knowledge of historic techniques of ship repair, wharf construction, and landfill.

Also reported in this chapter are studies of four military installations—

one of them devoted to defense, one to the storage of gunpowder, and the other two to the manufacture of munitions. One of the latter installations, although a cannon foundry during the Revolutionary War, had previously been the Bonnin and Morris Porcelain Factory, and the findings that the study of this site produced in some measure make up for the evidence of commerce and industry that lies buried beneath I-95. Investigation of the other military-industrial complex—the Frankford Arsenal—produced some evidence of what life was like in a military establishment of this sort during the nineteenth century. The story of Fort Mifflin's defensive role in the Revolutionary War is a particularly intriguing one, and the sad deterioration of the site in subsequent years is attested to by the physical evidence. Excavation of the fourth military site, this one in Franklin Square, revealed traces of a powder magazine dating from the Revolutionary War. Since Franklin Square is today at the approach to the Benjamin Franklin Bridge, it would not historically be considered part of the riverfront, situated as it is between Sixth and Seventh streets. The reason for including it in this chapter is its relation to the military theme so characteristic of the riverfront.

INTERSTATE-95: THE LONG AND THE SHORT OF IT

Southwark is the oldest of Philadelphia's many neighborhoods. Though today its eastern boundary is Front Street, its name once applied to all

the land from the Delaware River west to Sixth Street and south from Society Hill to Washington Avenue and beyond. Settled by Swedes in the

1640s, Southwark grew by leaps and bounds during the eighteenth century as shipbuilding and commerce boomed along the banks of the Dela-

ware River. The hardworking people who inhabited the tiny houses of this burgeoning neighborhood earned their livings in the maritime trades. They were the tradesmen and "mechanics"—shipwrights, ship chandlers, coopers, carpenters, caulkers, riggers, and makers of rope and sail—who, working alone or in small groups, helped forge the prosperity of the colonial city. Within less than a hundred years of the Revolution, however, the small riverfront workplaces where these "mechanics" had toiled had begun giving way to the edifices of large industries (Figure 5.1). By the mid-twentieth century, Delaware Avenue was lined with huge warehouses, sugar refineries, coal yards, and the like (Figure 5.2).

When Interstate-95 began cutting its long swath along the Delaware River in the late 1960s, it largely eradicated the heart of Philadelphia's waterfront district. The highway took with it not only many large, late nineteenth- and twentieth-century commercial structures along Delaware Avenue, but many rowhouses and older warehouses east of Front Street as well. It also had the unfortunate effect of creating both a physical and a psychological barrier to the river that was once the city's lifeblood. Forced to abandon their homes and having little legal recourse, since federal legislation on environmental impact had not yet been implemented, many of the residents of Southwark reacted angrily. One result was an epidemic of vandalism (Figure 5.3), which added to the constraints that already impeded archaeological work.

Meanwhile, some of the disgruntled residents of Society Hill had access to a different and more effective route for expressing their displeasure. As a result of the political clout of these Philadelphians, I-95 was designed partially underground, from Delancey Street north to Dock Street, covered overhead by small park areas. While the view and the feeling of access to the river here are undoubtedly more aesthetically pleasing than the brick wall and metal grates that separate the highway from Front Street both north and south, the consequences for archaeology were deleterious: the digging of the trench for the highway disrupted the stratigraphic context of many historic features and artifacts to be found there. In short, while sincere efforts were made at the time regarding the impact of the highway on archaeological resources, one inescapable fact remains: with the benefit of more than 20 years' hindsight (and the knowledge of the more rigorous ways in which the mandates of the National Historic Preservation Act of 1966 and the National Environmental Policy Act of 1969 are now implemented), such efforts fell woefully short.

The 1966–1967 Investigations

When I-95 cut its great gash through three hundred years of Philadelphia history, it attracted the attention not only of professional archaeologists, but also of that thorn in the professional archaeologist's side, the bottle collector. As it turned out, the professionals

Figure 5.3.

Vandalized row houses on Queen Street awaiting demolition as the Interstate-95 project gets underway. Vandalism—most of it by children and youths—was a constant impediment to archaeological investigation in Southwark. (Photo by J. L. Cotter)

Figure 5.4.

Bottle collectors at work between Delaware Avenue and Front Street in December 1974, after the roadway for Interstate-95 had been excavated. (Photo by J. L. Cotter)

who worked in the Southwark area in 1966–67 fared not nearly as well as the unauthorized collectors, who set to work at a later and more propitious time (Figure 5.4). Furthermore, the evidence of waterfront Philadelphia in the seventeenth and eighteenth centuries lay deeply buried beneath the right-of-way of the planned highway and could not be reached until the fill above it was removed. In 1966–67, although many buildings were removed, the fill was still in place, and the archaeologists could therefore do little more than test surface areas and record whatever features they observed (Figure 5.5). Attempts to use backhoes to open up test sections proved fruitless; the fill was so deep the machines could not penetrate to the level of the original dockfront area (Figure 5.6). In 1974, seven years after archaeological investigation in Southwark had gone as far as circumstances would permit, I-95 received its final authorization, and construction began immediately, allowing no opportunity to carry out further archaeological work.

Although the short report (Garvan 1972) that followed the 1966–67 investigations in Southwark summarized the project's methodology and research goals, it said little about what the archaeologists had found. The best information on these findings is contained in sketches of some of the artifacts drawn by Paul Huey (1967), who worked on the excavations while a graduate student at the University of Pennsylvania. From a maga-

zine article entitled "The Early Bird Gets the Worm" (Evans 1985), it seems fairly clear that the bottle collectors who went to work in 1974 did indeed get a very generous share of the "worms." Among the findings of the high school teachers, truck driver, and pet shop owner, who left their homes in New Jersey at five-thirty in the morning to descend on the pits and wells exposed by the bulldozers, were a number of intact bottles dating from the early eighteenth century. A broken bottle bearing the seal "Edward Roberts 1713" confirmed the date of the assemblage.

A major saving grace of the I-95 project was the historical and architectural information that the study produced (Garvan 1972:2–3). John Dickey, John Milner, and Margaret Tinkcom carried out this "aboveground" archaeology on some of the structures that lay in the path of the highway. The buildings whose history they researched and whose features

Figure 5.5.

Testing at Front and Spruce streets in 1967 after buildings had been cleared for Interstate-95. Here on the northwest corner in 1769 William West had a three-story house. Most eighteenth-century sites lay deeply buried under fill that was not removed until construction of the highway began in 1974. (Photo by J. L. Cotter)

they recorded (Tinkcom 1970) included the unpretentious but substantial rowhouses of Southwark on the east side of Front Street, as well as the warehouses of the riverfront (Figure 5.7). Some of these structures had been built in the early nineteenth century on the sites of seventeenth- and eighteenth-century houses and shops. The project architect, Robert L. Raley, made measured drawings and photographs of the buildings according to the standards of the Historic American Buildings Survey.* This historical and architectural material, which documents urban riverfront construction in the nineteenth century, constitutes a valuable resource for social and architectural historians and it forms a counterpoint to the sparse archaeological data retrieved from the I-95 strip. There, deeply buried, was the evidence of life along

* Raley's work is on file at the Library of Congress, and copies are available at the Philadelphia Historical Commission.

the Delaware in Philadelphia's early years; now dispersed, it is evidence of a missed archaeological opportunity.

The 1984 Sequel

Happily, the story of the archaeology of I-95 did not end in the 1960s. When plans were being made to build access ramps to I-95 in 1984, John Milner Associates contracted with the Pennsylvania Department of Transportation to carry out archaeological, architectural, and historical research mandated by the now more established National Historic Preservation Act of 1966 and the National Environmental Policy Act of 1969. Figure

5.8 shows the three proposed ramp areas that were studied: area A, a lot of land measuring 260 by 340 feet at the foot of Market Street; area B, a district known as "the Meadows," which lies east of I-95 between Delancey Street and Beck Street; and area C, a rectangular plot, also east of I-95, which is bounded by Washington Avenue, Morris Street, Delaware Avenue, and Front Street. Two reports came out of this research: Meyer and Cosans-Zebooker (1984) described the archaeological significance of the proposed ramp areas, and Cosans-Zebooker and Parrington (1984) described the archaeological investigations that took place. These two reports are the basis for what follows.

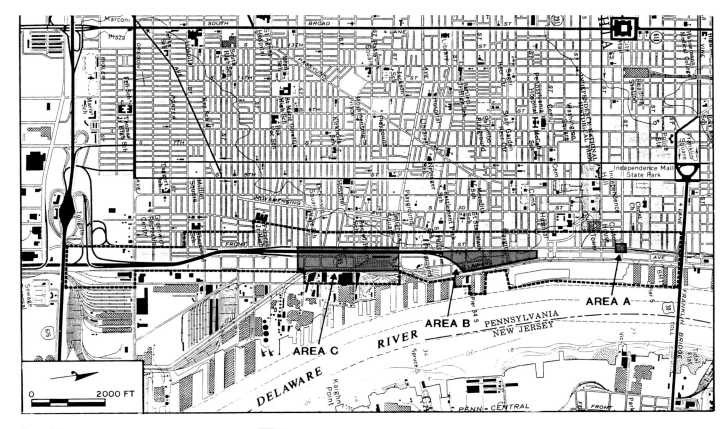

Figure 5.8.

Proposed areas for access ramps to Interstate-95. (From Meyer and Cosans-Zebooker 1984; courtesy of the Pennsylvania Department of Transportation, the Federal Highway Administration, and John Milner Associates)

 Primary Impact Area

Archaeological Significance

When William Penn first walked along the banks of the Delaware River in his green country town, those banks rose 20 feet above the river, overlooking sandy beaches in some areas and marshland in others. Penn's original plan was that all the terrain between the river and the banks should be common land. Before the end of the seventeenth century, however, the "common land" in the vicinity of areas A and B had been leased to merchants, who had begun to fill it and to build dwellings, shops, warehouses, and wharves along the Delaware. As methods of river dredg-

ing improved in the early nineteenth century, allowing earth from under the water to be reclaimed, the original wharves were torn down, earth was filled on site, and new wharves were built beyond the old shoreline in the vicinity of area B.

Area C, although a few blocks directly south of area B, is farther away from the river, since the river bends to the east at this point. All of area C originally consisted of marshland, but during the eighteenth century some of it was reclaimed as grazing land. During the nineteenth century, the section near the shoreline was heavily filled, and in the first decades of the twentieth century, the rest of the original marsh was filled to control the mosquitoes that bred there.

Presumably, area A must have been the most desirable of the three areas, for it was there William Penn first took up residence in his new colony. As noted in Chapter 3, before leaving Pennsylvania for the last time

in 1701, Penn deeded part of this land to his daughter Letitia. Later in the eighteenth century, the London Coffee House, a favorite meeting place for the merchants of the bustling colonial town, occupied a corner at Front and Market streets. Investigations during the 1970s of other properties in this neighborhood substantiated the historical and archaeological significance of area A (see discussions of 8 South Front Street and the High Ward in this chapter).

Historical research of areas B and C indicated that they, too, might contain important archaeological evidence. Both areas were part of the large tract of land that Queen Christina granted in 1653 to the Swedish settler Sven Shute, whose heirs—the three Swanson brothers of Wicaco—sometime in the 1660s divided the land among themselves. Although each of the brothers had a house lot on the site, where they presumably would have built log houses, the precise locations of these lots are unknown. In fact, the only known Swedish landmark in the vicinity is Gloria Dei Church, built in 1698–1700 on the site of the Swedes' old log blockhouse.

As early as 1701, numerous wharves were lining the riverfront, and as the merchants of the colonial city prospered and the economy boomed, ever-greater numbers of wharves jutted their wooden planks out into the Delaware, ready to unburden the tall-masted ships dotting the water of their cargoes of imported goods. By the 1730s, silhouettes of warehouses were competing with ships' masts for their share of the Philadelphia skyline, and the cobblestones of newly constructed streets and alleys were echoing with the clamor of sweating horses and swearing draymen carting goods to their destinations across the Meadows.

Shipbuilding also thrived along the banks of the Delaware throughout the eighteenth and nineteenth centuries, so much so that the river eventually became known as the "American Clyde" (Smith 1986:8). When the events of the 1770s created a need for warships, the machinery was already in place; it was a fairly painless process to switch over from building merchantmen to building armed frigates and sloops. After the war the nation's need for warships did not cease, although after World War II they were no longer built at Philadelphia. One of the most important shipyards of the late 1700s and early 1800s was, as shown in Figure 5.9, located just a few steps south of Gloria Dei Church. Its owner was Joshua Humphreys, who had designed several of the Continental Navy's warships and who was later the chief architect of the new Federal Navy's *Constitution* and other early frigates. Humphreys' own shipyard produced a number of the nation's earliest men-of-war (Smith 1986:132).

In addition to being important to the commerce of the city, areas B and C were of obvious military importance because of their strategic locations overlooking the river. In 1748, as a defense against French and Spanish privateers, two batteries were built along the riverfront. One of them, located near the foot of Lombard Street, was apparently a small and hastily built affair; the other—the Association Battery, located below Gloria Dei Church near the foot of Wharton Street—seems to have been more substantial, mounting as it did more than twenty-five cannons. The Association Battery (shown in Figure 2.13) was apparently abandoned sometime before the Revolutionary War as a result of the Quaker government's move to quash military expenditure. Later, however, part of the Association Battery's site was occupied by yet another military installation: the federal government's Philadelphia Navy Yard.

Figure 5.9.

Humphreys' shipyard, ca. 1799, with Gloria Dei Church in the background. The figure in the foreground may have been Joshua Humphreys himself. (Engraving by W. Birch & Son; courtesy of the Free Library of Philadelphia)

Figure 5.10.

The Navy Yard's twin ship houses, as shown in a watercolor painted by W. A. K. Martin in 1859. (Courtesy of Gloria Dei [Old Swedes'] Church)

Shortly after the turn of the nineteenth century, when the secretary of the navy decided it was high time for the young nation to have shipbuilding facilities of its own, the federal government acquired eighteen acres of land along the Delaware. The parcel of land was bounded by Front Street on the west and Ellsworth and Wharton streets on the north and south. For almost three-quarters of a century, the Navy Yard's twin ship houses, with their many-windowed roofs and sides, were prominent Philadelphia landmarks (Figure 5.10), and productive ones as well. Between 1815 and 1875, the Navy Yard launched some thirty-five men-of-war. After the facility moved to new quarters at League Island near the confluence of the Delaware and the Schuylkill in 1875, its former site was sold at auction in the Merchant's Exchange. The Pennsylvania Railroad paid one million dollars in cash for the site, whose waterfront equivalent today would be Pier 55 South (Smith 1986:133, 138–39).

The Civil War saw the creation of yet another sort of military establishment in the vicinity of area C: the Union Volunteer Refreshment Saloon and Hospital (Figure 5.11). Like its

Figure 5.11.

The Union Volunteer Refreshment Saloon and Hospital, as painted by Edward Moran in 1866. One of the Navy Yard's ship houses looms in the background. (Courtesy of the Philadelphia Maritime Museum: J. Welles Henderson Collection)

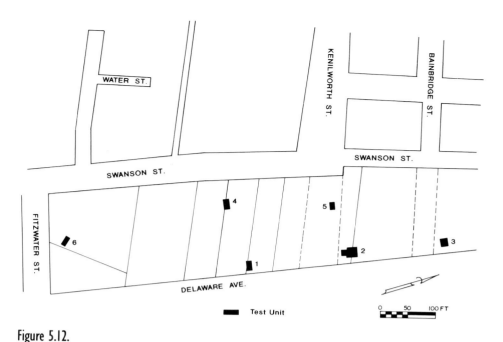

Figure 5.12.

Site plan, area B. (From Cosans-Zebooker and Parrington 1984; courtesy of the Pennsylvania Department of Transportation, the Federal Highway Administration, and John Milner Associates)

modern counterpart—the USO (United Service Organization) canteen—the saloon offered hospitality to lonely soldiers and sailors far from home, while the hospital provided medical care not easily available elsewhere in the city. The charitable establishment, one of several set up for the use of Union troops passing through Philadelphia on their way to the front, was the idea of Barzilai S. Brown, a Southwark grocer. It opened in 1861 in a small boat shop on Swanson Street at the edges of the Navy Yard and expanded as donations permitted. Here, men and boys, dusty and dirty from their travels, could spruce themselves up in the washrooms, post letters home free of charge, and assuage their hunger and thirst. What the quality of the liquid refreshment was is uncertain, but the food must not have been too bad; the saloon is reputed to have dispensed some 900,000 free meals (Smith 1986:138–39).

The Excavations

Although historical research established that all three areas contained sites of historical and archaeological significance, no fieldwork was conducted at area A, since final design plans called for little or no disturbance there. The fieldwork in the other two areas was preliminary in nature; its purpose was not to answer questions about the history and archaeology of the area, but to determine whether the remains of known historic sites survived below ground. Ten test units with an average size of 10 by 20 feet were dug by backhoe to assess the degree of disturbance in certain key areas (Figures 5.12 and 5.13).

The three test units dug along the east side of area B revealed the re-

Figure 5.13.

Site plan, area C. (From Cosans-Zebooker and Parrington 1984; courtesy of the Pennsylvania Department of Transportation, the Federal Highway Administration, and John Milner Associates)

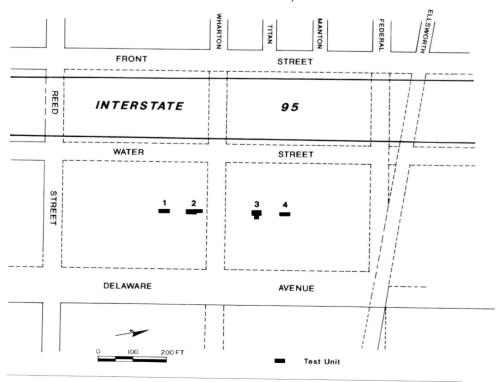

Figure 5.14.

Detail of wooden sill beam and cross beam foundation found in test unit 3, area B. (Courtesy of the Pennsylvania Department of Transportation, the Federal Highway Administration, and John Milner Associates)

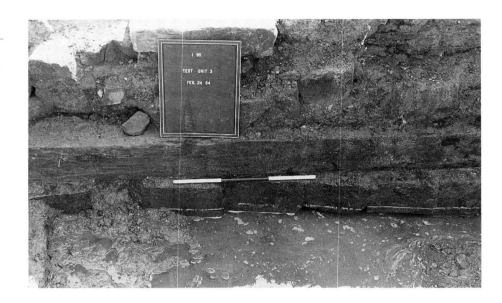

mains of massive timber and masonry wharves (Figure 5.14). These were in all probability the remnants of colonial wharves, which were buried under fill early in the 1800s when the shoreline was moved to the east and the land beyond the colonial pierheads was reclaimed. Although some nineteenth-century building took place on the pierheads, they still retain the potential to answer questions about eighteenth-century wharf construction and about techniques of land reclamation during the early years of the nineteenth century.

The test units in area C revealed such features of the old Navy Yard as access ways and housing for ships' supplies. The excavations here also demonstrated that over 6 feet of fill had been brought in to reclaim this marshy area in the nineteenth century. No evidence of the Association Battery was found, but traces may well still be there, buried beneath the large amount of fill covering the area. The site of the Union Volunteers Refreshment Saloon and Hospital could not be tested, as it was in current use;

however, given that none of the occasional construction that has taken place on the site since the Civil War has required a deep basement, it seems likely that the remains of the building still exist in a well-preserved state.

The 1988 Sequel

In 1988, the Pennsylvania Department of Transportation and the Federal Highway Administration selected a site on which to build access ramps from I-95 to Center City Philadelphia. The site chosen was in area B, bounded by South Street on the north and Catharine Street on the south. With construction of the ramps tentatively scheduled to begin in 1990, Louis Berger and Associates conducted extensive archaeological excavations in the autumn of 1988. The excavations concentrated on four areas located on approximately 1.8 acres of open land between I-95 and Delaware Avenue. As expected, the initial clearing of the fill by earth-

moving machinery revealed the foundations of large, nineteenth-century commercial buildings. Clearing of the rest of the fill by hand was a painstaking process, made even more difficult by the intricacy of some of the construction and by the presence of the water table just below the nineteenth-century foundations.

The research questions addressed by the excavations included some of the provocative issues raised by the preliminary testing done in 1984. Among these issues were the processes by which the riverfront was developed in the 1700s and the relationship between the domestic, commercial, industrial, and military components of the area. Another intriguing question—upon which the archaeological evidence produced to date has shed little light—concerns the nature of the Swedish settlement established here in the seventeenth century by Sven Shute and his heirs. It is expected that the report of the 1988 excavations (in progress) may provide archaeological answers to these and other questions.

WEST'S SHIPYARD AND ITS NEIGHBORS: FROM SAND TO ASPHALT ON THE "HERTZ LOT"

In August 1987 an asphalt-covered parking lot in an area east of I-95 had the distinction of becoming the first archaeological site to appear on the Philadelphia Register of Historic Places. A month later Carmen Weber, then archaeologist for the Philadelphia Historical Commission, began excavating the site, known at that time as the "Hertz lot." Her excavations showed, among other things, that despite the destructive impact of waterfront urbanization, intact physical evidence of the city's waterfront history does still exist there. The site, bounded by Water Street and Delaware Avenue and Vine and Callowhill streets, was first developed by Europeans in 1676, six years before William Penn's arrival in Philadelphia.

By 1690 this waterfront block contained not only two of the mainstays of life in the colonial city—a tavern and a shipyard—but a ropewalk and a public landing as well. Subsequent developments in the block during the eighteenth and nineteenth centuries reflect not only demographic trends in Philadelphia but also more general technological changes (Roberts, Cosans, and Barrett 1982). The historical and physical evidence recovered here has shed light on historic techniques of ship repair, wharf construction, and landfill.*

* Data for this account were supplied by Carmen A. Weber (personal communication and nomination form for the Philadelphia Register of Historic Places, April 2, 1987) and Weber (1988a).

From Sand to Asphalt: A Brief History of the Site

The broad, sandy shore of the Northern Liberties just beyond the city limit at Vine Street made it an ideal place for shipbuilding, and by 1676, even before the city was founded, one James West was running a shipyard there. Located next to a public landing at the foot of Vine Street, West's yard must have prospered, for in 1690 he acquired an abutting lot, thus adding 40 feet to the 60 feet of frontage he already owned on Front Street. From Front Street, West's lot, now 100 feet wide, ran 250 feet east to the river (Figure 5.15). Sitting on his newly acquired land was the Penny

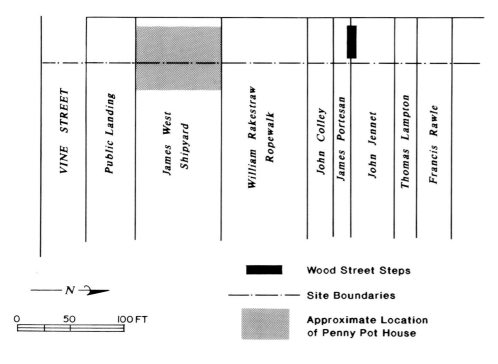

Figure 5.15.

West's shipyard and its neighbors, ca. 1690. (Courtesy of Carmen Weber)

Figure 5.16.

Section of *The South East Prospect of the City of Philadelphia,* by Peter Cooper, ca. 1720. Penny Pot House appears at the extreme right. (Courtesy of the Library Company of Philadelphia)

Figure 5.17.

The Penny Pot House and West's Shipyard. Scene dating from ca. the 1830s. (From Watson 1909:facing p. 153)

Pot House, a two-story brick tavern of "good dimensions." Under West's management, the tavern, too, became a thriving and well-known spot. In the municipal charter of 1701, William Penn made reference to it, decreeing that "the Landing places now & Heretofore used at the penny pot house &

Blew anchor [at Dock Creek] . . . be left open." The tavern also appears in Peter Cooper's 1720 view of Philadelphia (Figure 5.16), as well as in an old painting depicting the landing and the shipyard (Figure 5.17). Immediately north of West's property was the land of William Rakestraw, who in

1689 sought "Liberty to make ropes" there (City of Philadelphia: Minutes of the Board of Property, Book D, p. 28).

In the seventeenth century, West's shipyard repaired more ships than it built, and those built there must have been small, for with the help of seven workers, James West could finish one in a month. Some of West's workers boarded next door at his tavern, where they received part of their wages in drink. No doubt West was glad to pay his workers this way, as labor was relatively expensive; one ship cost him only £3 in timber but £30 for labor. West must also have found it a convenient way to pay, for he himself often received beer and food in payment for the work done at his shipyard. In 1701, for example, he received beer, flour, butter, sugar, and raisins in lieu of £39 in cash—the sum he had charged for a new sloop. With currency in short supply in early Philadelphia, such bartering was common (Dunn and Dunn 1982:21).

The West family continued to build ships on the property for the better part of the eighteenth century. James' son Charles, who inherited the shipyard in 1702, achieved renown as a shipwright with his construction of vessels weighing around 150 tons. By 1762, when Clarkson and Biddle published the map shown in Figure 5.18, the Wests had built a broad wharf extending out over the original shoreline. As can be seen in Figure 5.18, two similar land-fill developments had taken place elsewhere in the block: Hewling's Wharf appears next to West's, and at the northern end of the block near Callowhill Street is Shoemaker's Wharf. The original shoreline runs between them. Only three structures east of Water Street between Callowhill and Vine appear on this 1762 map.

Although Philadelphia grew rapidly both before and after the Revolutionary War, a glance at the 1762 Clarkson and Biddle map clearly indicates that prewar development in the Northern Liberties was relatively sparse. After the war, however, as

Figure 5.18.

Section of Clarkson and Biddle map, 1762. (Courtesy of the Library of Congress, Map Division)

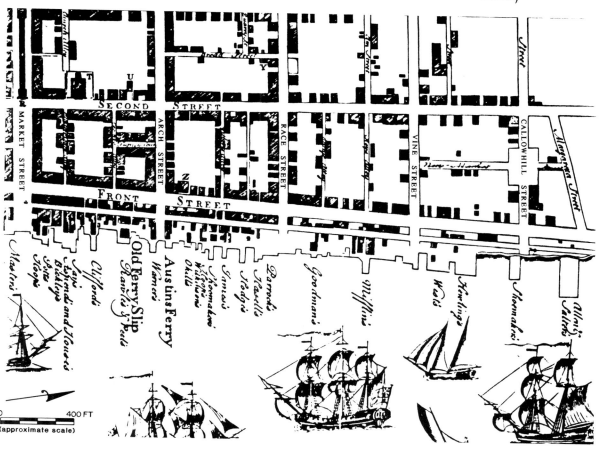

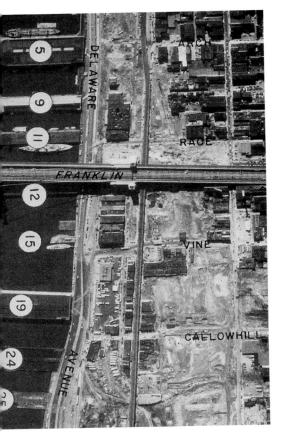

trade resumed and merchants prospered, the Northern Liberties, like the city itself, boomed. A map drawn in 1794 by A. P. Folie (Figure 5.19) shows a dramatic postwar increase in the number of wharves north of Vine Street. As more land in this area was reclaimed from the Delaware and more wharves extended farther out into the river, more structures were built along Water Street. These structures were used for a variety of purposes—commercial, industrial, and domestic—with one building often serving multiple functions.

The heterogeneous mix of occupations that characterized the densely populated blocks of Philadelphia proper in the 1790s also characterized the blocks of the Northern Liberties. In the increasingly populated water-

Figure 5.19.

Top, aerial view of the Hertz Lot site, where West's Shipyard was located, 1989; *bottom*, section of map drawn by A. P. Folie, 1794. (Courtesy of the City of Philadelphia)

front block between Vine and Callowhill streets, well-to-do merchants who imported china and exported lumber rubbed elbows with several laborers and ship joiners, a wood sawyer, a mariner, a shingle dresser, a baker, an innkeeper, and one "gentleman." Although the shipbuilding industry did not completely disappear from the area, commercial enterprises became more prevalent. It is significant that historic records describe William West, the great-grandson of the founder of West's Shipyard, as a merchant rather than a shipwright. While space-consuming shipyards were seeking more open areas south of the city and north of the Liberties, William West was busily building stores along an alley leading from Water Street to his wharf. Of the remaining shipwrights in the area in the 1790s, one was a man named William Taylor, who had owned property in the block since 1759.

As yet more land was filled and more wharves built in the first half of the nineteenth century, the block on which James West had established his shipyard in 1676 receded farther from the Delaware. With the center of maritime activity and trading now located to the east, merchants used the block primarily as a place for storing their goods. Among the stores and small warehouses at the southern end of the block in the early 1800s were those belonging to West's enterprising great-grandson William, who had by now entered the salt trade. At the northern end of the block on Callowhill Street, mariners, an oysterman, a waterman, and an innkeeper clustered in small buildings.

By 1859 the inhabitants of the small buildings on Callowhill Street were sharing the block with large warehouses, lumberyards, and open lots. The character of the block apparently remained much the same for many years, for in the late 1800s numerous small buildings still existed at the northern end of the block, while south of them were a coal yard, a fruit warehouse, and the Vine Street Market. By the early twentieth century, however, railroad tracks had covered everything in the block except some of the small structures on Callowhill Street. When Carmen Weber began her excavations in the asphalt-covered lot in September 1987, no physical trace of the block's long history remained above ground. The only structures standing on the site were a twentieth-century garage and a shed-like building.

The Excavations

In this study, as in most urban archaeological studies, the threat of development was the factor that prompted excavation. As can be seen in Figure 5.20, the proposed development did not affect the site of West's Shipyard directly, but rather a large part of the rest of the block. After two test trenches dug by backhoe in September 1987 revealed the interior wall of one early wharf and the exterior of another, the excavations intensified. By December 1987, when the field work ended, a team of six archaeologists had uncovered the remains of several more wharves and a ship's way, as well as numerous artifacts.

Documentary evidence and physical evidence from waterfront sites in other cities indicate that wharves were created by stacking logs to form walls, or bulkheads. Built out into the river from the shoreline, these walls formed three-sided boxes, which were then filled with debris to create a flat surface. Since this investigation was the first in Philadelphia to concentrate on riverfront wharves, one goal was to determine whether the techniques used in Philadelphia conformed to the patterns of landfill and wharf construction used elsewhere. It was also hoped that the study would produce data on the technology of early shipwrights.

The wharves uncovered in the small area shown in Figure 5.20 represent several building periods. The earliest wharf appeared to date from about 1750. Its long wall ran parallel to the shore, and the logs that formed it were held together with half-lap joints and had very little trim or finish (Figure 5.21). Some of the logs were missing, perhaps robbed for reuse

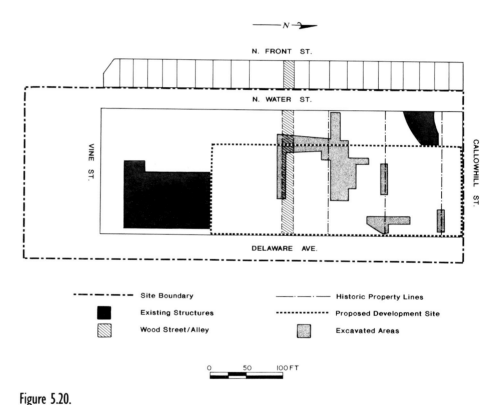

Figure 5.20.

Plan of the excavations at the Hertz Lot site. (Courtesy of Carmen Weber)

Figure 5.21.

Wharf bulkheads dating from about 1750 to 1800. (Courtesy of the City of Philadelphia)

Figure 5.22.

The ship's way: *left,* looking inland, with the late eighteenth-century wharf at left; *right,* looking toward the Delaware River and Pier 19. (Courtesy of the City of Philadelphia)

elsewhere. The fill, which created a flat surface between the interior of this wall and the shoreline, consisted of sand and gravel. Mixed in with the fill were various artifacts, among them ceramic sherds and wrought-iron nails, which provided a basis for dating the wharf.

The land on which this "long shoreline" wharf stood belonged from 1759 until 1797 to the shipwright William Taylor, who probably used the wharf for vessel repair. A common method of repairing ships in Taylor's day was to haul the vessel over on its side toward a wharf and then, working from small boats in the river, repair the hull. Such an operation was time-consuming and dangerous, sometimes causing the vessel more harm than good. Another common repair method was to "careen," or beach, the vessel. Both methods were more easily implemented with small ships and boats.

Another wharf, apparently dating from the late 1700s, had been built as an extension of the earlier one. Its long wall was built on top of the bulkhead dating from 1750, and it ran straight out from the shore rather than parallel to it. Like the earlier wall, it had half-lap joints secured by

wooden pins, or treenails. Since some of the logs in this wall had cuts not needed in the construction, it seems likely they were the logs robbed from the 1750 bulkhead. The bark still clinging to these logs two centuries later indicated many of them had been pine. One log, about 2 feet in diameter and over 10 feet long, may have been a chestnut. Ship ballast was evidently used as wharf fill, for among the artifacts found in the dark soil around these logs were cobble-stones and a type of limestone not found in the Philadelphia area.

Although historical records show that by the early 1800s the merchants on the site outnumbered the ship-wrights, a ship's way, sloping down toward the river and tentatively dated to the early 1800s, was found anchored to the side of the late eighteenth-century bulkhead (Figure 5.22). The presence of such a device, used to haul vessels out of the water and to launch them, was evidence that maritime industry continued here even as the shoreline moved farther east. The worn grooves in the two parallel wooden tracks of this ship's way and the distance between the tracks indicated that many small vessels, about 50 feet long, had been pulled or slid upright along the way in some type of wheeled cradle. It seems likely that some enterprising ship-wright, fed up with having to careen vessels or to haul them over on their sides in the water, had built this ship's way as an efficient and permanent means of repairing the small sloops

that commonly sailed the Delaware. Such vessels, which ferried passengers and goods across the river or to sea-going ships lying at anchor, were susceptible to borer worms and required frequent repair.

The type of ship's way found on the Hertz lot, tied into a permanent dock and wharf system and capable of being used over and over again, represents a significant departure from earlier technology. In the 1700s, ship's ways were apparently custom-made and used for the sole purpose of launching one particular vessel, after which the way was dismantled. The inefficiency of this method evidently did not come to national attention until the early 1820s, when Commodore John Rodgers began urging that the U.S. Navy build permanent marine railways for hauling ships from the water for rebuilding, repair, and storage. On January 27, 1823, in a message to a congressional committee in which he supported Rodgers' recommendations, President James Monroe noted that no permanent docks or ways then existed for vessel repair. Although the ship's way at the Hertz lot seems to have anticipated these national efforts, we have no way of knowing whether it was one of a kind or whether permanent ship's ways were common in early nineteenth-century Philadelphia. No other ship's way has been excavated in the city or, as far as we know, anywhere else on the East Coast. Such features are not indicated on maps, and the only painting of an early Philadelphia shipyard—the 1800 Birch print of Joshua Humphreys' shipyard shown in the preceding section (Figure 5.9)—provides little detail on the structure that is supporting the ship.

The methods used in constructing the ship's way differed from the techniques used in building the wharves that date from the 1700s. Exposure of 83 feet of the ship's way, including the shore end, showed that the pine logs used in the construction were finished and that they had common scarf joints, often used in shipbuilding, rather than half-lap joints. The scarf joints were secured with wrought iron spikes, which replaced the treenails used in the preceding century. The wrought-iron spikes were suggestive of the early 1800s date tentatively assigned to the ship's way, as were the artifacts found at the bottom of the way.

Washed in by the tide or dropped by a shipwright preoccupied in repairing a vessel, the artifacts lying in the ship's way were covered with dark silt. Even leather was well preserved in this anaerobic environment—the factor that also served to preserve the wooden wharves and way. The artifacts included copper nails, a boatmaker's ruler made of wood and brass, a wooden-handled chisel, a planing iron, leather shoes, bone button blanks and bone buttons, brass buttons and brass pins, copper cufflinks, beads of

faceted glass and jet, clay tobacco pipes, and a square lead token marked with an "X" (Figure 5.23). Such tokens were probably used as merchandise counters when ships unloaded their cargo; many similar items have been found near wharves in other cities. Not surprisingly, given the industrial nature of the site, ceramic pieces were relatively few. They included redware, creamware, porcelain, and transfer-printed pearlware; the last was the most recent type of ceramic found.

The finished pine logs, scarf joints, and iron fastenings that characterized the ship's way also characterized another early nineteenth-century feature: a bulkhead from a wharf that lay north of the ship's way (Figure 5.24). The logs at the top of this bulkhead, probably exposed at low tide, were more finished than those at the bottom, but the logs on its interior were unfinished. The bottom layer of fill here consisted of planks and stones. The stones had no doubt served as ship ballast and been lying conveniently to hand when the wharf was being built. Most of the fill, however, consisted of marine clays, apparently dredged elsewhere and brought here to be used in the construction. There were also pockets of wood waste, which no doubt came from the waterfront shops of coopers, shingle makers, or any of the many other nearby "me-

chanics" who worked with wood. Occasional pockets of dark silt contained various artifacts, no doubt representing redeposited trash heaps. The latest fill, which appeared to have been deposited in the 1840s, lay between the exterior of this bulkhead and the ship's way. Containing some very large, machine-sawn logs held together with machine-made iron spikes, this fill provided a final bit of evidence of a major change in technology.

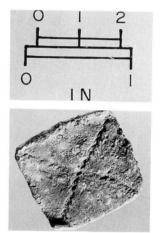

Figure 5.23.

Lead token used as a merchandise counter, found at the Hertz Lot site. (Photo by Carmen Weber)

Figure 5.24.

Bulkhead of a wharf dating from the early 1800s. Note the common scarf joinery. (Courtesy of the City of Philadelphia)

FRONT AND DOCK STREETS:
SOME OF THE EARLIEST EVIDENCE

From the earliest days of Philadelphia, the tidal basin into which the two branches of Dock Creek flowed was a hub of commerce (Hood 1971). South of it, across a mosquito-infested marsh, were the warehouses of the Free Society of Traders. Just to the north were the homes of several of the city's most influential merchants. As the neighborhood grew more densely populated in the course of the eighteenth and early nineteenth centuries, Dock Creek and its tidal basin were paved over, creating the irregularly shaped byway known as Dock Street (Figure 5.25). Like the rest of Society Hill, the area around Dock Street went into decline in the last half of the nineteenth century. Although much of Society Hill recovered as the regenerative spirit of Independence National Historical Park took hold in the 1960s, recovery for the irregular strip of land between Dock, Walnut, Front, and Second streets has been a rather recent phenomenon.

An archaeological investigation in 1968 (Liggett 1971a), prompted by the relocation of a sewer at Front and Dock streets, produced not only historical evidence of the sequential filling of Dock Creek and the tidal basin but also physical evidence of a causeway built across the marsh in the early 1700s. In 1984 Front and Dock streets, then occupied by a parking lot, again became the focus of archaeological investigation. The factor that prompted this investigation was the involvement of federal funding in a plan to build a hotel on the site. Carried out by John Milner Associates (Cosans 1984; McCarthy 1984b; McCarthy and Roberts [in preparation]), the investigation entailed his-torical research, field testing, and extensive excavation.

Historical Background

In 1682 James Claypoole, an energetic Quaker who ran a successful West Indian trading company in London, became a First Purchaser of land in Penn's colony. For the sum of £100, he acquired 5,000 country acres, additional acreage in the Northern Liberties, and two town lots. One town lot was on High Street; the other, with 102 feet of frontage along both Second and Front streets, ran east-west south of Walnut, in close proximity to Dock Creek (Nash 1986:345). Deciding to transfer his family and business to Philadelphia, Claypoole sent a servant ahead of him to construct a house at the southwest corner of Front and Walnut (Soderlund et al. 1983:179, 341).

Soon after Claypoole arrived in Philadelphia in the autumn of 1683, he wrote to his brother, a plantation owner in Barbados, describing not only the house that greeted him but also the commercial prospects of his Quaker neighbors and the optimism with which he embraced his new surroundings:

> My servant had built me a house like a barn, without a chimney, 40 foot long and 20 foot broad with a good dry cellar under it, which proved an extraordinary convenience for securing our goods and lodging my family, although it stood me in very dear. For he had run me up for diet and work near £60 sterling, which I am paying as money comes in

Figure 5.25.

Map of Front and Dock streets and environs. (From McCarthy and Roberts [in preparation]; courtesy of Rouse and Associates and John Milner Associates)

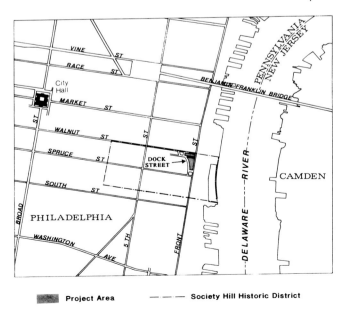

▬ Project Area   - - - - Society Hill Historic District

for goods. To this I built a kitchen of 20 foot square where I am to have a double chimney, which I hope will be up in 8 or 12 days. . . .

My lot in this place proves to be especially [good] for trade, one of the [best] in the city, and though I employ my time in serving the [Free] Society [of Traders], being treasurer, for which I have £100 sterling, yet my wife and children with my direction shall manage the business as well as if I did it myself. . . . So I desire thee, let us have a little trade together, and . . . if thou will take . . . 1000 or 2000 acres of land in this country, the sooner the better. For people come in so fast that it is like to be much dearer in a little time. It's judged about 1000 people came in 6 weeks, so that it is already double what it was, 1000 acres being now at £40 sterling.

Samuel Carpenter is next but one to me and is likely to get a great estate quickly. William Frampton is on the other side of me, building a great brewhouse. If I had time and could write, for [it is] cold, having no chimney, I would have filled some sheets . . . giving thee account of . . . our settlement, trade, and laws, etc. But now, . . . only this in short, I do believe it will prove a very healthy country, and that great improvements may be made in a few years by industry and skill. . . . (Soderlund et al. 1983: 340–41)

In most things, Claypoole proved an accurate prognosticator. Property did indeed become dearer, and Samuel Carpenter, who built the first wharf in the city in 1684 and added a limekiln to it in 1685 (Soderlund et al. 1983:369), soon amassed a considerable fortune. But as far as its being "a very healthy country," Claypoole was mistaken. He himself died in 1687, and his neighbor, Friend William Frampton, who built a bakery as well as a brewery, predeceased him by a year. In 1699 a fever swept through Philadelphia, taking several other Quaker merchants with it (Nash 1986:339, 355).

Short though Claypoole's life in Pennsylvania was, it was active. In addition to looking after his own busi-

ness and that of the Free Society of Traders, he was one of eleven colonists to whom Penn entrusted the management of his colony when he left for England in 1684. In his post as Commissioner of Property, Claypoole was responsible for allocating and selling land (Soderlund et al. 1983:387). One idea he promoted was that Dock Creek's swampy tidal basin could be turned into a harbor. By the early 1700s this notion had lost any supporters it might once have had. Wharves were by then jutting out into the Delaware, obviating the need for such a harbor, and with Dock Creek already reeking of sewage and offal, the idea of filling it and turning it into usable land had no doubt crossed more than one mind.

Claypoole was not around in 1693 to witness Edward Shippen's arrival in Philadelphia from Boston. Described as having "the biggest person, the biggest house, and the biggest coach" in the city, Shippen became mayor in 1701 by appointment of his friend William Penn, who had just granted the city a charter. Shippen's large house, located on Second Street near Dock Creek, bespoke the status of its Quaker owner, who in 1709 was one of the three wealthiest men in the city (Bronner 1982:34, 36, 63). But its spaciousness no doubt also had something to do with the size of Shippen's family, which, like everything else about him, was large. He fathered eleven children by three wives, becoming a father for the last time at the age of sixty-nine. Two of his older children, Edward, Jr., and Joseph, followed him from Boston to Philadelphia in 1704 (Nash 1986:339, 343, 358).

The character of the neighborhood near Front and Dock streets remained relatively unchanged throughout the eighteenth century, consisting primarily of a mix of middle-class artisans,

sea captains, and some well-to-do merchants. During these years, the two branches of Dock Creek were filled in, a section at a time (see Figure 4.12). The west branch was filled by 1757. The head of the northwest branch had presumably been filled sometime before 1740, when the block between Third and Fourth streets north of Walnut was developed. By 1769 it had been filled as far east as Second Street, and by 1784 all the way to the tidal basin. The basin was closed as far as Front Street between 1818 and 1821 and completely closed when Delaware Avenue was constructed in 1839 (Liggett 1971a).

As the nineteenth century progressed, the area around Front and Dock streets became increasingly commercial, with private residences and shops giving way to large warehouses and boardinghouses. The commercial trend continued into the twentieth century. Ultimately, in the 1960s, all the structures in the block bounded by Dock, Walnut, Front, and Second streets were demolished as part of an urban renewal program. After serving as a parking lot for a number of years, the site reverted in the late 1980s to one of its nineteenth-century uses. Serving again as a place of accommodation, it now houses a Sheraton hotel.

The Archaeological Investigations

In monitoring the contractor's machine excavations at Front and Dock streets in 1968, Liggett (1970c; 1971a) recorded a stone pier on the south side of Dock Street and a rather elaborate log causeway that extended 180 feet south of the pier (Figure 5.26). The causeway's bottom layer consisted of timbers laid lengthwise on pilings; lying across the timbers were several layers of logs and stringers, topped by

Figure 5.26.

Early eighteenth-century stone pier and log causeway uncovered south of Dock Street in 1968 by Barbara Liggett. (Photo by J. L. Cotter)

Figure 5.27.

Site plan of 1984 archaeological investigation at Front and Dock streets. (From McCarthy 1984b; courtesy of Rouse and Associates and John Milner Associates)

a surface layer of logs 6 to 8 inches in diameter. Beneath the bottom layer was a swamp of black organic muck, testimony to why a causeway was needed in the first place. Historical documents indicated the construction had taken place between 1718 and 1723.

When more sewer lines were dug in late 1969 and early 1970, Liggett (1971a, n.d.) recorded a stone pier on the north side of Dock Street, opposite the one uncovered in 1968. While the pier on the south side appeared to be an abutment for the 1718–1723 causeway, artifacts found around the pier on the north side indicated it had been built after 1750. The most likely explanation for the discrepancy in dates is that sections of the causeway were rebuilt in the course of the eighteenth century.

The purpose of the initial archaeological work carried out by John Milner Associates in 1984 was to identify and test areas of the site that had

been occupied in the seventeenth and eighteenth centuries. According to historical records, at least twelve lots had been occupied before 1700, and eleven more were in use during the colonial period. The testing indicated that a portion of the seventeenth-century ground surface survived in the southwest part of the study area (Figure 5.27). Also apparently surviving beneath the cellar floors of nineteenth-century commercial buildings were numerous eighteenth- and nineteenth-century privy pits (Cosans 1984; McCarthy 1984b).

After a large part of the site was mechanically excavated (Figure 5.28), the archaeologists examined a sample of the seventeenth-century ground surface and excavated the privy pits by hand. Somewhat unexpectedly, the ground surface in cellars D, G, and I (shown in Figure 5.27) yielded a number of prehistoric artifacts, most of them mixed in with historic material. However, a few prehistoric items came from deeper fill in cellar D; soil auger borings indicated this fill had come from a high, sandy bank in the immediate area. The inference was that the high ground had been the site of prehistoric occupation and that the fill was removed and used in reclaiming the swampy margins of Dock Creek in the early eighteenth century. Also supporting the notion that the prehistoric artifacts were discarded near the site rather than having been dug up and carted in from farther afield were the size and nature of the collection: eighteen stone tools, eighty-nine fragments of stone flakes and waste from tool-making, nineteen pottery sherds, and eleven fragments of fire-cracked rocks from a hearth. Of the stone artifacts, eight (7.5 percent) were projectile points. Although not unusually large, this artifact collection is probably the largest prehistoric one yet found in urban

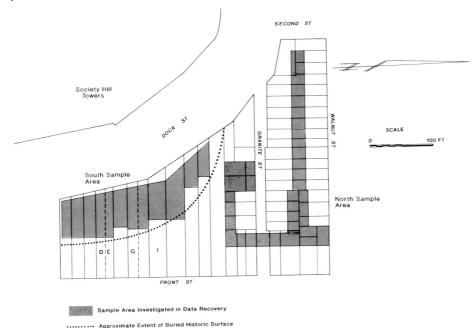

SECOND ST

Society Hill Towers

DOCK ST

GRANITE ST

WALNUT ST

SCALE
0   100 FT

South Sample Area

North Sample Area

D E   G   I

FRONT ST

▨ Sample Area Investigated in Data Recovery

⋯⋯ Approximate Extent of Buried Historic Surface

Philadelphia (McCarthy and Roberts [in preparation]).

The confluence of Dock Creek and the Delaware River was not a particularly strategic place for prehistoric habitation. More favorable locations existed at the Falls of the Schuylkill and at the confluence of the Schuylkill and the Delaware. One would expect sizable prehistoric occupation at these sites and perhaps a smaller, transient occupation at the mouth of Dock Creek. However, the fire-cracked hearth rocks suggested that occupation here was more than just transient. The rather high percentage of projectile points among the stone artifacts suggested that the site was used mainly for hunting, fishing, and other tasks related to food procurement, rather than for tool-making. The types of projectile points and ceramics found indicated the site was in use, at least intermittently, from the late Archaic-Transitional periods (ca. 2000–1400 B.C.) to A.D. 1600 or later (McCarthy and Roberts [in preparation]).

The earliest historical artifacts, dating from shortly after Philadelphia's founding in 1682, appeared on lots owned by Edward Shippen and Henry Flowers, another of the early settlers. The ceramics included redware, presumably made locally even at this early date, and some imported oriental porcelain and English tinglazed pieces. In all, the ceramic collection was rather mundane, perhaps reflecting the middle-class values of the early Quaker settlers as well as an initial lack of trade between the colony and England. A broken shell trade bead found in a trash pit suggested that trade with the Lenape during the late seventeenth century may have been more prevalent than previously suspected. Faunal remains also attested to the lifestyle of the early settlers. They apparently dined

Figure 5.28.

Sheraton Hotel site excavated to expose nineteenth-century foundations between Front and Dock streets, south of Walnut Street. Taken from the air during excavation, 1984. (Courtesy of John Milner Associates)

chiefly on beef, but some pig, sheep, chicken, goose, and fish bones, clam shells, and a rather large number of oyster shells testified to how they supplemented their diet (McCarthy and Roberts [in preparation]).

Cellars D, E, G, and I were once the backyards of Front Street houses. Upper layers of earth here attested to the sequential filling of Dock Creek. Beneath these layers were deposits of artifacts indicative of what went on in this neighborhood in the first half of the eighteenth century. In cellar I, bricks, nails, and utility ceramics were more prevalent than food remains, suggesting that this lot might have been used for some type of industry. In contrast, evidence of food preparation and consumption found in cellars D, E, and G indicated that much of the activity on these lots had been domestic (McCarthy and Roberts [in preparation]).

The bulk of the eighteenth-century artifacts came from three brick-lined privy pits (features 5, 6, and 9) and one brick-lined well (feature 30). Feature 5 dated from about 1730; the other three features appeared to date from about that time to the 1760s. Feature 5 was located on a lot that Joseph Shippen and his heirs owned from 1706 to 1754, and artifacts recovered from it attested to the lifestyle of a successful merchant. At the bot-

tom of feature 6 was a stock of creamware plates. They were apparently part of a merchant's faulty or outdated stock, an inference substantiated by many other whole or nearly whole ceramic vessels found elsewhere in this pit (McCarthy and Roberts [in preparation]).

Nineteenth-century features included twenty-seven brick-lined pits. This relatively large number of pits indicated an increasingly intensive use of land, as did the remains of a row of underground storage vaults that Jesse Godley built between 1849 and 1853. The granite-slab ceilings of "Godley's stores," as the vaults were known, served as the roadbed of Granite Street, which ran east-west across the block. Godley used the vaults as storage areas for his nearby warehouses. Other material evidence also substantiated the historical record of unceasing commercial activity in this area throughout the nineteenth century (McCarthy and Roberts [in preparation]).

Figure 5.29.

Aerial view of the riverfront, ca. 1970. The Benjamin Franklin Bridge is in the foreground. Above it on the right is Penn's Landing, dominated by a large boat basin. Running alongside Penn's Landing is Delaware Avenue, and to the right of it is land cleared for Interstate-95 construction. Part of the completed highway is visible in the upper right. (Courtesy of the Philadelphia Maritime Museum)

Figure 5.30.

Delaware Avenue, ca. 1890, looking north from the corner of Market Street. As early as 1800, narrow, rutted Water Street, created by the city's first merchants, was proving incapable of handling the traffic from the wharves and warehouses of the riverfront. In 1839 Delaware Avenue, 50 feet wide, was built with money that Stephen Girard, the wealthy merchant and financier, had left the city for that purpose. A few years after this photograph was taken, Delaware Avenue was widened again. (Courtesy of the Free Library of Philadelphia)

THE HIGH WARD: REFLECTIONS ON A CHANGING CULTURE

After the Benjamin Franklin Bridge between Philadelphia and Camden opened in 1926, the Delaware waterfront experienced a long, slow period of decline, evidenced by the progressive abandonment of the municipal and commercial piers that lined the river. Rejuvenation began in 1967 with plans for Penn's Landing—now a long, riverfront stretch containing quays, esplanades, condominiums, a museum, and a boat basin. Just about the time plans for Penn's Landing were getting underway, so were plans for the construction of I-95, which, when completed, would run west of Delaware Avenue (Figure 5.29). I-95 would thus sever the city from the artery that had linked it to the river. As can be seen in Figure 5.30, that artery has not always been the broad thoroughfare it is today.

In the late 1970s, to provide access to Delaware Avenue and the river in the vicinity of Penn's Landing, a bridge and pedestrian ramp over I-95 were constructed between Market Street and Chestnut. The construction affected twenty-one structures on the north side of the 100 block of Market Street and in the first block of North Front Street. One of these buildings had already been demolished; the other twenty were soon to suffer the same fate. All were potentially interesting from an archaeological and historical point of view; they stood in one of the oldest parts of the city, the High Ward, as this political district was called during the 1700s (Figure 5.31), when the town hall was at Market Street and Second.

In the first three months of 1976, the Philadelphia firm of Abraham

Levy Architect carried out a contract with the Pennsylvania Department of Transportation and the Pennsylvania Historical and Museum Commission for the archaeological investigation of these twenty-one buildings. Within the year, Herbert W. Levy, the architect and historic sites specialist who directed the investigation, and Charles E. Hunter, then a graduate student, had produced a report of the study (Hunter and Levy 1976). Hunter later used the data from this report

Figure 5.31.

The political wards of Philadelphia in the eighteenth century. The first town hall, whose arcaded ground floor served as a marketplace, was at Market Street and Second. (From Warner 1987)

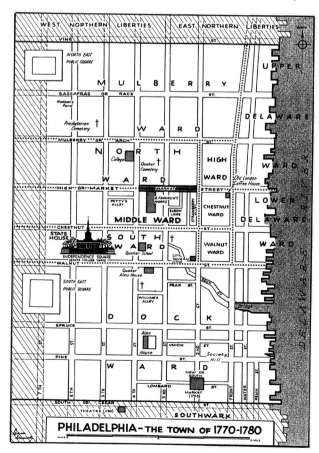

as the basis of a Ph.D. thesis (Hunter 1979). These two sources provided the data for the following account.

The Structures and the Artifacts

Although most of the twenty-one structures had been built as private residences with shops on the ground floor, all eventually gave way to wholly commercial buildings. This change in usage reflects a change in the character of the High Ward itself. Because the original architecture of the structures was basically unsuitable for warehousing and other commercial purposes, it was inevitable that this usage would also eventually decline. By 1976, when the buildings in this block of the old High Ward were slated for demolition, the neighborhood was undergoing yet another transformation, as riverfront enterprise began turning its attention to gentrified housing and services.

At the time of the investigation, the twenty structures still standing ranged in height from one to six stories, in width from 18 to 20 feet, and in depth from 80 to over 100 feet. The ground on which they had been built averaged 26 feet above mean low tide. All the structures were wood-framed with brick exteriors, and most had full, single-level basements. The structural evidence indicated that the houses had been constantly altered over the years. Interior walls and wall fragments of original houses were found in five of the buildings, but at only two of the buildings—those at 8 North Front Street and 131 Market Street—was there evidence of original eighteenth-century foundations.

The archaeologists uncovered nineteen privy pits within the block and excavated thirteen of them. These

Table 5.1. Artifacts and closing dates of pits in the High Ward.

Closing Date	Site of Pit	Artifacts
1760	121 Market Street	Cello-shaped Balsam of Life phial by Robert Turlington, dated 1750; kaolin pipe stems from three different zones, with average dates of 1743, 1745, and 1760; stoneware chamber pot and mug with mark of A. Duché, dating from 1730s; 3 mugs with cipher of Queen Anne, 1702–1714; other sherds of stoneware, slip-decorated combed ware, delft, and brown-glazed redware; William III halfpenny, 1689–1702; wine glass stems from 1685 to 1760, most of them earlier than 1725; 22 examples of McKearin bottle types, dates ranging from 1690 to 1730 and 1760 to 1770
1770	133 Market Street	Sherds of combed ware, delft, Chinese export porcelain, slip-decorated redware; 6 bone-handled knives; 1 cannon ball with diameter of 3½ inches; 1 1760–1770 (McKearin) bottle; 1 case bottle; small glass phials
1790	6 North Front Street	Sherds of combed ware, white salt-glazed stoneware plates (basket-weave molding), creamware plates (Royal pattern), delft, slip-decorated redware, brown-glazed redware, gray salt-glazed stoneware; fragments of case bottles; bottles of McKearin type 10 dating from 1790–1810
1790	8 North Front Street	Stoneware dating from 1680 to 1725 and later; white salt-glazed stoneware saucers, 1740–1770; creamware plates, 1770–1795 and later; Rhenish stoneware mugs, 1700–1775; other sherds of delft, Chinese export porcelain, slip-decorated redware; dip-molded bottles of McKearin type 10, 1790–1810; wine glass stems, 1735–1760
1800	135 Market Street	Redware; Chinese export porcelain; bottle of McKearin type 10, 1790–1810
1810–1825	121 Market Street	Many sherds of green and blue shell-edged pearlware plates, undecorated pearlware, redware, transfer-printed wares, and porcelain, with dates of 1800 to 1825; large quantity of glass fragments, with bottles dating from 1790 to 1810 or a little later; many animal bones and shellfish remains
1820–1840	139 Market Street	Many sherds of pearlware; green shell-edged transfer-printed with Chinese patterns, some hand-painted; bottle of McKearin type 11, 1820–1830
1820–1860	133 Market Street	Many fragments of kaolin pipes; several fragments of glass flasks
1825	105 Market Street	Polychrome pearlware (royal pattern) and blue, transfer-printed pearlware with Chinese patterns, 1800–1825; 6 redware chamberpots; slip-decorated redware plates; 1 redware mug; sherds of Chinese export porcelain; bottles of McKearin type 10, 1790–1810, and type 11, 1820–1830
1840–1870	121 Market Street	Transfer-printed "Spanish Convent" plate by Adams, 1840–1870; kaolin pipes, mid-1800s; Mexican 8-real coin of 1829; pocketwatch made by M. I. Tobias, Liverpool, 1810–1829; Dyottville bottles, 1850–1870; bottles of McKearin type 13, 1865–1875
1845	139 Market Street	Brown-glazed redware utility vessels; 1 sherd of combed ware; salt-glazed plate with basket-weave molding; ironstone china by Ridgeway, Morely, Wear and Co., Hanley, Staffordshire, ca. 1836–1842; sherds of pearlware and porcelain; bottles of McKearin type 11, 1820–1830 and later; liberty-head U.S. penny of 1815; fragments of 2 Rhenish stoneware vessels; 1 bottle neck from mid-1700s

From Hunter 1979.

thirteen pits yielded 20,220 ceramic sherds and an unspecified number of objects of glass and other materials. Hunter (1979) used the artifacts to establish closing dates for eleven of the thirteen pits. Table 5.1 lists both the closing dates and the artifacts. Hunter also used the artifacts to determine when the houses in the block had been built. He concluded that the earliest structure in the block had been built in 1703 at 101 Market Street and that the latest (the only one to have been added to the block in the nineteenth century) had been built in 1823 at 141 Market Street. In Hunter's opinion, the peak building period had been between 1770 and 1780, when eleven houses had gone up on the twenty-one lots. In addition to providing evidence of dates, the domestic artifacts found in the pits reflected the original use of the structures as private residences and small shops. A relatively large number of locally made ceramics and glass medicine bottles reflected the growth of local manufacturing during the first half of the nineteenth century.

An Interpretation of the Evidence

Hunter's goal in studying the artifacts recovered from the privy pits was to determine how they might reflect the settlement and growth of Philadelphia, the city's contacts with overseas markets, and the development of American manufacturing. He postulated that as a city and a port, Philadelphia would be fairly quick to reflect historic trends and events. His observations of the evidence from the High Ward led him to conclude that the artifacts found there reflected the following trends:

1682–1765:
Increasing importation of ceramics limits growth of domestic manufacture.

1765–1770:
Relations between England and the colonies deteriorate, leading to resolutions banning the importation of English goods. Domestic manufacture increases.

1770–1775:
Trade relations worsen. First and Second Continental Congresses meet. Domestic manufacture continues to grow.

1775–1781:
Revolutionary War is at its most active. Trade is disrupted. Conservative nature of artifacts from this period reflects the current political and economic stress.

1781–1783:
Peace is unconcluded, and there is less activity in the Philadelphia area. Mercantile uncertainty prevails.

1783–1810:
Philadelphia is the *de facto* capital of the nation, and the city's literary, architectural, and mercantile "golden age" begins. Importation of ceramics and other goods resumes.

1810–1817:
War of 1812–1814 disrupts technological development and growth of trade. Western lands are developing.

1817–1832:
Period of canal and railroad building occurs in Philadelphia area after 1823. Shipbuilding flourishes. Baldwin Locomotive Works opens in 1831. Domestic manufacturing becomes more sophisticated, and technology promotes more far-flung economic ties. High-quality ceramics become more abundant.

1832–1843:
Railroad and canal services expand, as do commerce and industry. Financial panic occurs in 1837.

1843–1880:
Philadelphia becomes increasingly urban. Philadelphia County and city are consolidated in 1854. Pennsylvania Railroad is chartered in 1846, and line from Philadelphia to Pittsburgh opens in 1854. Foreign trade is unsettled during Civil War, but industry in Philadelphia area expands dramatically. Economy experiences a downturn in the 1870s.

Hunter concludes that changes in patterns of artifact styles are, if anything, more conservative in periods of stress than at other times. His view is that "artifacts and features found in well-documented contexts can provide extensive information not only about the culture or period under study but also about the nature of archaeological methods and assumptions" (1979:278). However, he does not turn the quantified data over to the reader fully analyzed, nor does he address whether the artifacts really reflect the culturally disruptive events of the American Revolution, the Industrial Revolution, the Civil War, and the evocation of a metropolis. The reader may wonder whether even a complete series of artifacts in a pit filled incrementally from 1760 to 1900 (which has yet to be discovered in Philadelphia) would give any conclusive hints of historical events. They might only remain, as they were in the beginning, skewed markers of pooled individual tastes and the fortuitous circumstances of deposition. It remains the hope of archaeological researchers that sophisticated statistical analyses of artifacts may provide the means of at least setting forth probabilities with confidence, even accounting for, and projecting beyond, gaps in data. Fulfillment of this hope, as far as Philadelphia archaeology is concerned, is not yet at hand.

8 SOUTH FRONT STREET:
A STUDY IN CONTINUITY

One of the constants of urban life, as anomalous as it may sound, is change. Neighborhoods, like chameleons, are constantly adapting to the changing conditions of the environments that surround them. This evolution of the urban scene is, of course, reflected in the archaeological record—in the physical evidence of building, rebuilding, land modification, and reuse. Thus, for an archaeologist to chance upon an urban site that is characterized more by continuity than by change, especially in a neighborhood where marked change has taken place, is a rare opportunity indeed. Such an opportunity presented itself in the mid-1970s when 8 South Front

Figure 5.32.

A 1698 survey of the "Proprietaries Lot" and "Lettlia's [*sic*] Penn's Lotts." Presumably, this shows the proposed subdivision of Penn's lot, as it was not until 1701 that he actually deeded the land to Letitia. (Courtesy of the Historical Society of Pennsylvania)

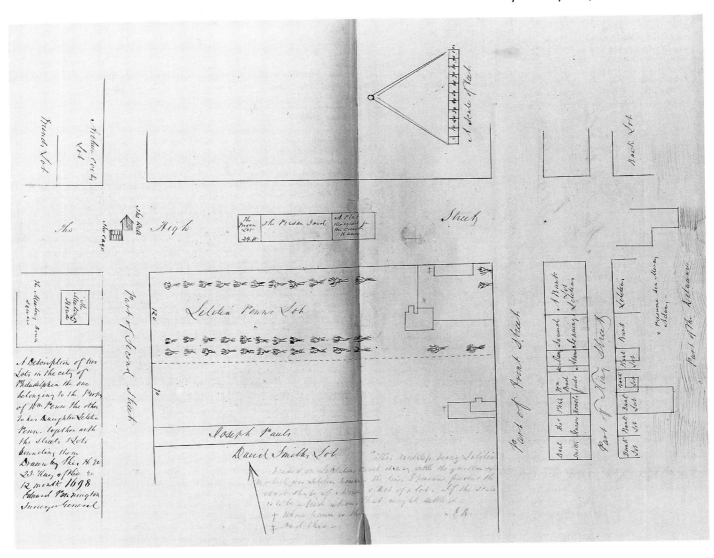

Street, a few steps south of Market, became the subject of an archaeological study. The goal of the study was to produce physical evidence that would illuminate the historical record of occupation of the same site by relatively few families and structures over a long period of time. Betty Cosans conducted the study; her site report (1976), together with a later general study of Front Street (Cosans-Zebooker 1985), form the basis for what follows.

The History of 8 South Front Street

For a hundred and fifty years, from 1683 to 1833, only three families were associated with 8 South Front Street: from 1683 to 1713, the Penns; from 1713 to 1736, the Yards; and from 1736 to 1833, the Bradfords. The site was initially part of a large parcel of land owned by William Penn. The piece of this parcel that Penn deeded to his daughter Letitia in 1701, with all the structures on it, included only the northern part of the property. As noted in Chapter 3, Letitia's lot extended 172 feet south from Market Street and 402 feet east and west between Front and Second streets. Figure 5.32, a 1698 survey of the property, shows a structure near the northeast corner of the lot, another structure fronting on Market Street near Front, and an orchard in the western part of the lot near Second Street.

Figure 5.33 shows the various subdivisions of neighboring properties that had taken place by 1701. That Letitia Penn's lot was not more substantially developed until the second decade of the eighteenth century may be partly explained by her father's circumstances at the turn of the century. At that time, William Penn was not only deeply in debt but also engaged

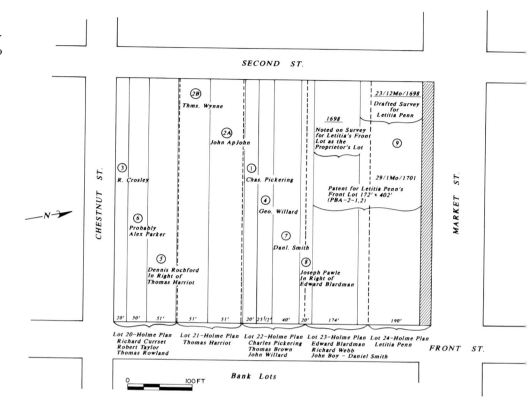

Figure 5.33.

Original lots shown on Holme's plan as they appeared in 1701 after subdivisions. (From Cosans 1976)

in a protracted financial battle with his business manager, Philip Ford—a battle ending in a lawsuit that sent Penn to debtor's prison. One of the issues in this dispute was whether an earlier agreement between the two men nullified Penn's right to grant the property at Front and Market streets to his daughter. Whether Penn's financial and legal troubles were at the root of the delay or not, it was not until 1713 that Letitia and her husband William Aubrey finally sold an undeveloped portion of their property for the sum of £255 to a bricklayer named Joseph Yard. Presumably, it was at about this time that Letitia built her own house on her portion of the lot.

Yard immediately began building three adjoining houses along Front Street, the middle of which was 8 South Front; no details of the con-

struction of these rowhouses have survived in the records. Upon Joseph's death in 1716, the property at 8 South Front Street passed to his son John. When John's mother died in 1736, the property was sold to Andrew Bradford, in whose family it remained for the next century. One of Andrew Bradford's descendants, Thomas Bradford, an ardent supporter of American independence who served in the militia as captain and lieutenant colonel, occupied the site for nearly fifty years, from 1779 to 1828. In 1833 his descendants sold the property to John Moss, a Philadelphia shipping merchant who three years later also bought the land on which the Walnut Street Prison had stood.

In addition to having belonged to only three families over a period of a hundred and fifty years, the lot at 8 South Front Street has for almost three hundred years had only two generations of buildings standing on it. The three adjoining houses that Joseph Yard erected in 1713 looked out toward the Delaware until 1834, when John Moss razed them. Although the buildings were altered between 1734 and 1756, when a kitchen and piazza were added, the core structures remained substantially unchanged until their demolition almost a century and a quarter after they were built. Moss replaced the eighteenth-century buildings with a four-story brick building, which still stands on the site today. In the ever-changing urban environment, this is an unusual record of stable property use—one that is rarely matched except by buildings of special historical or architectural significance.

Archaeology at 8 South Front Street

The excavations at 8 South Front Street indicated that Moss's 1834 building had incorporated much of Yard's earlier middle building, including most of the north and east foundation walls and part of the south wall. There was also evidence that the west part of the original cellar had been deepened, possibly at the time Moss razed the earlier buildings, which might explain the absence of any trace of the original west, or rear, foundation wall. Both the nineteenth-century west wall and the original foundation walls had been laid directly on undisturbed sandy, yellow-clay subsoil; a thin layer of mortar provided a firm base under the first course of stone. Although Moss seems to have made extensive use of Yard's

foundation walls, he apparently did not attempt to reuse all of the above-grade walls. While old joist pockets in the north wall indicated that he had used the original wall here, the absence of such pockets in the south wall suggested that he had razed and completely rebuilt this one.

Most of the archaeological attention focused on three pits found beneath modern concrete flooring in the basement. As shown in Figure 5.34, feature 1 extended partway under the foundation walls in the northwest corner of the building. The pit was about 4.5 feet in diameter and 20 feet deep, measured from the basement flooring. It was lined with dry-laid, handmade bricks set stretcherwise. Interestingly, two construction techniques had been used: in the upper half of the pit, the bricks were laid in a spiral, but in the lower half, they were laid in consecutive courses. The pit contained twelve layers of fill, several

of which yielded numerous artifacts. On the basis of its artifacts, one layer was tightly dated to about 1775–1785. Another, which contained approximately 200 reconstructible spirit bottles, appeared to be slightly earlier. One of the bottles found in this layer was dated 1769 and embossed with the name "J. Biddle"; although the Bradford family owned 8 South Front Street in 1769, J. Biddle was taxed as an occupant of the property in that year. The bottom layer of fill, consisting of highly organic black soil, contained a fair number of preserved wooden and leather objects, including a board with peg mortise, a turned wooden baluster, and no fewer than eight shoes. These artifacts, too, dated from the mid-eighteenth century.

Feature 2, another circular brick-

Figure 5.34.

Site plan and elevation, 8 South Front Street. (From Cosans 1976)

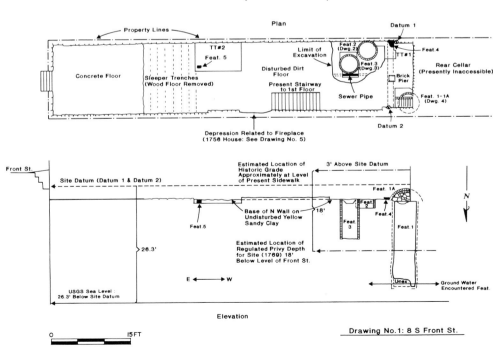

lined pit, was found along the south foundation wall near the southwest corner of the basement. It had an interior diameter of 3.75 feet but was only about 2.5 feet deep. Its dry-laid bricks, which were set stretcherwise in a spiral, appeared to be wasters that had been either overfired or underfired in the manufacturing process. As indicated in Figure 5.35, the pit contained a single deposit of dark-brown sandy soil, which yielded a fair number of artifacts. The artifacts, tightly dated to ca. 1720–1730, included a gray stoneware chamberpot bearing the mark "A.D.," indicating that it came from the stoneware kiln of Anthony Duché, near Fifth and Chestnut streets. Also found in feature 2 was a polychrome delft plate marked with the initials "G.R.," probably referring to George [Rex] I, who reigned from 1714 until 1727.

Feature 3 was just a little northeast of feature 2. This pit had an interior diameter of 3.3 feet and extended about 10 feet below the basement flooring. It was constructed of a single thickness of dry-laid bricks set in consecutive stretcher courses. Figure 5.36 shows the four soil levels recorded. Of these, level 2 yielded a relatively large collection of artifacts, including a British coin minted in 1734—proof that this fill had been deposited after that date.

Analysis of the data allowed for a reconstruction of the sequence in which the three excavated pits were used and the relationship between them. Feature 2 was apparently dug as a privy pit when Joseph Yard first built the house in 1713. Underfired or overfired waster bricks were not commonly used in privies in Philadelphia, but as a bricklayer, Joseph Yard must have had access to such wasters, which doubtless explains their appearance in this particular pit.

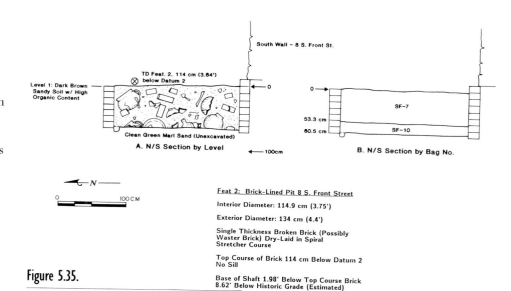

Figure 5.35.

Feature 2, 8 South Front Street, in section. (From Cosans 1976)

Figure 5.36.

Feature 3, 8 South Front Street, in section. (From Cosans 1976)

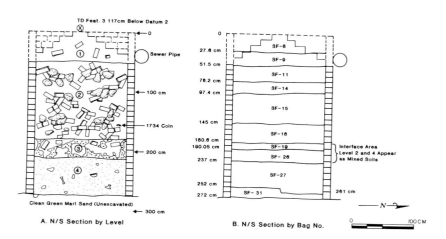

About a decade after its construction, feature 2 seems to have been abandoned and replaced by feature 3, which was dug almost directly beside it. The extreme shallowness of feature 2, which, if estimates of the original grade are correct, was no more than 8 feet deep, probably necessitated this shift. The new privy pit evidently extended more than 15 feet below the original grade and thus had almost twice the capacity of the first one.

Sometime between 1734 and 1756, when a kitchen wing was added to the property, the occupants of the house abandoned feature 3 and began using feature 1 as a privy pit. The latter may originally have been dug as a well, for it seems to have extended more than 26 feet below the original grade. With its greater depth, it would have served the needs of the site's occupants better than either of the previous privy pits. The health of anyone using water from wells in the vicinity of this deep privy pit would, however, have been ill-served. The artifacts in the upper and lower deposits of the pit indicated that feature 1 was in use for some forty years.

A complete analysis of the artifacts recovered during this investigation has not yet been undertaken; if and when it is, it will doubtless shed more light on the behavior of the people who lived at 8 South Front Street during the years the Yards and Bradfords owned the property. Even without such an analysis, however, this study has produced evidence of structural changes to an early Philadelphia site that has exhibited remarkable continuity over time. As such, it has added its own unique threads to the intricate web that constitutes the historical archaeology of the city.

FROM PORCELAIN ROSETTES TO BRASS CANNONS: THE STORY OF THE BONNIN AND MORRIS PORCELAIN FACTORY

In the brief two years it was in operation, from 1770 until 1772, the Bonnin and Morris Porcelain Factory, the first commercial attempt at making porcelain in the New World, demonstrated that American wares could rival those of the mother nation across the sea. The factory's subsequent conversion to a cannon foundry during the Revolutionary War was evidence that the shrewd inhabitants of New England did not hold an exclusive patent on that characteristic of American business and industry known as Yankee ingenuity. The buildings of the factory, long since razed, were in Southwark between Second and Front streets, south of Washington Avenue not far from the Delaware River.

The first archaeological investigation of the site was carried out by a class in historical archaeology at the University of Pennsylvania in 1967. Graham Hood (then a curator at the Yale University Art Gallery and later chief curator of Colonial Williamsburg), who had been researching the site and planning to test it himself, contributed to the investigation by providing data on the location of the factory and on its operation. The findings of the 1967 study were encouraging enough that Hood secured financing so that two graduate students—Paul R. Huey and Garry Wheeler Stone—could continue the investigation. In the summer of 1968, another Penn class joined Huey and Stone in excavating the site. The following account is based on the reports that came out of this joint archaeological enterprise (Hood 1969, 1972; Huey 1968a, 1968b; Lapsansky and Zakas 1968).

Commerce and Industry in Old Southwark: A Revolutionary Enterprise

On June 29, 1767, to the detriment of American trade and the benefit of British manufacture, the British Parliament passed the Townshend Acts, a new series of taxes to be imposed on the American colonies. The following summer, the colonies, already fuming at a variety of other impositions, retorted by declaring an embargo on all imported British-made goods. As a shrewd Philadelphia merchant and as

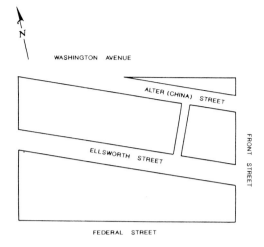

WASHINGTON AVENUE

ALTER (CHINA) STREET

ELLSWORTH STREET

FRONT STREET

FEDERAL STREET

Figure 5.37.

The locale of the Bonnin and Morris Porcelain Factory. The lot on which the factory stood was bounded on the north and south by Alter and Ellsworth streets, but where it lay between Front and Second streets is unknown. No picture of the factory or plan of the lot survives. (From Huey 1968b)

a loyal American patriot, George Anthony Morris was a staunch supporter of the embargo. Recognizing the commercial opportunity that the boycott might present, Morris formed a partnership with Gousse Bonnin for the purpose of establishing a porcelain factory, the first one in the colonies. Bonnin, recently arrived in Philadelphia from England, had been in business in Bow, near London, where fine porcelains were made, and he had gained some experience in the manufacture of ceramics.

As the 1760s drew to a close, Morris and Bonnin began erecting a factory on a lot owned by the Morris family. The lot is known to have been bounded on the south by Ellsworth Street (which was first called Wicaco Lane and later Prime Street) and on the north by Alter Street (which in tribute to the Bonnin and Morris venture was for a time called China Street), but just exactly where the lot sat between Front and Second streets

is uncertain (Figure 5.37). During the 1670s and 1680s, all the land in the vicinity was part of a large tract owned by the Swedish brothers, Swan, Oele, and Andries Swanson. The proximity of the eastern part of the Swansons' tract to the Delaware River made it particularly attractive for development, and eventually Swan Swanson's heirs sold several of the choice lots along the narrow road then known as Wicaco Lane to a saddler named Swen Bankson. In 1738 Bankson in turn sold off a 1½ acre lot to George Fitzwater, Philadelphia merchant and grandfather of George Anthony Morris. Fitzwater left most of the land to his daughter Martha Fitzwater Morris, who held the southern portion of it in joint tenancy with her son George and the northern portion in joint tenancy with her daughter Phoebe.

By July 26, 1770, George Morris and Gousse Bonnin had their factory standing. Its "sundry and spacious buildings" contained "three kilns, two furnaces, two mills, two clay vaults, cisterns, engines, and treading room" (Hood 1972:13). One building, no doubt the main one, was 80 feet long and 15 feet deep; three stories high and topped by a garret, it had 300 panes of glass gleaming in its windows. Of the two clay vaults, both of which were used for storing and ripening clay, one is known to have been situated under the east end of the factory. Outside the factory complex on China Street, a pump furnished the water the potters needed to soften and mix their clay.

Owing to numerous problems with finances, workmen, materials, and techniques, it was not until January 1771 that Bonnin and Morris announced the first successful production of their wares. By this time, however, they were facing a problem considerably more serious than the

others that plagued them. In 1769 the British Parliament had repealed all the Townshend taxes except the tax on tea, and in 1770 New York merchants had resumed trading with the British; the merchants of Boston and Philadelphia had soon followed suit.

Bonnin, the "acting proprietor," was having other problems as well. Although he held a 1769 patent for the exclusive manufacture of graphite crucibles anywhere in the American colonies or the rest of the British Empire for fourteen years, Bonnin had put his bets on porcelain as being the more profitable enterprise. After struggling to scrape clay from the banks of the Delaware between New Castle and Wilmington, as well as to muster garbage bones for calcining and a variety of other items necessary to the manufacture of bone porcelain, Bonnin came to the conclusion that the clay for which he yearned, clay that could withstand heat better than any material yet used in ceramic manufacture, was in South Carolina. In 1772, after a final labor dispute with the English potters who worked in the factory—and who had been warned by Wedgwood that they would starve in America—the luckless Bonnin gave up as "acting proprietor" and the next spring left with his family for England.

On December 21, 1772, having produced wares that were to become some of the rarest porcelain museum pieces in the world, the factory was put up at auction. On May 4, 1774, after a fourth attempt to sell the property at auction, the sheriff announced that Joseph Morris, father of George Anthony Morris, had bought the entire premises for £213.15.

Joseph Morris lost nothing on the bargain he had struck. After being leased to several short-term renters, the erstwhile porcelain factory came to the attention of the Pennsylvania Council of Safety. Appointed by the assembly in the summer of 1775 to look to the military requirements of the rebellious province, the Council of Safety had soon recognized the urgent need to secure sources of artillery. By 1776 it was funding the efforts of Captain Benjamin Loxley (the member of the Carpenters' Company who in 1768 had arranged the purchase of Carpenters' Court) and of an experienced brass-caster named James Byers to convert the Bonnin and Morris porcelain works into a foundry for casting brass cannons.

The conversion of the factory from the manufacture of dainty dishes to the casting of heavy cannon, though it did indeed require ingenuity and inventiveness, was not as impossible a job as it might sound. A number of the steps involved in manufacturing a brass cannon were familiar to the potter, and many of the implements, materials, and structures used in the porcelain factory were, with some clever adaptations, useful in the gun factory. The porcelain factory's supply of clay, for instance, was put to adaptive use. The first step in making the cannon, which in many ways was like making a molded clay pot, was to create a clay model of the cannon barrel. This the founders did by applying two coats of clay—the first, a soft clay tempered with brick powder; the second, a soft potter's clay well mixed with horse dung and hair or lint—to a bar of iron resting on an iron grate. A fire burning beneath the grate dried the clay as it was applied. Using a "modeling board" cut in the pattern of a cannon barrel, the founders smoothed and turned the clay model until it assumed the desired shape. When the surface was dry, they pinned to it plaster molds of the pan, the arms or handles, and whatever

ornamentation they might have had time for.

Next, the founders rubbed the model with tallow, covered it with four inches of luting loam—a cement of very fine, soft clay, strained and mixed with horse dung—and wrapped it with strong iron bands, over which they daubed yet more clay. As they crumbled and removed the interior of the dried and hardened model to obtain a hollow mold, the tallow prevented adherence to the luting loam. Using a windlass or tackle blocks, they lowered the hollow mold, well-reinforced with iron bands, vertically into one of the brick-lined pits that had formerly been used as a clay storage vault. After inserting a long iron core covered with a paste of ashes into the center of the mold to form the cannon's bore, they filled the pit with soft earth to provide firm support for the mold. The master founder then opened a spigot from an adjacent furnace, formerly used for firing porcelain and now for melting brass, and molten brass poured into the mold. After removing the iron core from the cooled casting, the founders trimmed the surface of the barrel, finished the bore in a boring mill, and drilled a vent hole. The cannon was then ready for mounting and testing.

An initial run of the foundry's finished product won Loxley the commission of major. It also won the confidence of the Continental Congress, which took over from the province the expense of operating the facility. When John Adams visited the foundry as a representative of the Congress on March 29, 1777, he was much impressed by it. Philippe Charles Tronson du Coudray, a learned and punctilious French engineer who had visions of becoming major general in supreme command of artillery and engineers, was, how-

ever, not impressed. As the foundry struggled with shortages of metal and attempted to melt down a shipload of French 1,000-pound cannons, each of which could be recast into three smaller, more maneuverable cannons capable of firing 6-pound shot, Coudray warned Congress that such a process was wasteful of the brass ingredients—the copper, tin, and zinc "so difficult to replace in this country." Emphasizing further that a botched brass mix could have disastrous consequences, causing the recast cannons to blow up, Coudray declared that these models "would be of a service as little durable as safe."

Despite Coudray's gloomy predictions, small brass 6-pounders and 8-inch mortars for the Continental Army continued to emerge from the foundry's casting pit, together with some iron work, until shortly before the British marched into Philadelphia on September 26, 1777. A few months earlier, on June 16, Commissary General Benjamin Flower had sent a warning to the foundry that it should be prepared to remove the operation as soon as the British reached the city. By the time the British arrived, Major Loxley was back on active duty, and James Byers had fled, leaving his tools, patterns, and metal at the foundry to be taken or destroyed. As it turned out, the equipment was not destroyed, and after Washington's army retook Philadelphia on June 18, 1778, Byers soon had the cannon foundry back in production.

With the demise of the munitions industry at the end of the Revolutionary War and the closing of the foundry, James Byers found himself with a broken contract and out of a job. The magnitude and effectiveness of French foreign aid in munitions doomed this nascent American industry until the War of 1812 loomed.

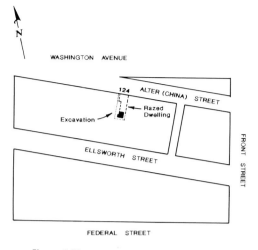

Figure 5.38.

Site of archaeological discovery at the Bonnin and Morris Porcelain Factory. Evidence of porcelain manufacture came to light at the rear of a vacant lot formerly occupied by a row house. (From Huey 1968b)

With no cannon to manufacture and with the British soon resuming their status as a strong competitive force in most lines of manufacture, the factory between Wicaco Lane and China Street languished. Ultimately, in the early 1800s, the factory's buildings were demolished and replaced by a row of wooden houses; these structures were to achieve fame as a sailors' brothel. They, too, in their turn came down, replaced in the 1830s by the red-brick rowhouses that now occupy part of the site of the first porcelain factory in the New World.

Archaeological Discovery

The students who conducted the first archaeological investigation at the site of the Bonnin and Morris Porcelain Factory in 1967 carried out more than a dozen tests in a narrow wedge of vacant land between Ellsworth and Alter streets, as well as in the backyards of Alter Street's early nineteenth-century rowhouses. In classic fashion, the very last scheduled field test produced the most interesting find. It occurred at the back of a narrow vacant lot that fronted on Alter Street (Figure 5.38). The lot, once occupied by a rowhouse, was at the time of the 1967 investigation a junkyard for the derelict trucks and other discards of a business next door (Figure 5.39). Here excavation revealed, at a depth of 13 inches from the surface, a 3-inch layer of wasters. It was filled with dozens of fragments of damaged sagger pots and at least one unglazed, molded fragment of bisque, as porcelain is called after it is fired and before it is glazed. The bisque fragment, also a waster spoiled in the process of production, had been fired once and, when discarded, had not yet been decorated. It, together with the sagger fragments, provided conclusive evidence of porcelain manufacture.

After the site had been cleared, further excavation by Huey and Stone and the summer class of 1968 produced some interesting additional evidence: more wasters of sagger pots and bisque, as well as plaster of Paris possibly used in molds. Figure 5.40 shows the excavated area and the stratigraphic position of the deposit. The sagger fragments, shown in Figure 5.41, gave a fair idea of the rough cylindrical vessels in which the porcelain was fired to safeguard it from the oxidizing and smudging flames of the furnace. The saggers, mostly of rough-fired pink clay and a few of yellow, ranged from 8½ to 14½ inches in diameter and from 2½ to 5¼ inches in height—ample enough to accommodate all the known Bonnin and Morris porcelain products.

In his study of the fragments of bone porcelain recovered from the site of the Bonnin and Morris factory, Graham Hood (1972) listed the sig-

Figure 5.39.

The lot as it appeared when first evidence of the Bonnin and Morris Porcelain Factory was found in 1967. The Bell Fuel Company, owner of the business next door to the site, was most cooperative in clearing the lot so that excavations could proceed in 1968. The 1967 excavation that produced the first evidence of porcelain manufacture was directly beneath the camera. Betty Cosans, then a Penn student, is at right. In the distance, on Carpenter Street between Front and Second, is Sparks' Shot Tower, a Philadelphia landmark since the early 1800s. (Photo by J. L. Cotter)

nificant examples. Perhaps the most significant were some bisque fragments of lattice-sided bowls with sprigs of rosettes on the interstices. As shown in Figure 5.42, the rosettes exactly matched those on a bowl at the Philadelphia Museum of Art. The museum's bowl, 6 inches in diameter and 2 inches high, had been assumed to be a Bonnin and Morris piece on the basis of the mark "P" that it bore; the matching bisque rosettes recovered from the site of the factory posi-

tively authenticated the museum example. Although Bonnin and Morris advertised in a Philadelphia newspaper of January 1771 that they would mark their wares with an "S," only three examples of this mark are presently known, and in each case the "S" is reversed so that it looks like a "Z." More often the Bonnin and Morris mark is "P." Whether the "S" stood for Southwark and the "P" for Philadelphia—or Pennsylvania—is unknown.

The last of the three Bonnin and

Morris sherds marked with a reverse "S" came to light in 1971 at Hanna's Town in Westmoreland County, Pennsylvania. Hanna's Town, a frontier settlement during the 1770s, was located along the route to Fort Pitt, as Pittsburgh was then known. The piece was among a number of Bonnin and Morris sherds, shown in Figure 5.43, unearthed by a team of excavators associated with the Society for Pennsylvania Archaeology. Hood (1972:34) noted that when analyzed by x-ray diffraction, the Hanna's Town sherds proved identical in paste composition to those recovered from the site of the Bonnin and Morris factory. He also noted that the design of the Hanna's Town sherds closely resembled that of a Bonnin and Morris fruit basket at Winterthur; interestingly, the design on this fruit basket matched that of a transfer-printed sherd found at the factory site. Other significant finds from the factory site included some molded sherds that bore a close resemblance to a sauceboat attributed to Bonnin and Morris, which is in the collection of the Brooklyn Museum, and sherds with painted scenes that matched corresponding parts of a molded-shell pickle tray in the collection of the Philadelphia Museum of Art.*

* When the study ended, Hood donated the fragments of saggers and porcelain found on the factory site to the Philadelphia Museum of Art, which has in its collection a representation of Bonnin and Morris finished ware.

Figure 5.40.

Bonnin and Morris Porcelain Factory. *Top,* the cleared site and excavated area looking north toward Alter Street in 1968; *left,* stratigraphy of the deposit. Undisturbed earth lay only 19 inches from the surface. Sagger deposit shows from 10 to 14 inches from surface. (Photos by J. L. Cotter)

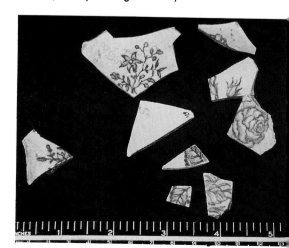

Figure 5.41.

Fragments of sagger pots found at the Bonnin and Morris Porcelain Factory. (Photo by J. L. Cotter)

Figure 5.42.

Comparison of a bisque rosette from the site of the Bonnin and Morris factory (at top) with the rosettes on a bowl owned by the Philadelphia Museum of Art. The museum's bowl had been assumed to be a Bonnin and Morris piece on the basis of its mark; the fragments of bisque from the factory site verified the assumption. (Courtesy of Graham Hood)

Figure 5.43.

Bonnin and Morris sherds found at Hanna's Town, Pennsylvania. One bears the mark "Z," the reverse "S" so far found on only two other sherds that could be attributed to Bonnin and Morris. (Courtesy of Margaret Fields)

Hood (1972) identified the types of vessels from which the sherds of the factory site had come. These included 4 fruit baskets with latticework joined by molded flowers, 4 medium-sized bowls, 15 small bowls, 13 cups, 16 punch bowls, and 26 sauceboats, 19 of which had floral molding. A number of sherds from various types of vessels had a molded "quilt" pattern resembling a chevron.

In addition to yielding substantial evidence of the products of the porcelain factory, the site between Ellsworth and Alter streets yielded some evidence of the cannon foundry that had served Washington's army. In a layer of mixed refuse deposited after 1772, Huey and Stone found drippings of molten brass as well as fragments of clay that differed in composition from the clay of saggers found in earlier deposits. This clay had probably been ground up with quartz and flakes of mica, mixed with water from the pump on old China Street, and furnished to the cannon founders as the tempered clay required for the cannon molds. In this deposit, Huey and Stone also found a French gunflint of the "spall," or single-flake, type—evidence at least of French munitions supply if not of

the presence of a Frenchman on the scene.* A flattened musketball of lead from the same deposit might have come from the gun of a Continental soldier, but it could just as well have been the product of Sparks' Shot Tower, a Philadelphia landmark ever since it began producing lead shot on Carpenter Street, just north of the factory, on Independence Day, 1808.

One thing the investigations of 1967 and 1968 failed to reveal was any structural evidence of the factory buildings or of their furnaces, kilns, and vaults; with luck, future excavations between Washington Avenue and Ellsworth Street may yet reveal these. The archaeological evidence these investigations did produce was, however, enough to authenticate extant museum examples of the products of the Bonnin and Morris factory, the first to produce porcelain in the New World. They also produced some evidence of that quality known as Yankee ingenuity as it was applied to converting a factory devoted to producing porcelain to one devoted to the manufacture of cannon.

* French gunflints, identified by a honey-colored flint as opposed to the dark-gray English flint, frequently are found wherever seventeenth- and eighteenth-century French trade and presence reached.

FORT MIFFLIN: FORGOTTEN DEFENDER

Fort Mifflin must be one of the nation's most neglected, unknown, and unvisited historic sites. It is also certainly one of the most important. Without it and the 350 men who defended it—most of whom died doing so—the American War of Independence might well have been lost before the autumn of 1777 was out. Today the old fort sits in a state of forlorn and ghostly isolation, looking out on the Delaware from the far reaches of the Philadelphia International Airport (Figure 5.44). While jumbo jets scream and whistle overhead, casting shadows on the decaying buildings that surround the parade ground, the grass on the embankments grows long and straight, untrampled by the feet of sightseers. The whole ghostlike establishment is kept barely together by the efforts of a small band of devoted volunteers.

Although some preliminary archaeological investigations have taken place on the site, plans for full-scale investigations have never been implemented, nor has the site received the restorative care and interpretation its history warrants. The city of Philadelphia has been the rather reluctant owner of Fort Mifflin since 1962, and very little in the way of restoration has taken place there since then. However, Fort Mifflin's slow and steady decline began long before 1962.

Fort Mifflin's History: From Heroic Stand to Seedy Limbo

In 1772, several years before the outbreak of war, the province of Pennsylvania, with the help of British engineers, began building a fort on an island in the Delaware River to ward off raiding ships.* Situated just below the mouth of the Schuylkill and composed of mud and silt, the aptly named Mud Island was separated from the mainland by a channel 500 feet in width, which long ago filled in (Figure 5.45). The British engineers had just managed to construct some barracks and officers' quarters and to face one wall of the fort with great blocks of carefully dressed local gneiss (Figure 5.46) when in 1773, due to lack of funds, the work ceased. Three years later it resumed, this time

* Historical data in this section are from Barnes (1956), Brumbaugh (1959), Campbell (1959), Corps of Engineers (n.d.), Martin (1979), Massey (1969), and Nelligan (1969).

under the direction of the Americans.

The completion of Mud Fort, as it was known, was the first piece of business the continental Committee of Public Safety addressed after its appointment by Congress in the summer of 1776. The committee's choice for directing this work was Thomas Mifflin, the able Pennsylvanian for whom the fort was renamed. Mifflin, an ardent Whig who had been active in the revolutionary movement from the beginning, had served as Washington's *aide-de-camp* in the first days of the war in 1775 and in 1776 was quartermaster general of the Continental Army. He was assisted in his work on Mud Island by the French engineer Philippe Charles Tronson du Coudray, who had shared with Congress his low opinion of the American effort to make cannon in the converted porcelain factory on Wicaco Lane. The punctilious Coudray died shortly before the fort was completed in 1777, and another French engineer, Col. François Louis

Figure 5.44.

View of Fort Mifflin from the air looking east toward the Delaware River, May 1977. (Photo by J. L. Cotter)

Figure 5.45.

Mud Island in 1777. The mainland long ago assimilated the channel that lay west of the island. This drawing shows the battle plan the British used to reduce Fort Mifflin in November 1777. (Courtesy of Huntington Library, San Marino, California)

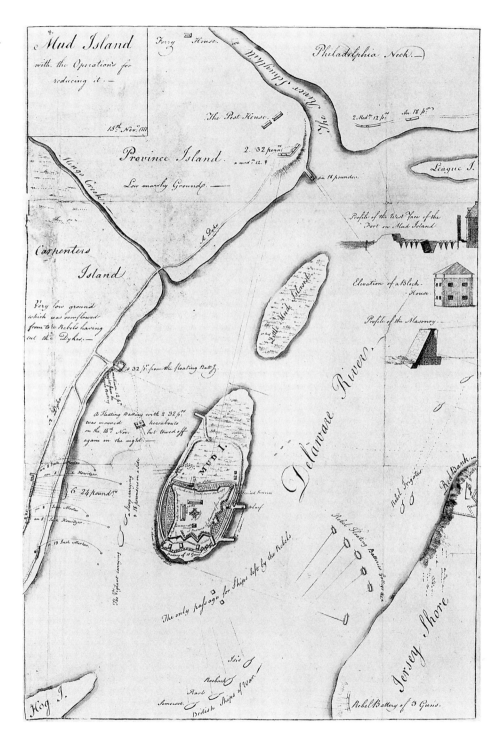

Teissedre de Fleury, replaced him. Fleury was at the fort through the battle that soon followed the fort's completion, and, like Coudray, he proved to be a tough taskmaster, vigilantly overseeing the enlisted men with cane ever in hand and never hesitating to use it.

The Committee of Public Safety had good reason for putting Mud Fort at the top of its agenda. In 1776 the outlook for the rebel forces was far from bright, and the arena of fighting had begun to shift south from New England. On August 27, 1776, soon after the committee was formed, Washington's army was defeated in the Battle of Long Island, and shortly thereafter the British occupied New York. On October 28, following the Battle of White Plains, Washington retreated to New Jersey, while the British, right behind him, proceeded to take Fort Washington and Fort Lee. After avoiding a direct attack by the British in the Battle of Princeton on January 3, 1777, Washington retreated to winter camp.

With the gap between Philadelphia and the British forces rapidly narrowing, the patriots on Mud Island worked feverishly to complete Fort Mifflin. With no time now to cut and fit stone, they finished the enclosure with timber palisades, adding timber blockhouses at three corners and banking earth to form ramparts and artillery platforms. They had just time to construct an abatis of half-trimmed trees, butts inward and branches pointing outward, to form a crude but annoying obstruction for the attacking force. The "finished" fort no doubt looked far more like a frontier fort thrown up as a defense against hostile Amerindians than like the original British plan or the French engineers' concept of it. It was certainly not equipped to take the punishment it would soon receive: the pounding of heavy ship's guns.

Figure 5.46.

The walls of Fort Mifflin. Ironically, the wall built by the British in 1772 was the only thing in the fort to withstand the British siege of 1777. The fort was rebuilt after 1798. (Photo by James L. Dillon; courtesy of the Philadelphia Maritime Museum)

Half a century after the fort first saw action, Joseph Plumb Martin, who enlisted in the Continental Army at the age of fifteen and was by the time he fought at Fort Mifflin a seasoned soldier of seventeen, recorded his opinion of the defenses:

Well, the island, as it is called, is nothing more than a mud flat in the Delaware, lying upon the west side of the channel. It is diked around the fort, with sluices so constructed that the fort can be laid under water at pleasure, (at least, it *was* so when I was there, and I presume it has not grown much higher since). On the eastern side, next the main river, was a zig-zag wall built of hewn stone, built, as I was informed, before the Revolution at the king's cost. At the southeastern part of the fortification (for fort it could not with propriety be called) was a battery of several long eighteen-pounders. At the southwestern angle was another battery with four or five twelve- and eighteen-pounders and one thirty-two-pounder. At the northwestern corner was another small battery with three twelve-pounders. There were also three blockhouses in different parts of the enclosure, but no cannon mounted upon them, nor were they of any use whatever to us while I was there. On the western side, between the batteries, was a high embankment, within which was a tier of palisadoes. In front of the stone wall, for about half its length, was another embankment, with palisadoes on the inside of it, and a narrow ditch between them and the stone wall. On the western side of the fortification was a row of barracks, extending from the northern part of the works to about half the length of the fort. On the northern end was another block of barracks which reached nearly across the fort from east to west. In front of these was a large square two-story house for

the accommodation of the officers. . . . In front of the barracks and other necessary places were parades and walks; the rest of the ground was soft mud. I have seen the enemy's shells fall upon it and sink so low that their report could not be heard when they burst, and I could only feel a tremulous motion of the earth at the time. At other times, when they burst near the surface of the ground, they would throw the mud fifty feet in the air. . . .

Our batteries were nothing more than old spars and timber laid up in parallel lines and filled between with mud and dirt. (Martin 1979:86–88)

As the autumn of 1777 approached, 350 uneasy men waited within this muddy, inadequately fortified enclosure for news of Washington's army. In the second week of September the news arrived: Washington's army had been routed on September 11 in the Battle of the Brandywine. Fifteen days later, on September 26, Sir William Howe's victorious army of 20,000 British and Hessian troops began marching into Philadelphia. With the population of the city then about 23,000, this sudden, dramatic increase placed the city—and the British commander—in desperate need of supplies. The week after the British occupied Philadelphia, Washington, in another losing battle, attacked them at Germantown. When that battle ended on October 4, Washington's army began its long westward retreat toward Valley Forge. Had Howe had the necessary supplies in hand, he could have gone after the retreating army and quite possibly put an end to the Revolution then and there. At that moment, however, Howe's supplies were aboard more than 250 British ships that were strung out in high impatience down the Delaware into the bay.

It was imperative for the British that their fleet, under the command of Howe's brother, Adm. Richard Howe, reach Philadelphia immediately. Ev-

ery day of delay would contribute more to the American cause. Howe, immobilized in Philadelphia, was unable to send troops to the aid of General Burgoyne at Saratoga, where very shortly, on October 17, General Gates' army would inflict a critical blow on the British. And, while Howe cooled his heels in Philadelphia waiting for his supplies, Washington's soldiers were able to steal a march on the farm foodstuffs in the countryside—foodstuffs that would just manage to sustain them in their winter camp at Valley Forge. Moreover, if the fleet did not reach Philadelphia before winter set in, harsh conditions might prevent Howe from seizing the opportunity to pursue his defeated enemy; in early October, however, that did not seem a very likely possibility.

The only things that stood between the British fleet and Philadelphia were two meagerly manned forts and the *chevaux-de-frise* the Americans had thrown up across the river. Consisting of heavy timber crates filled with rocks and chained together across the channel, the *chevaux-de-frise* were formidable-looking devices. Protruding from each crate was a heavy beam tipped with a barbed point of wrought iron, which was carefully poised to catch and rip the timber plank of any hull sailing against it. The *chevaux-de-frise* began upstream at Fort Mifflin, where the line of defense ran across the river to Red Bank, New Jersey; there Fort Mercer's strong earthworks rose against the shoreline.

Five miles farther down the river, at Billingsport, New Jersey, the British were already in possession of a smaller American fort. This one was to have guarded another line of *chevaux-de-frise* that connected with Billings Island on the Pennsylvania side of the river; it was, however, never finished.

Experienced military professionals that they were, the British had made short work of the Billingsport defenses even before the ramparts were complete. On October 9, in the face of a well-planned British attack, the defenders of the fort had spiked their guns and fled. But the *chevaux-de-frise* served their purpose. It was almost two weeks before the British were able to get by them and proceed to the upper defenses.

By October 21 they had arrived, and some 350 men at the Fort Mifflin garrison and 400 at Fort Mercer across the river suddenly found themselves staring out at the might of the British fleet lying within sight—but out of range—of their guns. In Philadelphia, just a few miles beyond the marshes surrounding Mud Island, Sir William Howe's crack army waited, outnumbering the combined forces of the two forts twenty-six to one. Plainly, it was not a question of which side would prevail, but of how long the Americans could hold out.

What the Americans within the forts were thinking or feeling as they waited for the attack is unknown. There is evidence, however, that a family named Bleakley who lived across the back channel a mile from Fort Mifflin were taking a rather nonchalant approach. Warned by the British that they had best evacuate their farmhouse before the attack began, the Bleakleys refused to budge. They changed their minds one day soon thereafter, when, seated at their dining table, they looked up to see a cannonball crashing through the wall. The farmhouse soon became known in Philadelphia as Cannonball House.*

* Some years ago the Daughters of the American Revolution had the Cannonball House moved from its original site to a spot across the road from the fort. There it still sits, hopefully awaiting the day when it and the fort are restored.

The first three movements of the British attack were intended to coincide for a quick knockout of the American defenses. On October 21 a force of two thousand Hessians ferried across the Delaware and marched via Haddonsfield, New Jersey, to attack Fort Mercer. The next day, no doubt to the astonishment of the attackers, the four hundred determined defenders of the fort beat them back, inflicting severe losses. Among the fatalities was Count Carl von Donop, who had led the Hessian troops.

Meanwhile, British forces had marched from Philadelphia to pound Fort Mifflin with mortar and cannon fire from across the channel behind the fort. At the same time, in the front of the fort, the British ships had drawn within range. The fort's wooden ramparts were soon wrecked, but the defenders fought on, augmented now by the efforts of the tiny Pennsylvania Navy. From behind the *chevaux-de-frise*, the navy's small gunboats sent a barrage of fire downriver at the British fleet. On October 23 luck and good aim on the part of the Americans inflicted heavy damage on six British warships. Both the *Augusta*, a 64-gun ship of the line, and the *Merlin*, a 16-gun sloop, ran aground. After the *Augusta* caught fire and exploded, the British gave a *coup-de-grace* to the *Merlin*. Then, not willing to risk another disaster, the attackers wisely withdrew.

It was not until November 10 that an all-out British attack began, with every shore and ship battery blazing. The British now threw almost everything they had into it, including additional shore batteries and stripped and lightened gunboats ready for shallow water. The great men-of-war, however, lay at a respectful distance, at extreme range. The carnage lasted for five days. Joseph Plumb Martin

(1979:92) gives us some flavor of it: "Our men were cut up like cornstalks. . . . I saw five artillerists belonging to one gun cut down by a single shot, and I saw men who were stooping to be protected by the works, but not stooping low enough, split like fish to be broiled." The men at Fort Mifflin kept their heads low all day, watching the 15-inch pine-log palisades splinter like matchsticks; at night they worked to repair them, sleeping only when exhaustion drove them to it. For sleeping space, they had a choice between the muddy ground of the fort or the barracks, but once entered there, according to Martin, few emerged alive, it being a favorite target of the British gunners. Martin (1979:89) recalled that in the two weeks he spent within the fort, he "never lay down to sleep a minute in all that time."

The day after the all-out attack began, the commander of the garrison, Lt. Col. Charles Smith, was seriously wounded and evacuated by night to Fort Mercer. Maj. Simeon Thayer took over the command. Noting there was not a single shot available for the fort's 32-pound cannon, and further noting that the British were being more than generous in their delivery of the needed ammunition, Thayer offered a gill of rum to any man who retrieved one of these cannonballs to be fired back at the enemy. Slogging through mud to retrieve them, many a man burned his hands on the British largesse. Martin (1979:90) recalled having seen "twenty to fifty men standing on the parade waiting with impatience the coming of the shot, which would often be seized before its motion had fully ceased and conveyed off to our gun to be sent back to its former owners."

By November 15, five days after the attack began, two British ships had managed to find a hole in the

chevaux-de-frise and to sneak up the back channel and situate themselves within a few hundred yards of the ramparts. At ten o'clock on the morning of that day, a British bugle sounded the commencement of the mightiest barrage of the eighteenth century. Every twenty minutes, one thousand cannonballs landed on Mud Island. By two o'clock the following morning, all but two guns in the fort were out of action and 70 percent of the defenders were killed or wounded. Major Thayer ordered the torch put to the wreckage that remained and prepared to evacuate his wounded to Fort Mercer, together with all the matériel that could be salvaged.

In the midst of all this, Joseph Plumb Martin, wits ever about him, remembered some hogsheads of rum in the fort and, needing his canteen to help himself to the spirits—"there being nothing to eat"—he looked for the messmate who had borrowed it. He found him, indeed, "but lying in a long line of dead men who had been brought out of the fort to be conveyed to the main, to have the last honors conferred upon them" (Martin 1979:93). Together with the other survivors, Martin then turned his attention to setting on fire all in the fort that would burn that night. When the weary men embarked in the three small boats that were to take them to the last refuge across the river, the flames rising from the fort illuminated their silhouettes, attracting British fire. Somehow, unharmed, they reached Fort Mercer. Four days later, on November 20, Fort Mercer also fell to the enemy. The blockade had been broken, but not in time to do the British very much good. The winter of 1777–78 soon set in, and the armies of both sides settled into winter camp. Having missed the chance to complete the American rout, General

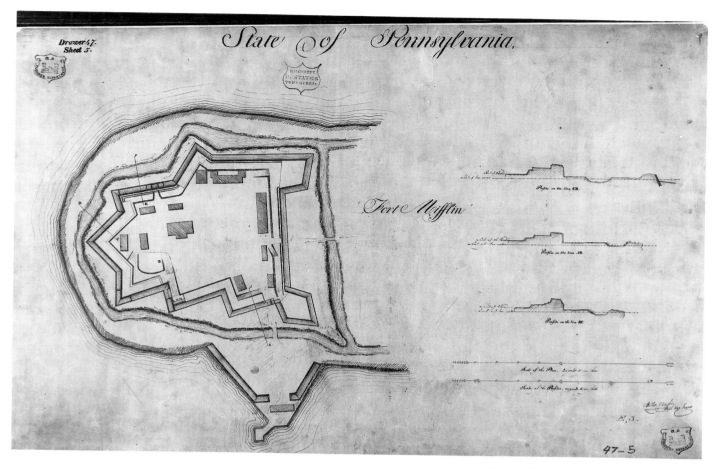

Figure 5.47.

Map of Fort Mifflin, 1819. (Drawn by Col. Louis Toussand; courtesy of the National Archives, RG 77, drawer 47, no. 5)

Howe took up all-too-comfortable quarters in Philadelphia, prompting Benjamin Franklin's famous remark that rather than Howe's taking Philadelpia, Philadelphia took Howe.

After the British surrendered at Yorktown in 1781, the fort on Mud Island lingered in its wrecked state for well over a decade. In 1793, as the new nation was awakening to its continuing need for defense, the Commonwealth of Pennsylvania appropriated $5,000 for the repair of the fort and secured for the job the services of Pierre Charles L'Enfant, designer of the city of Washington. It was not until 1798, however, during the administration of John Adams, that work began, and it was carried out under the direction of another French engineer, Col. Louis Touissand. The names of Adams and Touissand, carved into a marble keystone over one of the arched entrances to the fort, are still there, as is

the splendid Greek Revival house L'Enfant designed for the fort's commandant. Funds being short, the commandant's house was not completed until 1814, and today, funds apparently still being short, it is in very poor condition.*

By 1800 Touissand's workers had turned Fort Mifflin into a proper military installation. Leaving intact the stone wall the British had built in 1772, they reinforced the fort's earthen ramparts with rough stone walls faced with brick. Within the massive walls of the fort, they created six "bombproofs," well-insulated masonry chambers in which soldiers could live while the fort was under attack. Outside the walls of the fort—

* The commandant's house was severely damaged by fire on a cold day in the 1970s when a troop of boy scouts, ignoring instructions, entered it and proceeded to light a fire in a capped fireplace. The house still stands roofless, trees growing up under the beautiful woodwork of its elegantly arched doorways.

just across the road to the northeast— they built a two-story hospital with gable roof and galleries; the hospital was completed sometime before 1802. Touissand's workers also reconstructed, possibly on the original foundations at the edge of the parade ground, the soldiers' barracks Major Thayer had torched in 1777. Part of the soldiers' barracks that stand on the site today may date from 1798; the building was extensively repaired and renovated in 1835–36.

The renovation of the barracks was but one of several major changes the fort underwent during the 1830s and 1840s. New buildings that went up at this time included a storehouse, an arsenal, and an artillery shed for the storage of cannon; all these buildings still stand. They may have been built on the site of older buildings constructed in 1798, some of which are shown on an 1819 map of the site (Figure 5.47). Also still standing are a powder magazine, a blacksmith's shop, and the officers' quarters. The last structure dates from 1814, a reminder of the defense needs of the War of 1812.

The Civil War brought changes to the gun emplacements and to the interior of the fort's walls, as well as many other minor "modernizations." Across the moat that surrounds the fort, a demilune still contains granite gun platforms with circular iron tracks on which Civil War cannons once traversed. During these years the parade ground witnessed the execution of many deserters from the Union Army, and the damp, dim bombproofs echoed to the miseries of the Confederate prisoners who were confined there, some three hundred to four hundred at a time. The bombproofs were fitted out with wooden double-tier bunks—still preserved over a hundred years later—to accommodate the prisoners, who were secured behind massive, iron-studded timber doors.

With the advent of modern warfare in the twentieth century, Fort Mifflin became a military anachronism. In 1915 the War Department declared it a national monument, and, pending the presidential proclamation required to validate this designation, turned the site over to the Corps of Engineers for safekeeping. President Wilson, however, never got around to signing the proclamation; the U.S. involvement in World War I intervened, and the matter was forgotten. Had he signed it, it seems likely that Fort Mifflin would today be in the hands of the National Park Service, which, not long after it was established in 1916, began acquiring from the War De-

partment many of the nation's historic forts and battlefields.

In 1929 Philadelpia's mayor, Harry A. Mackey, and the Philadelphia Board of Trade asked the War Department to transfer the fort to the city's park department. When it became evident that the fort would require extensive—and expensive—repairs, the city began to back off. The project was ultimately abandoned.

Stuck with a historic relic that it was unable to use and that it was unauthorized to develop for public use, the Corps of Engineers maintained and policed the fort at bare-bones level. After housing an anti-aircraft battery in World War II and serving as a storage facility during the Korean conflict, Fort Mifflin deteriorated into what one Philadelphia observer described as a "seedy limbo." * In 1956 the General Services Administration authorized the transfer of the fort to the city of Philadelphia, but the city, parsimoniously measuring expenditure, did not take title until 1962. At the same time, the Corps of Engineers also ceased maintenance of the site. Thereafter, time and vandalism continued to decimate it.

At length, toward the end of December 1966, the city of Philadelphia began the restoration of Fort Mifflin by undertaking the conversion of the fort's storehouse. The converted storehouse was to serve as a building from which to pursue restoration and maintenance. Toward this end, architect G. Edwin Brumbaugh was hired in the late 1950s to develop plans for restoration of the fort. Brumbaugh, a fellow of the American Institute of Architects with a lively interest in archaeology, not only developed plans

* The observer was James M. Perry, who used the phrase in an article in the *Philadelphia Sunday Bulletin* of July 26, 1959.

for restoring the structures that survived on the site but also saw to it that in the summer of 1959 Lt. Col. J. Duncan Campbell, specialist in military archaeology, was hired to conduct a preliminary archaeological investigation. Several other authorized archaeological investigations, also of a limited nature, were to follow. In 1969 graduate students in archaeology at the University of Pennsylvania carried out an archaeological feasibility study for the city of Philadelphia, and in 1978 Barbara Liggett undertook a limited study for the Philadelphia Department of Recreation, which now manages the site. The reports of these studies (Campbell 1959; Cotter 1969; Liggett 1977, 1978d; Liggett and Laumark 1979; Thibaut 1975) provided the data for the following account.

Archaeology at Fort Mifflin

The 1959 Excavations

The first thing Lt. Col. Campbell demonstrated in the summer of 1959 was the aptness of the site's original name, Mud Fort. A map of the central parade ground sketched by Lt. Col. Charles Smith in 1777 showed crosswalks between four spaces marked "mud." As Campbell uncovered the postholes that once contained the supports for these wooden walks, it became evident that to extricate themselves from the ubiquitous mire, both the British and the Americans had dumped as much fill as they could into this central part of the fort.

The parade ground had a base of clay covered by a layer of sand and gravel that ranged from 4 to 24 inches in depth. Neither the clay nor the sand-and-gravel fill yielded any artifacts. Just above the sand and gravel

Figure 5.48.

A six-inch cannonball recovered from the moat at Fort Mifflin. (Photo by J. L. Cotter)

were intermittent traces of old sub-soil covered in places by as much as 18 inches of fill; the fill consisted of coal ash, mixed dirt and ash, brick rubble, and cinders mixed with pieces of iron. Campbell concluded that this fill was the wreckage of the 1777 bombardment and that it had been strewn over newly established topsoil. Here he found numerous eighteenth-century artifacts: buttons and insignia from uniforms, bullets, coins, pulleys from tackle gear, fragments of kitchen-ware and tableware, sherds of porcelain from the officers' quarters, and pieces of glass from bottles, tumblers,

and windows. The top layer consisted of from 5 to 12 inches of modern top-soil, which contained artifacts dating from after the time of the Revolution. Interestingly, Campbell found no cannonballs, suggesting that after the British evacuated Philadelphia in 1778, the Americans retrieved from the fort whatever ammunition they could. Exploration of the moat may yet yield a remarkable harvest of cannonball and shot. Figure 5.48 shows a 6-inch cannonball that some avoca-

Figure 5.49.

Plan of excavations carried out at Fort Mifflin in 1969. (Courtesy of the University Museum, University of Pennsylvania)

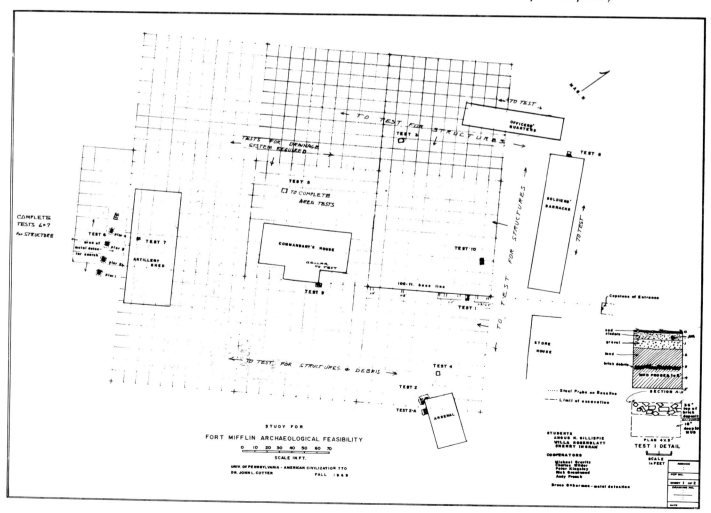

Figure 5.50.

Test 1 underway. Main gate of Fort Mifflin appears in background. (Photo by J. L. Cotter)

Figure 5.51.

Brick rubble dating from the siege of 1777 at the bottom of completed test 1, Fort Mifflin. (Photo by J. L. Cotter)

tional archaeologists, with the aid of a metal detector, recovered from the moat.

In addition to unearthing numerous artifacts, Campbell uncovered considerable structural evidence. Just south of the officers' quarters, he exposed part of the stone foundations of a building shown on the 1819 map of the site. Of all the structures subsequently removed from the site, this one, measuring 32 by 28 feet, was the largest. Further excavation at the northeast corner of these foundations indicated that a larger building, 40 by 36 feet, may have stood there. Campbell concluded that either the larger building had been erected over the smaller building's foundations, incorporating them on the south and west sides, or that the building had had double walls. The double walls would suggest that the building was used as a powder magazine.

A test trench 2 feet deep and running 140 feet from east to west in the northwest quarter of the fort failed to uncover evidence of the barracks the evacuating Americans burned to the ground in November 1777. West of the commandant's house, however, excavation revealed a portion of brick pavement, probably laid between 1835 and 1840. Between the commandant's house and the officers' quarters, Campbell also found an extensive, open brick drainage system.

The 1969 Excavations

The purpose of the feasibility study that the class from the University of Pennsylvania conducted in 1969 was to prepare for the city of Philadelphia a plan and cost estimate for a comprehensive archaeological investigation of the fort and features related to it. After examining the historical documentation and establishing a

grid of stakes inside the fort, the class, assisted by five students from the Episcopal Academy, carried out a series of ten tests in various parts of the site (Figure 5.49).

Test 1 was conducted along a baseline between the main gate and the commandant's house (Figure 5.50). It revealed essentially the same stratigraphy Campbell had noted a decade earlier: successive layers of clay, gravel fill, cinders, and sod. Here, however, at 3 feet below the surface and covered by 1½ feet of mud, was a layer of shattered brick. It rested on another layer of mud that was at least 5 feet deep. The evidence suggested that a brick walkway dating from the 1770s had predictably sunk into the mire and disappeared. Excavations nearer the center of the fort uncovered evidence of brick rubble dating from the destruction of the fort in 1777 (Figure 5.51).

Test 2 on the south side of the arsenal and test 9 east of the steps of the commandant's house revealed the brick drains of both structures. Some 30 feet northwest of the commandant's house, test 5 disclosed, at a depth of 1 to 2 feet, an assortment of domestic artifacts, mostly glass and ceramic and dating mainly from the middle to the end of the nineteenth century. The excavations did not, however, uncover evidence of the privy that had served the house.

As shown in Figure 5.52, test 3 at the southeast corner of the arsenal revealed traces of a brick wall set on a stone-and-mortar base. These were perhaps remnants of the original arsenal, which was destroyed in the siege of 1777. The earth in this vicinity yielded various iron artifacts dating from the same period (Figure 5.53).

Other structural evidence was found near the artillery shed. Some 15 to 20 feet behind the shed, at a depth of 1 to 2 feet, test 6 disclosed

the remains of five brick-and-stone piers that had supported the original artillery shed. Test unit 7, dug beneath the brick floor of the existing artillery shed, revealed a top layer of sandy fill, then the debris of a burned structure, another sandy layer, and, at the bottom, a layer of brick-and-mortar debris, possibly also part of the original artillery shed. Still more structural evidence—three large, flat stones, which may have been part of a former barracks—was found at the north end of the soldiers' barracks at a depth of 1.2 feet (test 8). West of the main entrance, test 10 revealed more tumbled bricks and foundation stones, also indicating an early structure.

Having tested the site as thoroughly as circumstances would allow, the class drew up a plan for a definitive archaeological investigation of Fort Mifflin. The plan was given to the city of Philadelphia, but it has never been implemented. It included the following recommendations:

1 Systematic testing of all the ground within the fort

a to locate the foundations of structures that stood on the site during the Revolutionary War, and

b to reveal the drainage system developed over time and now forgotten, so that the interior of the fort can be efficiently drained and the integrity of the ramparts maintained.

2 Draining, investigation, and restoration of the moat to its full depth, together with salvage of historical evidence.

3 Location, testing, and demarcation of the back channel that originally separated Mud Island from the mainland.

4 Location of the site across the back channel from which the British fired on the fort in 1777. (This site is known to have been southwest of the fort, and there, today, in a wooded area behind Strawbridge & Clothier's air freight

warehouse is a large gully, possibly indicating the outline of a British trench.)

5 Testing of the demilune outside the southeast gate of the fort and of the bridge to the demilune.

6 Testing of the commandant's house to determine whether it overlies an earlier, pre-1814 structure.

7 Investigations at the north and south ends of the 1814 officers' quarters to determine whether kitchen cellars were filled in because of flooding, which is known to have occurred within the fort. (Such filling did take place at Fort McHenry in Baltimore.)

8 Identification of the original water supply, whether by well, by cistern, or both.

9 Complete excavation of the site of the original artillery shed, identified in the feasibility study.

10 Investigation and interpretation of the hospital, built before 1802 just across the road from the fort to the northeast.

11 Investigation of the foundations of Cannonball House, originally located a mile from Fort Mifflin in the vicinity of the present Penrose Avenue sewage disposal plant, so that artifacts and other evidence can be conserved for interpretation.

Figure 5.52.

Test 3 showing remnants of what may have been the original arsenal at Fort Mifflin. (Photo by J. L. Cotter)

Figure 5.53.

Eighteenth-century iron artifacts found near the structural remains at Fort Mifflin shown in Figure 5.52. A metal detector was used to locate these objects. (Photo by J. L. Cotter)

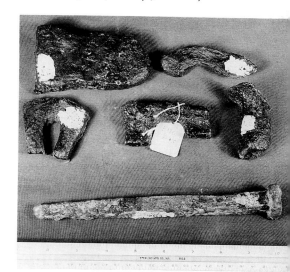

The 1978 Excavations

The goal of the limited study Barbara Liggett conducted in 1978 was to determine why the soil of the rampart at Fort Mifflin's north salient was sinking (Liggett and Laumark 1979). Excavations revealed a counterfort, or retaining wall, 12 feet high and made of cut and fitted limestone (Figure 5.54). The wall was securely based on timber cribbing, and at the bottom of it was a brick-and-stone drain. The

Figure 5.54.

Left, interior wall found beneath Fort Mifflin's north salient in 1978. (Photo by J. L. Cotter) *Below,* plan of north salient tests. (From Liggett and Laumark 1979)

wall and drain were built in the period after 1798, when the fort was reconstructed according to L'Enfant's 1794 plan. The outer facade of the wall was faced with brick—a fair protection until Civil War artillery demonstrated that a masonry structure could be reduced to rubble. Well-designed and well-built, the wall had stood fast, but the earth behind it had slumped.

Presumably, the earth behind the retaining wall had been scooped up from around the fort when the wall was built. From this earth, at a depth of 6 to 13 feet, Liggett recovered 228 ceramic and glass artifacts, all dating from before 1815. Creamware accounted for almost 40 percent of the artifacts, while pearlware accounted

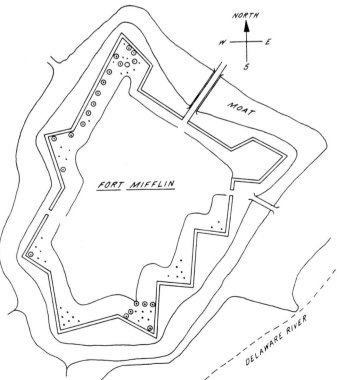

Record of probe and auger holes. Made for further evidence of counterfort construction. Circles are positive, dots are negative. Heavy masonry found in both Montressor and L'Enfant Sections.

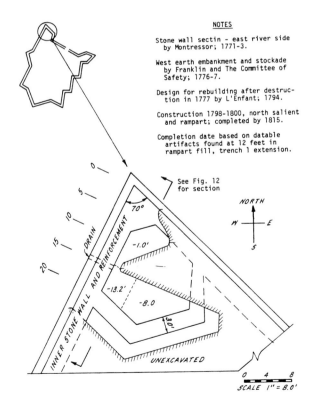

NOTES

Stone wall sectin - east river side by Montressor; 1771-3.

West earth embankment and stockade by Franklin and The Committee of Safety; 1776-7.

Design for rebuilding after destruction in 1777 by L'Enfant; 1794.

Construction 1798-1800, north salient and rampart; completed by 1815.

Completion date based on datable artifacts found at 12 feet in rampart fill, trench 1 extension.

Plan of Excavation at North Salient

for about 25 percent and earthenware for 21 percent. In the top 3 feet of fill were 2 gunflints, probably of French or Dutch make and dating from 1770 to 1800, as well as 2 bayonets. The lower fill yielded an iron cask in very bad condition, a uniform button with "US" molded on it, a sleeve or cuff button engraved with a cursive capital "J," and two molded clay pipe bowls. The shape of the pipe bowls indicated that they dated from the last quarter of the eighteenth century.

The conclusion of this study was much the same as one drawn by the feasibility study of 1969—namely, that the eighteenth- and early nineteenth-century designers and builders of the fort had fully understood that when erecting an enclosure of walls around an interior earth basin, it is necessary to pay careful attention to the installation and maintenance of drains. After the Civil War, however, as the quality of maintenance at the fort declined, the drains were neglected and ultimately forgotten. During World War I the parade ground was raised, burying the forgotten drains still deeper. Archaeological investigations at other forts, including Fort McHenry in Baltimore, have pinpointed the same drainage problems and the same history of careful original design followed by a declining level of maintenance.

As the twenty-first century approaches, the future of Fort Mifflin, the scene of a stand that altered the course of the American War of Independence, is dubious. There seem at present to be no guarantees that it will not be allowed to sink forgotten back into the mire from which it first rose.

THE FRANKLIN SQUARE POWDER MAGAZINE

Although the bicentennial fever that gripped Philadelphia in the early 1970s did little for Fort Mifflin's cause, it did have a salutary effect on Franklin Square, even if a temporary one. Envisioned by Thomas Holme as one of the five pastoral squares that would grace the center and each quadrant of Penn's "green country town," Franklin Square, located in the northeast quadrant, had by the 1970s undergone a series of transformations, none of them pastoral. In 1776 it was housing a powder magazine for the Continental Army. By 1926 it was at the center of a heavily trafficked area: the approach to the Benjamin Franklin Bridge. By 1966 it had become a drug-dealer's paradise.

In anticipation of the bicentennial of the nation, Philadelphia '76, which did much of the planning for Philadelphia's bicentennial celebrations, announced its plans to refurbish Franklin Square. Fearing that the refurbishment would destroy whatever traces of the old powder magazine might lie beneath the ground, Philadelphia '76 allocated funds for a preliminary historical and archaeological survey to the Museum Historic Research Center of the University of Pennsylvania. Carl Gatter, an interested researcher (Gatter 1975), and Dr. Richard Tyler of the Philadelphia Historical Commission were instrumental in initiating the archaeological effort and put research material at the disposal of the archaeologist in charge, Jeffrey L. Kenyon, from whose report (1975) the following derives.

The Historical Documentation

At the turn of the eighteenth century, memories of the Great Fire of London in 1666 were still fresh in the minds of many Philadelphians. Their concern about fire is reflected in their overwhelming use of brick as a building material; it is also reflected in their concern about the proper storage of gunpowder. By the 1720s stringent regulations governing the storage of gunpowder were already in force: powder in quantities greater than twelve pounds was to be stored in a dry, fireproof enclosure, and as further protection for people and property in the vicinity, the enclosure was to be designed to drive any accidental blast vertically rather than horizontally. Since many people found it difficult to comply with these regulations, petitions were soon circulating for the construction of a public powder magazine. Ultimately, in 1725, William Chancellor, sailmaker, was licensed to construct such a magazine east of Market Street, on the riverfront north of Pegg's Run, a waterway long since vanished underground.

Although Chancellor's magazine served the city until the Revolutionary War, it apparently fell short of the approved standards in several respects. In March 1776 Lewis Nicola, then in

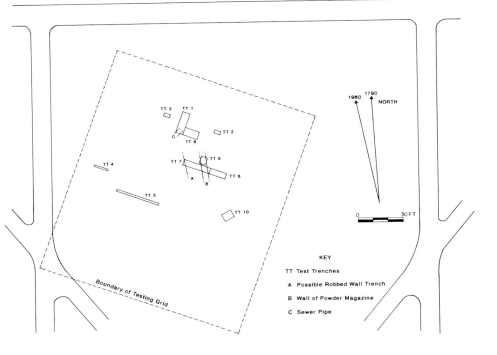

Figure 5.55.

Test trenches and structural features found in the north central section of Franklin Square. (From Kenyon 1975)

Figure 5.56.

Test trench 7 at Franklin Square in section. (From Kenyon 1975)

charge of the magazine, put the following petition before the Committee of Safety, a municipal body responsible for overseeing public safety in Philadelphia:

There is in this city a building of great public utility, but very unfit for the purpose for which it was erected, particularly at our present critical time, when some person enemical to the American Cause, may take an opportunity to distress us in a very material point, induced thereto from a dislike to ye brave resistance made by the Americans to the oppressive attempts on our liberties, or in expectation of an ample reward from a tyrannical ministry. The building I mean is our powder magazine, which is as badly situated as possible, in a low swampy place, unprotected by a surrounding wall or fence, & not secured from fire, accidental or designed, whereas magazines should, as much as possible, be placed in dry airy situations, so as to admit a free circulation & at the same time well guarded against fire.

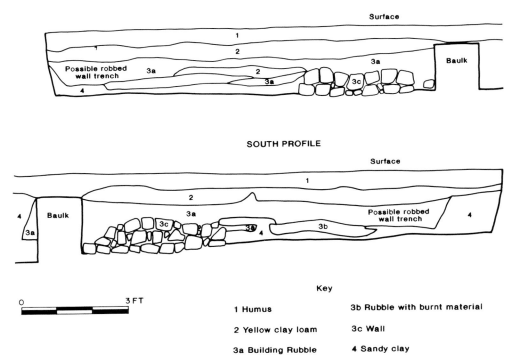

The most approved method of erecting magazines in Europe is the following:

The walls should be of a proper thickness, according to the intended size of the magazine, & well built to exclude all wet, with windows, or air holes, of a proper construction, . . . both under and above the floor, to admit a free circulation, yet exclude all possibility of inducing fire, and ye floor should have two wooden or iron gratings, and be raised at least one foot from the ground with a step of stone, the sil [sic] of the door should be of the same material. This free admission of air is necessary to keep the powder in a proper state, & preserve the casks which would be damaged by a confined damp air. As shingling is the only roofing used here, there should be at some distance underneath the roof an arch of brick or wood, if the latter, it should be covered with a coat about 5 or 6 inches thick of well tempered potter's clay, or fine mortar, so that if the roof took fire it might not communicate with the powder. The magazine should be surrounded by a good wall or fence, to obstruct all improper approach thereto. (Pennsylvania Archives, v. 4:715–16)

Subsequently, on April 16, 1776, the Committee of Safety passed a resolution to build a new magazine capable of holding a thousand barrels of powder and incorporating at least some of the features described by Nicola. By August the magazine was standing in Franklin Square. Except for an interlude during which the British were in control of not only the magazine but also the city, Capt. Joseph Stiles had charge of the facility until the late 1780s. By 1788 the storage capacity of the magazine had become inadequate, and Stiles requested permission to store excess powder in "a small frame house nearly adjoining the Magazine commonly called the Guard House." He described the state of the magazine in 1788:

The magazine is in length nearly North and South thirty-five feet, and in breadth sixteen feet, measur'd on the inside; the

height of the wall seven feet & eight inches. Under the floor the whole length of the building, and I judge about a foot above the ground, there appears a wall on which the sleepers rest, crossways of the building, those sleepers are many of them decayed by which means the floor is much settled yet it is in no ways damp. (Cited in Kenyon 1975)

Askew though his magazine may have been, Captain Stiles at least kept his powder dry. Not too many years after he lamented the state of his "sleepers," the magazine was closed, and in 1802–1806 a new storage facility was built near Gray's Ferry Road on the banks of the Schuylkill, far from the congested part of the city. In 1791 the old magazine in Franklin Square was serving as a storage depot for the oil used in the city's street lamps; sometime after 1811 it was demolished.

The Archaeological Investigation

To locate the Franklin Square powder magazine, Kenyon transferred the position recorded on historic maps to the present plan of the square, gridded the indicated area, and ran a soil resistivity test on it. Where the test indicated anomalies, he excavated (Figure 5.55). The strategy worked; test trench 7 dug in this area revealed wall fragments and demolition rubble.

Figure 5.56 shows test trench 7 in section. The table below summarizes Kenyon's findings.

Although time did not allow separation of the artifacts found in the internally striated demolition rubble, this rubble was clearly related to the 1776 powder magazine. In Kenyon's opinion:

. . . formal excavations would separate this material and provide information as to interior construction details and the chronology of use and demolition. It is hypothesized that the foundation base is from one of the main walls of the magazine, and that the filled trench to the west of this is from a robbed perimeter wall. The structure apparently had a stone footing with brick walls. The construction of the perimeter wall is unknown. It should be stressed that the above are only hypotheses, and that formal conclusions would have to await more extensive excavations. (Kenyon 1975:5)

Kenyon concluded his preliminary study by proposing a schedule of further excavations, but, to date, no further archaeological work has been conducted at Franklin Square. As a result of Kenyon's efforts, all that we know about the archaeology of Franklin Square is the tentative location of the magazine. The site, and perhaps other sections of the square itself, deserve more.

Stratum	Depth (in feet)	Date Range
Humus	Surface–0.6	Late 19th to mid-20th century
Clay loam	0.6–1.3	Late 18th to mid-19th century
Demolition rubble (internally striated)	1.3–2.7	1775 to 1825
Striated sandy clay	2.7 +	Sterile, undisturbed

From Kenyon 1975:5.

THE FRANKFORD ARSENAL: NEARLY TWO CENTURIES OF ARMING THE NATION

Like many other historic sites in Philadelphia, the Frankford Arsenal had an important influence not only on the city but on the nation as well. Almost from its inception in 1816, this military-industrial complex, situated along the Delaware River just north of Frankford Creek, was a leader in the field of munitions development and production. It also played a significant role in the industrialization of Philadelphia and was at one time one of the city's major employers. Among the many innovations spawned here were several early cartridge systems for breech-loading weapons, the Maynard priming system, the Frankford friction primer, and the recoilless rifle of World War II. Indicative of the growing importance of the arsenal was the growth of the site itself. When the arsenal opened in 1816, it occupied 20 acres; by the time it closed some 160 years later, it spread out over 110 acres, on which there were no fewer than 246 buildings.

In 1978, a year after the facility closed, John Milner Associates undertook a multidisciplinary investigation of the property under contract with

Figure 5.57.

Map of the Frankford Arsenal showing parade ground and early buildings. (From John Milner Associates 1979; courtesy of the Corps of Engineers, Baltimore District, Department of the Army, and John Milner Associates)

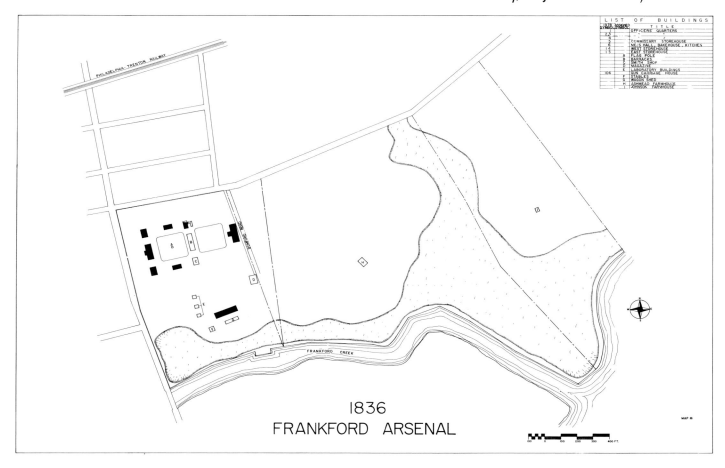

1836
FRANKFORD ARSENAL

the Baltimore District, Corps of Engineers. The goals of the archaeological aspect of the study were to locate and identify features shown on early maps of the site and to evaluate how the findings might be used in a program aimed at interpreting the arsenal's history. The report of this investigation (John Milner Associates 1979) is the basis for what follows.

The History of the Frankford Arsenal

By 1815 the Schuylkill Arsenal, which had been storing munitions for the nation's military forces since 1806, was no longer large enough to meet the needs of the burgeoning army, and its site along the Schuylkill River near Gray's Ferry Road was too close to the growing city of Philadelpia to make expansion feasible. That, in any case, was the conclusion of the recently formed federal Department of Ordnance, an independent bureau of the War Department charged with the procurement, repair, and storage of military weapons and ammunition. As part of its mission in 1815 to establish and administer ordnance depots throughout the country, the Department of Ordnance launched an intensive search of the Philadelphia area for a suitable location for a new depot. The following May, after more than a year's study and consideration of at least four properties, the department selected a 20-acre parcel of land along the Delaware River near Frankford Creek, north of the densely populated part of the city. Here there would be room for the storage depot to expand into an industrial complex, the waterways would provide access to iron and timber, and the arsenal could make use of the city's skilled work force and active gunpowder industry.

In the early decades of the nineteenth century, before the arsenal grew into a military-industrial giant, it consisted of a wharf and a handful of buildings—officers' quarters, a commandant's house, kitchens, storehouses, and a powder magazine. Most of these buildings were designed in the Federal style, and they clustered around a large quadrangle known as the parade ground (Figure 5.57). Some of them still stand. Among the early buildings that have vanished are a blacksmith's shop, built next to the parade ground in 1825 and demolished in 1883, and a two-story stone barracks, built in 1817 and demolished in 1891. The barracks, situated in the center of the parade ground, measured 100 by 33 feet. It had a slate roof, six bays, and a high basement. Surrounding the parade ground was a green area dominated by formal gardens, parks, and shade trees. A small farmyard with stables and poultry sheds occupied the southwest corner of the site. Although the complex retained this bucolic flavor throughout the 1800s, it retained its relatively diminutive size for little more than two decades.

After Capt. George D. Ramsey took command of the arsenal in 1838, the facility began expanding, and it was soon serving as more than just a storage depot and repair shop. It was now in the business of proofing powder, as well as testing various types of weapons, and its site had grown considerably; some 33 acres were now being used largely as a proving ground. By the early 1840s the arsenal was manufacturing large quantities of percussion caps, and, with the aid of new compressing machines, it was able to produce 40,000 lead balls in a single ten-hour day. By 1850 the Frankford Arsenal was widely recognized as the nation's foremost facility in the manufacture of percussion caps and small-arms ammunition.

In the decade or so before the Civil War, production at Frankford became highly mechanized. The facility's use of R. M. Bouton's single-operation machine to manufacture percussion caps necessitated the construction of a steam-powered factory, which was built in 1852 under the supervision of Maj. Peter V. Hagner, then in command of the arsenal. Other structures that went up on the site during the 1850s were devoted to manufacturing not only ordnance but also machines that would produce ordnance, and some of these machines were in continuous operation day and night. All told, the facility was at this time producing "bags, boxes, tin cases, caps, milling machines, friction tubes, and machines to make friction tubes" (John Milner Associates 1979:27). In short, the Frankford Arsenal was engaged in production for war.

After the outbreak of the Civil War, the Frankford Arsenal continued to manufacture percussion caps, paper fuzes for detonating explosives, cartridges, and other munitions. New construction aimed at minimizing damage from fire or explosion was, however, the major thrust of the arsenal during these years. Under the direction of commanding officer Maj. T. T. S. Laidley, several new buildings, including the Laidley Laboratories, in which cartridges were tested, had a "blowout feature": in an explosion, the roof and sides of the structure would collapse, but its iron framework would remain standing. Laidley was also instrumental in seeing that structural iron was used to "fireproof" several of the arsenal's new buildings.

In 1864 Lt. Col. S. V. Benet be-

Figure 5.58.

The Frankford Arsenal's rolling mill. Completed in 1866, the rolling mill was designed in industrial Italianate style by architect John Fraser. It influenced the design of most other buildings added to the military-industrial complex before World War I. (From John Milner Associates 1979; courtesy of the Corps of Engineers, Baltimore District, Department of the Army, and John Milner Associates)

came the eighteenth commanding officer of the Frankford Arsenal. His command witnessed one of the most ambitious construction projects ever undertaken at the facility: the building of a rolling mill to work copper and brass for cartridge production. Designed in industrial Italianate style by John Fraser, architect of the Union League's clubhouse on Broad Street, the rolling mill (Figure 5.58) took the better part of three years to build. It was not completed until 1866, a year after the Civil War had ended. Because production at Frankford dropped off dramatically in the postwar years, the rolling mill was not put to its intended use until the last decade of the nineteenth century. In the meantime, the mill—the arsenal's most imposing structure—served as a storage facility.

As production at the arsenal began declining in the late 1860s, scientific research and development intensified. Experiments were carried out on an early type of machine gun known as the Gatling gun and on "cannon percussion primers, sights, percussion fuzes and paper fuzes, explosive bullets, prismatic powder, Laidley (iron) targets, and tools" (John Milner Associates 1979:88). The post–Civil War years at the arsenal were also marked by considerable expansion of housing, including the construction in 1870 of a new barracks for single soldiers. Several buildings, among them the barracks built in 1817 in the center of the parade ground, were modified to house married soldiers and their dependents. Modifications made to the 1817 barracks included the installation in the basement of kitchens for each of six small apartments, all of which had two floors. The structure also had a piazza added to its front, or west, facade, and the yard behind it was the site of two privies and six sheds for coal or wood.

In the 1890s the Frankford Arsenal inaugurated a program for developing and testing smokeless powders. The program, directed by Capt. John Pitman in cooperation with the Du Pont Company, was aimed at achieving uniform ballistic qualities by testing powders at varying pressures and velocities. The testing was conducted in the Proof House, a newly built structure situated in the northeast part of the grounds. By the turn of the twentieth century, the various powders being produced required testing at longer ranges than those possible in the Proof House. As a result, the Sandy Hook Proving Ground in New Jersey took over this aspect of Frankford's role in ballistics engineering.

Frankford's waning role in ballistics testing was balanced by an increase in its manufacture of artillery ammunition and precision instruments. As the 1890s progressed, it became a leading producer of shrapnel, fuzes, and 2.3-inch ammunition shells and canisters. Putting the imposing old rolling mill to the use for which it was intended, it also led in the production of cartridges. By 1908 the creation of an Instrument Division and Optical Shop devoted to the manufacture of panoramic and telescopic sights had greatly increased the arsenal's capabilities.

The Frankford Arsenal played an important role as a producer of munitions in the two world wars of the twentieth century and in the Korean conflict. In 1939, as World War II loomed, the arsenal was making virtually all calibers and types of small-arms ammunition, and after the outbreak of the war, it increased its production dramatically. In fact, until private industry mobilized sufficiently to take up some of the burden, Frankford produced the lion's share of the country's ammunition. That private industry mobilized as quickly as it did in the 1940s was also owing in large part to the efforts of the arsenal, which not only shared advice and expertise with companies like Remington Arms and Western Cartridge, but also ran large programs to train private industries in the mass production of military ammunition.

While heavily involved in production during World War II, the arsenal continued to focus on research and development. It was instrumental in developing anti-aircraft and air-offensive weapons, and when a shortage of brass threatened the production of cartridge casings, it helped develop a steel casing, which it also manufactured. Perhaps the most notable invention to come out of Frankford during World War II was the recoilless rifle. The recoilless effect was achieved by allowing propellant gases to escape through exhaust vents in the rifle's breech. The special cartridge cases needed to allow some of the gases to be emitted rearward were also developed at Frankford.

When World War II ended, the Frankford Arsenal was the only plant in the country where military production was not curtailed. At this time, Frankford was ordered to "return to the pre-war role of keeping alive those phases of the munitions art that do not have a commercial counterpart" (John Milner Associates 1979:72). Once again, the arsenal concentrated on research and development, this time focusing on chemicals and special packaging for small-arms ammunition. It was, however, also instrumental in developing a catapult ejection system for jet aircraft. Even with a reduced workforce in this postwar period, the arsenal was employing more than 6,850 people.

When the Korean conflict began in the 1950s, the arsenal again expanded its production and for this purpose hastily added more than thirty structures to the site. Short-range light weapons and cartridges were typical of what Frankford produced during the 1950s. Because of major reorganizations in the U.S. Army during the 1960s and 1970s, almost all the arsenal's functions were gradually transferred to other installations. Finally, in 1977 the Frankford Arsenal—one of the most historically significant military facilities in the country—shut down its production lines forever. Today the arsenal is called the "Arsenal Business Center," and its buildings are being used by private companies.

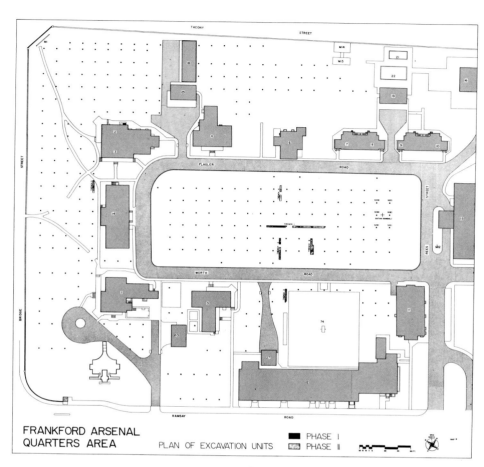

Figure 5.59.

Plan of excavation units at the Frankford Arsenal. (From John Milner Associates 1979; courtesy of the Corps of Engineers, Baltimore District, Department of the Army, and John Milner Associates)

The Archaeological Investigation

Of all the Frankford Arsenal's 110 acres, only the area around the parade ground had survived the years from 1816 to 1978 in largely untouched condition. Still green and harboring a fair number of rabbits, squirrels, and birds, it offered quite a contrast to the rest of the intensely developed site, much of it covered with

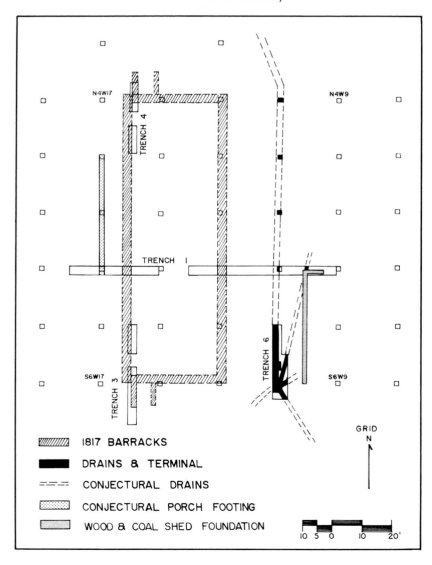

Figure 5.60.

Trenches dug in the vicinity of the 1817 barracks. (From John Milner Associates 1979; courtesy of the Corps of Engineers, Baltimore District, Department of the Army, and John Milner Associates)

▨▨▨▨ 1817 BARRACKS

████ DRAINS & TERMINAL

= = = CONJECTURAL DRAINS

CONJECTURAL PORCH FOOTING

WOOD & COAL SHED FOUNDATION

twentieth-century concrete and asphalt. Having been from the start the site of the arsenal's living quarters, the parade ground was, of course, significant in the early history of the facility. For that reason, and also because the area around the parade ground was largely undisturbed, it was there that archaeological excavations aimed at elucidating the arsenal's history began in the summer of 1978.

The search started with an attempt to find the remains of the original 1817 barracks and the 1825 blacksmith's shop. Sample testing of 340 units, each 2 feet square and part of the checkerboard grid shown in Figure 5.59, revealed the remains of the barracks, but it failed to turn up any evidence of the blacksmith's shop. The second phase of the investigation involved the excavation of large trenches in the area where the barracks had been found (Figure 5.60).

These trenches confirmed the barracks' documented dimensions of 100 by 33 feet. They also showed that the foundations were made of Wissahickon schist and mortar and were a sturdy 3 feet wide. Along the front, or west, foundation, three window sills, each made of brick and set in mortar on the schist of the basement wall, confirmed the existence of three of the six bays documented for the building. Interestingly, each of the sills had four small, diamond-shaped recesses, evidence that the windows were once covered by vertical iron bars. Some other unexpected and unrecorded details of the barracks' construction also came to light. Two sets of bulkhead walls, one on the north facade and one on the south, indicated that the basement could be entered from the outside. There was also evidence that the interior walls and bulkhead jambs of the basement had been heavily plastered and whitewashed and that

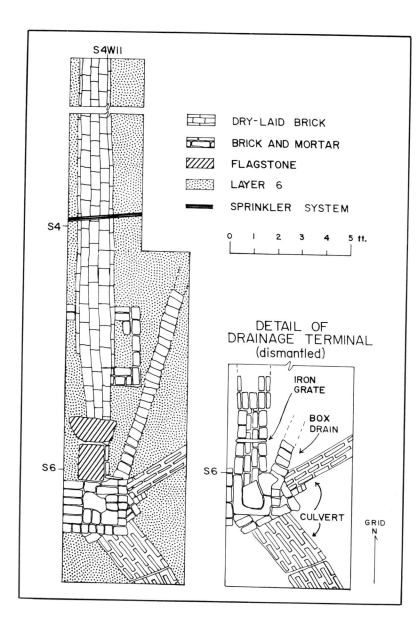

S4WII

DRY-LAID BRICK
BRICK AND MORTAR
FLAGSTONE
LAYER 6
SPRINKLER SYSTEM

0 1 2 3 4 5 ft.

S4

S6

DETAIL OF
DRAINAGE TERMINAL
(dismantled)

IRON
GRATE

BOX
DRAIN

S6

CULVERT

GRID
N

Figure 5.61.

Plan of culverts and drains found in trench 6. (From John Milner Associates 1979; courtesy of the Corps of Engineers, Baltimore District, Department of the Army, and John Milner Associates)

Figure 5.62.

Drain-and-culvert system in trench 6, looking south. (From John Milner Associates 1979; courtesy of the Corps of Engineers, Baltimore District, Department of the Army, and John Milner Associates)

the basement's floor had been brick, laid in a herringbone pattern on a firm, hard-packed base of sand.

Other evidence confirmed the record of alterations made to the barracks in the years following the Civil War. In a reversal of the frequent archaeological result of finding "everything but the kitchen sink," the archaeologists located a heavily corroded iron sink still securely bolted to the interior of the west foundation wall—testimony that after 1870 the basement had indeed been divided into kitchen units. Although its precise length was not determined, a small, brick porch footing made of

dry-laid stretchers set three rows wide and three courses deep offered convincing evidence of the piazza known to have been added to the front of the barracks. Probable evidence of the barracks' coal or wood sheds was found in the location documented for the sheds; in the yard east of the barracks, a trench revealed the remains of a thick brick-and-mortar wall. The bricks were set stretcherwise in six courses, about 17 inches deep. At least one end of this structure had apparently experienced some disturbance, for the wall terminated abruptly.

Another trench just east of the 1817

Figure 5.63.

Pedestal of triangular cannonball display. (From John Milner Associates 1979; courtesy of the Corps of Engineers, Baltimore District, Department of the Army, and John Milner Associates)

barracks (trench 6 in Figure 5.60) revealed a complex brick-and-mortar structure. As can be seen in Figures 5.61 and 5.62, it was obviously the remains of a drainage system for the barracks or parade ground, or both. Emanating from it at various levels and in various directions were four brick drains or culverts. Two of the culverts were arched and constructed of brick and mortar; the other two were box-shaped and primarily dry-laid. A 1904 map of the arsenal shows such a drainage system, but the archaeological evidence indicated that the lower portions of this system probably dated from the time when the barracks were built, ca. 1817.

Excavation of the earth adjacent to the parade ground revealed a small feature that one might expect to find only at a military installation or in a memorial park. It first appeared during the initial sample testing as a solid mass of stone-and-mortar rubble at a corner of a storehouse in the west end of the parade ground. Further exposure by a larger trench dug during the next phase of the investigation showed a triangle of stone approximately 6 feet long on each side (Figure 5.63). Initially perplexed as to the function of this feature, the archaeologists found a clue in a photograph of the storehouse taken about 1905. The photograph showed a large cannonball display at the corner of the building; what the archaeological evidence had confirmed was the triangular stone pedestal that once supported this display.

In addition to producing physical evidence of documented features, excavation revealed artifacts that provided information and clues about the undocumented behavior of the arsenal's military personnel and their families. By far the greatest number of artifacts was found in one distinct layer of the parade ground's generally nonuniform and complex stratigraphy. This layer, designated as layer 3, dated from 1817 to 1891, when the barracks was demolished. The layer above it, also distinct, was representative of the era from 1891 to 1970. Over both these layers was a deposit of recent fill, probably put there to level the parade ground.

The artifacts found in layer 3 reflected the general taste in ceramics that prevailed during the 74-year life span of the barracks; they included sherds of redware, pearlware, whiteware, yellow earthenware, and stoneware. Not surprisingly, layer 3 also yielded sherds of "military china," a utilitarian ware often referred to on residential sites as "hotel china." Since the barracks was the scene of residential life at a military-industrial complex, it is also not surprising that layer 3 yielded abundant evidence of clothing and personal and military activities. Some of this evidence is shown in Figure 5.64. Indicative of the activities of the children who lived on the site were a number of clay and glass marbles (Figure 5.65); a fragment of a toy lead soldier suggests that children then, as now, tended to emulate the behavior of their parents.

Figure 5.64.

Artifacts of clothing and personal and military activities. *Top (left to right),* brass folding-rule hinge, brass belt buckle, brass thimble, brass scabbard tip; *bottom (left to right),* brass remnants, gun flint. Other military objects found around the barracks included grapeshot, musketballs and cannonballs, cartridge casings, and bullets. (From John Milner Associates 1979; courtesy of the Corps of Engineers, Baltimore District, Department of the Army, and John Milner Associates)

Figure 5.65.

Artifacts of children. *Top (left to right),* clay marbles, lead soldier; *bottom (left to right),* glass marble, clay marbles. (From John Milner Associates 1979; courtesy of the Corps of Engineers, Baltimore District, Department of the Army, and John Milner Associates)

6

The City Beyond the Colonial Core

The meaning of the "city" beyond the colonial core is somewhat ambiguous, primarily because of the changes in Philadelphia's political boundaries effected by the Act of Consolidation in 1854. Until that time, the "city" meant the area between the Delaware and Schuylkill rivers bounded by South and Vine streets. Since then, of course, it has meant both the city and the county of Philadelphia. The "colonial core," on the other hand, has always been unambiguous, clearly signifying the blocks east of Seventh Street between Vine and South where Philadelphians clustered until the late 1700s.

Although many landmarks of the colonial core are still visible, the spaces beyond it (and even within it) had by 1850 changed to a degree that most colonial Philadelphians would have found hard to credit. As early as the 1830s, newly built canals and coal-burning factories, which could be, and increasingly were, situated well away from any source of water power, were starting to transform the landscape. Manayunk, a quiet hamlet along the Schuylkill in 1820, had by the 1830s become a booming mill town, and Bush Hill, Andrew Hamilton's former country seat at Spring Garden and Seventeenth streets, was functioning as a carpet factory. Bush Hill was but one of the many elegant country estates built in Philadelphia County during the colonial era that disappeared, together with acres of rich agricultural land and numerous working farms, as industrialization took hold in the first half of the nineteenth century.

In its reincarnation as a carpet factory (a highly successful one at that), Bush Hill was part of Spring Garden, a district carved out of the greenbelt of the Northern Liberties in 1813. In

1830 Spring Garden had just over 11,000 residents; by 1850 that number had grown to almost 59,000 (Warner 1987:51). Kensington, part of the Northern Liberties until 1820, experienced a similar pattern of growth. In 1850 these districts, both of them north of Vine Street between the two rivers, were among the most densely populated places in the Philadelphia region.

At the same time, industrialization was transforming the landscape within the original city limits. After the wooded land west of the colonial core was cleared during the Revolutionary War, most of it was taken up by pasture and large clay pits used by the city's fledgling industry of potters. Soon after the turn of the nineteenth century, those open fields began giving way to house lots and commercial buildings. As early as 1830, almost as many people were living west of Seventh Street as east of it (Wainwright 1982:280), and by 1850 the westward

rush to Broad Street and beyond was on. Within ten years, Rittenhouse Square would be the most prestigious address in Philadelphia, and the riotous expansion of the industrial city would be evident even on the other side of the Schuylkill. There, as elsewhere in Philadelphia County, farms, rural villages, and country estates vanished as horse-drawn streetcars appeared. Between 1850 and 1860 the population of West Philadelphia more than doubled, increasing from about 11,500 to almost 24,000, and that was but the beginning of development on the west bank of the Schuylkill (Warner 1987:51, 194).

Among the archaeological sites described in this chapter are a unique early eighteenth-century farm that somehow withstood the onslaught of development on the west bank of the Schuylkill; a complex of mills along Wissahickon Creek, where evidence of colonial industry surfaced; the forgotten burial grounds of two early

nineteenth-century churches, where excavation produced, among other things, evidence of how different the cultures of these congregations (one black and one white) were; an enormous public almshouse built in 1838, which by the end of the nineteenth century had taken on the characteristics of a general hospital; a hostel that sheltered the "fallen" women of Philadelphia from 1807 until 1916; a number of nineteenth-century neighborhoods variously characterized by mixed land use, social heterogeneity, social homogeneity, and ethnic clustering; an industrial site of the Victorian era; and an unknown burial ground where a prominent physician of the Victorian city engaged in some dubious dealings—of scientific and archaeological interest, of course. Taken together, these sites sketch a picture of how the green spaces that once existed beyond the city's colonial core evolved into the nineteenth-century industrial metropolis.

BARTRAM'S GARDEN: AN EARLY BOTANICAL VENTURE

Most of the farms that flourished on the outskirts of colonial Philadelphia have vanished, supplanted by monuments to nineteenth- and twentieth-century industry. It therefore seems particularly fortunate that one of the most unusual of these farms does still exist, though in surroundings its founder doubtless would not recognize. One of America's oldest surviving botanical gardens, Bartram's Garden occupies a site on the west

bank of the Schuylkill, which today offers views of oil refineries across the river, a gypsum plant to the south, and the gleaming glass and steel of the city skyline to the northeast. Begun in 1728 by John Bartram, an independent-minded if not eccentric Quaker farmer, the "garden," which is how Bartram referred to all his farm, has dwindled from about three hundred sprawling acres to ten acres of sloping wooded parkland. At the

top of the slope are a seventeenth-century farmhouse to which Bartram added his own distinctive touches—some of which remain an architectural enigma—a complex of outbuildings known as the seedhouse, and a large stone stable. Owned by the city of Philadelphia since 1891, maintained by the Fairmount Park Commission, and administered by the John Bartram Association, the property has in recent years been the focus

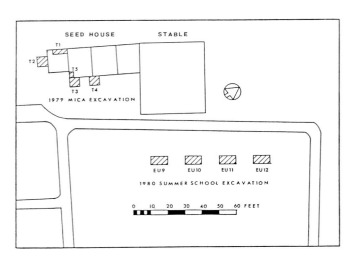

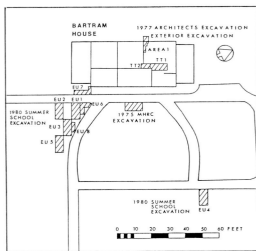

Figure 6.1.

Excavation sites at Bartram's garden, 1975–1980. (Courtesy of Joel Fry)

of several archaeological and architectural investigations (Figure 6.1). The following account is based on various historical, architectural, and archaeological studies conducted at the site, including Glenn (1978), Kenyon, Hunter, and Schenck (1975), Parrington (1979b; 1981a), and Fry (1986; in preparation).

John Bartram and His Legacy

John Bartram was born in 1699 in Darby, Pennsylvania, the son of English Quakers who had immigrated to Penn's colony shortly after its founding. Raised on a farm in Darby, he received only four or five years of formal education at the local Quaker school. Yet by the time he died in 1777 his reputation as a botanist was established on both sides of the Atlantic. Indeed, in the opinion of Carolus Linnaeus, the famed Swedish botanist, Bartram was "the greatest natural botanist in the world." By "natural"

botanist, Linnaeus meant self-taught, for what Bartram knew of plant life he learned from his own observations and reading. Hiring a tutor to teach him the Latin in which the botanical books of the day were written, he mastered the elements of the language within three months and as eagerly devoured books borrowed from learned friends, among them James Logan and Benjamin Franklin (Mower 1983; Bronner 1982:42).

With Franklin, who was seven years his junior, Bartram seems to have had a good deal in common—certainly an inquiring mind and a taste for learning, for he was instrumental in helping Franklin found the American Philosophical Society. Judging from Bartram's many other accomplishments and his extensive travels, he also shared with Franklin a prodigious amount of energy as well as the independent spirit characteristic of the American colonial. But unlike Franklin, Bartram confined his travels and his essential interests to North America. Although the popular taste dictated importing to the colonies all things European, Bartram concen-

trated on exploring native American flora. He began by studying the plant material in his own backyard, and eventually he traveled as far south as Florida, north to Lake Ontario, and west to the Ohio River. Bringing seeds, cuttings, and roots back to his farm on the Schuylkill, he studied and propagated the plants and ultimately exported to the Old World almost two hundred new species. While at home, he also pursued his interests in "soil fertilization, soil erosion, reclaimed marsh lands, improved crops and vegetables, cultivation of native grapes, and the introduction of certain fruit trees" (Mower 1983:1). In addition, he found time to use his knowledge of the medicinal properties of plants to help neighbors who could not afford to pay for medical treatment.

Among those who eagerly waited for Bartram's seed shipments to arrive in London was Peter Collinson, a Quaker wool merchant with an avid interest in botany. The two men corresponded for thirty-five years, and though they never met, they became close friends. Collinson introduced Bartram to a number of other influ-

Figure 6.2.

Facade of Bartram's house overlooking the Schuylkill. Bartram's granddaughter added the dormer windows and the one-story rooms on the north and south sides of the house in the nineteenth century. Otherwise, the house appears much as it did when Bartram died in 1777. (Courtesy of Joel Fry)

Figure 6.3.

Villa Sarego, designed by Andrea Palladio in the sixteenth century. The columns are reminiscent of those Bartram added to his house in 1770. (Courtesy of Alitalia)

ential English clients, and it was also owing to his intervention that King George III in 1765 appointed Bartram Royal Botanist, a post that earned him a stipend of £50 a year (Cheston 1953:13).

The farm at which Bartram conducted his botanical experiments was in the 1600s part of the northernmost Swedish plantation on the Schuylkill. Bartram bought the property for £45 at a sheriff's auction in 1728. It then consisted of just over a hundred acres and a small, gambrel-roofed stone farmhouse dating from about 1689. In the course of Bartram's lifetime, the farm grew to around three hundred acres, and as his fame spread, the site became a mecca for travelers both from the colonies and abroad who wished to see for themselves Bartram's renowned collection of native flora. These they found planted not according to any formal design but placed wherever they grew best.

The small Swedish farmhouse also grew, and, like the garden, the transformed dwelling revealed something of the character of its owner. Bartram apparently accomplished the additions

in two stages. A stone on the house facade inscribed with "1731" indicates that he and his second wife, the former Ann Mendenhall, had by then added a large kitchen with overhead chamber to the north side of the house. Other additions took place in 1770 when Bartram, then seventy-one years of age, gave the house an unusual classical facade by adding a centered, recessed porch set off by three columns (Figure 6.2). The columns, made of rough-cut drums of Pennsylvania schist topped by Ionic capitals, bear an interesting resemblance to those Andrea Palladio used at the Villa Sarego in Verona, one of the many villas and palaces he designed for wealthy Italians during the sixteenth century

(Figure 6.3). Whether Bartram ever saw any pictures of Palladio's work is unknown, but the Library Company of Philadelphia did have available Palladio's *Four Books of Architecture*.

Above Bartram's recessed porch is a second-floor bedroom framed in wood. The rest of the house front consists of cut and dressed schist laid with thick mortar joints. Around the corner, however, the side and back walls are more thriftily covered with stucco over rough, undressed schist, or "rubble." The stone frames of the symmetrically placed front windows are roughly carved to resemble baroque curves, and above the first-floor window of the study that Bartram added at the southeast corner of the

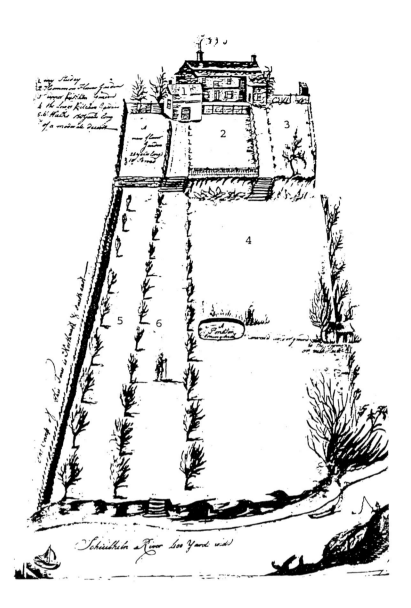

Figure 6.4.

Sketch John Bartram made of his house and garden in 1758. The study in front of the house was probably razed before the additions of 1770. Bartram's notations read: "1. My study; 2. common flower garden; 3. upper kitchen garden; 4. lower kitchen gardens; 5,6. walks 150 yds. long of a moderate descent." (Courtesy of the Earl of Derby, Knowsley, England, and Bartram's Garden)

Garden, no harm befell the property, and the Bartrams went on with business as usual (Mower 1983).

Bartram did not live to see the outcome of the Revolution. He died shortly after the Battle of the Brandywine in September 1777, leaving the house and garden to his son John, Jr. That William did not inherit the property is not too surprising, for William, his talents as a botanist notwithstanding, had already failed dismally in several business ventures underwritten by his father. William remained at the farm after his father's death, and together he and John, Jr., turned the garden into a commercial nursery, which they called John Bartram & Son. In 1783 they circulated an advertisement of their firm (Mower 1983). One of their early orders—no doubt a large and important one— came from Samuel Vaughan, who in the spring of 1785 planted Independence Square with a variety of trees purchased from the Bartrams.

After the death of John Bartram, Jr., the property passed to his daughter Ann Bartram Carr. Because of financial pressures, she sold it in 1850 to Andrew Eastwick, a self-made man who had made his fortune in Philadelphia's locomotive industry. Appreciative of the old house and garden and determined not to disturb them, Eastwick had his huge villa, which

house is the inscription, "It is God alone, Almighty Lord, the Holy One by me Ador'd—John Bartram 1770." The new study apparently eliminated the need for a small building at the front of the house that Bartram had used as an office or study. The latter, which appears in a sketch of the house and grounds that Bartram sent to England in 1758 (Figure 6.4), was probably razed before the additions of 1770 (Cheston 1953:27).

Bartram's family, like his house and garden, also grew. He had two children by his first marriage and nine by his second. William Bartram (1739–1823), the seventh of the eleven offspring, became a well-known botanist in his own right, displaying both an artistic and a scientific talent. He accompanied his father on many of his plant-collecting trips, including his exploration of Florida, which began in 1765 just after the elder Bartram's appointment as Royal Botanist. That appointment lasted for only a decade, for with the outbreak of the Revolution both the royal title and the stipend ended, as did Bartram's contacts with his English patrons. Little is known about Bartram's attitude toward the war, except for one letter in which he expressed grave concern that the British would destroy his "darling garden." Although British soldiers did indeed camp at Bartram's

was designed by Samuel Sloan, built in a cornfield just south of the garden. When Eastwick died in 1879, his family inherited the property, and eventually, in 1891, they put it up for sale. Thomas Meehan, once Eastwick's head gardener, was by then a successful Philadelphia nurseryman as well as a member of the City Council. An early champion of green spaces, Meehan was instrumental in persuading the city to purchase Bartram's Garden and to maintain it both as a historic site and a neighborhood park (Fry [in preparation]).

Twentieth-Century Investigations

Figure 6.1 shows the areas excavated in four investigations that have taken place at Bartram's Garden in recent years.* The first of these was a feasibility study conducted in 1975 under the auspices of the Museum Historic Research Center (MHRC) of the University Museum (Kenyon, Hunter, and Schenck 1975). It involved a search for subsurface traces of a central path in front of the house; such a path appears in historic photographs of the property.

This study was followed in 1977 by a full-scale architectural investigation of the house, which was carried out by John Dickey and Associates for the John Bartram Association. The object was to produce evidence that would aid in restoring the property and in interpreting its history. As reported by Glenn (1978), in their attempts to date sections of the house and to locate structural evidence, the restoration ar-

chitects conducted both interior and exterior excavations. They retrieved some artifacts but recorded only horizontal provenience. Since the stratigraphic positions of the artifacts are unknown, their archaeological significance is indeterminable.

In 1979 the Museum Institute for Conservation Archaeology (MICA) of the University Museum contracted with the John Bartram Association to make a study of the seedhouse for the purpose of locating physical evidence that would shed light on John Bartram's botanical activities (Parrington 1979b). Some of the outbuildings in the seedhouse complex date from John Bartram's occupancy of the premises, and some are much later. According to one of Bartram's descendants, these outbuildings had been used for the storage of botanical specimens (Cheston 1953:23), and the hope was that excavation would produce preserved botanical matter that would make it possible to define the kinds of seeds Bartram stored there. Unfortunately, the investigation produced no preserved seeds or pollen, and the evidence that was uncovered indicated that the part of the seedhouse under study had been built after Bartram's death in 1777.

This disappointment was tempered somewhat by the discovery of eighty-seven glass bottles in a trash deposit within the seedhouse. Dating from the late 1800s and early 1900s, they included 35 medicine bottles, most of which had contained large proportions of alcohol.* Among them were 7 Dr. Jayne's Expectorant bottles dating from the first decade of the twentieth century, 6 Lydia E. Pinkham's Vegetable Compound bottles, 6 Munyon's Paw-Paw bottles, 3 Bromo-Seltzer bottles, 2 Oxomulsion bottles,

1 Hankin's Specific bottle, and 1 Dr. Kilmer's Swamp-Root Kidney, Liver and Bladder Cure bottle (Parrington 1981a). It seems likely that the medicine bottles and other artifacts found in the trash pit were dumped there by workmen after the Fairmount Park Commission began restoring the seedhouse around the turn of the twentieth century.

The fourth archaeological investigation of Bartram's Garden took place in 1980 under the direction of Robert L. Schuyler. Carried out by students from the University of Pennsylvania, the excavations concentrated on two areas: the site of the old office or study, which was probably removed before Bartram added the classical facade to the house in 1770, and an

Figure 6.5.

The remains of a cobbled path, probably one of several symmetrical paths that John Bartram laid out through his garden in the mid-eighteenth century. (Courtesy of Joel Fry)

---

* A fifth, limited archaeological study by Joel Fry took place at Bartram's Garden in 1982 after heavy rains caused the brick paving northeast of the house to slump. Testing revealed a circular, brick-lined pit, apparently a cistern, but excavation to a depth of 14 feet produced only building debris from construction that took place on the property in the 1920s.

* See Chapter 11 for a discussion of the curative powers that manufacturers of these patent medicines claimed for their products.

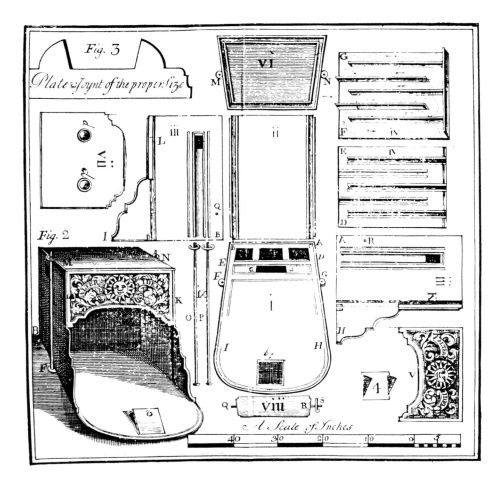

Figure 6.6.

Page from Franklin's *Account of the New-Invented Pennsylvania Fireplaces,* drawn by Lewis Evans, 1744. (Courtesy of the Historical Society of Pennsylvania)

open field east of the stable, where, according to historical records, a number of greenhouses once stood.

A robbed trench uncovered at the site of the study may well have held one of the building's foundation walls, for it seems likely that thrifty John Bartram would have reused all building materials salvageable from a razed structure on his property. Excavations in this area also revealed a number of garden features and postholes, but the most striking feature was a path running east toward the river from what may have been the front of the study (Figure 6.5). Neatly edged with shallow drainage troughs formed by cobbles set on end, the center of the path consisted of cobbles, brick fragments, and shells.

A series of widely spaced tests in the open field revealed parts of three structures. The only indication of the first structure was a stone wall, and the evidence of the second consisted

Figure 6.8.

Examples of unglazed earthenware flowerpots from the Bartram greenhouse. (Courtesy of Joel Fry)

Figure 6.7.

A Franklin stove plate found in the Bartram greenhouse. (Courtesy of Joel Fry)

of a foundation and a wall that had fallen as a result of fire. The remains of the third structure, however, clearly demonstrated that it had been a greenhouse—one that historical records indicated had been built in 1760–61. Constructed chiefly of brick and stone, it had had one sloping wall of wood framing that had held glass panes, and it had probably run 10 feet east-west and 30 or 40 feet north-south. It had been floored in stone and heated by stoves; a series of brick channels had funneled the heat through the base of the structure. The building was apparently destroyed sometime after 1838, perhaps about the time Eastwick acquired the property in 1850.

The area in and around the greenhouse site yielded some notable evidence: a plate from a Franklin stove, which had no doubt helped heat the building after it was first erected, and a host of horticultural artifacts that shed light on early nursery practices.* The plate from the "Pennsylvania Fireplace," as Benjamin Franklin called his 1741 invention, is very rare; only one other like it, housed in the Mercer Museum in Doylestown, Pennsylvania, is known to exist. Both are the front plates of what was essentially a six-plate stove (Figure 6.6), and each is decorated with a sun face flanked by a floral or leaf motif (Figure 6.7). The stove at Bartram's Garden was among the 140 Franklin stoves the Warwick Furnace in Chester County cast between 1760 and 1765. By the 1780s the Franklin

* Data on the stove plate and other artifacts from the greenhouse site were supplied by Joel Fry, who is analyzing them in conjunction with a doctoral dissertation at the University of Pennsylvania.

stove's susceptibility to corrosion had rendered it obsolete; even the inventor himself in his old age could not find an intact example.

The horticultural artifacts from the greenhouse included some 10,000 fragments of flowerpots, bell jars, greenhouse benches, watering devices, and other gardening accessories and tools. Reconstructions of over a hundred flowerpots indicated that four basic types had been in use: a large, tall, subconical nursing pot, a three-quarter or half pot, a standard pot less than half the size of the nursing pot, and a shallow pan or saucer for forcing plants (Figure 6.8). Made of unglazed earthenware, the flowerpots from Bartram's Garden suggest that some aspects of horticulture have changed very little over the past two centuries (Fry 1986).

THE GORGAS MILL COMPLEX: EARLY INDUSTRY ALONG THE WISSAHICKON

Although mills in the Philadelphia region reached their zenith in the days when the city was the nation's industrial leader, they were playing an important role in the local economy long before then. Early Swedish settlers, taking advantage of the swift descent of the streams of the Piedmont to the Fall Line, had set up water-powered mills even before William Penn had set foot on these shores. As Philadelphia grew in the eighteenth century and roads to markets improved, mills became more numerous. With the construction of canals to transport coal in the first half of the nineteenth century, mill towns began springing up along these waterways almost overnight. And as coal became more widely used, mills began appearing even where no water flowed. However, these symbols of the city's industrial past have received scant archaeological attention.* Manayunk, for example, one of the most important nineteenth-century milling centers, has to date been the focus of only one limited study.

Conducted by Liggett (1978b) for Philadelphia's Water Department, the Manayunk study monitored reconstruction and preservation of a small portion of the Manayunk Canal. Al-

* Some redress of this neglect has recently taken shape. In preparation for the annual meeting of the Society for Industrial Archaeology in 1990, hosted by the Oliver Evans Chapter in Philadelphia, the chapter has produced a survey of Philadelphia's historically significant industrial sites (Bowie 1990).

though the fieldwork was restricted by the size of the project area and the goals of the study, the archival research did produce some interesting data, including an 1848 survey listing the businesses in Manayunk. With twenty-three on the roster, Manayunk was quite clearly a flourishing nineteenth-century mill community. Liggett found very little documentation pertaining to the construction of the canal, but she nevertheless believes the original graphics for the canal's construction do exist and may be located in the archives of the Reading Company.

One exception to the general lack of archaeological research on the mills of Philadelphia is Jeffrey L.

Kenyon's 1974 study of the Gorgas Mill Complex, a mid-eighteenth-century flour-milling enterprise located along Wissahickon Creek in Fairmount Park. Kenyon, then Director of the Department of Education at the University Museum, chose the site as a place to implement an archaeological training program for high school students. Conducted within an interdisciplinary framework, the study used the techniques of the archaeologist, anthropologist, historian, botanist, and architect. The research objectives were to elucidate the physical development of the complex, the position of the complex in the regional economy of the eighteenth century, the archaeological potential of the complex, and the overall research potential of the Wissahickon

Figure 6.9.

Joseph Gorgas's house as it appeared in May 1974. The house and its outbuildings became known as the "Monastery." (Courtesy of the University Museum, University of Pennsylvania)

milling community. The study involved intensive research of secondary and primary documents pertaining to flour milling in general and the Gorgas Mill Complex in particular, as well as limited excavations along Wissahickon Creek. The following summary is based on Kenyon's report (1977b).

The Historical Record

In 1747 Joseph Gorgas began building a large, three-story private dwelling, the first structure at the Gorgas Mill Complex. Made of local Wissahickon schist, the house still stands on a high hill overlooking Wissahickon Creek (Figure 6.9). Interestingly, Joseph does not seem to have had clear title to the property, for the deed book indicates that his brother John actually owned the land. It is likely, however, that the brothers cooperated in developing the complex. Evidently a deeply religious man, Joseph Gorgas was intimately associated with the Church of the Brethren, a German sect of Seventh Day Baptists founded by Conrad Beissel, and for a while lived at Beissel's Cloisters in Ephrata in Lancaster County. Well before Gorgas finished building his house in 1751, the property was the scene of various religious ceremonies. One of the earliest ceremonies to take place there occurred at a spot along the creek, where, on December 25, 1723, the Church of the Brethren held its first baptismal service in America. Not surprisingly, Gorgas's house and its outbuildings became known as the "Monastery."

The Gorgas property was ideally situated for the development of a milling industry, since Wissahickon Creek's rather steep drop—approximately 90 feet over six miles from the Philadelphia County line to the creek's

outfall into the Schuylkill—ensures a constant flow of water. The Gorgas brothers were apparently able to recognize a good thing when they saw it, for by 1775 the site had not just one mill but two: a gristmill with three pairs of grinding stones and a sawmill, both made of the locally abundant Wissahickon schist. In addition, a dam was by then spanning the creek. Although not mentioned in the records, a headrace and tailrace had doubtless also been built to control the flow of water into and out of the milling dam.

By 1816 the complex had expanded to include several more stone buildings, among them a cooper's shop, corn crib, barn, and stable. Of the original structures, only the stable and Gorgas's house remain standing. Some time between 1800 and 1825, the gristmill was converted to a paper mill, and after the paper mill burned in the late 1840s, it was apparently rebuilt as a woolen mill (Figure 6.10)—an interesting example of the uses of water power available to numerous other mills along the Wissahickon. In 1891 the Fairmount Park Commission acquired the Gorgas property and still maintains title to it.

Location was not the only favorable factor in the development of the milling enterprise at the Gorgas Mill Complex. Until about 1730, inadequate roads had been a chief obstacle to the delivery of goods and services in the colonies, but by the mid-1700s they had greatly improved, allowing for the rapid and efficient transport of goods to the major markets. This improvement was particularly crucial to the development of the Gorgas Mill Complex and other milling enterprises along the Wissahickon, since until then the rather rugged terrain had been a serious hindrance to the marketing of goods. Moreover, with Philadelphia and other places in the colonies experiencing rapid growth throughout the eighteenth century, the demand for services and goods, particularly flour, was ever-increasing. By the 1740s flour had become an important commodity in the economy of the province and Philadelphia's most valuable export. In 1730 Pennsylvania produced 38,750 barrels of flour; in 1744 the yield was 165,967 barrels—an impressive increase in productivity in a period of just fourteen years. With the millers of the Delaware Valley supplying most of this flour, the Gorgas Mill Complex and other mills along the Wissahickon emerged as one of the most important eighteenth-century milling communities in America.

The Archaeological Study

Because of limited funding, Kenyon's investigation of the Gorgas Mill Complex was considerably more modest than originally planned, and the industrial components of the site ultimately received more attention than the domestic (i.e., the "Monastery"). As a result, most of the fieldwork took place along the bed of the creek in areas subject to heavy siltation during episodic flooding. The siltation proved to be a mixed blessing, for while it tended to preserve the structural remains, it also added to the difficulties of excavation; in some places, the alluvial deposits were more than 6 feet deep. Nonetheless, two areas of industrial activity did receive considerable archaeological attention: an unidentified structure partly visible along the creek, and the headrace, tailrace, and wheel housing of what was probably the original gristmill.

Kenyon initially assumed that the mysterious structure along the creek was the eighteenth-century sawmill, but the study yielded nothing to support this interpretation. Rather, the

evidence indicated the building had been used for some function that involved the production of heat. The building was 35 feet long and 23 feet wide; a pit appended to one end brought the total length to 44 feet. Among the features found within the main part of the structure were a forge grating and an ash pit, what appeared to be the base of a chimney, and two smaller features, both of which appeared to be casting boxes used in the production of small machine parts or tools. Kenyon concluded that the building had been a forge of some kind and that the pit had housed a wheel that generated power for a water-driven bellows.

Excavations at the probable site of the old gristmill revealed evidence of a headrace, tailrace, and wheel housing. A natural rock ledge formed part of the land-side retaining wall of the headrace; all the rest of the headrace and the tailrace were constructed of Wissahickon schist. The floor of the wheel pit had been raised more than once, perhaps because of technological innovations in the milling industry.

A fairly large number of artifacts spanning the eighteenth through twentieth centuries came to light along with the structural remains. However, it was impossible to tie these artifacts to the Gorgas Mill Complex, since all

Figure 6.10.

Nineteenth-century view of the mill at the Gorgas complex, showing the raceway to the old waterwheels and a steam plant that by 1875 had superseded them. (Courtesy of Mrs. B. Bacon Bostwick and the Fairmount Park Commission)

were found in several feet of alluvial silt. Deposited there when the Wissahickon flooded, they could have come from anywhere in the vicinity.

Perhaps the most important outcome of the Gorgas Mill study was the potential for research that it demonstrated. Clearly, at least some structural remains of eighteenth-century mills are still well preserved beneath the alluvial silts of the Wissahickon as it flows through Fairmount Park. This is due not just to the preservative nature of the alluvium but also to the protected status of the park. Although the area immediately surrounding the park has been intensively developed, the land within it has remained largely as it was in 1891, when the Fairmount Park Commission took it over. No doubt many other eighteenth- and nineteenth-century milling complexes in this area of "nascent industrialism" are at least as well preserved as the Gorgas Mill Complex.

THE FIRST AFRICAN BAPTIST CHURCH AND THE KENSINGTON METHODIST CHURCH: FORGOTTEN BURIAL GROUNDS

The congregations of the First African Baptist Church and the Kensington Methodist Church were formed at about the same time—the first decade of the nineteenth century—and both were located in Philadelphia County. Beyond that, the two seem to have had not much in common, an observation substantiated by evidence found in the burial ground of the First African Baptist Church. Their dissimilarities extend even to the way each church came into the archaeological limelight. When evidence of the First African Baptist Church cemetery first appeared, it took even the archaeologists who were on the scene by surprise, underscoring that most African-Americans in nineteenth-century Philadelphia were "people without a history." The investigation at Kensington, on the other hand, proceeded in a more orthodox fashion, beginning with an invitation from a bishop who wished to learn the truth about a bit of historical lore that had clung to the Kensington Methodist Church. Despite the differences in these investigations, they did have at least one element in common, for serendipitous discovery played a part in both.

The Cemetery of the First African Baptist Church: Physical Evidence of a "People without a History"

In November 1980 archaeologists from John Milner Associates were routinely monitoring construction of a part of the Commuter Rail Tunnel in Center City Philadelphia (see Chapter 6, "The Commuter Rail Tunnel"). Their attention was suddenly called to a discovery made by the operator of an earth-moving machine, which was steadily excavating a 30-foot gash on the south side of Vine Street between Eighth and Ninth streets. What the archaeologists saw 6 feet down in the ground was the end of a wooden coffin. Closer inspection revealed the skull of the occupant, as well as evidence of other burials. What the earth-moving machine had blundered into, and what the archaeologists were staring at, was a long-forgotten burial ground.

A trip to the archives established that the site had indeed been used as a cemetery and that the church that had used it was the First African Baptist Church, founded by an African-American congregation in 1809. To protect the site from any further disturbance, either from construction or looters, it was securely sealed. Ultimately, the cemetery was recommended for eligibility to the National Register of Historic Places, a determination that gave it temporary legal protection from any development, as it lay within a project area using federal assistance.

In 1983 Philadelphia's Redevelopment Authority, which owned the site, engaged John Milner Associates to excavate the cemetery and to remove all burials for scientific study.* Before the fieldwork began, arrangements were made with Dr. J. Lawrence Angel of the Smithsonian Institution to study

the skeletal remains, and permission to exhume them and to reinter them at another cemetery was obtained through a court hearing.* The preliminary work also included documentary research, which clarified insofar as was possible the history of the site, as well as the formulation of questions to be addressed in the course of the excavation. These questions, based on the documentary research, focused on acculturation, mortality, and health factors among the African-Americans of early nineteenth-century Philadelphia. With the preliminary work completed, excavation began in the summer of 1983 and ended a year later. Subsequently, a number of papers on various aspects of the First African Baptist Church Cemetery project have been published, including Parrington and Roberts (1984, 1990), Roberts (1984), Parrington, Pinter, and Struthers (1986), Parrington and Wideman (1986), Angel et al. (1987), and Parrington (1987). In addition, a 37-minute film of the project, entitled "Ground Truth: Archaeology in the City," was produced in 1988 by Silverwood Films of Philadelphia. The following account of the project, however, is based primarily on the three-volume excavation report (Parrington et al., 1989; Kelley and Angel, 1989).

Historical Background

The First African Baptist Church was located at Tenth and Vine streets until

---

* Other funding for the project was provided by the Federal Highway Administration, the Pennsylvania Department of Transportation, the William Penn Foundation, and the Barra Foundation.

* The remains of the individuals found buried at the site were reinterred in Eden Cemetery in Delaware County, where a memorial is proposed to mark their contribution to African-American studies.

1816, when a dispute led to a schism in the congregation. One branch stayed at that location; the other moved to Thirteenth and Vine. After losing its property at a sheriff's sale in 1822, the Thirteenth Street church moved again, this time to Eighth and Vine streets, where its pastor, Henry Simmons (Figure 6.11), owned property. Here the congregation worshipped, and here it buried its dead.

Beginning in 1838, the Board of Health repeatedly tried to close the burial ground because of overcrowding. The church resisted, and in 1841 Henry Simmons, as the owner of the ground, was summoned to appear at the Court of General Sessions. The outcome of this legal action is unknown, but the cemetery apparently continued in use; over a dozen burials occurred there in 1842. However, at some point before 1845, the cemetery did finally close, and church membership also declined. After Simmons died in 1848, the church seems to

have dissolved; in any event, it disappeared from the historical record.

In the 1850s a row of houses and a factory for making safes were built on the site. Some of these buildings stood until the 1960s, when they were demolished in preparation for eventual redevelopment. At the time of the chance discovery of the site in 1980, it was a parking lot being used as a staging area by the Commuter Rail Tunnel contractors.

Excavation: Burial Customs and Osteological Evidence

During the two seasons of excavation, the comparatively small site yielded over 140 burials. The presence of as many as five bodies in a single grave suggested that the Board of Health had had good cause for its concern about overcrowding. As shown in Figure 6.12, a number of the burials had been disturbed by the privies of

Figure 6.11.

Lithograph of the Reverend Henry Simmons, pastor of the First African Baptist Church. (Courtesy of the Historical Society of Pennsylvania)

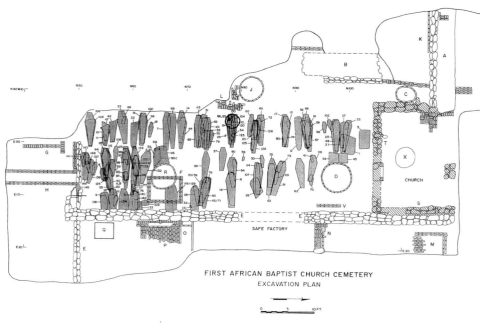

FIRST AFRICAN BAPTIST CHURCH CEMETERY
EXCAVATION PLAN

Figure 6.12.

Excavation plan of the cemetery of the First African Baptist Church, showing walls and pits impinging on some of the burials. (From Parrington et al. 1989; courtesy of the Redevelopment Authority of the City of Philadelphia and John Milner Associates)

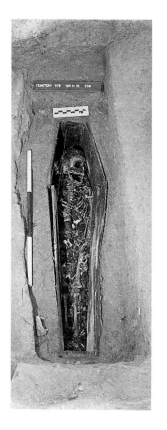

Figure 6.13.

Intact coffin found in the cemetery of the First African Baptist Church. Many of the coffins at deeper levels were well preserved. Typically, they had gabled lids made of four pieces of wood. (From Parrington et al. 1989; courtesy of the Redevelopment Authority of the City of Philadelphia and John Milner Associates)

the nineteenth-century rowhouses, as well as by the factory that had stood on the adjacent site. A few had also been disturbed by the tunnel construction, but the majority of them were relatively intact. At higher levels, the wood of the coffins had rotted, leaving organic stains marking the locations of the burials. Typically, the organic stain was in the shape of a hexagonal, pinch-toed coffin. At deeper levels, where the ground was moist, most of the coffins were still whole (Figure 6.13); it was thus possible to ascertain the kind of wood and the techniques used in making them.

Although most of the deceased had been buried in the Christian tradition—the body supine, hands by the thighs, and head to the west—variations that suggested the survival of African burial customs did occur. In eight cases, a single coin had been placed in the coffin near the head of the deceased; in six cases, a leather shoe had been placed on the coffin lid; and in two cases, a ceramic plate had been placed on the stomach of the deceased (Figure 6.14). The leather

Figure 6.14.

Adult female buried with a Chinese export porcelain plate on her stomach. (From Parrington et al. 1989; courtesy of the Redevelopment Authority of the City of Philadelphia and John Milner Associates)

shoes were found only at lower levels, where the moist conditions had preserved them; others at higher levels may not have survived.

These significant departures from the Christian burial tradition indicate that a fair proportion of the congregation of the First African Baptist Church retained memories of the burial customs of their homeland. The African belief was that death was a journey to an afterlife in the African homeland and that both the journey and the afterlife required material possessions. The shoes were probably symbolic of the journey, while the coins represented the fee for the return of the spirit to the homeland. The ceramic plates most likely were articles to be used in the afterlife; they may have had added significance as the last vessel used by the deceased, in which case they would have been thought to contain that person's energy or essence.

Osteological examination of the excavated remains showed that the average life expectancy was 14.39 years, although if individuals survived into adulthood, the average life expectancy was about 39 for females and 45 for males. Almost half the deceased were young children or infants, and many of them had died as a result of severe dietary deficiencies. Rickets, a disease caused by a deficiency of vitamin D or calcium, was common, and it was evident not just in infants but in older children and adults as well. One young woman appeared to have died in childbirth; she had been buried with a seven-month fetus in the crook of her left arm. Differences in the health patterns of men and women indicated their differing lifestyles. Men had a much higher incidence of degenerative joint disease than women, indicating that they had a harder physical lifestyle. But although they

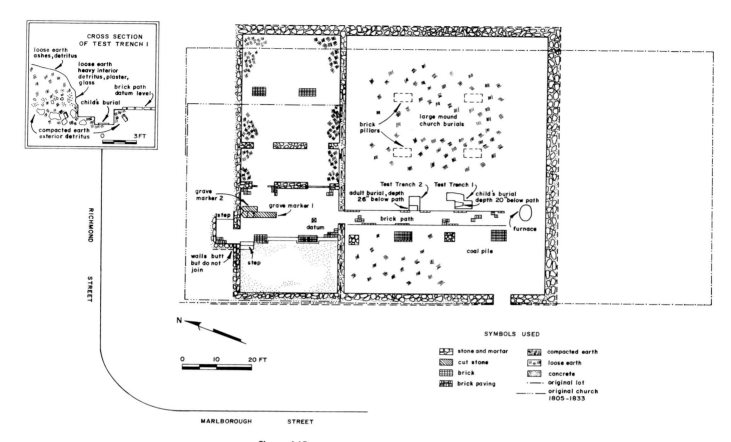

Figure 6.15.

Plan of the basement of the Kensington Methodist Church. (From Lapsansky and Cosans 1968)

had worked harder, a much lower rate of tooth decay indicated that men had enjoyed a better diet.

The pathologies of the children and infants are representative of health conditions among this segment of the African-American population during the time the cemetery was in use, but the adult pathologies reflect earlier conditions as well. The general picture that emerges from the skeletal analysis and the documentary research is of a highly stressed population with a very low standard of nutrition and health.

A Note on the Findings

The excavation of the cemetery of the First African Baptist Church resulted

in a good deal of published information about African-Americans in early nineteenth-century Philadelphia, as well as an extremely informative documentary film on all aspects of the project. It also produced physical evidence that acculturation of this segment of the population was at the time far from complete, that their standard of nutrition and health was low, and that their mortality rate was high. The paucity of historical documentation on African-Americans in the nineteenth-century city gives added value to these findings.

The Kensington Methodist Church: The Legend of the Indian Burial Mound

Although predecessors of the Lenape of the Delaware Valley may have exhibited some of the traits of the ancient Adena and Hopewellian people of the Ohio Valley, an interest in building burial mounds was not one of them. Nonetheless, a legend claiming that the Kensington Methodist Church at Marlborough and Richmond streets had been built over an Amerindian burial mound persisted for many years. Intrigued by this bit of lore, Fred Pierce Corson, bishop of the United Methodist Church in the Philadelphia area, in 1967 invited archeology students from the University of Pennsylvania to investigate the church's basement. In a series of unanticipated discoveries, the class solved the mystery of the mound and learned more about the church than anyone had thought to ask. The class report, written by Lapsansky and Cosans (1968), is the basis for the following account.

The Finds in the Basement

An inspection of the church's basement instantly proved that it did indeed contain an earth mound. Approximately 40 feet in diameter, the mound occupied a large part of the east side of the basement (Figure 6.15). Each of two tests at the edge of it produced a pinch-toed coffin. The first, uncovered at a depth of 20 inches, contained the remains of a child (Figure 6.16); the second, located at a depth of 26 inches, contained the remains of an adult. Together with the absence of any burial offerings, the nineteenth-century pinch-toed coffins ruled out the existence of an Amerindian burial mound, historic or prehistoric. Supporting evidence appeared in the form of two unset tombstones bearing the dates 1807 and 1812, which were found lying near the north foundation wall.

Historical Data and Structural Evidence

In quest of a conclusive explanation of the mound's origins, the class began searching the historical records. Although the church board denied them access to the church's records, an explanation was soon forthcoming. Deeds in the city's archives and a history of the church written by a nineteenth-century pastor (Swindell 1899) proved

Figure 6.16.

At the edge of the "mound" in the basement of the Kensington Methodist Church, a child had been buried in a small pinch-toed coffin. The coffin was replaced after the archaeological test was completed. (Photo by J. L. Cotter)

Figure 6.17.

An 1800 view of Kensington on the Delaware River with the port of Philadelphia in the background. (Engraving by W. Birch & Son; courtesy of the Free Library of Philadelphia)

particularly helpful. Scharf and West-cott's (1884) omission of any mention of the legend of the burial mound in their *History of Philadelphia, 1609–1884*, also provided a significant clue. These authors were greatly interested in Shackamaxon, as Kensington was originally known, and had they heard of the legend as they were writing their volume in the 1880s, they would no doubt have noted it in their account of the Kensington Methodist Church.

According to the pastor's history, the Kensington Methodist Church originated in 1801 when sixty members of St. George's Church at Fourth Street near Arch broke off from that congregation and formed a Methodist group called the "United Society of the People." For several years the new congregation held services near the Delaware River in Kensington (Figure 6.17) in the shade of the tree where Penn's legendary treaty with the Lenape was supposedly signed, and in bad weather they gathered in a nearby carpenter's shed. After convincing the trustees of St. George's to purchase a 60-by-120-foot lot at the corner of Marlborough and Richmond streets, the congregaton erected a church there in 1805. The front of the church faced west on Marlborough Street, and toward the back of the church, the east side of the lot was set apart as a burial ground.

The burial ground remained in use until a new church was built on the site in 1833. That church, like the present one, faced north on Richmond Street. Because of financial problems, the east side of the basement was not finished until 1835, and when it was, it had no entrance from Marlborough Street. In 1853 the rebuilding of this second church produced the present structure, and since then no other construction has taken place on the site.

The structural evidence confirmed the historical data. The investigation showed that the partition wall and the foundation walls on the west side of the basement were definitely older than the foundation walls on the east; they may date from the 1833 church and possibly even from the 1805 structure. Moreover, as Figure 6.15 shows, when the dimensions of the 1805 church are superimposed on those of the present one, parts of the walls coincide.

Laying the Legend to Rest

Taken together, the historical data and structural evidence suggested only one thing: the builders of the 1853 church had created the mound by piling the earth they excavated for the wall trenches in the center of the basement rather than hauling it away—a familiar practice among cost-cutting builders of the time. Deposits of trash from the frequent refurbishing of the interior had added to the mound's size (see cross-section in Figure 6.15). An organ cello stop found near the bottom layer of interior trash dated that layer as after 1873, which is the year the first organ was installed in the church. The clay and ashes found in the top layers of the mound were no doubt the result of two things. When a coal-burning furnace was installed around the turn of the twentieth century, it entailed digging a foundation and laying a brick path to it. Trash from that construction no doubt wound up in the mound, and ashes from furnace cleanings must surely have added to it.

Although the origin of the mound had been explained, the legend that it was an Amerindian burial mound had not. A possible explanation now occurred to the class. By the last half of the nineteenth century, word of the Hopewellian burial mounds had spread up the tributaries of the Ohio River into Pennsylvania. The church history described sharp rises and declines in the membership during this time. So if around 1900 a new parishioner with a speculative knowledge of Amerindian burial mounds seized upon the mound in the church basement to initiate the legend, no one in a position to contradict the claim may have been around. Whatever the case, the romance of archaeology came rather early to Kensington.

A SITE FOR A NEW CONVENTION CENTER: OF ALMSHOUSES, TRAINS AND TERMINALS, AND SHELTERS FOR FALLEN WOMEN

In the mid-1980s, Philadelphia's plan to erect a new convention center required an environmental impact statement on each of the three sites under consideration. The sites were the area in West Philadelphia where the present Civic Center now stands overlooking the Schuylkill River (Figure 6.18); Franklintown, an irregularly shaped area north of Race Street between Fifteenth and Twentieth streets, which includes Logan Square (Figure 6.19); and the Reading site, bounded roughly by Market, Race, Eleventh, and Thirteenth streets and so-called because of the presence of the old Reading Railroad's terminal (Figure 6.20).

As part of the environmental impact statements, John Milner Associates conducted studies of the architectural and archaeological resources of each site. The purpose of these preliminary, or Phase I, studies was to determine which properties within the three sites had cultural resources significant enough to merit their eligibility for the National Register of Historic Places. Although the initial studies involved no fieldwork, they did involve considerable historical research, and to date they have resulted in four reports (Meyer and Parrington 1983; Cosans-Zebooker, Meyer, and Young 1985; Cosans-Zebooker and Meyer 1985a, 1985b). A subsequent report (Blomberg [in preparation, a]), in progress at the time of this writing, addresses the results of archaeological data recovery excavations at the Reading site, the site ultimately selected for construction of the new convention center.

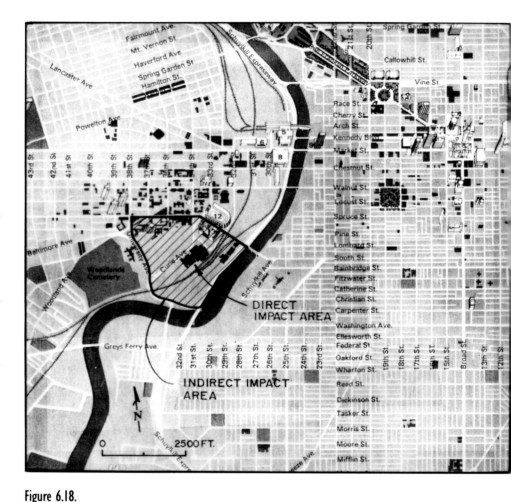

Figure 6.18.

Map of the proposed site in West Philadelphia for a new convention center. (From Cosans-Zebooker and Meyer 1985a; courtesy of the Philadelphia Industrial Development Corporation and John Milner Associates)

Other archaeological studies in recent years have focused on sites adjacent to those proposed for the new convention center. One such site was occupied in the nineteenth century by an enormous public almshouse; another was home to a shelter for "fallen" women. Together with John Milner Associates' cultural resource evaluations of the proposed convention center sites, and the report on the Reading site currently in preparation, these studies of adjacent sites have enhanced our knowledge of Philadelphia neighborhoods over the centuries.

West Philadelphia

The evaluation of the cultural resources of the West Philadelphia site was limited to the area covered by the Civic Center. Because of the center's deep basement, Cosans-Zebooker and Meyer (1985a) concluded that no significant archaeological resources were likely to have survived. However, this part of West Philadelphia has an interesting history, and it is likely that physical evidence of that history does still exist in the immediate vicinity of the Civic Center. No formal archaeological excavations have ever been carried out there, but the area has been the focus of another archaeological survey, as well as of some artifact salvage.

The Blockley Almshouse

The Blockley Almshouse was built in 1838 across the street from where the Civic Center now stands, and the last above-ground vestiges of this institution did not disappear until 1959. In the mid-1980s the University of Pennsylvania set forth a proposal to build medical facilities on the site. Because the project was expected to

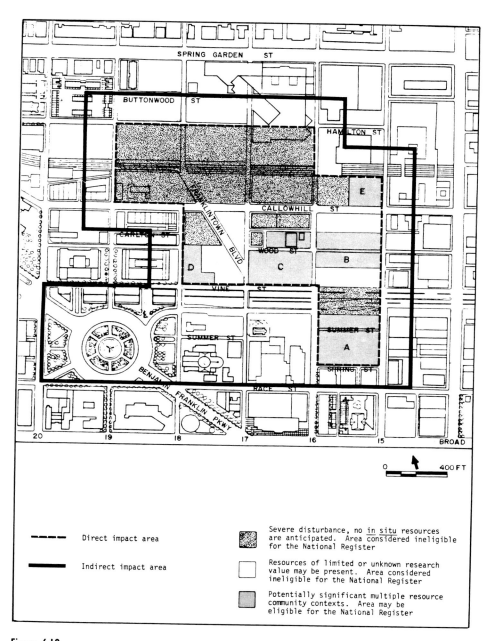

Figure 6.19.

Map of the proposed site in Franklintown. (From Cosans-Zebooker and Meyer 1985b; courtesy of the Philadelphia Industrial Development Corporation and John Milner Associates)

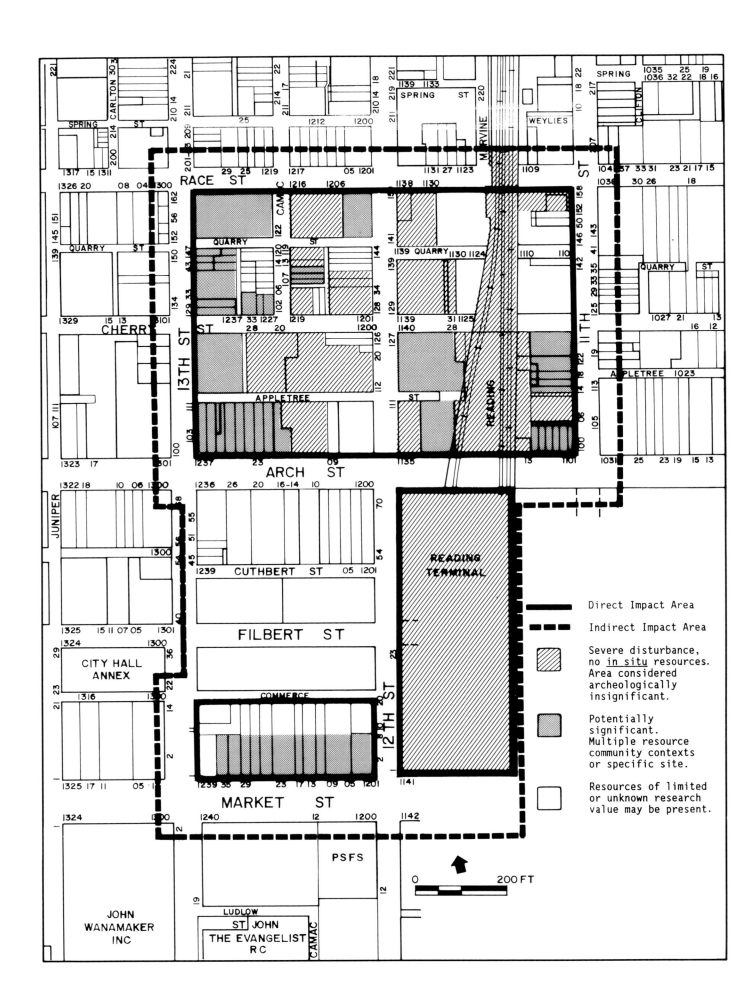

Direct Impact Area

Indirect Impact Area

Severe disturbance, no _in situ_ resources. Area considered archeologically insignificant.

Potentially significant. Multiple resource community contexts or specific site.

Resources of limited or unknown research value may be present.

0   200 FT

Figure 6.20.

Map of the proposed Reading site. (From Cosans-Zebooker, Meyer, and Young 1985; courtesy of the Philadelphia Industrial Development Corporation and John Milner Associates)

receive some federal assistance, it required an archaeological survey. The survey was carried out by Parrington and Lind (1985), whose research is reflected in this account.

In 1735 Andrew Hamilton, designer of the Pennsylvania State House and owner of Bush Hill, purchased 300 acres of land west of the Schuylkill River in Blockley Township. The land included the present sites of Woodlands Cemetery, the Civic Center, and adjacent parts of the University of Pennsylvania campus. After Hamilton died in 1741, his son James inherited the property, operated it as a working farm, and built upon it a farmhouse known as Woodlands; greatly altered, the house still stands at Woodland Avenue and Fortieth Street. Most of the area around Hamilton's property was rural, although a few small villages, including Hamilton Village and Mantua, were soon dotting the landscape (Cosans-Zebooker and Meyer 1985a:14–16).

Woodlands took on its present architectural characteristics in 1788, when William Hamilton, Andrew's grandson, expanded and remodeled it into a handsome, early Federal mansion. Within little more than half a century of the remodeling, however, both the gracious mansion and all the rest of the estate had passed out of the Hamilton family. In 1829 the city of Philadelphia bought more than half of the original 300 acres, where it soon began erecting the Blockley Almshouse, and in 1843 Woodlands

Cemetery bought the mansion and all the acreage around it.

The Blockley Almshouse was the third and last in a series of city almshouses, the first having been built from 1730 to 1733 between Spruce, Pine, Third, and Fourth streets, and the second in 1767 on Spruce Street between Tenth and Eleventh. Such institutions were a rare and purely urban phenomenon in America during the 1700s; until the 1800s, most of America's poor and sick were cared for by family or neighbors (Rothman 1971:30–31). Although Philadelphia was one of the few places to provide almshouses in the eighteenth century, it apparently did not do so with any great alacrity. The public almshouse of the 1730s had become hopelessly overcrowded before the 1767 one was built, and an increase in the value of the land on which it stood doubtless also played a role in its relocation to the west. The same factors seem to have operated in the building of the Blockley Almshouse. By 1828 the 1767 almshouse had reached the saturation point, and Tenth and Eleventh streets were no longer the city's outskirts. In an attempt to remedy the re-

current problem of overcrowding (and no doubt also to capitalize on the value of the land), the "Guardians for the Relief and Employment of the Poor of the City of Philadelphia" in 1829 purchased 187 acres of the Hamilton estate in Blockley Township (Lawrence 1905:81).

The monumental structure that William Strickland designed for this site was intended to end overcrowding of the public almshouse for all time. Occupying ten acres, it consisted of a quadrangle bounded by four buildings, each 60 feet wide and over 500 feet long (Figure 6.21). With its Doric portico and eight unfluted columns, the facade of the building was no doubt meant to instill awe and respect in the unfortunate individuals who passed through its portals. A nearby burial ground for the indigent, situated where Franklin Field (Penn's athletic stadium) now stands, must have added to the gloom of the picture. However, with social conditions

Figure 6.21.

The Blockley Almshouse as it appeared in August 1853. (Courtesy of the Library Company of Philadelphia)

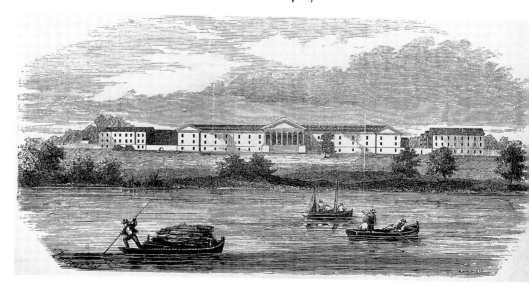

in nineteenth-century Philadelphia being what they were, the original intent of the Blockley Almshouse was soon defeated. In 1875 the almshouse had 3,000 inmates (Rosenthal 1963: 21–22), and by the end of the 1800s a plethora of ancillary structures had been built to accommodate the ever-increasing number of paupers.

In the course of the nineteenth century, the almshouse changed. Rather than being an institution for housing and feeding the poor, it became something more akin to a general hospital. This transition was officially recognized in 1903, when the institution became known as the Philadelphia General Hospital. In the meantime, the University of Pennsylvania, which moved to West Philadelphia in 1872, had purchased most of the 187 acres of the almshouse tract for its expanding campus. The university began gradual demolition of the old almshouse/hospital buildings in the 1920s, and by 1959 the last of them was gone.

Although few, if any, traces of the nineteenth-century almshouse complex exist above ground, evidence of the paupers buried there has occasionally surfaced in the course of construction work around Franklin Field. Parrington and Lind (1985) concluded that an area with particular potential for archaeological research is the site where the southwest building of the complex stood. This building served as a "lunatic asylum" during the nineteenth century, and the land in front of it appears to have been relatively undisturbed as the complex underwent development. Until water closets were installed in the 1850s, this yard had held privies, and after they were filled in, it became an exercise yard for the inmates. Such deposits could shed light on the behavior and activities of a nineteenth-century "minority group"

who have to date received little archaeological attention. In addition, deposits of trash in this area could contain evidence of innovations in medical care during the nineteenth century; the stratigraphic positions of such artifacts as medicine bottles, syringes, cupping glasses, and lancets could indicate the time at which particular medical practices were abandoned and replaced by new ones. Unfortunately, Ward and McCarthy (1990), in a follow-up Phase II study of the site, found that the area had been disturbed largely by various construction activities throughout the long history of the site. Consequently, no such evidence of early medical practices was found to have survived in one rather localized area near the site of the former Blockley Almshouse.

The Hilton Hotel Site

In 1894 the city of Philadelphia conveyed to the University of Pennsylvania a tract of eight acres bordering the almshouse site. This tract is presently occupied by the University Museum and by Penn Tower, a high-rise building constructed in 1973 as a Hilton hotel. The construction of the hotel, which entailed deep excavation, provided the opportunity for an archaeology class at the University of Pennsylvania to engage in some on-site observation and salvage. Bulldozers had excavated the site to an average depth of 30 feet, with piling holes extending to 35 feet below grade. Many layers of fill were observable on all sides of the pit, but no intrusive pits appeared at the bottom. The class retrieved a large collection of artifacts from the fill both at the bottom of the pit and at the sides (Figure 6.22). The artifacts indicated quite clearly that the site had been used as a dump in

the late nineteenth century. It was also evident that as trash filled the site, the steep natural slope of the land toward the Schuylkill had been leveled.

Mark Ohno, one of the class members, added to the collection of artifacts items he had retrieved after dump trucks hauled them away from the site. He subsequently spent a year analyzing the entire collection and produced a report describing his findings (Ohno 1978). Of the selection of intact or nearly intact artifacts (mostly bottles), the most popular by far were patent medicine bottles. They comprised 37 percent of the sixty-two identifiable bottles. Spirit and beer bottles accounted for only 12 percent, and the remainder had contained soda, food, cosmetics, and the like. Tempting as it might be to associate these artifacts with the almshouse, Ohno's documentary research indicated that the site was used as a "public dump" in the late 1800s. The fill therefore could have come from anywhere in the Philadelphia region; it is most likely, however, that it came from West Philadelphia.

Franklintown and the Area around Logan Square

Franklintown North and South

The area of Franklintown north of the old city limit at Vine Street was originally part of the Manor of Springettsbury, a large tract of land belonging to William Penn and his family. This area, like all of the rest of Franklintown—and indeed like most of the Philadelphia region—remained undeveloped throughout the colonial period, with cleared land devoted chiefly to grazing livestock and growing crops. In the 1790s Robert Morris proposed

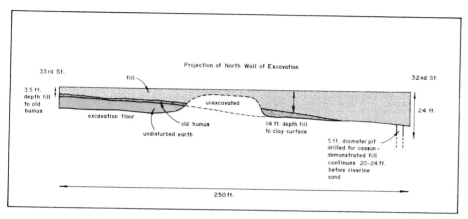

Figure 6.22.

Top, artifacts found in a nineteenth-century dump on a construction site behind the University Museum, adjacent to the old Blockley Almshouse in 1973. (Photo by J. L. Cotter) *Bottom,* construction excavation section showing extent of fill. (From Ohno 1978)

freight yards and railroad depots built over them would have destroyed any traces of their original occupants. Indeed, another archaeological testing program at the intersection of Seventeenth and Callowhill streets confirmed the presence of extensive twentieth-century disturbances (Parrington, Cress, and Tidlow 1986).

Logan Square and Vicinity

Because Logan Square was outside the part of Franklintown that would have been directly affected by the construction of a convention center (had this site been the selected alternative), it did not figure largely in John Milner Associates' evaluation and report. As a result of another construction project, however, an unusual site just off Logan Square became the subject of a full-scale archaeological investigation in 1988. As that investigation progresses, we may get a glimpse into the lives of members of a minority group about whom nineteenth-century historians tended to be rather reticent.

As the square that Thomas Holme laid out for the northwest quadrant of the city, Logan Square was, of course, situated well beyond the colonial core. It was not until the 1860s and 1870s, when the Cathedral of Saints Peter and Paul and the Academy of Natural Sciences were built, that it began taking on its present imposing charac-

a plan to build a canal that would have run through Franklintown. The canal was to have linked the Delaware and Schuylkill rivers, but although it appears on several maps of Philadelphia drawn about 1800, no concrete evidence confirming that it was ever built exists (Cosans-Zebooker and Meyer 1985b:20).

The completion in 1834 of the Columbia Railroad, which ran between the Susquehanna River and a terminus on the outskirts of the city near Franklintown, spurred the area's development, and when that development came, it was heavily industrial in nature. Manufacturing firms were quick to set up shop in the northern part of Franklintown close to the railroad facility. Among the most prominent of the firms in this part of the district of Spring Garden were William Sellers' Machine Tool Company, the Norris Locomotive Works, and the Baldwin Locomotive Works. By the late 1800s, Baldwin had become one

of Philadelphia's largest industrial plants, covering a nineteen-acre site and employing nearly three thousand workers (Cosans-Zebooker and Meyer 1985b:21–22).

Many of the employees in the factories of the northern part of Franklintown doubtless lived in the southern part of the area, a neighborhood of predominantly working-class residences. As shown in Figure 6.19, John Milner Associates recommended five of these residential blocks as eligible for the National Register of Historic Places. These areas were thought to have considerable archaeological potential in that they could provide information about the spatial patterning and demography of a sizable portion of Philadelphia's industrial work force during the nineteenth century (Cosans-Zebooker and Meyer 1985b:40–42). The industrial sites in the northern part of the area were not recommended for the National Register of Historic Places because it appeared that the

ter. For some fifty years before that time—as well as for some fifty years after—Logan Square had as a neighbor a hostel that sheltered the "fallen" women of Philadelphia. Located in the western part of the block between Twentieth and Twenty-First streets north of Race, this asylum was another of the good works of Bishop William White, patriot of the American Revolution and creator of the Protestant Episcopal Church in the United States. Together with George Williams, a civic-minded Philadelphian, White founded the Magdalen Society, which maintained the hostel for prostitutes from 1807 until 1916. Over the years, the hostel housed as many as eighty women at a time, and after 1838 some of the women who died there were buried on the premises.

Although Logan Square had undergone some startling changes even before the Magdalen Society vacated its premises in 1916, more dramatic changes were yet to come. In 1917 construction of the Benjamin Franklin Parkway began, and by 1927 the Free Library of Philadelphia was lending its imposing facade to Logan Square. In 1934 the Franklin Institute, founded for the promotion of science in 1824, took up its present quarters in the block where the Magdalen Society had held forth for over a century.* For a number of years the forgotten site of the Magdalen Society's old building was marked by two of the institute's outdoor exhibits: a Boeing 707 airplane and an Atlas rocket. One can but wonder what the "fallen" women of nineteenth-century

Philadelphia might have thought of these soaring twentieth-century symbols.

In 1988, the Franklin Institute began constructing an addition on the piece of open land where the airplane and rocket had stood. The Magdalen Society's shelter might well have remained forgotten and buried, since no archaeological review was necessary prior to the excavation for the construction. In fact, the hole was already 12 feet deep and a block long when a newspaper reporter began inquiring about what cultural resources might have existed on the site. The Franklin Institute was quick to acknowledge that significant archaeological resources might be present. Its administrators immediately halted the excavation, while Carmen Weber (1988b), archaeologist for the Philadelphia Historical Commission, did a quick review of the historical data to confirm the archaeological significance of the site. Consequently, the institute contracted with the Clio Group to test the site to determine whether any archaeological resources might have survived disturbances that occurred there in the last few decades, including the driving of deep footings to hold the Boeing 707.

As a result of the testing, the investigation moved into a Phase II evaluation under the direction of LuAnn DeCunzo who, as principal archaeologist, followed up Weber's initial archival research with an exhaustive insight into the Magdalen Asylum operation. Although only 10 percent of the site remained to be investigated, much of this was representative of the earlier years of the nineteenth century. Here the artifacts reflected a large proportion of inexpensive white wares—creamware and pearlware—and little bottle glass; the ceramic and other artifact evidence suggested strongly that the inmates received nu-

merous "hand-me-downs" from the concerned gentry of Philadelphia.

At some point in asylum history between 1830 and 1850, the deposition of trash, perhaps with compost for the garden, ceased. The record indicates an extensive garden tended by men hired as gardeners (hard work was unbecoming to women in the eyes of contemporary gentility), and in the 1830s the practice of placing the graves of deceased inmates in the garden area was initiated, to continue over a decade. The archaeological evidence indicates the diet at the asylum favored beef, followed by pig, sheep, and chicken, with oysters the most popular shellfish.

According to the historical record, the asylum enforced a no-smoking regulation from 1821. By the end of the century, the asylum purchased jumping rope and put up a swing. In 1903 the women spent much of the year scraping and painting the interior walls, while hired workmen put up wallpaper and painted the outside. In 1914 the women played in the February snows with their sleds. In 1916–17 architect John T. Windrim was hired to design an addition to the asylum for conversion of the property to City Domestic Relations Courts, and the Magdalen Society Asylum passed into history (DeCunzo et al. 1989:221–25). The burials and the bulk of archaeological evidence became demolition and construction fill of the twentieth century.

The Reading Site

The Reading site, ultimately Philadelphia's choice as the place to build a new convention center, experienced its first wave of development between 1800 and 1820. Most of the buildings constructed at this time were private

* The founder of the Franklin Institute was Samuel V. Merrick, an engineer and industrialist who was also responsible for the building of Philadelphia's first gasworks (see Chapter 6, "The Point Breeze Gas Works"). From 1825 until its move to Logan Square in the 1930s, the Franklin Institute occupied the neoclassical building at 15 South Seventh Street where the Atwater Kent Museum now resides; the building was designed for the Institute by John Haviland.

residences, but a few were devoted to light industry and commerce. In the 1830s the neighborhood acquired a few institutions, includng the Grace Episcopal Church, built at the corner of Twelfth and Cherry streets in 1833, and the Lying-In Charity, an obstetric facility chartered in 1832 and located in the first block of North Eleventh Street. Several other medical institutions were located close to the neighborhood; among these were the Philadelphia College of Pharmacy, founded in 1821, and the Pennsylvania College of Dental Surgery, chartered in 1856 (Cosans-Zebooker, Meyer, and Young 1985:26; Richardson 1982:244; Geffen 1982:322).

By 1860 the Franklin Farmers' Market—a replacement of the old High Street market sheds, which were demolished in 1853—was conducting business at Twelfth and Market streets. In 1891, when the Reading Railroad began building its terminal on that site, the market was given space under the train shed. Although the Reading Company ceased to be a railroad company some years ago, the market, now known as the Reading Terminal Market, continues to flourish in the same spot it has occupied for so many years. With its vibrant mix of colors and tongues and its direct antecedents going back to the days of William Penn, it is an engrossing expression of Philadelphia's link to the past as well as of Philadelphia's culture today.

In the late nineteenth century, with City Hall going up a few blocks to the west and the Reading Terminal emerging in all its Italian Renaissance splendor on Market Street (Figure 6.23), the architecture in the area became quite diverse, and the character of the neighborhood changed rapidly. Most of the residences on the major streets gave way to commercial enterprises, and large commercial loft

buildings, some with highly ornamented facades, appeared on the sites of many of the early nineteenth-century structures (Meyer and Parrington 1983:4). As the area grew increasingly commercial, burlesque theaters, houses of prostitution, and cheap rooming houses and hotels became more numerous. Institutions such as the Grace Episcopal Church apparently did not adapt to the neighborhood's changing character, for they eventually moved elsewhere (Cosans-Zebooker, Meyer, and Young 1985:27).

John Milner Associates' initial investigation of the cultural resources of the Reading site entailed the evaluation of the archaeological significance of more than two hundred properties. Of these properties, twenty-two were recommended as potentially eligible for the National Register of Historic Places (see Figure 6.20). They included the site of the Grace Episcopal

Figure 6.23.

The Reading Terminal in 1909. In the foreground is the "Head House," which contained waiting rooms and offices. Now refurbished, it provides access to the commuter train station on the lower level. Behind it at street level is the market, and above that are the old train platforms covered by the train shed. When completed, the arched shed was the largest single-span structure in the world. A landmark on the Historic American Engineering Record, the shed remained in use until the commuter rail tunnel was completed in 1984; it is expected to be used again in the new Pennsylvania Convention Center. (Courtesy of the Free Library of Philadelphia)

Church, marked by a parking lot at the southeast corner of Twelfth and Cherry streets, and twenty-one properties along Arch and Eleventh streets, where doctors, dentists, and druggists had lived and practiced their professions in the mid- to late 1800s (Cosans-Zebooker, Meyer, and Young 1985:90). These twenty-one properties were recommended as potentially eligible not as individual sites but as part of a multiple resource, a nineteenth-century "doctors' row." The rest of the properties included in the evaluation were judged ineligible for the National Register, chiefly because they were thought to have limited research value or because documentary sources indicated that any archaeological evidence on these sites was most likely disturbed or destroyed.

Discrepancies in historical records indicated that the site of the Grace Episcopal Church could contain significant archaeological evidence. According to the church's records, thirty-three bodies were buried in an unspecified number of vaults at the church and were reinterred at Woodlands Cemetery when the church vacated the site in 1911. According to the cemetery's records, however, the remains of only sixteen individuals were reinterred. If human remains do still lie beneath the site at Twelfth and Cherry, they have the potential to provide information on nineteenth-century health, nutrition, and mortality.

The clustering of medical institutions around the neighborhood accounts for the number of doctors, dentists, and druggists who lived and worked in small enclaves in the 1100 and 1200 blocks of Arch Street and in the first block of North Eleventh Street during the last half of the nineteenth century. Among the prominent physicians who either lived or had their offices in these blocks were Dr. Walter Williamson, cofounder in 1848 of the Homeopathic Medical College of Pennsylvania, and Dr. H. N. Guernsey, a faculty member at the same institution. The twenty-one properties comprising the "doctors' row" of this area were thought to be archaeologically significant because of their potential for shedding light on Philadelphia's nineteenth-century medical community, which counted among its achievements the development of new approaches to pharmacology and homeopathic medicine. Cosans-Zebooker, Meyer, and Young (1985:90–91) suggested that an archaeological investigation of a sample of these properties, particularly of their privy pits, could produce a wealth of new data on the private (as opposed to the public) practice of medicine, including approaches to diagnosis and cure.

Because the Reading site was chosen as the site for the new convention center, John Milner Associates undertook intensive archeological investigations there in 1988 under the direction of Michael Parrington and William R. Henry, Jr. Before the land north of the Reading Terminal was cleared of existing buildings, archaeologists excavated seven nineteenth-century privy shafts and two backyard midden areas along the 1100 block of Arch Street and the 200 block of North Twelfth Street. Considerable material evidence was found, particularly in some of the privies, pertaining to the medical practices of the doctors, dentists, and druggists who lived and worked in the area in the nineteenth century. Accordingly, the report on the results of the excavations (Blomberg [in preparation, a]) focus on the nature of those practices, as well as on factors of privy construction, depositional processes, and the nature of block- and/or site-related fill contexts. In an effort to ascertain the nature and extent of medically related deposits in the excavated privies, Blomberg (in preparation, a) also undertook hemoglobin analysis of several soil samples from some of the features, the first such analytical application to historical archaeological deposits undertaken in the United States. As of this writing, the results are still pending.

VINE STREET FROM RIVER TO RIVER: MIXED NINETEENTH-CENTURY NEIGHBORHOODS

Vine Street, the northern boundary of Penn's green country town until 1854, was by 1948 inadequate to handle the amount of traffic flowing over it, and so the "Vine Street Expressway" was constructed to expedite traffic between the Delaware and the Schuylkill rivers. By the early 1980s, this artery was in serious need of improvement, and plans for its reconstruction called for an environmental impact statement. As part of that effort, John Milner Associates contracted with the Pennsylvania Department of Transportation for an archaeological evaluation of nineteen city blocks bounded by Callowhill and Race streets on the north and south and stretching from Delaware Avenue west to Sixteenth Street (Figure 6.24). The evaluation involved detailed historical analyses of each of these blocks, and its findings prompted some selective archaeological testing. As in the study of the sites for a new convention center described in the preceding section, the purpose of the evaluation was to determine which sites had archaeological resources potentially eligible for the National Register of Historic Places. Although the evaluation concluded that ten of the nineteen blocks were potentially eligible for the National Register, the Pennsylvania State Historic Preservation office ultimately determined that only four blocks were potentially eligible. Roberts, Cosans, and Barrett (1982) conducted the evaluation, and their report is the basis for the following account.

Historical Background

In the 1790s the new Commonwealth of Pennsylvania initiated a building boom in the undeveloped lands north of the city limits by selling off large parts of the Northern Liberties to pay off debts from the Revolutionary War. Soon thereafter, the eastern part of that area was the center of some rather noxious crafts and industries (Scatchard and Scatchard 1978), whose malodorous fumes had become unwelcome in the densely populated blocks within the city limits. Among this offensive cluster were tanners and other leather craftsmen, butchers, glue makers, tallow chandlers, candle makers, soap boilers, sugar refiners, distillers, and brewers. The area was not purely industrial and commercial, however. In fact, like most other

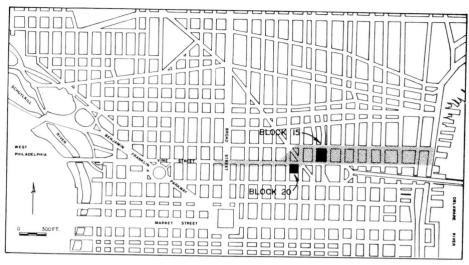

Vine Street Corridor

Figure 6.24.

Blocks potentially affected by the reconstruction of the Vine Street Expressway. Circled numbers indicate the blocks evaluated for archaeological resources. (From Roberts, Cosans, and Barrett 1982; courtesy of the Pennsylvania Department of Transportation, the Federal Highway Administration, and John Milner Associates)

neighborhoods in the study area, it was characterized throughout the 1800s by a mixture of residences and businesses. As might be expected, a mixed residential-commercial-industrial community of this sort was inhabited mainly by families of modest means, and it had few churches, libraries, courthouses, or hospitals. The market stalls at Callowhill and New Market streets were its focal point. By the end of the 1800s, the character of the community had become less mixed; by then, the industrial components were predominating.

The twentieth century saw few changes in this general pattern of land use throughout the study area. It did, however, see several large-scale construction projects that had profound effects on the character and prevailing street patterns of particular neighborhoods within the area. These projects included the construction of the Benjamin Franklin Bridge to New Jersey in the 1920s, the Vine Street Expressway in 1948, and Interstate-95 in the 1960s and 1970s. Recent improvements to the Vine Street Ex-

pressway, now completed, had similar effects.

The Archaeological Evaluation

With archaeological testing impossible in most places because of the existing expressway and standing buildings, the evaluation concentrated heavily on historical documents. It resulted in the analyses of three aspects of the area's history: land use and development, street development, and the socioeconomic characteristics of the various neighborhoods. The information derived from these analyses formed the basis for making recommendations about the eligibility for the National Register of Historic Places of each block in the study area.

The City Beyond the Colonial Core   **299**

Land Use and Development

The analysis of land use and development resulted in the identification of over 1,000 potential archaeological sites within the study area. Although land *use* and *development* may appear to be relatively synonymous terms, the analysis showed that the people who owned and developed the land were frequently not the people who occupied and used it. In fact, until 1860 only 10 percent of the property owners in the study area occupied their own premises. By 1860, 915 sites had been developed as residences, but many of these residences were undoubtedly also the sites of craft shops and light industry. The area at that time had 56 industrial sites, but only two blocks were characterized as heavily industrial. They were block 1, bounded by Delaware Avenue and Front, Callowhill, and Vine streets, and block 5, bounded by Second, Third, Callowhill, and Vine streets.

Ten public and private institutions had been scattered throughout the study area. They included churches, schools, a charitable institution, and two cemeteries, one of which belonged to the First African Baptist Church, discussed earlier in this chapter. The presence of only ten institutional sites in such a large area is a testament to mixed land use—commercial, industrial, and residential—and to the modest incomes of most of the residents of these neighborhoods.

The analysis of land use and development also identified twenty-one public accommodations, including taverns, hotels, and livery stables. One of the earliest sites within the study area was the Penny Pot House; as described in Chapter 5, this tavern, dating from the 1680s, was located near the Delaware River at the foot of Vine Street. Most of the other public accommodations in the area had been clustered in the block bounded by Third, Fourth, Callowhill, and Vine streets. Among the other types of archaeological contexts identified in this analysis were courts, alleys, interior streets, and potentially significant topographical features.

Street Development

Several subway tunnels run through the study area, and where they exist, any archaeological evidence has no doubt been destroyed. However, the analysis of street development suggested that the study area may still have beneath its streets and alleys numerous archaeological features, such as the foundations of old buildings, the remains of early road surfaces, and fragments of early sewer, water, and gas mains. Because market stalls, like the one at the intersection of Callowhill and New Market streets, were often located in the roadways, subsurface traces of them may also still exist.

Many of the alleys that date from the early nineteenth century were jointly developed by the owners of the abutting properties, and most of them have probably remained within a foot of their original grade. Because nineteenth-century repaving efforts generally consisted of replacing worn surfaces, they would have fostered retention of the grade at a relatively stable level. A study of these early nineteenth-century alleys could therefore provide an idea of the level of historic grades.

Socioeconomic Characteristics

The application of a socioeconomic ranking scheme to the study area was in some ways the most ambitious aspect of the evaluation. Based on a ranking scheme developed by the Philadelphia Social History Project (Hershberg 1976; Hershberg and Dockhorn 1976), this analysis was designed to identify the kinds of people occupying the study area, to isolate clusterings of similar groups of people, and to provide a basis for selective archaeological testing. Because the Philadelphia Social History Project focused exclusively on the nineteenth century, it offered a potentially good data base for the Vine Street area, whose development took place almost entirely within that century (Barrett 1982).

Various documentary sources (e.g., federal censuses, tax assessors' records, business directories, manufacturing censuses, and surveys of Philadelphia's black population) for the years 1841, 1850, 1860, and 1870 provided a wealth of socioeconomic information. It was possible to ascertain the name, age, place of birth, race, economic status, and occupation of household members for each of these four years. Once all the base data were collected, they were categorized according to the ranking scheme devised by the Philadelphia Social History Project. This scheme, which focuses on occupation as a variable, is as follows:

1 High white-collar and professional occupations (particularly merchants, doctors, clergymen, and dentists).

2 Low white-collar and proprietary occupations (shopkeepers, business owners, accountants, clerks, etc.).

3 Skilled craftsmen (e.g., carpenters, shoemakers, machinists).

4 Unskilled workers with specified occupations (e.g., ditch diggers, carters, porters).

5 Unskilled workers with no specified occupations (i.e., laborers).

6 Unskilled workers who do not fall into either of the preceding two categories (e.g., mill worker, factory worker).

7 Occupations for which only the work site was specified (e.g., shop, mill, liquor store).

8 No reported occupation (e.g., gentleman or retired).

9 Catch-all category for occupations about which not enough is known for specific classification.

When the data were plotted on base maps of each block in the study area, they formed a mosaic of socioeconomic information for each of the four years to which the data apply. The results of the socioeconomic analysis indicated that the neighborhoods of the study area at mid-nineteenth century were fairly heterogeneous in terms of the occupations of their residents. A large percentage of the residents in each neighborhood were skilled craftsmen and white-collar workers, both "low" and "high." Although unskilled workers were generally less numerous than the skilled and white-collar workers, they, too, were uniformly distributed.

By 1860 the area apparently had undergone some changes. Unskilled workers had become more numerous, and ethnic clustering had begun to characterize various neighborhoods. Although more than half the residents of each block were native-born, at least three ethnic concentrations were evident. German immigrants clustered in the area just west of Ninth Street and north of Vine, Irish immigrants were prevalent near Broad and Vine streets, and a strong concentration of African-Americans lived along the south side of Vine Street between Ninth and Tenth streets in an area known as Liberty Court.

Archaeological Testing

As noted earlier, only four of the nineteen blocks in the study area were ultimately determined potentially eligible for the National Register of Historic Places. One of these blocks (block 18) was considered archaeologically significant because it contained the cemetery of the First African Baptist Church. Since that cemetery was slated to become the subject of the full-scale excavation described earlier in this chapter, it obviously required no additional investigation. Another of the four recommended blocks also required no immediate fieldwork, as it lay outside the area that would be disrupted by the reconstruction of the expressway. This was block 1, bounded by Delaware Avenue and Front, Callowhill, and Vine streets, and significant because of the colonial development that took place there. It was subsequently excavated in 1987 (see Chapter 5, "West's Shipyard and Its Neighbors").

Because the expressway's reconstruction would have disrupted or destroyed potential archaeological resources in the other two blocks recommended for the National Register, these blocks did require archaeological testing to determine whether such resources existed. They were block 15, bounded by Seventh, Eighth, Callowhill, and Vine streets and potentially significant because of the recorded presence of a Moravian church and cemetery; and block 20, bounded by Ninth, Tenth, Vine, and Race streets and potentially significant primarily for the African-American enclave known as Liberty Court (see Figure 6.24).

Block 15

Originally a small piece of the Penn family's Manor of Springettsbury, block 15 was part of a parcel of land granted to Joshua Lawrence in 1734. In 1786 the Moravian Church bought a section of the block at Vine and Franklin streets and established a church and cemetery there, but most of the block was not developed until the 1800s. When it was developed, it was mixed in character, containing both light industries and residences. Many of the residences were occupied by white-collar workers, among them merchants, doctors, dentists, and clergymen.

Using historical documents as a guide, Cress and McCarthy (1985) excavated nine test units in block 15 (Figure 6.25). All the units measured either 5 or 10 feet by 20 feet and were dug where records indicated the Moravian cemetery and the backyards of private residences would have been. Some of the units were excavated to a depth of more than 12 feet. Two yielded evidence of the foundations or cellars of industrial buildings, probably warehouses, and two produced structural evidence of residences. The remaining five test units produced numerous nineteenth-century artifacts, all of which were found in redeposited, heavily disturbed fill.

Cress and McCarthy (1985:14–27) found no evidence of the Moravian cemetery. Interestingly, they also found no evidence of privy pits or wells. They concluded that massive redevelopment of the block in the late nineteenth century and the twentieth century had caused subsurface disturbance great enough to destroy the integrity of most of the archaeological evidence. They also speculated that when the Moravian church moved away from the neighborhood in about 1890, it may have removed and reinterred any remains buried on its former site. Whether that was so or not, it was clear that no archaeological resources that would make block 15

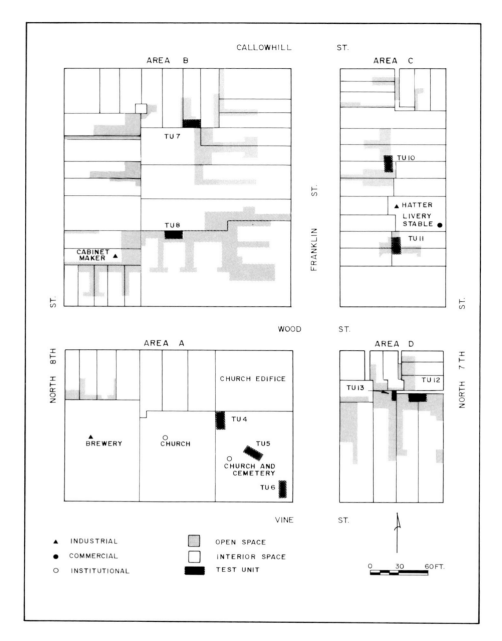

Figure 6.25.

Excavation plan of block 15, showing sites recorded in historic documents. (From Cress and McCarthy 1985; courtesy of the Pennsylvania Department of Transportation, the Federal Highway Administration, and John Milner Associates)

eligible for the National Register of Historic Places remained intact.

Block 20

The results of excavations in block 20, conducted by McCarthy (1984c), were quite different from those in block 15. Here, three deep test units, each 10 by 20 feet, revealed a clay pit, intact cellars, and undisturbed backyard deposits. The clay pit may have been the work of the first owner of the land in and around block 20—one Thomas Coates, "brickmaster," who in 1735 was granted a large parcel of land that included this block. Although Coates probably used the land for his business, he never developed it to any great extent. By 1860, however, block 20 contained thirty-two properties, most of them residences. In the 1840s the block was inhabited mainly by white-collar professionals and skilled craftsmen, but by the 1860s and 1870s most of its residents were unskilled workers, primarily African-Americans who lived in Liberty Court

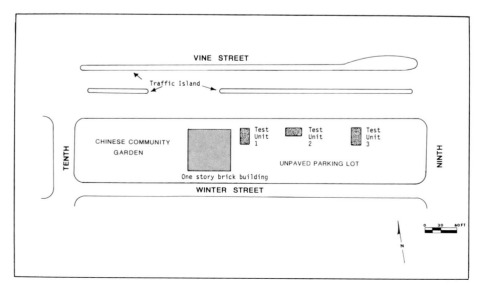

Figure 6.26.

Locations of test trenches and excavation units in block 20. (From McCarthy et al. 1987; courtesy of the Pennsylvania Department of Transportation, the Federal Highway Administration, and John Milner Associates)

and Irish immigrants who lived in Java Court, another small enclave within the block.

The most significant finds in block 20 were several intact backyard deposits that had been sealed under layers of fill. Revealed in several excavation units and test trenches (Figure 6.26), these deposits were associated with properties that had fronted on Java Court and Winter Street. They included many artifacts dating from the early to mid-nineteenth century, among them fragments of whiteware, creamware, pearlware, glass, and clay pipes. McCarthy (1984c:26) successfully argued that these artifacts were rare survivors in an urban core such as block 20 and constituted archaeological resources significant enough to qualify the site as eligible for the National Register of Historic Places. Recommending a full-scale archaeological excavation, McCarthy pointed out that together with the artifacts and structural evidence produced by the field testing, additional evidence found in privy pits and wells could provide rich insights into the working class of Philadelphia in the mid-nineteenth century.

Data Recovery

Subsequent data recovery excavations of block 20 were conducted in 1985. While the yard deposits identified in the evaluation of the block were found to be part of a sheet midden that predated the residential development of the block, seven brick-lined privy shaft features, four box drains, and a large pit were excavated, containing artifacts associated with the historic residents of the block. In addition, a burial pit was encountered behind one of the Liberty Court residences that contained the remains of five African-Americans. Prior to the construction of Liberty Court,

property in the western portion of the block was owned from 1810 to 1822 by the First African Baptist Church, located at Tenth Street. The church subsequently moved to Eighth and Vine streets, where a larger sample of the church's deceased members was investigated in the mid-1980s (see Chapter 6, "The First African Baptist Church"). The burials were apparently associated with the congregation. During the construction of Liberty Court, they were most likely exhumed and relocated to the pit behind the residences (McCarthy et al. 1987).

In addition to the potential to provide important time-depth information about the health and well-being of Philadelphia's free-black community in the early nineteenth century, the excavation also provided evidence of the material lives of the residents of Liberty Court. While portions of a high-status "flow-blue," transfer-printed pearlware tea set were recovered, the overall composition of the recovered assemblage was very much like that recovered from a mid- to late nineteenth-century African-American site in Washington, D.C. (McCarthy et al. 1987:76–77, 80–81). This finding suggested that nineteenth-century African-Americans in different cities were more comparable in their life-styles and life experiences than their closest neighbors, reflecting their social isolation from the larger community (McCarthy et al. 1987:104–6).

Construction Monitoring

When construction in 1987 began to uncover numerous archaeological features and artifacts, the Pennsylvania Department of Transportation expanded John Milner Associates' role to include monitoring excavation work and recovery of important ar-

chaeological data in cooperation with the highway construction throughout the new expressway project area. Through the end of 1989, ongoing monitoring of excavations resulted in identification and recording of 71 features, most of which were brick-lined privies. Of this total, 18 features were found to contain significant artifact assemblages, some of which dated from the eighteenth century. These features were excavated by the archaeologists, the artifacts were recovered for analysis, and a report will be prepared after the excavation work and monitoring are completed in the early 1990s.

Since burials associated with the First African Baptist Church were discovered during the block 20 data recovery, and since approximately one-half of the property owned by the church on Tenth Street from 1810 to 1822 had been sealed under the east-bound lanes of Vine Street when the road was widened in the late 1940s, John Milner Associates was also retained by the Department of Transportation to archaeologically examine the remainder of the historic church property for additional burials when traffic was re-routed during the course of the construction of the new Vine Street Expressway. In the early spring of 1990, this field investigation was completed, and more than ninety additional burials were ultimately excavated, thereby providing perhaps an unprecedented opportunity to compare two related African-American burial populations from the First African Baptist Church. As of this writing, detailed comparative analysis is underway, and the results are expected to shed considerable additional light on the characteristics of African-American burial practices, acculturation, and health throughout the first half of the nineteenth century in Philadelphia.

THE NINTH WARD: NINETEENTH-CENTURY SANITATION PRACTICES

Philadelphia's Ninth Ward includes the section of Center City now occupied by the Gallery, a multilevel, multiblock, indoor shopping mall on East Market Street. The first part of the Gallery was completed in 1977, and in the early 1980s a parking garage and an extension known as Gallery II were added. Because federal assistance was involved, an architectural and archaeological evaluation of the area that would be affected by the

Figure 6.27.

Map of the Ninth Ward study area and surroundings. (From Schooler and Roberts 1979; courtesy of the Market Street East Development Corporation and John Milner Associates)

new construction took place in 1979. Undertaken by John Milner Associates for the Market Street East Development Corporation, the evaluation determined that the area had little of architectural merit, but that it might contain significant archaeological resources. Consequently, several properties between Market and Arch streets in the vicinity of Tenth and Eleventh became the focus of archaeological excavations (Figure 6.27). The reports of the evaluation (Schooler and Roberts 1979) and the excavations (Roberts and Cosans 1980) provided the data for the following account.

Land Use and Development in the Ninth Ward

In the 1780s both Adam Guier and John Morgan bought lots from the Commonwealth of Pennsylvania in the section of Philadelphia now subsumed by the Ninth Ward. Four of Guier's lots were at the southwest corner of Arch and Eleventh streets; all six of Morgan's were at the northeast corner of Market and Eleventh. All the lots were fairly large: Guier's extended some 300 feet south from Arch Street to Filbert Street, and Morgan's extended the same distance north from Market Street to Filbert.

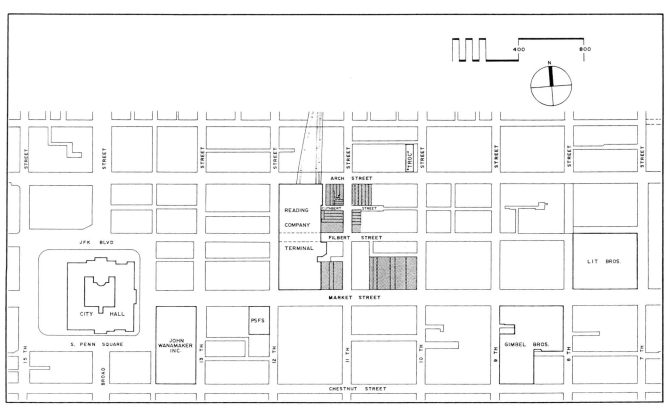

Although apparently a man of some means, Adam Guier was not a particularly prominent Philadelphian. A grazier by occupation, he immediately began using most of his new land for pasture. However, he also built a house at the corner of Eleventh and Filbert streets, which he presumably occupied himself. When he died, the property passed to his son, Adam Guier, Jr., who in 1811 subdivided the northern part of it into building lots. Guier, Jr., sold these lots with the stipulation that within two years of the purchase date, the new owners had to develop the properties. Most, if not all, of the purchasers apparently complied with this stipulation, for by 1815 each lot was occupied by a two- or three-story brick dwelling. The younger Guier also created an alley 30 feet wide that ran in an east-west direction at the rear of his Arch Street properties. Originally known as Mary Street, the alley was later renamed Cuthbert Street.

In contrast to Adam Guier, John Morgan, a renowned physician, was a prominent Philadelphian. Generally recognized as the first American expert in medical history and education, he was responsible for the establishment of a medical school—the first in the colonies—at the College of Philadelphia in 1765. Later, during the Revolutionary War, he served as the Continental Army's director-general of hospitals. Morgan died soon after he bought the six lots at Market and Eleventh streets, and the distinction of developing them fell to one George Hunter, who purchased them from Morgan's estate with an entrepreneurial gleam in his eye. By 1825, brick dwellings much like those erected on Guier's Arch Street lots a decade earlier were standing on Morgan's former lots.

Of the original brick dwellings built on Guier's and Morgan's former property, only one was still standing in 1979. It was located at 1100 Arch Street on land that once belonged to Adam Guier (Figure 6.28). The rest of these structures met their demise in the late 1800s and early 1900s, when large commercial structures were built on their sites. The Reading Terminal, erected 1891–1893, still stands where Guier's livestock used to graze.

The Excavations

The excavations in the Ninth Ward had two goals: to test the accuracy of a model for predicting location and other characteristics of subsurface pits (Schooler and Roberts 1979:170–74), and to produce physical evidence of the cultural behavior of a segment of Philadelphia's nineteenth-century population about whom the historical record says little. However, the most important result of the excavations was information pertaining to a waste-disposal practice in the nineteenth-century city.

The Predictive Model

The predictive model that Roberts and Cosans tested during excavations in the Ninth Ward was designed to pinpoint the above-ground location of privy pits and to indicate the extent to which these features survived below ground, as well as the degree of disturbance they were likely to have suffered.* Above-ground locations were

* A "predictive model" is essentially an informed guess, based on ecological and historical data, as to where archaeological sites and features may be found.

Figure 6.28.

Southwest corner of Eleventh and Arch streets in 1979. 1100 Arch Street is in the foreground. (From Roberts and Cosans 1980; courtesy of the Market Street East Development Corporation and John Milner Associates)

inferred from various nineteenth-century maps, including the Hexamer and Locher maps of 1857 and the Jones map of 1875, which show small squares or rectangles detached or semi-detached from the principal buildings of various properties. Roberts and Cosans hypothesized that these squares and rectangles represented outhouses below which presumably would have been privy pits. Figure 6.29, which was used as a guide in the excavations, shows the squares and rectangles superimposed on a map of the project area.

The predictions of the depth of the pit shafts took into account two factors: the 1769 "privy depth ordinance" (*Pennsylvania Gazette*, November 16, 1769), which, to protect groundwater from pollution, set the maximum depth of privy pits at 20 feet; and the knowledge that historic grade and contemporary grade in Center City

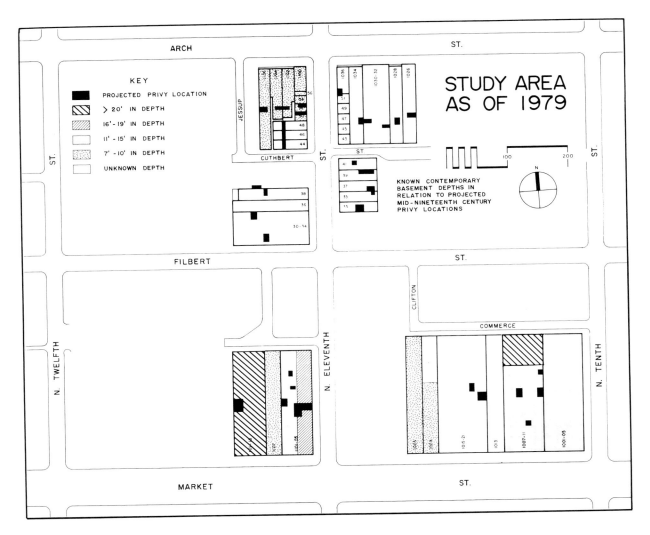

Figure 6.29.

Projected locations of privy pits in the Ninth Ward. (From Roberts and Cosans 1980; courtesy of the Market Street East Development Corporation and John Milner Associates)

Philadelphia are roughly equal. To arrive at a prediction of how many feet of the pit were likely to have survived the construction of basements in the late 1800s and early 1900s, the depth of contemporary basements was subtracted from the maximum 20-foot depth set by the 1769 law.

Application of the predictive model succeeded in locating only one of the pits suggested by the small squares and rectangles appearing on the old maps; it was found in the basement of 50 North Eleventh Street. This disap-

pointing performance may indicate that the hypothesis about the function of the squares and rectangles was wrong. However, it could also indicate that the maps were inaccurate; privies and water closets may have been razed, removed, and replaced so often that the cartographers simply could not keep up with them. As a result, it was concluded that data from deeds, probate courts, insurance surveys, and other such sources may prove to be more reliable indicators of the location of such archaeological features.

The model also failed in its predictions about depth. None of the privy pits excavated to their full depth conformed to the 1769 regulation; all were more than 20 feet deep. Apparently, Philadelphians in the 1800s, at least those who resided in the Ninth Ward, were ignoring the 1769 ordi-

nance, and no one was enforcing it. One explanation may be that after a public water system was installed in the early 1800s, concern about polluting the groundwater subsided.

Site-Specific Artifacts and Waste-Disposal Practices

Excavations in the Ninth Ward produced many ceramic artifacts of many different patterns—so many, in fact, that it was most unlikely all of them could have come from the properties where they were found. The inability to tie the artifacts to the people who lived on the sites obviously dashed any hope of shedding light on the cultural behavior of individual householders. Nonetheless, the artifacts, together with some structural evidence, did shed light on a general cultural practice: a method of waste disposal that archaeologists had not noted before.

One clue to this practice was the unusual construction of four of the seven privy pits uncovered in the course of the excavations. These unusual pits had two shafts, the upper one larger in diameter (5½ feet on average) than the lower (3 feet on average), and at the interface of the shafts was a lip or sill that supported a wooden plank (Figure 6.30). The plank loosely covered the opening to the narrower shaft below, and the evidence strongly suggested that it was used as a receptacle for broken glass and ceramics placed there to aid in the percolation of liquid waste. The prototype for this kind of construction is the French drain, which uses gravel and stones, rather than glass and ceramics, to facilitate drainage.

Resting on the wooden plank of one of these four pits was a three-foot deposit containing over 17,000 artifacts. Most of the artifacts consisted of broken ceramics, and they had been printed or painted in more than sixty different patterns. Sixty different sets of dishes is considerably more than even the wealthiest household in nineteenth-century Philadelphia could be expected to have possessed. The only explanation seems to be that the householder, or more likely laborers hired by the householder, deliberately deposited these broken ceramics in the pit as a percolation aid. Some of the ceramics may have come from the household, but it seems probable that many of them were either imperfect products discarded by manufacturers or items broken in transit from England and obtained at the docks.

Although the artifacts found in the privy pits of the Ninth Ward cannot

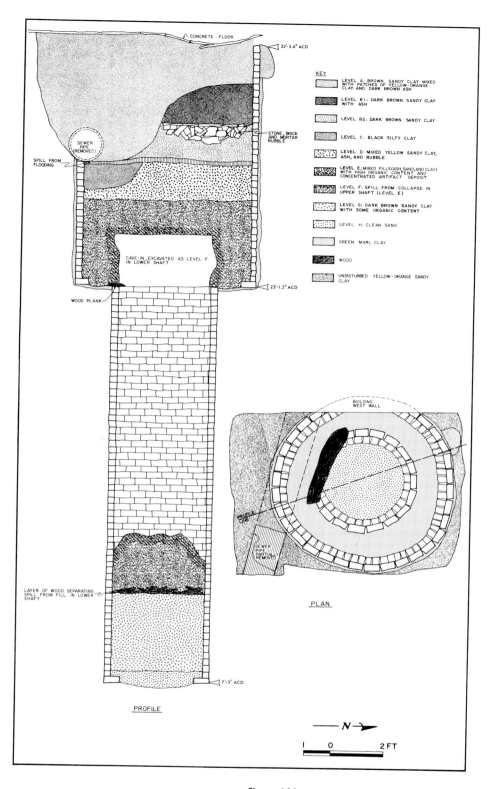

Figure 6.30.

Profile and plan of pit at 50 North Eleventh Street, showing wooden plank and other construction features. (From Roberts and Cosans 1980; courtesy of the Market Street East Development Corporation and John Milner Associates)

tell us anything about behavior in individual households, they do provide a fair idea of the time this waste-disposal practice was in use. With few exceptions, the artifacts in the percolation fill dated from between 1820 and 1850, suggesting that the practice was in use from the time the first dwellings were built on these sites.

The Ninth Ward is certainly not the only site, urban or rural, to have confounded archaeologists' ambitions by yielding artifacts that do not seem site-specific. Investigations of agricultural fields have often produced artifacts that seem completely unrelated to the local history. The answer here may be exactly the same as the answer to the puzzle of the Ninth Ward artifacts: they are in all likelihood not site-specific. A common destination for the waste cleaned out of Philadelphia's privy pits in the nineteenth century was a farmer's field, where it was spread and dug into the earth as a composting agent (Thibaut 1982:204–6; Roberts and Barrett 1984). If the contents of the pits of the Ninth Ward are any indication, such deposits would have contained an abundance of material that traveled a long and circuitous route before reaching the farmer's field.

THE COMMUTER RAIL TUNNEL: OF SCHOOLBOY PRANKS AND OTHER SITE-SPECIFIC MATTERS

Large engineering projects involving the demolition of buildings and the machine excavation of huge mounds of earth have an uncanny fascination for many people. Archaeologists, too, are fascinated by this kind of activity, but for different reasons. For the archaeologist, a major disturbance of the urban environment means an opportunity to learn about the past. The "Center City Commuter Rail Connector," an underground link between the old Pennsylvania Railroad and the old Reading line, was an engineering project large enough to capture the imagination of both archaeologists and the general public. Completed in 1984, this vast project included the construction of a tunnel in the area bounded by Eighth and Nine streets and Race and Brown streets (Figure 6.31). Provision was made for a brief initial historical survey (Levy 1978), and subsequent monitoring and excavation were carried out by John Milner Associates under contract to the City of Philadelphia. The report of the archaeological findings, written by Cosans-Zebooker and Barrett (1985), is the basis for the following account.

Historical Background

A small part of the study area lay within the original city limits, but most of it was in the Northern Liberties, in the section that in 1813 became the district of Spring Garden. Although some of the land here was being used in the late 1600s, no intensive development took place until the nineteenth century. During the colonial era, potters dug clay pits in the fields that then dotted the landscape, but as Philadelphia grew in the course of the eighteenth century, the clay pits were filled in. References to "tenements" and "messuages" in property deeds dating from the early nineteenth century indicate that the area had by then begun to witness the building of domestic structures.

As houses began springing up, so did a number of commercial enterprises and a few institutions. In the nineteenth century the area had two public schools, two hotels, livery stables, a church cemetery, a fire company, carpentry shops, potters' shops and shoemakers' shops, bakeries, soap and candle factories, confectionaries, coal yards, railroad facilities, and a public market on Spring Garden Street. With the development of Chinatown in the southern part of the area in the late 1800s and early 1900s, Chinese restaurants began to appear.

One block in the study area—the 300 block of North Ninth Street—contained a distinctly homogeneous social group. Here upper-class merchants and other wealthy individuals had clustered in the first half of the nineteenth century. Elsewhere in the area, no one social group stood out.

Most of the houses were small, three-story brick or frame buildings with rear yards containing privies, and most were occupied by more than one family; houses that fronted on courts and alleys shared a backyard. Of the two public schools in the area, one was the John Quincy Adams Public School, erected on the east side of Darien Street below Buttonwood Street in 1852–53. The church cemetery mentioned above was the one belonging to the First African Baptist Church at Eighth and Vine, discussed earlier in this chapter.

The Archaeological Findings

Archaeological excavations in the area began in June 1979 and ended in November 1980. The major discoveries included the site of the church cemetery, which subsequently became the focus of another archaeological study; a clay pit, which contained the debris of eighteenth-century potters; and 103 brick- or wood-lined privy pits, which yielded an enormous number of artifacts. The goal in analyzing the artifacts was to identify social differences among the people who had owned them. Obviously, to achieve such a goal, one must first of all solve the puzzle of who, in fact, did own them.

That conundrum has, of course, confounded many an archaeological study. With more than one family sharing a single dwelling and only one privy in the backyard, who could be certain about which family had deposited which trash in the backyard pit? The puzzle becomes even more intricate when the privy was shared by multiple dwellings, for such a privy was probably filled with the discards of many households. The fill, placed there when the pit was closed or as a percolation aid when it was cleaned, may have come from the households of the neighborhood, or, as noted in the study of the Ninth Ward, it may

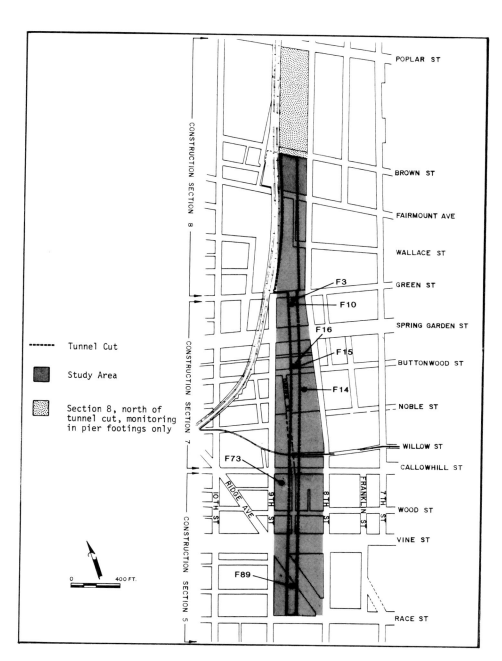

Figure 6.31.

Map of the north end of the Commuter Rail Tunnel showing the study area and tunnel cut. (From Cosans-Zebooker and Barrett 1985; courtesy of the City of Philadelphia and John Milner Associates)

have come from the docks or from the waste heaps of nearby potters' shops. This study was fortunate in being able to establish a few definite links between the artifacts and their owners.

Schoolboy Pranks

The more unlike the neighbors the occupant of a site is, the greater the possibility of identifying site-related material. Institutional sites such as schools are particularly promising in this regard, and indeed the John Quincy Adams Public School lived up to the promise. A circular, brick-lined privy pit (feature 14 in Figure 6.31) was found where historical records indicated the school's detached, unheated toilets had been. The pit yielded a large number of artifacts that were obviously school-related. Among these site-specific finds was a small wooden box tied with leather straps and containing slate pencils, lead pencils, penholders and nibs, a sponge, and a small ink bottle (Figures 6.32 and 6.33). The box was obviously not store-bought, and it is easy to imagine some proud parent making it for a child.

It may be that the handmade box represents a parent's pride in a child. The place where it was found, however, suggests another facet of human behavior. The box was obviously in good condition and so had not been discarded as trash. Its small owner may accidentally have dropped it down the privy, but given the sometimes malevolent nature of school children, it could also have been deliberately thrown there as a prank. Many of the other artifacts found in the privy pit could also have been deliberately thrown there by the pranksters of the John Quincy Adams Public School. Among the toys and trinkets found in the pit were china doll heads, the handle of a jump rope, a pocketknife, and several earthenware cups bearing instructive mottoes. These artifacts, which provide a glimpse of the lighter side of nineteenth-century school life, help dispel some of the Dickensian gloom so often associated with schools of this period.

Figure 6.32.

Child's school box found in feature 14 at the site of the John Quincy Adams Public School. (From Cosans-Zebooker and Barrett 1985; courtesy of the City of Philadelphia and John Milner Associates)

Figure 6.33.

Contents of the school box: penholders, pen points, lead pencils, slate pencils, a small ink bottle, and a sponge. (From Cosans-Zebooker and Barrett 1985; courtesy of the City of Philadelphia and John Milner Associates)

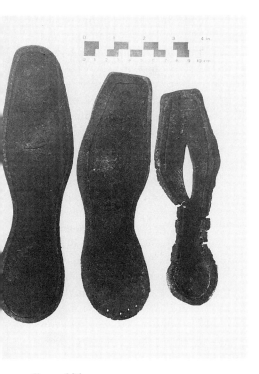

Figure 6.34.

Leather soles and insoles found in feature 3. (From Cosans-Zebooker and Barrett 1985; courtesy of the City of Philadelphia and John Milner Associates)

A Trifle for Eliza and Other Site-Specific Matters

Feature 10, one of the seven privy pits found at 814–816 Spring Garden Street, yielded at least one artifact that most assuredly had belonged to a former occupant of the site. The artifact, a small wooden box that had contained a whetstone, was marked "D. W. Clark." Clark was a carpenter who had lived at the site until 1834; he may also have been the source of some wood shavings found in feature 10.

The ownership of a white earthenware cup found in feature 3, another of the pits at 814–816 Spring Garden,

was less certain, but it is tempting to link it with a lady named Eliza Newell, who lived at the site with her husband John in 1850. On the cup, transfer-printed in red, was the inscription, "A Trifle for Eliza." Although the other 305 ceramic items found in feature 3 suggested that the pit was in use from 1820 to 1840, it is not impossible that it was still open in 1850, when the Newells lived there. The pit may well have been filled over a period of time extending beyond 1840. The pieces of shoe leather shown in Figure 6.34, which were among the 105 pieces of leather found in the pit, support this supposition, for in 1841 shoemakers were living on the site.

Several pits contained pottery wasters, sometimes in fairly large numbers. In the case of feature 73, a privy pit located at 332 Darien Street, there appeared to be a connection between the wasters found in the pit and the property owner. The artifacts suggested that the pit was filled between 1820 and 1840; historical records showed that in 1835 John Halfline, "brickmaster," lived at 332 Darien Street and that in 1841 he had a pottery at 41 Ridge Road.

Artifacts found in feature 89 at 217 Schell Street suggested a tie to the Chinese comunity that began developing in that area in the late 1800s and early 1900s. (The 200 block of Schell Street, which ran north-south between Race and Vine, was removed when Ridge Avenue was extended and hence does not appear on Figure 6.31.) Feature 89 had been filled during the early twentieth century, and among the objects found there were a number of porcelain bowls, a porcelain soup spoon, two bamboo objects resembling chopsticks, and faunal remains that contained a high percentage of pig bones. Given that pork is a

popular Chinese staple and that the other artifacts also suggested oriental origins, the evidence of a link between feature 89 and the Chinese population was fairly compelling. Unfortunately, because of illegibility in the census records, it was impossible to determine who was living at 217 Schell Street in 1910; in 1900 it was occupied by an African-American family named Small. The records for 1910 do indicate, however, that two Chinese families lived somewhere in the block and that both were in the restaurant business.

Artifacts from pits in the 300 block of North Ninth Street reflected the high social status that historical records ascribed to the residents of that block in the first half of the nineteenth century. Among these status symbols were matching sets of ceramic teaware and dinnerware and pieces of hand-painted porcelain and pearlware. The correlation between the historical record and the physical evidence suggested that the artifacts had come from the households in the immediate area. In many other cases, however, the artifacts appeared to have come from farther afield.

Communal Filling

Several pits contained large numbers of artifacts; Feature 3's yield of 3,591 was not unusual. Volumes like these suggest that the artifacts came not from one household but from multiple households in the community or even from farther away. Even the pit at the John Quincy Adams Public School appeared to have been communally filled; although some of the artifacts found there were definitely site-specific, others clearly were not.

Cross-mends between pits provided more evidence of communal

filling; pieces of vessels found in feature 15 matched those found in feature 16. Features 15 and 16 were on abutting properties (813 and 815 Buttonwood Street), suggesting that the trash was stored in backyard middens until it was thrown away. John Halfline's wasters may also have found their way into neighborhood privy pits. As a potter, he would proba-bly have been glad to contribute his discards to the cleaning or closing of his neighbors' privies.

A Concluding Note

The communal filling of privy pits appears to have been a widespread practice, and it obviously makes the task of tracing artifacts to the individuals who discarded them difficult, if not in most cases impossible. Nonetheless, as this study demonstrated, if the source of the artifacts is sufficiently distinctive, links between the artifacts and their owners can be established, and when they are, they can add to our knowledge of the lifestyles of the past.

THE POINT BREEZE GAS WORKS: ARCHAEOLOGY WITHOUT DIGGING

Remnants of the Point Breeze Gas Works, built between 1851 and 1854 on Passyunk Avenue near the east bank of the Schuylkill River, still stand as visible reminders of Philadelphia's industrial past. That aspect of the city's history has received relatively little archaeological attention, and the physical evidence of it grows ever scarcer as the twentieth century draws to a close. An above-ground study of the Point Breeze Gas Works in 1977 therefore represents a significant contribution to the archaeological record. The study marshaled the historical evidence, produced measured drawings of an existing building, and resulted in the serendipitous discovery of photographs that document production at the gasworks from 1897 until 1930. Found moldering under a tarpaulin beneath a leaky roof at Point Breeze, the photographs now reside in the archives of the city of Philadelphia. The reports of the study (Orr 1977; Orr and Levy 1985; Cotter and Orr 1975:10) provided data for the historical account that follows.

The City's First Gasworks: A Light "Most Clear, Bright, and Dazzling"

The technology of using gas for lighting was developed and perfected in England in the early years of the nineteenth century. By the 1820s, gaslights were in general use there, illuminating homes, streets, and factories. American observers, greatly impressed with this new technology, returned home from England determined to promote and develop it. As early as 1803, a Philadelphian by the name of Benjamin Henfrey was urging the city councilmen to develop a system of gas lighting by extracting gas from coal and burning it at the top of octagonal towers. The idea did not take. Concerned about nauseous odors, explosions, and a litany of other perils, the council long remained chary of authorizing the manufacture of gas for public use.

The private sector was more venturesome. William Strickland's design for the Masonic Hall, built in 1809 on Chestnut Street, included a plant for manufacturing gas. By 1816 Charles

Figure 6.35.

Samuel V. Merrick (1801–1870), engineer, industrialist, and designer of Philadelphia's first gasworks at Twenty-Third and Market streets. (Courtesy of the Franklin Institute)

Willson Peale had installed a retort in the tower room of Independence Hall to produce gas lighting for his museum on the second floor of that august building. And when the second Chestnut Street Theatre opened in 1822 with a gas generator on the premises, audiences blinked in astonishment at the gas lighting. Even a private residence at 200 Lombard Street boasted its own gas generator.

By 1834 Samuel V. Merrick (Figure 6.35), a prominent engineer and manufacturer of fire engines who was also the founder of the Franklin Institute, had had enough of the city councilmen's pusillanimous nonsense. He ran for councilman himself, was elected, and set about amending the situation. Within two years, the city's first gasworks was standing at Twenty-Third and Market streets near the Schuylkill River. Designed by Merrick, who used London's Regency Park Gas Works as his model, the gasworks included a retort house with 30 retorts (Figure 6.36), a purifying house, a meter room, a laboratory, and two gasholders. With its great smokestacks shaped like Doric columns and its cast-iron trussing (Figure 6.37), the gasworks had a flourish that was a bellwether of the industrial architecture to come.

The gasworks first began producing illuminating gas from soft coal in February 1836. With shops and entryways to homes alight, Philadelphians marveled. One diarist described the light as the "most clear, bright, and dazzling" he had ever seen. A year later the first gas street lamps went into operation, lighting up Second Street from South Street all the way to Vine. Dazzled though Philadelphians may have been, the light produced by the first gaslights was in fact yellow, smoky, and polluting. In the 1840s the invention of the atmo-

Figure 6.36.

Interior of the retort house at the city's first gasworks. The retorts were chambers in which soft coal was heated and decomposed into gas. (From *Gleason's Pictorial* April 2, 1853, p. 216)

Figure 6.37.

Exterior of the city's first gasworks. The fluted columns of the smokestacks appear at left; to the right of them are the gasholders, or storage tanks, with their cast-iron trussing. (From *Gleason's Pictorial* April 2, 1853, p. 216)

spheric burner resulted in cleaner combustion and a brighter light, but this technology, which introduced air into the gas stream just below the flame, did not come into general use until the 1850s.

The gasworks began as a semiprivate corporation, built with private capital and managed by twelve trustees elected by the city councilmen. The original corporation dissolved in 1841 when the city bought out the rights to the gasworks from the stockholders and took over the management entirely. As the demand for gas grew dramatically within the next decade, the city commissioners added several new structures to the gasworks in an effort to step up production. By 1850 the plant had four retort houses and eleven gasholders, with a total capacity of 1.68 million cubic feet.

Despite the plant's tremendous increase in capacity between 1836 and 1850, John C. Cresson, who had succeeded Merrick as chief engineer of the gasworks, recognized that the facility would soon be unable to meet the demands of the city's rapidly growing population. At mid-century the area west of Broad Street was beginning to experience development, and more and more miles of gas mains were being laid beneath the city's streets. By 1853 almost ninety miles of mains were supplying illuminating gas to nine thousand customers. Gas furnaces and stoves, although not yet in general use, were not unknown, and they would certainly not be long in coming. Cresson himself may have heard of a Moravian named Z. A. Winsler, who in London in 1802 gave dinner parties at which food was cooked on a gas stove in a gas-heated room. In the middle years of the nineteenth century, however, such use of gas was still a rarity in Britain and all but nonexistent in America (Derry and Williams 1960:513–14).

Around 1850 Cresson began pressing the city to build another gasworks beyond the city limits. Although Cresson's foresight in this regard makes it tempting to credit him with great vision, his devotion to his chosen field apparently caused him to have a few blind spots. In 1861, speculating about proposed improvements in gas technology, he noted that these ideas "do not bear upon their face the evidence of absurdity, or impracticability, such as one attached to the famous project of electric lite, so much agitated a year or two back." Cresson was not alone in his partiality to the use of gas for lighting; it monopolized the attention both of the public and of inventors, in America and abroad, for many years. By the turn of the century, however, the electric light would have put the gaslight on a permanent back burner.

The Gasworks at Point Breeze: An Industrial Site of the Victorian Era

With more foresight than their reticence about the use of gas would imply, the city fathers in 1815 bought seventy-five acres of land fronting on the Schuylkill at Point Breeze, two and a half miles south of the first gasworks at Market Street. Construction of the Point Breeze Gas Works began on this site in 1851, and the plant was for the most part complete three years

Figure 6.38.

The Point Breeze Gas Works as shown on the Hopkins ward map of 1876. The original four buildings appear in a row along Passyunk Avenue. The long rectangle by the number 260 is the first retort house, the "L"-shaped structure is the purifying house, the small rectangle is the meter house, and the single circle is the first gasholder. (Courtesy of the City Archives of Philadelphia)

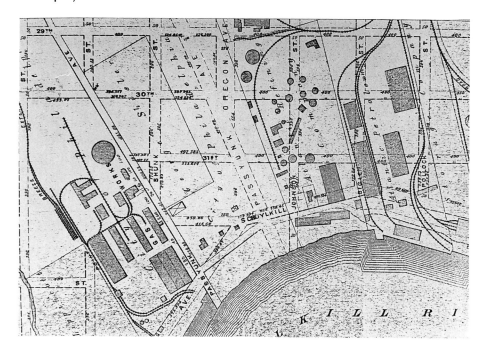

later. The original complex consisted of a retort house, purifying house, meter house, and gas holder (Figure 6.38). Designed in Victorian Gothic according to John Cresson's specifications, the buildings were made of gray granite and had cast-iron roof trusses covered with slate. Of these structures, only the meter house and the purifying house still stand.

Figure 6.39.

Switching locomotives at the Point Breeze plant in 1903. (Courtesy of the City Archives of Philadelphia)

Figure 6.40.

The first retort house at the Point Breeze Gas Works. This photograph was taken about 1860 by John Cresson's son Charles, who was assistant engineer of the plant. (Courtesy of the Library Company of Philadelphia)

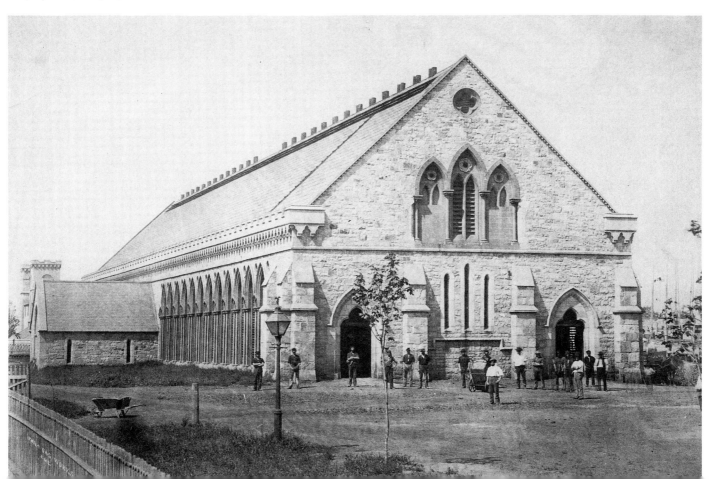

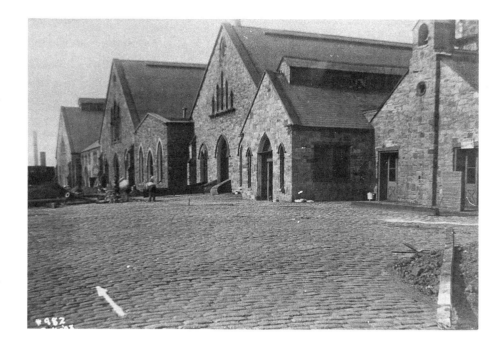

Figure 6.41.

Buildings at the Point Breeze plant in 1903. The purifying house appears at far right. (Courtesy of the City Archives of Philadelphia)

Figure 6.42.

Gasholder at Station "A" (Market Street) in 1903. (Courtesy of the City Archives of Philadelphia.)

Cresson's specifications for the new gasworks were a model of scientific planning for economy of operation. Barges unloaded their freight of bituminous coal at a wharf at the foot of Passyunk Avenue, where it was stored in stone sheds. From there, horses pulled cars of it to the retort house; later, steam engines replaced the horses (Figure 6.39). The retort house had seventy-two retorts, each holding 250 pounds of coal. Feeding the coal into them was hard work, especially in the hot and humid Philadelphia summers, and Cresson planned the building with the workers' comfort—and efficiency—in mind. All the arched windows along its sides had slatted blinds that could be opened for air in the summer (Figure 6.40). Openings along the high ridge of the roof pulled the hot air from the retorts skyward, creating a draft that drew fresh air in through the open windows.

Pneumatic pumps were used in propelling the gas produced by the burning coal to the purifying house, an L-shaped structure located 100 feet east of the retort house (Figure 6.41). After the gas was condensed and purified in that structure, it was passed through the meter house, where meters registered the gas production and clerks recorded it. It then went into the gasholder, the largest one built to that date. Surrounded by twelve cast-iron towers connected by openwork girders, the holder had a diameter of 160 feet and a capacity of 1.8 million cubic feet. Construction of the holder was almost complete when, on February 21, 1854, a snowstorm caused its partial collapse. This disaster, later attributed to shoddy materials and workmanship, delayed the completion of the gasholder for two years. But it did not delay produc-

Figure 6.43.

Detail of the Point Breeze meter house. (Photo by J. L. Cotter)

tion of gas at the Point Breeze facility. The gas produced there was funneled through a connecting main, completed in 1852, to the holders at the original gasworks on Market Street, over two miles away (Figure 6.42).

In 1860 several new structures were added to the complex. They were made of brownstone rather than granite, but in all other respects they resembled the original structures. Of the two original buildings still standing, the meter house is the more spectacular example of Victorian industrial architecture (Figure 6.43). With its gray granite, lancet windows, and arched doors, it so resembles a chapel that engaged couples over the years have asked to use it for weddings. In 1862 the meter house underwent some renovations, including the addition of stepped buttresses to the upper part of its outer walls. Reflective of Victorian ideas about industrial buildings, the purpose of these buttresses seems to have been nothing more than cosmetic.

The Point Breeze Gas Works survived the introduction of the electric light; in fact, as gas furnaces and stoves came into use, it became one of the world's major generators of gas. But the introduction of natural gas to Philadelphia in 1948 foretold the imminent demise of the old facility. After a brief standby period, the manufacture of gas from coal ceased. The site is an important one because, as Orr and Levy (1985:3) note, "the development and success of the gas works affected the lives of every Phila-

delphian. It created revolutions in domestic and public social activity."

Today not a trace remains of the original gasworks at Twenty-Third and Market streets. Its site has been gouged by the deep basements of large buildings. Its disappearance, together with the possibility that the photographs of Point Breeze might well have moldered away had this study not resulted in their chance salvage, is a reminder of how fragile the record of our industrial heritage is.

THE "SAPONIFIED" MAN AND WOMAN: SOME VICTORIAN ARCHAEOLOGY

Although planned, systematic archaeology in Philadelphia began in the 1950s at Independence National Historical Park, many accidental discoveries of an archaeological nature no doubt took place long before then. Few of them, however, were ever recorded. One early accidental archaeological discovery that has been documented—or at least partially so—took place during Philadelphia's Victorian era, and the story as it thereafter unfolded has some intriguing Dickensian overtones.

In 1875, under conditions that remain rather cloudy, two recently disinterred bodies came into the possession of Dr. Joseph Leidy (1823–1891), distinguished professor of anatomy at the University of Pennsylvania Medical School and president of the Academy of Natural Sciences of Philadelphia. The exposed burials were the extraordinarily well preserved and abundant remains of a man and woman. Their stout, if not obese, bodies had been laid to rest in earth under conditions that rendered the fat into adipocere, a soaplike substance that arrests the bacterial action of decay.*

Leidy presented the male body, complete with the well-preserved stockings that adorned it (Figure 6.44), to the Wistar Museum at Penn's medical school, where it was displayed with a label that read:

Body of Wilhelm von Ellenbogen, who died of yellow fever in 1792 aged 63 years. The fat is converted into adipocere, an ammonical soap. A so-called petrified body. Presented by Dr. Joseph Leidy

When the Wistar Institute revised the museum's displays in 1958, it gave the "saponified man" to the Smithsonian Institution in Washington, D.C., where it is now part of an exhibit of human mummification in the American Museum of Natural History.

Leidy presented the female body to the College of Physicians of Philadelphia for display at its Mütter Museum, which for well over a century has housed a remarkable collection of medical memorabilia.* There she still rests, exhibited under a glass case (Figure 6.45). The label on the body originally read:

Body of a fat woman changed to adipocere; "Petrified body." The woman, named Ellenbogen, died in Philadelphia of yellow fever in 1792 and was buried near Fourth and Race Streets. The process is as follows: The nitrogeneous tissues give off ammonia, this attacking the fat of the body forms a hard soap. The form is well preserved. Presented by Dr. Joseph Leidy

McFarland's Search

In 1942 Dr. Joseph McFarland, a pathologist who was curator of the Mütter Museum as well as a fellow of the College of Physicians, completed a long and painstaking study of the story of the saponified couple who "died of yellow fever in 1792" and their departure from a burial ground "near Fourth and Race Streets." In an article describing his research, McFarland (1942:138–43) recalled how he had first heard the story of Dr. Leidy's finds in the autumn of 1885, when as a medical student at Penn, he had attended some of Leidy's lectures. Among other former medical students who had also heard the story "from Leidy's lips" were Dr. William Hunt, who recounted it in a newspaper article in 1896, and Dr. Guy Hinsdale, who shared his reminiscences with McFarland in a letter in October 1941.*

As a pathologist, McFarland noted that the "woman named Ellenbogen" seemed "to have been buried without an undertaker's skill . . . for it is nude, the jaw has fallen, and the toothless mouth gapes widely open." He found "few anatomical landmarks." The breasts, "once prominent, are as in old age, now flattened against the chest wall. They, and the long thin

---

* This phenomenon, long familiar to forensic specialists, was first documented in Paris in the last half of the eighteenth century. One twentieth-century authority, Dr. A. Keith Mant (1957:18), describes adipocere as a product of decomposition that "consists essentially of a mixture of fatty acids formed by the post-mortem hydrolysis of body fats together with the mummified remains of muscles, fibrous and nervous tissues, and a little soap." Mant also notes that although adipocere formation is usually regarded as "a phenomenon of late decomposition, . . . [it] normally commences rapidly after death."

* The Mütter Museum, located at 19 South Twenty-Second Street, was founded in 1858 when Dr. Thomas Dent Mütter, former professor of surgery at Jefferson Medical College, presented his teaching collection to the College of Physicians of Philadelphia. The College of Physicians, itself a venerable institution founded in 1787, added to the collection over the years, so that the museum now has an astounding variety of exhibits, ranging from the skeletons of a giant and a dwarf to items demonstrating the development of patent medicines.

* Hunt's account appeared in the *Philadelphia Public Ledger* on January 16, 1896. Gretchen Worden, curator of the Mütter Museum, who generously supplied data for the present account, notes that McFarland's recollections are somewhat distorted versions of Hunt's and Hinsdale's.

---

hair tied with a ribbon, are all that remain to determine the sex." He judged that the lady had "had a plump figure, but was old, and probably ugly, with a nut-cracker profile at the time of her death" (McFarland 1942:139).

Although the male was labeled as "von Ellenbogen" and the female as "Ellenbogen," McFarland assumed they were either husband and wife or brother and sister. He began his research by using the surname to look for further clues to their identity. Finding none in the records of the Mütter Museum or of the Wistar Museum, he started combing the city archives. There he found no indication that any deaths due to yellow fever had occurred in Philadelphia in 1792. Moreover, in the published lists of names of the thousands of people who did die of yellow fever in the great epidemic of 1793, neither a single "Ellenbogen" nor "von Ellenbogen" appeared. Nor did such a name appear in any of the three volumes of B. Strassburger and J. Hinke's *Pennsylvania German Pioneers*, or in the lists of all the ship passengers who debarked in Philadelphia before 1794, or in I. D. Rupp's *Collection of Upwards of Thirty Thousand Names of German, Swiss, Dutch, French, and Other Immigrants in Pennsylvania*. The names also were not in the first Philadelphia Directory, published in 1791, or in the editions of 1792 and 1793.

The name "Ellenbogen" first appeared in the Philadelphia Directory for 1836, and there it appeared twice. It also appeared twice in the Philadelphia City Directory for 1935–36 and in the Philadelphia telephone directory for 1941. Upon contacting the contemporary Ellenbogens, McFarland learned they were cousins descended from "country Dutch"; their

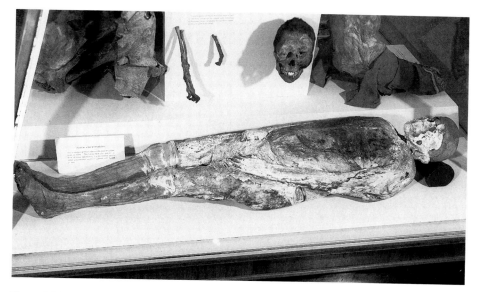

Figure 6.44.

The "saponified" man. (Courtesy of the National Museum of Natural History, Smithsonian Institution)

Figure 6.45.

The "saponified" woman, whose body has no doubt grown a bit darker over the years, since the glass case over her has not completely withstood the incursion of Philadelphia soot. (Courtesy of the Mütter Museum, College of Physicians of Philadelphia)

ancestors had lived near Danville and had had little or no connection with Philadelphia.

Having gone down that blind alley, McFarland next tried to identify the burial ground, described by the label on the female body as being "near Fourth and Race Streets." In the eighteenth century, as now, the blocks near Fourth and Race contained a number of churches, and no fewer than three of these were German: St. Michael's Lutheran Church, the German Reformed Church, and the Zion Lutheran Church. Parishioners of St. Michael's, at Fifth Street and Appletree Alley, may have been buried in the churchyard, but McFarland's examination of church records revealed no Ellenbogens or von Ellenbogens in that congregation or in any of the others. Moreover, he discovered that the burial grounds of the other churches were located at some distance from the churches themselves. Parishioners of the German Reformed Church, on Race Street near Fourth, may have been buried in Franklin Square, two blocks west of the church. (However, an excavation of a portion of Franklin Square in the 1970s, described in Chapter 5, produced no evidence of bodies, saponified or otherwise.) The burial ground of the Zion Lutheran Church had been between Race and Vine Streets just east of Eighth. (This burial ground was in the block next to the cemetery of the First African Baptist Church, and of the many burials excavated there in 1983–84, none showed any evidence of saponification.)

McFarland himself had long believed the cemetery was on Broad Street below Chestnut. In Hinsdale's opinion, however, it was near Third and Pine. In short, the location of the cemetery remained a mystery. But

McFarland's discovery of a receipt that Leidy had given the Mütter Museum gave him a few more leads. Dated November 18, 1875, the receipt acknowledged that Leidy had received from the Museum of the College of Physicians $7.50 in payment for "expenses on the procural of an adipocere body." To this, Leidy had added a note:

The above amount is one-half of the sum paid persons through whose connivance I was enabled to procure two adipocere bodies, one for the College of Physicians, the other for the University. J. L.

Taking a clue from the 1875 date on the receipt, McFarland searched the city records to find whether any cemetery had been abandoned in that year and whether the Board of Health had at any time in the 1870s given permission for the removal of bodies from a cemetery. Once again, McFarland drew a blank.

However, Leidy's admission of the "connivance" of the persons who unearthed the bodies and made them available to him—at a price of $15—suggested a new angle, and McFarland began formulating a theory. For this, he drew not only on his own memories of his former professor and the lectures he had heard in 1885, but also on Hinsdale's recollections of Leidy and those Hunt had published in 1896.

According to McFarland's theory, workmen engaged in some kind of street construction had accidentally dug up the bodies, possibly together with others. As one of the framers and backers of Pennsylvania's 1867 "Anatomical Act," Leidy had to have been fully aware of the legal status of the bodies. The act, designed to end grave robbing and the sale of bodies to phy-

sicians and medical schools, set forth a number of regulations pertaining to exhumation and reinterral. In the case of authorized removal of a body for medical purposes, it specifically stated:

Each body shall be used only for the promotion of medical science within this state, and whosoever shall use such body or bodies for any other purpose, . . . and whosoever shall sell or buy such bodies or in any way traffic, in the same, shall be deemed guilty of a misdemeanor, punishable by a term not exceeding five years at hard labor in the county jail.

Although Leidy may indeed have intended the bodies for the promotion of medical science, he had to stretch the financial involvement a bit. His former students recalled Leidy's mentioning in his lectures that he had claimed the bodies as his relatives and had paid "the costs incurred" in their removal to the museums. However, his former students were also familiar with a story that Leidy had paid an initially adamant work boss to allow the bodies to be hauled away from the scene in a wagon Leidy had hired for the purpose.

Having theoretically reconstructed how Leidy came into possession of the bodies, though not where they were found, McFarland had only one more thing to explain: the surnames on the bodies. For this, McFarland, Hunt, and Hinsdale also had a theory. Dr. Leidy, of German extraction, was possessed of little humor, and what little he had was notoriously heavy. Predictably, in his lectures on the human skeleton, he would be moved to observe that the part of the elbow where the ulnar nerve passes by the bone of the upper arm is commonly referred to as the funny bone, at which point he would inquire if anyone could state the scientific name for the upper arm. Going along with the weighty gag, his students would refrain from answering, so that Leidy could say, with a great beam on his face, "The humerus!" With the ulnar nerve and humerus thus permanently fixed in his students minds as one of the good doctor's witticisms, it was but a small step to recall that the German word for elbow is *Ellenbogen*, and the mystery of why this name did not appear in the records is dispelled. This may well have been the most enduring of Dr. Leidy's witticisms, and, we can only hope, the least lively.

Postscript

In 1987, diagnostic-imaging techniques shed new light on the story of the saponified couple. Using portable radiographic equipment, technicians from Jefferson University's College of Allied Health Sciences tested the remains of the saponified woman. The results showed that the woman was toothless and that her lower jaw had been damaged. All other bones, however, were in excellent condition; there was no evidence of arthritis or other pathological changes due to aging. The conclusion was that she had been about forty years of age. The most significant result, however, was the discovery of six straight pins—two near the head, two near the right elbow, one near the groin, and one near the left ankle.

The straight pins had obviously been used to pin a shroud around the body, a common practice well into the nineteenth century. More important, however, these pins, which had solid heads, were of a type not manufactured before 1824.* They therefore put the fiction that the couple died in the late 1700s permanently to rest.

Additional evidence of a nineteenth-century burial date came in the form of two four-hole buttons—probably cuff buttons, since they were found near the wrists. Four-hole buttons were more common in the nineteenth century than in the eighteenth.

As technology becomes more sophisticated, more clues to the mystery of the saponified couple may yet emerge and ultimately clarify Dr. Leidy's strange account. How involved his harmless fiction of convenience and humor became calls to mind Sir Walter Scott's cautionary words (*Marmion*, stanza 17):

> Oh, what a tangled web we weave,
> When first we practise to deceive.

* The Ellenbogen reference in the 1836 Philadelphia City Directory could therefore match the burials, if "Ellenbogens" they were.

7

Germantown

WYCK: GERMANTOWN'S OLDEST SURVIVING HOUSE

STENTON: JAMES LOGAN'S COUNTRY ESTATE

GRUMBLETHORPE: GERMANTOWN'S FIRST SUMMER HOME

THE DESHLER-MORRIS HOUSE:
THE NATION'S FIRST "SUMMER WHITE HOUSE"

CLIVEDEN: WOUNDED VETERAN OF THE REVOLUTIONARY WAR

THE STORY OF HOW AN UNKNOWN BRITISH SOLDIER OF THE BATTLE OF GERMANTOWN REGAINED HIS IDENTITY

Until the industrial age caught up with the settlements in Philadelphia County, most of them were obscure farming villages. Germantown, however, was a unique exception. Settled in 1683 by Quakers, Mennonites, and other religious dissenters of Dutch and German backgrounds, this small community, situated six miles northwest of Center Square, quickly established its own industrial economy, and in doing so it became well known up and down the eastern seaboard for the excellence of the goods it produced.

Francis Daniel Pastorius (1651–1719), a learned lawyer from Frankfurt am Main, was Germantown's first spokesman. In the fall of 1683, on behalf of the Dutch and German settlers, he negotiated with William Penn for the grant of Germantown's 6,000 acres. According to Pastorius, the first Europeans to inhabit these 6,000 acres were "mostly linen weavers and not any too skilled in agriculture" (Soderlund et al. 1983:356). Their skill at weaving was such, however, that the women of Philadelphia were soon clamoring to buy their "pure fine linnen cloth" at the semiannual Philadelphia fairs (Bronner 1982:62). In relatively short order, this fine stuff was known and in demand throughout the colonies.

By March 1684 the industrious Germantowners had so often traversed the sloping path to Philadelphia, two hours away, that they had, in Pastorius's words, "trodden [it] out into good shape." Forty-two in all in the winter of 1683–84, they lived along a main street and a cross street in twelve dwellings set on three-acre lots (Soderlund et al. 1983:356). By 1700 the main street was a mile long, and despite the settlers' alleged lack of agricultural skill, it was studded with orchards (Dunn and Dunn 1982:

Figure 7.1.

The market shed at Market Square. The firehouse with its cupola appears to the right. (From a painting by William Britton, ca. 1820; courtesy of the American Federation of Arts)

25). This street, now known as Germantown Avenue, became the main route from Philadelphia to Reading, Bethlehem, and other points northwest of the city.

In 1689, two years before Germantown received a borough charter entitling it to its own local government and market, it set aside a plot of land on the west side of Germantown Avenue at Queen Lane for public buildings, a market, and a burial ground. For whatever reason, this public common was never put to its intended use. In 1704 another common was laid out, and it has been Germantown's focal point ever since. Occupying a half acre on the east side of Germantown Avenue at Schoolhouse Lane, Market Square, as it is known, was in the early eighteenth century the site of a prison, stocks, public scales, and a public well. Sometime before 1745, it also became the site of a market shed, and in 1814 a firehouse was built there as well. In poor condition by the early 1800s, the market shed was razed by order of the Germantown Council in 1850 (Tinkcom 1967:69–72). In the mid-1960s an archeological discovery in the north end of the square of six brick pedestal footings, each about 3 by 4 feet and

set about 5 feet apart (Foley 1965), provided positive proof that this market shed, like New Market in Society Hill, had been built in the European manner, open at the sides with two parallel rows of brick pillars supporting a gable roof (Figure 7.1).*

After receiving its borough charter in 1691, Germantown elected Pastorius as its first mayor. A pious man, Pastorious was also a scholar, a linguist, an author, a teacher—both at the Quaker school in Philadelphia and in Germantown—and a member of the Pennsylvania Assembly. For all that, he may have been a disappointed man, for his vision of a "small separate province" within Pennsylvania for his fellow German nonconformists was never fulfilled. It seems more likely, however, that Pastorius passed to his great reward comforted by the knowledge that his reason for wanting a separate province, to "better protect ourselves against all oppression," was a well-established

---

* Foley's excavations (1965:6) also showed that a road had once led from Germantown Avenue to the north side of the market shed. Made of graduated layers of gneiss and schist, with the smallest rocks forming the bottom layer, the road appeared to have been constructed in the "telford" style, so-called because of Thomas Telford (1757–1843), the Scottish engineer who developed it.

precept in Penn's colony (Soderlund et al. 1983:358).

Although "wedged in among the English" and not as German as Pastorius might have had it, colonial Germantown had a decidedly more Germanic flavor than colonial Philadelphia. The first place of worship in the village was a log meetinghouse built by Dutch- and German-speaking Quakers in 1686. By 1726 both the German Reformed Church and the German Lutheran Church had congregations in the community. And by 1753 a German-language newspaper published in Germantown claimed a readership of four thousand (Bronner 1982:47; Thayer 1982:87).

German immigration slackened after the first wave in 1683, but in 1727 it began to pick up again, and by midcentury it was at high tide. Of the some 37,000 Germans who arrived in Philadelphia between 1749 and 1754 (Wokeck 1986:261), many were skilled artisans who gravitated to

Germantown. While these newcomers were swelling the ranks of the town's middle class, some other trends were becoming evident. Emulating in Germantown the example Penn had set at Pennsbury Manor, men who had prospered in the city built handsome mansions in the midst of large plantations. Others, intent on escaping the heat and smell of the city in summer, built somewhat more modest seasonal homes; elevated some 200 feet above Center Square, the settlement had a cooler and kinder summer climate than Philadelphia. In November 1793 George Washington, whose memories of Germantown included the defeat he suffered there in 1777 at the hands of the British army, sought refuge from the yellow fever then terrorizing the city in a comfortable home just off Market Square. When Washington returned with his family to the same house the following summer, his presence enhanced Germantown's reputation as a choice summer retreat.

With train service between the northwestern suburbs and Philadelphia well established by the 1840s, Germantown began experiencing a building boom, one that signaled its transition to a commuting suburb. Property values soared, and Italianate villas became the rage. Adding to Germantown's numbers in the mid-1800s were some new English immigrants; knitters of what became famous as "Germantown woolen goods," these artisans had lost their jobs in England when the machines of the industrial age replaced them (Geffen 1982:311, 326–27). Succeeding years brought other ethnic groups to Germantown, Italian, Irish, and African among them. As more and more African-Americans moved west and north out of the city in the course of the twentieth century, they became Germantown's largest ethnic group.

Despite efforts at redevelopment in recent years, Germantown has many visible reminders of urban blight and industrial decay. It also has, however, a remarkable collection of handsome and carefully restored historic houses. The unique history of each of these properties reflects some phase of Germantown's past; taken together, they paint a picture of Philadelphia over the centuries. The archaeological investigations described in this chapter have added intimate, small-scale detail to that collective history. Figure 7.2 shows the locations of the properties that were the focus of these investigations, superimposed on an 1808 map.

Figure 7.2.

Archaeological sites in Germantown superimposed on an 1808 map. (Courtesy of the Library Company of Philadelphia)

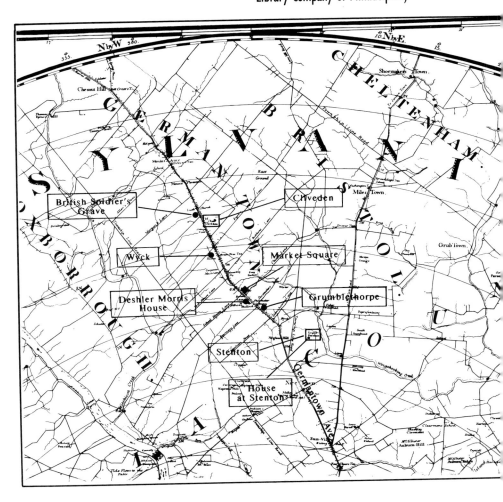

WYCK: GERMANTOWN'S OLDEST SURVIVING HOUSE

Wyck is the oldest structure still standing in Germantown and among the oldest in Philadelphia.* It started out about 1690 as the unassuming homestead of Hans Milan, a Dutch Quaker whose fifty acres of land extended from Germantown Avenue west toward Wissahickon Creek. With its thick walls constructed of the local stone, Wyck kept Milan and his family warm in winter and cool in summer. Although enlarged and altered over the years, Wyck continued to perform the same function for nine generations of Hans Milan's descendants. During those years, the house witnessed its full share of history, including the sufferings of British soldiers wounded in the Battle of Germantown and a visit many years after the Revolutionary War from the Marquis de Lafayette, one of America's most revered war heroes. The last of Milan's descendants to live at Wyck was Robert B. Haines III, whose widow created the Wyck Charitable Trust in 1973 and deeded the property to it. The Germantown Historical Society has maintained the property since that time.

Today, Wyck sits behind a tall picket fence at 6026 Germantown Avenue on two acres of ground covered by lawns, gardens, a carriage house, and various other outbuildings (Figures 7.3, *top*, and 7.4). A large stone structure northwest of the house, constructed as a barn in 1796, has served as a private residence since the

* The name "Wyck" may derive from the Amerindian *wickwam*, meaning house, or from *wyc* or *wic*, a Saxon suffix denoting mansion or village, as in "Berwick" (Heckewelder 1819:413–14; Claussen 1970:2–3). *Wyck* in Dutch (*wijk* in modern Dutch) means district, ward, quarter, or parish, as Milan knew (Paul Huey, personal correspondence, 1991).

CIRCA 1700   CIRCA 1730

CIRCA 1770

Figure 7.3.

Top, Wyck, the house from the lawn, south elevation 1989. (Photo by J. L. Cotter) *Bottom,* conjectural north elevations (Drawing by M. A. Bower 1979)

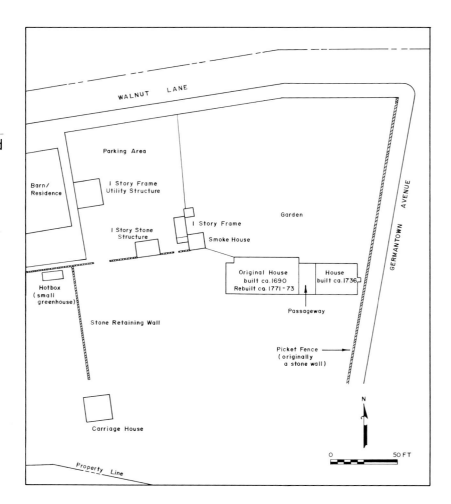

Figure 7.4.

Plan of the grounds at Wyck. (From Cotter and Hall 1979)

WALNUT LANE

Parking Area

Barn/ Residence

1 Story Frame Utility Structure

1 Story Stone Structure

1 Story Frame

Smoke House

Garden

Original House built ca. 1690 Rebuilt ca. 1771-73

House built ca. 1736

Passageway

Hotbox (small greenhouse)

Stone Retaining Wall

Picket Fence (originally a stone wall)

GERMANTOWN AVENUE

N

Carriage House

0   50 FT

Property Line

1890s.* In 1979 students from the University of Pennsylvania conducted an archaeological feasibility study of the property; the report of this study (Cotter and Hall 1979) provided the basis for much of what follows. Another archaeological study took place at Wyck in 1980; the findings of this study, conducted by Parrington (1980b), are also described in this section.

Highlights of Wyck's History: From Quaker Plain to Quaker Wet

The complex story of how Wyck evolved from Hans Milan's modest stone house into the spacious and lovely place it is today apparently began about 1715 when Milan built a house just east of his own for his daughter and her husband, Dirck Jansen.† A carriageway 18 feet wide leading to a barn or stable originally separated the two houses. At some point, however, a second-floor room was built over the carriageway to connect the two dwellings at the roofline. The result was a single structure 80 feet long, with its front facing south and an open carriageway running through it at ground level. This alteration probably took place while Caspar Wistar (1696–1752) was living at Wyck (see Figure 7.3, bottom). After arriving in Philadelphia from Germany with his brother John in

* Pioneering what was to become familiar as the adaptive use of historic buildings, Mantle Fielding, a Philadelphia architect and art historian, converted the barn to its present usage in 1891.
† Gaps in the historical record make it possible to put several different interpretations on the early history of Wyck. The interpretation given here, based on Lloyd (1986), seems the most likely one.

1727, Wistar had soon married the Jansen's daughter Catherine.*

By the time of the Revolution, the carriageway had been enclosed and a floor laid to form a broad passageway through the center of the house. This alteration was most likely the work of the Wistars' daughter Margaret and her Quaker husband, Reuben Haines. Although Margaret did not inherit Wyck until her mother's death in 1786, she lived there with her husband and children well before that time.

Before the property could undergo

* Born Wuester, Caspar Wistar changed the spelling of his surname after arriving in Philadelphia, where he made glass and buttons. His brother John, who chose to spell his name Wister, was the builder of Germantown's first summer home (see "Grumblethorpe: Germantown's First Summer Home," below). Two other well-known bearers of these names were the namesake of the Wistar Institute, anatomist Caspar Wistar (1761–1818), an important figure in Philadelphia's early medical community, and the novelist Owen Wister, great-great grandson of John Wister and author of *The Virginian*, published in 1902.

any other major alterations, Wyck found itself on October 4, 1777, while the Battle of Germantown raged around it, serving as a field hospital for the British army. Dark stains on the floors of the house are said to be the marks, apparently ineradicable, of the blood shed that day as the limbs of British soldiers were amputated. It is also said that the soldiers who died at Wyck on October 4, 1777, were buried west of the carriage house in an area now occupied by a vegetable garden.

During the 1790s a number of changes took place at Wyck. They included the construction in 1794 of a brewery north of the house; the construction in 1796 of the present barn/ residence, which may have been built over or near the foundations of the original barn; the construction, also in 1796, of a small wooden firehouse, which until about 1856 stood northeast of the house on Germantown

Avenue; and the stuccoing of the exterior stone of the house itself in 1799 (Group for Environmental Education 1984:20). In 1824, a year before the Marquis de Lafayette came to call, Wyck underwent yet more alterations, this time under the direction of one of Philadelphia's most renowned architects, William Strickland.

The Brewery at Wyck

The story of how Quaker-owned Wyck came to be the site of a brewery should perhaps begin with the Green Tree Tavern. This establishment was built directly across the street from Wyck by Daniel Pastorius, grandson of Germantown's first leader, in 1748, shortly before Reuben Haines, husband of Hans Milan's great-granddaughter, took over the operation of a Philadelphia brewery. No doubt Daniel Pastorius's enterprise played at least some part in Friend Haines' decision. Still standing at 6023 Germantown Avenue, the Green Tree Tavern is interesting not just for this connection but also because it is a good example of Germantown's early architecture. Unlike Wyck, whose front faces south, the tavern faces the main street,* as most Germantown houses did. Because the south sides of the houses were visible to people coming up the hill from Philadelphia, these sides were usually finished in the same way as the fronts. Thus both the front and the south side of the Green Tree Tavern have a pent eave and a heavy Georgian cornice and are made of cut and dressed stone, while the other two sides lack these features and are made of undressed rubble.

Reuben Haines' involvement with Philadelphia brewing began when he advanced credit to a brewer named

* The Green Tree Tavern is now used as a church building.

Timothy Matlack. Matlack had built a brewery and malthouse at 145 Market Street sometime between 1746 and 1750, but despite Philadelphia's abundant supply of taverns (117 in 1758) and its tradition of brewing dating to 1683, Matlack's business failed to prosper. By 1751 he was in debt not only to Haines but also to Haines' father-in-law, Caspar Wistar. Matlack's indebtedness to Wistar may have stemmed from his having bought bottles for his beer from the glassworks Wistar owned in Alloway, New Jersey.* In any event, Wistar and Haines forced Matlack to share control of the business in 1751, and in 1754, after Matlack's death, Haines took over the management of the brewery, which he operated profitably for many years under the name of Reuben Haines and Son.

Although members of the Society of Friends discouraged the making, sale, and consumption of spirits in the province of Pennsylvania, they promoted the making of beer. Rather conveniently, several of them also profited from this occupation; Reuben Haines was certainly not the first or last Quaker to do so. As early as 1683, a Quaker named William Frampton was building a "great brewhouse" near Front and Walnut streets (Soderlund et al. 1983:341). In 1687 Friend Anthony Morris built a brewery in the same neighborhood; by the twentieth century Morris's brewery was the oldest continuing business in America. William Penn, who described William Frampton as an "able Man," also described the beer that Frampton, Morris, and other Philadelphia brewers of the 1680s produced:

Our DRINK has been Beer . . . made mostly of Molasses, which well boyled,

* Using the excellent silica found in the riverbeds of New Jersey, Wistar's plant produced window glass and bottles. Established in 1738, it was the first glassworks in New Jersey.

with Sassafras or Pine infused into it, makes very tolerable drink; but now they make Mault and Mault Drink begins to be very common, especially at the Ordinaries and the Houses of the more substantial people. (Baron 1962)

The American brewing industry was destined for a decline after the Revolutionary War ended, for as trade revived, imported spirits—particularly West Indian rum—became plentiful and cheap. In these troubled postwar years, the brewery of Reuben Haines and Son received some free publicity, no doubt welcome even if it came at the cost of a rather un-Quakerly display. On July 4, 1788, Philadelphia staged a grand parade—one of the most spectacular ever held in a city that became famous for its parades—to "honor the establishment of the Constitution of the United States" (Cotter and Hall 1979:163). Thereafter, a local newspaper reported that Reuben Haines had headed the delegation of brewers, all of whom had marched with "ears of barley in their hats, and sashes of hop vines, carrying malt shovels and mashing oars [and] a standard . . . decorated with the brewers arms and the motto, . . . 'Home brew'd is best'" (Cotter and Hall, 1979:163). This bit of publicity may have had something to do with another of the brewery's coups: an order of beer in 1792 from President George Washington himself.

Of Reuben and Margaret Haines' offspring, the one who seems to have taken the greatest interest in brewing was Caspar Wistar Haines (1762–1801). In the 1780s Caspar was in business with his father at the family brewery on Market Street, and in 1794, a year after he inherited Wyck, he began building a brewery complex on the property. Situated north of the house, the complex included a 50-by-22-foot stone malthouse with kiln, a 22-by-20-foot stone brewhouse, and a 22-by-15-foot wooden mill-house. Soon after the brewery was completed, Caspar transferred the operation of Reuben Haines and Son from Philadelphia to Wyck.

The building of the brewery at Wyck may have signified prescient caution and economizing on the part of Caspar Wistar Haines, for between 1810 and 1820 the production of beer in America declined drastically (Baron 1962:124). More likely, however, it signified financial success, for in the 1790s Caspar had the means not only to build the brewery but also to implement a number of other changes at Wyck. In 1796 he built the large barn that presently serves as a residence; in the same year he gave the Middle Ward fire company a piece of land on which to build a small fire-house; and in 1799 he had the exterior of the house stuccoed.

After Caspar Wistar Haines died in 1801, Wyck passed to his son, Reuben Haines, Jr. (1786–1831). Apparently more interested in horticulture and natural history than in brewing, and perhaps also in reaction to the slump of the brewing industry, Reuben, Jr., inaugurated the practice of leasing the brewery to outsiders. Although the cost of repairs to the brewery ate up most of the rental income, this practice continued for almost a decade after Reuben's death. The last brewer to lease the facility at Wyck was Thomas Ladley, who died in 1840. At that point, twenty-year-old John Smith Haines, Reuben's son, was master of Wyck, and he decided to dismantle the brewery. His reasons for doing so are interesting. He noted that the brewery was a nuisance to neighbors, probably because of its fragrance, and that it attracted the idle and worthless among them. Most telling, perhaps, he noted that "troubled times and quite a few temperance societies" ac-counted for a loss of business (Claussen 1970:156).

When John Smith Haines gave up the unprofitable brewing business, he made quite sure—in good, thrifty Quaker style—to salvage every stone of every building in the complex. He may later have had some regrets, for in the 1850s, as large-scale brewing technology was introduced, the American brewing industry revived. However, he could have comforted himself with the knowledge that after 1840 Quakers were conspicuous by their absence among the ranks of American brewers. In any case, it would have been difficult for Haines to resurrect the brewery, since nine years after he razed it, he and other members of his family laid out a public street over part of the site. Known as Walnut Lane, this street connects Germantown Avenue with Wayne Avenue. The Haineses' motive in developing Walnut Lane may have been related to the land speculation afoot in the 1840s as Germantown entered its suburban phase.

Alterations of the 1820s and 1830s

In 1820 Reuben Haines, Jr., and his wife Jane gave up their house on Chestnut Street in Philadelphia to take up permanent residence at Wyck. Reuben did so "without one single feeling of regret." Jane, on the other hand, found the accommodations not entirely to her liking, complaining that if the drafts in the old house were not quickly repaired, "we shall all be congealed to statues." Once Haines set about fixing the house, he found the state of repair so poor he decided it would be folly to attempt to "patch the patches" and so initiated a thorough renovation (Mackenzie 1979: 60, 89). On May 23, 1824, he wrote to his wife about the alterations then under way: "Thee very well knows few if any ever begin a career of vice, or commence the repairs of an old Building, that stop exactly at the point they intended" (Wyck Archives). Haines' evident desire to see an end to the extensive renovations at Wyck in 1824 was no doubt related to the presence of the aging Marquis de Lafayette in Philadelphia that year. By the time Lafayette graced Wyck with his presence at a reception held there in his honor on July 25, 1825, the old house was spruced up, presumably to Haines' liking.

Reuben Haines, Jr., was certainly not the "wettest" Quaker around— "wet" in the sense of being ostentatious—but he obviously had a good deal of pride in his house, as well as the means to indulge it. The architect he engaged to direct the renovations at Wyck in 1824 was William Strickland, one of the foremost architects of the day. When those renovations began, workmen on Chestnut Street were just putting the finishing touches to one of Strickland's most famous buildings, the Second Bank of the United States. Within a few years, Strickland would also have to his credit the steeple at Independence Hall and the Merchant's Exchange.

Strickland's renovations at Wyck included turning the broad passage-way in the center of the structure into a "living hall." Here Strickland installed an architectural feature familiar in the twentieth century but novel at the time: sliding glass double doors, which look out over lawns and gardens at either end of the room (see Figure 7.3, top). A letter in the family archives at Wyck, written while the renovations were going on, mentions that Strickland's workmen were conveniently dumping their debris over the garden wall behind the carriage house. No doubt Reuben Haines, Jr., made quite sure all litter was out of sight by the time the Marquis de Lafayette arrived on July 25, 1825. An ardent horticulturist, Haines also would certainly have ensured that the gardens visible from his new first-floor room were in peak condition. The Haines family's interest in horticulture evidently continued after Reuben's death in 1831, for in 1835 a greenhouse was built on the property. This structure was torn down in 1912.

Archaeology at Wyck

The observation of Reuben Haines, Jr., about the seemingly unending nature of careers of vice and repairs of old houses applies equally well to archaeological pursuits. The two investigations described here were followed in 1982 by a third, when the Wyck Charitable Trust, in anticipation of building a greenhouse on the grounds, commissioned archaeologist Elizabeth Righter to search for traces of the 1835 greenhouse. Righter's (1982) results were largely negative and are not reported here.

The Feasibility Study of 1979

The object of the feasibility study was to develop recommendations for future investigations. After observing the house and other structures on the grounds and exploring some of the vast number of documents at Wyck, Penn students under the direction of Cotter and Hall (1979) tested various parts of the property. As shown in Figure 7.5, test A focused on finding evidence of the old firehouse; the results there were negative. Tests B–E and G, which concentrated on the site of the brewery, had a more rewarding

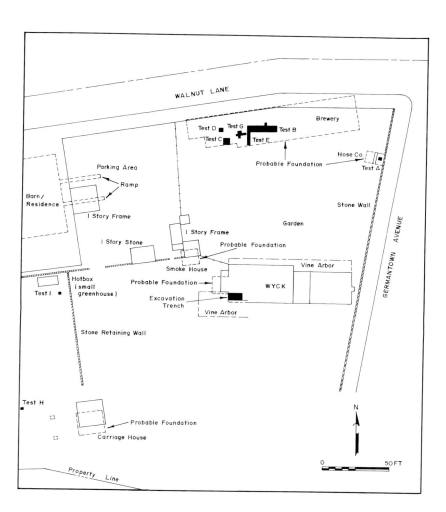

Figure 7.5.

Test locations at Wyck. (From Cotter and Hall 1979)

outcome. Test F (not shown in Figure 7.5) took place in the vegetable garden 91 feet west of the carriage house, where British soldiers are reputed to have been buried in October 1777, but it yielded only a twentieth-century drain pipe. Tests H and I were soil-section tests.

Test B, a 10-by-3-foot trench dug about 10 feet south of the sidewalk on Walnut Lane, produced the major find: a large cache of broken green bottles buried under 14 inches of soil (Figure 7.6, *bottom*). Embossing on many of the bottles announced they had been made by the Phoenix Glass Works of Millville, New Jersey, which by 1900 was one of the biggest manufacturers of glass in the country. Mixed in with the bottle glass were a few ceramic items and some unmistakable evidence of demolition: fragments of brick, mortar, stone, window glass, and cut nails. Shown in section

as feature 5 in Figure 7.6 (*top*), this cache of artifacts resembles a wall trench, with one straight side clearly defined.

Clearly, feature 5 had been part of the wall of a brewery building. John Smith Haines had taken care to remove the stones of the building, but he had left the demolition debris and discarded contents of the building behind. Since this appeared to have been the south wall of the building, whatever else remains of that structure must now lie under Walnut Lane to the north and perhaps extend even under the buildings on the other side of that street.

It was hoped that in addition to defining soil strata, tests I or H might reveal traces of the dump Strickland's

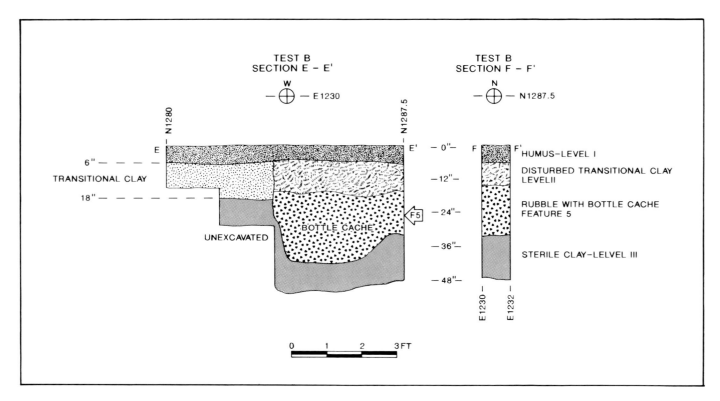

Figure 7.6.

Top, profile of test B, feature 5; *bottom,* beer and lotion bottles from test B, feature 5. (From Cotter and Hall 1979)

workmen created behind the garden wall during the renovations of 1824. Unfortunately, no such evidence appeared. The only other evidence of note was a sloping brick drain 4½ feet long located in test G. The bottom of the drain lay 16 inches below the surface. Since the drain appeared to have been constructed before the debris of feature 5 was deposited, it may have served a structure that occupied the site before Caspar Wistar Haines built the brewery there.

The study ended by making the following recommendations for future investigations:

1 Further research in the estimated 45,000 documents at Wyck to shed more light on past lifestyles there. These documents contain references to the life of children at Wyck (their crafts, hobbies, and so on), to daily housekeeping routines, and to household furnishings and utensils, as well as the dates these items were purchased and their cost.

2 Documentary research to clarify how Hans Milan's original fifty acres, which stretched west from Germantown Avenue toward Wissahickon Creek, diminished over the years to Wyck's present two acres.

3 Excavation under the sidewalk of Walnut Lane to disclose more of the brewery complex and, should the opportunity arise, excavation beneath the street itself to disclose all or most of the complex.

4 Testing in the cellar of the original half of the house (allegedly located west of the center passageway), which could help resolve questions about construction dates.

5 Excavations in the basement of the barn/residence and in the area around it. Such excavations could produce evidence of the original barn and of the evolution of farming practices at Wyck.

6 Further testing in the vegetable garden west of the carriage house for traces of burials said to have occurred in that area during the Battle of Germantown.

7 Extension of the search for the dump created by Strickland's workmen during the renovations of 1824, since it could contain informative artifacts.

8 More extensive testing to locate the remains of the firehouse.

The 1980 Study

While carrying out some renovations in 1979, the Wyck Charitable Trust uncovered a stone wall within a room on the south side of the house, just in front of the kitchen (Figure 7.7). In initiating the study conducted by Parrington (1980b), the trust had three specific goals in mind: to define the edges of the wall, to determine the relationship between the wall and the main house, and to date the wall on the basis of the artifacts found near it.

The wall was made of irregularly shaped pieces of Wissahickon schist held together by a light-gray mortar. It was aligned in the same direction as the house and clearly butted up to the wall of the house, suggesting it was a later construction. The artifacts found in the wall trench supported this suggestion, for they dated from the first half of the nineteenth century. However, just exactly when and why this wall was built remains a mystery.

Among the artifacts found in the wall trench were several sherds of hand-painted creamware vessels; one had been lettered "Golden Flowered Henbane." These vessels had been part of a set of "botanical ware," which was made in the Swansea potteries in Wales from about 1800 to 1810 (Godden 1965: plate 565). Documents at Wyck record that the Haines family bought a set of botanical ware in 1816, and, in fact, some pieces of this set are still in the collection at Wyck. The sherds found in the wall trench undoubtedly had been part of that set. It is rather unusual to be able to make such a direct correlation between the artifacts found at a site and the his-torical record. In this case, it was possible because of the extensive documentation available at Wyck and because the high cost of the botanical ware ensured that the purchase would be noted in the family accounts.

Several other ceramic pieces provided more evidence that the wall had been built in the first half of the nineteenth century. One of these pieces—a fragment of creamware impressed with the mark "Vedgwood"—also provided evidence of sharp practice among nineteenth-century potters; in an attempt to cash in on Wedgwood's popularity in the nineteenth century, many manufacturers used trademarks similar to his. This particular piece may have been made by William Smith and Company of Stockton-on-Tees in Yorkshire sometime around 1840 to 1850. Among the other pieces of supporting evidence were three matching sherds of a pearlware plate with a transfer-printed Chinese motif. This plate had been made by John and William Ridgway, who were in business together from 1814 to 1830 (Godden 1964: 534, 734).

Although the goals of this study were limited, the excavation did demonstrate that this section of the house has a good deal of potential for providing more information about Wyck's history. Little more than 10 percent of the earth beneath this room was excavated, but within this small area—just over 8 by 4 feet—more than 250 artifacts appeared. It seems likely that the area was used as a place to dump trash from the adjacent kitchen. The unexcavated portion of the room may well contain artifacts and food remains that could shed light on the lifestyles and eating habits of past residents of Wyck.

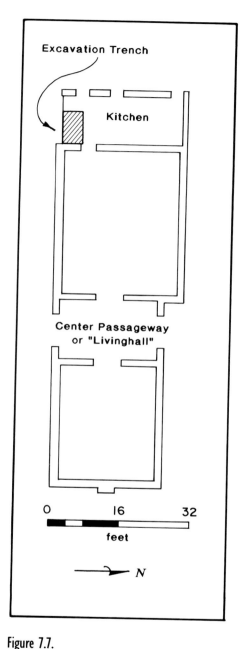

Figure 7.7.

Plan of Wyck showing location of excavation trench for stone wall. (From Parrington 1980b; courtesy of the Museum Institute for Conservation Archaeology, University of Pennsylvania)

STENTON: JAMES LOGAN'S COUNTRY ESTATE

Built in 1728, Stenton was one of the first large country estates created by wealthy Philadelphians intent on living the life of the landed English gentry. Its founder was James Logan (1674–1751), who had come to America to serve as William Penn's secretary.* Logan's stately mansion sat in the midst of 500 rural acres. It now sits at Windrim Avenue and Eighteenth Street surrounded by busy streets, a six-acre city park, and an iron fence. Inside the fence, in strange juxtaposition to the fine Flemish bond of the mansion, is a rustic log cabin, painstakingly hauled there in 1969 in the name of conservation. Originally the dwelling of a Quaker family, the cabin was built in 1755–56 at Sixteenth and Race streets, where the Friends Select School now stands; today it is the quarters of Stenton's resident manager. Among the other structures on the grounds around the mansion are a large eighteenth-century stone barn, an old kitchen-greenhouse complex, a privy, and a toolshed that was once an ice house (Figure 7.8).

Between 1868 and 1908, the city of Philadelphia gradually took over the block of land on which Stenton sits and converted it to a public park. Stenton and its outbuildings, which lie in the northwest part of the block, are administered by the National Society of the Colonial Dames of the Commonwealth of Pennsylvania. Since the late 1960s, the society has sponsored a number of archaeological investigations at Stenton.

* Logan named Stenton after his father's birthplace in Scotland. His father was an impoverished schoolmaster (Bronner 1982:40–41).

Stenton's Founder and His Progeny

James Logan may have been colonial Philadelphia's most intellectual citizen. He was certainly far from its most endearing. The son of poor but educated Scottish Quakers who had emigrated to northern Ireland before his birth, Logan emigrated to Philadelphia in 1699 as William Penn's secretary. He was evidently quite a satisfactory employee, for when Penn sailed from Philadelphia to England for the last time in 1701, he not only invited the twenty-seven-year-old Logan to take over the tenancy of the Slate Roof House, but also made him his personal representative in America.

A serious man, if not a dour one, of great ability and brilliant intellect, James Logan had a strong acquisitive streak and a talent for manipulation. These qualities, combined with the influence and power he wielded as Penn's agent, were destined to make him a very wealthy man. By 1749 he owned 18,000 acres of prime land in Pennsylvania and New Jersey, not to mention his cash reserves and securities (Bronner 1982:41). In the course of his long career, Logan held many public posts. He was mayor of Philadelphia, member of the governor's council, acting governor, judge, and chief justice of Pennsylvania's supreme court. But it was as Indian agent and commissioner of property that Logan made his fortune.

In his role as Indian agent, Logan prospered as a fur merchant. Establishing his own trading post in the province, he resurrected the fur trade with the Lenape—a trade that had gone into decline along with the Dutch and the Swedes after Penn's settlers arrived. The Lenape, too, would soon go into decline, with a good deal of help from James Logan, Commissioner of Property for the Province of Pennsylvania. Penn's ship had scarcely cleared Cape Henlopen before Logan was enmeshed in land deals that would result in the rapid disappearance of the Brandywine band from the Delaware Valley, and more land for eager colonists such as Logan to acquire. The most famous—more aptly, infamous—of Logan's land deals was the Walking Purchase of 1737, in which Logan conspired with Penn's son Thomas to cheat Amerindians in the Forks of the Delaware area out of many thousands of acres of prime land. That may have been the last of Logan's land deals with the Amerindians, since shortly thereafter there were none left in the Delaware Valley, but other dealings almost as unsavory preceded it (Jennings 1986:206–9).

If Logan was lacking in scruples, he was certainly not lacking in taste. Stenton is not only the first example of Georgian architecture in Philadelphia; because of its owner's Quaker restraint and aesthetic sense, it may, in its simple, elegant symmetry, also be one of the most compelling (Figure 7.9). Sturdy brick pilasters accentuate its corners, and the Flemish-bond pattern of its brickwork and the modillions along the cornice beneath the eaves of its hipped roof provide ornamental relief. A staircase and fireplace occupy the spacious center entry hall of the house, and on the second floor above them is the large front

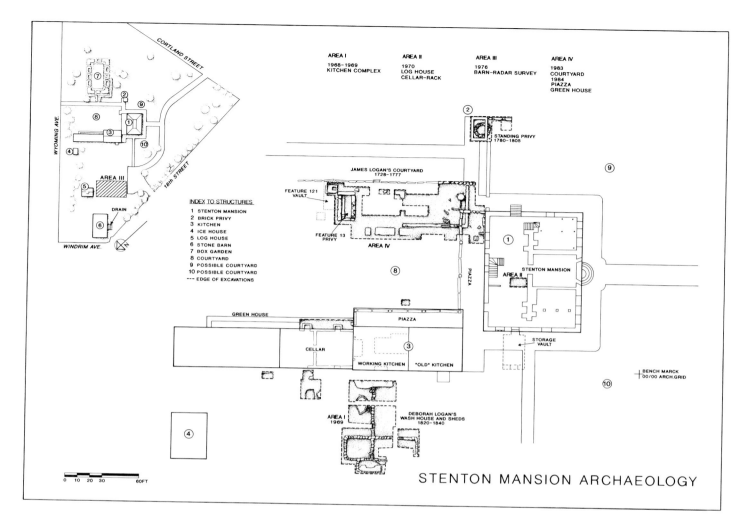

Figure 7.8.

Plan of the grounds at Stenton. (Courtesy of John Dickey)

Figure 7.9.

The mansion at Stenton. (Photo by J. L. Cotter)

room Logan used as a library. Here, no doubt, Logan spent some of his happiest hours, sequestered from the world and engaged in the intellectual pursuits that were his true passion. Fluent in at least six languages and a mathematician as well, Logan had by the time of his death in 1751 amassed a library of some 2,500 volumes, one of the largest and finest libraries in the colonies. Today, the "Loganian Library" remains largely intact at the Library Company of Philadelphia (Bronner 1982:42).

Logan was also greatly interested in plant life and agriculture. That he had a barn standing on his plantation at Stenton by 1724, four years before he built the mansion, indicates the importance he attached to this aspect of his estate (Smith 1976:45). By 1740 he evidently had also built a greenhouse behind the kitchen (Barbara Liggett, personal communication, 1987). Logan's plant experiments at Stenton ultimately brought him to the attention of the renowned Swedish botanist, Carolus Linnaeus (Bronner 1982:42). Although the praise Linnaeus bestowed on Logan's work was not quite as lavish as the praise he heaped on Logan's protégé, John Bartram, it was enough to ensure Logan's reputation as a botanist.

Neither of Logan's two sons shared his intellectual bent, though one of them did appear to share his acquisitive instincts; this was William, who by 1740 was a successful merchant and a leading figure in Philadelphia's business community (Bronner 1982:42; Nash 1986:340). Between 1756 and 1760 William Logan apparently undertook some new construction at Stenton, including building a new privy at the rear of the mansion behind the kitchen and greenhouse (Barbara Liggett, personal communication, 1987). William died in 1776,

and for the rest of the Revolutionary War period the estate was in the hands of a caretaker. During that time, it served as headquarters for both Gen. Sir William Howe and General Washington.

By the 1780s Stenton was in rather run-down condition, and Dr. George Logan, James' grandson, was its master. He made various improvements to the property, which evidently included tearing down the privy William Logan had built and erecting the one that still stands on the property (Barbara Liggett, personal communication, 1987). George Logan inherited not only his grandfather's estate but also his interest in agriculture and plant life. His experiments at Stenton ranged from improving pig feed to improving soil by applying lime and gypsum. He must have become quite noted for his success in these endeavors, for on July 8, 1787, George Washington, a keen gentleman-farmer himself, went to Stenton for dinner and a discussion of methods of soil improvement. George Logan was also something of an inventor; a plow he designed was impressive enough that Thomas Jefferson ordered one like it for his friend James Madison (Smith 1976:45).

In his grandfather's barn at Stenton, George Logan stored barley, buckwheat, oats, rye, flax, timothy, corn, hay, and blue grass. The barn also sheltered his various farm animals—pigs, sheep, cattle, oxen, and horses—as well as his race horse, Eclipse. The night of April 24, 1787, must therefore have been a grim one at Stenton, for the next day, Sarah Logan Fisher, George's sister, wrote in her diary, "Heard this morning that Dr. Logan's barn and stables and 20 tons of hay was burnt and lost last night" (Smith 1976:46). Apparently undaunted, George Logan had by Sep-

tember 17 of the same year replaced the barn with the one that now stands on the property (Figure 7.10).

Stenton remained in the Logan family even as industrial Philadelphia encroached around it. The last member of the family to live there was Gustavus Logan, who, with the estate already greatly diminished, vacated the premises sometime around 1876.

Archaeology at Stenton

Archaeology at Stenton began in 1966 with a feasibility study conducted by students from Temple University under the direction of John L. Cotter. The recommendations that came out of this study prompted the Society of the Colonial Dames to authorize a number of archaeological investigations in ensuing years (Stoddart and Engle 1983).

Investigations of 1968–70

In 1968, in anticipation of the gift of the log cabin that now sits on what is left of the Logan estate, Barbara Liggett and Betty Cosans investigated the site designated for the cabin. They found nothing there to indicate any prior construction.

Between 1968 and 1970 Liggett and Cosans also tested the cellar of the mansion and an area on the north side of the kitchen. The study in the cellar focused on a wooden wine rack Ivor Noël Hume, archaeologist at Colonial Williamsburg, had noticed lying near the foot of the stairs; because restoration at Williamsburg required such an item, he was interested in obtaining more data on it. In the fill beneath the wine rack, Liggett and Cosans found, among other items, a piece of shell-edged pearlware dating from ca. 1810, at first blush suggesting that the rack had been placed there after that date. However, the marks from the rack's original hinges were much like those made by door hinges on the third floor of the mansion; those doors date from 1730 to 1740. So it is possible the rack was built before 1740 and moved after 1810 to its present location. While investigating the wine rack in the cellar, Liggett and Cosans also took the opportunity to disprove a legend that a "secret tunnel" had once led from the cellar of the mansion to the barn. Structural evidence was quite conclusive that no such escape route had ever existed (Liggett 1970d).

In their excavations on the north side of the kitchen, Liggett and Cosans unearthed a complex of stone walls that suggested that the first outbuilding James Logan erected behind his kitchen was a washhouse. He evidently then built a greenhouse behind that and eventually adjusted the floors of these two outbuildings so they would be even with the floor of the kitchen. The washhouse was later removed to allow for the expansion of the greenhouse. Of the 32,039 artifacts recovered in these excavations, about 53 percent consisted of earthenware, about 17 percent were organic materials, and 16.5 percent were architectural items, mostly nails. Given the eighteenth- and early nineteenth-century dates of most of the artifacts found here, it is strange that stoneware accounted for less than 1 percent of the total, as did clay tobacco pipes. Given the social status of the residents of Stenton, it is also strange that porcelain represented only 2.7 percent of the total. Excluding window glass, glass items accounted for 4 percent; most numerous among these items were fragments of spirit bottles (Liggett 1970d).

Investigations of 1975

Having decided in 1974 to restore George Logan's stone barn, the Society of the Colonial Dames contracted with the Museum Historic Research Center of the University Museum to investigate the site. In 1975, in an effort to produce data that would aid in an authentic restoration, a team of researchers (Kenyon et al. 1975; Bevan and Kenyon 1975) excavated an area beneath the barn. They found evidence that a central corridor had once run the length of the structure. They also found that the barn had originally had two doors on its west side, five small doors on its east side opening onto the barnyard, and an upper floor used for threshing and storing hay. The conclusion was that George Logan's barn had been typical of the kind of barn built in southeastern Pennsylvania in the early years of the republic. Further excavation outside

Figure 7.10.

The barn at Stenton. (Photo by J. L. Cotter)

the barn showed that the "secret tunnel" of legend, already disproved by Liggett and Cosans, was, in fact, an arched brick drain. The drain had been designed to channel runoff from the mansion away from the barn so that the water would not undermine the barn's foundations.

Because the Society of the Colonial Dames was eager to have information not just about the barn but also about other areas of the property that might contain significant archaeological evidence, Kenyon and Bevan (Kenyon 1976, 1977a; Kenyon and Bevan 1977) conducted another study at Stenton

in 1975. The object of this study was to determine how effective a ground-penetrating radar device was in detecting subsurface features and artifacts. Commonly known as soil-scan radar, the device was developed by Geophysical Survey Systems to detect thin ice during oil explorations in the

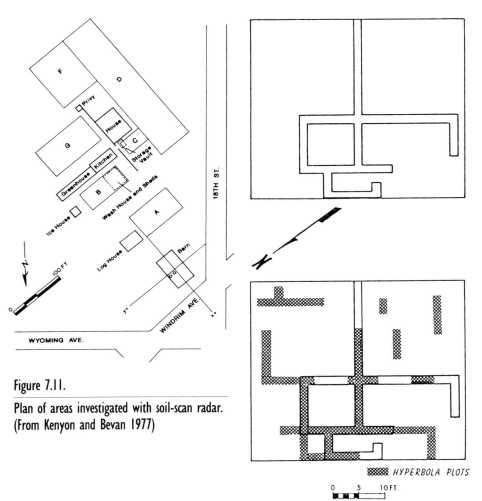

Figure 7.11.

Plan of areas investigated with soil-scan radar. (From Kenyon and Bevan 1977)

Figure 7.12.

Top, schematic diagram of stonewall complex; *bottom,* same diagram with plot of radar echoes superimposed. (From Kenyon and Bevan 1977)

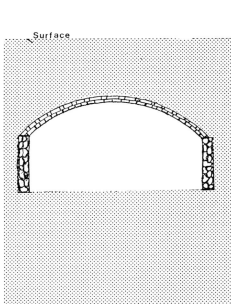

Vault; NE–SW Section

Figure 7.13.

Northeast-southwest cross-section of the underground storage vault at Stenton. (From Kenyon and Bevan 1977)

Arctic. It uses high-frequency electronic equipment, which is dragged over the ground in a cart, to transmit short electrical pulses, or echoes, via an antenna to a graphic recorder. When the electrical pulse exceeds a set threshold, indicating that the radar has picked up an anomalous feature, the recorder notes the length of the signal by etching a vertical line on electrosensitive paper. The device thus produces a profile proportional to the dimensions of the detected features.

To see whether the radar device would pick up such anomalous subsurface features as dense artifacts or wall trenches less dense than the surrounding earth, Kenyon and Bevan tested the equipment in areas where they knew such features existed (Figure 7.11). One of these areas was the complex of stone walls Liggett had excavated on the north side of the kitchen in 1970. The subsurface features detected by the soil-scan radar were congruent with Liggett's graphic plan of the excavated area (Figure 7.12).

Investigations of 1981–82

In 1981–82 Liggett did some additional work at the rear of the mansion, including excavating the pit beneath the existing privy. Built in the late 1700s or early 1800s while George Logan lived at Stenton, the privy itself measured 5 feet by 9 feet and was 8 feet high; the pit beneath it was 6 feet in diameter and 18 feet deep. Near the top of the pit and offset from it, Liggett found a rectangular brick chamber with an opening 1.3 feet wide; she speculated that it might have been a drain for flushing. The evidence from the privy and the area around it led Liggett to conclude that sometime between 1756 and 1760 William Logan dismantled the original privy and built his own, which was in turn dismantled when George Logan built the present one.

Additional excavation along a 50-foot line between the kitchen and the privy revealed the remains of a garden wall, which had apparently run

from near the rear of the mansion to the privy. This trench also revealed two stone foundation walls from unrecorded structures and an underground storage vault that seems to have been in use from about 1730 through 1760 (Figure 7.13). Many of the artifacts Liggett unearthed in these excavations dated from the mid- to late 1700s. The fragments of ceramics found suggest that the Logans preferred those made by Wedgwood rather than those of Liverpool manufacture (Babara Liggett, personal communication, 1987).

Liggett also tested an area abutting the kitchen, which she identified as the site of James Logan's original greenhouse, or "Orangerie." Built on a stone foundation, the greenhouse had apparently had two windows and a door on the side facing the barn, and two windows on the opposite side. Evidence found in the well of one of the windows indicated the greenhouse was built about 1740 (Barbara Liggett, personal communication, 1987).

GRUMBLETHORPE: GERMANTOWN'S FIRST SUMMER HOME

When the number of German immigrants landing in Philadelphia began to increase in 1727, among the first to arrive were two young brothers named Wuester. John, then nineteen years old, changed the spelling of his surname to "Wister," Caspar opted for "Wistar." Caspar, who married the granddaughter of Hans Milan of Wyck, embarked on a career as a glass manufacturer (see Chapter 7, "Wyck").

John became a wine merchant. By 1741, at the age of thirty-three, John was prosperous enough not only to own a sizable house at Fourth and Market streets, but to buy 200 acres of upland in Germantown. Three years later, he built a summer home there at what is now 5267 Germantown Avenue. The first summer home in Germantown, it set a trend that continued into the nineteenth century, as

other well-to-do Philadelphians, fleeing the city in summer, followed Wister's example.

The local folk of Germantown originally referred to John Wister's summer home as Wister's "Big House," presumably to distinguish it from the somewhat smaller tenant house Wister built right next door. In the early 1800s, the whole property became collectively known as "Grumblethorpe"

Figure 7.14.

Grumblethorpe, Wister's "Big House," with the tenant house on the left. (Photo by J. L. Cotter)

when Charles Jones Wister, Sr., John Wister's grandson, named it after a contemporary novel. The fanciful name stuck, and Grumblethorpe it is today.

After John Wister died in 1789, Grumblethorpe passed to his heirs and remained in the family until 1940, when the Philadelphia Society for the Preservation of Landmarks took it over. By then, much of Wister's original 200 acres was gone, and both the main house and the tenant house had suffered the indignities of fashionable "modernization." Nonetheless, the

houses were intact enough to be restored to their original appearances in 1957, and though the double lot behind the houses ended in a railroad right of way, traces of the remarkable garden planted by Wister's offspring could still be seen.

In 1977 the Philadelphia Society for the Preservation of Landmarks invited students from the University of Pennsylvania to conduct an archaeological study at Grumblethorpe, and the following summer another group of Penn students took up where the first group had left off. The report of these studies (Cotter and students 1978a) was the basis for the following account; the historical data in the report were derived largely from Wister (1866) and Jellett (1904).

From Summer Home to Historic Home: A Brief History of Grumblethorpe

Built in 1744, both Wister's "Big House" and his tenant house are in most respects typical of other Germantown houses of that time, although the "Big House" does have a few flourishes reflecting its original use as a summer home. Both houses are made of the local Wissahickon schist, dressed in the front but untrimmed in the rear, and both are relatively unsophisticated in their design (Figure 7.14).

The main house has a frontage of about 43 feet on Germantown Avenue and a depth of about 34 feet, while the tenant house is about 32 feet wide and 28 feet deep. The houses sit quite close to the road, and the area in front of the main one was—and is once again—paved with brick, a luxury in the days before sidewalks. On the paving were some settles, or long benches, surrounded by a red-painted railing that kept wandering cows at bay. The pent eave around the front and south side of the house was intended to provide some protection from the elements. On the second floor over the pent eave at the front, a small door opens onto a balcony. The shingled roof has no dormers; windows on either side of the chimneys in the gable ends provide light for the garret.

The main house has two front doors, both split in the middle so either half can be opened to let in the air; the upper half may also have served to frame a pretty face, for such doors are sometimes called "courting doors." The door on the right is the main entrance, leading into a hall with a stairway to the upper floor. To the right of the hall is the "east parlor," and behind that is the library. The door on the other side of the house opens into the "west parlor," and behind that is the dining room. A wing behind the dining room contains the kitchen and pantry.

During the Revolutionary War, Wister's "Big House" was a center of activity, some of it martial, much of it social. In October 1777 it served as the headquarters of British Gen. James Agnew. According to legend, after Agnew was wounded in the Battle of Germantown, he was brought back to the "Big House" and laid on the floor of the west parlor; there the blood from his fatal wounds supposedly soaked into the floorboards, leaving indelible stains. A year or so after this event, according to a diary kept by

John Wister's granddaughter Sally, the atmosphere at Grumblethorpe was a good deal less morbid. Young American officers were then apparently flocking to the "Big House" and, in company with Sally's father Daniel, playing an occasional practical joke on the more pompous of their comrades (Federal Writers' Project 1988:479).

Charles Jones Wister, Sr., the grandson who named Grumblethorpe in the early 1800s, was something of a Renaissance man. An outstanding horticulturist, a botanist, and a founder of the Academy of Natural Sciences of Philadelphia,* he was also interested in astronomy and meteorology. Unfortunately, he was interested in building as well. Between 1806 and 1808 he "modernized" both the main house and the tenant house in the Federal fashion. Off came the pent eave of the "Big House," and up on the roof went dormer windows. Pebble-dashed stucco covered the schist at the front of the house, and a new door flanked by columns replaced the "courting door" at the main entrance. The other old door gave way to a window. Similar fashionable "improvements" took place within.

The grounds, however, came to life during the tenure of Charles Jones Wister, Sr., and even today show evidence of his work. Ginkgo trees, which he imported from China, still grow in the backyard, a beautiful beech still graces the garden, and wisteria, named after him, still clambers over an arbor. Some of the fruit trees and grape vines he planted were productive for well over a century. His flower garden, originally measuring 450 by

80 feet, had beds of varying shapes edged with boxwood, with picturesque paths wandering through them. The plants that grew there included everything from native wildflowers and herbs to exotic imports. A corner of the property was reserved for a vegetable garden and a berry patch.

During the time Charles Jones Wister, Sr., lived at Grumblethorpe, he added some outbuildings to the property and made alterations to others. Figure 7.15 shows the approximate locations of most of these features. Wister himself noted some of these changes in his "Garden Book," and his son Charles Jones Wister, Jr. (1866), duly recorded them for posterity:

1809: Oct. 5th. Began to dig the ice house (first in Germantown). . . .
1819: Built shop over summer kitchen for clock making and experiments. . . .
1822: Built second barn. . . .
1834: Observatory erected on top of the smoke-house for transit instrument, telescope and astronomical clock.

Among the features Wister, Sr., did not mention were a double-doored stone privy, plastered on the outside, which still stands behind the kitchen; a well near the kitchen door, where the wooden pump can still be seen today (Figure 7.16); another well that served the tenant house; two gazebos, or summer houses, one in the garden and the other near the barn; a carriage house; a cider mill; a chicken coop; a corn crib; and a number of wooden beehives. The beehives were probably scattered throughout the garden. Whatever remains of the carriage house, the barn, and the gazebo near the barn is now buried off the property beneath the pavement of a school yard.

How exactly Charles Jones Wis-

* The Academy of Natural Sciences of Philadelphia was established in 1812. Another of its founders was Reuben Haines, Jr., who moved to Germantown in 1820.

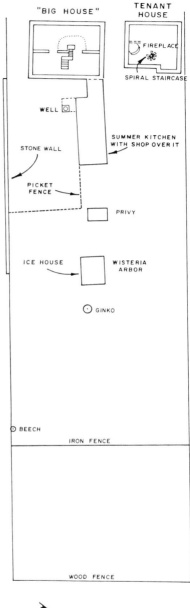

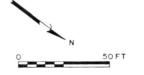

Figure 7.15.

Locations of structures at Grumblethorpe. The land on which the barn, carriage house, and second summer house stood is no longer part of the property. (From Cotter and students 1978a)

ter, Sr., divided his time between his garden, his observatory, and his shop over the summer kitchen is uncertain. It seems safe to assume, however, that he spent a good deal of time in the shop industriously pursuing his varied mechanical interests. The walls of the room were hung with woodworking and metalworking tools of almost every description, antiquated models as well as up-to-date ones. Here the gentleman hobbiest could try his hand at the craft of the carpenter, the blacksmith, the tinker, the engraver, the glazier, the painter, and the clockmaker.

Charles Jones Wister, Jr., evidently inherited some of his father's love of mechanical things. As a boy, Charles, Jr., learned the skill of repairing clocks and watches, and it became one of his favorite pastimes. No doubt his neighbors were partial to this pastime, too, since he cleaned and repaired their clocks and watches free of charge. Charles, Jr., must also have been popular with Germantown's younger crowd, for another of his hobbies was making steel-pointed tops out of non-splitting dogwood. Flung into the ring with artful violence by the expert juvenile top-spinners of Germantown, Wister's tops were known for wreaking havoc on those of lesser quality.

After Charles Jones Wister, Jr., died in 1910, his father's tools remained gathering dust in the workshop until 1925, when Alexander and Owen Wister donated two truck loads of them to the Mercer Museum in Doylestown.* There they continue to make a significant contribution to the museum's collection of "Tools of the Nation's Makers."

When the Philadelphia Society for the Preservation of Landmarks ac-

* Alexander and Owen Wister were the grandsons of Charles Jones Wister, Sr. Owen Wister, well-known author of *The Virginian,* never resided at Grumblethorpe.

quired Grumblethorpe in 1940, it began painstakingly restoring Wister's "Big House" and tenant house to their original appearances. The restoration of the main house, completed in 1957 under the direction of architect George Clarence Johnson, included removing the stucco on the house front, repairing the schist, and replacing nineteenth-century roof slates with hand-split shingles. The pent eave was reconstructed, as were the second-floor balcony and first-floor "courting doors." Windows reappeared in their original sizes with panes of blown glass. Layers of paint on the exterior trim were stripped to reveal the original color, and the trim was duly repainted a brownish red. Inside, the woodwork reverted to its original blue, and eighteenth-century mantles appeared where Victorian ones had been. Antique hardware or hand-forged replicas replaced machine-made pieces. Even the paving was restored to its original appearance, authenticated by fragments of brick found beneath the sidewalk and in the cellarway. By the time the restoration was complete, Wister's "Big House" looked as much like it did in 1744 as careful research and hard work could ensure.

Archaeology at Grumblethorpe

In 1977 Penn students tested four areas of the earth floor beneath the cellar of Wister's "Big House" (Cotter 1977; Figure 7.17). The tests showed no evidence that an earlier floor had lain beneath this one. The fill consisted of clean sand that varied in depth from 3 to 12 inches. This uneven fill lay directly on top of solid Wissahickon schist, indicating that the builders of the house had cut a shelf for the basement right out of the native rock. Remarkably, the well, situated only 18 feet from the rear wall of the cellar, proved to be more than 20 feet deep and at the time of the study contained 10 feet of clear water. Evidently, the rock formation must slope sharply in this area.

In contrast to the cellar of the "Big House," which is unpaved except for a small brick apron near the cellar stairs, the cellar of the tenant house is covered with cemented brick. No tests were carried out there, but the class did record the cellar's unusual spiral staircase. Its center post consists of the trunk of an oak tree, and oak risers are doweled and set into it. Another noteworthy rustic oddity in the tenant house is the untrimmed, round oak log that serves as a mantle over the kitchen fireplace.

Figure 7.16.

Rear of Wister's "Big House." The well appears in the angle of the house and rear structures, with the wood framing of the workshop over the summer kitchen visible to the right. Part of the privy can be seen at extreme right. (Photo by J. L. Cotter)

Tests in the garden revealed evidence of a path 12 to 14 feet inside the fence on the north side of the double lot (Figure 7.17). The path had ostensibly led from the back door of the tenant house to the barn and outbuildings that once stood in the rear of the property. The evidence consisted of a bed of ashes about 4½ feet wide and 2 to 4 inches deep, set on top of a narrower layer of small schist stones. The stone layer ranged from 5 to 10 inches deep, and at a depth of 7 inches it contained a 5-inch iron spike. The spike was very corroded, but it appeared to be hand-wrought; together with a sherd from a redware bowl found in the same spot, it indicated the path had been laid in the eighteenth century.

Documentary research helped pinpoint the site of the ice house that Charles Jones Wister, Sr., built in 1809. In his study of the property in 1904, Edwin Jellett described "an elevated square [as] the site of the early ice house . . . covered by an arbored

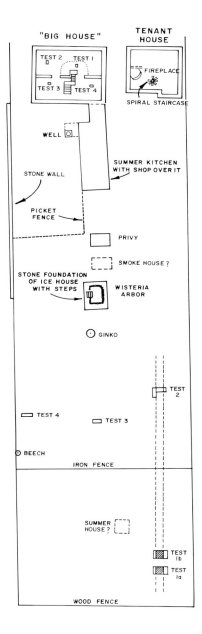

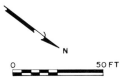

Figure 7.17.

Test locations at Grumblethorpe. (From Cotter and students 1978a)

Figure 7.18.

Plan and profile of the ice house. (From Cotter and students 1978a)

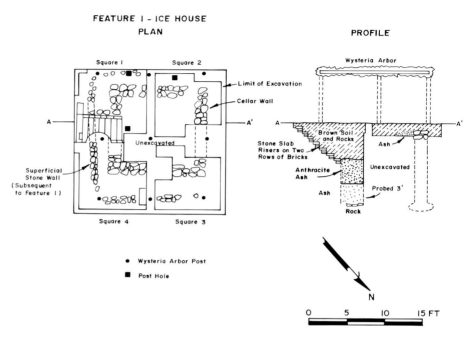

FEATURE I - ICE HOUSE

Figure 7.19.

Steps leading down into the ice house. (Photo by J. L. Cotter)

wisteria tree." When students inspected the area beneath the wisteria arbor in the backyard in 1978, they found the well-mortared stone walls of a structure that had measured 13 by 13 feet (Figure 7.18). The walls were 20 inches thick, and although the area was excavated to a depth of only 8 feet, probing indicated that the walls extended at least 11 feet into the ground and that the floor of the ice house consisted of solid rock. Outside the southeast wall, a stairway made of stone slabs and brick had seven risers descending to a depth of 5 feet (Figure 7.19).

The fill in the stairwell and top five feet of the ice pit consisted of brown soil and rocks. The fill in the next 3 feet of the pit consisted of anthracite ashes and clinkers from a fireplace or furnace. Very few artifacts were found in the fill, but all dated from the late nineteenth century, indicating the ice house was closed and the pit filled at

that time. This date coincides nicely with Jellett's observation that the ice house was no longer in use in 1904, and with an entry in the "Garden Book" kept by Charles Jones Wister, Sr., indicating that in 1853 it *was* still in use; in December of that year, Wister noted that he had "filled the ice house" (Cotter and students 1978a).

The study concluded with recommendations for further testing to locate the other vanished features and outbuildings of Grumblethorpe's double lot. Toward this end, in 1989 the Morven Research Group in Landscape Archaeology conducted extensive archaeological and historical investigations related to the garden sequence at Grumblethorpe (Bescherer et al. 1990). Tests indicated six periods between 1744 and the present and continuous reworking of the garden landscape, with renewed paths alternating in elevation with raised and lowered flower beds.

THE DESHLER-MORRIS HOUSE: THE NATION'S FIRST "SUMMER WHITE HOUSE"

Following in the footsteps of his uncle, John Wister, David Deshler began building a summer home in Germantown in the 1740s—a project he did not actually complete until 1772. Deshler's house was located a few blocks north of his uncle's "Big House," almost opposite Market Square at what is now 5442 Germantown Avenue. It achieved fame as the temporary residence of President Washington in the autumn of 1793 and the summer of 1794. In the 1830s Samuel Morris, a Philadelphia businessman, bought the historic property, and it remained in the Morris family until the late 1940s, when it became part of Independence National Historical Park. By that time, the house had had additions, and additions to the additions.

In 1976, before it began restoring the house to its late eighteenth-century appearance, the National Park Service contracted with Daniel G. Crozier of Temple University to conduct an archaeological investigation of the property. The work that preceded the restoration involved not only excavation but also considerable research into the architectural development of the house. Crozier's report (1978a) provided the basis for much of the following account.

From Summer Cottage to the "First Summer White House": How the Deshler-Morris House Grew

Just when David Deshler began laying the foundations for his house is uncertain, but by 1750 he had erected a modest structure two stories high

and one room deep, with a center chimney. For some reason—perhaps to allow for later expansion or perhaps for privacy—Deshler chose to set this little house back from the road and to have its front facing south rather than looking out on the busy scene in Market Square across the way.

A merchant trading in goods from India, Deshler was by 1772 prosperous enough to be able to add an entire new house to his original cottage. The new house fronted on the main road and connected with the original structure in the rear. Like Wister's "Big House," it was two stories high, with a garret at the top, and it had chimneys and windows in its gable

ends and no dormers in the garret. There, for the most part, the resemblance between nephew's 1772 house and uncle's 1744 house ended. Deshler dressed up the front of his new house with stucco ruled to look like stone, painted its trim white, and gave it a dentiled cornice ornamented with modillions and a classical doorway flanked by Tuscan columns and

Figure 7.20.

The Deshler-Morris House after restoration by the National Park Service. (Photo by Thomas Davies; courtesy of Independence National Historical Park)

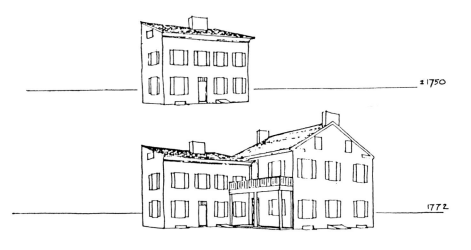

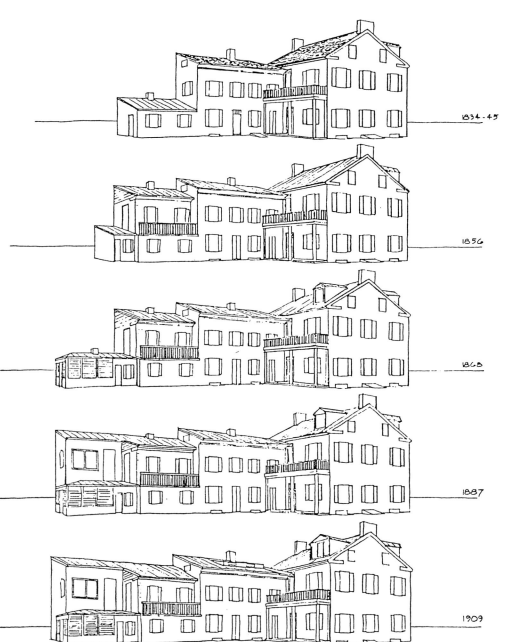

Figure 7.21.

Sketches of the Deshler-Morris House as it appeared in 1750 and 1772. (From drawing by M. Adlerstein; courtesy of the National Park Service)

Figure 7.22.

Development of the Deshler-Morris House, 1834–1909. (From drawing by M. Adlerstein; courtesy of the National Park Service)

topped by a pediment. Such architectural embellishments around doorways were by then fairly common in Philadelphia but rare in Germantown. Figure 7.20 shows the house front after restoration.

Deshler's plan for a center door and hall in his new house was another departure from Germantown tradition; like Wister's "Big House," most Germantown houses of the time had more than one front door. Deshler's center hall widened out beyond the front rooms on either side of it to accommodate a graceful stairway. Running through to the rear of the house, the hall opened onto an inviting little porch at the angle of the original cottage and new house; over the porch was a banistered balcony (Figure 7.21). The woodwork and fireplace mantles in the interior, like the paneled front door and shutters, were the best that colonial craftsmen could produce. The house was equipped with fine furniture, silver, and dinnerware. In the grounds around the house, Deshler planted orchards, vineyards, and gardens.

By 1793 Deshler's house and grounds must have matured and mellowed to an elegant state, for when At-

Figure 7.23.

The Deshler-Morris House in 1885, from the garden. (Courtesy of Elliston P. Morris)

torney General Edmund Randolph was looking for a place to house President Washington in November of that year, it was Deshler's house he chose. Washington had left Philadelphia to go to Mount Vernon in September, as was his usual custom. In September 1793, however, as the yellow fever epidemic raged, his departure from the city caused a good deal of consternation. While Philadelphians felt bereft of Washington's stolid and comforting presence, the man himself fretted at Mount Vernon about whether Congress would be able to reconvene as planned in Philadelphia in December. Physicians said the rains of autumn would quell the epidemic, but the rains never came; a drought that had begun in summer after an unusually wet spring continued through October. The result was a large number of stagnant pools of water, ideal breeding places for the disease-bearing mosquitos. Against the advice of the few officials who still hung on in the temporary capital, Washington set out on October 28 bound for Germantown, where Randolph had secured quarters for him at David Deshler's house. Just as Washington was bidding farewell to his family at Mount Vernon, a fortuitous frost was hitting Philadelphia, causing the epidemic to abate (Miller 1982: 182, 185–88).

The president arrived in Germantown on November 1 and opened his office in Deshler's house the next day. On November 10, a brisk autumn Sunday—again against advice—he rode into Philadelphia to survey the scene for himself. What he saw must

have heartened him, for on returning to Deshler's house he sent out word that Congress should meet as planned in Philadelphia in December. Washington himself left Germantown for Philadelphia in early December (Miller 1982: 188). The next summer, when another, less virulent epidemic of yellow fever struck Philadelphia, Washington returned to Deshler's house with his family. Henceforth, the house could lay claim to being the nation's "first summer White House."

Among the activities in which George and Martha Washington engaged during their stay in Germantown in the summer of 1794 were attending services in a church on Market Square and entertaining Martha's grandson and his schoolmates at tea. The grandson, George Washington Parke Custis, was then attending nearby Germantown Academy, where classes were held year-round. The Washingtons' penchant for sharing their tea with hungry schoolboys came to light in a story told by Samuel Morris's grandson. In the 1860s, as a child of eight or nine, Morris's grandson and his sister had been left alone in the house for a few hours on a summer Sunday afternoon when the doors were left open for ventilation and callers were welcome. One of

their callers that day was an old gentleman in his eighties named Jesse Walm. He told the children he had come to pay a last visit to the little parlor at the rear of the main house where as a boy he had taken tea with his schoolmate Custis and the Washingtons, at the president's insistence.

Samuel Morris was apparently instilled with some of the patriotic fervor and national pride that gripped America in the 1820s. After buying Deshler's historic house in the 1830s, he took exception to the unkempt nature of neighboring Market Square, with its decaying market shed, and in an effort to beautify it had trees and shrubs planted there (Tinkcom 1967: 72). Nor did Morris neglect his own property. After 1834 he added dormer windows to the front of the house and a one-story kitchen at the rear. The kitchen, built in 1839, and the dormers in the front were but the first in a series of additions and alterations (Figure 7.22). By 1856 the kitchen had a second story with balcony, a small one-story washhouse had been appended at the rear, and the doorway of the original cottage had been altered. By 1868 the rear of the main house had a dormer window, and the one-story washhouse had been enlarged. By 1887 the washhouse had a second story. And by 1909 an extension had been built along the north side of the house (not visible in Figure 7.22), and the dormer at the rear of the main house was larger. Figure 7.23, a photograph of the rear of the house in 1885, gives some idea of what the property was like at that time.

Archaeology at the Deshler-Morris House

The limited, specific purpose of Daniel Crozier's archaeological work at the Deshler-Morris House was to ensure

that the restoration of the house to its late eighteenth-century appearance would not disturb any unknown structural feature. The work was directed to designated parts of the site, including a part of the cellar beneath the original cottage and an area just outside the cellar, but it focused mainly on areas cleared when the nineteenth-century additions were demolished (Figure 7.24).

Crozier (1978a) succeeded in uncovering three features. Structure 1, located where the washhouse had stood, was a circular brick pit, mortared on the outside but dry-laid on the interior. It had a diameter of more

than 6 feet, and at a depth of 7 feet it terminated in bedrock (Figure 7.25). Its function was somewhat puzzling. One might expect to find a cistern collecting rainwater near a washhouse, but cisterns usually had mortared brick sides and floors. Also, if it had originally been a cistern, it must no longer have served that purpose after the washhouse was expanded and built over it in 1868. It might then have been used as a cold cellar for storing perishable foods. In any event, when pipes for a town water supply were installed, they weakened the pit to the point of collapse, and a mortared brick arch was built to support

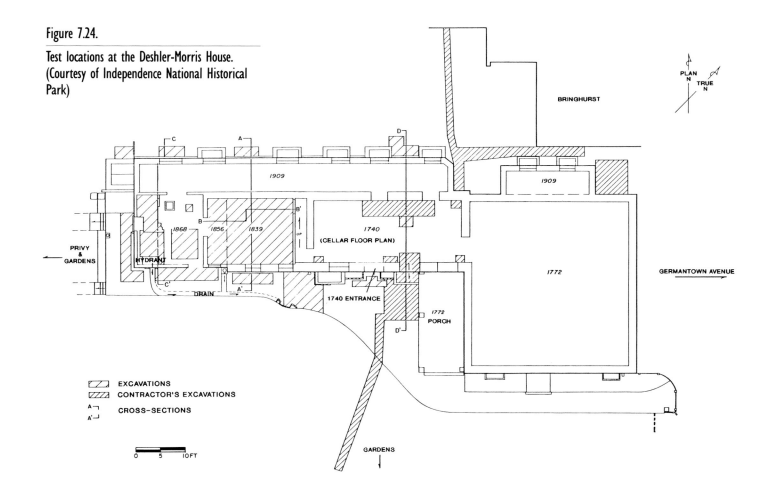

Figure 7.24.

Test locations at the Deshler-Morris House. (Courtesy of Independence National Historical Park)

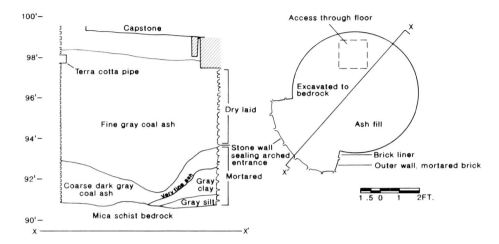

Although Crozier's investigation had a narrowly defined purpose, his findings enabled him to make recommendations for future archaeological studies of the Deshler-Morris House and its grounds. Among these recommendations were the following:

1 Further testing of the garden to determine historic grade and to uncover more of the eighteenth-century garden paths. Definition of the paths would provide an idea of the arrangement of the plantings.

2 Use of electronic sensing equipment to identify additional features.

3 Soil analysis.

4 Investigation of a privy, built in 1884, which still stands west of the house.

5 Compilation of a photographic record of all aspects of the house and grounds.

As always, archaeological work at a historic site is work in progress, as long as the site exists. The Deshler-Morris House currently awaits the implementation of some or all of Crozier's recommendations.

the capstone. After 1909 the pit was used, as abandoned pits usually were, for the deposit of coal ash.

Structure 2 was another circular, brick-lined pit, and although it was not fully excavated, its function seemed fairly clear. Its location between the original cottage and the 1839 addition indicated it had been used as a cistern to collect rainwater draining from the roofs above it. Structure 3 was the base of a brick stove in the 1839 kitchen; its upper part had been removed in 1949 by personnel from the National Park Service. Not surprisingly, given the amount of construction west of the original cottage during the nineteenth century, all the artifacts recovered here were found in mixed deposits and dated from the early 1700s to about 1865.

Crozier also uncovered traces of a flagstone walk buried beneath brick debris in front of the original cottage. The artifacts found in this area suggested that David Deshler had laid this walk at the time he built the cottage. In the garden south of the house, Crozier found evidence of a gravel walk below the level of a nineteenth-century brick path, as well as a trash deposit.

CLIVEDEN: WOUNDED VETERAN OF THE REVOLUTIONARY WAR

Built in 1763–1767, Cliveden was the most elegant country estate Germantown had yet seen, and indeed one of the most elegant in all the colonies. Its owner was Benjamin Chew (1722–1810), an eminent lawyer who from 1774 to 1776 was chief justice of the supreme court of the province of Pennsylvania. Ten years after Cliveden was completed, both the mansion and its master took some hard knocks. An avowed Loyalist, Benjamin Chew was exiled to New Jersey in 1777 (Tinkcom 1982:131), and on October 4 of that year, Cliveden became the scene of some of the sharpest fighting that took place in Germantown that day. Although neither Cliveden nor Chew emerged from the war unscathed, both survived to witness happier days.

After Chew's death in 1810, his long line of descendants lived at Cliveden for more than a hundred and fifty years. During that time, the estate dwindled from its original sprawling acreage to its present six acres of park land at 6401 Germantown Avenue. In 1972 the Chew family presented Cliveden to the National Trust for Historic Preservation. Six years later, plans to restore the kitchen and the cold frames in the garden and to reconstruct a shed that was once attached to the barn called for documentary and archaeological research, and Lynne G. Lewis, archaeologist for the National Trust, carried out a series of excavations. Lewis's report (1979) provided data for the following account, as did Tinckom's (1964) historical treatise on the estate.

Cliveden: Suitable Surroundings for "a Constellation of Beauties"

With the help of a local master carpenter named Jacob Knor, Benjamin Chew began designing the mansion at Cliveden in the early 1760s. What emerged in 1767 was one of the finest examples of Georgian architecture in America (Figure 7.26). Projecting from the front of the mansion is a central pavilion with two pediments, the lower one topping a doorway flanked by Doric columns. The dressed schist, limestone belt course, and heavy modillioned cornice of the facade create an impression of stability and strength, while the uneven line of the chimneys, dormer windows, urns, and pediment along the roof provides a lighter, contrasting note. The rubble of the side walls of the mansion is covered with stucco scored to simulate stone; the rear wall is plain rubble. Furnished with the best of the Philadelphia cabinetmaker's craft and adorned with handsome wainscoting, cornices, and moldings, the interior of the mansion is as elegant as the facade. Separating the center hall from the stairway is a screen of finely fluted Doric columns. The hall, the largest room in the mansion, was probably the most elaborate hall in the colonies (Group for Environmental Education 1984:27).

Behind the mansion are two "dependencies": a kitchen just to the north and another outbuilding to the south

Figure 7.26.

The mansion at Cliveden. (Photo by J. L. Cotter)

Figure 7.27.

Plan of the grounds at Cliveden. (From Lewis 1979)

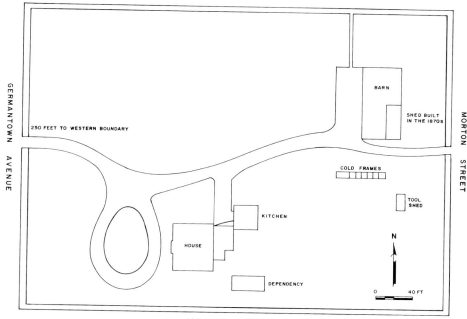

(Figure 7.27). A two-story addition was built between the main house and the kitchen in 1856, and at the same time the barn was enlarged. In the 1870s a shed was added to the southeast corner of the barn. Among the other structures on the estate in the nineteenth century were a smokehouse, a henhouse, a gazebo, and some cold frames.

The gardens Chew planted at Cliveden in the 1760s were destined to become the backdrop of romantic assignations, for as four of Chew's thirteen daughters (he had one son) grew into young ladies, suitors trotted up the hill from Philadelphia hell-bent for Cliveden. In the estimation of Abigail Adams, who observed the Misses Chew at one of Martha Washington's weekly Philadelphia soirées in the early 1790s, they were "a constellation of beauties" (Miller 1982:179). Among the Chew family's memorabilia are some mementos of Miss Peggy Chew's wartime romance with Capt. John André, a dashing British officer who captured the heart of more than one Philadelphia belle during the British occupation of the city.*

---

* Among the other Philadelphia belles who consorted with André and his fellow British officers was Peggy Shippen, great-great granddaughter of the first mayor of Philadelphia. After the Continental Army retook Philadelphia in 1778, the lovely Miss Shippen married the American Major-General Benedict Arnold, who was then serving as military commander of Philadelphia. Through his bride, Arnold met Captain André and embarked upon the double-dealing that would soon earn him lasting notoriety (Tinkcom 1982:143–44). In 1779, with some ill-gotten gains garnered from profiteering in Philadelphia, Arnold bought his bride a magnificent mansion in East Fairmount Park. Known as Mount Pleasant, the mansion was built in 1762 by John McPherson, a Scottish sea captain turned privateer (Federal Writers' Project 1988:552–53).

On October 4, 1777, with Benjamin Chew exiled to New Jersey and the rest of the family absent from the estate, Cliveden became a refuge and fortress for five or six small companies of British soldiers under the command of Lt. Col. Thomas Musgrave. Caught behind the line of Washington's advance down Germantown Avenue toward Howe's forces at Market Square, Musgrave's contingent of about a hundred British soldiers barricaded themselves behind Cliveden's stout walls. In their desperate attempts to dislodge the British, American troops bombarded the mansion with cannon, blowing in its front door and leaving permanent scars on its stone walls. When Musgrave refused to surrender, Continental soldiers stormed the mansion, intent on setting it on fire. Easy targets, they were shot in their tracks, and as the tide of the main battle turned and Washington's army retreated back up Germantown Avenue, bodies of dead Continentals lay scattered about Cliveden's grounds.

After the Battle of Germantown ended, Chew sold, and thirteen years later repurchased and further repaired, the mansion. After the war

ended, Benjamin Chew, despite his Tory sympathies, regained his former prominence in Philadelphia's social and political circles. On May 18, 1787, President Washington himself attended the wedding of one of Chew's daughters. The wedding took place at 110 South Third Street in a townhouse Chew had bought from John Penn in 1771. Chew's next-door neighbor on Third Street was Samuel Powel, last mayor of Philadelphia before the Revolution and a staunch supporter of the revolutionary cause. In 1789, when Powel was again elected mayor, the atmosphere of reconciliation created by the ratification of the federal Constitution was such that even a known former Loyalist such as Benjamin Chew could be elected a city councilman (Miller 1982:167 [amended by Jennifer Esler, Director of Cliveden, by correspondence, 1989]).

Archaeology at Cliveden

Lewis's investigation at Cliveden in 1978 concentrated on three areas: the southeast corner of the barn, where a shed had been built in the 1870s; the cold frames; and the kitchen dependency (Figure 7.28). The shed had been destroyed in the course of the twentieth century, and at the time of the excavation, plans were being made to reconstruct it and put it to practical use. The fill around the southeast corner of the barn where the shed had stood yielded 5,250 ceramic sherds. These sherds ranged in date from the early 1700s to the 1900s.

The 6,566 artifacts found in the vicinity of the cold frames suggested that these structures had been built in the early 1800s and that when they fell into disuse, the spot had become a dump for animal bones and other kitchen refuse. Predictably, most of the 2,321 ceramic sherds found beneath the cold frames were coarse earthenware fragments of flowerpots, but pearlware and whiteware were also well represented, each accounting for 13 percent of the ceramic count (Lewis 1979).

Excavations adjacent to the kitchen produced 65,904 ceramic sherds that dated from the mid-1700s to the late 1800s. As might be expected, most of these domestic discards were of fine quality. Creamware accounted for 36 percent, pearlware for 29 percent, and coarse earthenware for only 19 percent. The pearlware found here indicated that the Chews had a definite preference for the green shell-edged type—an observation confirmed by the ceramic wares that survive intact in the mansion. In this regard, the Chews differed from most of their contemporaries, for green shell-edged pearlware was generally less popular than blue. Lewis found little stoneware of any kind and, rather surprisingly, not one sherd that she could attribute to a chamber pot. Of the 4,581 glass sherds, some were from pharmaceutical and condiment bottles, but most were the fragments of wine bottles.

The only piece of evidence of the hot and heavy fighting that took place at Cliveden during the Battle of Germantown was a solitary gun flint; not so much as a single cannonball or musketball appeared. The most likely explanation for this lack of evidence is that most of the fighting took place at the front of the mansion. Among the other artifacts Lewis recovered were five beads and the fragments of fifteen toys. The toys included seven clay marbles and one glass one, a lead soldier and two lead firemen, and a horse and its rider. In all, the evidence indicated that the Chews, as befitted the conservative and the wealthy, discarded few of their personal possessions, that they lived well, and that they and their servants broke a moderate amount of choice wares.

Figure 7.28.

Site plans of the kitchen dependency and cold frames at Cliveden. (From Lewis 1979)

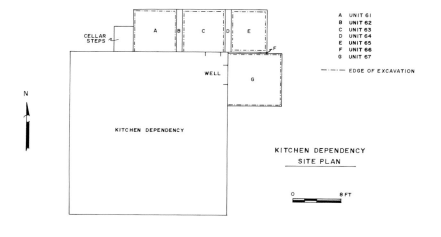

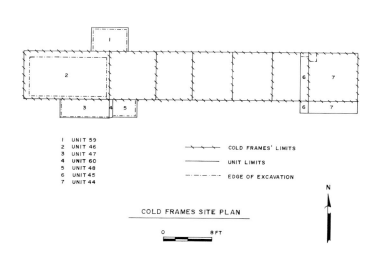

THE STORY OF HOW AN UNKNOWN BRITISH SOLDIER OF THE BATTLE OF GERMANTOWN REGAINED HIS IDENTITY

In November 1985, in the course of renovating an early twentieth-century post office at the corner of West-view and Germantown avenues, construction workers digging around the foundations of the old building came upon a skeleton buried in the muddy earth. They prudently notified the county coroner, who in turn enlisted the services of Alan E. Mann, a physical anthropologist, and Janet Monge of the University Museum of the University of Pennsylvania. Osteological examination and archaeological analysis, coupled with historical sleuthing and good luck, succeeded in identifying the remains as those of an unknown British soldier who died in the Battle of Germantown on October 4, 1777. Rather amazingly, given that more than two centuries had elapsed since the battle, the researchers ultimately were able to discover even the name of the unknown soldier. Among the historical sleuths were Brian D. Crane, a student of historical archaeology at Penn who wrote a thesis on the subject in 1986, and Stephen Gilbert, a high school teacher in Rio, Wisconsin, who, as a dedicated historical researcher of the Revolutionary War, became fascinated with the case when he read a newspaper account of it. Obviously, the researchers' success depended to some extent on a knowledge of the Battle of Germantown.

The Battle

After routing Washington's army in the Battle of the Brandywine on September 11, 1777, and occupying Philadelphia on September 26, Gen. Sir William Howe found himself in a vulnerable position. The city was desperately low on provisions, and Howe's own supplies were still en route to him by sea. Before vacating the city, the Americans had done all they could to ensure that Howe's supplies would not get up the Delaware; *cheveaux-de-frise* were strung across the river,* and determined Continental soldiers waited in forts from Billingsport north to Fort Mifflin and Fort Mercer for the approach of the British fleet. To reduce these defenses, Howe had to deploy troops from Germantown, where he had posted the main body of the army to guard Philadelphia against assault by Washington's army. Howe's own headquarters were at Stenton, while Lord Cornwallis was in command in Philadelphia.

With the British forces stretched thin between Germantown and the Delaware, General Washington decided to take advantage of the situation by launching an attack at Germantown on October 4. Washington's plan called for a two pronged-approach (Figure 7.29). The main body of the army, under the command of Generals Wayne, Sullivan, and Conway, was to march down Germantown Avenue to attack the British center. Meanwhile, three other columns, under the command of Generals McDougall, Greene, and Stephen, were to attack the British right. The center of the British line was near Market Square, but two British light infantry regiments—the 40th and

> * As noted in Chapter 5, *cheveaux-de-frise* were heavy timber crates filled with rocks and chained together across the river. Protruding from each crate was a heavy beam tipped with a sharp iron point.

52nd—were stationed well forward of the British center in present-day Mount Airy. A detachment of pickets assigned to guard these two regiments was posted on the property of Jacob Gensell, an immigrant from Württemburg, at what is now the corner of Westview and Germantown avenues.

With a dense fog enveloping Germantown on the morning of October 4, the Americans had the advantage of being able to come at the enemy under cover. However, as "Mad" Anthony Wayne's troops advanced through Mount Airy, they disregarded orders and opened fire on the sentries who were guarding the 40th and 52nd Light Infantry Regiments. Thus alerted, the 40th and 52nd came forward to engage what they thought was a small American force. Surprised to find themselves outnumbered, they fell back toward the British center, leaving some men dead on the Gensell property. Together with about a hundred soldiers of the 40th. Lt. Col. Thomas Musgrave retreated into Cliveden and held out there against troops diverted from General Sullivan's column throughout the ensuing battle.

Although the diversion of Sullivan's men caused that column to lose some of its momentum, things initially went well enough for the Continental Army. As Greene's column and the main body of the army converged on Market Square, they were actually driving the enemy before them, giving Howe reason to consider retreating from Philadelphia altogether. At that instant, however, disaster struck. Gen. Adam Stephen, having fortified himself far too well with liquor, got lost in the fog, came up behind the American line, and ordered his troops to fire. Thinking they had been out-flanked, the Americans fell back in panic and confusion, and Howe succeeded in driving them from Germantown, thus starting them on their way to winter camp at Valley Forge. The disgraced Stephen was subsequently court-martialed, found guilty of having been "disguised in liquor," as the eighteenth-century euphemism had it, and dismissed from the Continental Army.*

Despite the outcome of the battle, the Americans' conviction that they were on the verge of victory did much for their morale and impressed the French enough that they signed an alliance with the American government the following year. The determination of the attack was also sufficiently impressive to cause Howe to withdraw his forces into Philadelphia, where, as Benjamin Franklin observed, Howe's luxurious lifestyle had an unexpected effect, for the conquered city soon conquered Howe (Van Doren: 1956:585).

Of the approximately 10,000 British and Hessian soldiers and 10,000 Americans who saw action at Germantown, 71 British and Hessians and 152 Americans were initially killed in the fighting. Later, however, as others died of their wounds, the numbers rose to about 500 British

* Stephen, who had served honorably with the British at Fort Duquesne in 1755 and with Washington at Princeton and Trenton earlier in the Revolutionary War, defended himself stoutly at the court-martial, something he apparently continued to do until his death in 1791. A letter to Robert Carler Nicholas dated December 15, 1777, in which Stephen details his defense, is on file at the Historical Society of Pennsylvania. After returning to the Bower, his home in what is now West Virginia, Stephen resumed his role of respected landowner and went on to lay out the town of Martinsburg near his plantation. To this day, West Virginians regard him as a possible scapegoat for the American disaster at Germantown (Nelson 1976:186–94).

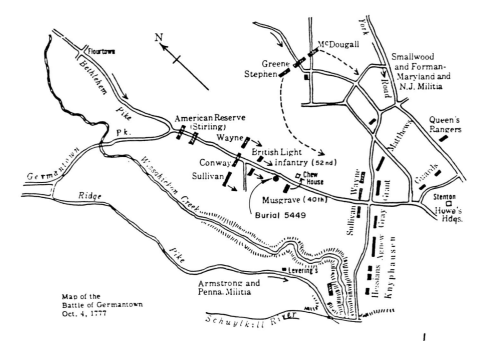

Figure 7.29.

Map of the battle of Germantown. The soldier at the right wears the uniform of a sergeant of the British 52nd Light Infantry Regiment. (Map adapted from Reed 1965:219; figure of British soldier from McGregor and Molls 1975: figure 25)

and Hessians dead and 1,000 Americans (Crane 1986:10–13). Those killed in battle were apparently buried where they fell. Watson (1909) refers to eye-witness accounts of burials of British pickets on the Gensell property, owned in the nineteenth century by Philip Weaver. Similarly, the Reverend Francis Heyl (1917) relates that Major Witherspoon, son of a signer of the Declaration of Independence, was killed by a cannonball on Weaver's property and buried with six other soldiers in front of Weaver's house. Major Witherspoon's remains were later removed to New Jersey (Crane 1986:13).

The Detective Work

The skeleton unearthed on the former Gensell/Weaver property in 1985 lay in an extended position at an angle to the foundation wall of the old post of-

fice building. Both its feet were missing, probably only recently destroyed by the excavations involved in renovating the building. Alan Mann and Janet Monge found four metal buttons along the midline of the skeleton and at the wrists, as well as a number of artifacts in the surrounding soil. The mixture of artifacts indicated that the earth around the skeleton had been considerably disturbed. Mingled with some sheep and cow bones were a number of cut nails; a badly cor-

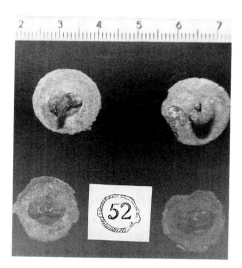

Figure 7.30.

The four buttons found on the skeleton. The inset shows the pattern and number "52," which appeared after the buttons were cleaned. (Courtesy of the University Museum, University of Pennsylvania)

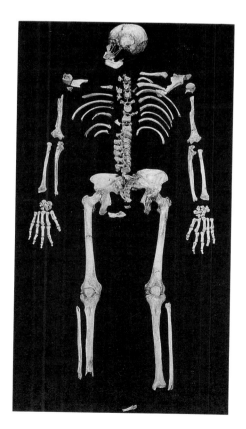

Figure 7.31.

The skeleton. (Courtesy of the University Museum, University of Pennsylvania)

roded metal disk 9.5 centimeters in diameter; fragments of late eighteenth-century earthenware, porcelain, and clay pipe stems; and some nineteenth-century pottery, glass, and machine-made nails.

The four metal buttons provided an important clue to the identity of the deceased. After cleaning them in a solution of dilute acid and removing the corrosion, Mann and Monge were able to discern a design on the buttons. All had a simple pattern around the edge, and the number "52" appeared in relief on the faces of them (Figure 7.30). One of the buttons without the "52" had a white metal shank; the other three had iron shanks. Uniformly 0.9 centimeters in diameter, all the buttons contained lead and a large quantity of tin, the ingredients of pewter—and of British army buttons in the late eighteenth century.

Osteological examination and measurements of the fairly intact cranium and of the fragments of vertebrae, scapulae, ribs, pelvis, and arm and leg bones indicated that the deceased had been male, thirty to forty years old, between 5 feet 6 inches and 5 feet 8 inches tall, and extremely muscular (Figure 7.31). He had suffered from some arthritis, but the bones showed no evidence of trauma or disease that would have caused his death. Here in all probability was a very robust British soldier of the 52nd Light Infantry, one who had endured heavy back packs and slept on hard surfaces in the field.

With this information in hand, Brian Crane (1986) took up the trail. He learned that the 52nd Light Infantry Regiment had been formed only

shortly before it came to America in 1775 and that it returned to England in 1778. He also discovered that the British Public Record Office has a remarkably extensive amount of data on the British armed forces, dating as far back as the seventeenth century. Using some of these data, Frey (1981), for example, had been able to determine that of the four regiments of British infantrymen serving in America in 1782, 48 percent were between the ages of thirty and forty and 13 percent were over forty. Encouraged by these findings, Crane wrote to the Public Record Office in London requesting information that might throw light on exactly who among the overwhelmed British picket died in Germantown on the foggy morning of October 4, 1777. Unfortunately, what came back from London were four pages of information pertaining to a contingent of the 52nd Light Infantry that served in New York in 1777.

Meanwhile, in Wisconsin, Stephen Gilbert had read a newspaper report of the discovery of the unknown British soldier in Germantown. He persuaded a friend in London to go to the British Public Record Office to look up entries for the contingent of the 52nd Light Infantry Regiment that fought in the Battle of Germantown in 1777. Thus the robust, heavy-muscled, British infantryman, dead and forgotten for over two hundred years, finally regained his identity. The records for June 25 through December 24, 1777, revealed that a soldier from a company of the 52nd led by Capt. George Hamilton had been killed on October 4, 1777. His name was John Waite. Private Waite was reinterred in the British plot of Northwood Cemetery at Fifteenth and Haines streets, with military honors and an Episcopal minister presiding, on November 2, 1986.

PART III

Archaeological Sites in the Surrounding Counties

8

Bucks County

PENNSBURY MANOR: PENN'S
ARCHAEOLOGICAL PROBLEM

FALLSINGTON: "THE TOWN TIME FORGOT"

THE WYNKOOP HOUSE: A MODEST DUTCH
DWELLING IN THE HINTERLANDS

TREVOSE, THE GROWDEN MANSION

Bucks County was created in March 1683, when the first provincial assembly voted to divide Penn's colony into Bucks, Chester, and Philadelphia counties (Figure 8.1). Like the other counties, Bucks served not only as a source of food for Philadelphia, but also as the site of various early industries. In 1679 the first permanent European colonists in this area—a group of English Quakers from West New Jersey—ventured across the Delaware to establish a little community called Crookhorne on the Fall Line opposite present-day Trenton. By 1692 Crookhorne was part of Falls Township, one of the recently formed political subdivisions in the lower part of Bucks County. Three miles inland in the northern part of Falls Township, another little settlement was evolving around a meetinghouse English Quakers had built in 1690; this village became known as Fallsington.

Also in Falls Township, but lower down beyond the great bend of the Delaware, was Pennsbury Manor, William Penn's country seat. Although Penn set aside manorial lands for himself and his family in all of Pennsylvania's three counties, it was only in Bucks County that he actually developed an estate. No doubt Pennsbury Manor's access to the Delaware River was a drawing card. From there Penn was able to avoid the bumpy byways of the interior (then little more than narrow Amerindian paths worn by centuries of travel) and commute to Philadelphia by water, rowed along in his river barge.

Not many would-be lords of the manor followed Penn north from the city to the banks of the Delaware in Bucks County; nor, for that matter, did many of them gravitate south to the Delaware in Chester County. Finding the climate of the riverfront not very conducive to comfort or health,

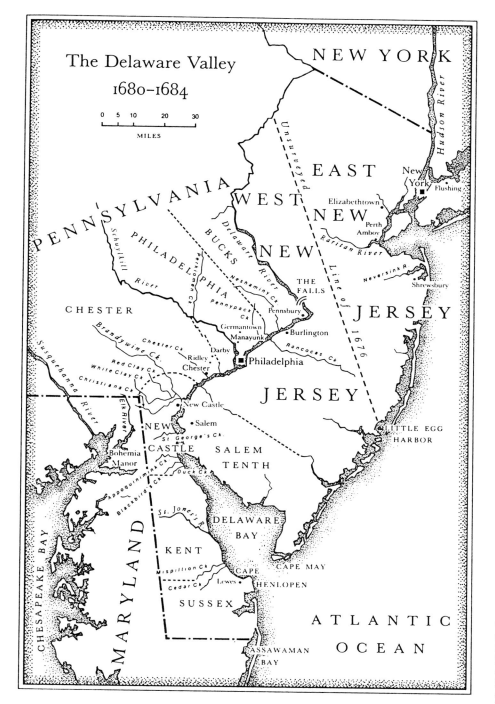

The Delaware Valley 1680-1684

0 5 10   20   30
MILES

Figure 8.1.

The Delaware Valley, 1680–1684, showing the three Pennsylvania counties created in March 1683. (From Soderlund et al. 1983:175)

the majority of wealthy Philadelphians, eager to duplicate the English manor in the Pennsylvania countryside, headed for the wooded elevations west of the city. Thus most of Bucks County was left to the yeoman-types who had inhabited it even before William Penn arrived.

Tax and probate records for the 1680s and 1690s confirm the yeoman status of the great majority of inhabitants not just of Bucks County but of Chester and Philadelphia counties as well. Inventories show that farmers in the counties generally had large tracts of undeveloped land, simple household furnishings, and not much livestock. The nabobs in the city, on the other hand, had "silver spoons, linen cloths, walnut chairs, and black slaves," and they paid almost twice as much in taxes per capita as their country cousins (Dunn and Dunn 1982:24–25).

Except where the Lenape had already done the work for them,* the pioneering farmers of Bucks County had to clear their land of virgin tim-

---

* According to Henry Mercer (1923), the Lenape settlement of Playwicky was located near Langhorne, where Simon Vanartsdalen established a farmstead in 1770. During a historical and archaeological study of the property (Auerbach and Marshall 1983; Lazenby and Landis 1983), an oval-shaped, charcoal-filled trench marked by postholes, together with aboriginal tools and waste flakes, came to light. This charcoal-making feature could have been historic or prehistoric in origin. The purity of the charcoal and the intermixing of clay pipe fragments dating from the late 1600s or early 1700s suggested that it dated from historic times, but its characteristics did not conform to any of the historically documented techniques for making charcoal.

ber before doing any intensive farming. On this fertile land, they grew a variety of crops, among them corn, oats, and potatoes, but wheat was their cash crop (Davis 1876:712). Without these farmers and the foodstuffs they produced, Philadelphia would not have grown and prospered as it did. With their abundant crops, the farmers prospered, too, soon building commodious barns and replacing the log cabins in which they first lived with sturdy stone farmhouses, many of which still adorn the landscape.

As farmers cleared more land, planted more fields of wheat, and built more substantial structures, entrepreneurs erected water-powered gristmills and sawmills along Bucks County's many creeks. As early as 1693, Samuel Carpenter, the wealthy merchant who built the Slate Roof House in Philadelphia, owned shares in some of these mills (Dunn and Dunn 1982:23). Gradually, a medley of craft shops also came into existence.

In the early 1700s, a sizable group of Dutch who had earlier settled in East New Jersey and in New York's Hudson River Valley and Long Island joined the first settlers of Bucks County. They bought land primarily in the southwest part of the county in the townships of Middletown, Northampton, Southampton, and Bensalem. Their presence contributed to the ethnic and religious diversity that came to characterize all of Penn's colony—a diversity that Francis Daniel Pastorius likened to that of Noah's ark (Soderlund et al. 1983:356). English Quakers and Dutch Reformed in Bucks County soon had as neighbors German Lutherans, Welsh Baptists, English Methodists and Anglicans, and

Scots-Irish Presbyterians* (Davis 1876:59–61, 319).

Starting with Penn's probable reason for creating an estate at Pennsbury Manor—and even before—transportation was a key to the development of Bucks County. Over the centuries, the Lenape had created a network of overland paths that followed the most easily navigable contours of the terrain in eastern Pennsylvania. Later, the European settlers, eager to get their produce to market at Philadelphia and Bristol, built roads over these narrow trails. The river, of course, continued to be an important means of transport, and before long, inns and taverns were clustering around the numerous boat and ferry landings on the Delaware to cater to the needs of tired, thirsty travelers. In time, some of these landings developed into villages.

By 1831 the Delaware Division of the Pennsylvania Canal was passing through Bucks County. Built to connect with the Lehigh Canal at Easton and to transport coal to Philadelphia, the canal also gave the farmers in the area more efficient means of getting their grain and other products to market. By 1850, however, Bucks County was no longer a major supplier of agricultural products. Intensive farming had depleted the soil, and overwhelm-

* The Reverend William Tennent, a well-known early Presbyterian in Bucks County, argued—to the distaste of many Presbyterian clerics in the city—for emotion in religion. In 1727, near Neshaminy, Tennent built "Log College," a rustic structure where he trained young men for the ministry. It faded from the scene in 1747 when the Presbyterian synod formed the College of New Jersey at Elizabethtown, an institution known today as Princeton University (Bronner 1982:48; Federal Writers' Project 1988:664).

ing competition was arising in the Midwest, where railroads were enabling pioneering farmers in the fertile heartland to speed their produce to eastern markets. The railroad came to Bucks County, too, initiated by the Philadelphia and Trenton Railroad in the 1830s; the North Penn Railroad between Philadelphia and Bethlehem followed in 1857 (Davis 1876:748, 750, 866).

Like the river that drew Penn to Bucks County in the seventeenth century, the transportation networks of the twentieth century drew middle-class commuters. By World War I, Bucks County's population was fast increasing. It took a jump after World War II, when Falls Township became the site of Levittown and the U.S. Steel Fairless Works; the latter burgeoned and languished in the course of just a few decades. In the 1970s, after Interstate-95 linked Philadelphia with Trenton, Bucks County's population jumped 15 percent. A high growth rate has continued to characterize Bucks County, and today many an old farmer's field is covered with housing developments, suburban shopping malls, and so-called corporate parks.

The archaeological sites investigated in Bucks County, though relatively few, reflect important facets of the area's development. Among them are Pennsbury Manor, the prototype of the wealthy gentleman's country seat; Fallsington, an early Quaker village; the Wynkoop House, an eighteenth-century Dutch homestead; and Trevose, the Growden mansion, one of the few large estates besides Pennsbury Manor to be built in Bucks County during the colonial era.

PENNSBURY MANOR: PENN'S ARCHAEOLOGICAL PROBLEM

Pennsbury Manor, the embodiment of Penn's belief in the goodness of country life, had its beginnings in 1683 and reached its prime about 1700; yet by 1830 only foundation traces remained. Nonetheless, in reconstructed form, Pennsbury Manor, like a few other of Penn's guiding lights, endures. Left in the care of trusted servants when Penn departed for England in 1701, the estate fell into disrepair after Penn failed to return. By the time of the Revolution the manor house was so deteriorated that Penn's descendants had it pulled down, and in 1792 they sold off the land—300 acres, all that by then remained of the original manorial lands (Davis 1876: 192, 787). Among the succession of owners was the Crozier family, who built a house on the foundations of the original manor house in 1835. In 1886 the Croziers sold the estate, and by 1930 it was in the hands of the Warner Company.

In 1932 the Warner Company gave the Commonwealth of Pennsylvania ten acres of land, including the site on which the Crozier house then stood, to be preserved as a memorial to William Penn (Melvin 1940:143). The ten acres have since grown to forty-three, and today—thanks to a reconstruction of the original manor house, outbuildings, and landscape undertaken by the Pennsylvania Historical and Museum Commission in 1933—the site looks much as it did during Penn's lifetime, when forty acres were cleared. The reconstruction was not completed until 1942. Interestingly, Pennsbury Manor was also the focus of a detailed "Historic Structures Report" (Tidlow et al. 1987), perhaps the first such study of a recreated historic property undertaken in this country.

Albert Cook Myers, who did the historical research for the reconstruction, found a wealth of data about the building of the manor but little pertaining to its actual appearance. Here Donald Cadzow, archaeologist for the reconstruction, fared somewhat better, producing physical evidence of such details as the English bond of the manor house's exterior brick. The physical evidence, coupled with the discovery in 1934 of a small drawing of the house, helped R. Brognard Okie, the architect for the project, produce an architectural rendering of the manor house (Figure 8.2). Had Penn seen Okie's reconstruction (Figure 8.3), its eighteenth-century overtones would probably have surprised and delighted him. But, as we shall see, one or two facets of the actual construction impressed him otherwise.

Figure 8.2.

Right, drawing of manor house found on a 1736 map of Pennsbury Manor. (Courtesy of the Historical Society of Pennsylvania) *Below,* architectural rendering of reconstructed manor house, based on 1736 map figure and archaeological evidence. (Courtesy of the Pennsylvania State Archives, Pennsylvania Historical and Museum Commission)

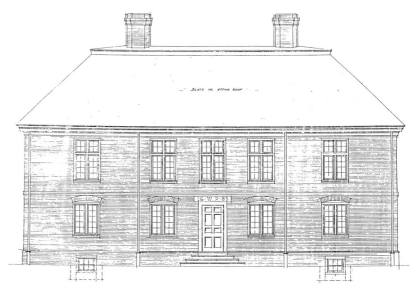

Penn's Country Estate: "A Sweet Place and Retired"

A measure of William Penn's affection for Pennsbury Manor can be gleaned from the documents he wrote in August 1684 as he hurriedly prepared to leave for England to defend his colony's borders against Lord Baltimore's claims. Writing aboard the *Endeavor* just before she sailed down the Delaware, Penn scratched out a brief set of instructions for the provincial council, dashed off an informal will, and quickly penned a rather disjointed letter to his wife Gulielma in England. In the midst of his haste, however, he somehow found time to prepare a detailed list of instructions for Ralph Smythe, the gardener at Pennsbury Manor, telling him how to fence the courtyards, what to plant in "the garden by the house," how to gravel the walks, and even cautioning him to "remember to make both wine and vinegar." Penn's letter to Gulielma also reflects his attachment to Pennsbury Manor, for in this moment of leavetaking, he tells her he would "think well of thy coming and living here [at Pennsbury], where a sweet place and retired is provided for thee and thine" (Soderlund et al. 1983: 387–93).

The idea of a country estate in his new colony seems to have been in the forefront of Penn's mind almost from the moment Charles II granted him a charter in March 1681. A month later, Penn appointed his cousin William Markham to be his deputy governor in Pennsylvania and sent him off with instructions to begin purchasing land from the Lenape and also to look about for a suitable site for Penn's own manor house (Peare 1957; Davis 1876:55). The very first purchase Markham negotiated, formally acknowledged in July 1682 by twelve Lenape leaders, included the 8,400 acres in Bucks County on which Penn began building a large brick manor house in 1683 (Soderlund et al. 1983:155). The manorial lands spread over the Lenape hamlet of Sipaessing, and when Falls Township was created, they occupied almost half of it (Davis 1876:50).

Before building at Pennsbury, Penn apparently had to purchase some of his plantation from a cantankerous character named Thomas King. King had already cleared and fenced some fields, planted a peach orchard, and built a corn crib and one other structure on the property. The latter was probably a barn or house, for it had a key which, to the outrage of Penn's steward, James Harrison,* King kept. That was not the only cause of Harrison's outrage. King also

---

* James Harrison died in 1687 and was buried in the Pemberton Family cemetery, near Pennsbury Manor, on land now occupied by the Fairless Steel Works. The construction of the steel factory in 1950 prompted the cemetery's removal, which was monitored by John Witthoft. Witthoft (1951a:21–31) noted the presence of thirteen graves, all aligned north–south. Most notable were the remains of an Amerindian who had been buried face down after being shot at close range at least four times.

Figure 8.3.

The reconstructed manor house front, riverward view. (Courtesy of Pennsbury Manor)

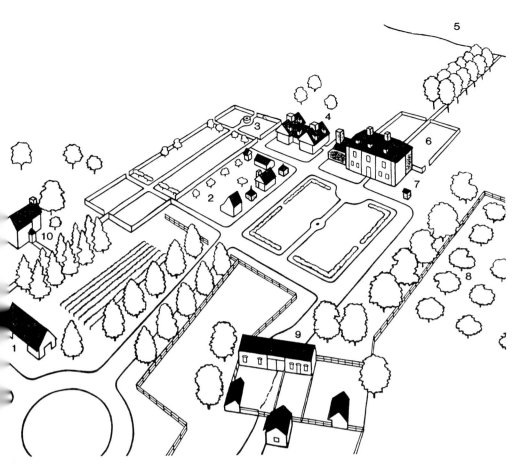

Figure 8.4.

Map of the reconstructed grounds at Pennsbury Manor: *1*, shed for river barge; *2*, outbuildings, including joyner's shop, icehouse, smokehouse, woodshed, and plantation office; *3*, kitchen garden; *4*, "Bake and Brew House"; *5*, Delaware River; *6*, formal gardens; *7*, manor house; *8*, orchard; *9*, barn, other farm buildings, and blacksmith's shop; *10*, house built by the Crozier family in 1835 and moved during the reconstruction. (From a drawing by John Tracy; courtesy of the Pennsylvania Historical and Museum Commission)

destroyed the corn crib and tore down much of the fencing so that wandering cows and pigs could help themselves to Harrison's newly planted crops. "Besides that," the irate and frustrated Harrison wrote to Penn, "he does it in contempt and to provoke" (Soderlund et al. 1983: 351–52).

With such hindrances, progress at Pennsbury Manor was no doubt not as rapid as Penn would have liked. Although he visited the site frequently in 1683 and 1684 to check on the construction, he did not take up residence there until his second visit to America in 1699–1701, and then he did so only in the warmer months when the Delaware was not frozen. As Pennsbury's main thoroughfare, the Delaware dominated the landscape in the seventeenth and eighteenth centuries, and it continues to do so today. The reconstructed house looks out upon the river, with a tree-lined alley leading from the formal

gardens in front of the house to a stone landing at the river's edge. The house has a large center hall dividing the family parlor from the proprietor's parlor and bedchamber. Three more bedrooms and a nursery occupy the second floor, with servants' quarters and workrooms located in the attic and in a first-floor wing. The original hipped roof of the main house had a leaden reservoir, whose leakage was ultimately the ruination of the place (Davis 1876:90).

When Penn left for England in 1684, the manor house and its outbuildings were not yet complete, and in 1685 he wrote to James Harrison urging him to "finish what is built as fast as it can be done" (Davis 1876: 91). He also sent him an English bricklayer, three carpenters, four servants, and a wheelwright to assist with the work. Among the outbuildings Penn wanted Harrison to build were a kitchen, a washhouse, a brewhouse, and a stable for twelve horses.

Copious other instructions followed, including an order to replace the front door of the manor house because "the present one is most low and ugly." The house front no doubt had other embellishments as well, for in yet another letter to Harrison, Penn wrote, "Pray don't let the front be common" (Davis 1876:90–91, 181). The carpentry work for the new front door and other embellishments was probably done on the premises by a "joyner." Among the outbuildings now on the property are an icehouse, a smokehouse, the steward's "plantation office," and a blacksmith's shop (Figure 8.4); they have not been verified, archaeologically or historically.

In Penn's absence, Ralph Smythe, together with several other gardeners, dutifully fulfilled Penn's directives for the grounds. After terracing the land in front of the house, Smythe laid out a broad gravel path from the front door down to the river and lined it with poplars. He also planted the kitchen garden with vegetables, herbs, and fruits, and laid out the formal walled gardens in a geometric pattern; there carefully clipped evergreen shrubs and imported English flowers mingled with the most beautiful of the native wildflowers. Shade trees and an orchard of apple, peach, plum, pear, and cherry trees grew elsewhere on the estate, and paths through the forest offered views up and down the river. Although no landscape archaeology addressing the identification of garden evidence has been done here to date, Thomforde (1986) has listed every plant mentioned in the William Penn correspondence.

The animals on the premises included not only cows, sheep, and work horses but also some fine, well-bred horses Penn brought from England. Although Penn rode his horses about the countryside, he traveled to Philadelphia and other places on the Delaware by water. The river barge he had made for his personal use had a mast and sail, an awning to protect passengers from the sun, and a crew of officers and six oarsmen (Davis 1876:183–84). The voyage to Philadelphia took about five hours.

Although Pennsbury Manor bustled with activity for several years after Penn's departure in 1684, it had fallen into disrepair by the time he returned in 1699 with his second wife Hannah, his twenty-one-year-old daughter Letitia, and his infant son John, born in February, 1700, at the Slate Roof House. John, the only one of Penn's children to be born in America, spent his first two summers at Pennsbury. After refurbishing the buildings and plantation, the Penn family apparently led a very comfortable, if not luxurious, life at Pennsbury Manor. The household furnishings, like everything else about the place, were of excellent quality, although not extravagant. Penn's lifestyle, while less lavish than that of most gentlemen of his rank, was nonetheless far more lavish than the plain style of most of his Quaker contemporaries.

Visitors to Pennsbury Manor, Lenape among them, were frequent, and all were treated with generous hospitality. For his Lenape guests, Penn bought small amounts of brandy and rum and on one occasion ten pence worth of tobacco, even though he thought smoking almost as evil a habit as swearing. The steward bought flour by the tun and molasses by the hogshead. The cellars of the manor house were amply stocked with imported wines. What beer the plantation's brewhouse did not produce was brought from Philadelphia; cider was made from apples grown on the premises. Five-foot sturgeons and a variety of other fish came in abundance from the Delaware. Beef, smoked venison, shad, and pork were imported from Philadelphia, candles from Boston, butter from Rhode Island, and the luxuries of tea and coffee from New York (Davis 1876:93, 180–81).

Penn left Pennsbury Manor in 1701 fully expecting he would one day return and make it his permanent residence. He apparently clung to that notion for several years, for as late as 1708 he wrote to James Logan instructing him to "let William Walton, that comes from Bristol, keep all in order til we come" (Davis 1876:191). Penn, of course, never did return, and by 1709 the place was already beginning to crumble. Within one hundred and twenty years, it would be gone, only to be resurrected some one hundred and twelve years later.

Archaeology at Pennsbury Manor

Comparatively little is known about the archaeological work Donald Cadzow conducted under the aegis of the WPA at Pennsbury Manor between 1932 and 1936. Like some other archaeologists of the 1930s,

Cadzow was apparently of the opinion that a reconstruction based on the excavated evidence obviated the need for a detailed report. In any event, he never produced one. However, some information on Cadzow's excavations is available from other sources (Steinmetz 1932; Anonymous 1934, 1938; Myers 1937; Okie 1941; Weaver and Kolb 1983a, 1983b).

According to these secondary sources, Cadzow not only uncovered the 60-by-40 foot foundations of the original manor house, which are recorded on engineering drawings; he also found evidence of the English bond pattern of the exterior brick, the remains of fireplaces and a bake oven, and a great deal of hardware for windows and doors, as well as many nails. Just east of the manor house, he located the site of the "Bake and Brew House," where interior drains and an iron hoop from a ripening vat also came to light. Cadzow may well have missed numerous small artifacts, since footage of the project contained in the State Archive film, *The Beginnings of the Commission's Historical Restorations*, shows that he screened some of the excavated fill with a coarse mesh. It is also possible that he unearthed Amerindian artifacts predating William Penn's ownership of the land, but no evidence, either physical or documentary, remains to attest to any such discovery.

The lack of information on Cadzow's work at Pennsbury in the 1930s prompted the Pennsylvania Historical and Museum Commission to sponsor another archaeological investigation of the site in 1978. The purpose of this work, carried out by Becker (1978b), was to locate evidence not only of Penn's outbuildings, paths, and roadways, but also of Amerindian occupation of the site. Although test trenches dug near the house produced no traces of old structures, paths, or roads, they did demonstrate that the reconstruction of the terraced land in front of the house accurately reflected the topography of 1700. Becker also unearthed a fairly large number of artifacts dating from the time of William Penn through to the twentieth century. However, the mixed contexts in which all the artifacts appeared limited their usefulness in interpreting the history of the site.

Excavations undertaken at Pennsbury Manor by Kardas and Larrabee in 1986 fared somewhat better. A series of excavation trenches placed in the front and back yards of the Manor House revealed intermittent evidence of an intact seventeenth- and/or eighteenth-century living surface that escaped the massive landscaping activities undertaken in the 1940s. In addition to the recovery of several hundred artifacts, mostly bits of ceramic and glass, Kardas and Larrabee's excavations also revealed "a rectangular pit or bed. . . , a clay walkway or walk foundation, gravel paths, and brick concentrations," all also in all likelihood dating to the 1680–1730 time period. Several prehistoric artifacts were also found, including one Late Woodland grit-tempered, incised potsherd (Kardas and Larrabee 1986:63–64).

The only evidence of aboriginal oc-cupation Becker (1978b) found in his inspection of the fields around the manor was a fragment of a banner-stone—a type of ground stone with a hole drilled through it that Amerindians of the Archaic and Transitional periods used to weight their atlatls, or spear-throwers (see Figure 1.6). This artifact, which appeared between the orchard and the house, predated any Lenape occupation of the site by at least two thousand years.

In 1981 Cushman and Roberts undertook another archaeological investigation at Pennsbury Manor. Like Becker, they were interested in locating evidence of prehistoric Amerindians or of the Lenape who lived at the historically documented village of Sipaessing before William Penn bought their land. Although Cushman and Roberts closely inspected the surface of fifty-seven cultivated acres and excavated nine test units, they found no subsurface features and slightly less than two dozen Amerindian artifacts. The artifacts included waste flakes of flint, jasper, quartz, and quartzite, pieces of projectile points, and a large flake of quartz-ite that showed signs of heavy wear (Cushman and Roberts 1981:54–56). None of these artifacts unequivocally demonstrated Lenape occupation of the site. Likewise, investigations con-ducted by Jordan and Lazenby (1983) in cultivated fields about 2,000 feet west of Pennsbury failed to turn up any evidence of the Lenape although, again, sparse evidence of earlier Amerindians was found.

The failure of these researchers to find evidence of the Lenape may indicate that Sipaessing was located farther from Pennsbury Manor than historical records suggest. However, the mixed contexts noted in Becker's study make it quite clear that the excavations and reconstruction of the 1930s caused subsurface disturbance in the area around Pennsbury Manor, and evidence of Sipaessing could have been a casualty of that disturbance. Archaeological excavation, like any disturbance of the earth, may uncover evidence of the past, but in doing so it also destroys the integrity of that evidence. If an adequate record is not made as archaeological work progresses, the result will be a loss to scholarship, regardless of how authentic the reconstruction of a historic site may be and of how much archaeology contributed to it. Although Cadzow produced numerous letters and memoranda providing minimal information on his findings (Tidlow et al. 1987), he regrettably failed to produce a unified or formal report on the results of his work.

FALLSINGTON: "THE TOWN TIME FORGOT"

Four miles from Pennsbury Manor in the northern part of Falls Township is the historic village of Fallsington. Before 1690, when a group of English Quakers built a meetinghouse there, Fallsington was probably nothing more than a scattering of log cabins.

The quiet little community that began growing up around the meetinghouse no doubt experienced some excitement in the summers of 1700 and 1701, for during his sojourns at Pennsbury Manor William Penn attended services there.

During the next hundred years, Fallsington developed along much the same lines as many other Bucks County towns, with stone houses replacing the first log structures and craftsmen settling in to supply the needs of the farmers in the neighboring countryside. In the nineteenth century and on into the twentieth, Fallsington remained a quiet village outpost, well removed from the urban centers of Philadelphia and Trenton. By the early 1950s, however, it was feeling the pressure of suburban development. Three miles to the south, Levittown had arisen, a phenomenon that helped the population of Falls Township skyrocket from about 3,000 in 1950 to 29,082 in 1960 (DeCunzo and Sanford 1978).

In 1954, to preserve the village's historic core from encroaching development, a group of concerned citizens founded Historic Fallsington, Inc. This organization has since acquired and restored several of the village's historic buildings, some of which now operate as museums. Soon after its formation, Historic Fallsington, Inc., rescued its first property—an eighteenth-century dwelling known as the Burges-Lippincott House—from possible demolition. Six years later it purchased the eighteenth-century Stage Coach Tavern, and by 1969 it was the owner of four more properties, including the Moon-Williamson House, a log cabin built about 1685, and the Gambrel Roof House, built as a Quaker meetinghouse in 1728. In 1972 Fallsington was declared a historic district and placed on the National Register of Historic Places.

Today, as the traveler from Philadelphia enters Fallsington after having passed miles of suburban sprawl to get there, the transition is abrupt and startling. Fallsington does indeed seem to be, as the brochure of Historic Fallsington, Inc. describes it, "the town time forgot." Despite the many miles of new and used car lots, shopping malls, and fast food restaurants on nearby Route 1, one can easily imagine eighteenth- and nineteenth-century travelers happily pulling up at the Stage Coach Tavern.

Figure 8.5.

Fallsington's third meetinghouse, constructed in 1789. (Courtesy of LuAnn DeCunzo and Douglas Sanford)

Over the years since its inception, Historic Fallsington, Inc., has sponsored several archaeological investigations. In 1978 its board of trustees accepted the proposal of Lu Ann DeCunzo and Douglas Sanford, then students in the Department of American Civilization at the University of Pennsylvania, to conduct an archaeological feasibility study of the community. DeCunzo and Sanford's report (1978) provided the basis for the following account.

History of Fallsington

The Quaker meetinghouse around which Fallsington first grew was built on land Samuel Burges gave to the Falls Meeting in the late 1680s. On April 3, 1689, the meeting agreed to build a structure 25 feet long and 20 feet wide, but just where on Burges's gift of six acres the notes of the meeting do not specify. Six months after having ordered 25,000 bricks for the building, the meeting

learned that the bricks were of inferior quality. The Friends thereupon cancelled the order and hired a carpenter to build the entire structure of wood.* The carpentry work cost £41 and was paid for partly in wheat, worth 9s/3d a bushel (Davis 1876: 105). Completed in July 1690, the wooden meetinghouse had a first floor gallery with bannisters and a chimney lined with sawn boards (DeCunzo and Sanford 1978). Later, the members of the meeting built an 18-by-20-foot stable to shelter their horses in bad weather.

* The Friends' refusal to use the inferior bricks contrasts with later practice in Philadelphia. In the 1800s, builders in Philadelphia often used poorly fired bricks in interior masonry and masked them with a veneer of better ones, a practice that threatens the integrity of many old buildings in the city today.

Figure 8.6.

Map of Fallsington village: *1*, Gillingham's General Store, now the headquarters of Historic Fallsington, Inc.; *2*, Burges-Lippincott House; *3*, house built by John Merrick in 1788; *4*, Hough House; *5*, Gambrel Roof House, the village's second meetinghouse, built in 1728; *6*, schoolmaster's house, built in 1758; *7*, third meetinghouse, built in 1789; *8*, fourth meetinghouse, built in 1841; *9*, Stage Coach Tavern; *10*, three Federal houses, built ca. 1830; *11*, Episcopal church, built in 1876; *12*, library, built in 1879; *13*, the "Manor House," front section added to older (ca. 1700) rear section in 1816; *14*, the Moon-Williamson House. (Courtesy of Historic Fallsington, Inc.)

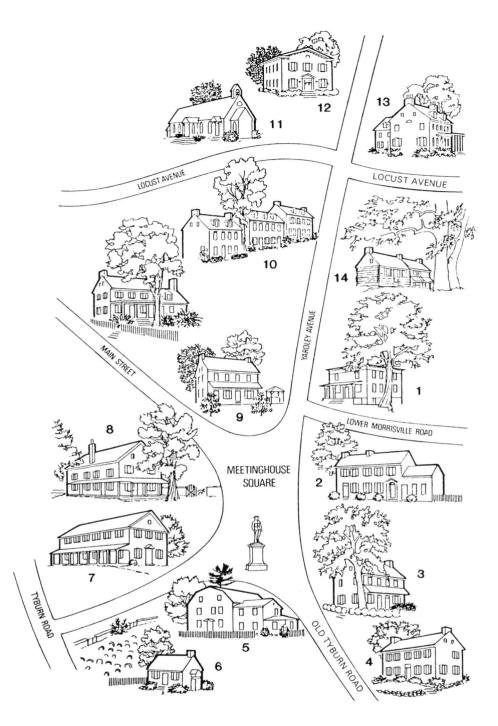

Although the wooden meetinghouse of 1690 no longer stands, three of its successors do. By 1728 the Falls meeting had outgrown the 1690 meetinghouse, and at the cost of £1,000 it built a new one of stone. The old wooden one was soon thriftily converted to a school. The second meetinghouse probably acquired its gambrel roof in 1758 when the meeting repaired it. In the same year, the meeting also built a small stone house for its schoolmaster. By 1789 the meeting had outgrown the gambrel-roofed meetinghouse, and it built a third one, shown in Figure 8.5.

Disagreement over doctrinal matters within the Society of Friends led to the construction of a fourth meetinghouse in 1841. In 1827 the society had experienced the "Hicksite-Orthodox Separation," a schism not mended until recent years (Wainwright 1982: 296). Led by Elias Hicks, the traditional Hicksites objected to what they perceived as the Friends' reliance on the Bible rather than on inner light as the primary spiritual source. In

1841 the Hicksites of Fallsington built their own meetinghouse almost next door to the one dating from 1789 (Figure 8.6). The 1841 meetinghouse is still in use, while the 1789 one serves as a community center. The 1728 gambrel-roofed meetinghouse, which over the years served as a boarding school, day school, library, and dental parlor, was converted to apartments in 1940.

How much of a settlement existed around the meetinghouse that Fallsington's first settlers built is uncertain. No doubt, however, whatever structures existed in the vicinity before 1690 looked much like the Moon-Williamson House, shown in Figure 8.7. Built in two sections, the older part, in the front, dates from about 1685 and with its log construction shows a Swedish influence; the addition in the rear is typical of the frame dwellings of early English settlers. The house derives its name from Samuel Moon, a carpenter who bought it in 1767, and from Miss Mary Williamson, who owned it in the 1870s and bestowed on it some Victorian touches, removed in restoration.

The Moon-Williamson House is a rare specimen of the log dwellings built by early settlers in the Delaware Valley. As communities developed and farmers and craftsmen prospered, most log cabins gave way to stone houses. Stone houses were not, however, the only harbinger of development in Falls Township. Roads were soon leading from the Falls of the Delaware to the meetinghouse at Fallsington and connecting mills and artisans' shops with the ferry to New Jersey. In 1766 Daniel Burges, one of Samuel Burges's descendants, contributed to Fallsington's development by subdividing his land and selling it off as one-acre town lots.

One of the first owners of Burges's subdivided land was John Merrick, a cordwainer by trade. In 1768 Merrick bought a two-acre village tract that contained a small stone house, and by 1781 he was operating a tannery at the rear of the premises. About 1783, when one of his daughters married a man named Jessie Hough, Merrick enlarged the house (Figure 8.8), and in 1788 he built another one next door. By the 1790s he was prosperous enough to purchase house lots just northwest of the tannery for his other three daughters and their husbands.

When John Merrick died, his son-in-law Jessie Hough took over the operation of the tannery, which was owned and run by Merrick's descendants until it went out of business in the 1860s. The next-to-last owner was Joseph Howell, who oversaw the business from his home in Trenton, a little over three miles away. When Howell died in 1853, the estate of two stone houses and "all the old tannery

Figure 8.7.

The Moon-Williamson House, dating from about 1685. (Courtesy of LuAnn DeCunzo and Douglas Sanford)

Figure 8.8.

The Hough House. The smaller section was built before 1768. John Merrick added the larger section about 1783. (Courtesy of LuAnn DeCunzo and Douglas Sanford)

buildings, waggon house and stabling thereunto belonging" passed to his son Eseck. Eseck lived in Fallsington, but not at either of the two houses he inherited. Amassing a considerable fortune as a banker, he lived at the so-called Manor House, one of Fallsington's most gracious old homes, until his death in 1887.

Although Fallsington was a quiet backwater during the nineteenth century, it was at the same time a busy, self-sufficient little community. Coaches traveling between Philadelphia and Trenton made regular stops at the Stage Coach Tavern, as did farmers from upper Bucks County en route with their produce to boat landings along the Delaware. Established in 1798 in an old stone house on Fallsington's Meetinghouse Square, the Stage Coach Tavern became known after the Civil War as the National Hotel. Another active nineteenth-century establishment just off Meetinghouse Square was Gillingham's General Store; this emporium was also the village's post office. The community boasted three blacksmiths, three wheelwrights, a carriage painter, a broom maker, a cordwainer, various cabinetmakers and milkmen, and a library founded in 1800 with a total of 238 volumes. The Fallsington Library Company housed its books in different village homes until 1879, when Isaiah Williamson, a local farmboy who made his fortune as a Philadelphia merchant, donated money to erect a library building.

For a small village, Fallsington has an extraordinarily diverse collection of architecture. The fine Georgian doorway of the Burges-Lippincott House was probably the work of Joseph Kelly, a carpenter who owned the property at the end of the 1700s. Built before the Revolutionary War by a descendant of Samuel Burges, the house

was enlarged in the 1830s when Dr. Henry Lippincott added a small office to it. The Federal style made its appearance late in Fallsington, at about 1830, when a master carpenter built three townhouses along Yardley Avenue. Greek Revival houses began appearing after 1850, followed by houses built in the Victorian Gothic style. An 1876 Episcopal church is an interesting example of "cottage Victorian," while the library built in 1879 shows the lingering influence of the Classical Revival.

Archaeology at Fallsington

Although DeCunzo and Sanford (1978) evaluated forty-six sites in and around Fallsington's historic district for future research and archaeological potential, they spent most of their time testing two particular sites. The first was the presumed site of the meetinghouse of Fallsington's early settlers, built in 1690. The minutes of the meeting suggested that the meetinghouse had been built right next to the original burial ground off Meetinghouse Square. In the east wall that surrounds that burial ground, De-Cunzo and Sanford found pockets for construction beams. Although systematic probing of this area at 3-foot intervals failed to reveal any conclusive pattern, testing of a nearby area did reveal what appeared to be more than half the foundation walls of an 18-by-14-foot building.

The second site tested was in the rear of the Hough House, where John Merrick and Jessie Hough operated a tannery in the late 1700s; other of Merrick's heirs continued the operation until the 1860s. Although the account books kept by Merrick's descendants provide some valuable in-

formation about the tannery, they throw little or no light on the physical appearance of the tannery's structures and equipment. However, an inventory of the property made in the early 1790s lists a currying shop, a beam house, where hides were dehaired with beaming knives, a bark mill, and a drying shed, as well as a variety of tools and equipment, including stoves, oil jars, currying knives, and fourteen vats. A description of Fallsington written in her remarkably active old age by Louise Watson White (1859–1955), a Fallsington native, mentions "an old tanyard filled with row upon row of vats with passageways between" and a long shed for drying hides. Still evident in the yard, though now encased in concrete and surrounded by loose fieldstones, is the spring that provided water for the tannery.

Archaeological investigation of the tannery site could establish only the ruins of a 23-by-18-foot stone structure and a series of impressions in the earth in a low-lying area 220 feet east of the Hough House. The impressions appeared to have been made by a row of four vats. The area around these impressions was evidently used as a dump for household trash even while the tannery was in business; here, beneath layers of rubble, loam, and fill containing numerous artifacts of the late 1800s and early 1900s, DeCunzo and Sanford found fragments of lead-glazed earthenware, slipware, and gray salt-glazed stoneware dating from the late 1700s or early 1800s. Another test in this area revealed a layer of planks or boards; lying about 2½ feet from the surface, they could have served as the flooring beneath a vat.

DeCunzo and Sanford concluded their study by making a detailed set of recommendations for future archaeological research to the trustees of Historic Fallsington.* They recommended an interdisciplinary approach to the research, including taking into account oral history, as told by long-time Fallsington residents, and the

* In 1982, four years after she and Sanford concluded their study of Fallsington, DeCunzo became executive director of Historic Fallsington, Inc. Under her direction, the archaeological program at Fallsington was innovative and active. In 1985, when the organization was planning a major rehabilitation of the 1728 Gambrel Roof House, DeCunzo directed a summer staff of over forty volunteers in excavating test areas around the house and in the cellar beneath it. The local teenagers and senior citizens who made up most of the staff also processed the artifacts they recovered (LuAnn DeCunzo, personal communication, 1985).

study of documents, houses, and artifacts as a means of understanding the traditional crafts practiced in pre-industrial Fallsington. Their proposal also specified the requirements of a thorough investigation of the tannery site.

In 1986, Kardas and Larrabee conducted limited archaeological investigation at the Moon-Williamson House. A series of archaeological trenches and smaller shovel tests placed on all four sides of the house revealed a partially intact yard deposit dating to the late eighteenth century, as well as a nineteenth-century flagstone walkway and a twentieth-century brick walk (Kardas and Lar-

rabee 1986:45, 51–52). Nearly all recovered artifacts dated to the late eighteenth and early nineteenth centuries. They were not sparse, averaging more than 11 per square foot of excavated area, reflective, no doubt, of the intensive use of the farm dwelling early on in its history (Kardas and Larrabee 1986:39, 52). As is common at such historic properties, most of the artifacts were ceramic and glass fragments, with a few clay pipe fragments and nails also found. A brass ring and stamped copper buckle, both dating to the late eighteenth century, and two stone projectile points, both dating to the Archaic period, rounded out the Moon-Williamson artifact collection.

THE WYNKOOP HOUSE: A MODEST DUTCH DWELLING IN THE HINTERLANDS

Built sometime between 1727 and 1739, the Wynkoop House stood at the intersection of Holland Road and Route 332 near Richboro in Northampton Township until 1958—a stone testament to a Dutchman's desire to bestow an air of permanence on his settlement in the wilderness of Bucks County. The Dutchman in question may have been Gerardus Wynkoop, or it may have been his son and namesake, the second Gerardus Wynkoop, or it may have been his grandson Nicholas—or possibly all of them together. In 1739 Nicholas built a rather grand stone house known as Vredens Hoff less than a quarter of a mile away from the earlier structure. Both houses passed out of the Wynkoop family, and during the nineteenth and twentieth centuries, they

were owned by at least twelve different parties. Vredens Hoff (meaning Verdant Court) burned down in 1911, but the Wynkoop House hung on, remaining in relatively good shape until the late 1930s. By the mid-1950s, however, it was in such bad shape that it had become a public hazard, and in 1958 it was pulled down.

In 1976–77, at the request of Joseph A. Fleuhr III, who had acquired the site and wished to learn more about its history before he built on it, students from Bucks County Community College, under the direction of Lyle L. Rosenberger, excavated the cellar of the Wynkoop House. Rosenberger's report (1977) provided data for the following account.

History of the Wynkoop House

The first Gerardus Wynkoop, also known as Garret Wynkoop, was one of the fairly large number of Dutch settlers who migrated from East New Jersey, Long Island, and the Hudson River Valley to the southwest part of Bucks County in the early 1700s. His father, Cornelius, had immigrated from the Netherlands to New York in the seventeenth century. When Gerardus arrived in southeastern Pennsylvania with his wife and children in 1717, it was still a frontier land where Lenape roamed the thick virgin forests. First settling in an area that is now part of Montgomery County, Gerardus moved to Northampton Township in Bucks County in 1727,

THE WYNKOOP HOUSE

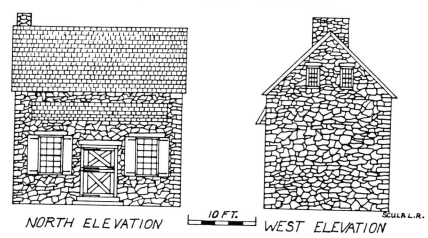

NORTH ELEVATION   10 FT.   WEST ELEVATION

SCUL R. L.R.

Figure 8.9.

The Wynkoop House. (From Rosenberger 1977)

Figure 8.10.

Archaeological features at the Wynkoop House: *A,* cellar; *B,* chimney base; *C,* stone steps; *D,* concrete slab; *E,* stone pile; *F,* foundation of cistern or outbuilding. (From Rosenberger 1977)

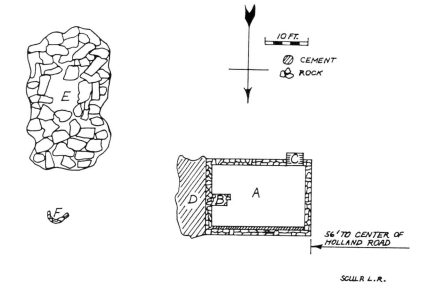

10 FT.

CEMENT

ROCK

56' TO CENTER OF HOLLAND ROAD

SCUL R. L.R.

where he bought from Edward Weston 521 acres of land along Neshaminy Creek. What sort of house he built after taking possession of the land is unknown; it could have been a log cabin, or it could have been the stone dwelling that became known as the Wynkoop House. In any event, in 1738 he conveyed 260 acres of his tract to his grandson Nicholas, the offspring of the second Gerardus Wynkoop (Davis 1876:358). There Nicholas proceeded to build Vredens Hoff.

The second Gerardus Wynkoop achieved a certain amount of fame in local circles as an ardent advocate of the revolutionary cause. But of all the Wynkoops, the best known was Nicholas's son Henry, who by the age of forty had become a respected judge

in the Bucks County court system. Henry was born in 1737, two years before his father built Vredens Hoff, and according to local tradition, his birthplace was either the Wynkoop House or a nearby log cabin. Like his grandfather, Henry was dedicated to the Revolution. A lieutenant in the Continental Army, he was also involved in the political meetings that preceded the Declaration of Independence in Philadelphia in 1776 and

a member of the first U.S. Congress that met in New York in 1789. He is said to have been a personal friend of such luminaries as Washington and Hamilton (Davis 1876:358). No doubt Henry did his entertaining not at the modest Wynkoop House but at his father's more regal manse.

The Wynkoop House was a simple structure (Figure 8.9). Measuring 24 feet 6 inches by 18 feet 9 inches, it had one large room on each of its two floors. The chimney was located on the east wall, and each floor had a fireplace. The house had a full cellar, and its pitched roof was covered with wooden shingles. The exterior fieldstone and red sandstone were laid in a random pattern, although all lintels and corner quoins were carefully dressed in rectangular shapes. The house exhibited certain Dutch characteristics, such as a double-hung door whose top and bottom sections could swing independently of each other, a full cellar, and one room per floor, but it was not classically Dutch in character. A shed was added to the east wall, probably in the late 1800s or early 1900s. When the house was pulled down in 1958, its cellar was filled in with the building rubble—the stones and wood laboriously cut out of the Bucks County wilderness of the early 1700s.

Archaeology at the Wynkoop House

The archaeological investigation of the Wynkoop house, done largely on a volunteer basis, was limited to twenty days. The goals were to record whatever structural features or architectural details might be encountered and to retrieve artifacts dating from the time the Wynkoops occupied the house. Although Rosenberger (1977) and the sixteen students who made up the research team excavated only in the cellar, they examined the area outside it. Among their findings to the

east of the house were the partial foundations of a cistern or outbuilding and a large pile of stones (Figure 8.10).

In removing almost 2,000 cubic feet of fill and building debris from the cellar, the team also uncovered a chimney base inside the east wall, a set of six stone steps in the south wall, and a concrete slab outside the east foundation. The concrete slab was obviously the floor of the shed added to the house in the late 1800s or early 1900s. Among the items found in the rubble was a large sandstone drain basin weighing between 300 and 400 pounds; it had probably been used to drain water away from the kitchen. Also found were several slabs of concrete with the words "Vredens Hof" impressed in letters two inches high. These items were obviously of relatively recent manufacture and intended for ornamentation, but whether they belonged to the Wynkoop House or had come from Vredens Hoff is open to speculation.

Of the several hundred artifacts recovered, the vast majority were found near the east and west foundation walls, a pattern that was almost assuredly the result of the techniques used in razing the house. The artifacts dated from the early 1700s to the mid-1900s; most, however, dated from the turn of the twentieth century. The earliest item found was the pewter handle of a fork or spoon. Ceramics included the usual sherds of local redware and whiteware. One

whiteware sherd dating from the early 1800s was decorated with a sketch and the words "Salem Witch" and "Old Witch House." All of the many pieces of glass from spirit and medicine bottles that appeared had been manufactured in the late 1800s or in the 1900s. The earliest of the fifteen coins found was an 1851 Liberty-head copper penny; the latest was a 1923 Indian-head nickel.

Not surprisingly, Rosenberger's team also retrieved numerous architectural items: wrought and cut nails, strap hinges, spike hinge hooks, and L-shaped spikes, as well as pieces of window framing, beams, joists, studding, shingles, and baseboard molding. Many of these items were original to the house. Interestingly, the team also found a stone door frame with hinge pins for top and bottom strap hinges set in lead. Rosenberger's interpretation of this item was that it provided positive proof that the Wynkoop House had had a double-hung Dutch door.

Given that the razing of the Wynkoop House had so severely disturbed the site in 1958, it was almost inevitable that no matter what Rosenberger's team found, it could not shed much light on the habits of the house's original occupants or even its later ones. Nonetheless, the investigation did shed some light on the vernacular architecture of a house built by pioneering Dutchmen in the frontier country of Bucks County in the early 1700s.

TREVOSE, THE GROWDEN MANSION

Joseph Growden was one of the First Purchasers of land in Penn's colony, and, as can be seen in Figure 8.11, his estate was a considerable one. Almost rivaling Pennsbury Manor in size, it occupied nearly half of Bensalem Township. Located in Trevose, a town named after the Growden Mansion and plantation, the estate has been whittled down over the years to a mere twelve acres, and the area around it is now almost as full of houses as it was of trees when Joseph Growden first saw it (Figure 8.12).

The mansion, too, has apparently experienced some changes. As shown in Figure 8.13, the Growden Mansion today has three stories, a hipped roof, and a coating of stucco over its exterior stone. It also has two flanking dependencies—one a kitchen, the other an office; both have gable roofs and are made of undressed stone.

With its classical tripartite plan, the Growden Mansion is one of the earliest examples of Palladian architecture in the Delaware Valley. The exact date of the mansion's con-struction has, however, been something of a mystery—one on which an interdisciplinary investigation managed to shed some light. The investigation came about as a result of Bensalem Township's plan to open

Figure 8.11.

Detail from Thomas Holme's map of "Ye Improved Part of Pensilvania in America," published about 1700. Growden's land appears near the center of the picture. (Courtesy of the Library of Congress, Map Division)

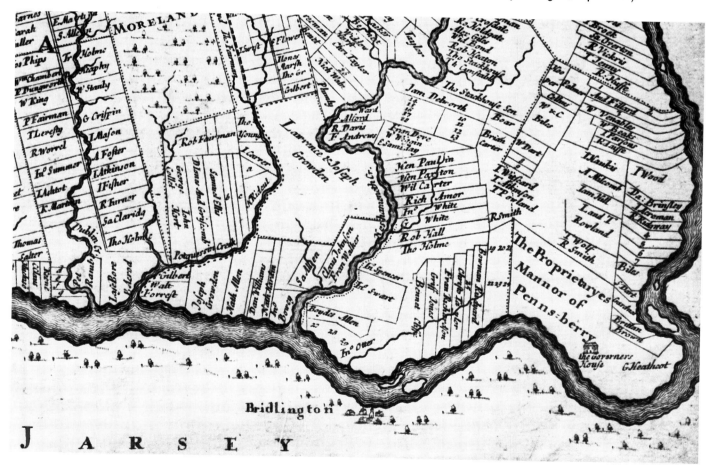

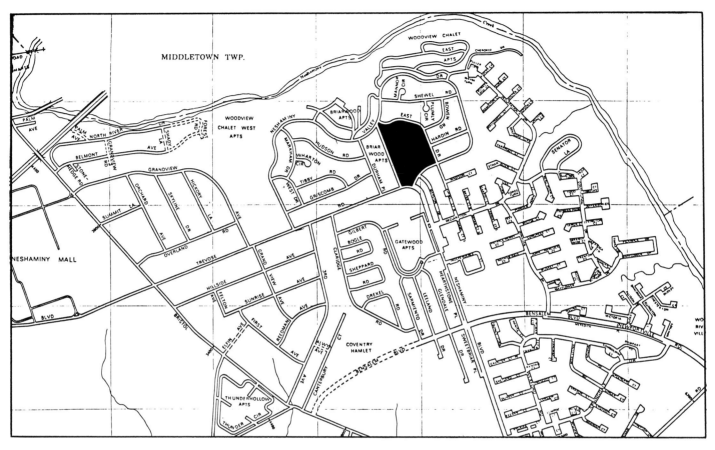

Figure 8.12.

Map of Bensalem Township showing the present boundaries of the Trevose property. (From Schooler, Bourke, and Righter 1983; courtesy of the Supervisors of Bensalem Township and John Milner Associates)

the estate to the public. Carried out for the township by John Milner Associates (Schooler, Bourke, and Righter 1983), it entailed historical, architectural, and archaeological research. It also demonstrated that archaeology can sometimes be as useful for what it fails to uncover as for what it does uncover. Schooler, Bourke, and Righter's report (1983) was the basis for the following account.

The Historical Research

Joseph Growden was one of the most influential men in Penn's province. Among the posts he held was that of chief justice of Pennsylvania. He was also a Quaker, and, quite appropriately, the original name for his plantation of 5,000 acres in Bucks County appears to have been "Bensalem," meaning "Hill of Peace." The evidence for this comes in a deed dated February 12, 1688, in which Growden referred to the 202 acres he was selling as "part of the Manor of Bensalem." It was apparently not until Bensalem Township was formed in 1692 that Growden changed the

name of his plantation to Trevose, the name of his homestead in England (Davis 1876:142–43).

When Joseph Growden died in 1737, Trevose passed to his son Lawrence. Like his father, Lawrence was a person of some renown, serving as a provincial judge and as the speaker of the provincial assembly in 1739. Lawrence's daughter Grace married another speaker of the assembly, Joseph Galloway, who held that office in 1774. As noted in Chapter 3, it was because of Galloway's apparent pacifism and suspected Tory leanings that the members of the First Continental Congress rejected his offer of the State House as a meeting place and chose Carpenters' Hall instead. Grace Growden Galloway inherited Trevose upon her father's death in 1770, and it remained in the Galloway family until well into the nineteenth century.

The long-held assumption has been that Joseph Growden built the mansion that now stands at Trevose. In his *History of Bucks County . . .*, written in 1876, William Watts Hart Davis states:

Soon after his arrival [Joseph Growden] built himself a beautiful residence on . . . his manor in Bensalem. . . . It was rather baronial-looking for a country dwelling at that period. An engraving of 1687 represents a large two-story stone house, with attic, divided by a hall through the middle, portico at the front door, pointed stone, pitch roof, and nine windows and door in front. At either end was a wing that contained dining-room, kitchen, servants' quarters, office, etc. . . . A small fire-proof office to the

right . . . still bears the marks of British bullets fired by a plundering party in 1778. The walls of the main building remain, but it has been greatly changed by its present owner. . . . [T]he outside has been covered with a coat of plaster, and a story added. . . . (Davis 1876:143)

To this, Davis adds, "Gabriel Thomas speaks of the Growden residence in 1696 as 'a very noble and fine house, very pleasantly situated, and likewise a famous orchard, wherein are contained above a thousand apple trees.'"

Although it does indeed appear that Joseph Growden built a mansion on his plantation soon after he bought the land, Schooler, Bourke, and Righter discovered a bit of evidence that suggests the house now standing at Trevose was a second-generation rebuilding, the work of Growden's son Lawrence. The evidence appeared in the *Pennsylvania Gazette*

of February 27, 1788, in a public notice pertaining to Joseph Galloway's "lease for life" of the estate:

Trevose, . . . the ancient seat of Joseph Growden, Esq., formerly Chief Justice of Pennsylvania, succeeded by his son Lawrence Growden, Esq., one of the assistant Judges of the Supreme Court, on which are erected an elegant mansion house, *built by the latter* [italics added], in the modern stile, four rooms on a floor, with kitchen and out offices, . . . two good barns, stables and many other useful buildings and erections, a large and good garden and orchards, abounding with the best fruit trees . . . in whole 422¼ acres and 22 perches of land. . . . This estate is subject to a lease for life of Joseph Galloway, Esq. . . .

Although this item does not specify when Lawrence Growden built or rebuilt the mansion, certain facts, as well as architectural details of the house itself, suggest that the date

Figure 8.13.

Trevose, the Growden Mansion. (From Schooler, Bourke, and Righter 1983; courtesy of the Supervisors of Bensalem Township and John Milner Associates)

would have been about 1740. For one thing, Lawrence left Pennsylvania in 1715 and did not return to live in the Philadelphia area until 1732. For another, he did not hold title to the property until after his father's death in 1737, and it seems unlikely that he would have undertaken such a project until he did have clear title. Schooler, Bourke, and Righter (1983:119) suggest it may not have been until 1741, when Lawrence married the wealthy Sarah Biles, that the construction or renovation began.

Archaeology at Trevose

One goal of Schooler, Bourke, and Righter's archaeological investigation at Trevose was to unravel a mystery presented by two nineteenth-century drawings of the mansion. One, a print done by Sartain in 1858, shows a connecting passageway between the mansion and the kitchen dependency (Figure 8.14). The other, a copy of a pen-and-ink sketch drawn about 1850, shows no connector. It was possible, of course, that both drawings were accurate, that the passageway shown in the Sartain print was built after 1850 and before 1858. At the time of the investigation, a passage-

way did indeed connect the mansion and kitchen, but the architectural evidence indicated it had not been built until the 1890s; it also appeared to have been built for temporary use only, for it was deteriorated beyond salvage.

Excavation of two test units near the existing passageway failed to uncover evidence of any foundations or soil disturbance, which would in all probability have been present in these areas had the passageway shown in Sartain's print existed (see TU-1 and TU-2 in Figure 8.15). While this absence of evidence was significant, equally significant was a discovery made in test unit 1 (TU-1). At about

Figure 8.14.

Trevose, rendered by Samuel Sartain, 1858. (From Wood 1870)

2 feet from the surface, Schooler, Bourke, and Righter encountered what they believed was the eighteenth-century surface. It consisted of hard-packed, silty clay with thin pockets of humic material clinging to it. Although this layer contained few datable artifacts, the layers above it contained many artifacts that dated from the early nineteenth century and possibly even from the eighteenth, thus supporting the contention that the bottom layer of hard-packed clay was the original grade level. Running through the bottom layer in a north-south direction about a foot west of the kitchen was a small trough. About 2 inches wide and 1 inch deep, the trough was clearly the result of rain dripping from the overhanging kitchen roof—sure proof that no passageway had preceded the existing one. The drip line, sparsity of humic material, and clayey consistency of the soil also indicated that considerable erosion was taking place at the time the original surface was exposed.

Schooler, Bourke, and Righter found evidence of the original grade in several other test units around the property. They also found what may be the sites of outbuildings not documented in the historical records. However, the principal contribution of archaeology to this interdisciplinary study was in demonstrating, both by what it failed to uncover and by what it did uncover, that the Sartain print was inaccurate and that until the late 1800s there had been no protected access to the kitchen dependency.

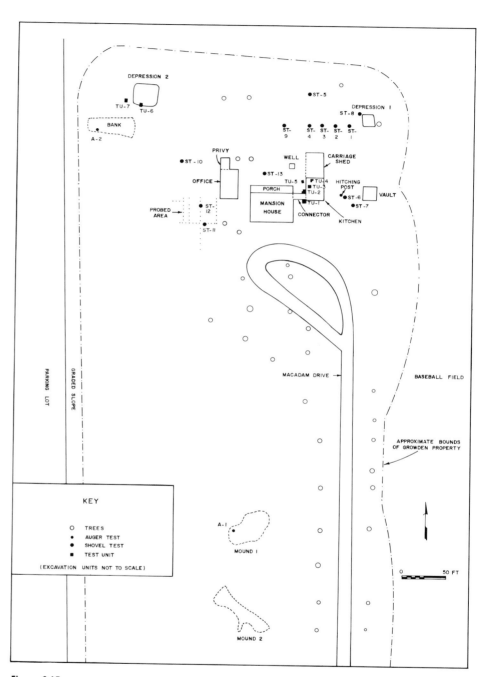

Figure 8.15.

Site plan of Trevose. (From Schooler, Bourke, and Righter 1983; courtesy of the Supervisors of Bensalem Township and John Milner Associates)

9
Montgomery County

HARRITON: WITNESS TO NATIONAL
AND PERSONAL FRUSTRATION

GRAEME PARK: FROM MALT HOUSE
TO GEORGIAN MANSION

HOPE LODGE: OF LEGENDS
AND UNCERTAIN ORIGINS

THE PETER WENTZ FARMSTEAD: GERMANIC
INFLUENCE IN THE DELAWARE VALLEY

THE HIGHLANDS: SOCIAL STRATIFICATION
IN FORT WASHINGTON

Montgomery County, itself the result of a revolution of sorts, came into being at the end of the Revolutionary War. In 1782 farmers in the western reaches of Philadelphia County, fired by the spirit of independence then abroad and availing themselves of their new political voice, began agitating for the creation of a separate county. At the head of their list of grievances was paying taxes for benefits disproportionately bestowed on Philadelphia city dwellers, but they also objected to having less than their fair share of representation on the governing councils of Philadelphia County. Moreover, for many of them the county seat in Philadelphia was simply too far away. On September 10, 1784, after considerable bickering over boundaries, the state assembly voted to create Montgomery County along the boundary lines shown in Figure 9.1. By 1790 the new county had a total of twenty-eight townships, including Lower Merion.

Lower Merion Township was originally part of the Welsh Tract, or "Barony," a parcel of 40,000 acres that William Penn granted to a group of Welsh Quakers in the early 1680s. When the boundaries of the three original counties were established in 1683, the Welsh Tract was divided between Chester County and the part of Philadelphia County that ultimately became Montgomery County. Merion Township wound up in Philadelphia County; Haverford and Radnor Townships, also part of the Welsh Tract, went to Chester County. Whereas most settlers gravitated toward places already settled by the early Swedes, Dutch, and English, the Welsh Quakers, because of their determination to live as a group and Penn's granting of that wish with the Welsh Tract, found themselves plunging into the untouched wilderness of Merion, Haverford, and Radnor (Smith 1862: 147–48, 165).

Sometimes called the "key to the Keystone state," Montgomery County has a remarkably diverse collection of historic sites—a diversity that reflects the characteristic Pennsylvania blending of nationalities and religions. The region had a large number of Welsh Quakers, of course, but there were representatives of many other sects and backgrounds as well. "Germans"— actually a Protestant medley of Swiss, Rhinelanders, Holsteins, Palatines, Silesians, and Netherlanders (National Heritage Corporation 1975: 6)—were particularly prominent in this area. Careful farmers whose methods of crop rotation and fertilization ensured the earth's productivity for over two centuries, the Germans settled on independent farmsteads scattered across the countryside. Widely dispersed farming communities characterized the region for many years. It was not until the nineteenth century that Montgomery County had towns of any real size.

The mixture of social classes so evident in the early (and even the later) city of Philadelphia was also evident in this agricultural hinterland. Although the large majority of people were "dirt farmers," who lived by tilling the land, the area was also the home of a fair number of "gentleman farmers," large landowners who were also city merchants, professionals, and statesmen. Mill owners, tavern-keepers, ironmasters, artisans, and miners and other laborers made up most of the rest of the population.

In addition to having at least one early log house that has withstood the

Figure 9.1.

Contemporary map of Montgomery County.

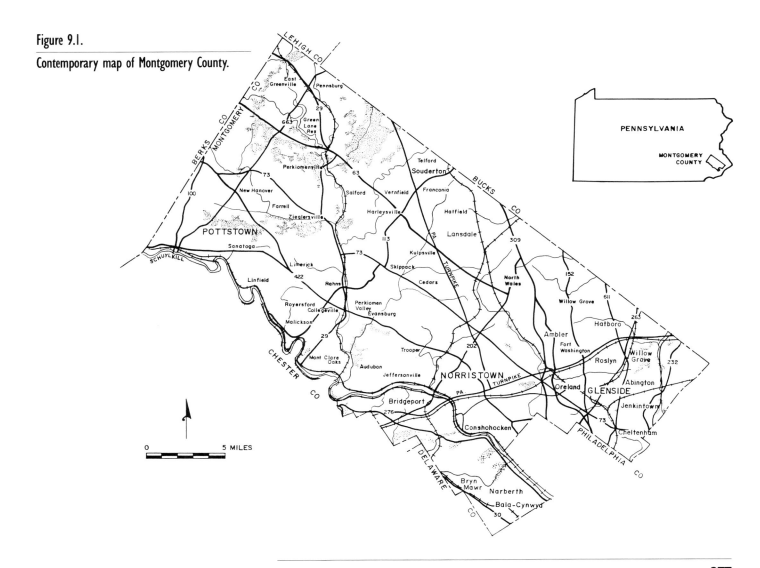

test of time, Montgomery County has a number of eighteenth-century stone mansions. One of these impressive places began as part of a distillery—a Scotsman's dream of combining lucrative enterprise with the making of good whiskey. Other early industrial and commercial sites, some of which still stand, include the gristmills and paper mills that cropped up along the county's abundant streams; the taverns and inns that appeared at crossroads as highways were built; kilns that burned local limestone into the mortar used in Philadelphia buildings (Basalik 1984); marble quarries (one of which produced the blue marble of the mantle in Jefferson's room at the Graff House); copper, lead, and iron ore mines; and iron forges. All these enterprises were, of course, on a small scale, often family-owned and -run.

During the Revolutionary War this part of the Philadelphia region saw considerable action. Washington planned and staged the Battle of Germantown from the Peter Wentz Farmstead in Worcester Township, and his defeated soldiers later wended their way through this countryside en route to Valley Forge. Among several reminders of the presence of Washington's army in Montgomery County are earthen fortifications that still stand near the town of Fort Washington. Another military site from yet another war was located in present-day La Mott, where African-American troops trained during the Civil War at a facility known as Camp William Penn.

In the first half of the nineteenth century, Montgomery County witnessed the building of the Schuylkill Canal and, of more lasting importance, the building of several railroads. Among the first was the Philadelphia, Germantown & Norristown Railroad, which connected the county

seat at Norristown with the city of Philadelphia. As the railroads brought products from other parts of the country, introducing an element of competition, some of Montgomery County's small colonial industries went into decline. In their stead came manufacturing plants that converted raw materials imported to the county into many different products. By 1858 sixteen mills along Mill Creek in Lower Merion Township were manufacturing everything from cotton and flour to gunpowder and paper, and tanneries and iron and textile mills were spread throughout the county. As agriculture declined and business and industry took over, towns developed around the plants in these rather widely dispersed locations (Alderfer 1951:176–78, 201–5).

In the late nineteenth and early twentieth centuries, Montgomery County became something of a mecca for Philadelphia's self-made merchant-princes. Among those who built their palaces along Old York Road were John Wanamaker, John Stetson, William Elkins, and Peter A. B. Widener. Elkins started out as a grocer and Widener as a butcher; as partners, they made a fortune in Philadelphia's traction industry. Widener built one of the most elaborate structures of all: the Versailles-like Lynnewood Hall, which boasted 110 rooms, including a huge ballroom and art gallery. Ogontz, home of the notorious financial buccaneer Jay Cooke, was scarcely less pretentious (Burt and Davies 1982:484–85; Abernethy 1982:532). Situated near Washington Lane in Cheltenham Township, it was visited on several occasions by Cooke's friend, President Ulysses S. Grant, whose son attended Cheltenham Military Academy, an institution that stood opposite Ogontz from 1875

until 1910.* Another of Cheltenham Military Academy's students was the poet Ezra Pound, whose parents lived in nearby Wyncote from 1891 until 1930.

It could be said that Montgomery County's modern era began with the introduction of railroads in the 1830s. However, it was some time before it acquired the middle-class suburban aspect that in large part characterizes it today. Among those who sped the transformation along were William Elkins and Peter Widener, who in the 1880s began speculating in Montgomery County real estate. Other wealthy men followed their example, buying up large tracts of land and selling it off in suburban-sized plots. As a result, by the late 1890s hundreds of houses were being built, a movement that gained increasing momentum in the next century.

Relatively little of Montgomery County's considerable archaeological potential has been tapped. Among the historic sites that have received archaeological attention are Harriton, a stone house built by a Welsh Quaker in 1704; the Peter Wentz Farmstead, built in 1758 by a second-generation German on land amassed by his father; and three stately eighteenth-century mansions, one of which began as a distillery.

---

* A public school now occupies the site of Cheltenham Military Academy. It became the focus of archaeological study in the 1960s, when Emmanuel Kramer, a teacher in the Cheltenham public schools, led his high school students in uncovering the foundations of the old military academy. The excavation, which took place in a shallow crawl space in the school's basement, produced thousands of artifacts, including numerous buttons and buckles from military uniforms. Since then, Kramer has trained and led other high school classes in archaeological investigations of historic sites in Montgomery County (Kramer 1979, 1982), Independence National Historical Park, and Germantown, where students found evidence of original grades and features at the Maxwell Mansion.

HARRITON: WITNESS TO NATIONAL
AND PERSONAL FRUSTRATION

In 1704 a Welsh Quaker named Rowland Ellis built himself a stone house in the part of the "Welsh Tract" now known as Lower Merion Township. He called his house Bryn Mawr, meaning High Hill, after his ancestral home in Merionethshire, Wales. The town that subsequently grew up near Ellis's house took its name from it. It was the small vanity of Richard Harrison, Jr., a Maryland tobacco planter who later in the 1700s acquired Ellis's property, to rename the house Harriton. The most famous occupant of Harriton was, however, neither a Harrison nor an Ellis, but Charles Thomson (1729–1824), who played an important role in the American Revolution.

The house that Rowland Ellis built at what is now the junction of Old Gulph and Harriton roads has sturdy walls of schist and a T-shaped plan, with two rooms in the front and one in the rear. Its tall chimneys, steeply pitched roof, flaring pent eave, and squat dormer windows reflect a definite Welsh influence (Figure 9.2). A one-story stone solarium has been added to the west side of the house, and behind it is a large, three-story addition built in 1926. A stone privy, which may date from 1704, stands about 10 feet behind the modern ad-

Figure 9.2.

Harriton. The "cave," or root cellar, appears at left. (Photo by J. L. Cotter)

dition (Figure 9.3). About 50 feet away from the house, dug into the side of a terrace, is a stone-lined root cellar (Figure 9.4); it is no doubt the "cave" that Charles Thomson's diary notes was constructed at Harriton in the spring of 1799. Also standing on the property is a large tenant house covered inside and out with modern trim; some documentation suggests the modern trim masks an early log construction.

Although Rowland Ellis's original stone house has been enlarged, the acreage around it has been greatly reduced. A considerable plantation during the tenure of Richard Harrison, Jr., Harriton today has but sixteen acres. Lower Merion Township acquired the property in 1969, and it is now maintained by the Harriton Association. In 1976 the association authorized students from the University of Pennsylvania to conduct an archaeological feasibility study of the property.* Bruce C. Gill, the curator-director of the Harriton Association, participated in the study and provided data for the historical account that follows. The archaeological data are from the class report (Cotter 1976).

Harriton's Most Famous Occupant

On September 1, 1774, Hannah Harrison, who inherited Harriton from her father Richard Harrison, Jr., married Charles Thomson, a Philadelphia merchant who had started out as a schoolmaster. They could not have had much of a honeymoon, for four days later the First Continental Congress elected Thomson as its secretary. Like its choice of Carpenters' Hall over the State House, the Continental Congress's choice of Charles Thomson as secretary was an indication of which way the political wind was blowing. Known as a committed, hard-core radical, he was the scourge of the city's conservatives.

Thomson began his political activity early on in the events leading to the Revolution. In November 1767, when the British government imposed the Townshend duties on the colonies, he was one of the few Philadelphia merchants who at once actively re-

Figure 9.3.

The privy at Harriton. (Photo by J. L. Cotter)

* Charles Kolb (1971), of Bryn Mawr College, had previously conducted an excavation of a large trash midden at Harriton, but since Kolb's analysis determined that the midden dated between 1900 and 1915, his study, regrettably, offers little toward the early history of the site.

Figure 9.4.

The "cave," or root cellar. (Photo by J. L. Cotter)

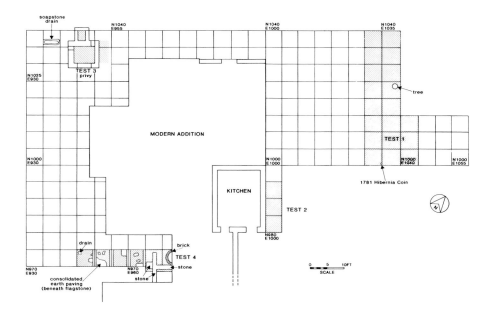

Figure 9.5.

Plan showing four of the six test sites at Harriton. (From Cotter 1976)

lished in 1808, his translation failed to attract many readers and soon sank like a stone into ecclesiastical history.

Archaeology at Harriton

In the summer and fall of 1976, students from the University of Pennsylvania conducted a total of six archaeological tests at Harriton (Figure 9.5). The purpose of test 1 was to find traces of a small structure that appears east of the house in an undated photograph of the property. Although nineteen 5-foot squares were stripped to undisturbed earth at 6 to 7 inches below the surface, no structural evidence appeared. However, one of the squares near the driveway did contain an Irish colonial coin dated 1781 and marked "Hibernia, George Rex III." A few feet away from where the coin was found was a posthole 18 inches deep, and at the bottom of this hole were some soapstone fragments. The hole had probably contained a hitching post that was braced by the soapstone fragments.

The purpose of test 2 was to determine whether any unrecorded structural features existed beyond the kitchen walls, but it produced no evidence of such features. Test 3, which was intended to throw some light on the date of the privy's construction, was somewhat more productive. Made of fieldstone and framed in oak, the privy measured 8 by 8 feet, and its interior walls were plastered and whitewashed. It had a steeply sloping roof, a pediment projecting over the entrance, and a window in its east wall.

sisted the new taxes; it took considerable prodding and a good six months for others to do so. And after Paul Revere rode into Philadelphia in May 1774 with the news that the British were about to close the port of Boston because of that city's famous "tea party" and presented a plea for help from Bostonians, Thomson became one of the leaders of the movement that resulted two years later in the nation's Declaration of Independence (Tinkcom 1982:115, 119).

Competent and conscientious, Thomson unstintingly served the new republic until 1789, often at his own expense. In addition to being congressional secretary, he acted as secretary of foreign affairs. Among his many contributions was conceiving the symbol used on the great seal of the United States—the bald eagle that holds an olive branch and arrows in its claws. The greatest disappointment of Thomson's life was his failure to win appointment as secretary of state in Washington's first cabinet. In 1789,

having dutifully notified Washington of his election as president, Thomson retired to Harriton at the age of sixty.

It has been said that Charles Thomson knew more and said less about the Revolution than any man who lived through it. During his years of service to the congress, he kept a secret journal of congressional business, but when John Jay and others asked him to write a history of the American Revolution based on his journal and vast personal knowledge, he not only declined but also burned the journal and all papers relating to his official duties. While no doubt a loss to future historians, this action did earn Thomson the accolade of being the "most discreet, judicious" figure to take part in the Revolution. Despite his refusal to write about the things he knew best, Thomson did pursue another literary project before his death at Harriton at the age of ninety-four. Although not a member of any church, he spent nine years working on a new English translation of the Bible. Pub-

Figure 9.6.

Cleanout at the rear of the Harriton privy. (Photo by J. L. Cotter)

room of the original T-shaped house, produced some structural evidence for which no documentary explanation exists. In the angle between the front and rear of the original house was a T-shaped configuration of mortared stone walls. One wall extended 8 feet out from the rear room, and at about 5 feet it intersected with another wall that connected with the front part of the house. The purpose of these walls remains a mystery, as does the purpose of a 5-foot arc of bricks found against the cellar wall of the rear room. Although it appeared that the arc of bricks might have been a vent, no opening was found in the cellar wall. The earth in this area had been greatly disturbed during the construction of 1926, and no eighteenth-century artifacts or soil zone was found.

Test 5, conducted beneath the pent eave at the front of the house, was unsuccessful in its effort to uncover the eighteenth-century drip line, possibly indicating a gutter on the eave. Test 6 focused on the stone-lined root cellar, or "cave," dug into the terrace 50 feet southwest of the house. It was hoped that artifacts found here would reflect how this structure may have been used. However, no artifacts appeared, and the only thing that could be concluded from this test was that the floor of the cave had been kept exceptionally clean.

Its oak laths were secured mainly with square-headed, hand-wrought nails. The door had strap hinges, and the ceiling and floors were made of tongue-and-groove fir boards. Sometime after plumbing was installed in the house in 1926, the privy had been converted to a potting shed.

At the rear of the privy was an opening to facilitate cleanout (Figure 9.6), a familiar feature of outhouses in the "Dutch" country of southeastern Pennsylvania, where farmers generally cleaned their privies after dark and dispersed the spoil in the nearby fields (Long 1963). The waste-collection box was 4 feet deep, measured from ground level, and at its bottom was a sloping stone to facilitate access and removal of contents. The box was filled with leaf mold and fragments of early twentieth-century milk bottles and tin cans. The latest date on any of these items was 1925, indicating that the privy fell into disuse very soon after plumbing was installed in the house in 1926. Sometime before 1926 the floor of the collection box had been covered with a layer of concrete spread over a base of small, flat fieldstones. A thin, flat fragment of window glass and a square-headed, hand-wrought nail appeared among the fieldstones; below the stones was undisturbed earth. Since no physical or documentary evidence of any other privies ever having been built at Harriton has yet been found, it would appear that Rowland Ellis built this privy at the same time he built his stone house in 1704.

Test 4, placed west of the rear

GRAEME PARK: FROM MALT HOUSE
TO GEORGIAN MANSION

Graeme Park is an unusual eighteenth-century estate with an extraordinarily well documented history. Located about a half mile west of Route 611 on County Line Road in Horsham, it began in 1721–22 as a distillery, a sideline of the province's enterprising governor, Sir William Keith. When Dr. Thomas Graeme, who had married Keith's stepdaughter, bought the property in 1739, he turned the building that Keith had probably used as a malt house into an elegant Georgian mansion. Originally occupying 1,200 acres of land, some of it no doubt in Bucks County, the estate by 1778 had been reduced to 600 acres, and by 1958 it had dwindled to 44 acres, all of them in Montgomery County.

Upon Graeme's death in 1772, the estate passed to his daughter Elizabeth, whose financial distress in the 1780s forced her to sell off more of the land. After Elizabeth died in 1801, Samuel Penrose, a Quaker farmer, bought what was left of the estate, and by 1821 he and his family had moved into a complex of new dwellings they had built on the premises. In 1920 Welsh Strawbridge acquired Graeme Park, where he and his family resided in the buildings erected by the Penroses. Thus Graeme's Georgian mansion, unoccupied but well-maintained for over a century, escaped modernization.

In 1958, when the proposed extension of an airstrip at the abutting Willow Grove Naval Air Station was threatening the property, the Strawbridges gave the Commonwealth of Pennsylvania the mansion and 42 acres surrounding it. Since then, under the auspices of the Pennsylvania Historical and Museum Commission, which administers the property, Graeme Park has been the subject of several archaeological studies.

History of Graeme Park

Sir William Keith (1669–1749), the offspring of a Scotsman who became a baronet in 1663, inherited his title in 1721. By that time his once rich and powerful family had lost both lands and fortune. His impoverished state did not, however, seem to deter Keith from taking financial risks. He was strangely anticipatory of the fast-moving American opportunist of the late nineteenth and twentieth centuries, and he also seems to have had just the right mix of prestige, courtly manners, and democratic affability to win influential friends and impress people of all classes. He may, in fact, have been something of what today would be called a "con man," though he was apparently one with quite a few redeeming features. The astute Benjamin Franklin remembered him as the mentor who sent the young printer Franklin to London to buy himself a press, but who neglected to give him funds or letters of introduction.

In 1714, when Keith was forty-five years old, Queen Anne appointed him surveyor-general of the "royal customs" in the American colonies, a post he lost a year later when the Hanovers came to power. In the interim, he had stayed at the homes of various planters and gotten a taste of opulent plantation life. Finding himself without a job in 1715, he went to Philadelphia to inquire about the position of lieutenant governor (Esther

1966a, 1966b). After mustering high-ranking friends to intercede with the provincial council on his behalf, Keith received the offer of the post on February 25, 1716. He thereupon sailed for England, where he collected his family, household goods, appointment from William Penn, and enough money borrowed from friends not only to pay for the return passage but also to set himself up in style in Philadelphia.

Accompanying Keith on the return voyage in the spring of 1717 were his wife, the widowed Ann Newberry Driggs; their four sons, the youngest of whom was born on the ship; his wife's daughter Ann, age seventeen; and the young Ann's future husband, Dr. Thomas Graeme, then twenty-nine years old. In Philadelphia the Keiths rented a succession of fashionable houses, among them two of the most imposing then standing in the city: the Slate Roof House, built in 1687 on Second Street near Walnut by Samuel Carpenter and later leased to both William Penn and James Logan, and the Edward Shippen House, built in 1693 on Second Street near Dock Creek by the man who became the first mayor of the city.

After William Penn died in 1718 and his sons began vying for the proprietorship of Pennsylvania, Keith, who was as usual living above his salary and means, took steps to ensure his own financial future. Among his money-making schemes—none of which prospered—were real-estate speculation along the Susquehanna River, the establishment of a town at Easton, an iron furnace, a copper mine, and "Fountain Low," the distillery he built in Horsham in 1721–

Figure 9.7.

Graeme Park: *top,* front of mansion, facing north; *bottom,* rear of mansion, facing south. (Courtesy of the Pennsylvania State Archives, Division of History)

22 (Esther 1966a:3). His plans for Fountain Low were apparently based on his recollections of the hospitality he had enjoyed at various prosperous American plantations in 1714–15. Never one for thinking small, Keith hoped to prosper enough by the making of whiskey to be able to create an American estate that would rival those of the English aristocracy. Though the distillery did not bring him the financial rewards he hoped, we can presume, or at least hope, that it produced acceptable whiskey, for Keith delighted in sending samples of it to his friends.

Just exactly how Keith came into possession of the 1,200 acres on which he built Fountain Low is a bit foggy. According to some sources, he bought the land from Andrew Hamilton for the sum of £500. According to others, he shrewdly acquired it as payment of a debt owed not to him but to the government—a matter of back taxes owed by the estate of Samuel Carpenter, who when he died in 1714 owned a large part of Horsham Township. Whatever Keith paid or did not pay for the land, he spent £2,000 developing it. On the premises were a small distilling complex, a large building possibly used both as a malt house and a part-time residence, a "Long House for accommodation" (presumably for the distillery workers), an overseer's house, slave quarters, and a barn, stables, and other small farm buildings. In addition, as governor of the province, Keith saw to it that a road (now part of Route 611) was laid out to connect Fountain Low with Philadelphia, twenty-six miles away.

After the good Governor Keith issued paper money without consulting the Penn family, James Logan and others who believed Keith was promoting the interests of the common people at the expense of the proprietor began urging the Penns to remove him from office, and in June 1726 they did just that. More bad press followed in November 1727 when Governor Gordon, Keith's successor, accused him of having used crown funds to develop Fountain Low. Meanwhile, Keith had taken up residence at the distillery in Horsham and, testifying to his popularity among the voting public, had been elected to the provincial assembly. In March 1728, leaving his wife behind him, Keith sailed for London to answer the demands of his creditors. In Britain he managed to get himself elected to parliament as the representative from Aberdeen and, in a final bit of self-promotion before dying as a debtor at Old Bailey at the age of eighty in 1749, to write *The History of the British Plantations in America with a Chronological Account of the Most Remarkable Things* (Esther 1966a:4–6).

By 1737 Lady Ann Keith, whom Sir William left behind at Fountain Low in 1728, had managed to sell the property and to move into the townhouse rented by her daughter and her increasingly respected and affluent son-in-law, Dr. Thomas Graeme. After Graeme bought Fountain Low in 1739 and renamed it Graeme Park, Lady Ann returned to the estate, where she died the following summer at the age of sixty-three; she was buried in the Christ Church burial ground in Philadelphia.

Like Sir William Keith, Dr. Thomas Graeme was a Scottish Presbyterian, but there the resemblance ended. Graeme became port physician for the city of Philadelphia—an important post in those epidemic-ridden times, entailing responsibility for ensuring that all ships entering and leaving the port were free of contagious disease. Well-respected for his pioneering quarantine practices, he was also on the first staff of the Pennsylvania Hospital, a member of the provincial council, a justice of the Pennsylvania Supreme Court, and a fellow of the American Philosophical Society. Sadly, despite Graeme's medical skill, only three of his eight children lived past childhood.

Under Graeme's care and supervision, Sir William's industrial enterprise became a country estate that reflected the affluence and social status of its owner. There was little Graeme could do to the unusual exterior of the mansion to disguise its industrial origins; its exceptionally narrow windows, general lack of symmetry, and Swedish gambrel roof were dead giveaways (Figure 9.7). Inside, however, with the use of fine paneling, wainscoting, and Dutch tiles or marble trim around the fireplaces, he was able to transform the unusually high-ceilinged rooms into elegant Georgian salons (Figure 9.8).

Figure 9.8.

Marble-trimmed fireplace and paneling at Graeme Park. (Courtesy of the Pennsylvania State Archives, Division of History)

Figure 9.9.

Map of Graeme Park, 1967. (Courtesy of the
Pennsylvania Historical and Museum
Commission)

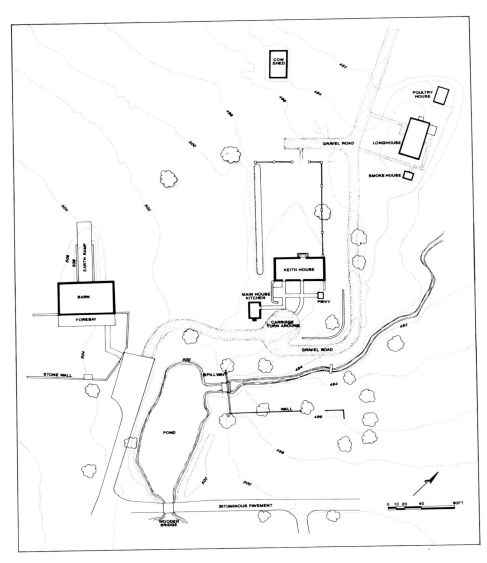

Here, in the summer months, Graeme and his youngest child, Elizabeth, who became his hostess after his wife's death, entertained some of the most eminent Philadelphians of the time, among them Benjamin Franklin. With Philadelphia a long twenty-six miles off, guests often stayed for weeks at a time and sometimes wore out their welcome.

Elizabeth, a poetess, seems to have had not the best of judgment when it came to men. After a romance with Benjamin Franklin's son William left her heartbroken, she married—against her father's wishes—Henry Hugh Ferguson, a Tory who enlisted under the British colors during the Revolutionary War. When Howe evacuated Philadelphia in June 1778, Ferguson sailed for England, and Elizabeth never saw him again. Coupled with her romantic foibles, she also had the poor judgment in October 1777, just after the Battle of Germantown, to deliver a note from the Rev. Jacob Duché, rector of Christ Church, to General Washington, then encamped in Towamencin about ten miles west of Graeme Park. Having read Duché's note, which suggested that Washington take advantage of the peace terms Howe was offering, Washington soundly berated Mrs. Ferguson and turned the letter over to Congress, an action that soon had some unpleasant consequences for the mistress of Graeme Park (Alderfer 1951:111, 131–32).

On September 17, 1778, with Elizabeth herself now under suspicion of treason, the colonial government con-fiscated Graeme Park as property belonging to the traitor Henry Hugh Ferguson. This seizure resulted in an exhaustive inventory of all "the sundry household goods and chattels" in the house.* The inventory also noted

* "An Inventory of the Sundry Household Goods and Chattels found in the House of Hugh Ferguson of Grame Park Taken This Seventeenth of September 1778" contains one of the most complete descriptions of the contents of a historic house existing in the Philadelphia region. It is available in the *Pennsylvania Archives*, 6th series 1906 (12):653–60.

that the estate then contained 600 acres of land, a three-story house, and "a barn, stable, and other buildings." By way of a somewhat skeptical-sounding postscript, the appraisers of the estate added, "Elizabeth Graeme Furgusson says she only has 12 sheep and 11 hogs." Although the colonial government allowed Elizabeth to remain at Graeme Park, it sold off most of her belongings at auction. In 1781 the supreme court absolved her of the charge of high treason and returned her land to her. By then £3,000 in debt, she began selling off parts of the estate.

The federal tax census for 1798 shows that Graeme Park then contained two stone houses, one being the mansion, which is described as measuring 56 by 25 feet and having thirty-nine windows. The other, two stories high, was 30 by 60 feet and had fifteen windows; it was presumably the erstwhile distillery's "Long House for accommodation." Also on the premises were a one-story stone kitchen measuring 20 by 15 feet and a 40-by-50-foot frame barn. Of these buildings, only the mansion was still standing when the Strawbridge family presented Graeme Park to the Commonwealth of Pennsylvania in 1958. The property did, however, contain a barn built in 1850 (Figure 9.9).

Archaeology at Graeme Park

Soon after the Pennsylvania Historical and Museum Commission took over the administration of Graeme Park in 1958, J. Duncan Campbell conducted the first archaeological investigation of the property. As part of a plan for restoring the estate, Campbell's work focused on locating the sites of razed buildings. Campbell's initial exploration was followed by a number of other archaeological studies (Hally 1961, 1962; Witthoft 1964; Borstling 1965a; Deihl and Fidler 1965; Esther 1966a, 1966b, 1967; Warfel 1985; Kardas and Larrabee 1986); not all of them succeeded in producing significant data.

About 25 feet south of the mansion, Campbell (1958) uncovered the foundations of the 20-by-15-foot kitchen (Figure 9.10). Here a layer of dark topsoil contained a number of twentieth-century artifacts, beneath which

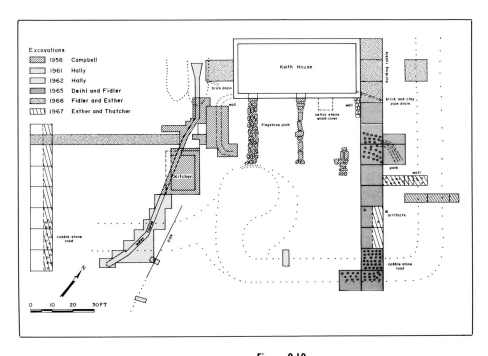

Figure 9.10.

Plan of selected excavations at Graeme Park. (From Esther 1967)

was a layer of light-colored dirt containing artifacts of eighteenth-century date. From the debris, Campbell concluded that the kitchen had been deteriorating for several years and was then pulled down all at once, after which the light-colored dirt was brought in to cover the site; the razing was probably done after 1801. Campbell found no brick debris whatsoever, indicating that the kitchen had been made exclusively of stone. The only explanation for the absence of a fireplace seemed to be either that the bricks had been salvaged or that a large walnut tree then standing at the north end of the kitchen was obscuring it. Campbell also noted a watercourse with a partially mortared floor that ran through a corner of the kitchen; apparently emanating from the nearby pond, it could have provided the kitchen with fresh water or served as a drain.

The date of the kitchen's con-

struction was fixed by historical evidence. An advertisement appearing at the time Lady Ann Keith was selling the property in 1737 makes no mention of the kitchen; a letter from Ann Graeme to her daughter Elizabeth on August 20, 1762, asks for postponement of a visit because masons and carpenters were then at work in the kitchen. With the help of historical documentation and the archaeological data produced by Campbell's investigation, the one-story stone kitchen has since been reconstructed.

Campbell believed that the purpose of a stone wall with curved ends extending from the south corner of the mansion was to screen the kitchen from the house and that the wall was probably built at the same time as the

Figure 9.11.

Excavations of the "smokehouse" at Graeme Park. (From Esther 1967)

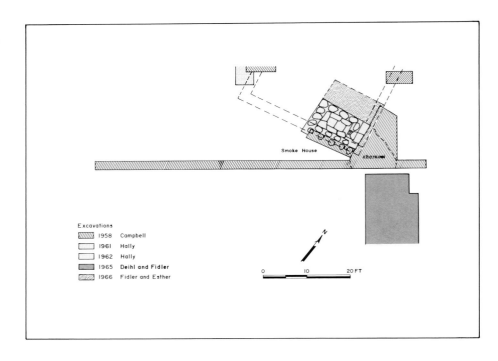

kitchen. He found evidence of a similar wall extending from the east corner of the mansion. He also found flagstone walks in front of the two doors on the southeast side of the mansion, indications of a cobblestone road and turnaround, and evidence of two structures. One of the structures may have been the eighteenth-century barn; evidence of it consisted of a line of rock rubble beginning 110 feet northwest of the mansion. Campbell tentatively identified the other structure, located 100 feet north and 100 feet east of the mansion, as a "tenant house."

Hally (1961, 1962) extended Campbell's excavation of the water course, tracing it both north and south of the kitchen. From the evidence, it was unclear whether Graeme had had the watercourse laid in 1762, as part of his kitchen construction, or whether it had been built earlier, possibly in 1721–22 to supply Sir William Keith's whiskey distillery. If it had been laid earlier, Graeme obviously put it to good use by placing the kitchen over it. The watercourse reappeared at the northern edge of the pond, and a depression that looked like a ditch suggested that it continued through the area around the barn.

After excavating the structure Campbell had tentatively identified as a "tenant house," Hally concluded it had been a smokehouse. It measured 9 by 11 feet, its stone rubble flooring was less than a foot deep, and it had an iron grate over a shallow stone box set just inside the east foundation wall (Figure 9.11). Although the structure appeared to have been made chiefly

of wood, some brick rubble indicated that the lower walls around the grate had been made of brick. Esther's work on the site of this structure in 1966 led her to conclude that it might have been built sometime between 1755 and 1772. If so, it would probably have been ready for the post-1801 demolition of the kitchen documented earlier by Campbell.

Hally also excavated the site of another razed structure. Located 143 feet northwest of the mansion, this one had been made of stone, was almost 34 feet square, and appeared to have been built in the first half of the eighteenth century. It had a half basement, which was at its greatest depth 3 feet from the original surface. An opening in its east wall led to a carefully constructed drain; an opening in the west wall suggested there had been access to the shallow basement from the outside. Just exactly what this structure was used for is uncertain. Among Hally's other finds were further traces of the cobblestone

road Campbell had begun uncovering in 1958 and evidence of a garden wall northwest of the house. A garden wall appears in the same location in a 1725 print of Graeme Park.

Beyond the spillway of the pond south of the mansion, Fidler and Esther found three stone retaining walls, which appeared to have been built after 1755 (Esther 1966b). In their exploration of the cellar floor of the mansion, they discovered a recess that bore a resemblance to the seventeenth-century cooling pits found at Jamestown (Cotter 1958: 138, 140).

Esther (1967) attributed the inability of archaeological studies at Graeme Park to produce evidence of the "Long House" or other vanished buildings of record to nineteenth-century salvage. According to her theory, as deteriorating buildings were razed during the 1800s, some building materials may have been saved and reused. Esther found support for her theory in John Fanning

Watson's report of his visit to Graeme Park in 1855; Watson (1909) recorded no eighteenth-century buildings on the grounds other than the mansion.

According to Esther (1966a), the archaeological data indicate two main building periods at Graeme Park: 1722–1728 by Sir William Keith and 1755–1770 by Dr. Thomas Graeme. Esther notes, however, that between 1739 and 1755, under Graeme's supervision, the grounds may have undergone some improvement. Of the features identified by the archaeological investigations, none (excluding the mansion, of course) can be assigned definitely to the earlier period, although the 34-foot-square structure Hally found was apparently built before 1755. Only the kitchen can be

definitely assigned to the later period. Among those that could have been built in either period are the smokehouse, the garden wall, and the watercourse, which was most likely extended to serve new structures as they were built.

Building on the work of the earlier researchers at Graeme Park, Kardas and Larrabee (1986) concentrated their investigation on the north side of the house in an effort to define a formal garden known from historical documents. Here, the placement of five archaeological trenches revealed at least two, and possibly three, poorly preserved brick walkways, along with several unpaved path remnants, and defined a portion of a stone rubble perimeter wall, thus confirming the

presence and location of the formal garden (Kardas and Larrabee 1986: 61–62). Although artifacts were sparse, nearly all dated to the eighteenth century and included, for the most part, bits of glass and ceramic. A small eighteenth-century gentleman's pocketknife, however, was also found (Kardas and Larrabee 1986:55). Interestingly, distributional analysis of the artifacts strongly indicated long-term meticulous care of the garden; artifacts were found to cluster along the edges of the walkways, suggesting frequent sweeping of the walks (Kardas and Larrabee 1986:48). Apparently, the Keiths and Graemes were a tidy lot.

HOPE LODGE: OF LEGENDS AND UNCERTAIN ORIGINS

Hope Lodge, a particularly stately and serene Georgian mansion (Figure 9.12), sits on a broad, expansive tract off the Bethlehem Pike near the Skippack Pike and Wissahickon Creek. The early history of the house is far less well documented than that of Graeme Park and other historic sites in Montgomery Country. Its exact date of construction is unknown, and there is even some question as to who built it. Given these loopholes, it is perhaps not surprising that the history of Hope Lodge has been heavily interlaced and larded with legend. The legends range from the credible, if unsubstantiated, to the patently far-fetched.

The mansion is said to have served as a field hospital for Continental soldiers wounded in battle, as head-

quarters for both Gen. George Washington and Gen. Nathanael Greene, and as a station for the underground railroad during the Civil War. It is even said that Washington, in an uncharacteristic burst of effrontery, rode his horse straight through the mansion from back door to front (Wallace 1962:117, 135). One thing about the history of Hope Lodge that does seem certain is that it derived its name from Henry Hope, of the same family as the Hope Diamond. However, in another quirk of Hope Lodge's history, Henry Hope never lived there.

After having at least five different owners in the eighteenth century, Hope Lodge came into the possession of Jacob Wentz in 1832, and it remained in his family for almost a cen-

tury. In 1957 the Commonwealth of Pennsylvania acquired the property, and the Pennsylvania Historical and Museum Commission has administered it since that time.

The Early History of Hope Lodge

Whitemarsh Township, in which Hope Lodge is located, began as William Penn's grant of 5,000 acres to Major Jasper Farmer and one—or perhaps two—of his six sons in 1685 (Figure 9.13). Farmer, a British army officer, had emigrated from Cork, Ireland, with his large family and twenty workmen and servants. Although he sent his workers out from Philadelphia to develop a large plantation,

Farmer died before he could take up residence there. His widow, Mary, however, who appears to have been a rather indomitable sort, did move to the Whitemarsh wilderness, where from 1687 until her death in 1696 she managed the estate herself and apparently made quite a tidy living operating lime kilns and selling the crushed calcined lime they produced in Philadelphia at six pence a bushel (Alderfer 1951:33, 85).

In addition to her pioneering effort at farm industry, Mary Farmer was apparently also responsible for building the first gristmill in the area (Wallace 1962:123). Standing on the banks of Wissahickon Creek, Farmer's gristmill was a focal point for the farmers in the surrounding countryside and, as such, it led to a bit of road-building. Although Bethlehem Pike was an extension of the road from Philadelphia through Germantown, Skippack Pike, which was constructed before 1713, seems to have come into existence largely as a result of Farmer's gristmill.

Upon Mary Farmer's death, her son Edward inherited 3,750 acres of the original grant, including the land on which Hope Lodge now stands. Edward Farmer would presumably have had a house somewhere on his vast acreage, but whether it was the grand house that became known as Hope Lodge is uncertain. If Farmer did build the mansion, he was evidently no longer in possession of it when he died in 1745, for his will makes no mention of it (Wallace 1962:126). The construction of the mansion is generally attributed not to him but to Samuel Morris, a Quaker farmer and miller who became something of an entrepreneur. In 1740 Morris bought a 50 percent interest in Farmer's gristmill, which included a 50 percent interest in the 150 acres on which Hope Lodge was built. The next year Morris apparently bought out Farmer's interest in the land, for in a later mortgage agreement that documents Morris's purchase of a Philadelphia bank from Farmer, he put up the land as surety, noting that he "bought [it] from Edward Farmar in 1741" (cited in Liggett 1975: 59–60).

Samuel Morris never married. Beyond that, little is known of his life. More, in fact, seems to be known about his death. Because he died intestate, an innkeeper named Peter Adams, who was with Morris at the time of his death, was called upon to make a deposition for the records of Philadelphia County. Adams testified that he was summoned to "the house of Samuel Morris" when the latter was taken ill and that he stayed with him until the end. In the wake of the legal proceedings, Samuel Morris's brother Joshua came into possession of Morris's house and land. Joshua Morris never lived there, and in 1776, in the midst of the Revolution, he sold the estate to William West.

West had emigrated from Ireland to Pennsylvania in 1750. By the time the Revolutionary War broke out, he had become a prosperous merchant and was cutting quite a figure in the

Figure 9.12.

Hope Lodge. (Courtesy of the Pennsylvania State Archives, Division of History)

higher echelons of Philadelphia society. At about the same time, West's nephew, named after him and known as William West, Jr., was embarking on a career as an intelligence officer for the Continental forces.

West's country estate was the scene of some minor skirmishes between Washington's troops and the British in the late fall of 1777, but there is no evidence that the mansion ever served as a military hospital or headquarters. In December Washington's men withdrew from their positions on three hills overlooking the mansion (which came to be known as Militia Hill, Camp Hill, and Fort Hill) and started on the final leg of their journey to winter camp at Valley Forge. The British withdrew to the occupied city of Philadelphia, where William West, Jr., apparently played a major role in the underground campaign waged to dislodge them (Wallace 1962: 134–36).

William West died on October 28, 1782, evidently hoping that his nephew would take up residence at his country estate. That was not to be, however. After the war, William West, Jr., resigned from the army and became involved in black-market trade in the West Indies, an activity that ultimately led to his being accused of treason. The charges were dropped, and shortly thereafter West, Jr., moved to Baltimore, never having lived for any length of time in his uncle's country mansion.

In 1784 Henry Hope of Holland acquired the property from West's estate and gave it to his cousin as a wedding gift. The cousin, James Horatio Watmough, had only recently arrived in North America, but it was not his first visit. Born in Nova Scotia, Watmough at the age of eight had been sent to England for his education. Upon reaching adulthood, he went to work for his cousin's firm,

Hope and Company. However, he was not pleased with certain familial arrangements Hope had in mind for him, and in 1782 he left England for America. The disagreement between the cousins could not have been very serious, for Watmough not only accepted Henry Hope's generous gift but also named the property after him.

Settling into Hope Lodge with his bride, Watmough ultimately became a prominent and prosperous Philadelphia banker. According to a 1798 tax assessment, the property then had, in addition to the mansion, a 40-by-23-foot stone barn, a stable, a hay house, and a stone-working shop; no doubt it had some elegant formal gardens as well. Watmough died in 1812, leaving a will so confusing the courts declared he had died intestate. Hope Lodge remained in the hands of Watmough's four children until 1832, when the estate was deeded to Jacob Wentz, whose family retained title to it for almost a century (Wallace 1962: 138–42).

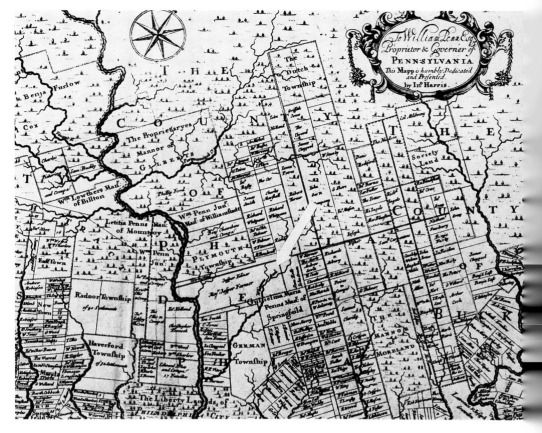

Figure 9.13.

The Farmer tract, shown on the John Harris edition of Thomas Holme's map of Pennsylvania, ca. 1690. Its size rivals that of "German Township," just south of it. (Courtesy of the Library Company of Philadelphia)

Archaeology at Hope Lodge

Shortly after Henry Borstling (1965b) completed a largely inconclusive resistivity survey at Hope Lodge, Barbara Liggett (1967) contracted with the Pennsylvania Historical and Museum Commission to carry out a series of archaeological excavations at Hope Lodge and at two areas near the estate. One of these nearby areas, on the opposite side of Bethlehem Pike from Hope Lodge itself, was the site of the gristmill Mary Farmer is credited with having built on the banks of Wissahickon Creek in the late 1600s. An early nineteenth-century gristmill known as Mather Mill now occupies the site. Liggett excavated three test trenches here in the hope of determining how the original millrace was built and when it was closed. She was also interested in discovering the purpose of what appeared to be a terrace on the bank of the creek. Although she did not find answers to all her questions, she did uncover at about 10 feet from the surface part of a stone feature, around which she also found some early artifacts. Ligget concluded that the stone feature could have been part of the wall of the late seventeenth-century millrace.

The other nearby area was at the edge of the Hope Lodge property, just off Bethlehem Pike at the front of the mansion. Here a stone sill in a retaining wall had given rise to the assumption that this was where the estate's original driveway had been. The archaeological evidence proved otherwise: a 13-by-15-foot excavation unit revealed what appeared to be a footpath rather than a driveway. The path was made of a thin layer of gravel and crushed limestone laid directly on an old humic surface, and a large, flat fieldstone found with it indicated it had had some steps. Analysis of the mortar that held the fieldstones together demonstrated that the steps, and probably the path, had been laid after 1832.

Liggett continued her search for the original driveway onto the estate itself, where she had noted a shallow depression running between the retaining wall and a terrace in front of the mansion. Although Liggett found no evidence of the driveway or even of a continuation of the footpath, she did uncover near the front of the mansion a low wall, which she at first thought was a step placed there for the convenience of passengers alighting from carriages. However, further excavation and probing demonstrated that this feature, found about 2 feet from the surface, was a retaining wall that largely encircled the mansion. It had

probably been built after 1840 and fallen into disuse in the late 1800s; by the early 1900s it had been covered with gravel and buried. The most enigmatic find of Liggett's entire investigation of Hope Lodge also occurred near the front terrace; here a test trench revealed the nearly complete skeleton of a mature female pig.

Liggett's excavation of nineteen trenches of varying sizes in the formal garden on the south side of the mansion demonstrated that this area had been used for at least two different purposes. Shallow root molds spaced 5½ feet apart indicated that at one time, probably before the mansion was built, it had been a cornfield; a series of terraces indicated that it had later been turned into an elaborate formal garden. Liggett recorded three major changes to the landscape: the ground had been leveled when the mansion was built; later, the stone retaining wall of the front terrace had been extended around the side of the house; and later still, a new series of terraces and stylized gardens had been superimposed on earlier ones.

Liggett excavated eight units near a flagpole northwest of the house, where, according to oral tradition, an old stable had been. At about a foot below the surface, she found what appeared to be one or possibly two stone floors. The "flooring" consisted of jumbled rocks overlain by gravel. Among the few artifacts found here were some horseshoes, suggesting this may indeed have been the site of a stable; however, it could also have been a courtyard. Whether a courtyard or a stable, it had occupied an area about 40 feet long and 25 to 30 feet wide.

In an attempt to date the existing barn, Liggett tested the area around it. Here she uncovered several walls, some projecting from the walls of the barn. Some of these features had

probably been barnyard walls or the walls of attached sheds, but others appeared to be foundation walls, indicating that the barn had once been larger and of a different shape. Supporting this theory was the presence of a considerable amount of demolition debris. However, test trenches in this area produced little evidence that this had been the site of the barn described in the 1798 tax assessment of Hope Lodge; most artifacts recovered here dated from the mid-1800s to the late 1800s. But in the east wall of the barn itself, Liggett found mud-and-straw mortar, suggesting that this part of the barn had been built before 1800 and was no doubt part of the barn mentioned in the 1798 tax assessment. Liggett hypothesized that shortly after Jacob Wentz acquired the property in 1832, he had added an extension and bay door to the south side of the barn, and that sometime between 1850 and 1900 one of the Wentzes had built a similar addition on the north side. Liggett also found the circular remains of a silo with a diameter of about 10 feet, but she was unable to date it.

Evidence of the Wentz family's occupation of Hope Lodge—and of their material culture—was found in abundance in a well near the mansion. Evidently dug in the late 1800s and about 25 feet deep, the well was nearly overflowing with artifacts dating from about 1880 to 1920. In addition to containing ample evidence of the dairy George Wentz had operated in the early 1900s, the well contained a porcelain doll, a ceremonial sword sheath, assorted cutlery, a coffee pot, several toy guns, a rake, two pitchforks, several files, a pair of pliers, two shovels, a scythe, sickle blades, several clocks, two watches, and a number of metal figurines, including a small bronze mule, souvenir of the 1901 St. Louis World's Fair.

THE PETER WENTZ FARMSTEAD: GERMANIC INFLUENCE IN THE DELAWARE VALLEY

Situated on Schultz Road near the Skippack Pike in Worcester Township, the Peter Wentz Farmstead today consists of sixty-seven acres, a stone farmhouse built in 1758, a barn, and some other outbuildings. The site is an interesting example of how the German settlers of Pennsylvania lived and the ways in which they adapted to the culture of their new surroundings. The blending of old culture with new is particularly evident in the architecture of the farmhouse (Figures 9.14 and 9.15). Its builder, Peter Wentz, Jr., was the American-born son of one of the many German Protestants who immigrated to Pennsylvania in the course of the eighteenth century. It is not known from which of the "German" countries the elder Peter Wentz hailed,

but, like many of his fellow immigrants, he chose to settle not in a town or village but on a farmstead in the upper reaches of the Philadelphia region.

Industrious and frugal, Peter Wentz, Sr., prospered to the extent of being able to leave his offspring sizable pieces of land. The 300 acres he left to Peter Wentz, Jr., remained in the Wentz family until the late eighteenth century. However, the longest ownership of the Peter Wentz Farmstead was not by the Wentzes but by another family of German descent, the Schultzes, whose ancestor Melchior Schultz bought the property in 1794. The farmstead remained in the Schultz family for a hundred and fifty years. In 1970 the Commissioners of Mont-

gomery County acquired the buildings and sixty-seven acres that today comprise the farmstead and embarked on an ambitious program of restoring the site and interpreting its history.

History of the Peter Wentz Farmstead

In 1711 the elder Peter Wentz bought a 50-acre tract in Towamencin Township. By 1715 he had acquired three more tracts, bringing his land holdings to 334 acres. By 1738 he owned an additional 656 acres, on which he

Figure 9.14.

South elevation of the house at the Peter Wentz Farmstead. Built by the son of a German immigrant, this farmhouse, with its rough stone walls, balcony, and pent eave, shows a mix of colonial and German influences. (From National Heritage Corporation 1975; courtesy of the Commissioners of Montgomery County and the National Heritage Corporation)

built himself a house. So well did he build that it still stands on what is now called Fisher Road. The elder Wentz made his last land purchase in 1743, when he bought 956 acres abutting the property on which he had built his house. Within these 956 acres, in Worcester Township, his son Peter soon developed his own farmstead (National Heritage Corporation 1975:8).

When the elder Peter Wentz died in 1749, his sons, daughters, grandsons, and granddaughters inherited his property. Figure 9.16 shows how the 956 acres of his last land purchase were divided among his offspring. Peter Wentz, Jr., had apparently begun developing the 300 acres he inherited even before his father's death. About 1744 he built a stone barn and a log house on his future inheritance; portions of the barn still stand, and the log house probably survived until about 1875. A gristmill whose ruins can still be seen across Schultz Road from the farmstead may have been built on the log house's foundations (Figure 9.17).

After Peter Wentz, Jr., came into his inheritance, he went to work in earnest, building the nine-room stone farmhouse that still stands on the property. Finished in 1758, the house was one of the largest and grandest the neighboring countryside had yet seen (National Heritage Corporation 1975:11). In the autumn of 1777 it was still apparently among the most imposing, for it was the place George Washington chose to use as headquarters before the Battle of Germantown.

By 1784 Peter Wentz, Jr., had dissolved his inheritance, parceling his 300 acres out among various buyers. In 1771 Nicholas Hoffman bought a large piece of the land, in 1774 Wentz's son John bought two additional parcels, and in 1784 Devault Beiber bought the farmhouse and all that

Figure 9.15.

West elevation of the house at the Peter Wentz farmstead. (From National Heritage Corporation 1975; courtesy of the Commissioners of Montgomery County and the National Heritage Corporation)

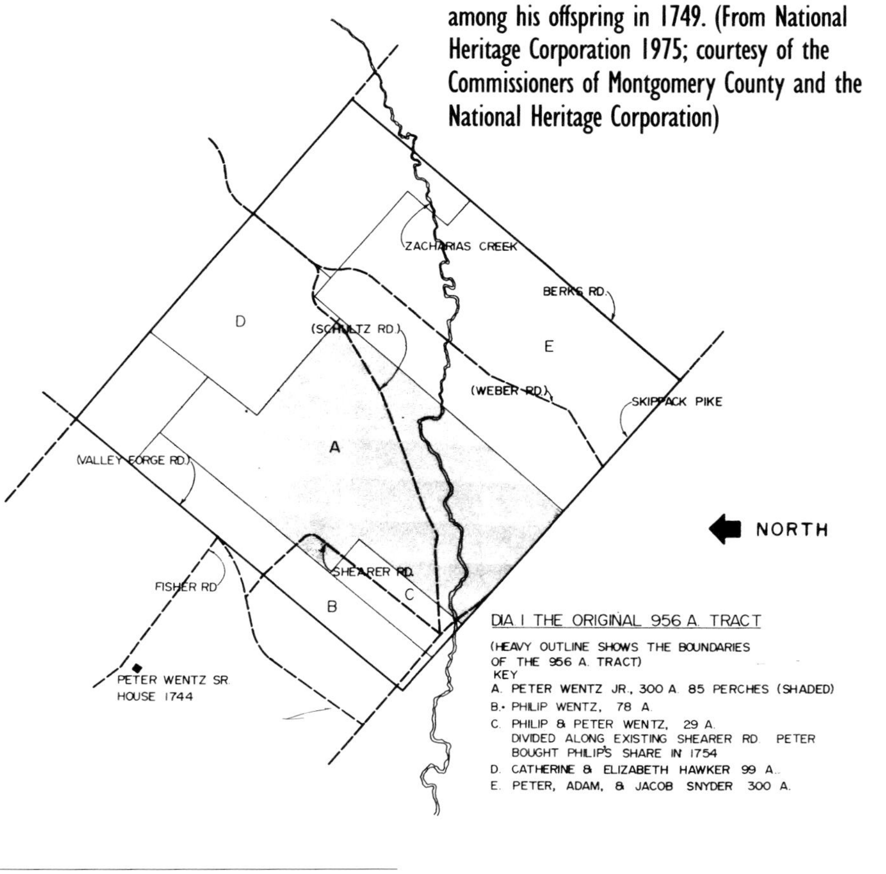

Figure 9.16.

Division of the elder Peter Wentz's 956 acres among his offspring in 1749. (From National Heritage Corporation 1975; courtesy of the Commissioners of Montgomery County and the National Heritage Corporation)

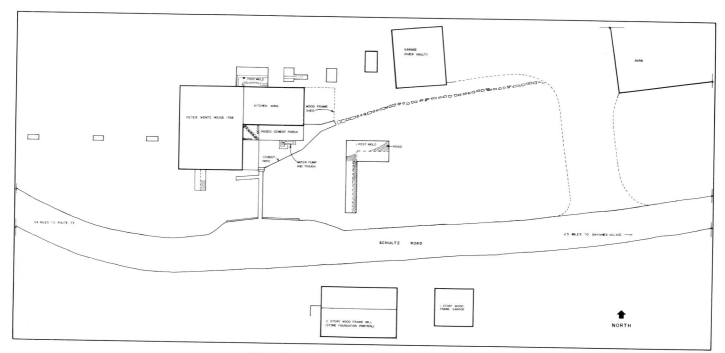

NORTH

Figure 9.17.

Map of the Peter Wentz farmstead, showing the site of the mill across the road from the farmhouse. (From National Heritage Corporation 1975; courtesy of the Commissioners of Montgomery County and the National Heritage Corporation)

Figure 9.18.

Dissolution of the younger Peter Wentz's property, 1771–1784. (From National Heritage Corporation 1975; courtesy of the Commissioners of Montgomery County and the National Heritage Corporation)

was left of the land (Figure 9.18). Whether Peter lived at the farmstead between 1784 and his death in 1793 is unknown. However, the year after Peter's death, Devault Beiber sold the farmstead to Melchior Schultz, whose family owned it until 1944.

Archaeology at the Peter Wentz Farmstead

Since the Commissioners of Montgomery County acquired the Peter Wentz Farmstead in 1970, they have sponsored a number of archaeological investigations, all of them part of the overall plan for accurately restoring the property and interpreting its history. The first investigation, conducted in 1973 by the National Heritage Corporation (1975), produced evidence that the road that passes by the farmhouse once ran considerably closer to it than it does today. Excavation southeast of the house revealed at about a foot below the surface a stone roadbed, which had probably been ballast for an earlier road or cartway. Artifacts found below the stones dated from about 1775 to 1825. The dates of the artifacts, together with

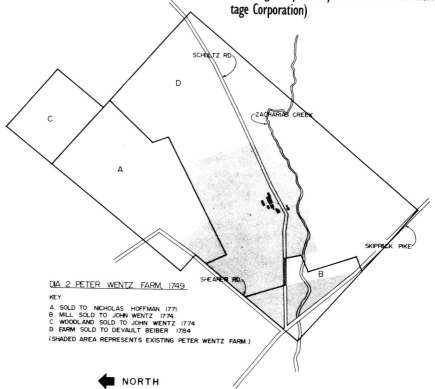

DIA 2 PETER WENTZ FARM, 1749

KEY

A. SOLD TO NICHOLAS HOFFMAN 1771
B. MILL SOLD TO JOHN WENTZ 1774
C. WOODLAND SOLD TO JOHN WENTZ 1774
D. FARM SOLD TO DEVAULT BEIBER 1784
(SHADED AREA REPRESENTS EXISTING PETER WENTZ FARM.)

← NORTH

the presence in the roadbed of a large tree some hundred years old, indicated that the old road had fallen into disuse about 1850 (National Heritage Corporation 1975:173).

The National Heritage Corporation's study also focused on the kitchen wing of the farmhouse (Figure 9.19). Until about 1870, when the kitchen was remodeled, part of the wing had been a "breezeway" between the house and kitchen. The evidence showed that the north wall of the kitchen was original and largely intact, except for a new door and window. The massive dry-laid stone wall, 22 inches thick, that divides the wing into east and west halves, was also original and had been the west wall of the kitchen. Somewhere along this wall there would have been a door opening onto the breezeway. The south wall, however, from the dividing wall to the main house, dated from an 1870 remodeling (National Heritage Corporation 1975:176).

In 1975 Elizabeth Righter of Jack McCormick and Associates excavated an area north of the house where the original kitchen garden would presumably have been planted. Righter found three postholes suggestive of the kind of fence early Pennsylvania Germans typically built around their gardens. Such gardens were square and had picket fences around them; the pickets were attached to posts, which were generally hewn from locust or chestnut trees and spaced 11 feet apart. Righter was able to extrapolate from the positions in which she found the three postholes that there had been others and that all had been spaced 11 feet apart. However, the postholes, about 14 inches in diameter, contained the remains of cedar posts, rather than locust or chestnut, and the artifacts found around them suggested that the posts had been erected in the early 1800s. It

seems likely that they were replacements of earlier ones and that the postholes were evidence of an early garden fence (Righter 1975:1–5).

In 1976 Righter continued her investigation of the farmstead, this time focusing on the ruins of the gristmill across Schultz Road and on the early road the National Heritage Corporation had begun uncovering three years before. Excavation indicated that the gristmill, known to have been intact as late as 1893, was built on the foundations of an earlier structure, possibly the log house built about 1744 by Peter Wentz, Jr. The earlier structure had probably measured about 16 by 16 feet; the gristmill superimposed on it had been 16 by 40 feet. The most striking feature of the earlier structure was a collection of elongated stones set in a clay fill; it looked rather like part of a cobbled street. It could have been a hearth, but there were no signs of its having been subjected to fire (Righter 1976: 14, 19).

As shown in Figure 9.20, Righter's excavation of ten trenches southeast of the house demonstrated that the old road or cartway had extended from a cul-de-sac on the east side of the house at least as far west as an existing shed, a distance of more than 400 feet. The width of the cartway varied from 33 feet at its widest point to 15 feet at its narrowest. In some places the stones of the roadbed overlay a 2-inch bed of shale chips; in others they did not. The stones varied in size from less than 1 inch to up to 9 inches, with the smaller ones serving as packing for the larger ones. Found in a layer of earth above the stones was an English copper halfpenny dated 1861, proof that the cartway had been built before that date. The cul-de-sac on the east side of the house measured roughly 35 feet per side and was set on a bed of flat stones; growing in a ragged ring

around it were some wild tulips and grape hyacinths. The evidence suggested that the cul-de-sac may have been a courtyard during the eighteenth century (Righter 1976:6, 7, 14).

In 1984, after a garage about 70 feet beyond the kitchen wing had been razed, John McCarthy of John Milner Associates excavated the roughly rectangular ruin that appeared when the modern debris was cleared away. The structure measured about 25 feet by 18 feet and was divided into two sections. The north section, which had rubble walls extending about 4 feet below grade, had apparently been built first. Part of this section had a cellar roofed over with flat stones. Entry to it was through the south section, where there were two more cellar chambers and a staircase to the outside. The chambers in the south section—one about 5 feet deep, the other about 8 feet deep—had vaulted roofs of stone and brick. The mortar in the north section indicated it had been built in the early 1800s, and it may have been used as an icehouse. The purpose of the south section, with its vaulted chambers, was unclear, but this section, too, may have been built before 1825; found in one of the building trenches was a redware jug with a green-mottled glaze—a type of ceramic made in Philadelphia between 1800 and 1830. Portland cement found in the south section indicated it had been rehabilitated in the late 1800s, and it is likely that the chambers here may then have been used as root cellars (McCarthy 1984a:6).

McCarthy's excavation of two trenches near the "icehouse/root cellars" revealed the remains of a dry-laid, 12-by-7-foot stone foundation with a smaller foundation projecting from its south side. The main foundation was only about 2 feet deep; this depth, as well as the dry-laid con-

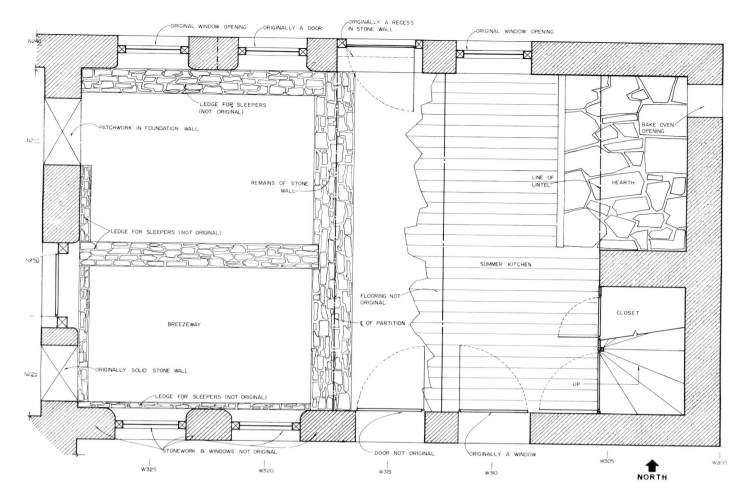

Figure 9.19.

Plan of the kitchen wing at the Peter Wentz Farmstead. (From National Heritage Corporation 1975; courtesy of the Commissioners of Montgomery County and the National Heritage Corporation)

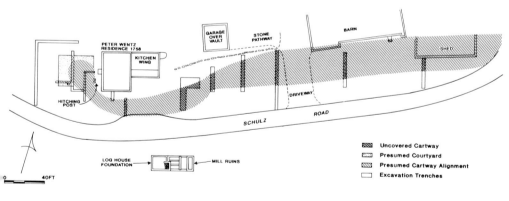

Figure 9.20.

Excavation plan showing the old road between the cul-de-sac and the shed at the Peter Wentz Farmstead. (From Righter 1976; courtesy of the Commissioners of Montgomery County and Jack McCormick and Associates)

struction, indicated it had supported a light structure—one that was probably made of wood and that was in all likelihood a privy. The projecting foundation was suggestive of the kind of waste-collection box found behind the privy at Harriton (see Chapter 9, "Harriton"). Although Pennsylvanian German privies were usually only about 5 by 7 feet, the larger size of

the one McCarthy uncovered would not have been out of keeping with the size of the Peter Wentz Farmstead (McCarthy 1984a:10–11).

At the Peter Wentz Farmstead, as at many other historic sites in the Philadelphia region, the data produced by archaeological investigations contributed to an accurate restoration of the site. Today the

kitchen wing of the house looks much as it did in 1758, as do the gardens and some of the outbuildings. Although these studies were oriented more to structures than to the people who inhabited them, they nonetheless threw some light on the way those people lived.

THE HIGHLANDS: SOCIAL
STRATIFICATION IN FORT WASHINGTON

At different times during the first half of the nineteenth century, three of the wealthiest men in southeastern Pennsylvania were the owners of the Highlands, a country estate built in the uplands of Montgomery County in 1795–96. Now situated on 43 acres at 7001 Sheaff Lane in Fort Washington, the estate originally consisted of 330 acres, a large and elegant mansion, a fine three-story stone barn, an octagonal two-story springhouse, an icehouse, an elaborate formal garden (requisite status symbol of the gentleman farmer), and a tenant farmhouse (Figure 9.21). As usual, the lives of the wealthy owners of the estate are fairly well documented, while those of the tenant farmers are historically anonymous. The mansion still stands, but evidence of the tenant house, like its occupants, has gone to ground.

By the 1970s the Highlands had become a state-owned property administered by the Pennsylvania Historical and Museum Commission and maintained by the Highlands Historical Society. Under the aegis of these organizations, the long-forgotten tenant house came in for its full share of archaeological attention. In 1976, in conjunction with a doctoral dissertation at the University of Pennsylvania, Joseph Hall IV conducted a comparative study aimed at elucidating the lifestyles of the first three

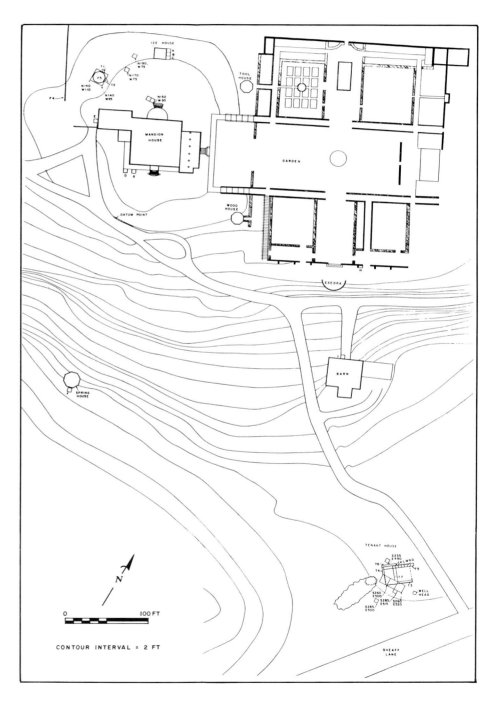

Figure 9.21.

Plan of the Highlands. (From Hall 1978)

Figure 9.22.

The mansion at the Highlands. (Photo by Joseph Hall IV)

owners of the mansion and of the tenant farmers who lived at the Highlands during the same period. In 1978 Richard H. Jordan of the Department of Anthropology at Bryn Mawr College undertook an archaeological investigation that included additional excavation of the tenant farmhouse. The following account summarizes the results of the historical and archaeological research reported by Hall (1978) and Jordan (1978).

The Highlands and Its Historical Context

In 1795 Anthony Morris, a wealthy Quaker businessman as well as one of the new republic's most prominent statesmen, bought 300 acres of the highest land east of the junction of Skippack and Butler pikes. Christening his estate "the Highlands," Morris proceeded to build a thirty-two-room mansion on a hilltop overlooking

Whitemarsh Valley. Completed in 1796, the mansion, made of cut schist, incorporated some architectural details of the Federal style, then popular in Philadelphia (Figure 9.22). By 1805 the estate had a tenant house, occupants unknown. The tenant house stood almost 600 feet southeast of the hilltop mansion on the lower ground near the entrance to the estate.

As the descendant of a family of aristocratic Quakers, it was not unusual for Anthony Morris to build a fine country house; the precedent had been set at Pennsbury Manor over a century before. But the final impetus for Morris's decision was probably related to his serving as Speaker of the House of Representatives while the federal government was quartered in Philadelphia in the 1790s. As House speaker, Morris no doubt felt it incumbent on him to have a country estate where he could entertain the leading figures of the land in suitable style; among his guests at the Highlands were Thomas Jefferson, James

Madison, and James Monroe. As a resident of Philadelphia in the 1790s, Morris was no doubt also glad to have a country place where he could retreat when yellow fever threatened.

The motives of the next two owners of the Highlands in acquiring and maintaining a country estate seem to differ in some respects from Morris's motives—and to reflect the changing mores of the times. Daniel Hitner, the land-rich scion of an established local family of German descent who succeeded Morris as owner of the Highlands, may have seen in his purchase the opportunity for making a quick profit. In any event, he was not in possession of the estate for very long, for in 1813 he sold it to its third owner, George Sheaff, who retained ownership until just before his death in 1851.

In addition to having made a fortune by importing wine and spirits to Philadelphia, Sheaff had married Anne Catherine Muhlenberg, offspring of the Reverend Henry Muhlenberg, who was well known for his role in establishing the German Lutheran Church in Philadelphia in the 1740s. Like Anthony Morris, Sheaff no doubt saw the Highlands as an appropriate backdrop for one of his wealth and social position. In the course of his tenure there, however, Sheaff may also have come to view it as something of a bulwark against the egalitarianism that characterized the nation during the Jacksonian Age. When Alexis de Tocqueville visited the United States soon after Jackson assumed the presidency in 1829, he commented on the withdrawal of the American aristocracy, noting that:

. . . the wealthy members of the community have abandoned the lists, through unwillingness to contend, and frequently to contend in vain, against the poorer classes of their fellow-citizens. They concentrate all their enjoyments in the privacy of their homes, where they occupy a rank that cannot be assumed in public; and they constitute a private society in the State, which has its own tastes and pleasures. (Tocqueville 1949 [1835]: 209)

Among George Sheaff's private "tastes and pleasures" was his two-acre formal garden, which he enclosed with the crenelated walls that surround it today.

Although the battlements of George Sheaff's garden walls no doubt signified his nurture of aristocratic privilege, they do not seem to have signified his complete withdrawal from the "lists." He was apparently first and foremost a shrewd entrepreneur, not above paying his neighbors for their services in his stock in trade—wine and spirits. He actively maintained his social and business connections in the city, and when plans were being made to bring the railroad out to Germantown, George Sheaff was at the fore-

front of the movement, serving both as a founding member and the secretary of the Philadelphia, Germantown & Norristown Railroad in 1831.

When Sheaff sold the Highlands shortly before he died in 1851, he advertised the estate as appealing to "gentlemen desirous of purchasing a permanent country residence in Pennsylvania" (Hall 1978: 37). Among the amenities described were a turnpike within a mile of the property and two railroads within five miles; moreover, "an omnibus passes the gate morning and evening every day, from the Exchange, and the Philadelphia morning papers are received by mail every morning at 7 o'clock" (Hall 1978: 260). Suburbia was coming of age and looking forward to the twentieth century, when most country estates would become white elephants, carved into subdivisions by hard-pressed owners or turned over to public agencies for tax benefits.

Archaeology at the Highlands

The 1976 Study

The object of Hall's study of the Highlands in 1976 was to determine differences in the material culture of the occupants of the mansion and of the tenant house by comparing the artifacts each group left behind in the years 1796–1851 (Hall 1978). Underlying Hall's thesis was the correlation between ownership of high-quality ceramics and high socioeconomic status demonstrated in numerous archaeological studies of eighteenth-century sites. His expectation was that a wide range of good imported British and Chinese ceramics at the tenant house would reflect the movement toward egalitarianism in America in

the first half of the nineteenth century and the new enfranchisement of "the poorer classes," to use Tocqueville's terminology.

Hall (1978) retrieved the artifacts he used in his study by excavating a number of test pits near the mansion and near the razed tenant house (see Figure 9.21). Despite the vast differences in the wealth of the occupants of the mansion and tenant house, the pits at both places contained the same types of ceramics. In each case, coarse earthenware accounted for about 25 percent of the total. The rest of each collection consisted of refined British earthenware and porcelain. But although the same types of ceramics appeared in each collection, there were significant differences. Statistical comparison showed a high percentage of imported British pearlware and creamware of good quality at the tenant house; at the mansion, there was a plainer assemblage of edge-decorated creamware and a higher percentage of polychrome porcelain.

Given that no cross-mends between the two collections appeared, it seems most unlikely that the tenant farmers' ceramics had originated at the mansion and been donated when chipped or fished out of a trash heap when broken. The statistical differences between the two collections were another strong indication that the tenant farmers had bought their own ceramics; not a single sherd of the gaudy Dutch glazed, hand-painted polychrome pearlware found in the pits at the tenant house appeared in the pits at the mansion. The pits at the tenant house contained no matching sets of ceramic tableware, suggesting that the farmers had bought a single, good ceramic piece whenever they could afford it.

From these findings, Hall concluded that egalitarianism of a sort—and social stratification of a definite kind—was indeed in evidence at the Highlands in the first half of the nineteenth century. He interpreted the artifacts found at the tenant house as reflecting the buying power of the newly aspiring "poorer classes" and those found at the mansion as reflecting the tendency of the elite to cling to the older symbols of their status and to shun the new ceramics available to their servants. In short, in Hall's view, the physical evidence supported the contention that Americans in the Jacksonian Age celebrated equality while living in a society stratified according to wealth and family background. But if most could not be wealthy, they manifested no desire to level society by the kinds of civil strife that shook France in 1789, most of Europe in 1848, and Russia in 1917; rather, they strove to attain the symbols that had traditionally been available only to the rich.

The 1978 Study

Two years after Hall concluded his study of the Highlands, Richard Jordan (1978), under contract to the Commonwealth of Pennsylvania, conducted another study of the property. His agenda included excavating the site of the tenant farmhouse and its well, and testing the ruins of a greenhouse. The farmhouse had been 36 feet long and 18 feet deep and oriented so that its length faced the winter sun (see Figure 9.21). Its foundation walls consisted of well-dressed Wissahickon schist, carefully mortared and extending 4 feet beneath present ground level. A layer of ash encountered at a depth of 18 inches, especially heavy at the west end of the house, suggested that the structure had been made of wood and had burned to the ground. Although Jordan did not quantify the artifacts he found around the house foundations, he did describe pearlware and glass as common, creamware as rare, and whiteware and mocha earthenware as somewhere in between. The glass included fragments of wine bottles, perfume bottles, medicine bottles, and drinking glasses; window glass was also common. Among the other artifacts retrieved here were a silver chain link, a single white clay pipe stem, and buttons of shell, bone, and brass. Because the depth of the well presented too great a danger, Jordan excavated only the top 5 feet. Here he found 1,800 artifacts, most of them fragments of glass bottles and jars manufactured in the twentieth century.

The greenhouse was located 30 feet west of the toolhouse that stands on the edge of the formal garden (see Figure 9.21). The ruins consisted of three parallel rows of rocks, and their spacing suggested a structure 50 feet long and 20 feet wide or wider. Jordan found the heaviest concentration of artifacts along the exterior of the north foundation wall and inside the northwest corner of the interior. The artifacts, totaling over 600 and dating from the early to mid-1800s, included an unspecified number of glazed ceramics and colored glass fragments; a decorated kaolin pipe stem; square nails, screws, hinges, and latches, all made of iron; a well-crafted ivory-handled knife; a U.S. three-penny coin, dated 1852; and a bottle marked "W. C. Montgomery's," which purported to contain a hair-restoring fluid. Jordan's report makes no mention of any window glass found on this site—a curious bit of negative evidence for a greenhouse.

Jordan concluded his study by recommending the permanent cataloguing, conservation, and storage of the some 5,000 to 6,000 artifacts then at the Highlands. He also recommended that excavation of the existing features continue.

10

Chester and Delaware Counties

In September 1789, five years after Montgomery County came into existence, the state assembly voted to create Delaware County by dividing Chester County along the boundary lines shown in Figure 2 in the Introduction. The new county was the result of a protracted and heated dispute over the location of the original county seat at Chester. For people in the western part of the area, it was a long journey to that town at the county's southeastern border, and they lobbied strenuously for the removal of the county government to a more central location. The "removalists" won the battle when West Chester became Chester County's seat in 1786. But the war was not over. As the residents of Chester and the southeastern part of the county began experiencing some of the inconvenience their western neighbors had previously felt, they launched a campaign that led, after much petitioning, to the formation of Delaware County, with the town of Chester serving as its county seat.

Although in most respects Chester County and its spinoff followed the same course of development as Bucks, Philadelphia, and Montgomery counties, at least one difference is discernible. The early Swedish influence in this area was marked, as a few of the sites described in this chapter testify. In 1643 Johan Printz, the third colonial governor of New Sweden, installed his seat of government on Tinicum Island, thereby establishing the first permanent European settlement within the present bounds of Pennsylvania. Here Printz built a log fort, as well as a residence known as the "Printzhof." Described by a contemporary as "very handsome," with "a fine orchard, a pleasure house and other conveniences," the Printzhof was no doubt a far cry from the rough log cabin in which the typical Swedish settler lived (Smith 1862:31).

The Swedes seem to have been a rugged and independent lot who preferred life on isolated farms scattered along the area's many creeks to life in villages or towns. Twice—once in 1657 and again in 1660—they successfully resisted the efforts of the Dutch, who were by then masters of the Delaware Valley, to concentrate them in one or two villages (Smith 1862:72, 77). This preference for rural life was evidently shared by the English and Welsh Quakers who began settling in Chester County in the early 1680s, for although these newcomers arrived in ever-increasing numbers, no towns of any size appeared. Even the county seat of Chester failed to grow. Founded as the Swedish hamlet of Upland in 1644, Chester received a borough charter in 1699 entitling it to a weekly market and two annual fairs. But despite these prerogatives and the growth of the county's population, Chester's population remained static throughout the 1700s. Chester County was not alone in its failure to produce prospering market towns; none of the neighboring counties did, either. One reason for this failure was the proximity of the great market town of Philadelphia (Dunn and Dunn 1982:24).

The city of Chester may well retain archaeological traces of its market house and other early structures,* but most of the log cabins of the Swedes of the countryside seem to have vanished, leaving few traces behind. The

Figure 10.1.

"Swedish Cabin" on Creek Road, Clifton Heights, Upper Darby Township. The cabin's log construction, proportions, and roof treatment are typical of structures built by Swedes in the 1600s. However, the earliest artifact recovered by students from the University of Pennsylvania working under the direction of Robert Schuyler in 1980 dated from the late 1700s. In 1988 a group of volunteers directed by Glenn Sheehan of the archaeological consulting firm of SJS had similar results: their earliest find was a coin minted in 1770. (Photo by J. L. Cotter)

Morton Homestead is an exception, and for many years it was thought that the "Swedish Cabin," a log structure on the banks of Darby Creek in Upper Darby Township, was also. However, limited archaeological investigations of the Swedish Cabin in the 1980s cast considerable doubt on that theory (Robert Schuyler, personal communication, 1981; Glenn Sheehan, personal communication, 1988). The earliest artifacts recovered dated from the late 1700s, and the structural evidence tended to discount the possibility that the cabin had been built in the 1600s and moved to its present site at a later date. Despite its early Swedish characteristics (Figure 10.1), the cabin was apparently built on the site sometime after 1750.

In addition to having more Swedes than most places in the Philadelphia region, Chester County, with a good part of the Welsh Tract lying within its bounds, had a heavy concentration of Welsh Quakers as well. German

* In conjunction with a plan by the Pennsylvania Department of Transportation to improve access of commercial traffic to Chester along Route 291, Parrington and Schenck (1982) conducted an archaeological survey of the affected area. They identified four sites as having archaeological potential: the site of a market house that stood in Chester's Market Square from 1744 until 1857 and the sites of three houses, two of them apparently built before 1700 and the other during the 1700s.

settlers, however, seem to have been relatively few, many of them having gravitated to the upper reaches of the Philadelphia region, where Montgomery County was the ultimate beneficiary of their careful farming methods. The smaller number of Germans in both Bucks and Chester counties may account for the early decline of agriculture in both places. As early as 1804 a good part of the land in Chester County had been "farmed out," a condition ameliorated when the practice of applying lime to the soil was introduced (Smith 1862:350).

The mills of Chester County never experienced the same lapse as its agriculture. With six major creeks—Brandywine, Chester, Ridley, Crum, Darby, and Cobbs—draining into the Delaware, and French Creek and other streams draining into the Schuylkill, the county was ideally suited to water-powered industry. The first mill, "doubtless the most useful institution in the country" (Smith 1862: 120), was built on Cobbs Creek about 1644. Known as Swedes' Mill, it was still grinding flour in 1695, by which time an additional five mills were in operation. By 1730 the county had a paper mill, and by 1750 it also had an iron forge and a mill for slitting and rolling iron. By 1810 it had a woolen factory, and within fifteen years of that date—even before steam engines came into general use in the area—it had no fewer than 200 mills, producing everything from flour, snuff, and sawn lumber to textiles, paper, gunpowder, nails, knives, and linseed oil (Smith 1862:38, 191, 258–59, 353, 356–57, 383).

Where there are mills, there are roads, ferries, and bridges to get to them; where there are roads, ferries, and bridges, there are taverns to cater to the people who traverse them; and where there are taverns, villages are likely to grow up around them. That

tale of development Chester County shared with all its neighbors. It also shared in providing a backdrop for the Revolutionary War. In addition to having been the site of the Battle of the Brandywine and the Continental Army's winter camp at Valley Forge, it was the scene of many another less well known war drama, including that of Yellow Springs, a once-fashionable spa near Valley Forge that became the site of a military hospital in 1778. Samuel Kennedy, the owner of Yellow Springs, not only donated his land for the hospital, he also served as a surgeon there and, contracting a "putrid fever" from one of his soldier patients, many of whom suffered from smallpox and typhoid, gave his life to the cause (Roark 1974:31). Descriptions of the physical appearance of the hospital indicate that Kennedy and the military men who planned it had an enlightened view of treating illness and injury among battle-weary soldiers. Facing south, the large, three-story frame structure was light and airy and "commodiously divided into dining rooms, drawing rooms and chambers." Despite the enlightened approach, numerous men died; many are said to have been buried in a meadow in front of the hospital (Futhey and Cope 1881:101).*

---

* When the hospital closed in 1781, Yellow Springs reverted to its prewar role as a spa. It served again as a military hospital during the Civil War and as an orphanage thereafter. After the hospital burned in 1902 and was rebuilt, it served as an art school and, before it burned again in the early 1960s, as a film studio. In 1974 the Yellow Springs Foundation acquired the 152-acre tract, and in the same year Kenyon and Hunter (1974) conducted an archaeological feasibility study, using historical documentation to identify areas for future excavation and research. In a follow-up study, Kenyon, Thibaut, and Schenck (1977) discovered that the hospital's foundations extended no more than a foot into the ground, suggesting that the hospital had been erected in haste. These excavations produced no evidence of medical practice during the Revolutionary War; the earliest artifacts dated from the 1800s.

The archaeological sites described in this chapter span the years from 1642 through the early 1800s.* They reflect not only the early presence of Swedes in this area but also the lifestyle of the Welsh Quakers and English settlers who joined them in the early 1680s. Among the sites are a crude stone cottage hastily built by the manager of a mill in 1683, an early mill village, an eighteenth-century farmhouse, and two grand country mansions, both of which started out in a rather modest way. The major site described in the chapter is Valley Forge, the revolutionary war encampment that became the symbol of America's determined struggle for independence.

---

* At the time of this writing, substantial archaeological investigations were nearing completion, as several primarily nineteenth-century sites were located in the path of the Mid-County Expressway (also known as the Blue Route), a north-south artery built by the Pennsylvania Department of Transportation to connect the Pennsylvania Turnpike with Interstate 95. These sites were identified during an initial Phase 1 survey by McCarthy and Graff (1983). The archaeological studies, conducted by CHRS and John Milner Associates, included, among others, detailed investigation of the Isaac Free Site, a late nineteenth-century industrial worker's house (Cress et al. [in preparation, c]); the Bailey Tenant Site, a nineteenth-century African-American–occupied tenant house (Cress et al. [in preparation, a]); the Charles Brown Site, a late nineteenth- and early twentieth-century site associated with Trinity U.A.M.E. Church (Cress et al. [in preparation, b]); a prohibition-era speakeasy dump (Cress et al. [in preparation, f]); the Sloan Springhouse, associated with the nineteenth-century Lamb Tavern (Cress et al. [in preparation, e]); the Rhoads Whetstone Factory Complex, a late nineteenth-century rural manufacturing enterprise (Cress et al. [in preparation, d]); and the Taylor House, a late eighteenth- and early nineteenth-century tenant farmstead (Cress et al. [in preparation, g]). Also investigated were the site of a nineteenth-century rural watertower, a Victorian residence, and portions of an eighteenth-century village named Avondale, which was associated with the well-known Thomas Leiper Industrial Complex (Basalik et al. [in preparation]).

THE PRINTZHOF: A HEAVY MAN
WITH A HEAVY HAND

The Printzhof, home of the Swedish colonial governor from 1643 until 1653, is one of the few early Swedish sites in the Delaware Valley well-documented by historical records. The structure stood on Tinicum Island near present-day Essington—an area that has suffered selective disturbance over the years (Figure 10.2). The site has thrice been the focus of archaeological study. In 1937, the tricentennial of the Swedish presence in the Delaware Valley, state archaeologist Donald Cadzow directed a team of WPA employees in an excavation intended to uncover the structural remains of the Printzhof. Although Cadzow did locate what he believed were the foundations of the house and its related structures, no report of his findings exists, nor did plans to reconstruct the buildings materialize. Almost forty years later, in 1976, the Pennsylvania Historical and Museum Commission sponsored a re-excavation of the site, with the aim of verifying Cadzow's conclusion that this had indeed been the site of Governor Johan Printz's home. Marshall Becker (1977a, 1977b, 1978a, 1979) carried out this work. Investigations were continued in 1989 for the Commission and the American Swedish Historical Museum by MAAR Associates, in association with Frens and Frens. At this writing, the latter work has not been completed.

Johan Printz and His New World Domain

On November 1, 1642, Johan Printz, lieutenant colonel in the Swedish cavalry and the newly commissioned governor of Queen Christina's American colony, sailed for the New World with his wife and daughter, a lieutenant governor, a secretary, a chaplain, a surgeon (who also doubled as a barber), about two dozen soldiers and their officers, a number of settlers, and a formidably detailed list of instructions from his royal employer.[*] The bottom line of that list was that New Sweden should show a profit.

Among the matters to which Printz was to attend were increasing the fur trade with the Lenape and securing their friendship by selling them goods

[*] Data for this historical account are from Smith (1862:28–69 passim).

"at lower prices than those they receive from the Dutch of Fort Nassau, or from the English their neighbors." He was also "to work underhand as much as possible, with good manners and with success" (Smith 1862), to remove the English from the Delaware River; in this undertaking—the only thing on which it seems the Swedes and Dutch could agree—Printz had the full support of the Dutch. In addition, Printz was to promote the development of agriculture among his people (first the cultivation of grain to feed themselves and then the cultivation of tobacco for export); to ensure "a good species" of sheep so that fine wool might be sent back to Sweden; to search for minerals and metals; and to inquire into the establishment of fisheries.

In choosing Tinicum as his seat of government in February 1643, Printz chose well, for another of his instructions was to "shut" the Delaware

Figure 10.2.

Site of the Printzhof in 1966. The depression in the foreground is from Donald Cadzow's excavation in 1937. (Photo by J. L. Cotter)

River to the Dutch traders. Tinicum Island, which then jutted out into the river, not only gave Printz a commanding position on the Delaware but also was close enough to the Dutch trading post at Fort Nassau (just south of present-day Camden, New Jersey) to allow him to keep an eye on Dutch movements.

As energetic as he was huge—reputedly some 400 pounds—Printz executed his duties so satisfactorily that within nine months of his arrival in the New World, the Swedish crown awarded him and his heirs the whole of Tinicum Island. After arriving at Tinicum, Printz built a log fort, known as New Gottenburg, and a log residence for himself and his family, which he called Printz Hall, or Printzhof. As noted by Becker (1979:16), Printz evidently built well, possibly on the order of a Swedish "gore" (manor house) after the first wooden structures were rebuilt following an accidental fire on November 23, 1645. Printzhof stood for more than 160 years after rebuilding, ultimately succumbing to fire in the early 1800s. Designed to defy attack, it was two stories high and had at least two fireplaces, made of pale-yellow bricks. Signifying the affluence of its owner were the glass panes in its windows and the draperies and library of its interior. Around Fort New Gottenburg, settlers (presumably those who accompanied Printz to the New World) established a number of small farms.

After Fort New Gottenburg burned in November 1645, Printz quickly rebuilt it. Meanwhile, he had seen to it that a gristmill, the same one that became known as Swedes' mill, was built on the banks of Cobbs Creek, and he had also established at least two more strategically placed forts. In 1646 he had a church erected on Tinicum Island. It was consecrated on

Figure 10.3.

Right, foundations of the Printzhof: *A,* probable first structure, built in 1643–44, with corner fireplace *e* and door *g.* The structure may have expanded as shown by *B,* when rebuilt after the fire of 1645; *h* would have been another corner fireplace. *C* was a later addition, as was *d,* which may have been another fireplace. (From Becker 1978a) *Below,* drawing by Robert Waddington, WPA General Foreman, showing the excavated "Foundations of Printz House" in 1937. (From a photostat supplied by the Pennsylvania Historical and Museum Commission)

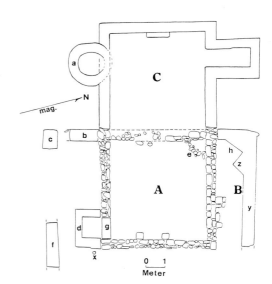

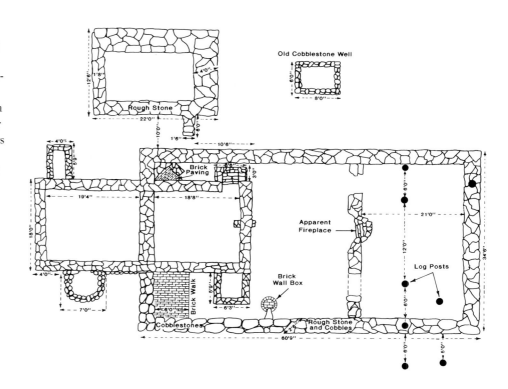

September 4 by the Reverend John Campanius, who the same day also consecrated a burial ground near the river. It is said that some Lenape attended Campanius's first church service and were much awed by the length of time he talked as well as by the utter silence of those who listened to him.

Printz's accomplishments were no small feats in a thickly wooded wilderness where the only highways were the Delaware, the Schuylkill, and their tributaries. They are all the more remarkable in view of the amount of time he spent bickering with the Dutch. Evidently brusque, dictatorial, and high-handed, Printz not only offended the Dutch personally; far worse, he also made serious inroads on their trade with the Lenape. Nonetheless, Printz somehow managed to avoid all-out war with them. Under his governorship, Swedish farmsteads slowly increased in size and number; meanwhile, of course, the lands of the Lenape decreased. On at least one occasion in the late 1640s, a number of Lenape leaders verbally took the Swedes to task, pointing out that while the Dutch had been in their presence for almost thirty years and had never taken land from them, the Swedes, only recently arrived on the river, had already taken and settled much of their land. Somehow, Printz managed to avoid bloodshed with them, too.

Bored at last with diplomacy and the lack of military activity, or perhaps discouraged by the scarcity of supplies and settlers arriving from Sweden, Printz resigned his post and returned to his homeland in late 1653—just in time to miss the fireworks that erupted under the governorship of his successor, John Rising. Immediately upon his arrival in May 1654, and in apparent violation of his instructions from the Swedish crown, Rising took possession of Fort Casimir, a weakly manned Dutch trading post at present-day New Castle, Delaware. The result was that Dutch trade and authority on the river were crippled. The Dutch response to this action was over a year in coming, but when it did, in the form of a well-equipped armada commanded by Peter Stuyvesant, it put an end to the Dutch and Swedish disputes. The Dutch victors apparently inflicted a good deal of punishment on their

Swedish foes. At Tinicum Island, where Printz's daughter had remained after his departure, the soldiers allegedly drove off the people who lived outside the fort, plundered their belongings, destroyed their crops, and killed their cattle. The amount of damage they inflicted on the fort itself is unknown, but if the Dutch did not destroy it, they subsequently allowed it to decay. Printz's daughter continued to live on the island for some years, but in greatly reduced circumstances.

Archaeology at the Printzhof

Although Donald Cadzow's notes on his fieldwork at Tinicum have not yet been found, a measured drawing by his WPA foreman (Figure 10.3, *bottom*) as well as some photographs and film footage of the excavation do exist. With these visual records and the evidence of the exposed foundations, Marshall Becker was able to reconstruct some of Cadzow's methodology. It appeared that in stripping topsoil from the park area, Cadzow had uncovered the foundation walls of the Printzhof* and then probed alongside them, mixing the artifacts in the fill layers; it also looked as if all the foundation stones had been reset. How many artifacts Cadzow removed is unknown; those that have not been lost are in the collection of the American Swedish Museum in Philadelphia (Figures 10.4–10.7). Although Cadzow had sorted the artifacts into cate-

* However, in 1970, a University of Pennsylvania class under the direction of John L. Cotter (King and Hancock 1970) examined the site and concluded that the foundations were probably of an eighteenth-century, not a seventeenth-century, house. As corroborative evidence, further tests by Frens and Frens and MAAR Associates in 1989 suggested that the foundations were associated with the Taylor family, landowners in the 1700s (Dale Frens, personal communication, 1990).

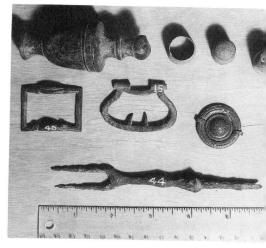

Figure 10.4.

Artifacts from the Printzhof: *from top left,* brass finial, three brass thimbles, two buckles and a boss of brass, and a two-tined iron fork. (Photo by J. L. Cotter; courtesy of the Swedish Museum, Philadelphia)

Figure 10.5.

Wrought-iron claw hammer and lock from the Printzhof. (Photo by J. L. Cotter; courtesy of the Swedish Museum, Philadelphia)

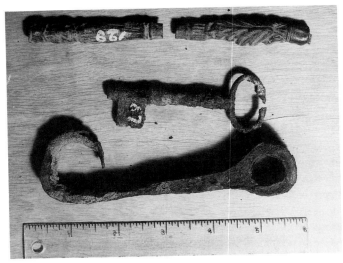

Figure 10.6.

A knife with engraved bone handle and a collection of pipes from the Printzhof. The two pipes at lower right are probably of Lenape origin. (Photo by J. L. Cotter; courtesy of the Swedish Museum, Philadelphia)

Figure 10.7.

Brass instrument handles, an iron key, and an iron door hinge from the Printzhof. (Photo by J. L. Cotter; courtesy of the Swedish Museum, Philadelphia)

Figure 10.8.

The "witch bottle" found at the Printzhof. (From Becker 1978a)

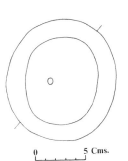
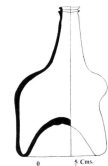

gories, he had given only a few of them provenience labels. Without field notes, the labels were of little use.

In re-excavating the site, Becker re-located two features Cadzow had noted. One was a small pit outside the southwest corner of the foundations of what is presumably the Printzhof (see Figure 10.3). Buried upside down in the pit, together with a bird bone and a redware sherd, was an olive-green bottle that dated from about 1740 (Figure 10.8). The bottle was sealed with a wooden plug, and inside it were six brass pins. It was apparently a so-called witch bottle (Becker 1978a), intended to counteract the power of a witch; pins were thought to be effective in warding off such evil. That the bottle had been buried near a chimney foundation may suggest that whoever put it there was trying to prevent the witch's spirit from coming down the chimney. Fear of the supernatural was common in the early eighteenth century, as evidenced by laws of that date that prohibit the practice of witchcraft in Pennsylvania.

The other feature that Becker re-located was a pit at the northwest corner of the foundations. The pit contained both colonial and Lenape artifacts, indicating considerable contact between the two groups during the seventeenth century, and indeed historical references bear out that the Lenape were frequent visitors at the Printzhof. Among the items of probable Lenape origin were several effigy pipes and pipe fragments, a stone celt, and a number of small animal bones. Becker (1977a:45) also uncovered the complete skeleton of a dog beneath several layers of fill containing items of European manufacture, as well as a series of empty graves, apparently dug by the Lenape for flexed burials. The graves were located between the Printzhof and the river's edge. Because the graves contained no skeletal remains, Becker concluded that either Cadzow had removed the remains in 1937 or the graves had never been used for burials. Numerous yellow bricks found scattered throughout the site may have been made in Sweden or Holland and exported to the New World, but the evidence for this is not conclusive.

While archaeology at the Printzhof has added to our knowledge of life in the Delaware Valley in the seventeenth and eighteenth centuries, the site has more potential still for shedding light on the interaction between the early Swedish settlers of Pennsylvania and the native Americans who greeted them on their arrival. It may also contain evidence of the Lenape who occupied or traversed the site before the Swedes arrived.

THE MORTON HOMESTEAD AND THE MORTONSON HOUSE: THE OLD SWEDES AT HOME

The Morton Homestead might more aptly be called the Mortonson Homestead, for it was built by Morton Mortonson, Sr., a Swedish immigrant, about 1654. The name "Morton" was bestowed on it as the result of a legend that came into existence during the last half of the nineteenth century. According to the legend, the homestead—a log cabin standing near the banks of Darby Creek along what is now Route 420 in Ridley Township—was the birthplace of John Morton, one of Pennsylvania's nine signers of the Declaration of Independence. Although Morton (who like other members of his family dropped the suffix "son" from his surname) was a great-grandson of Morton Mortonson, Sr., the legend had no basis in fact. However, it became so well entrenched that when the Commonwealth of Pennsylvania restored the dilapidated property and dedicated it as a memorial to John Morton in 1938, an official marker proclaimed it to be the revered signer's birthplace. It was not until 1957, after several title searches, that the Pennsylvania Historical and Museum Commission retracted the claim and gave the old cabin its present, more innocuous appellation (Springer 1967:29–32).

The Mortonson House, located in Norwood Borough near the confluence of Muckinipattus and Darby creeks, has also been the subject of a good deal of confused legend, and, rather ironically, it might more aptly be called the Morton House. Because the initials "MM" are set in dark-glazed bricks in the outside wall of its kitchen chimney, the house has traditionally been attributed to Morton Mortonson, Sr., and therefore regarded as one of Delaware County's oldest historic sites. In fact, it seems to have been built sometime after 1758 by Morton Morton, another of Mortonson's great-grandchildren (Springer 1967:33–34). Although it cannot claim to be among the county's earliest landmarks, the Mortonson House has many intriguing architectural features. Juxtaposed with the rustic Morton Homestead, it is also an interesting illustration of how far a Swedish immigrant's offspring had come in just over a hundred years.

Both the Morton Homestead and the Mortonson House have been the subject of archaeological study. In 1978, when a large sewer main was being laid near the Homestead, Mid-Atlantic Archaeological Research (MAAR) conducted an investigation of that part of the site.* After the Norwood Borough Council undertook a restoration of the Mortonson House in 1965, the house, by then on the brink of collapse, claimed the attention not only of archaeologists (Cosans 1969) but of architects as well.

The Properties of Morton Mortonson, Sr., and His Offspring

Morton Mortonson, Sr., born a Swedish subject, immigrated to America sometime before 1654, bringing with him his oldest son, Morton Mortonson, Jr., who was then about eight years of age. It is not known how Mortonson, Sr., first came into possession of his land, but on May 18, 1672, Francis Lovelace, colonial governor under the Duke of York, issued a patent confirming the grant of 200 acres to Jan Cornelius, Mattys Matty-

* A minor archaeological monitoring effort was undertaken in 1986 at the Morton Homestead by Joiré and Roberts during the construction of additional utility lines, but no archaeological features relating to the early occupation of the site were found. Additional research has also recently been undertaken at the Morton Homestead by MAAR Associates, but at the time of this writing, it had not been completed.

son, and Morton Mortonson in "Amosland," as much of Ridley Township was then known. By 1675, when Walter Wharton surveyed the property and found that it contained 728 acres rather than the 200 described in the confirming patent, Mattys Mattyson was no longer in the picture (Springer 1967:3–5). Jan Cornelius occupied the "upper" part of the tract, near Muckinipattus Creek; Mortonson lived on the "lower" part, where sometime about 1654 he had built the south section of the log cabin that still stands there. In 1694, after Jan Cornelius died intestate, his son Andreas Johnson sold to Morton Mortonson all that remained of Cornelius's land (MAAR 1978:62–63).

By the late 1690s Mortonson's small log cabin was housing himself, his wife, his son Andrew, his son Mathias, and Mathias's wife and young children. Morton Mortonson, Jr., and the rest of the elder Mortonsons' offspring had by then moved away from home. To accommodate Mathias's growing family (five children under the age of six by 1700), another log cabin was built next to the original one in 1698 (Springer 1967:6). The narrow space separating the two houses was later enclosed by stone walls and roofed over (Figure 10.9).

Three years before he died in 1706, Morton Mortonson, Sr., deeded the homestead to his son Mathias and gave his son Andrew, then newly married, 257 acres of land farther up Darby Creek in present-day Norwood Borough. Part of this acreage was from Mortonson's original grant; the rest was from the acreage he had bought from Andreas Johnson in 1694. Here, a little more than a mile east of the homestead, Andrew died in 1722, leaving a house, a widow, and five daughters, but no will. The court divided his estate among his

daughters, awarding Lydia, the youngest, the house and the land around it. Sometime between 1734 and 1741, Lydia married Morton Morton, grandson of Morton Mortonson, Jr. Lydia died in 1756, and on August 8, 1758, Morton Morton married Mary Boon of Darby. Presumably soon thereafter, he built on the property, near the juncture of Darby Creek and the Muckinipattus, the well-proportioned, two-story brick house that ultimately became known as the Mortonson House (Springer 1967: 8, 33–34).

Mathias Mortonson died just a few years after his father. The old homestead then passed to his son Andrew and next to his grandson Jonas. In 1779 Jonas sold it to a cousin named Sketchley Morton. Sketchley owned the homestead for only five years, selling it in 1784 to Joseph Hoof and Benjamin Ford, the first owners who were not direct descendants of Morton Mortonson, Sr. By that time, the property had already entered its first commercial phase, as evidenced by a ferry that in the 1760s plied back and forth across Darby Creek from a land-

ing at the homestead (MAAR 1978: 64, 68).

The homestead was apparently serving as a landing place for wayfarers on Darby Creek from an early date, for in 1687 a road was laid out from Springfield to "ye landing Place by the maine creeks Side beyond Morten Mortensons House" (Springer 1967:8; Figure 10.10). The road cut through several farms, to the disgruntlement of some farmers, who repeatedly expressed their objections by throwing roadblocks in the way of travelers. As a result, a new road, still known as Amosland Road, was laid out in 1726 (Springer 1967:7). By 1848 the course of this road in the vicinity of the homestead had been altered so that it no longer took the extended jog shown in Figure 10.11 but ran in a relatively straight line to the landing at the creek (MAAR 1978: 69–70).

Although Morton Mortonson's property had a landing place at least as early as 1687, the first record of a

Figure 10.9.

The Morton Homestead. (Photo by J. L. Cotter)

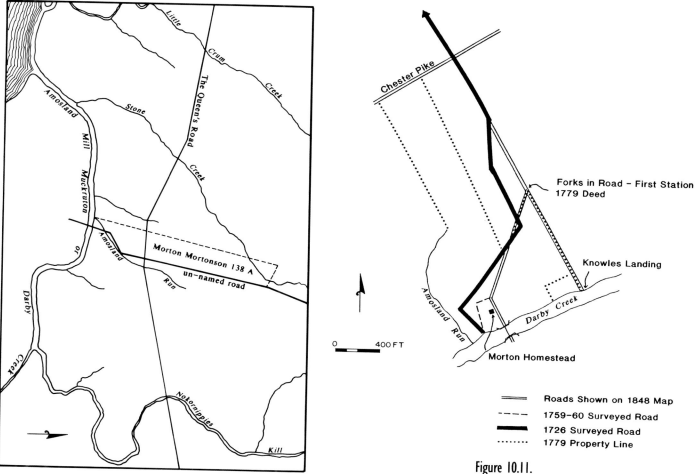

Figure 10.10.

Road built in 1687 from Springfield to the landing place on Darby Creek. The road runs along the 138-acre tract on which Mortonson, Sr. built his log cabin. (Courtesy of the Historical Society of Pennsylvania)

Figure 10.11.

Known road locations, 1726–1848. (From Mid-Atlantic Archaeological Research 1978)

Legend:
- ⎯⎯ Roads Shown on 1848 Map
- – – – 1759–60 Surveyed Road
- ▬▬ 1726 Surveyed Road
- ·········· 1779 Property Line

ferry at the landing does not occur until 1768. In that year, William Smith of Ridley Township was assessed for eight acres of land, three head of cattle, and a ferry at the landing. Jonas Morton was the owner of the homestead at that time, and he evidently leased a part of the property to Smith. For some unknown reason, the ferry went out of operation in 1771 and was not re-established until after Joseph Hoof and Benjamin Ford bought the homestead from Sketchley Morton in 1784. The deed described the property as "a certain messuage or tenement and tract of land there-

unto belonging with a ferry thereon established on Darby Creek." Two years later, Hoof petitioned for a license for a ferry and a "house of entertainment," the first reference to a tavern at the homestead site. Until 1848, when a bridge near the landing rendered it obsolete, the ferry operated continuously under a series of different owners. By the time of its demise, it had become known as Morris' Ferry, in token of George and Amos Morris, two of the entrepreneurs who owned the homestead in the first half of the nineteenth century (MAAR 1978:67–69).

Archaeology at the Morton Homestead

The sewer main that prompted the archaeological investigation at the Morton Homestead in 1978 was to be laid parallel to Darby Creek and to intersect the spot where it was thought William Smith's eighteenth-century ferry had anchored (Figure 10.12). Archaeological excavation of a 20-by-140-foot trench along this path revealed, at nearly 8 feet below existing grade, what were doubtless the remains of a log road. The archaeologists' report (MAAR 1978:23) described the road's construction (see also Figure 10.13):

1. Four logs or sections of logs (9″ to 12″ in diameter) were laid down perpendicular to the creek bed and spaced from 3.5 to 4 feet off center. These logs appear to have been stripped of their bark.
2. Split logs were then laid atop and nailed fast with hand wrought spikes driven into the underlying logs. Only one row of nails remained to be recorded (3 spikes) although a careful examination of the entire exposed roadbed was made with a metal detector. The split logs appear to have been the outer surfaces of large logs taken from a saw mill. The bottoms were relatively flat although the top surfaces, including numerous knots, formed a rough corduroy surface.
3. Small post pilings were then driven into the muck and clay at irregular intervals alongside of the shortest logs in the road. To these pilings (and possibly to the split logs) were fastened slivers or split sections of logs that served as road curbs. The presence of pilings and curbs (only one section was found in place) reduced the width of the road bed to 15 feet.
4. The entire substructure was covered with gravel to form a relatively smooth surface. The gravel had, for the most part, been washed away after the road was abandoned but sufficient amounts were found between the logs to determine its use as road fill.

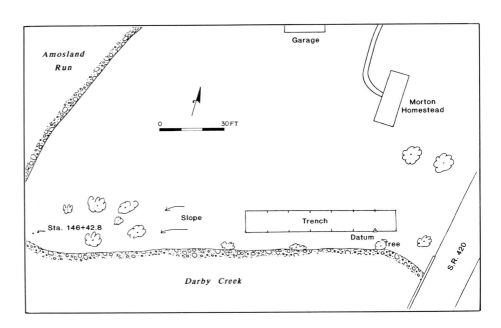

Figure 10.12.
Plan of excavation at the Morton Homestead. (From Mid-Atlantic Archaeological Research 1978)

Figure 10.13.
Log road to the ferry landing at the Morton Homestead. (From Mid-Atlantic Archaeological Research 1978)

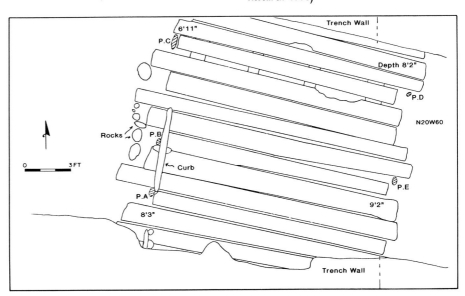

The relatively steep pitch of the road (roughly 1 to 10 feet down toward Darby Creek) supported the conclusion that this log road had led to the ferry landing.

The log road was embedded in a layer of black organic muck, overlaid by an extensive series of later fills, one as recent as 1955. Artifacts found in the layer of muck dated from about 1720 through the early 1800s; most of them had been made after 1750.

They included the usual collection of creamware, pearlware, and salt-glazed stoneware, mainly in small sherds. Although very little glass was found, the artifacts did include an intact eighteenth-century scent bottle. Among the other noteworthy finds were an Irish halfpenny minted in 1749, the bone handle of an eighteenth-century toothbrush, and a nineteenth-century wooden shuttle for weaving nets.

The layer of gravel fill above the

log road contained a silver coin, probably minted during the reign of George II (1727–1760); a brass button and a pewter one, both made in the eighteenth century; and several prehistoric stone artifacts, including a broken projectile point. The prehistoric objects had doubtless been dug up elsewhere along with the gravel and hauled to the site to be laid down on top of the log road (MAAR 1978: 33–34).

Although the investigation produced no artifacts that could have belonged to Morton Mortonson, Sr., or to his son Mathias, it did document a feature that was part of everyday life at the Morton Homestead from the 1760s until 1848—the road down to the ferry.

Archaeology at the Mortonson House

When Morton Morton had his mason set his initials, which were also those of his second wife Mary, into the chimney wall of the kitchen wing of his new house sometime after 1758, he could hardly have anticipated the mystification that would ensue in the nineteenth and twentieth centuries, or the sad state into which his house would lapse. Morton died in 1781, and the property remained in his family until 1873, when J. Washington Gesner sold it to Charles McClees. Ultimately, after a series of owners, the house was abandoned in the late 1930s, and the land around it became a municipal park. Thereafter, the house, which had already suffered from "modernization," suffered from neglect and vandalism as well.

Originally a finely proportioned, two-story brick building with an attached one-story kitchen wing, the house had its symmetry destroyed sometime during the nineteenth cen-

tury when a third story of inferior brick was added to the main house and a wooden second story was plunked atop the kitchen (Springer 1967:33). By the time the Norwood Borough Council came to the rescue of the house in 1965, the wooden addition to the kitchen wing had already taken care of itself. In crumbling, however, it had also taken with it the original story below, so that all of the wing left standing was the huge chimney marked "MM" (Figure 10.14).

John Dickey, the architect engaged to carry out the restoration, and Charles Peterson, the Philadelphia architect who gave the house a close inspection in 1969, agreed that the main part of the house had been erected sometime before 1763, that it was perhaps begun as early as the 1730s, and that considerable alteration had occurred in the 1800s (Lewis 1969). In his notes to Mary Butler Lewis, the first archaeologist to work on the project, Peterson commented on the pre-Georgian look of the house and the features that gave it a distinct character: the three brick bonds (Flemish,

English, and common) on the north wall of the kitchen wing; the rich moldings of the main house's mantles and paneling; and, particularly, the evidence in the brickwork on the south elevation of the main house of a second-floor balcony. Peterson noted that although balconies were once common in Philadelphia, few examples remain. One such example is the reconstructed balcony at Grumblethorpe in Germantown.

Although it was clear that the main house had been built after 1730, and most likely after 1758, the gambrel roof of the kitchen wing—still outlined on the exterior wall of the main house—and the primitive look of the kitchen's exterior brickwork suggested that this wing might have been built earlier. A primary object of the archaeology was to determine whether that was indeed the case. Mary Butler

Figure 10.14.

The Mortonson House in June 1969. An "M" and the line of a second "M" are visible in the kitchen chimney, between brace bars. (Photo by J. L. Cotter)

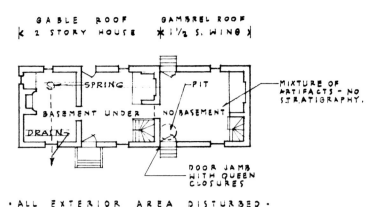

Figure 10.15.

Plan of the Mortonson House. Excavation outside the house was fruitless because the entire area had been filled in the early 1940s. (Courtesy of John Dickey)

Lewis began the investigation in the spring of 1969; it was completed after her death by Betty Cosans.

The kitchen wing had no basement. Two plank floors, long since rotted into wood dust, had been laid one on top of another. The top planks had rested on wooden sills and run in the direction opposite that of the ones beneath; the latter had been set on stone supports. The top floor apparently was laid at a considerably later date than the bottom one. A pit about 3 feet wide and 2 feet deep in the southwest corner of the kitchen crawl space contained an abundance of artifacts mixed with brick and mortar debris (Figure 10.15); the artifacts and debris were evidently deposited at the same time. Artifacts ranged in date from about 1760 to 1850 and included U.S. coins minted in 1803, 1804, and 1821; a George II halfpenny, its date illegible; a large amount of creamware, perfected by Josiah Wedgwood in 1760; and a large amount of pearlware, introduced by Wedgwood in 1780 and produced until 1850 (Cosans 1969).

The south foundation wall of the

kitchen had been entirely rebuilt, apparently long after the main house was built, and it lacked the shelf for supporting joists found on the north wall of the kitchen. The evidence showed that the north wall had been built at the same time as the main house. Matching layers of paint appeared on both sides of a door frame in the common wall between the kitchen wing and the house. Moreover, the artifacts found in the kitchen and house presented much the same profile. Well over a thousand sherds from the site were analyzed, and they all dated from about 1730 to 1930, with a modal range of 1810 to 1840; stoneware and delft accounted for very little of the ceramic collection, but creamware dating from about 1760 was remarkably abundant (Dickey 1975:2, 3). Further proof that kitchen wing and house were built simultaneously was a jamb Dickey discovered in the southeast corner of the house. Built directly into the fabric of the main house, it had been the jamb of a kitchen door to the outside.

A great flood in 1843 was probably why the south wall of the kitchen was

rebuilt. Whoever did the work had used old material and not been a very skilled mason. Because the new wall did not reach the floor joists, earth and a few large stones had been shoveled into the crawl space and the joists laid down over them. More evidence of probable flood damage and subsequent repair appeared in the cellar beneath the main house. The floor of the cellar consisted of schist leveled off along the edges with stones and broken bricks, but in the southeast part of the cellar the floor was considerably eroded, possibly because flood water had poured through the cellar windows. Suggestive of repair work was an aqua-blue beer bottle mortared into the base of the chimney in the northeast corner of the basement; the bottle dated between 1840 and 1865. Deposits of glass and ceramics dating from about the same period were also found near the northeast cornerstones of the house. Another item of note in the cellar was a spring that emerged from the schist. The spring had originally had a circular stone-lined collecting basin and a wooden overflow pipe that exited through the south wall, but these items had been replaced with a twentieth-century iron cylinder and a 4-inch soil pipe (Lewis 1969:2).

The architectural elements of the house discovered in the course of the investigation—among them mantle-pieces, outside benches, and the second-story balcony noted by Peterson—suggest a lifestyle that probably would have been quite foreign to Morton Morton's great-grandfather. To architect John Dickey (1975:4–5), they also suggested "a man in control of his environment, who was able to place windows, doors, and balconies where he wanted them, and include a whole waterfall of mouldings under the mantel shelves."

THE GRANGE: A WELSH QUAKER
ESTATE AND ITS EVOLUTION

Remote from walks where noise and revels reign,
And fierce ambition fires the phrensied brain,

. . . .

Where woe-fraught Health declines her languid head,
And hearses black-rob'd bear the thronging dead;
Remote from town with all its clamorous train
Its veteran vices, wiles and galling pain,
Grange lies—luxuriant in fair rural scenes,
Gay plumy groves, bright lawns, and velvet greens,
Proud forests humming to the hollow gale,
And craggy steeps dark frowning o'er the vale

. . . .

—Dr. Charles Caldwell, "Grange," ca. 1798

No doubt Henry Lewis, the staid Welsh Quaker who in 1682 built what ultimately became known as the Grange, would not have recognized his property from this flight of poetic fancy. No doubt, too, the poet, who was a frequent visitor at the Grange in the 1790s, would have had a difficult time equating the subject of his poem with the Victorian splendor, complete with gingerbread, shown in Figure 10.16.

Situated on a hilltop overlooking Cobbs Creek in Haverford Township,* the Grange began as a modest stone cottage called Maencloch (meaning Redstone), after Maenclochog, Henry Lewis's birthplace in Narberth Parish, Pembrokeshire, Wales. During the colonial period, it was transformed into a gentleman's country estate, and about the time of the Revolution it was host to such illustrious figures as Benjamin Frank-

* Today the Grange is approached by Myrtle Avenue near Township Line Road in Penfield.

Figure 10.16.

The Grange as it appeared in April 1978. (Photo by J. L. Cotter)

lin, Robert Morris, and generals Washington and Lafayette. It was, in fact, because of Lafayette, whose home in France was called the Grange, that the estate received its present name in the 1780s. It received its Victorian embellishments in the 1850s and 1860s.

Haverford Township acquired the estate from its last private owner in 1974 and, with the help of the Friends of the Grange, has maintained the property since that time. As part of the Friends' continuing program of conservation, a class from the University of Pennsylvania undertook an archaeological feasibility study of the property in 1978. The report of that study (Cotter and students 1978b) provided the basis for the following account.

History of the Grange

Henry Lewis, a member of the carpenters' guild in his native Maenclochog, was in the vanguard of Welsh Quakers who settled the Welsh Tract, the 40,000 acres of wilderness in Haverford, Radnor, and Merion townships that William Penn conveyed to them as a group. After exacting from Penn his promise that their individual plots of land would be grouped together and making their purchases through Lewis David, Penn's land agent in Wales, Henry Lewis and a few other Quakers left the poverty of their homeland and the persecution their sect suffered there and sailed for the New World in 1682. Lewis, his wife Margaret, and their three children settled on a 250-acre tract in Haverford Township. With ever more Welsh Quakers fleeing poverty and persecution, the wilderness around the Lewis homestead soon gave way to cleared land and farms.

Within little more than a year of their arrival, they had a number of neighbors (Smith 1862:148, 478).

Henry Lewis lived for only six years after settling in Pennsylvania. During that time, he helped found the Haverford Friends' Meeting, served as a "visitor of the poor and the sick," and was on the first grand jury to convene in Philadelphia. His son Henry, who inherited Maencloch in 1688, achieved some renown, serving as a member of the provincial assembly in 1715 and again in 1718. During the younger Henry's tenure of the property, it grew from 250 acres to 350. Maencloch passed out of the Lewis family, and out of its phase as a working farm, in 1749 when Henry Lewis III, yeoman of Haverford, sold it to Capt. John Wilcocks.

Renaming the property Clifton Hall, Wilcocks transformed Lewis's stone house into the summer mansion shown in Figure 10.17. He also created formal gardens with fountains and pools, had a scenic walk three-quarters of a mile long cut through the slope of the surrounding hillside, and added a greenhouse, hothouse, and dairy. It is said that to keep his considerable number of slaves busy, Wilcocks had them dig a ditch around the entire estate (Smith 1862:394).

In 1761 Wilcocks sold Clifton Hall to Charles Cruickshank, a wealthy Scot only recently arrived in America. Early in the 1770s Cruickshank enlarged the mansion, and probably about the same time he also enlarged the greenhouse and enhanced the beauty of the grounds by extending the woodland walks, adding plantings, and terracing the formal gardens (Figure 10.18). In addition, through his purchases of abutting land, Cruickshank increased the acreage of the estate, which by now included one or

Figure 10.17.

The Grange in 1770, when it was known as Clifton Hall, as depicted by Charles Cruickshank, who owned the estate from 1761 to 1782. (From Smith 1862:393)

more tenant houses. In short, Cruickshank created the colonial country estate *par excellence.*

John Ross, a prosperous Philadelphia merchant, married Cruickshank's daughter Clemantina in 1768, and in 1782, when Cruickshank returned to Scotland, Ross bought Clifton Hall from him. A prominent figure in the American Revolution, Ross actively backed Robert Morris in his efforts to finance the war and also served as a muster-master of the 1776 Committee of Public Safety in Philadelphia and as a Continental agent in Nantes. It was because of his wartime associations that the estate had so many distinguished guests.

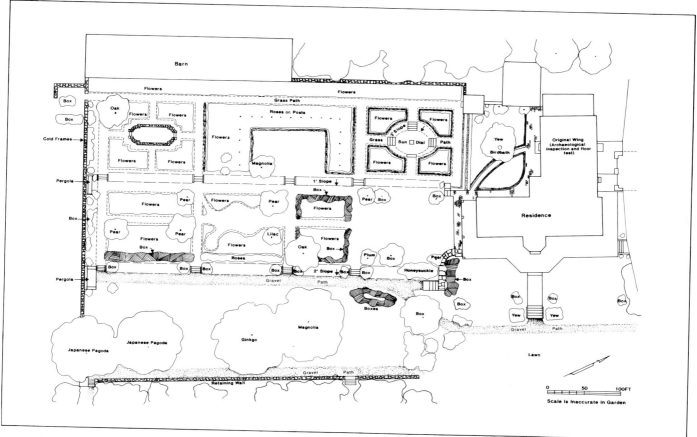

Figure 10.18.

Terraced gardens at the Grange in 1939. (Courtesy of Friends of the Grange)

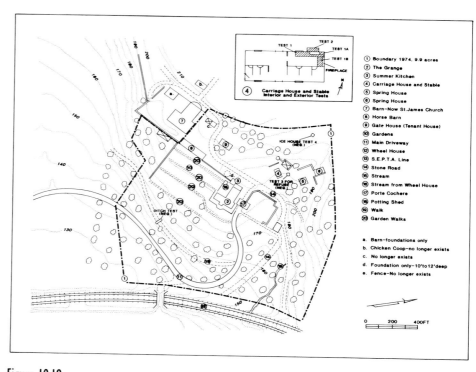

Figure 10.19.

Plan of the Grange in 1974. (Courtesy of Friends of the Grange)

After the war, Ross's fortune apparently continued to grow, for he not only increased the size of the Grange to 600 acres, but in 1791 built a fine new townhouse for himself at Second and Pine streets, just across from New Market. However, the recession of 1797, which ultimately put Robert Morris in debtors' prison, was also Ross's undoing. When he died in 1806, his heirs were left with large debts, a lavishly furnished townhouse, an exquisite country estate, and trunks full of worthless Continental currency. In 1810 Ross's son-in-law sold the Grange to John Brinton, who six years later sold it to Manuel Eyre, a partner in the Philadelphia shipping firm of Eyre and Massey. Eyre owned and occupied the Grange until his death in 1845.

In 1850 John Ashurst, Manuel Eyre's son-in-law, bought the estate, which by then included only 103 acres of land, and with the help of architect John E. Carver set about turning the Colonial mansion into a Victorian retreat. Among the Victorian embellishments that followed was a *porte cochere* designed in 1863 by John McArthur, Jr., architect of Philadelphia's City Hall. After Ashurst's death in 1892, his family retained the mansion for a number of years but sold off a sizable part of the land to a railroad company, as evidenced by the suburban line that still skirts the estate. After the Ashursts' tenure, the Grange had but two more private owners: Loren M. Downs, from 1905 until 1913, and Benjamin R. Hoffman, from 1913 until 1974, when Haverford Township acquired the property. Figure 10.19 shows the features of the 9.9-acre estate in 1974, as well as a few features that long ago disappeared.

Archaeology at the Grange

The primary objective of the 1978 archaeological study of the Grange was to find evidence of Henry Lewis's original stone dwelling (Cotter and students 1978b). Inspection of the cellar walls of the mansion failed to reveal any such evidence. Moreover, tests beneath the thin layer of cement that served as the cellar floor revealed no earlier flooring or any stratigraphy in the earth. Apparently, the earth had been leveled before the cement was poured.

The next tests took place at the carriage house, a structure that appears at first glance to be purely Vic-

Figure 10.20.

Tests in the carriage house at the Grange. Possible sill wall can be seen dimly at left, beneath the window. (Photo by J. L. Cotter)

torian but whose doors and stair rail date from the eighteenth century. While half of the carriage house is devoted to stalls, a room in the northwest corner has domestic features, including a blocked stone fireplace and an adjoining corner nook that might once have been a flight of stairs. The fill in the corner nook contained sherds of creamware, stoneware, and export porcelain dating from the mid- to late 1700s, as well as a copper penny coined at the first U.S. Mint on North Seventh Street in 1797 (see Chapter 4, "The U.S. Mint"). The tests here also revealed what may have been a sill that once supported floor joists (Figure 10.20). No artifacts of the early 1700s or late 1600s were found in conjunction with this wall, but until the feature is completely excavated, the possibility that it was part of Henry Lewis's stone house cannot be ruled out.

Four test units excavated on the grounds of the estate produced nothing out of the ordinary. One of these tests, conducted well south of the mansion beyond the terraced gardens, was intended to produce evidence of the ditch Wilcocks' slaves are alleged to have dug around the estate in the 1750s. Neither the test nor inspection of the surrounding area revealed any traces. According to Smith's *History of Delaware County*, however, parts of the ditch were still visible in 1862, and many people then living could recall when the outline of the entire ditch could be traced.

THE CALEB PUSEY HOUSE:
A DURABLE QUAKER RUSTIC

Caleb Pusey (1651–1727) was a somewhat better known personage than his fellow Quaker and contemporary, Henry Lewis. In addition to being the manager of the Chester Mills—an important post in the first days of the province, when much depended on getting corn ground and lumber sawed—Pusey served as a sheriff of Chester County, a justice of the county court, and a member of the provincial assembly and the executive council. He was also instrumental in drawing the circular line that in 1701 divided Pennsylvania from Delaware (Patterson 1962a, 1962b). If we are to judge by Pusey's rustic house (Figure 10.21, *top*), which has stood since 1683 near Chester Creek in Upland on the northern outskirts of Chester, Henry Lewis's lost stone house in Haverford Township was probably quite modest. But rough as Pusey's dwelling was, it was on at least one occasion visited by none other than William Penn himself.*

In 1962, in conjunction with plans to restore the house, the Friends of

* A comparable stone house was built from 1678 to 1684 by the Swedish immigrant Jan Boelsen on the Schuylkill River opposite Peter's Island. It is now in Fairmount Park, occupied by the Friends of Philadelphia Parks (Figure 10.21, bottom). Future archaeological investigation is being contemplated at the time of this writing.

the Caleb Pusey House asked the Archaeological Society of Delaware to excavate the site. For the next four and a half years, volunteers working on a part-time basis under the direction of Allen Schiek carried out a series of excavations both inside and outside the structure. Meanwhile, research into the history of the property was ongoing.

Caleb Pusey: From Last Maker to Mill Owner

Caleb Pusey was born in England in 1651 and for the first thirty years of his life lived in Chipping Lambourn, Berkshire. A Quaker by conviction and a last maker by trade, he gave up the shoe business in 1681, when Penn advertised land at affordable prices

Figure 10.21.

Top, the Caleb Pusey House as it appeared during archaeological excavation in the cellar area, June 10, 1962; *bottom,* the Jan Boelsen Cottage, built from 1678 to 1684 on the west side of the Schuylkill River opposite Peter's Island, in Fairmount Park, as it appeared in 1989. (Photos by J. L. Cotter)

in his new American colony. Pusey promptly became a First Purchaser, acquiring 250 acres of Pennsylvania for the sum of £5. Before leaving England, he secured not only a wife, Ann Stone Worley, but also a berth in the New World. In partnership with nine other men, Pusey entered into an agreement to erect "one or more water mills" in Pennsylvania. The partnership was divided into thirty-two equal shares, and William Penn "was to have and bear five parts thereof, both in profit and loss" (Smith 1862:147). Pusey—a junior partner, owning only one share of the thirty-two—was elected manager of the enterprise.

Arriving in America before William Penn, Pusey and his wife settled in Upland, a village settled by Swedes almost forty years earlier. After Penn arrived in the autumn of 1682, he granted Pusey warrants for twenty acres of land on which to build the mills. The land, which Pusey called Landing Ford Plantation, came in two parcels and was located on both sides of Chester Creek near Pusey's own 250 acres in Upland (Smith 1862: 147). By the time 1683 was out, Pusey had built not only a gristmill but also a house.

From the looks of the house, it would appear that Friend Pusey was more concerned with his milling enterprise than with his domicile. A two-story stone structure, the house was crudely (and apparently hastily) built. It has two sections, each with one room per floor (Figure 10.22); the sections were probably built only a few years apart. The whole structure measures 46 by 18½ feet, and its walls are 18 inches thick. It originally had a bake oven, a large walk-in fireplace, and a pitched roof. A gambrel roof was added to one section of the house at a later date, presumably to provide more headroom upstairs; another afterthought was a window in one of the gable ends. When the original stones in the walls of the house fell out, the holes were roughly patched with bricks. In this rather primitive establishment William Penn is known to have dined in 1699 (Patterson 1962a, 1962b; Albrecht 1972).

The mill that Pusey built in 1683 was the first new one in Chester County since 1644, when Swedes' Mill was built on Cobbs Creek. As manager of the milling enterprise, Pusey must at times have felt a kinship to Job. Soon after he built the first gristmill and dam, they floated away in a flood. He doggedly rebuilt them and at the same time constructed a sawmill. When the second dam broke in yet another violent flood,

Figure 10.22.

Cross-sections, plans, and elevations of the Caleb Pusey House. (Courtesy of the National Park Service and Price and Dickey, Architects)

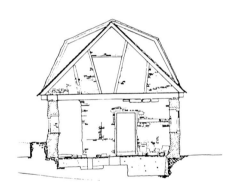

CROSS SECTION THROUGH WEST END
LOOKING EAST

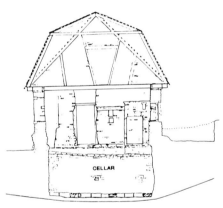

CROSS SECTION THROUGH EAST END
LOOKING WEST

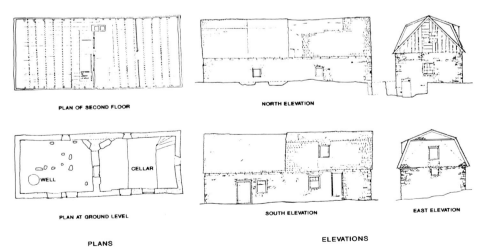

PLAN OF SECOND FLOOR

NORTH ELEVATION

PLAN AT GROUND LEVEL

SOUTH ELEVATION

EAST ELEVATION

PLANS

ELEVATIONS

Pusey decided to build a millrace farther upstream, which necessitated the purchase of additional land. The expense of constructing the millrace and maintaining the buildings exceeded the mills' profits, and as a result the partnership fell into debt to Robert Turner. Pusey, who by then owned five of the company's thirty-two shares, and William Penn, with his five shares, were the only two of the partners who paid their part of the debt to Turner. In 1692 Turner sued the other partners for nonpayment, and when the court could find no buyer for the property, Turner was awarded twenty-two shares in the partnership. In the same year, however, Samuel Carpenter bought all of Turner's shares, and from 1692 until 1705 Carpenter, Pusey, and Penn were the owners of the Chester Mills (Smith 1862:563–64).

In addition to coping with natural disasters and threats of bankruptcy, Pusey also had to deal with competition. In 1687 he petitioned the county court "against Thomas Coborne for setting a water mill above him upon Upland Creek" (Smith 1862: 161–62). A number of Coborne's upstream neighbors came to his support, pointing out to the court the great need for a mill in their part of the county, and Pusey consequently lost his case. By 1717 Pusey had evidently had enough of life in Upland, for in that year he moved to East Marlborough Township in Chester County, where he died ten years later (Albrecht 1969:8).

Archaeology at the Caleb Pusey House

The west section of Caleb Pusey's house has no cellar beneath it; the floor joists rest on stone sleepers.

Here in the 1960s Schiek and his volunteers found a dry-laid stone well 3 feet in diameter, together with a handmade iron pulley wheel and a well-preserved pump casing made of a reamed and squared tree trunk. Under the east section of the house, they found a small cellar, 15 by 8 feet and 7 feet deep; a circular stairway provided access to it. Probably once used as a root cellar, it had been totally filled in about the turn of the twentieth century. The fill had clearly come from a trash heap; it was laden with artifacts, and most of the oldest objects were found in the top layers. Among the artifacts was a large copper still, badly flattened and damaged. It may well have belonged to Caleb Pusey himself, for an inventory of his property records his possession of such an item. Other possible evidence of Pusey's industry was a section of a millstone that had been used to patch a quoin (Schiek 1974:296, 297; Albrecht 1972:4, 8, 18, 21).

Another forgotten cellar appeared beneath the extreme east end of the house. Measuring 34 by 17 feet and 6 feet deep, this cellar had evidently been destroyed by fire, for many of the artifacts found here were severely warped and fused. The artifacts suggested that the fire had occurred sometime before 1800. Among the items recovered were lumps of antimony sulfide, two clay crucibles of a type used in assaying, apothecary jars, a glass pestle, and a small brick pedestal, possibly the base of a laboratory work table—in all, strong evidence that some type of scientific experimentation had taken place on the premises (Albrecht 1972:13–15).

The artifacts recovered from the Caleb Pusey House numbered in the thousands and were exceptionally diverse. They included everything from flint projectile points and a sleigh bell

to beads, buttons, buckles, thimbles, and shoe fragments. Of the 205 coins found, the earliest was an English halfpenny dated 1681; the latest, a U.S. penny dated 1951. Among the most unusual coins were one struck in 1693 during the reign of William and Mary; a 1680 Spanish four-real piece made of tin or pewter, probably counterfeit; and a silver twopenny coin known as maundy money, specially minted for the king of England to distribute to the poor on Holy Thursday. The many different places in which these coins had been minted—among them Peru, Mexico, France, and several of the American colonies—reflects the lack of a standard national currency in colonial America, where just about any type of coinage was legal tender. Surprisingly, chemical and x-ray analyses of the copper coins showed that metallurgical processes had changed very little over a 150-year period; the copper content remained nearly constant at 90 percent (Schiek 1974:302–3; 1969).

The seventy-one thimbles included in the artifact collection presented something of a mystery; sixty-eight of these items were made of brass, one of German silver, and two of plastic. Although it was learned that sewing classes met at a nearby school in the mid-nineteenth century, that fact alone did not explain how such a large number of thimbles came to be deposited at the Caleb Pusey House (Scheik 1974:303).

Among the other brass objects in the collection was a spoon handle, whose origin was almost indisputable. Marked with the initials of both Caleb and Ann Pusey, it had doubtless belonged to the house's first owners. An x-ray analysis of the brass spoon and of a brass candlestick and key suggested that these items had been made in Britain; the proportions

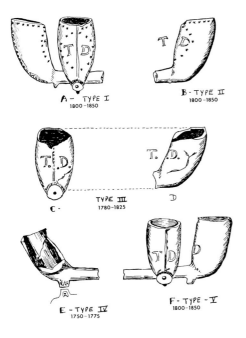

A - TYPE I
1800-1850

B - TYPE II
1800-1850

TYPE III
1780-1825

C -

T. D.

D

E - TYPE IV
1750-1775

F - TYPE V
1800-1850

Figure 10.24.

Pipes attributed to Tippett and Evans, ca. 1690–1725. (From Alexander 1978)

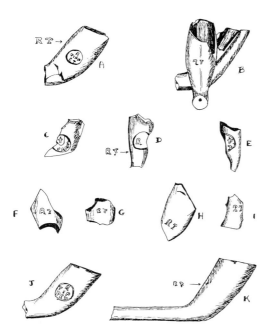

Figure 10.23.

Pipe fragments found in excavations at the Caleb Pusey House: five of the variations on the mark "TD." (From Alexander 1978)

of the alloys used in them corresponded to those in authenticated British specimens. Most of the pewter items subjected to the same kind of analysis, among them fragments of spoons and a plate, appeared to have been made in America; they had less than the 90 percent of tin found in British pewter. The one silver item analyzed—a spoon—was 95 percent pure silver; it had probably been made in Britain about 1850 (Carlson 1974:328).

Toys, both intact and in pieces, appeared in abundance. They included porcelain dolls; a lead Indian, horse, and jockey; handmade bone dominoes; a metal whistle; a miniature oxcart made of slip-glazed red clay; and 427 marbles of various kinds—

molded and blown glass, adobe, glazed clay, and white ceramic. Also found were slates and slate pencils, a jew's harp, and three little potties. Two of the latter had light brown globs of glazed clay adhering to their interiors, no doubt intended as visual inducement to small toddlers undergoing the rigors of toilet training (Schiek 1974:303; Albrecht 1972:20). Evidently, children were abundant at the Caleb Pusey House throughout most of its history.

The excavations produced a remarkable collection of clay pipe fragments. Over 2,300 in all, they dated from the seventeenth century to the early twentieth and had been made in at least eight different countries: England, Scotland, Ireland, the Netherlands, Germany, France, Japan, and the United States. The pipe bowls included twelve or more variations of the mark "TD" (Figure 10.23). Originally the insignia of Thomas Dormer, a pipe maker in late eighteenth-century London, this mark became very common as pipe manufacturers everywhere modified or copied Dormer's style. Probably the most important items among the pipe collection were the fragments of eighteen bowls and stems that Alexander (1978), who analyzed the entire collection, attributed to Tippett and Evans, the foremost pipe manufacturers in Bristol during the seventeenth and eighteenth centuries. As shown in Figure 10.24, Tippett and Evans put their marks either on the back of the pipe bowl or on the side.

Although almost all the artifacts at the Caleb Pusey House were found in disturbed contexts, they nonetheless included items that could almost certainly be tied to their owners. All in all, they provided a valuable glimpse of everyday life as it was lived in this house for almost three centuries.

RIDLEY CREEK STATE PARK: THE COLONIAL PENNSYLVANIA PLANTATION AND SYCAMORE MILLS

Ridley Creek State Park encompasses 2,606 acres of rolling meadows and woodland, most of it in Edgemont Township south of the West Chester Pike (Figure 10.25). Once an area of working farms and small water-powered mills, the park has several interesting historic sites. Among these are an old mill village called Sycamore Mills (formerly called Bishop's Mills) and the "Colonial Pennsylvania

Plantation," a farm owned and worked by the same Quaker family for over a hundred years. The Bishop's Mill Historical Institute now operates the plantation as a demonstration of farm life in southeastern Pennsylvania in the late eighteenth century. Also of interest is the Hunting Hill mansion. Now used as the park office, the mansion was built around an eighteenth-century stone farmhouse by the

Jeffords family in 1914. Until the Commonwealth of Pennsylvania bought the land for the park in the 1960s, the Jeffords owned 2,200 acres of it; the rest was divided among six much smaller estates. The park was opened to the public in 1972 and

Figure 10.25.

Map of Ridley Creek State Park. (Courtesy of Ridley Creek State Park)

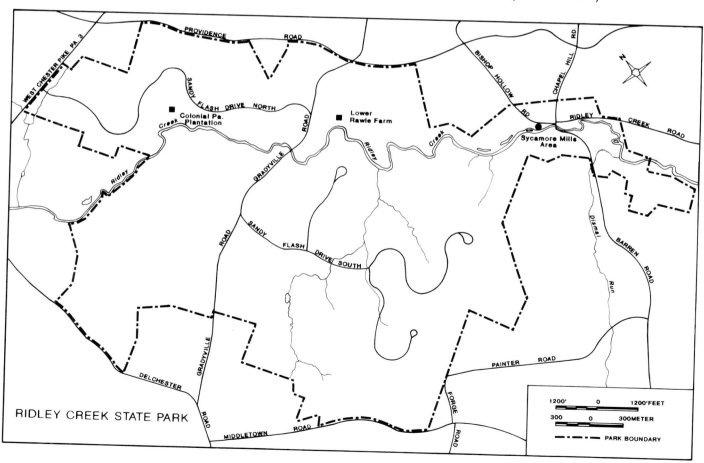

since 1976 has been a historic district on the National Register of Historic Places.

The sites in Ridley Creek State Park have been the focus of a good deal of historical and archaeological research. There have been numerous studies of the plantation and the mill village—an unusual level of attention, given that the people who lived on these sites were for the most part plain working folk, not very prominent in the historical record. One interesting study (Callender et al. 1975) involved a survey of the buildings of nine farms within the park's confines. The findings showed that the builders had paid attention to topography, climate, and various other constraints. Most farmhouses and barns faced south for warmth in winter and were often built into a gradient as protection from the north wind. The proximity to water was also an important consideration in the positioning of the buildings. The typical farmhouse was Georgian in plan, had had additions and modifications, and was separated from the barn by outbuildings.

Other research has shown that the typical farm in Edgemont Township during the late eighteenth century had between 110 and 120 acres of land and that the household might number as many as fifteen people—an extended family plus a few servants. The farmers were most often English Quakers, and like farmers in out-of-the-way places everywhere, they were generally preoccupied with the land on which their existence depended and unaware of remote world affairs until those affairs affected them directly.

In most respects, the Colonial Pennsylvania Plantation fits the profile of farm life formulated by the building survey and the historical research. Although it has been the subject of more study than the mill village in Ridley Creek State Park, the mill village also offers some intriguing research themes, among them early industry, rural economy, vernacular architecture, and preservation history (Herman 1976). The following account summarizes the findings of a few of the studies of both farm life and mill life along Ridley Creek.

Farm Life

History of the Colonial Pennsylvania Plantation

The original owner of the land on which this farmstead was built was a Quaker named Thomas Duckett, who received a grant of 300 acres in Edgemont Township from William Penn in 1686. Duckett in turn sold the land to another Quaker named Barnaby Wilcox, whose heirs sold it to yet another Quaker, Ralph Lewis, in 1701. The original core of the farmhouse now standing on the site was not built until about 1705, during the tenure of Ralph Lewis, and it is unclear whether Duckett or Wilcox ever lived on their land in Edgemont Township. In 1684 both men were members of the Friends' newly formed Haverford Monthly Meeting, and the first of those monthly meetings took place at "the house of Thomas Duckett, which was located on the west bank of the Schuylkill, a short distance above the . . . Market street bridge" (Smith 1862:149). The notes of the Haverford Monthly Meeting for October 1684 record that both Thomas Duckett and Barnaby Wilcox were charged with finding suitable places for burying the Quaker dead. With that, both men seem to fade from the historical record, an anonymity that also cloaked later owners of this farm in Edgemont Township.

In 1720 Ralph Lewis's son Evan sold the farmhouse and eighty acres of land to Joseph Pratt, a Quaker of Middletown Township. Over the next 103 years, four generations of Pratts lived there, expanding both the house and the acreage. By 1776 the Pratts' farm was larger than most farms around it. Living there were two grandparents, two parents, three daughters, four sons, two slaves, and an indentured servant. Interestingly, the number of slaves and indentured servants in this Quaker household was the same in 1776 as in 1720, even though the size of the place had increased.

The farmhouse, facing south and with thick walls of schist, sits on a hillside where the slope behind it protects it from the north wind (Figure 10.26). By 1836 the dwelling had undergone six major renovations, first expanding east from the original core and then west, so that the structure now measures about 70 feet by 25 feet. The last renovation was the work of Philip Bishop, who bought the property from the Pratts in 1833. It involved raising the roof of the kitchen at the west end of the house to two and a half stories. The kitchen has a stairway to the second floor and, on its west wall, a walk-in fireplace 12 feet wide. Attached to the kitchen is a "still room," which sits over a root cellar. The still room contains a beehive bake oven and was used for storing preserves, dried herbs, and firewood. A well is conveniently located in front of the kitchen door. The kitchen has no cellar; the main house has a full one.

Just 30 feet west of the kitchen is a stone springhouse (Figure 10.27). Used for storing dairy products and meat, it is built into the hillside and sits over a slowly flowing brook.

Figure 10.26.

The farmhouse of Joseph Pratt at the Colonial Pennsylvania Plantation in 1985. (Courtesy of Ridley Creek State Park)

Figure 10.27.

The springhouse at the Colonial Pennsylvania Plantation. (Courtesy of Ridley Creek State Park)

Figure 10.28.

Map of the Colonial Pennsylvania Plantation: *1*, farmhouse; *2*, still room; *3*, springhouse; *4*, stone cabin; *5*, wagon shed; *6*, barn; *7*, Ridley Creek. (Courtesy of the Bishop's Mill Historical Institute)

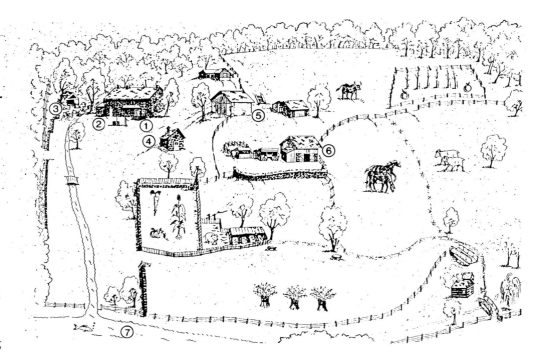

Chores that require a constant fire, such as candlemaking and laundry, were done in the open air under the shelter of the springhouse's extended roof. The loft may have housed slaves or servants.

The farm's present 112 acres contain a number of other outbuildings (Figure 10.28). A stone cabin situated between the house and barn is the oldest structure on the property, but whether it was first used as a dwelling is uncertain. Evidence of a thatched roof suggests that once may have been the case, but the evidence is far from conclusive. It was in any event later used as a smokehouse. The barn, 170 feet southeast of the house, is positioned on the hillside so that wagons could pull up to the second level and unload grain directly into the loft.

Two Archaeological Studies

In 1974 Helen Smith, staff archaeologist for the Colonial Pennsylvania Plantation, tested the earth beneath the kitchen floor of the Pratts' old farmhouse. The soil was hardpan and orange-yellow in color, with a patch of dark brown in the northeast corner where the foundations of a bake oven had once stood. Because of water seepage, large stones and stacks of smaller stones had been placed under the floor beams as supports. The stones may have formed the original floor of the kitchen.

Figure 10.29.

Stone-lined box with an iron pipe at the bottom at the Colonial Pennsylvania Plantation. (Photo by J. L. Cotter)

The artifacts that appeared in the soil beneath the stone supports provide an interesting glimpse of what the residents of the farm did as they gathered around the fireplace in the kitchen. A good many children had evidently played marbles in front of the fire and done their lessons there as well. Here Smith (1974a, 1974b, 1974c) found 138 marbles and 52 lead pencils, as well as 50 beads, 503 buttons, 61 sherds from clay pipes, and 37 coins. Among the miscellaneous objects in Smith's collection were parts of spoons and forks, a sleigh bell, keys, and numerous glass and ceramic items, including pieces of a child's tea set and the bottom of an olive-green glass vessel that may have been made about 1730. Most of the artifacts dated from about 1850 to 1900, but those found in an area along the north wall included some that dated as early as 1825.

Among the marbles were ones made of clay, glass, and ceramic; the glass and ceramic marbles had probably been made between 1846 and 1858. Clay pipes ranged in date from the 1820s to the early 1900s. The number of buttons that found their way through the cracks in the floorboards is a little short of spectacular. They were made of wood, bone, white china, black glass, and vulcanized rubber. The process for making vulcanized rubber was not patented until 1839; white-china buttons were available commercially after 1840; and black-glass buttons were popular from about 1875 until 1910. The coins ranged in date from a George III halfpenny minted in the 1770s to a Lincoln penny dated 1944; the 1944 coin was the latest object found. Judging from the number of coins recovered, the occupants of the house were as careful with their money as they were careless with their buttons.

Smith (1974a) also tested the basement beneath the main house. There she found only nine marbles, two lead pencils, and four coins—clearly indicating where most of the household activity took place. In all, Smith's explorations beneath both the house and the kitchen produced very few artifacts dating from the early eighteenth century.

In 1975, in the hope of locating more eighteenth-century artifacts, students from the University of Pennsylvania tested an area on the hillside behind the farmhouse, where there was a circular, stone-lined cistern.* Although they found no evidence dating from the eighteenth century, they did discover a previously unrecorded aspect of farm life in the nineteenth century. A 2½-inch iron pipe, laid below the frost line, connected the cistern to the stone-lined box shown in Figure 10.29. The box was located 72 feet uphill from the cistern. Measuring about 3.5 feet by 4 feet, it had a stone lid and was covered with a shallow earth fill. The iron pipe, which ran through the bottom of the box, appeared to be part of an aqueduct—a theory that further exploration confirmed.

At the very top of the hill, an iron pipe connected to a small, hidden fresh-water spring. Between the spring and the first box near the bottom of the hill were three similar stone-lined boxes, spaced at irregular intervals, as well as another circular, stone-lined cistern.† It was now evident that this

* The full report of this study is given in Cotter and students (1975).
† In tracing the pipe up the hillside, the class also discovered a stone-lined pit measuring 20 feet across and 10 feet deep—evidently a defunct lime-kiln—and the remains of a portable sawmill. Evidence of the sawmill consisted of 13 feet of track, the debris of the "donkey cart" on which logs had been moved to the circular saw, and pieces of abandoned machinery. The machinery dated from the last half of the nineteenth century, indicating that the slope was still heavily wooded at that time.

had been a supplementary water supply for the farm, with water from the distant spring running downhill through iron pipes past a succession of stone boxes and two cisterns for accumulating water. The aqueduct probably provided the farm with water in winter when the stream by the springhouse froze over. The purpose of the stone boxes, however, remained rather mysterious until a year later, when two students (Danko and Matthews 1976) continued their study of farm life by undertaking an oral history of Lower Rawle Farm, another of the old properties within Ridley Creek State Park.

An Oral History: Recollections of Farm Life along Ridley Creek

Lower Rawle Farm bears a close resemblance to the Colonial Pennsylvania Plantation, even to having the same kind of aqueduct system. The aqueduct remained in use on the Rawle property until 1950, when electric power finally arrived there and water could be conveniently pumped. A former resident of the Rawle house told Danko and Mathews (1976) that it had been his job to check the pipes of the aqueduct when the water failed to reach its destination, which in the twentieth century at the Rawle house had been the second-floor bathroom. He described how he did it and the kind of things that blocked the flow of water:

"I'd put my ear to the ground to see if the water was flowing. One time we had an eel the size of the pipe stuck in the intake. Usually the pipes clogged at the beginning because of leaves and mud."

Another informant, who had for years helped farm families in the area maintain their equipment, not only explained how the pipes were cleaned but also dispelled the mystery of the stone-lined boxes. When asked what purpose these things had served, he replied:

"So they could get in there to break the pipe apart to clean it out. Because if they made it one big, long pipe, they wouldn't be able ever to get it cleaned out. . . ."

"How did they clean it?"

"With rods, what they call chain links. . . . The rods . . . would have a knuckle on each end. You keep pushin' it in, pushin' it in. See?"

Danko and Matthew's (1976) informants also confirmed the impression that the kitchen was the center of life in farmhouses along Ridley Creek. The kitchen was "where we kids got the most together, because that's where we had to do our lessons," and it had a long table to accommodate the many people who lived in the house. In winter, bedrooms were bitterly cold and habitable only in a featherbed. The parlor went unused in wintertime "because it was too cold in there and you'd have to build a fire in the fireplace. It took too much wood, too much wood cuttin'." The pump outside the kitchen was called a "cucumber pump":

"Why did they call it a cucumber pump?"

"Because it was always painted green. Never saw them no other way and that's the only thing they were known as—a cucumber pump."

Mill Life

History of a Mill Village

By 1725 a gristmill and a flour mill were standing on the banks of Ridley Creek in the village now known as Sycamore Mills. They remained small enterprises until 1755, when Thomas Bishop began buying into them and his son Thomas, Jr., began improving them. Under the management of Thomas Bishop, Jr., the complex expanded to include a mill for rolling and slitting iron, a wheelwright's shop, a blacksmith shop, and other craft shops catering to the needs of farmers in the neighboring countryside.

In 1825, at the zenith of the Bishop family's fortunes, Amor Bishop owned twenty acres of land, a gristmill, a sawmill, a rolling and slitting mill, a stonesmith shop, a countinghouse, two houses, two stables, a barn, and a springhouse. His father also owned several houses and outbuildings. Amor's gristmills were then producing as much as 10,000 bushels of grain a year, while the annual yield from his rolling and slitting mill was a hundred tons of iron.

By 1826 the mill village had expanded as far as it ever would. It was too far away from the new canals and railroads and from the source of raw materials to compete with iron-processing mills in those favored locales. The *coup de grace* came on Saturday, August 5, 1843, when a hurricane dumped sixteen inches of rain on the area in less than three hours. The violent flood that ensued carried the mills and those who remained in or near them off to their destruction (Herman 1976:5–8). Thereafter, the village reverted to its earlier role as a place for grinding grain and sawing lumber for custom work. When the mills that housed these small industries burned in 1901, the village passed out of its industrial phase.

In 1905 revival of the village seemed imminent. With the arts and crafts

Figure 10.30.

Mill worker's house, built ca. 1800–1810, in Sycamore Mills. (Courtesy of Ridley Creek State Park)

movement of the early twentieth century then in full swing, H. H. Battles bought the buildings of the mill village with the intent of converting them to craft shops and residences (Herman 1976:28, 35). He also planned to reconstruct the burned mills. After an energetic start lavishly praised in local newspapers, Battles' project lost momentum in 1911, and a few years later he sold out his holdings in the village.

Although the mills of the village have disappeared from sight, many of its early domestic structures still stand. They include the rather spacious, stuccoed-stone house Amor Bishop built for himself in 1822, as well as four of the tiny stone houses the Bishops built for their mill workers (Figure 10.30). Amor Bishop's house, located northeast of the old mill site on the opposite side of Ridley Creek, closely resembles the farmhouses in the area; its style is perhaps best described as "vernacular Georgian." The date of its construction is still visible on a stone set in its west gable. Near Bishop's house are the shell of an enormous stone barn and a dilapidated wooden wagon shed set on brick pillars.

A Study of Mill Workers' Artifacts

In 1973 a fire gutted one of the small stone houses once inhabited by the workers of Bishop's Mills. Subsequently, McCarthy (McCarthy n.d.; McCarthy and Moffet 1980) excavated the site and analyzed the recovered artifacts by comparing his pattern with Stanley South's (1977) Carolina pattern. The results, shown in Table 10.1, demonstrate a moderate but significant difference between this mill worker's home and the home depicted by South's model, which is supposed to represent life in relatively established settlements along the Eastern Seaboard in the eighteenth and early nineteenth centuries.

The "kitchen" artifacts listed in Table 10.1 consisted mainly of ceramics. McCarthy and Moffet (1980) further analyzed the ceramics according to group and type. Table 10.2 shows

Table 10.1. Comparison of artifacts from Sycamore Mills with South's range for the Carolina pattern.

Group	Number	Percentage	South's Range
Kitchen	2,935	48.16	51.8–69.2
Architecture	2,940	48.24	19.7–31.4
Furniture	76	1.25	0.1–0.6
Arms	50	0.82	0.1–1.2
Clothing	20	0.32	0.6–5.4
Personal	9	0.15	0.1–0.5
Tobacco pipes	6	0.10	1.8–13.9
Activities	58	0.96	0.9–2.7

From McCarthy and Moffett 1980:71.

Table 10.2. Ceramics from Sycamore Mills by group and type.

Group and Type of Ware	Count	Percentage
Highly decorated		
Transfer-printed	89	4.10
Hand-painted	27	1.24
Porcelain	16	0.74
Bennington	13	0.60
Jackfield	4	0.18
Group percentage		6.86
Lightly decorated		
Banded	43	1.98
Edge	8	0.37
Sponge	8	0.37
Slip	28	1.29
Group percentage		4.01
Undecorated		
Plain dining	1,283	59.10
Utility	652	30.03
Group percentage		89.13

From McCarthy and Moffett 1980:72.

the results of this analysis. The mean date of manufacture of these wares was 1822.9. Since the house that had stood on this site was built no later than 1814, most of the artifacts were apparently deposited as trash in relatively short order.

As compared with their peers in the city, the workers of Bishop's Mills seem to have had a fairly modest collection of domestic belongings. It is unfortunate that no collections of artifacts from the mill owners' homes are as yet available for comparison.

WAYNESBOROUGH: THE ESTATE OF GENERAL "MAD" ANTHONY WAYNE

Our streets, for many days, rang with nothing but the name of General Wayne. You are remembered constantly next to our good and great Washington, over our claret and Madeira. You have established the national character of our country; you have taught our enemies that bravery, humanity, and magnanimity, are the great national virtues of the Americans.

—Gen. Nathanael Greene, letter to Anthony Wayne,
after the Battle of Stony Point

General Wayne had a constitutional attachment to the sword, and this case of character had acquired strength from indulgence.

—Gen. Henry "Light Horse Harry" Lee, in Robert Debs Heinl, Jr.,
The Dictionary of Military and Naval Quotations

The subject of this adulation and restrained censure, Revolutionary War general "Mad" Anthony Wayne, was born in the mansion known as Waynesborough in Paoli, Chester County, on January 1, 1745. The mansion, begun on a relatively modest scale by Wayne's grandfather about 1724, expanded several times under the ownership of many generations of Waynes. The last member of the Wayne family to live there was William Wayne, who in 1965 sold the property to Mr. and Mrs. Oren W. June. The estate had by then seen better days, and in restoring it the Junes used a large collection of Wayne family documents and old paintings of the house to good advantage. Waynesborough has since become a National Historic Landmark.

In 1974, at the invitation of the

Figure 10.31.

Rear of the mansion at Waynesborough with the original wing of the house at right. (Photo by J. L. Cotter)

Junes, students from the University of Pennsylvania conducted an extensive series of archaeological tests at Waynesborough. The object of the testing was to locate the sites of structures known to have once stood on the property. It was also hoped that the excavations might produce artifacts attesting to life on the estate in the eighteenth century. The following account is derived from the summary report of the study (Cotter 1975).

History of the Site

"Mad" Anthony Wayne's grandfather, also named Anthony, was a native of County Wicklow, Ireland. A military man himself, he commanded a squadron of dragoons under William of Orange in the Battle of the Boyne in 1690. He emigrated to America in 1724, bringing considerable resources with him. Shortly after his arrival, in exchange for assuming a debt of £125 owed by Thomas Edwards and wife, he acquired 386 acres of land in Easttown Township, Chester County. He promptly paid off the debt to gain full possession of the land. The small wing on the east side of the mansion probably dates from just after his purchase in 1724 (Figure 10.31). The mansion's central block was built about 1735, and other major additions were made in 1792 and 1902.

Isaac Wayne, "Mad" Anthony's father, was also a soldier. In 1755, after the French and Indians defeated Gen. Edward Braddock's British troops in western Pennsylvania, Isaac left for the French and Indian War and fought in it as a British captain until its end in 1760. In the meantime, young Anthony—ten years old when he saw his father off to war—was entrusted to the care of his uncle, Gilbert Wayne, and enrolled in the country school of which Gilbert was master. A letter

Gilbert wrote to his brother Isaac in 1757 attests to Anthony's military inclinations from an early age. Gilbert observed that Anthony would "never make a scholar" and was distracting his schoolmates by staging battles and seiges in the schoolyard: "During noon, in place of the usual games or amusements, he has the boys employed in throwing up redoubts, skirmishing, etc." Gilbert concluded by warning his brother that unless Anthony paid more attention to his books, he would be dismissed from the school.

By the time Anthony Wayne died at a military post on Lake Erie in 1796, he was the much revered commander-in-chief of the U.S. Army. His early military career, however, had some rather low points. On the night of September 20, 1777, he was encamped near his home at Paoli with 1,500 men under his command. Informed by local Tories of the exact position of Wayne's division, General Howe dispatched a sizable attacking force. Taken by surprise, Wayne's men retreated, and when the so-called Paoli Massacre was over, American casualties numbered somewhere between 150 and 300; the British listed but 7 dead. In the aftermath, with rumors and accusations hanging heavy in the air, Wayne demanded—and received—a court martial. Wayne's spirited appeal of his case in October 1777 included such phrases as, "I rest my honor and my character, which to me are dearer than life." The court unanimously concluded that Wayne "had done every thing to be expected, from an active, brave and vigilant officer" and exonerated him completely (Smith 1862:315–16).

After Wayne led his troops in the Battle of Monmouth in New Jersey on June 28, 1778, he again came under personal attack, for some months later Gen. Charles Lee publicly questioned his courage and stability dur-

ing that fighting. This time Wayne's reaction was to challenge his detractor to a duel. Somehow, the duel was avoided without sacrifice of honor, and both men lived on to fight other battles. Wayne's greatest triumph, in fact, occurred just six months after this affair ended, when on July 15, 1779, he led the American forces to an important victory at Stony Point, New York.

It seems unlikely that the testy and vigorous General Wayne would have had much time or inclination to devote himself to improving his family estate, and indeed only one of the major renovations that took place there after 1735 occurred during his lifetime. The first renovation, in 1735, involved the addition of a large, rectangular block of undressed schist to the small, two-story house Wayne's grandfather had built, also of undressed schist, in 1724 (Figure 10.32). The new addition was three stories high and had two dormers on the front (i.e., south) side of its wood-shingled, pitched roof and three in the rear. A center hall ran, and still runs, through this portion of the house from front to back, where a door opens onto a covered porch; the porch leads onto an open terrace. On either side of the center hall are two rooms separated by a fireplace. Access to the cellar beneath this part of the house is through stairs in an opening along the west wall. Interestingly, the cellar stairs have stone ramps on each side of them; the ramps allowed barrels, restrained by ropes, to be easily rolled down into the cellar.

In 1792 a one-story kitchen wing was added at the northeast corner of the main house, and in 1860 a second story was added to it. The years 1870–1890 saw a number of minor changes. The original large stone chimneys of the house were replaced with smaller ones of brick topped with tall chimney

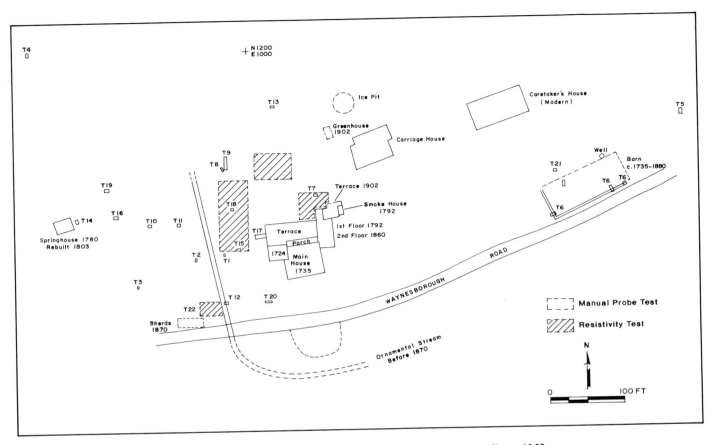

Figure 10.32.

Plan of Waynesborough, showing archaeological test sites. (From Cotter 1975)

Figure 10.33.

Test 18 at Waynesborough. Beneath 15 inches of new topsoil, the old terrace extended to a depth of 48 inches from the surface. (From Cotter 1975)

pots (not all of which survived seventeen winters). A lightning rod came and went. At the front of the house, a wrought-iron fence replaced an earlier picket one, which had already replaced a board one. And all wood trim in sight, originally white, was painted blue. Inside, the dividing wall between the first-floor rooms on the west side of the main house was removed to create one large Victorian parlor.

In 1902 T. Mellon Rogers, architect of Independence Hall fame, came on the scene to add his own inimitable touches. Had Rogers stopped at adding a terrace, which subsequently became a laundry room, life for future restorers of the estate would probably have been a good deal easier. Rogers, however, saw fit to impose his concept of a Colonial house on the Wayne mansion. Although the brick chimneys gave way to stone ones that resembled the originals, the new ones were topped by flagstone wind deflectors. The dormer windows in the roof were treated to rather elaborate pediments, and their panes, originally four over four, became six over six. On the second floor of the west wall of the original 1724 structure, a window appeared where one had never been. Inside, Rogers did the house a favor by replacing the wall between the two first-floor rooms on the west side of the main house. But he also obliterated a number of original wallpapers and paint colors. The last change to occur before the Junes began restoring the mansion in the late 1960s was undertaken by William Wayne, who simplified the dormers by removing Rogers' pediments.

The outbuildings of the estate have, of course, also been altered over the years. A 1783 survey map shows the mansion, a springhouse, a coach barn, and a barn spread out along Waynesborough Road. The barn was at least as large as the house itself. In 1974 the barn was no longer a part of the landscape, and a sizable, two-story carriage house stood in the rear of the house. The springhouse, a stone structure rebuilt at least twice, collapsed sometime after 1967.

Archaeological Testing

Figure 10.32 shows the locations of the twenty-two test trenches Penn students dug at Waynesborough in 1974 in an effort to verify structures documented as having once stood on the property. The major find occurred 300 feet east of the house, where a series of tests (all designated as test 6) revealed the south and west foundation walls of a barn that had stood there from about 1735 to 1880. The walls were 12 inches wide, extended into the earth for 20 inches, and were topped with 2 inches of humus. The area apparently had been recently leveled and filled.

Test 17, west of the original part of the house, revealed the fieldstone foundations of the estate's first bake oven. The oven had evidently extended about 5 feet beyond the wall of the house and been 5 to 6 feet wide. It had ostensibly vented into the house chimney. Its iron doors may have opened inside or outside the house, or both. The principle in using ovens like these was to get the interior bricks hot by lighting a fire within, raking the hot ashes out, and, using a long-handled wooden shovel called a "peel," inserting the goods to be baked well back on the oven floor. The service door and chimney draft were then shut until the food was cooked.

Test 18 (Figure 10.33) showed that this area west of the house had recently been covered with 15 inches of topsoil to create a terrace. Beneath the topsoil was an older terrace that extended 48 inches beneath the surface. At the bottom were late eighteenth- and early nineteenth-century sherds. Other sherds of the same date were located in test 1, where the topsoil for a terrace was also evident.

Test 12, near Waynesborough Road, produced a remnant of a rock structure—possibly a wall for a canal—as well as some eighteenth-century artifacts. Test 22 was an effort to determine whether the rocks found in test 12 were actually part of a canal wall; historical documents at Waynesborough contain references to a "stream next to the house" and "the large stream" farther down, as well as to water being channeled from three springs. The rocks proved to be not part of an upright wall but rather a rock lining for the sloping bank of a canal. The rock lining on the canal's east bank may have been constructed in the late 1700s or early 1800s, but the Portland cement found lining the west bank was definitely manufactured after 1846 and probably much later.

The amount of structural evidence produced by these preliminary tests indicated that a more extensive investigation of the grounds at Waynesborough could have some interesting results. The tests also demonstrated that the grade at Waynesborough had changed drastically over the years; the ground level near the 1724 house in the vicinity of test 17 was 48 inches above undisturbed earth, and in test 22 it was 69 inches above. The most notable negative result of the study was the failure of widespread probing to find traces of a tannery that historical records indicated had stood where tests 10, 11, 16, and 19 were placed.

VALLEY FORGE: A
NATIONAL ICON UNCOVERED

In a hilly, wooded area near the junction of the Schuykill River and Valley Creek (Figure 10.34), the Continental Army found a defensible site to spend the winter of 1777–78. The site, known as Valley Forge, was a long, safe eighteen miles northwest of Philadelphia, but close enough to allow the Continentals to keep an eye on the British, who, after routing them at the Brandywine and mauling them at Germantown, had occupied the city. At Valley Forge, General Washington, his staff, and his soldiers experienced varying degrees of shivering hope in an epic contest of endurance with the elements, the enemy, and deficient supplies and pay.

Even in the rather cynical late twentieth century, Americans tend to respect and even revere Valley Forge as a symbol of the nation's spirit. It was not always so. When the Continental Army marched off from the scene of its wintry nightmare in June 1778, frugal farmers speedily swarmed over the fields, salvaging everything useful in sight. Logs from the huts where soldiers had shivered through the winter were soon housing chickens and livestock or finding their way into split rail fences. Only the foundations of small fireplaces remained to signify the suffering of the winter of 1777–78, and they, too, gradually faded from view as the woods regrew around them. When George Washington returned to muse over the campsite ten years later, he found "all the Works . . . in ruins; and the Incampments in woods where the grounds had not been cultivated."

The sentiment that led to the restoration of the encampment at Valley Forge was no more immediate in gathering than was the idea of memorializing Independence Hall. And the factor that spurred the latter movement—Lafayette's triumphal return to Philadelphia in 1824—seems to have kindled some interest in Valley Forge. The first recorded suggestion . to preserve the site was made in 1828. With travel up the Schuylkill then still by barge and the state of the roads offering little inducement to make the pilgrimage from Philadelphia, the idea lay dormant for almost half a century. Meanwhile, dedicated antiquarians and collectors of relics occasionally visited the site, acquiring a few things the farmers had missed half a century before.

In 1876, with the Centennial Exposition taking place in Philadelphia, patriotic reflection, together with the main line of the Reading Railroad and its nearby station, brought an influx of pilgrims to Valley Forge. Two years later, when the centennial of Washington's evacuation of the camp was

Figure 10.34.

Map of Valley Forge, showing archaeological sites.

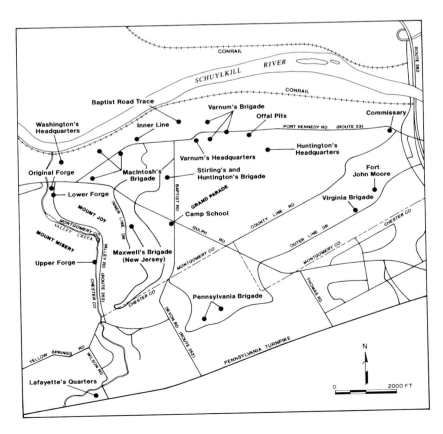

celebrated on June 19, 1878, patriotism burst into flame, fanned by the oratory of Henry Armitt Brown, speaker on that memorable occasion. The Valley Forge Centennial and Memorial Association was speedily formed and managed to raise $3,000 of the $6,000 necessary to purchase the farmhouse that had been Washington's headquarters and one and a half acres around it; the balance was secured by a mortgage. As with most drives to memorialize a hallowed spot, interest waned as obligations grew. The property would have been lost had the Patriotic Order of the Sons of America not come to the rescue in 1885 and paid the mortgage in full (Wildes 1938:295–98).

In 1893 the Commonwealth of Pennsylvania passed an act "to acquire, preserve and maintain forever, the Revolutionary camp ground at Valley Forge for the enjoyment of the people of the State" (cited in Ralph and Parrington 1979). The Valley Forge Park Commission was formed to manage the park, which it continued to do until the bicentennial of the nation in 1976. On July 4 of that year, the park was turned over to the federal government, and since then the park, known as Valley Forge National Historical Park, has been administered by the National Park Service.

Valley Forge in the Winter of 1777–78

It seems unlikely that the soldiers who straggled into the wooded hills of Valley Forge on December 19, 1777, got a very warm reception from the local residents. It was because of Washington's army that several of them had lost their means of livelihood just a few months before. In September the British had blown up the dam across Valley Creek and destroyed the village's iron forge, gristmill, and sawmill to prevent their being of use to the Continentals. Local farmers, too, were no doubt not very welcoming. Most of them were disinterested in the war and found it irksome to have it deposited right on their doorsteps. Moreover, a few farmers would soon be ousted from their homes when high-ranking officers commandeered them for their quarters.

If the soldiers' reception was frigid, the air on December 19 was not any less so. A light snow covered the ground, and a cold wind was blowing. Joseph Plumb Martin, that ubiquitous young soldier of the Revolutionary War, was among the 12,000 soldiers who shuffled into Valley Forge that day, and he later had this to say about the experience:

We were now in a truly forlorn condition—no clothing, no provisions and as disheartened as need be. We arrived, however, at our destination a few days before Christmas. Our prospect was indeed dreary. In our miserable condition, to go into the wild woods and build us habitations to *stay* (not to *live*) in, in such a weak, starved and naked condition, was appalling in the highest degree. . . . But we were now absolutely in danger of perishing, and that too, in the midst of a plentiful country. We then had but little and often nothing to eat for days together; but now we had nothing and saw no likelihood of any betterment of our condition. Had there fallen deep snows (and it was the time of year to expect them) or even heavy and long rainstorms, the whole army must have perished. Or had the enemy, strong and well provided as he then was, thought fit to pursue us, our poor emaciated carcasses must have "strewed the plain." (Martin 1979:102–3)

By nightfall on the first day, Martin, resourceful as ever, had managed to dine on a small pumpkin heated on a flat rock and to get a swig from a reluctant soldier's canteen, though for the swig he had to part with his last three pence.

The first order of business of any army in a new encampment is to get under shelter—any shelter—especially in cold weather. The soldiers pitched all available tenting immediately, but it was far from enough. Some men huddled under arbors of branches covered with brush and leaves. Whether the "habitations" Martin referred to were such makeshift shelters or the log huts Washington immediately ordered his men to build is unclear. But until the soldiers were settled in these huts, which ultimately numbered about two thousand, Washington himself braved the elements under his "marquee," a large tent usually used for staff conferences and dining.

It was not until early January that the commander-in-chief folded his tent and moved into Isaac Potts' farmhouse, a two-story stone structure whose front room Washington used both as office and bedroom. Measuring just 24 by 33 feet, the farmhouse was inadequate as a military headquarters, and as the winter wore on, Washington had a little log house built next door for use as a dining room. After its construction, Martha Washington, who had arrived at Valley Forge in February, noted that the addition "has made our quarters much more tolerable than they were at first." Meanwhile, Lafayette had moved into a very decent house south of Valley Forge, as had French engineer Louis L. Duportail, who laid out the camp but escaped having to live in it.

Washington's orders for setting up the camp, based on Duportail's plans, were designed to make the camp as strong as possible, and his Orderly Book, on file at the National Archives,* shows that they were very explicit:

[Huts] fourteen feet by sixteen each; the sides, ends, and roofs made with logs; the roofs made tight with split slabs, or some other way; the sides made tight with clay; a fireplace made of wood, and secured with clay on the inside, eighteen inches thick; this fire-place to be in the rear of the hut; the door to be in the end next the street; the doors to be made of split oak slabs, unless boards be procured; the side walls to be six feet and a half high. The officers' huts are to form a line in the rear of the troops, one hut to be allowed to each general officer; one to the staff of each brigade; one to the field officer of each regiment; one to the staff of each regiment; one to the commissioned officers of two companies; and one to every twelve non-commissioned officers and soldiers.

Given the hilly terrain and other constraints under which they worked, the soldiers laid their huts out in remarkably straight lines. Their only equipment was whatever hardware and tools the quartermaster could muster, and their materials were the rocks they had to wrest out of the earth and the trees that towered above them. Moreover, many of them were town-bred and had no experience or skill in building. One explanation for the neat rows formed by the huts, or at least by those of General Muhlenburg's men on the outer line of defense, lies in this passage from Muhlenburg's Orderly Book, on file at the National Archives:

The Gen'l promises to reward the Party in each Reg't who finishes their hutts in the most Nicest & most workmanlike manner with 12 Dollars and as there is reason to believe that Boards fore covering may be found scarce and difficult to be got he offers 100 dollars to any Officer or Soldier who in the opinion of three Gen'ls . . . shall substitute some

* On December 18, 1777, while at Gulph Mills, Washington issued these orders (cited in *The Picket Post*, July 1944, pp. 9–10).

other covering that may be cheaper and Quicker made and will in every Respect answer the End.

The twelve-dollar prizes were duly won, but the record is dim as to whether anyone snagged the one-hundred-dollar prize by coming up with an idea for the roof.

With such encouragement, and with the winter wind howling about their poorly clad bodies, the soldiers soon denuded the forests of Mount Joy and Mount Misery, as the two most prominent nearby slopes were known. The wood not only served to shelter the men but also to warm them and whatever food they could lay their hands on, which was at the best of times very little and at other times desperately little. Joseph Plumb Martin was a member of one of the foraging parties sent out soon after the army's arrival at Valley Forge to comb the countryside for farmers with food and persuade them to part with it—as forcefully as need be. The first victims of starvation as the winter wore on were the horses of Gen. Henry Knox's artillery brigade; several hundred of them died.

Another telling statistic of the winter of 1777–78 is that at one point four thousand men—a third of the army—were listed as unfit for duty because of inadequate clothing. Although on October 2, 1779, Washington ordered that the uniforms of all branches of the service be blue, with different-colored jacket facings designating the different state regiments, at Valley Forge circumstances did not permit such distinctions. The soldier's uniform Washington then favored, because of its cheapness and durability and, above all, because of its effect on the enemy, by now grown respectful of the woodsman's marksmanship, was the hunting shirt of deerskin, dyed homespun breeches, and leggings.

The job of the brigade quartermaster was formidable. He not only had to find axes, nails, pails, tin canisters, camp kettles, and straw bedding for his brigade; he also had to find hospital supplies. Washington's orders were that all brigades were to have two "Flying Hospital Hutts," each 25 by 15 feet and 9 feet high. They were to be located near the center of the hut line and no more than 100 yards from the brigade, if the terrain permitted. In these hospital huts an estimated two thousand men died of typhus, dysentery, and pneumonia in the winter of 1777–78.

Ingenuity was at a premium, and at any moment, any one of the many soldiers with special skills might be called upon to offer his services. Men who had been carpenters, blacksmiths, wheelwrights, ropemakers, and leather workers in peacetime found themselves in great demand. One day, this enigmatic appeal for a very specialized skill appeared in Washington's Orderly Book:

If there are any persons in the Army who understand making thin paper, such as bank notes are struck on, they are desired to apply immediately to the Orderly Office, where they will be shewn a sample of the paper—Officers commanding Regiments are to publish this on Regimental Orders. . . .

Since no follow-up to this document appears in the records, we are left to speculate on the success, to say nothing of the purpose, of the quest. The most satisfactory answer seems to be that it was part of a plan to deceive the enemy by counterfeiting a document or bank note.

As the months wore on and cold weather turned to warm, nature provided another unpleasantry: poison ivy. Martin (1979:110) records relieving himself of "the itch" by applying a salve of tallow and sulphur. Almost two hundred years later, archaeologists, suffering from the same itch, found a bit of sulphur on a hut floor. Martin, and many others like him, may have contracted his case in the spring while engaged in digging offal pits and defensive ditches and earthen forts. To avoid unhealthy contamination as the weather warmed in late March and early April, Washington ordered that offal pits be dug and that teams of trash collectors keep "the streets and alleys of the camp free from all kinds of filth. . . . All bones and putrid meat, dirty straw and any other kind of filth to be every day collected and burnt." The defensive ditches and earthen forts Washington thought prudent to add should the fair weather entice Howe out of his comfortable lair in Philadephia. According to an eye witness (Auburey 1923:170–71), these defenses were very slight: "The ditches were not more than three feet deep, and so narrow, that a drum-boy might with ease leap over."

In the early months of 1778, poor discipline and morale—and the possibility of mutiny—presented far greater threats than Howe. That mutiny was averted and the ragged army turned into a unified fighting force was owing in large part to the efforts of Prussian drillmaster Friedrich von Steuben. The effect of months of von Steuben's daily drilling was evident as the men marched out of Valley Forge in orderly columns, heads held high, on June 19, 1778.

Archaeology at Valley Forge

The Valley Forge Park Commission, charged in the 1890s with the management of the park, ultimately perceived its mandate not only as preservation and maintenance, but also, and perhaps more strongly, as restoration. In undertaking to restore

the camp to its 1777–78 appearance, the commission set itself quite a task. In the more than one hundred years since Washington and his army had decamped, local residents had gone uncooperatively about their business, salvaging logs from huts, plowing over the entrenchments, and erecting new domestic and industrial structures. During the early twentieth century, the commission, undaunted, set about razing the contemporary village of Valley Forge.

In the process of demolishing a dam erected for a cotton mill, the restorationists unearthed what were probably the remains of an iron forge that had been rebuilt after the Revolutionary War. Because this material was unrelated to the winter of 1777–78, it was judged not worth preserving. However, the discovery seems to have sparked the commission's inter-

est in reconstructing a forge of the Revolutionary War period on Valley Creek. This idea led to the first formal archaeological excavations in the park—a search from 1929 to 1931 for the site of the forge the British destroyed in September 1777 (Clarke 1929; Schenck 1984; Stone 1984: 115–19). The work produced an embarrassing abundance of forges, including the "Lower Forge," on the east side of Valley Creek not far from Washington's headquarters, and the "Upper Forge," farther south on the west side of the creek (see Figure 10.34).

Covered by 7 feet of silt, the waterwheels and other wooden machinery of the Upper Forge, a stone structure

Figure 10.35.

Map of Upper Forge, from excavations carried out from 1929 to 1931. (Courtesy of Valley Forge National Historical Park)

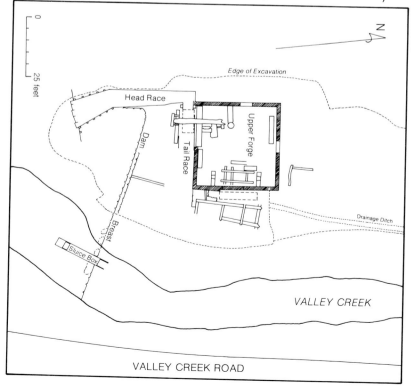

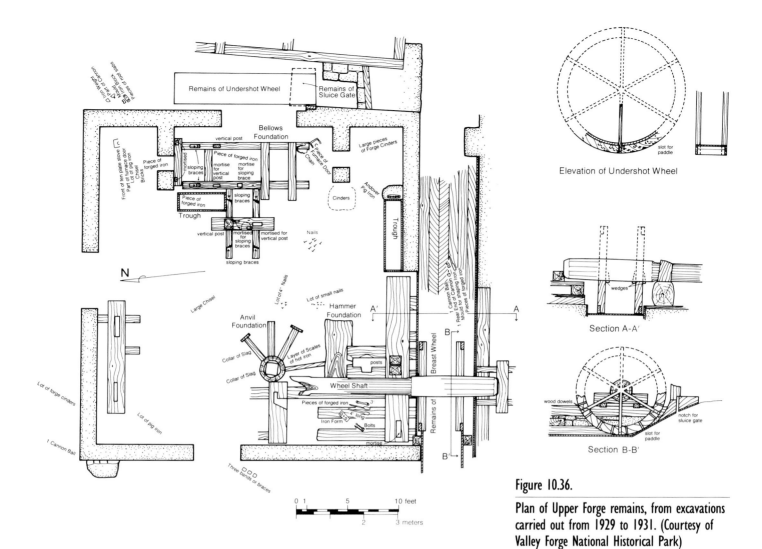

Figure 10.36 labels:
Remains of Undershot Wheel
Remains of Sluice Gate
Bellows Foundation
vertical post
mortised
sloping braces
mortise for vertical post
mortise for sloping brace
Large pieces of Forge Cinders
Piece of forged iron
Bricks
Front of ten plate stove
Part of furnace door
Lot of pig iron
Chisel
Piece of forged iron
Piece of Pump Door Chain
Cinders
Andover Pig Iron
Trough
Piece of forged iron
sloping braces
vertical post
mortise for sloping braces
mortise for vertical post
sloping braces
Nails
N
Large Chisel
Lot of 4" Nails
Lot of small nails
Anvil Foundation
Hammer Foundation
A'
A
B'
B
1 Cannon Ball
1 Rear End of Cannon
Mould for shaping iron
Pieces of forged iron
Breast Wheel
Trough
Collar of Slag
Layer of Scales of hot iron
Collar of Slag
posts
Lot of forge cinders
Lot of pig iron
Wheel Shaft
Remains of
Pieces of forged iron
Iron Form
Bolts
mortise
1 Cannon Ball
Three bands or braces

Elevation of Undershot Wheel
slot for paddle
wedges
Section A-A'
wood dowels
notch for sluice gate
slot for paddle
Section B-B'

0 1   5   10 feet
2   3 meters

Figure 10.36.

Plan of Upper Forge remains, from excavations carried out from 1929 to 1931. (Courtesy of Valley Forge National Historical Park)

about 35 feet square, were exceptionally well preserved (Figures 10.35 and 10.36). This early archaeology was of exceptional quality, too, and included one of the first applications of dendrochronology in historical archaeology. The archaeologists sent sections of timbers from the two forges to the Museum of Northern Arizona, where it was concluded that the Lower Forge was twenty-three years older than the Upper Forge.

Although the plan to reconstruct a forge was never carried out, the excavation of the Upper Forge must have served as advertisement for the "goods" archaeological excavation can produce, for in the next forty-five years the park witnessed a remarkable amount of excavation. The quality of the work was as varied as the reasons for undertaking it. It ranged from avocational explorations done with

metal detectors to work undertaken for teaching purposes and for producing evidence for reconstructions. All of it was done in the context of individual projects with site-specific goals. It was not until the National Park Service took over the administration of the park in 1976 that a unified research plan was formulated.*

The National Park Service took the very sensible first step of assembling an inventory of what it had by commissioning the Museum Applied Science Center for Archaeology of the University Museum to compile infor-

* The National Park Service has also played an educational role at the park. In the late 1970s park personnel instructed students from Lower Merion High School in archaeological purpose and practice. The students, already carefully trained in archaeological methods by their classroom teacher, Stephen McCarter, contributed their skilled labor to fieldwork at Valley Forge.

mation on all previous archaeology at Valley Forge (Schenck 1978). The work also included a geophysical survey that used radar and resistivity devices to identify archaeological remains (Ralph and Parrington 1979; Parrington 1979c). One unfortunate finding of the geophysical survey was that the ground had been severely disturbed over the years, particularly during the 1950s and 1960s, when numerous utility lines were laid to accommodate International Boy Scout Jamborees held at Valley Forge.

The forges that gave the site its name, the farmhouses that housed Washington and his officers, the slight earthen defenses behind which the army huddled—all have come in for their share of archaeological scrutiny over the years. Work at the Upper Forge, begun in 1929–1931, continued in 1966, when interest in reconstructing a forge resurfaced. At that time, Ditchburn (1966:3–4) re-excavated the Upper Forge and found it to be essentially as recorded in 1929–1931, though somewhat damaged by intermittent flooding. In 1984 Helen Schenck submitted a sample of the iron artifacts recovered in the 1929–1931 excavations to a metallurgical analysis. The samples contained large amounts of carbon, suggesting that either the refining process at the forge was inefficient or that the forge had been making "German steel," a product with a high amount of carbon, the ingredient that gives steel its strength (Schenck 1984, 1988; Schenck and Knox 1985, 1986).

The farmhouses that have received archaeological attention include the Isaac Potts House, site of Washington's headquarters (Hunter and Packard 1973b); the David Stephens House, site of Varnum's headquarters (Warfel and Kent 1975; Hunter and Packard 1973a); the Maurice Stephens House, site of Huntingdon's headquarters (Kerrigan and Packard 1973; Shuster 1975; Warfel and Kent 1975); and the Samuel Packard House, site of Duportail's and Lafayette's quarters (Webster 1966; Shuster 1976). Among the fortifications that have been studied are the ditches of the inner line of defense (Jordan and de Toledo 1976; Bevan 1984) and Fort John Moore, excavated by J. Duncan Campbell in 1948. Other excavated sites include the Commissary and the Camp School (Barrett and Packard 1973a, 1973b) and even one of the army's offal pits (Olsen 1964; Campbell 1966).

While these excavations have produced valuable information, much of the best information about life at the encampment has come from the sites of private soldiers' huts. The first ex-cavations of these sites took place in the early 1960s, and they came about when it became clear that documentary evidence alone could not answer all the questions that arose as the huts were being reconstructed. Were all the huts really alike? Just how did the numerous unskilled and few skilled workmen of Washington's army build them? What was life like in the huts? What did the soldiers who lived in them do to wile away the time? What objects would have been in their possession? These were among the questions excavations of the hut sites were intended to answer. The first ex-cavations focused on the site where Maxwell's New Jersey Brigade had encamped. Since then, the sites of various other brigades have also been excavated.

The Encampment of the New Jersey Brigade

In 1962 John Witthoft and J. Duncan Campbell collaborated in excavating the floors of five huts the men of Maxwell's Brigade built in 1777–78. The construction of the huts appeared to conform to General Washington's orders. Three of the huts were in a line, and each appeared to have measured 16 by 14 feet. The centers of the hearths were 27 feet apart. The other two huts were in a line just behind the first row. Measuring 12 by 12 feet, they had apparently been occupied by officers. The backs of the huts, where the fireplaces were located, faced northeast, a reasonable winter orientation. One of the officers' huts had its chimney in a corner rather than centered on the rear wall (Campbell 1962).

The objects found in the floors and fireplaces of the five huts paint a picture of what a soldier in Washington's army was using—and losing—as, in between reveille, von Steuben's daily drills, and taps, he suffered the misery and boredom of camp life. The objects included a fish hook, a penknife, numerous wrought-iron nails, musket balls, gunflints, small buckshot, parts of bayonet scabbards, buttons, a British penny of 1773, and sherds of glass and glazed earthenware. The loss of the ammunition and gunflints must have been purely accidental, for any soldier found wasting such items was subject to thirty-nine lashes. Moreover, no soldier would have thrown away a gunflint; the firing device of his musket was vital to his survival. Some of the musket balls were suspiciously tool-marked, suggesting that they may have been handled by surgical instruments and that a hospital hut had been located nearby. The variety of the buttons Witthoft and Campbell recovered substantiated the historical facts that the uniform of the Continental "G.I." was unlikely to be "government issue" and that at Valley Forge ill-clad soldiers were apt to be wearing anything they could lay their hands on.

The Encampment of the Pennsylvania Brigade

In 1966 graduate students from the University of Pennsylvania, under the direction of John Cotter (1966c), identified and mapped several hut sites and excavated two of them.* The sites were located in the area designated on Duportail's plan of the encampment as the site of the Pennsylvania Brigade. They were marked by a series of depressions in the earth next to a hillside.

At the east end of one of the two promising sites chosen for excavation

---

* Contributing their labor to the excavation were Stanley Landis, avocational archaeologist; William Richard Gordon, arms expert, member of the Valley Forge Park Commission, and treasurer of the University of Pennsylvania; and Gordon's teen-age son.

Figure 10.37.

Hut site of the Pennsylvania Brigade. Digging around the tree roots for evidence of the hut required patience, and entailed some pain. The bandage on the arm of the shoveler in the rear covers a case of poison ivy that required a day of hospitalization. (Photo by J. L. Cotter)

was a sizable oak tree, approximately sixty years old. As the slow work of recording the excavation with measurements and photographs progressed, it was evident that a concentration of flat stones—apparently the base of a fireplace wall—was appearing directly beneath the roots of the tree. Leaving enough roots to save the tree while removing enough earth to reveal the stones required considerable patience (Figure 10.37), but at length there appeared a collection of flat stones spread like a dropped deck of cards. South of them were more stones, evidently the base of the other wall of the fireplace, and in the area between the two stone bases were traces of calcined bones in soil that deepened into fine, gray-brown wood ash.

More careful testing revealed nothing identifiable as a hut floor. One side of the floor had apparently slid down the slope of the hill. The other side, dug into a niche in the hill, was equally elusive. In the niche was a clutter of flat rocks, probably fallen there after having been used to shore up a log wall. Artifacts, too, were initially elusive. It took a metal detector to produce the first one—an iron file looking so much like the rat-tail ones still sold in hardware stores it was at first thought to be modern. It turned out, however, to be a genuine memento of activity in the hut, and its loss probably gave rise to some muttered curses, for a good file was a useful army tool. Soon after the file appeared, the floor level, particularly

around the fireplace, yielded a number of other artifacts: two coins, three plain pewter buttons, two lead buttons, a brass button, a sherd of English creamware, buckshot, three lead musket balls together with some melted lead from the hearthside industry of casting them, and—most intriguing of all to the members of the team then suffering from poison ivy— a pellet of sulfur as big as the tip of a small finger. In addition to Joseph Plumb Martin's mention of using a sulfur salve to relieve the "itch," medical records of the Continental Army show that the quartermaster was ordered to supply sulfur for use in treating skin disorders.

Excavation of the second hut site progressed more rapidly. The first thing to appear was a well-defined fireplace, nearly intact. Its slightly spread stone wings were at the widest point 5 feet apart, and it had been about 2½ feet deep. In places, the fireplace walls had been less than a foot thick—considerably less than the 18 inches Washington's regulations called for, but safe enough for small fires. It is unlikely that any soldier would have endangered a hut he had had to build with his own hands by making a recklessly large fire with wood he had had to procure and chop himself. Although no well-defined floor level appeared, the floor had

evidently consisted of gray earth sprinkled in places with small flat stones; the stones had been thrust into the mud between the wall logs as caulking against the weather.

The finds from the floor of this hut, some of which are shown in Figure 10.38, included an assortment of beef, fowl, and rabbit bones; six wrought-iron nails; three lead musket balls; a bone button blank; eight pewter buttons, one inscribed "USA"; four copper or bronze buttons; a brass button; a brass shoe buckle; a two-tined fork with a piece of its bone handle; four sherds of lead-glazed earthenware; a few fragments of glass, probably from spirit bottles; and the glass signet from a ring on which were inscribed several Masonic emblems. The single brass button turned out to be from a uniform of Valley Forge Military Academy (founded 1927), and when the glass signet appeared a few inches away from it, it was greeted with some skepticism, for the chances seemed to be that it, too, was of twentieth-century origin. A few years later, however, an excavation at a Revolutionary War site in South Carolina produced an identical glass signet (Baker 1972). Modest though these finds were, they do give a glimpse of soldiers breaking their shoe buckles, losing their buttons and an occasional fork, and breaking some humble earthenware

Figure 10.38.

Artifacts found at a hut of the Pennsylvania Brigade. A glass Masonic signet button is at the bottom center. (Photo by J. L. Cotter)

and bottles—typical activities of the humdrum of military life since time immemorial.

Encampment of the Virginia Brigade

Beginning in 1972–73, as plans were being made to construct a parking lot on a level stretch of ground where the Virginia Brigade had once had their huts, another series of excavations took place. Carried out by archaeologists from the Pennsylvania Historical and Museum Commission and students and staff from the University of Delaware, the University of Pennsylvania, and the National Park Service the work resulted in a number of reports (Egloff, Packard, and Ramsay n.d.; Packard 1972, 1973; Cotter 1972; Hall 1972a, 1972b; Parrington 1979d, 1979–80; Parrington, Schenck, and Thibaut 1984; Orr, Blades, and Campana 1985).

The excavations succeeded in locating seventeen huts, four pits, and numerous artifacts of the Revolutionary War. In this area, soil discoloration marked the places where vertical wooden posts had stood. The posts

may have framed the huts, or they may have supported bunks. To allow more headroom, the floors of the huts had been hollowed out to depths ranging from 8 inches to 18 inches, a common practice but one that was thought unhealthy; it was specifically prohibited the year after Washington's army left Valley Forge. The dimensions of these hollows varied from 12½ by 12 feet to 7½ by 6½ feet. The huts themselves may have been much larger. The orientation of the fireplaces was irregular, to say the least, with little apparent attempt to comply with Washington's order that fireplaces should be in the rear of the huts. The arrangement of the lines of the huts also seemed to deviate from plan.

Evidence from the Huts: A Summary

The orderly layout of the huts of Maxwell's New Jersey Brigade and the irregularity of the huts of the Virginians is a reminder that although Washington was attempting to create a unified army at Valley Forge, his soldiers came from different parts of the country with distinctly different cultural behaviors. Conditions at each brigade encampment also depended to a certain extent on the whims of

the individual brigade commander, who was in total control of the supplies his men received. Thus neither Washington's orders nor the contemporary account of a soldier in one particular brigade can be relied on to give a picture of what the entire encampment was like.

The artifacts recovered from the hut sites reinforce the bleak picture painted by historical accounts of the encampment at Valley Forge. The great majority of objects were issued by the army for military use or subsistence; lead musket balls, gunflints, and other kinds of military items predominated. Very few personal possessions appeared—a few coins, a thimble, a penknife, a ring, and some marbles. What little the soldiers had came almost exclusively from the quartermaster, and those items were generally in such short supply that what one soldier lost was presumably soon found and used by another.

One item that does seem to have been in plentiful supply was the lead musket ball. Almost 250 of these items were recovered from the various encampment sites. About 60 percent of them were .75 calibre, suitable for use with muskets of both British and American make; the rest were .69 calibre, the size used with the French-made Charleville musket. A good many musket balls had tooth marks on them. One explanation may be that "biting the bullet" was common practice when punishment was being administered (Hanson and Hsu 1975: 80–81). Another theory is that soldiers bit into the musket balls in the hope that when they hit their mark, they would add infection to the wound (Witthoft 1951b:60–61). Whatever the reason, over 10 percent of the musket balls had tooth marks on them, so the practice seems to have been fairly common.

THE BARNS-BRINTON HOUSE: ARCHAEOLOGICAL EVIDENCE OF OLD U.S. ROUTE 1

The Barns-Brinton House is located in Pennsbury Township along U.S. Route 1 near Chadds Ford, Pennsylvania. Unfortunately, little of the site's history is known, and for this reason the property probably possesses little regional significance. However, with the urging and financial assistance of the Chadds Ford Historical Society, the house underwent a substantial restoration in the 1970s, and today it appears much as it must have looked in the early eighteenth century, when it was built.

The Barns-Brinton House is a two-and-one-half-story brick structure, measuring 20 by 40 feet in plan, with two rooms on the first floor and three on the second. The house originally (and as restored) had pent eaves along the entirety of the east, west, and south facades and along the majority of the north facade. A lean-to shed was originally along the north wall. Significantly, there are two ornamental diamonds in the brickwork forming the west gable (Anderson 1959), an embellishment not appearing on most eighteenth-century Chester County houses. Prior to its restoration, the house retained much of its original fabric, trim, and hardware, an obvious inducement to its restoration.

What little is known of the history of the Barns-Brinton property indicates that the house may have been built as early as 1704 or 1705, but more likely not until ca. 1717–1722 (Anderson 1959; Macdonald and Townsend 1975:1). However, it is known that William Barnes purchased the property between 1704 and 1715 from Peter Dicks, Jr. Be- tween 1722 and 1731, William Barnes maintained a tavern license for the property, and presumably operated it as an inn for travelers along the old Baltimore Road. While it may have continued in use as a tavern beyond 1731, records do not indicate this (Anderson 1959). By 1753, the property had been sold to James Brinton, and the property was to remain in the Brinton family for the next 106 years. Subsequently, the property changed hands several times, until its recent purchase by the Chadds Ford Historical Society. Although the records are unclear, it is likely that the property functioned as a tavern or inn for only a short time, and that it functioned primarily as a residence for the ma-

Figure 10.39.

Barns-Brinton House, Chadds Ford, as it appeared ca. 1900. (Courtesy of the Chadds Ford Historical Society)

jority of its owners and occupants until its purchase by the Historical Society.

Archaeological excavations at the Barns-Brinton House were undertaken on three separate occasions (Macdonald and Townsend 1975; Townsend 1979; Henry and Roberts 1986), with the goals of each centered primarily on the provision of archaeological evidence to assist in architectural restoration efforts undertaken by the Chadds Ford Historical Society. Initially, questions concerning the presence and configuration of an early porch or stoop and the elevation of original grade were addressed archaeologically (Macdonald and Townsend 1975). The second investigation was designed to build upon the results of the first, specifically to aid in an interpretation of the original appearance of the area south of the house (Townsend 1979:3), where the original U.S. Route 1 (Baltimore Road) was located. Route 1 still passes by the house, but on the north side. The third investigation (Henry and Roberts 1986) was a minor archaeological monitoring effort during reconstruction of a small retaining wall. No significant archaeological features were excavated during this work.

While the identification of an early front porch remained problematic, due to the presence outside the front door of a recent "cement slab laid upon a deep bed of stone rubble" (Townsend 1979:20), at least three other features important to the historic interpretation of the property were identified during excavations. The first of these was identification of the original Baltimore Road, the northern edge of which was found to be approximately 30 feet from the south elevation of the house. Although several layers of road surfacing, or metalling, were identified by excavation, none, alas, could be posi-

tively identified as dating to the early eighteenth-century origins of the house. However, the horizontal placement of the original highway was identified, a location that probably did not shift dramatically through time. Indeed, a photograph taken ca. 1900 (Figure 10.39) shows a dirt road in a position that approximates the 30-foot distance from the south elevation of the house confirmed archaeologically.

The remaining two features of importance identified by excavation at the Barns-Brinton House are both low stone retaining walls of dry-laid construction. The earliest of the walls is aligned parallel to the old Baltimore Road, approximately four feet north of the northern edge of the road. Stratigraphic and artifactual evidence strongly indicates that this wall dates to the origins of the house in the early eighteenth century, and was built to isolate the Barns-Brinton property from the Baltimore Road (Townsend 1979:20). Another retaining wall was also found paralleling the Baltimore Road and located approximately 10 feet from the northern edge of the road. Stratigraphic evidence places this wall later in time than the other wall, probably at the turn of the nineteenth century (Townsend 1979:21). It appears that at the time this retaining wall was built, the earlier wall was dismantled, and possibly robbed of its stone to construct the new one.

Artifact recovery at the Barns-Brinton House was disappointing. While a relatively large sample of artifacts dating to the nineteenth and twentieth centuries was recovered, very few clearly dating to the eighteenth century were found. Those artifacts that could be associated with the early occupation of the house consisted principally of small ceramic sherds, among them a fragment of delft, and some eighteenth-century wine bottle necks.

Nineteenth-century artifacts of note included a pair of unglazed porcelain male and female figurines, an iron scissors, and a small pocket knife constructed in the shape of a Victorian-style woman's shoe (Townsend 1979:9). While artifacts such as these proved useful in assigning relative dates to several of the site's strata, none, unfortunately, were of interest or significance to the restoration and development efforts of the property.

The picture that emerges from the limited excavations undertaken at the Barns-Brinton House reveals a considerably more idyllic scene than that evident at the site now. Today the site is subject to the continuous sounds of heavy truck and automobile traffic roaring by on Route 1 within 10 or 15 feet of the northwest corner and rear elevation of the house. Indeed, the orientation of the house to contemporary traffic patterns along Route 1 is anomalous, since Route 1 is a new alignment that bears no direct relationship to the historic placement of the house. As noted earlier, however, excavations confirmed the existence and location of an earlier Route 1 (Baltimore Road) about 30 feet from the south (front) elevation of the house, and between the house and the road was found evidence of two successive retaining walls. It is perhaps not too great a leap of faith to suggest that behind the retaining walls were well-kept lawns and gardens throughout much of the eighteenth- and nineteenth-century history of the Barns-Brinton House, lawns and gardens that the retaining walls were designed to mask from the "offensive" horse-drawn traffic along the original road. The truly offensive traffic of the contemporary U.S. Route 1 could hardly have been envisioned by William Barnes and subsequent owners of the property during the eighteenth and nineteenth centuries.

PART IV

Archaeological Perspectives

II

A Retrospective View:
Interpreting the Evidence

If the task of the archaeologist ended with retrieving the material evidence of past cultures from the earth, one could say without reservation that archaeology in Philadelphia has been eminently successful; the volume of evidence produced in this city and its immediate environs has been staggering. The archaeologist's goal, however, is not merely to amass evidence but to explain what the evidence means, and explanation of this sort requires careful analysis. To make logical inferences about the nature of past lifeways from a collection of broken ceramics, rusted utensils, robbed trenches, and the like, the archaeologist must describe each piece of evidence in terms of its spatial and temporal characteristics and classify it in a way that allows comparison with other artifact collections. As noted several times elsewhere in this volume, archaeology in Philadelphia has been generally lacking in this regard; most artifact collections in this well-excavated city have not been thoroughly analyzed.

One reason for this shortcoming is that, to date, archaeology in Philadelphia has been practiced almost exclusively on an ad hoc, catch-as-catch-can basis. Perhaps because archaeologists have been too busy digging, artifacts have too often sat gathering dust on a laboratory shelf once the fieldwork phase of an investigation has ended. Only in rare instances has there been systematic analysis aimed at establishing correlations or incongruences between the archaeological data and the historical record. Even at Independence National Historical Park, where the National Park Service has sponsored numerous archaeological investigations, data analysis has generally accomplished little beyond answering the elemental questions of site identity that have been the usual focus of work there.

The difficulty in interpreting the significance of Philadelphia's archaeological data is compounded by the inaccessibility of the data. Reports of the investigations have for the most part never been published, and no central repository for either the reports or the artifacts exists. The storage facility the city maintains at the Atwater Kent Museum for artifacts collected from municipally owned sites is not yet permanent, and with other artifact collections scattered throughout the city and no one curator in charge of them, monitoring is sometimes remiss. At least one artifact collection—that assembled at the Man Full of Trouble Tavern by students from the University of Pennsylvania in 1966—has been accidentally lost, once again thrown away as trash.

The problem of scattered, inaccessible data has been somewhat ameliorated in recent years as various organizations have made an effort to provide computerized inventories of the storage locations of their artifact collections and reports. Outstanding among these efforts was one that began in 1979, when the National Park Service commissioned a study designed to synthesize data from all archaeological excavations conducted to that date within Independence National Historical Park. Carried out by Hall and Schenck (1979), the study resulted in the creation of archaeological base maps that show the locations of excavations within the overall park, as well as more detailed maps of excavated features at the park's most significant sites. In addition to giving very brief synopses of the excavations, Hall and Schenck's report has a tabular appendix that lists the name of the principal investigator of each excavation, the date of the work, the title of the report, and a code identifying the site's location on the base maps.

Among Hall and Schenck's recommendations for future synthesis of park data were a study that would correlate stratigraphic profiles of park excavations, the creation of a central repository for all archaeological records, the construction of historic base maps depicting the park at particular time periods, and the periodic updating of their base maps and report to incorporate new archaeological data. The last recommendation received some attention in the 1980s when, as part of a museum internship at Independence National Historic Park, Steven Patrick (1987) produced a report with appendices citing the storage locations of all artifacts, field notes, reports, and archaeological maps and drawings then in the park's collection. Hall and Schenck's base maps and report, together with Pat-

rick's work, have brought considerable order to the huge amount of data available at Independence National Historic Park, providing a useful planning tool for future archaeological endeavors. But valuable as these studies have been in making the park's archaeological data more accessible, they did not accomplish much in the way of data analysis.

Thus, at Independence National Historic Park, as elsewhere throughout the city, we have a vast amount of the material evidence of Philadelphia's past available, but in the absence of comprehensive analyses that would allow for comparison of individual data collections, we lack any precise basis for interpreting it. Despite this lack, the evidence often seems to speak for itself and even in its unanalyzed state adds a unique dimension to our understanding of how Philadelphia evolved over the centuries. Not only does it include details not recorded in historical documents; it also occasionally strikes a contradictory note, making statements that challenge some of our traditional assumptions about the past. Generally, however, the archaeological evidence suggests a clear correlation with the cultural themes documented in Philadelphia's historical record. The most obvious of these correlations and contradictions are recapitulated in the pages that follow.

STRATIFICATION AND THE OPEN SOCIETY

Aside from a few aboriginal artifacts and a few traces of the Swedish settlers of the mid-1600s, the archaeological story of Philadelphia barely gets underway until the early eighteenth century. At that point, the material evidence starts confirming the historical impression of a society clearly stratified into social classes but nonetheless open—open in the sense of religious freedom and a constant intermingling of people from all walks of life.

Religious freedom fortunately has been an enduring characteristic; just a stroll through the city will confirm the diversity of Philadelphia's religious sects and how long they have been around. But in the mid-nineteenth century, as the Industrial Revolution separated the haves from the have-nots, the mixed character of Philadelphia's neighborhoods changed. Streets where middle-class artisans and upper-class merchants once lived and labored gave way to blocks of warehouses and other industrial buildings. As the well-to-do segment of the population fled west to Rittenhouse Square or the suburbs, elegant eighteenth-century homes near the Delaware became commercial properties or unsanitary tenements for the city's growing number of poor. By 1930 Philadelphia had become, in the words of Sam Bass Warner, Jr. (1987:171), a "core city of poverty surrounded by a ring of working-class and middle-class homes." The material evidence also confirms the start of that trend.

Evidence of Stratification

Death may recognize no social distinctions, but in Philadelphia the rites of passage did. The paupers found buried in Washington Square went into the ground *en masse,* wrapped in canvas shrouds without benefit of coffins; in times of epidemic, some of the city's nabobs went to meet their Maker in much the same fashion. Although the poor African-Americans of the First African Baptist Church were indeed buried in coffins, the coffins were simple pinch-toed boxes, sometimes heaped five to a grave. In contrast, at St. Paul's Church, we find the upper-class Episcopal denizens of Society Hill ensconced in elaborate "caskets," resting inside costly vaults.*

* In 1989 church historian Bruce Gill and National Park Service architect Penelope Batcheler also

Quakers, eschewing the pomp and circumstance that characterized the funeral rituals of Anglicans in the early 1700s, buried their dead with plain gravestones or with none at all, and sometimes, for economy's sake—as at the Arch Street Meeting House—they superimposed one grave on top of another.† The gravestones of other religious sects in Philadelphia during the late 1700s and early 1800s were not much more elaborate than those of the Quakers. Consisting usually of rather simple, thin, upright slabs of marble with gracefully curved tops, they lacked the motifs of death's head, cherub's head, and willow tree that characterized gravestones in New England from the seventeenth through the nineteenth centuries (Deetz 1967: 31). After about 1830, affluence and status seeking in Philadelphia joined forces to produce memorials and mausoleums of the highly ornate type still on view at Laurel Hill Cemetery.

We have considerable archaeological evidence of the lifestyles of Philadelphia's upper and middle classes from the late 1600s through the 1800s, but relatively little of the lifestyles of what Tocqueville called the "poorer classes." The evidence indicates that early Quakers lived as plainly as they were buried, but that as they acquired some wealth, they were not above indulging in a worldly display of their new social status, a precedent the Lord Proprietor himself set early on in the life of the colony when he built Pennsbury Manor. The rather mundane collection of ceramics found at Front and Dock streets attests that the

identified a series of intact brick vaults under the memorials of the church yard cemetery of Christ Church at Second Street near Market.
† This was a familiar practice in other crowded urban cemeteries. Huey (personal correspondence, 1991) mentions superimposition of burials in the old Dutch Reformed cemetery in Albany, New York, which lacked additional space.

earliest Quakers adhered to a simple lifestyle—possibly because of their middle-class values, but possibly also out of necessity, for in the 1680s trade with England was probably minimal. Further evidence of the way early Quakers lived was found in Independence Square, where excavations revealed the tiny foundations of narrow houses built by Welsh Quakers in the late 1600s. Caleb Pusey's rustic house on the banks of Chester Creek still stands in testimony to the quality of Quaker life in the frontier settlement of 1683. It is in marked contrast to another monument to Quaker life: Stenton, the manor house James Logan erected in 1728. Wyck, though not quite as grand as Stenton, also reflects changes in the Quaker way of life as they prospered in the course of the eighteenth and early nineteenth centuries.

A comparison of the architectural features of the Morton Homestead, possibly dating as early as 1654, and the Mortonson House, probably built about 1760, indicates the differences between the lifestyles of early Swedish settlers and those of their descendants little more than a century later. The Grange—transformed from a modest stone cottage to a magnificent country estate in the 1700s and "Victorianized" after 1850—is a manifestation of the wealth and tastes that defined Philadelphia's upper class during the eighteenth and nineteenth centuries. At the Bishop White House, authentically restored with the help of archaeological findings, we have a testimony to the lifestyle of a distinguished member of the non-Quaker segment of the Philadelphia Establishment from 1788 to 1836, a period that spans both the Federal era and the presidency of Andrew Jackson (1829–1837). Just down Walnut Street from the good bishop's house, at the McIlvaine House where William B.

Fling lived from 1826 until 1855, we have evidence of a thrifty and middle-class lifestyle; ceramics were modest, shoes were thrown away only when well worn, and little of value was lost in the privy.

A comparison of ceramics from the mansion and the tenant house at the Highlands suggests that even in the egalitarian days of the Jacksonian Age, Philadelphia society remained clearly stratified, but it also suggests that the "poorer classes," rather than rebelling against the system, strove to emulate the tastes of the upper class—and sometimes had the means to do so. Judging from the ceramics found at the mill village in Ridley Creek State Park, workers in rural mill villages were less well off during the Jacksonian Age than either tenant farmers at such places as the Highlands or workers in the city.

At a time when most colonists' idea of a proper garden was probably a plot planted with vegetables with a fence around it to keep out the neighbor's marauding pigs, William Penn was directing the creation of an elaborate formal garden at Pennsbury Manor. Gardens of this type would soon become the requisite status symbol of the gentleman farmer. Archaeological investigations at Stenton, Grumblethorpe, the Deshler-Morris House, Hope Lodge, the Highlands, and Waynesborough have produced evidence of vanished greenhouses, garden paths, terraces, and retaining walls.* The garden excavated at the Peter Wentz Farmstead was presumably not a formal garden but the utilitarian kind of kitchen garden planted by German farmers; postholes in the

earth suggested that a picket fence had surrounded the plot. Another exception to the notion of garden as status symbol was the garden John Bartram planted in 1728. Begun as a scientific enterprise, it soon became a commercial one and is today one of America's oldest surviving botanic gardens and first commercial nurseries.

Although taverns abounded in colonial Philadelphia, construction during the late nineteenth and early twentieth centuries obliterated many of these sites. Archaeologists have investigated only two of them. One—the City Tavern, built in 1773 and reputed to be the most genteel such establishment in town—failed to yield any material evidence of its early history. But if we are to judge by the evidence obtained from the other site—the Man Full of Trouble Tavern—taverns, like many other aspects of Philadelphia life, were stratified according to social class. It seems unlikely that Thomas Jefferson, for all his democratic fervor, would have been at ease in a humble establishment such as Man Full of Trouble, where glasses seem to have been at a minimum and drink poured out of the keg or bottle into leather cups, pewter mugs, or wooden vessels was the usual mode of service.

Diet, too, seems to have varied according to social class. Bones and shells dug up at Front and Dock streets indicate that from the very first days of the settlement, the upper and middle classes of Philadelphia were eating quite a healthy and varied diet. That artisans and other members of the city's middle class continued to eat well during the eighteenth century and on into the nineteenth is suggested by food traces found in privy pits at Franklin's rental houses on Market Street and at the McIlvaine House. Bones from privy pits at Independence Square support the im-

pression of a generally well-fed population with a marked fondness for beef. However, we also have evidence that some people ate better than the general population and that others ate far less well. Whoever dined on the meat from the bones found at New Market East was eating very well indeed in the late 1700s—better than the middle-class artisans and merchants who lived in Franklin's rental houses. On the other hand, osteological examination of the remains found at the burial ground of the First African Baptist Church showed that the diet of members of this congregation from about 1822 to 1845 was poor, to say the least; average life expectancy was 14.39 years, and dietary deficiencies were the cause of death of many of the children and infants buried there.

Philadelphia's caste system was evident even in prison. The ceramics found at the Walnut Street Prison attest to high living on the part of some of the inmates, most likely those in the debtors' part of the prison, and plain living on the part of others, most likely those who labored in the prison's workshops. That the artifacts do not reflect actual privation on the part of any of the inmates is no doubt a reflection of the Quakers' push for penal reform.

Evidence of an Open Society and Social Change

Even without taking into account any evidence dug from the earth, just a glance at the houses still standing in Society Hill—or merely a consideration of their former occupants—is enough to confirm the theory that Philadelphians from all walks of life rubbed elbows on a daily basis until well into the nineteenth century. The modest house at 310 Cypress Street, which was both home and shop for

---

* In the densely populated city, intact physical evidence of old gardens is—not surprisingly—exceedingly scarce. At Independence Square, archaeologists found only meager evidence of the landscaping done by Samuel Vaughan in 1784–85.

generations of artisans and tradesmen after 1785, is half a block away from the freestanding mansion at 321 South Fourth Street, whose occupants between 1786 and 1837 included two of Philadelphia's most prominent citizens: Col. Henry Hill and Dr. Philip Syng Physick. In the block where New Market East now stands are the elegant townhouse built in 1791 by John Ross, a wealthy merchant whose country estate at the time was the Grange, and the twin Harper Houses, former residences of artisans whose shops were in the interior of the block. In the 300 block of Walnut Street are the Bishop White House and the McIlvaine House, occupied between 1826 and 1836 by representatives of two distinct social classes.

Outside of Society Hill, archaeo-logical evidence from the block where the first U.S. Mint stood from 1792 until 1833 also suggests a daily intimacy between the privileged and the not-so-privileged classes, as well as the mix of domestic and commercial or industrial sites that characterized so many other blocks in preindustrial Philadelphia.

That Philadelphia neighborhoods changed with the advent of the industrial age is attested by evidence from several archaeological studies. The High Ward, once a mixed neighborhood of residences and shops, became an area of warehouses, as did the part of Society Hill around Front and Dock streets. Boardinghouses of diverse character were part of Society Hill in the eighteenth century, and they were still to be found there in the middle of the nineteenth. But by the second quarter of the twentieth century, the respectable little boardinghouse Mrs. Relf had run in the late 1700s at 301 Pine Street—now known as the Kosciuszko House—was being used as a bakery. By 1870 the Bishop White House had already entered its commercial phase.

Block 20 of the Vine Street study (at Tenth and Vine streets), occupied by a mix of professionals and skilled workers in the 1840s, was by the 1860s the home of unskilled immigrants who clustered in ethnic groups in small enclaves within the block. The study conducted in the area affected by the Commuter Rail Tunnel produced yet more evidence of the growing ethnicity of Philadelphia neighborhoods in the late nineteenth century.

SANITATION AND HEALTH CARE

Considering the state of sanitation in Philadelphia during the eighteenth and nineteenth centuries, the wonder is not that so many people died in epidemics but that so many survived. The archaeological record attests time and again to the ways in which Philadelphians, against the dictates not only of eighteenth-century city ordinances but also of common sense, polluted their environment. At the Bishop White House, we see a well, a cistern, and a cold cellar for food storage placed just a few feet from a privy sewer that flowed out into Dock Creek. At Independence Square, we find an abandoned well illegally being used as a privy pit, with the waste undoubtedly seeping into the groundwater. For more evidence of this method of contaminating potable water, we have only to turn to the cellar of 8 South Front Street, where for about forty years in the middle of the eighteenth century the inhabitants used an old well, sunk more than 26 feet into the earth, as a privy pit. And in the Ninth Ward of the 1800s, we find Philadelphians cavalierly ignoring the 1769 "privy depth ordinance"; all the privy pits excavated at this site exceeded the maximum 20-foot depth set by law.

The communal use of privies, of which we also have considerable archaeological evidence, no doubt played a role in the spread of bacterial infection. However, as evidence from Area F, the Ninth Ward, and various other sites attests, eighteenth- and nineteenth-century Philadelphians did periodically clean their privy pits and also sometimes placed broken ceramics in the shafts to aid in percolation. The waste removed in the cleaning was apparently hauled to the countryside and dumped.

The problem of where and how to dispose of mountains of miscellaneous trash may sometimes seem as if it originated in the late twentieth century, but the amount and kinds of trash—from the wreckage of structures to kitchen garbage and false teeth—that archaeologists have found in abandoned wells, privy pits, cisterns, and other features all over Philadelphia indicates otherwise. This exceedingly well-documented method of waste disposal probably did not help the sanitation problem. In any case, the smell of rotting garbage must surely have contributed to the malodorous air in early Philadelphia—although it was, of course, not the only source of the stench.

Among the prime offending sources was Dock Creek, which received not only offerings of the kind emanating from the Bishop White House but also offal from the tanneries situated along it. Dock Creek was not the only stream in the city used in this fashion, and the *Aedis aegypti* mosquitoes that spread yellow fever must have found them hospitable breeding places. Marshy areas with poor drainage, abundant in the Philadelphia area, were another excellent breeding ground for mosquitoes; with the drainage problems so evident at Fort Mifflin, it is a wonder the Continental soldiers who died there in battle in the autumn of 1777 did not die of yellow fever instead.

Medical care in Philadelphia was better than in most places, but it nonetheless involved some "cures" that were as uncomfortable and debilitating as the ailments they were supposed to cure. As a result, the city had its share of charlatans and quacks. While we have little material evidence of the practices of bona fide physicians in early Philadelphia,* we have ample evidence of the success of the charlatans and quacks. Bottles that once contained the patent medicines concocted and peddled by these enterprising individuals have appeared at sites all over the city; evidently, when it came to health care, both those who could afford doctors and those who could not resorted to patent medicines. No doubt part of the appeal of these nostrums was their alcoholic

* The report of archaeological investigations undertaken at the Pennsylvania Convention Center site (Blomberg [in preparation, a]), however, holds promise of shedding considerable light on this topic.

content, but their soaring sales during the nineteenth century can also be attributed to vigorous marketing and advertising.

At the forefront of the shady world of quack medicine in nineteenth-century Philadelphia were William Swaim, Thomas Dyott, and David Jayne. Swaim appeared on the Philadelphia scene in 1820, when he introduced his "Panacea," a concoction of sarsparilla and oil of wintergreen laced with a substantial amount of alcohol and an even more sinister ingredient: a form of mercury called corrosive sublimate. The alcohol no doubt explains the popularity of Swaim's Panacea, but the corrosive sublimate is strange, to say the least, in a product that claimed to cure mercury poisoning in addition to numerous other ills. Swaim marketed his Panacea in impressive octagonal bottles of green glass with raised lettering. Another of his products—this one claiming to dispel parasitic worms—was sold in an oval bottle labeled "Swaim's/Vermifuge/Dysentry/Choleramorbus/Dyspepsia" (Parrington and Schenck 1979:78–79).

Despite the opposition of Philadelphia's medical establishment to Swaim's products, and despite the price of his products—three dollars a bottle for the Panacea—they were evidently popular; fragments of bottles that contained Swaim's products appeared at Area F (Parrington 1980c: 35–42) and the Ninth Ward (Roberts and Cosans 1980:149–50). Thanks to the aggressive sort of advertising shown in Figure 11.1, to the gullibility of the American public, and to the not unpleasant (if not exactly salutary) effects of his products, William Swaim had by 1850 amassed a fortune estimated at half a million dollars (Young 1974:56–85).

Dr. Thomas Dyott arrived in Phila-

delphia from England in the 1790s. Starting out as a manufacturer of patent medicines, he eventually acquired a glass factory near Kensington. Known as the Dyottville Glass Works, the factory employed about 200 "apprentices," or children, and 100 adults. With a chapel on the premises, three Sunday services, prayer meetings held on weeknights, a temperance society, and a policy of "extra rewards and compensation to such as

Figure 11.1.

Early twentieth-century patent medicine bottle label. (Courtesy of W. W. Norton & Company and Schlesinger Library, Radcliffe College)

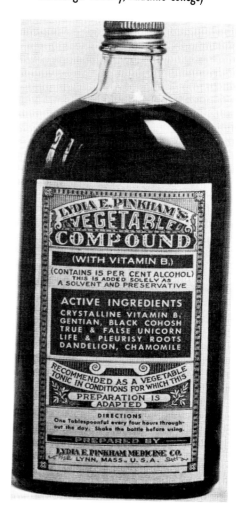

were faithful and did over-work" (Scharf and Westcott 1884:2299), the Dyottville Glass Works was apparently a curious establishment. Its products included some very superior flasks, three of which came to light during excavations in the Ninth Ward (Young 1974:31–37; Roberts and Cosans 1980:151–52). The factory closed down in 1859 when its proprietor was found guilty of fraudulent insolvency and jailed. It reopened under new management three years later.

Dr. David Jayne's name first appears in the Philadelphia City Directories in the 1830s. By 1849 he had become wealthy enough to erect the city's first "skyscraper." The eight-story building, which stood on Chestnut Street near Third until 1957, had a Venetian Gothic facade made of granite, a roof adorned with an observation tower and sculptured mortars and pestles, and the name of its proprietor emblazoned beneath the roof line. The original architect, William L. Johnston, died while the building was still under construction, and Jayne promptly hired Thomas U. Walter, one of the most prominent architects of the day, to replace him (Geffen 1982:312). Jayne's fortune was owing to the popularity of his "Expectorant," a product that was still being made in the early 1900s. The collection of thirty-five medicine bottles found at Bartram's Garden included no fewer than seven of Dr. Jayne's Expectorant bottles (Parrington 1981a:36). The same kind of bottles have turned up as far afield as the sites of nineteenth-century mining camps in the far west (Toulouse 1970:63–64).

In comparison with the claims of some of his competitors, Dr. Jayne's claim that his Expectorant would cure respiratory diseases seems rather mod-

est. A preparation called Ozomulsion was advertised as a remedy for "Consumption, Coughs, Colds, Whooping Cough, Bronchial Affections, Asthma, La Grippe, Pneumonia, and all Pulmonary Diseases, also for Scrofula, All Blood Disorders, Chronic Catarrh, Nervous and General Debility, Sleeplesness [sic], Night Sweats, Fevers, Rickets or Softening of Bones in Children, Anaemia or Thin Blood, Loss of Flesh, and All Conditions of Wasting" (Cramp 1921:99). Ozomulsion was obviously very handy stuff to have around, but for those suffering from rheumatism, gout, and lumbago, Hankin's Specific claimed to be the answer. For those afflicted with dyspepsia, nerve, heart, or stomach disorders or merely in need of a laxative, there was Munyon's Paw-Paw (Derner 1968:17, 66). Bromo-Seltzer was advertised as a treatment for mental exhaustion, brain fatigue, and headache, and until government regulations in the 1920s made the company modify its claims, Lydia E. Pinkham's Vegetable Compound was promoted as a cure for "female complaints" and for kidney ailments in either sex (Stage 1979:92, 198). The collection of medicine bottles from Bartram's Garden included examples of all these products.

With the exception of alcohol, the ingredients in most nineteenth-century patent medicines were fairly innocuous. But the alcohol content was often quite high. When analysed in 1913, Lydia E. Pinkham's Vegetable Compound contained 19.3 percent alcohol; Dr. Kilmer's Swamp-Root Kidney, Liver and Bladder Cure contained about 9 percent (Stage 1979:183; Cramp 1921:207). The demand for the latter product became so great that the company built a five-story factory with an automated bottling line capable of turning out two thou-

sand bottles an hour (Wilson and Wilson 1971:124).

Curiously, although archaeologists in Philadelphia have paid considerable attention to many aspects of sanitation and health care, they have paid little attention to just how people kept themelves clean enough to be socially acceptable. No doubt some of the crocks, vats, and kettles found on Philadelphia sites were used to hold liquid home-made soap, hot water for laundry, and soiled cloth diapers or other items awaiting laundering, but since these vessels could have been used for a variety of other purposes, none can be definitely identified with sanitation. The purpose of a toothbrush is hard to mistake, and many made of bone or wood with a grid of holes for holding pig bristles have appeared at early domestic sites in Philadelphia. Toothbrushes have been part of the kit of the genteel since the seventeenth century; for the poor and Amerindians, a frayed twig probably sufficed. Toothpicks were another fairly common aid to dental hygiene. Some were made of ivory or precious metals; others, of wood splinters. The curry comb, a finetoothed comb used not for dressing the hair but for combing parasites out of it, was yet another well-known item of personal hygiene. Strangely, although wash basins have been found in great numbers in Philadelphia, no wooden or tin bathing tubs have apparently ever come to light, though they were no doubt often kept in bedrooms and next to kitchen hearths or stoves. Also strange is the fact that archaeologists heretofore have not noted a usage familiar to a few living memories; namely, that covered ceramic crocks and metal pails were clandestinely used to soak sanitary cloths, a practice to be kept from the notice of men and children.

COMMERCE AND INDUSTRY

Commerce and industry in the Philadelphia region are older than the city itself. The fur trade with the Lenape and other Amerindian groups had its origins in the sixteenth century, and shipbuilding and water-powered mills were part of the regional economy even before William Penn arrived However, we have little or no physical evidence of these early commercial and industrial enterprises and relatively little of the vast number that followed. Archaeology in Philadelphia began with a focus on domiciles and public buildings of the Colonial and Federal eras, and as a result, the sites responsible for generating the city's wealth were largely neglected. Many such sites were lost during the construction of Interstate-95; others have simply disappeared in the continuous building and rebuilding that has characterized Philadelphia over the centuries. Nonetheless, given the number of commercial and industrial sites that once existed, they are probably still the largest thematic topic remaining for the archaeologist in Philadelphia to explore—and, given their role in the development of the Philadelphia region, they are also likely to be one of the most informative. Even the meager amount of evidence from the small fraction of commercial and industrial sites that archaeologists have investigated paints a picture, if a skeletal one, of Philadelphia's growth into an industrial giant in the course of the eighteenth and nineteenth centuries.

Evidence of the techniques of wharf construction and landfill that Philadelphians used as they began moving the shoreline of the Delaware farther east in the mid-1700s came to light near the site of West's shipyard on Delaware Avenue north of Vine Street. Excavations in this vicinity also produced some information on historic techniques of ship repair. To the south, test units dug in areas proposed for access ramps to Interstate-95 revealed remnants of other colonial wharves that had been buried beneath fill in the early 1800s. These test units also revealed traces of the first Philadelphia Navy Yard, built by the federal government south of Wharton Street soon after the turn of the nineteenth century. Continuing investigation there promises to shed even more light on these early remnants of Philadelphia's commercial heritage.

Two other early government enterprises of which we have some physical evidence are the first U.S. Mint on North Seventh Street and the Frankford Arsenal. Evidence from the block in which the mint had been located attests not only to the metallurgical experimentation that went on there from 1792 until 1833 but also to the kinds of ceramics in which merchants in the block dealt in the first half of the nineteenth century. While excavations at the Frankford Arsenal did not produce information of an industrial nature, they did shed light on the quality of domestic life at a military-industrial complex of the nineteenth century. Some scant evidence of another, even earlier military-industrial enterprise—a cannon foundry of the Revolutionary War—turned up at the site of the Bonnin and Morris Porcelain Factory in Southwark.

The introduction of gas lighting in Philadelphia in 1836 signaled a revolution in the domestic and commercial life of the city, and the above-ground study of the Point Breeze Gas Works assembled the historic evidence of how this industry evolved. Although the study involved no excavation, it nonetheless resulted in the recovery of some valuable artifacts: a series of photographs documenting production at Point Breeze from 1897 to 1930.

We also have a little evidence of the evolution of the local ceramics industry. The late seventeenth-century ceramics found at Front and Dock streets, consisting chiefly of locally made pottery and a few imported pieces, suggest that in the first years of Penn's colony, at least one settler was taking advantage of the minimal amount of trade with England by making and selling redware. The trivets, kiln bricks, and vast number of wasters found at Franklin Court presumably attest to the industry of the rapscallion John Rogers, who, as Deborah Franklin's first husband, seems to have operated a kiln on the premises in the 1720s. Although Anthony Duché was making stoneware not far from Franklin Court during the same period and pieces of his products have turned up at sites all over Philadelphia, no sign of his kiln has ever appeared. In fact, the only kiln site other than Rogers' t[…] have been archaeologically investigated in Philadelphia is the Bonnin and Morris Porcelain Factory. Ther[…] a small deposit of damaged sagger[…] pots and bisque attested to Gouss[…] Bonnin's efforts in the early 1770[…] make porcelain as fine as any im[…] ported from the Old World.

The study of the area affecte[…] Commuter Rail Tunnel produc[…] evidence of the work of a nin[…] century potter: one John Hal[…] in 1841 had a kiln on Ridge[…]

Excavations in this area also indicated that the tradition of artisans working out of small shops in their own homes, begun when the city was first founded, was still thriving in the first half of the nineteenth century. Among the artisans who were plying their crafts in this area were a number of shoemakers and at least one carpenter. The privy pit at 310 Cypress Street in Society Hill yielded more evidence of this continuing tradition. Here, between 1840 and 1850, two Irish immigrants—one a shoemaker, the other a printer—left unmistakable signs of their trades.

Even some of the country estates of the eighteenth and nineteenth centuries had industrial or commercial components. This rather strange juxtaposition of genteel country life and business enterprise was probably not unrelated to the profit motive that characterized Penn's colony from its inception. At Wyck, elegantly refurbished by Reuben Haines, Jr., just in time for Lafayette's visit in the mid-20s, we have evidence of a brewery operated on the grounds from until 1840, when a loss of business ought about by "troubled times e a few temperance societies"

(Cotter and Hall 1979:197) resulted in its closing. Graeme Park, which dates to 1720, was another scene of early industry. It was, in fact, originally built as a whiskey distillery, although a water course that may have served the distillery is the only physical evidence we have of this usage.

Mills were, of course, a cornerstone of Philadelphia's industrial heritage, but we have scant physical evidence of them. Although in the 1680s Caleb Pusey was making his livelihood as the manager of a milling enterprise in which William Penn himself owned shares, excavations focused not on the mills, which were located along Chester Creek, but on Pusey's nearby humble house. There, the only evidence related to Pusey's milling enterprise was a section of a millstone used in repairing the cellar. Similarly, excavations at the mill village in Ridley Creek State Park focused on domestic life rather than on the industries that thrived there in the late eighteenth and early nineteenth centuries. On the banks of Wissahickon Creek across the road from Hope Lodge in Montgomery County, some limited testing produced possible evi-

dence of the gristmill Mary Farmer built there in the late 1600s. Farther down Wissahickon Creek, in Fairmount Park, excavations at the site of the eighteenth-century Gorgas Mill Complex produced evidence of the headrace, tailrace, and wheel housing of a long-vanished mill, as well as some evidence of an old forge. Forges, too, were a vital part of the colonial economy, and archaeological studies in Chester County of the ones that gave Valley Forge its name have added significantly to our knowledge of eighteenth-century iron technology.

Rounding out the inventory of commercial and industrial sites that have received archaeological attention are the tannery that John Merrick and his heirs operated at Fallsington from the 1780s until the 1860s and the Walnut Street Prison. Although a prison may seem like an improbable commercial setting, evidence from the one that once stood on Walnut Street attested to the nail-making, button-making, stone-sawing, and tailoring in which the inmates engaged as they experienced the Quakers' enlightened version of rehabilitation in the late eighteenth and early nineteenth centuries.

BEHAVIOR

akers of the first es enacted re- w of socially equently, avior was , the early every- d sod- Road. ing,"

drunkenness, incest, polygamy, and "rude sports, plays, and games" (George, Nead, and McCamant 1879: 133, 135, 190). Given the sweep of these laws, violations were no doubt common, but, as Burnston (1982) has pointed out, when behavior that violates the social norms is successfully concealed, it becomes "historically in-

visible." It comes to light only when the archaeologist hits upon evidence of its having occurred.

Archaeological evidence of deviant behavior has to date been relatively rare in Philadelphia, but that is not to say such behavior was a rare occurrence. The privy, of course, would have been a likely spot to hide the *corpora*

View ctives

delecti of all kinds of misdeeds, ranging from the accidental breakage of household goods to far more serious matters. How many of the broken ceramics archaeologists have fished out of these pits were deliberately put there by guilt-ridden children or servants trying to escape the consequences of their misadventures we shall never know. But it would appear that mischief, rather than misadventure or guilt, accounts for the presence in the privy pit at the John Quincy Adams Public School of a child's school box and several toys and trinkets—all in rather good condition.

Among the clearest pieces of evidence of deviant behavior in colonial Philadelphia are the remains of a seven-month fetus and a full-term infant found in the Quaker Meeting House privy pit at New Market East. As noted in Chapter 4, stillborn infants or infants who died shortly after birth were customarily buried in churchyards. The reason these little bodies were concealed in the pit at the Quaker Meeting House seems to be that they were murdered or conceived out of wedlock, or both. The penalty for infanticide was hanging, and the consequence of bearing an illegitimate child was social ostracism.

We also have three pieces of pornographic material from early Philadelphia, items that were no doubt not acceptable in polite society. Two of them—pipe tampers showing a nude male and female in connubial embrace—were identical except that one was made of brass and the other of pewter. That one dated from the eighteenth century and the other appeared in a nineteenth-century deposit indicates that this particular pornographic item was quite a popular piece over quite a long time. The brass tamper was dug out of a privy pit at New Hall in Carpenters' Court, scene of the First Continental Congress; the pewter one came from 310 Cypress Street, home of Irish immigrant artisans after 1840. The third pornographic item— a wooden phallus—appeared in a privy pit near the East Wing of Independence Hall. Just exactly how or why these items wound up in privy pits is anyone's guess.

Evidence of another kind of forbidden activity came not from a privy pit but from the demolition rubble at the site of the Walnut Street Prison. Excavations there produced, among many other things, five bone dice. The inmate who made these dice had clearly been intent on violating the prison's ban on gambling. Only one of the dice had "spots" drilled into it; the rest were unfinished, suggesting perhaps that to avoid detection, the inmate had hastily disposed of the evidence.

Witchcraft was taken very seriously in early eighteenth-century Philadelphia, and the all-encompassing laws of the province naturally included a prohibition of it. Not too surprisingly, we have no evidence demonstrating how witches plied their craft, but we do have evidence of a related practice. The olive-green bottle dating from about 1740 that appeared upside down in a pit at the Printzhof was a so-called witch bottle, intended to counteract the power of a witch. The brass pins inside the bottle were thought to be effective in warding off evil. The pit containing the bottle, which also contained a bird bone and a redware sherd, was located near the base of a chimney, suggesting that whoever buried the bottle there was trying to keep the evil spirit from coming down the chimney.

Excavation in Independence Square produced another bit of evidence not forthcoming from the historical record. In this instance, it was the provincial government itself that was responsible for the deviation from strictly proper behavior. When the government decided to build a wall around its land at Independence Square in 1739, the property line was very irregular, with a dip to the north occurring more or less in the middle of the plot. Since it would have been impractical to build a wall that followed such an irregular line, historians had assumed the wall was built in a straight line across the northernmost part of the property line. However, excavation of the wall showed that it ran in a straight line across the southernmost property boundary, thus enclosing almost 15,500 square feet of privately owned land. In the twentieth century this action would no doubt have been viewed with consternation as governmental encroachment on the private domain.

SPORTING PHILADELPHIA

Material evidence of some human activities is so evanescent that a few mementos are the best the archaeologist can hope to encounter. Sporting events, at least in early Philadelphia, are one such activity. The Greeks and Romans may have built their stadiums and athletic equipment to last; colonial Philadelphians did not. Nonetheless, from the days when wealthy roués flaunted Quaker mores by betting on the horses and jockeys that raced up and down Sassafras Street—eponymously renamed Race Street—to the present, sports have been an important part of Philadelphia culture. Thus, although evidence of early sporting sites and artifacts in Philadelphia is lacking, this topic deserves at least a passing nod. Fortunately, of athletics after about 1850 we have considerable memorabilia, not least of which is the photographic record.*

Evidence—or Lack of It—of Early Sporting Philadelphia

Although horse racing was probably the most popular spectator sport in colonial Philadelphia, we have no physical evidence of it. No vestige of the track on Race Street or of another early, makeshift track—this one around Center Square—remains. Center Square ceased to function as a racetrack around 1800, when the little Greek temple Benjamin Latrobe designed as the pumphouse for the city's first waterworks was installed there. Bull baiting, bear baiting, and cock fighting, also popular spectator sports, have left equally slim pickings for the archaeologist.

*This section is based on Cotter (1985).

One other early spectator sport may hold out a hair more hope for archaeology. Equestrian performances were viewed inside circular buildings known as hippodromes, and the best hippodrome in Philadelphia is still standing. Not too long after opening in this capacity in 1809, the Walnut Street Theater—the oldest continuously operated theater in the English-speaking world—was adapted to its present usage. Although the auditorium has been rebuilt three times, the old hippodrome's classical facade remains intact.

A few ancient skates may remain to attest to the popularity of ice skating in early Philadelphia, but we have nothing except written documents to attest to the popularity of swimming. Here, as in so many other things, Benjamin Franklin was expert. Not only did the fourteen-year-old Franklin invent a pair of hand-held wooden palettes to give him more purchase on the water as he swam; as an elderly diplomat, he amazed Parisians by casting off his clothes and swimming briskly in the Seine. However, we have not a shred of physical evidence to attest to Franklin's physical prowess in the water.

We obviously also have no physical evidence of the earliest versions of baseball. Baseball rules were not codified until the 1840s, but the game began evolving in the late 1700s from cricket and another English import known as rounders. The boys of Philadelphia played rounders on sandlots using a bat and a leather-covered ball of twine wound around a cork core, but in contrast to later baseball players, they ran the bases clockwise.

Archery was popular among the aristocracy in England at least as

early as the days of Edward III (1312–1377), and tennis came into vogue in the 1500s. Henry VIII (1491–1547) is known to have complained of the expense of keeping Ann Boleyn in archery equipment, but he evidently did not balk when it came to building a tennis court for himself at Hampton Court Palace in 1529. In colonial Philadelphia, however, archery and tennis were all but unknown. By the early 1700s even the fast-vanishing Lenape had forsaken the bow and arrow for the gun. Had the busy colonists had more time for avocational pursuits or had there been an established, leisured aristocracy, we might have some hope of occasionally recovering a well-preserved wooden bow or tennis racket.

As it is, the archaeological record of sports and sporting equipment remains all but blank until the last half of the nineteenth century, and for knowledge of this facet of early Philadelphia culture we must turn to historical documentation and period paintings. Delft tiles of the seventeenth and eighteenth centuries depicting children at play, such as those shown in Figure 11.2, are another excellent archaeological reference.

Evidence of Sporting Philadelphia after 1850

Football is an old game that did not reach Philadelphia until the late nineteenth century. Its rowdy beginnings can be traced to the fourteenth century, when Edward III briefly prohibited it because it impeded the progress of archery. Two centuries later, it was evidently still thought of as the rough-

Figure 11.2.

Blue-and-white delft tiles of 1675–1750 showing children at play. The games and sports of children in the American colonies were much the same as those played by their European peers. (Photo by Eric Mitchell; courtesy of the Philadelphia Museum of Art, gift of Anthony N. B. Garvan)

Figure 11.3.

The University of Pennsylvania football team of 1878. The football, held by the coach in top hat and cutaway, is rounder than it is today, but more pointed than the sphere with which the game was first played. The players wore no helmets or padding. (Courtesy of the Archives of the University of Pennsylvania)

Figure 11.4.

Boat houses on the east bank of the Schuylkill, 1878. The University of Pennsylvania's house is in the foreground. (Courtesy of the Archives of the University of Pennsylvania)

and-tumble game of unruly gangs; in *King Lear* (act 1, scene 4), Shakespeare has the Earl of Kent give Oswald his due with the epithet, "you base football player." By 1876, however, football was vying with rugby for favor at the University of Pennsylvania. Football lost, only to win first place in campus popularity before the turn of the twentieth century.*

* Football at Penn, together with all other sports played there over the years, owes much to the ever-visionary Benjamin Franklin, whose *Proposals Relating to the Education of Youth in Pennsylvania*, written in 1749, included the admonition that to keep students "in Health, and to strengthen and render active their Bodies," they should engage in "Running, Leaping, Wrestling, and Swimming, etc" (Van Doren 1956:189–91).

The football with which the game was first played was a sphere, but by 1878 it had already begun developing a more oval shape (Figure 11.3). By the turn of the twentieth century, it had acquired the pointed ends that characterize it today. The pointed ends made it more truly a game of chance, for with the rounded shape, it was easier to predict how the ball would bounce. Although a few tired, sagging old leather bags linger on the trophy cases at Penn's Palestra to remind us of how football was first played, the original playing fields at Penn have vanished, supplanted in the late 1890s by Franklin Field, the most enduring of the University's athletic arenas.

The earliest surviving playing fields in the Philadelphia area are at the Germantown Cricket Club, established in 1854 to replace a short-lived club of the same name that had disbanded a few years earlier (Geffen 1982:331). The Germantown Cricket Club's tennis courts are as ready for play today as they were when Bill Tilden used them in the 1920s. But the turnvereins—athletic clubs dedicated to the fitness of Philadelphia Germans in the last half of the nineteenth century—have vanished, as has Connie Mack Stadium in North Philadelphia, where the Philadelphia Phillies made some baseball history in the first half of the twentieth century.

Rowing on the Schuylkill, first organized in 1854 by the Barge Club of the University of Pennsylvania, has been memorialized not only in the paintings of Thomas Eakins but also in the Victorian boathouses that still line the east bank of the river. The boathouses are the oldest architecture of this type in the nation (Figure 11.4). Cycling, introduced to America about the time of the Philadelphia Centennial Exposition of 1876, has also been an enduring sport, and some of the high wheelers that preceded today's sleek models are still around to attest to the sport's beginnings.

Basketball, one sport to have originated in the United States, came into being in December 1891 on the gym floor of the International YMCA Training School (later Springfield College) in Springfield, Massachusetts. It was the brainchild of James Naismith, a Canadian teacher, who, to improve the coordination and skills of his jaded gym students, put a half-bushel peach basket on a wall and gave them a ball to lob into it. The game caught on quickly. The original eighteen players were whittled down to five to a team, and an iron hoop with a closed net replaced the basket. Soon tiring of poking the ball out of the net with a pole, the players cut the net open at the bottom. The rules of the game were published in January 1892. Within two years basketball had become an international sport, and by 1896 it was a permanent part of the athletic program at the University of Pennsylvania. Figure 11.5 attests to its popularity among the youngsters of the area in 1909.

Photography has come a long way since the photograph shown in Figure 11.5 was taken. Today's video equipment—and audio equipment—can capture vignettes of human behavior with an accuracy unlikely to be matched by artifacts dug from the earth. Depending on their durability, which depends on the archival care they receive, such records may be among the most valuable artifacts ever handed down from one generation to another.

Figure 11.5.

The "Runts" of the Germantown Boys Club in 1909. These basketball aficionados posed in the best manner of the sports heroes of the day. (Lantern slide by Marriot C. Morris, copied by Brian Peterson; courtesy of the Germantown Historical Society)

12

A Prospective View:
Directions for Future Research

ARCHAEOLOGICAL RESOURCES OF THE
DELAWARE RIVER: SUBMERGED SITES AND
SHIPWRECKS

TRANSPORTATION NETWORKS

INDUSTRIAL SITES

A CONCLUDING NOTE ON THE FUTURE
OF PHILADELPHIA'S ARCHAEOLOGY

*The history of archaeology in the City of London recalls the story of the Siby-
line Books. Knowledge is offered to each generation at a price—and is destroyed
when the price is not paid. The price rises for each generation . . . and the
remaining store of information diminishes. None has yet been prepared to
pay in full. . . . If ever a generation arises that is prepared to pay the full
price of a total scientific excavation over whatever area is then available,
complete pages of the book will be won. By that time very few pages indeed
will remain.*

—Ralph Merrifield, 1965, quoted in Biddle, Hudson, and Heighway
(1973)

A good many pages of Philadelphia's
archaeological record have been won.
A good many have been lost; before
the implementation of the National
Historic Preservation Act of 1966
and the National Environmental Protection Act of 1969, the wholesale
disturbance or destruction of archaeological sites was not uncommon. But
despite such losses and the constant
building and rebuilding Philadelphia
has experienced over the years, a considerable amount of the material evidence of the city's past no doubt still
lies hidden and buried, awaiting sal-
vation or destruction.

Anyone inclined to dismiss the archaeological potential of a historic site
because of the construction that has
taken place on it should heed the lesson afforded in the summer of 1988,
when no fewer than seventeen artifact-
laden pits appeared on a tract of land
previously judged so disturbed as to
be not worth a preliminary archaeological survey. The tract, at the northwest corner of Fourth and Chestnut
streets, had during the nineteenth and
twentieth centuries accommodated
massive buildings with deep basements.* Because of the likelihood that
the deep basements had destroyed all
archaeological resources, the construction of the new Omni Hotel and
parking garage began without the
usual documentary research. As it
turned out, six of the seventeen pits uncovered as bulldozers started digging
below the old foundations contained
an extraordinarily rich collection of
eighteenth-century artifacts. The collection included some of the most interesting eighteenth-century ceramics
ever found on a Philadelphia site,
among them pieces of stoneware and
heretofore unrecognized examples of
black manganese decorated earthen-

---

* Among these buildings was the Provident Life
and Trust Company, designed by Frank Furness
and James Windrim.

ware from the pottery kiln Anthony Duché operated near Fifth and Chestnut streets from the 1720s to 1762.* In the opinion of David Orr, Regional Archaeologist for the National Park Service, these colonial trash pits were the most data-packed ones yet uncovered in Philadelphia.

The identification of these pits and subsequent recovery of the artifacts came about by chance. Had some interested members of the staff at Independence National Historical Park not been keeping an unofficial eye on the local scene and alerted officials when they spotted the pits, the artifacts would have been obliterated. As it was, their prompt action resulted in equally prompt archaeological excavations. How much evidence has been lost under similar but less fortunate circumstances is open to speculation (Palmer 1979).

If what remains of Philadelphia's archaeological resources is not also to be lost to the wrecking ball of prog-

* Information supplied by John Milner Associates from report in progress (Blomberg [in preparation, b]).

ress, identification of what and where the untapped resources are is essential. Between 1979 and 1984, prompted by environmental concerns and the necessity of complying with federal legislation, five regional planning studies (Gilbert/Commonwealth Associates 1979; Cee Jay Frederick Associates and John Milner Associates 1981; LeeDecker 1983; McHugh 1983; Cox 1984) addressed this issue. One of these studies (LeeDecker 1983) explored the great potential for prehistoric and historic sites in Fairmount Park, which with its protected status has been largely undisturbed since the 1890s. The others focused on known and potential archaeological sites in and along the Delaware River and Bay.

While all these regional planning studies were pioneering efforts and contributed to the identification of Philadelphia's archaeological resources, the ones by McHugh and Cox are of particular interest because of the light they shed on the city's maritime past and on man-made changes to the shoreline and bed of

the Delaware River, changes that also affected the condition of archaeological resources. The Delaware was, of course, an extremely important— indeed, a determining—factor in the region's development, but before McHugh's and Cox's studies, submerged sites and shipwrecks and the processes that changed the river's configuration had received little or no archaeological attention. Other historically significant factors have been similarly neglected (Garvan 1963). Transportation networks, for instance, so vital in the city's development, have to date been the focus of scarcely any archaeological research, nor have the industries, schools, churches, and theaters of eighteenth- and nineteenth-century Philadelphia received their quota of attention. Unless such resources are singled out for study and potential sites inventoried, the archaeological record will be forever missing some important pages. This chapter discusses just a couple of these relatively uncharted areas, with the hope that future researchers will be inspired to explore them.

ARCHAEOLOGICAL RESOURCES OF THE DELAWARE RIVER: SUBMERGED SITES AND SHIPWRECKS

In the wake of the National Historic Preservation Act and the National Environmental Policy Act in the late 1960s, many government agencies conscientiously embraced the legislative mandate that they assess the effects of their programs on the natural and cultural environments. One agency to do so was the Philadelphia District, Corps of Engineers, which since 1885 has been responsible for

overseeing all dredging and construction in the Delaware River and Bay. In 1983, as the Corps was preparing to dredge sediment from some of the Delaware's navigational channels and anchorages,* it commissioned GAI Consultants to identify cultural resources in these waters and

* Anchorages are areas away from the main navigational channel where large ships can await clearance to dock their cargos.

also in the land areas where the Corps was proposing to dump the dredged material (McHugh 1983). Although McHugh did not identify any archaeological sites in the Pennsylvania part of the study area, he did identify the processes, including dredging and the disposal of waste material, that have modified both the shoreline and the bed of the Delaware River. These processes obviously have im-

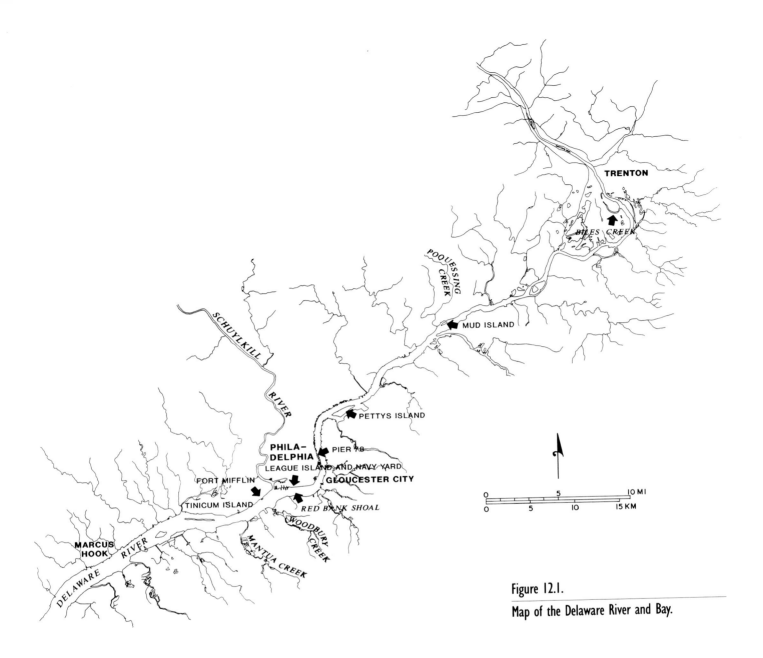

Figure 12.1.

Map of the Delaware River and Bay.

portant implications for the survival of archaeological resources.

A year after McHugh's study, the Pennsylvania Historical and Museum Commission sponsored another study that involved an evaluation of the cultural resources of the Delaware. Carried out by J. Lee Cox, Jr. (1984), under the auspices of the Philadelphia Maritime Museum, the study not only identified submerged archaeological sites but also formulated a model for predicting the possible locations of such sites. In addition, like McHugh's study, it reviewed the history of man-made changes in and along the Delaware.

Changes in the Delaware

As the Dutch and Swedes who plied the Delaware River in the early seventeenth century discovered, travel on that river could be treacherous. With the ebb and flow of the tides constantly changing the contours of the river bottom and creating hazardous shoals, much depended on the skill of the individual pilot (McHugh 1983: 27–28). The harried pilots had little other than their own skill to rely on, for early aids to navigation on the Delaware were rudimentary, consisting chiefly of buoys marking the position

of shoals and other navigational impediments. During the Revolutionary War, these impediments included the formidable *chevaux-de-frise* that the defenders of Philadelphia had strung across the river (Cox 1984:67–68).

Although some dredging of the Delaware took place in the early 1800s, it was done on a relatively small scale until the 1870s. By that time, ships had become larger and the navigational problem was even more acute, but technology had also progressed to the point that some large-scale answers to the problem were possible. Schooner's Ledge, a particularly troublesome rock reef eighteen miles below Philadelphia, was blasted out of existence, and Mifflin Bar and Pettys Island (Figure 12.1), both opposite Philadelphia, underwent extensive dredging (Cee Jay Frederick Associates and John Milner Associates 1981; Heite 1982). Projects of this size ultimately created a disposal problem. Much of the dredged material was initially dumped near Fort Mifflin and League Island, but by the 1890s these areas had filled up and the spoil was being dumped on the river bottom itself, away from established shipping channels and anchorages (McHugh 1983:28).

In 1887, two years after the Corps of Engineers assumed primary responsibility for dredging and construction in the Delaware, a conference on harbor improvements was held in Phila-

delphia. Foremost on the agenda was the inability of the port of Philadelphia to accommodate large, sea-going cargo vessels. To resolve the problem, a plan was formulated to extend the wharf line farther out into the river, but it was clear that to implement this plan, two large islands opposite the city—Smith's Island and Windmill Island (Figure 12.2)—would have to be removed. Public outcry against the removal of the islands was such that the issue dragged on unresolved for several years. Finally, in 1893, a new plan evolved; it called not only for the removal of Smith's and Windmill islands but also for additional dredging in the channel at Pettys Island. In implementing the plan, the Corps of Engineers dredged 21,500,000 cubic yards of material (McHugh 1983:31, 132).

By 1900 the Corps of Engineers

was engaged in excavating a channel 30 feet wide from Philadelphia to the sea at Bombay Hook, Delaware. This project, together with other harbor and channel improvements, necessitated the creation of six new disposal areas in various parts of the riverfront. At about the same time, fifteen new land areas created with material dredged from the river appeared at League Island, where new piers and retaining walls were being built at the Philadelphia Navy Yard (McHugh 1983:29, 134).

During the past century—indeed, ever since the Corps of Engineers took

Figure 12.2.

View of Smith's and Windmill islands in 1890. Baths and beer gardens made Smith's Island a popular summer resort for working men and their families during the nineteenth century. (From Cox 1984)

over harbor improvements in 1885—modifications to the Delaware River have been unceasing, with the result that the appearance of the river has been altered substantially. McHugh (1983:26) has summarized the processes involved in these changes:

- Infilling or diking of low-lying areas
- Stabilization of the river banks
- Excavation and subsequent widening and deepening of navigational channels and anchorages
- Partial or complete removal of islands
- Construction of submerged piers to control currents, of bridges with piers embedded in the river, and of wharves, slips, basins, and other harbor facilities
- Disposal of dredged spoil and of urban and industrial wastes, resulting in creation of man-made land

Both McHugh (1983:42–43) and Cox (1984:70 ff.) concluded that significant archaeological resources are unlikely to be found in submerged sites subjected to long-term dredging, such as navigational channels and anchorages, and in submerged sites where natural features like shoals and rock reefs have been removed. They also concluded that such resources are unlikely to be found in land areas along the shoreline where dredged material has been dumped or construction has taken place; however, it is likely that the dumping of spoil and formation of man-made land could just as well help to preserve a site as to destroy it.

Submerged Sites and Shipwrecks

Cox's identification of submerged sites and shipwrecks in the Delaware depended almost entirely on documentary research. He did, however, also conduct a brief reconnaissance of the river. The only shipwreck he found was a small, nineteenth-century sailing vessel submerged and lying in two pieces near the mouth of Woodbury Creek in New Jersey, nearly opposite Fort Mifflin. The vessel apparently had been a two-masted wooden schooner, about 30 to 50 feet long (Cox 1984:161). Among the artifacts Cox recovered from the wreck were a cast-iron tea kettle, a pair of coal tongs, an iron anchor, and an iron spike. The artifacts are now housed at the Philadelphia Maritime Museum. The Mantua Anchorage Wreck, as the site was christened, was the first entry in the Pennsylvania Historical and Museum Commission's recording system for underwater archaeological sites.

Of the more than 140 ships documented as having been wrecked or run aground in the Delaware, the precise locations of only a small fraction are known (Cox 1984:170–76). One of the most interesting of these vessels is the British frigate *Augusta*. Hit by a barrage from the Pennsylvania Navy during the battle of Fort Mifflin in October 1777, the *Augusta* ran aground on the Red Bank Shoal just downstream from Fort Mercer. After she caught fire and exploded, the British abandoned her, leaving the Americans free to salvage whatever they chose. Thereafter, the vessel remained largely untouched, even though partly visible, until 1867. By that time, rumor had it that gold had been on board, and a small group of entrepreneurs succeeding in raising and moving the wreck to Gloucester City, New Jersey. The entrepreneurs found no gold at all, but according to an early twentieth-century account, they did find the following:

A lot of silver spoons, marked "H.W. 1748," with a coat of arms consisting of an ancient-shaped cross, an old English Bull's Eye watch, 7 guinea pieces bearing the vignette of George III and with dates ranging from 1760 to 1770, some Spanish silver-dollars, 3 guns of heavy calibre, which now lie on the beach at Red Bank, about 60 tons weight of balls, and about 100 tons of Kentlidge iron (ballast). . . . The vessel had been constructed of Irish oak and joined with trunnels of the same material. The timber is today pronounced as good as when put together (Quoted in Cox 1984:81)

Soon after the *Augusta* arrived in Gloucester City, her owners decided to fence her in and charge admission to see her. Interest waned within a few years, and the exhibition fell into disrepair. Shortly thereafter, a heavy storm washed the frigate to a nearby beach. The remains of the *Augusta* are said to be still partly visible from Market Street in Gloucester City at low tide (Cox 1984:82).

Four other derelict vessels lie near Pier 78 at the foot of Mifflin Street in South Philadelphia. One is the wreck of a paddle-wheeled steamboat whose iron hull can be seen from midships to bow at low tide; her identity is unknown, but she was apparently built in the last half of the nineteenth century. The other three vessels lie buried in mud and are visible only in aerial photographs. All are wooden-hulled schooners. One, the *Francis J. McDonald*, was built in 1917 at Noank, Connecticut. The others, the *Albert D. Cummins* and the *Marie F. Cummins*, were built in 1920 at Beaumont, Texas. The *Albert D. Cummins* may be the best-preserved four-masted schooner in the country (Cox 1984:82–83, 156).

Another iron-hulled, paddle-wheeled steamboat lies near the mouth of Biles Creek not far from the U.S. Steel Fairless Works in Bucks County. Within Biles Creek itself are the wrecks of several late nineteenth- and early twentieth-century canal boats. When built in 1857, the steamboat was christened the *John A. Warner* but was renamed the *Burlington* in 1905. After running passenger excursions between Philadelphia and Trenton for many years, the *Burlington* met her end when she foundered on a submerged cable from a dredging barge in 1910 (Cox 1984:85, 128).

The vast amount of dredging of the Delaware since the 1870s has no doubt disturbed a good many submerged sites and shipwrecks. However, only a few instances of such disturbances have been documented. In 1941, while dredging near Hog Island, workers came upon a site that contained a number of artifacts but no timbers. The artifacts included a hand-forged anchor weighing 40 pounds, approximately 280 pounds of copper sheeting, a hand-forged brass spike, numerous hand-wrought nails, an iron cannonball, a copper spoon, and a brass collar button marked "USNYN, 1871." In 1948 two more shipwrecks came to light as workers were dredging near Woodbury Creek and Mantua Creek on the New Jersey side of the Delaware. Only the wreck near Woodbury Creek was documented. Sunk in about 6 feet of mud, the vessel, estimated to have been at least 200 feet long, had evidently been a supply or merchant ship. The site yielded nail kegs, table knives, hand scythes, brass locks and keys, pewter plates, hinges, a harpoon, hoes, copper tea kettles, bottles, ceramics, and silver shoe buckles. The present whereabouts of the artifacts are unknown, but a cursory analysis of the bottles and ceramics at the time they were recovered suggested that the vessel dated to the late seventeenth or early eighteenth century; the style of the pewter plates suggested Dutch origins (Cox 1984:84–85).

Predicting the Locations of Submerged Archaeological Resources

In formulating his model for predicting the locations of submerged sites and shipwrecks, Cox (1984:123–29) took into consideration such factors as historic population density, transportation activity, shipwrecks that have been historically documented but never found, characteristics of the river, dredging and other disturbances, and development likely to take place in the future. Using this model, Cox suggested that the area of the Delaware between Marcus Hook and Allegheny Avenue in Philadelphia has a "medium-high" potential for the presence of submerged cultural resources. The reason Cox did not assign a "high" potential to this area is not that it is likely to lack resources but that intensive dredging in this vicinity has probably seriously disturbed or destroyed many of these resources. Because the river from Philadelphia north to Trenton has experienced less dredging and because a thick coat of sediment has probably protected submerged resources in this part of the river, Cox ranked it as having high potential.

Although Cox gave the Delaware from Marcus Hook to Allegheny Avenue only a medium-high ranking, he did point out three specific sections in this part of the river that have an unusually high potential for archaeological research (Cox 1984:87–89, 125). The site near Pier 78 off the foot of Mifflin Street, where the three wooden-hulled schooners lie, is noteworthy because vessels of this type have not been made in many years, and study of them could provide information on a vanished aspect of shipbuilding. The channel behind Tinicum Island is, according to Cox (1984:88), "the single largest 'undis-

turbed' portion of river bottom on the Pennsylvania side of the river below Trenton"; it has also been the scene of much historic activity. In 1777 two British ships used it as cover for their approach on Fort Mifflin, and in the same year an American ship was scuttled in the channel near the mouth of Darby Creek. The back channel of Pettys Island has also witnessed a good deal of history, and despite the dredging that has taken place there, the nearby tidal flats have remained largely undisturbed. At least two historic vessels were abandoned at Pettys Island, and both may still lie there, protected beneath at least 10 feet of river silt and possibly also some dredging soil. One is the *Alliance*, a frigate used in the Revolutionary War and scrapped in the late eighteenth century. The other is a steamboat designed by John Fitch, the gentleman who invented the steamboat and sent the first one chugging up the Delaware in 1786.

Cox (1984:86, 128) singled out two areas of the river north of Philadelphia as being of particular archaeological significance. One is the area around Biles Creek where the wreck of the *Burlington* lies. In this vicinity, the British sank six American sloops and schooners in May 1778. Because the small channel behind Biles Island has never been dredged, the chances of locating some or all of these vessels would seem to be relatively good. The other significant area in this part of the river is around the mouth of Poquessing Creek and the nearby small back channel of Mud Island (not to be confused with the Mud Island south of Philadelphia where Fort Mifflin was built). This area has been called a "historic graveyard for vessels," and limited dredging here has reputedly resulted in the recovery of various artifacts.

TRANSPORTATION NETWORKS

Streets, alleys, and turnpikes, bridges and causeways, wharves and piers, ferry and boat landings, canals and towpaths, trolley tracks, train tracks—all are the telltale signs of development, and in Philadelphia they tell the story of the industrial path this city took. Yet in a place that at around the turn of the twentieth century had as many as 400 trains arriving and departing in a single day, a complete streetcar and suburban rail system, two rivers bustling with ferries and cargo ships, miles of wharves and piers, and streets already becoming jammed with automobiles, transportation networks have received precious little archaeological attention. They are, in fact, one of the most glaring lacunae in Philadelphia's archaeological record. Indeed, to date only one archaeological treatise on Philadelphia's transportation networks has been formally published (Parrington 1983).

There are a few other exceptions to this neglect, among them the studies of the Sansom Street cartway in Area F (see Chapter 3, "The McIlvaine House Privy and Area F"), the causeway at Dock Creek (see Chapter 5, "Front and Dock Streets"), and the wharves near West's shipyard (see Chapter 5, "West's Shipyard and Its Neighbors"). Archaeological investigation has also led to the discovery of a telford-style road underlying Market Square in Germantown (see Chapter 7, "Germantown"), an old road at the Peter Wentz Farmstead (see Chapter 9, "The Peter Wentz Farmstead"), a log road leading to a ferry landing at the Morton Homestead (see Chapter 10, "The Morton Homestead"), and the original U.S. Route 1 (Baltimore Pike) at the Barns-Brinton House (see Chapter 10, "The Barns-Brinton House"). But given that transportation networks were the vital connecting link between the eighteenth- and nineteenth-century industries on which Philadelphia's wealth was based, the amount of archaeological research devoted to them seems to border on the trivial.

Future research into Philadelphia's transportation networks could take many directions. Among the numerous unexplored topics are the evolution of street design; the paving of streets with cobbles, Belgian blocks, creosoted wooden blocks, bricks, macadam, and concrete with asphalt topping; the installation of gutters and sewers to drain the streets; the laying of tracks for horse-drawn and motorized vehicles; and the myriad types and designs of the vehicles that used the streets, from horse-drawn railway streetcars and bicycles to motorcycles and automobiles.

Indeed, so little archaeological research has been devoted to transportation in Philadelphia that little remains to be said, except to express the hope that the situation will be amended in the future. There seems to be some prospect of that happening in the not-too-distant future, since the Oliver Evans Chapter of the Society for Industrial Archaeology has published a district-by-district inventory of industrial sites in the Philadelphia region (Bowie 1990). This publication gives a long-overdue focus to the transportation networks that were the lifeline of industrial Philadelphia.

INDUSTRIAL SITES

Although the industrial sites of Philadelphia have received less archaeological attention than their role in the city's history would warrant, they have fared somewhat better than transportation networks. Nonetheless, there are still many gaping holes in this chapter of Philadelphia's archaeological record. Among the neglected sites are such industrial monuments as the Schuylkill Canal and the manufacturing enterprises it served, the numerous shipyards that once lined the Delaware, and various defunct industries situated within the city's park lands. In the planning study Lee-Decker (1983;5–7) conducted for the Fairmount Park Commission, he pointed out the great untapped archaeological potential of areas along Wissahickon Creek, Cresheim Creek, Tacony Creek, Pennypack Creek, Cobbs Creek, and the Schuylkill River. Of the many industries along these waterways during the eighteenth and nineteenth centuries—textile mills, gristmills, dye works,

Figure 12.3.

Fairmount Waterworks in 1978. The Philadelphia Museum of Art occupies the hill where the waterworks' reservoir was located. In the 1980s the city began restoring the buildings of the complex. (Photo by J. L. Cotter)

Figure 12.4.

Plan of the Fairmount Waterworks. (From Cosans-Zebooker and Parrington 1983; courtesy of the City of Philadelphia and John Milner Associates)

breweries, papermills, and sawmills among them—to date only the Gorgas Mill Complex has been the subject of focused archaeological investigation (Kenyon 1977b).

Not all the gaps in the archaeological record of Philadelphia's industries are due to neglect. As the Appendix points out, some sites simply fail to yield much useful data. For instance, limited testing by Cosans-Zebooker and Parrington (1983) at the Fairmount Waterworks (Figure 12.3), perhaps the best-known and best-documented industrial site in the city,* produced no trace of the Jonval turbines and other pumping machinery known to have been used there. But—in testimony that archaeology at a historic site is always work in progress—later excavations did. The Jonval turbine system was installed in the New Mill House of the waterworks complex in 1851 (Figure 12.4). In 1911, two years after the waterworks closed, scrap merchants re-

* As noted in Chapter 2, the Fairmount Waterworks was designed by Frederick Graff in 1815 (Parrington 1984b) to replace the pumphouse that Benjamin Latrobe had designed for Center Square some fifteen years earlier. The Historic American Engineering Record maintains measured drawings of all the buildings in the waterworks complex.

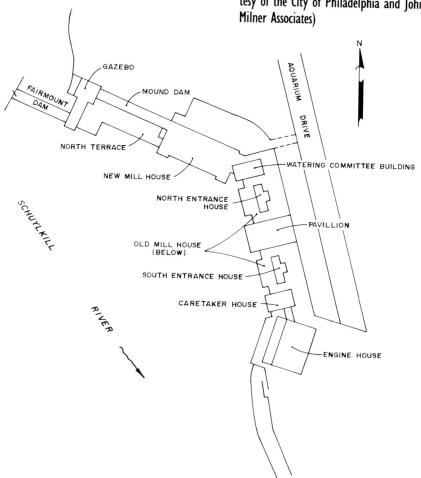

moved 1,323,245 pounds of iron and 8,376 pounds of brass from the New Mill House, which the city was then converting to an aquarium. Although Cosans and Parrington's limited excavations led them to conclude that the scrap mechants of 1911 had done their work too well, Joel Fry (1988), under contract to the Philadelphia Water Department, excavated parts of what were apparently eight of the twelve wheel blades and rim of a Jonval turbine's upper, stationary, 8-foot wheel. The parts appeared in 4 feet of clay fill in a pump well connected to the turbine system. They were an important find, since the wheel blades had been one of the few undocumented segments of the pumping system at the New Mill House.

Ironically, one Philadelphia industry that has suffered a rather profound neglect is one whose products are of the greatest interest to archaeologists. While ceramics of local manufacture have turned up at practically every historic site excavated in Philadelphia and have been the object of considerable study because of their usefulness as indicators of date and status, the places where these items were made—with the notable exceptions of the Bonnin and Morris Porcelain Factory and John Rogers' kiln in Franklin Court—have received scant archaeological attention. This general neglect of kiln sites is particularly ironic, since a good deal of historical documentation about the pottery industry in Philadelphia from colonial times through the nineteenth century is available.* A study by Bower (1975, 1985) researched Philadelphia's ceramic industry from 1683 to 1775;

two studies by Myers (1977, 1980), focused on this industry in the Middle Atlantic region; and one by Giannini (1981) illuminated the life and career of one of Philadelphia's earliest and best-known potters, the Huguenot immigrant Anthony Duché.

Because pottery kilns posed a fire hazard, all seven potters who worked in Philadelphia between 1683 and 1720 were located on the outskirts of the city in the area west of Fourth Street and north of Vine. By 1720, however, Anthony Duché had set up his stoneware kiln closer to the city, near the northeast corner of Chestnut Street and Fifth. The first documentation of Duché's presence in Philadelphia shows that in 1705 he married a fellow Hugenot, Ann Doz, but he appears not to have begun operating his kiln until 1720, by which time he was one of nine Philadelphia potters. As the city expanded and imports failed to meet the increasing demand for ceramics, the number of Duché's competitors grew; from 1720 until just before the Revolution, at least twenty-four potters were plying their trade in Philadelphia. The large number of Duché's wares excavated at Philadelphia sites attests to his continuing popularity and success despite increased competition. Like other local potters, Duché had the advantage of being able to undercut the prices of the imports, but he also must have had an unusually good sense of the local taste in ceramics. This saga of colonial enterprise ended shortly after Duché's death in 1762. In January 1763, as the sale of his property was pending, the pottery burned to the ground (Bower 1975:6–7, 12; Giannini 1981).

After a lull during the turmoil of the Revolution, Philadelphia's pottery industry regained its vitality. When the embargo of 1807 and Non-Intercourse

Act of 1809 cut off the supply of fine imported ceramics, local potters moved to fill the void. These attempts at making fine earthenware were of short duration. After the war with England ended in 1815, imports flooded into the country again, and local potters were unable to compete either in price or in quality. Abandoning the "carriage trade" to the competition, established potters returned to making their traditional utilitarian redwares. In 1826, however, William Ellis Tucker decided to renew the Bonnin and Morris tradition of making fine porcelain in Philadelphia. Tucker opened his porcelain factory in a former waterworks building at Twenty-Third and Chestnut streets (Myers 1980:5–7, 24). Apparently, at least one of the problems that had plagued Gousse Bonnin—undermining by English competitors—plagued William Ellis Tucker as well. According to Tucker's brother, the "man who placed the ware in the kiln was employed by some interested parties in England to impede our success" (Barber 1909:128–29). Although Tucker put an end to the sabotage, his porcelain factory never succeeded commercially. After he died in 1832, the factory limped on until 1838, when it ceased production altogether.

Although we have documentary evidence of Tucker's factory and Duché's kiln and physical evidence of their wares, we have no archaeological knowledge of these sites and very little of the other potteries that existed in Philadelphia in the eighteenth and nineteenth centuries. Nor do we know much about how these wares were made; technology during this period was a closely guarded secret. Information derived from excavation of kiln sites could therefore fill an especially regrettable void in our industrial knowledge of the city.

---

* See Chapter 6, "Vine Street," for what may be an eighteenth-century brick clay pit of Thomas Coates beneath Vine Street and the same chapter for similar clay pits at the Commuter Rail Tunnel site.

The manufacture of chemicals is another important local industry of which we have considerable documentary evidence but little or no archaeological evidence. In tracing the life and career of John Harrison, a chemist whose business ultimately merged to become Merck and Company, Zimmt (1981) identified the Philadelphia sites Harrison occupied in the course of his long career. Born in 1773 to Quaker immigrants, Harrison was apprenticed to a "chymist," or druggist, at the age of fourteen. By the time he was twenty, he was in business with Samuel Betton selling chemicals and drugs at 10 South Second Street. Although most of the products Betton and Harrison sold were imported, small quantities of some items, such as nitric acid and oxide and chloride of mercury, were made on the premises.

By 1806 Harrison was in business for himself at 75 North Fifth Street. Two years later he had moved to a location "near 121 Green Street" (Zimmt 1981:16), three blocks north of Vine not far from the Delaware River. There he had a leaden chamber capable of producing 3,500 carboys of sulfuric acid per year. In 1809, after a fire had destroyed the factory on Green Street, Harrison moved his op-eration to the Northern Liberties, near Frankford Avenue and Second Street.

In 1814 Harrison demonstrated his penchant for innovation by installing at his plant in the Northern Liberties the first still ever to be lined with platinum.* The platinum acted as a catalyst in producing sulfur trioxide from sulfur dioxide gas reacting with oxygen. Made with the help of Dr. Eric Bollman, a German chemist, Harrison's platinum-lined still weighed 700 ounces, held 25 gallons of sulfuric acid, and ran uninterruptedly for fifteen years.

After Harrison died in 1833, his sons continued the business under the name of Harrison Brothers. By 1851 the plant had expanded into a complex of buildings at Fitler and Hancock streets between Front and Second—an area that would subsequently become heavily industrial. Ultimately, after various changes in partnership, Powers, Wrightman, and the youngest brother, G. L. Harrison, emerged as Merck and Company. Archaeological evidence of the products made on the various premises occupied by John

---

* When first identified in 1750, platinum was cheaper than gold. In Spain, to prevent its being used to debase gold, it was separated from Colombian gold and thrown into rivers (Zimmt 1981:25).

Harrison's enterprise would undoubtedly add a new dimension to the history of the chemical industry in Philadelphia. The remaining Harrison brothers built a large, modern plant between the Schuylkill and Grays Ferry Avenue from 1864 to 1898, and in 1916 sold out to Du Pont (Zimmt 1981:17–20).

Other gaps in the archaeological record of Philadelphia's industries are too many to enumerate here, but with the work of the Oliver Evans Chapter of the Society for Industrial Archaeology has been doing since its founding in 1984, the future for this area of study looks hopeful (Bowie 1990). Another encouraging note for industrial sites is the growing amount of adaptive reuse of nineteenth-century industrial structures in the "Old City" section of Philadelphia. The conversion of buildings such as the Wireworks in the 300 block of Race Street to apartments and condominiums preserves their attractive exteriors as a pleasing feature of the streetscape. However, it also dramatically alters their interiors. Historical and archaeological inquiry into such buildings and photographs of their interiors before construction work begins would be a useful contribution to the archaeological record.

A CONCLUDING NOTE ON THE FUTURE OF PHILADELPHIA'S ARCHAEOLOGY

Although Philadelphia has been the subject of more archaeological study than any other major city in North America, much more obviously remains to be done. Equally obviously, not all of it will get done, at least in the foreseeable future. Archaeologists are therefore faced with setting some priorities.

While this chapter has pointed out a few directions for future archaeology in Philadelphia, it should not be forgotten that at its present state of development, archaeological excavation destroys a site even as it results in the recovery of artifacts and the recording of other data. Excavation is certainly justified when development is threatening a site or when it can answer worthwhile research questions, but its justification is questionable when the site can be preserved as is to await future excavation, which will no doubt be conducted with better, less destructive methods.

It would therefore seem that money now spent on excavating protected archaeological sites, such as those located on government-owned park lands, might be put to better use if channeled into the analyses of existing artifact collections. As pointed out in Chapter 11, in the absence of comprehensive analyses, the data are limited in their usefulness. With such analyses as a basis for comparison, we would be in a position not only to infer more about the broad cultural patterns of Philadelphia's past, but possibly also to gain some insights into urban life throughout America in the eighteenth and nineteenth centuries. Archaeological data, if properly retrieved and cared for, do not go bad, and using modern techniques to analyze them can be fruitful, as demonstrated by Schenck's work at Valley Forge in 1984 (see Chapter 10, "Valley Forge"); the artifacts Schenck submitted for metallurgical analysis had been excavated more than half a century earlier. The re-evaluation of the remains of the "saponified" woman in 1987 (see Chapter 6, "The 'Saponified' Man and Woman") is but one of many other illustrations of the value of using modern techniques to analyze old evidence.

Conserving archaeological data and making them readily accessible are among other top priorities for future Philadelphia archaeology. One way of achieving both these ends would be to create a central repository for the data. In addition, to make sure that archaeological findings are available, contracts for archaeological investigations should provide for the prompt and funded dissemination or publication of the results of data analysis. Last but far from least on the list of archaeological priorities is the need for a comprehensive base map of the Philadelphia region referencing historical data to known and potential sites and showing the locations of all such sites. Such a map would not only consolidate the archaeological data and make them more accessible; it would also be a large step toward making sure that the physical evidence of Philadelphia's past does not vanish.

Appendix
Minor Archaeological Investigations
in the Philadelphia Region

Investigations undertaken to comply with federal legislation by locating, identifying, and evaluating archaeological resources occasionally fail to find any resources; more often, perhaps, the resources that are found have been so disturbed or are so insignificant they warrant no further exploration. Studies not prompted by legislative mandate also sometimes fail to produce much positive archaeological or historical information. Negative though the results of such investigations may be, they can inform the archaeologist not only of the settlement preferences of prehistoric and historic populations but also of the nature and extent of disturbances in particular areas. Thus the "minor" investigations summarized in the pages that follow constitute valuable links in the archaeological record of the Philadelphia region. Figure A.1 shows the sites on which these investigations focused.

Figure A.1.

Sites of minor archaeological investigations in the Philadelphia region.

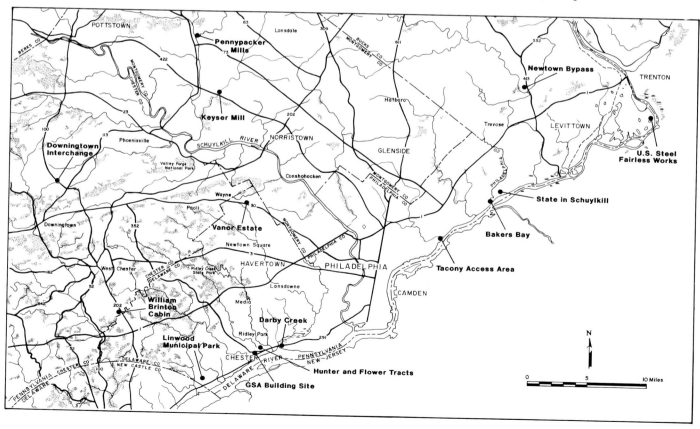

Philadelphia County

Tacony Access Area

Investigators: Thomas and Archibald (1981).

Purpose of Investigation: Survey of archaeological resources in an area along the Delaware River where the Pennsylvania Fish Commission was planning to develop a boating and recreational facility.

Methods Used: Documentary research, informant interviews, and subsurface testing.

Summary of Findings: Existence of archaeological resources unlikely, because until about 1942, when the area was extensively filled, it consisted of marsh and open water.

Montgomery County

Keyser Mill

Investigators: Knecht and Jordan (1984).

Purpose of Investigation: To minimize disturbance to potentially significant archaeological resources in advance of efforts by the Pennsylvania Department of Environmental Resources to stabilize the mid-nineteenth-century mill. Specifically, surviving evidence of the millrace and hydropower system was sought.

Methods Used: Subsurface testing, both interior and exterior to the mill.

Summary of Findings: All traces of the original tailrace were gone, and twentieth-century modifications to the mill had compromised the integrity and research value of surviving mill elements—in particular, twin wheel wells and associated dressed timbers.

Recommendations: No significant archaeological resources were present.

Pennypacker Mills

Investigators: Parrington and Hoffman (1984); Hoffman (1984).

Purpose of Investigations: To provide a preliminary evaluation of archaeological resources that may be present in an approximately 140-acre tract that forms part of the 260-year-old Pennypacker* estate (Parrington and Hoffman 1984), and to provide a site-specific survey for archaeological resources potentially affected by the construction of a new parking facility and access road (Hoffman 1984).

Methods Used: Documentary research, informant interviews, field reconnaissance, and subsurface testing.

Summary of Findings: Five prehistoric archaeological sites were identified on the tract, ranging from the Early Archaic through the Late Woodland periods. An ephemeral historic archaeological component was also identified to the south of the Pennypacker house, and a few Revolutionary War–period artifacts were also reported from the property.

Recommendations: Recommendations for the responsible management of all identified archaeological resources were made.

Bakers Bay

Investigators: Schiek and Brown (1985).

Purpose of Investigation: Survey of archaeological resources on a seventeen-acre tract at the juncture of Poquessing Creek and the Delaware River, where a housing development was being planned.

Methods Used: Documentary research, field reconnaissance, and subsurface testing.

Summary of Findings: Historical documentation of colonial farming, a ferry landing, a fishing wharf, and three country estates of the late 1800s and early 1900s; structural evidence and artifacts of the three country estates and of aboriginal occupation.

Recommendations: Further evaluation of the aboriginal site and the three country estates,

---

* Samuel Pennypacker was a prominent judge, and a noted historian, bibliophile, and antiquarian, who went on to become governor of Pennsylvania from 1903 to 1907.

---

and continuation of the search for the ferry landing and fishing wharf.

Bucks County

U.S. Steel Fairless Works

Investigators: Kardas and Larrabee (1982).

Purpose of Investigation: Assessment of the archaeological potential of two sites that U.S. Steel was proposing to fill with hazardous and residual wastes.

Methods Used: Documentary research, predictive modeling of locations of archaeological resources, field reconnaissance, and subsurface testing.

Summary of Findings: Previous disturbance of nearly three-quarters of the study area; privy pit and well shaft indicating a farmstead dating to at least 1832; five prehistoric stone artifacts, suggesting a more intensively occupied site east of the study area along the Delaware River.

Recommendations: Protection of the farmstead and the margin of the prehistoric site during development and use of the landfill sites.

Newtown Bypass

Investigator: Wilson (1982).

Purpose of Investigation: Evaluation of archaeological, architectural, and historical resources as part of an environmental impact statement required by state highway construction.

Methods Used: Documentary research, field reconnaissance, and subsurface testing.

Summary of Findings: Fifteen farmsteads dating to the early or mid-1800s still standing; nineteenth-century mills standing on three of the farmsteads; four historic roads; a stone bridge built in 1875; a schoolhouse; two twentieth-century dumps.

Recommendations: Eligibility of the farmsteads and mills for the National Register of Historic Places and avoidance of the resources during construction.

State in Schuylkill Fishing Club

Investigator: Parrington (1981b).

Purpose of Investigation: Salvage of silver and other items from a fire-gutted building that a historic social club, founded in 1732, had occupied since 1944; determination, based on the amount of silver missing, of the possibility that the fire had been deliberately set to conceal a burglary.

Methods Used: Inspection of the shell of the structure and supervision of the removal of debris and of the artifact salvage.

Summary of Findings: Three layers of artifacts, consisting of a bottom layer of melted and distorted nineteenth-century silver and ceramics from first-floor display cases, directly overlaid by what remained of the modern possessions of a young couple who had lived on the second floor, directly overlaid by an institutional ceramic dining service that had been stored on the third floor*; arson unlikely in view of the amount of silver recovered.

Chester County

Downington Interchange

Investigators: Basalik and Brown (n.d.).

Purpose of Investigation: Archaeological survey of a right-of-way proposed in a state highway improvement project.

Methods Used: Documentary research, field reconnaissance, and subsurface testing.

Summary of Findings: Historical documentation of early farming, of a late nineteenth-century farmstead with several structures partially overlapping the study area, and of a tannery just south of the study area; no physical evidence of archaeological resources within the right-of-way, although adjacent areas contained structural evidence of a nineteenth-century house and barn, artifacts

---

* This investigation provides an interesting object lesson in the pitfalls of archaeological interpretation. Contemporary knowledge of the site made interpretation of the deposition of the three layers simple, but without it, an archaeologist might infer three separate historical occupations of the site.

---

indicating the presence of another farmstead, and two flakes of quartz possibly suggesting a nearby Amerindian encampment.

William Brinton Cabin

Investigator: Becker (1980a), at the invitation of the Chester County Historical Society.

Purpose of Investigation: Location of a site where, according to local oral tradition, the first European-built structure immediately south of West Chester stood in the 1600s.

Methods Used: Historical research of primary documents and oral tradition, subsurface testing, aerial photographs, and proton magnetometer and resistivity testing.

Summary of Findings: Site, although documented, not located owing to imprecise, inaccurate documentation.

Delaware County

Vanor Estate

Investigator: Townsend (1976).

Purpose of Investigation: Evaluation of the historical and archaeological resources on a seven-acre tract owned by the U.S. Forest Service but formerly part of a large country estate that dates to at least the mid-1700s.

Methods Used: Documentary research, field reconnaissance, and subsurface testing.

Summary of Findings: Evidence of twentieth-century structures only; no evidence of significant historical or archaeological resources.

Hunter and Flower Tracts

Investigator: Thomas (1978).

Purpose of Investigation: Evaluation of the archaeological resources on two tracts of land where a tank-storage farm and a gas-processing plant were planned.

Methods Used: Documentary research, field reconnaissance, and subsurface testing.

Summary of Findings: Historical documentation of the use of both tracts as farmsteads during the 1700s and 1800s; structural evidence of the ruins of a house, barn, outbuilding, and possibly a springhouse on each property; evidence indicating the possible presence of artifacts in undisturbed contexts at each ruin.

Recommendations: Protection of the farmsteads from disturbance by the planned development or, if disturbance is unavoidable, more in-depth research to evaluate the archaeological significance of the farmsteads.

General Services Administration (GSA) Building Site

Investigator: Cosans (1982).

Purpose of Investigation: Survey of archaeological resources on a small, vacant lot in the city of Chester, where the GSA was planning to erect an office building.

Methods Used: Documentary research, field reconnaissance, and subsurface testing.

Summary of Findings: Historical documentation that the lot was undeveloped until about 1870, after which several brick rowhouses had stood on it until Chester's urban renewal program resulted in their razing in 1972; physical evidence that grading and filling had severely disturbed the site and that no significant archaeological features survived intact.

Linwood Municipal Park

Investigator: Townsend (1983).

Purpose of Investigation: Survey of the archaeological resources on a nineteen-acre municipal park slated for extensive improvement.

Methods Used: Documentary research, field reconnaissance, and subsurface testing.

Summary of Findings: Historical documentation that the site had from about 1870 to about 1918 contained the barn and outbuildings of a farmstead; no documentation of any previous development; physical evidence that scraping and regrading for the park after 1918, the laying of numerous utility lines, and erosion and soggy conditions had destroyed the integrity of any archaeological resources the site might have contained.

Darby Creek

Investigator: Mid-Atlantic Archaeological Research (1977).

Purpose of Investigation: Survey of archaeological resources in an area along the north side of Darby Creek near its confluence with the Delaware River slated for a new sewer force main.

Methods Used: Documentary research, field reconnaissance, and subsurface testing.

Summary of Findings: Historical documentation of eighteenth- and nineteenth-century farming and farmsteads, a gristmill, early roadways, an eighteenth-century ferry landing, and an eighteenth-century tavern. In addition, a small historic artifact midden consisting of redwares, whitewares, bottle glass, nails, kaolin pipe stems and bowls, and a crucifix was discovered between Interstate-95 and Wanamaker Avenue, near Swarthmore. Minimal evidence for a Late Woodland Amerindian occupation was also found.

Recommendation: Recommendations for further research of the artifact midden were offered.

Glossary

Archaeological / Geological

alluvial: Clay, sand, gravel, or rock material deposited by running water.

anthracite coal: Hard, lustrous natural fuel, longer-burning and hotter than bituminous coal because it contains less volatile matter.

anvil stone: A stone with a flat or cupped surface on which seeds or nuts are cracked or ground with a hand-held smooth stone.

argillite: A compact rock metamorphosed from clay cemented by silica.

artifact: Object made or adapted by man.

atlatl: Flat or rounded shaft with a hook in one end to receive the hollowed end of a projectile shaft, enabling the holder to propel the weapon with great force.

balk: Unexcavated area between excavated grid units at a site, left to provide a stratigraphic section.

biface: Worked on both sides to fashion an object, here of stone.

bituminous coal: A soft coal that yields less heat and burns more quickly than anthracite coal.

bola stone: Two or more round stones tied together and thrown at an animal so as to entangle it and bring it down.

carbon 14 (radiocarbon dating): Isotope of carbon rendered radioactive in the high atmosphere, which, falling to earth, is found in the remains of organic substances. Because its half-life is known, C_{14} can be used to date a substance by measuring its diminished radioactivity.

celt: Stone implement with a ground edge, usually hafted in a wood shaft like a mattock or chisel, and used principally to trim or hollow out wooden objects, here by the Amerindians.

chalcedony: Translucent, colored quartz stone with the properties of flint—e.g., conchoidal (shell-like) fracture.

chert: A flint-like rock characterized by conchoidal fracture, rendering it useful in making artifacts by flaking, like the chalcedony of which it is mainly composed.

city datum: In Philadelphia, an elevation reference 2.25 feet above mean high water mark at the foot of Chestnut Street, with reference to the Delaware River.

cross-mend: Sherds from different strata or site locations matched to indicate portions of a single vessel.

dolomite: A limestone or marble rich in magnesium carbonate.

ecology: The pattern of relationships between organisms and their environment.

ethnology: The analytical and comparative study of historic human groups.

fall line: The line joining the rapids on rivers falling to the sea and marking the limit of navigability for each river.

feature: Soil disturbance or man-made (or adapted) construction.

flint: Hard siliceous stone, occurring in nodules in limestone formations, that is characterized by a conchoidal fracture ideal for making aboriginal flaked tools and gunflints, and for producing sparks when struck by iron or steel.

gabbro: A granular igneous rock composed of calcium carbonate, ferrous magnesium, and other minerals.

gneiss (Baltimore gneiss): Foliated granitic rock.

grade: An original surface before deposition or erosion has changed it. In archaeology, a historical surface of reference.

granite: A hard igneous rock with a crystalline texture used for building.

grave offering: Artifacts buried with the dead.

grid system: Method of excavation in which features, artifacts, and excavation areas are related to the coordinates of the grid.

Holocene: Recent. Generally, after the glacial age.

hominid: Any of a family of primates comprising the ancestors of modern man.

Homo sapiens: Species name of modern man: *Homo* for the genus, *sapiens* a specific epithet meaning wise—sometimes doubled to *sapiens sapiens*.

indenture: A contract binding one person to work for another for a given period of time in exchange for keep and training.

jasper: An opaque, compact, variety of stone stained with various colors (red, green, yellow, etc.) and having the conchoidal fracture characteristic of flint, making it useful for flaked artifacts.

limestone: A water-deposited rock formation consisting of the calcium carbonate of shells and corals; may be cut for building stone or crushed and burned to make lime for mortar.

lithic: Stone, as applied here to materials used for making artifacts.

longhouse: Long communal dwelling of the Late Woodland Amerindians extending into the time of contact, notably among the Iroquois.

longitudinal profile: A section through the longest axis of an archaeological feature.

matrilineal: Tracing of descent through the mother's line.

mean ceramic date: The midpoint between the earliest and latest ceramic dates at a site, based on the known range of manufacturing dates. In practice, the sherd count for each ceramic type is multiplied by the known median date for each type, and the quotients are added. The resultant sum is divided by the sum of the sherds to obtain the median date of the site.

mica: A transparent mineral silicate crystallized in planes and separating into many thin leaves.

midden: A deposit of household refuse.

Piedmont: Land lying at the base of a mountain range; also, physiographic region in which most of the area discussed in this book occurs.

Pleistocene: In general, pertaining to the glacial and interglacial episodes of the Quaternary.

post mold: A stain in the earth left by the mold of a structure post that rotted away, revealed by careful excavation.

quartz: Hexagonal crystals of silicon dioxide, often colorless and transparent, with limited conchoidal fracture; difficult to flake or grind for shaping into artifacts.

quartzite: A hard, metamorphosed quartz sandstone with a conchoidal fracture useful in making flaked stone artifacts.

rhyolite: Acidic volcanic rock; the lava form of granite.

robbed trench: Traces observable in the ground when a wall has been removed.

rockshelter: A shallow cave with a sheltering overhang permitting a protected living space.

sachema (sachem): Chief of a confederation of Algonquian tribes of the Mid- to North Atlantic coast.

savanna: Subtropical to temperate grassland that may have intermittent tree growth.

seine: A large net with sinkers at one edge and floats on the opposite edge that hangs vertically in the water. When the edges are pulled together or the stone edge is raised, fish are trapped.

serpentine: A friable metamorphic building stone essentially composed of a hydrous magnesium silicate, having a dull-green mottled color. It is

noted for its limited weathering capability.

shale: Metamorphosed clay, mud, or silt, finely laminated, the minerals of which are essentially unchanged from the time of deposition.

sherd: Fragment of a vessel of any material.

Sinanthropus pekinensis: Species name of pre-sapiens human (living about 500,000 years ago) found in the entrance areas of limestone caves north of Beijing (Peking), China.

soapstone: A soft stone with a soapy feel containing principally talc and characterized by durability when exposed to heat and cold. Used for cooking vessels, griddles, and building trim.

soil resistivity test: A method of locating archaeological features by inducing a small electrical charge through the ground and measuring the resistance between the points of induction.

stratigraphy: Term used to describe archaeological layers (strata).

subsistence mode: The main elements of the means for existence of a group—here, the food, shelter, and artifacts of daily life.

taiga: Subarctic land beginning where the tundra ends and characterized by a moist environment dominated by spruces and firs.

terminus post quem: Date *after* which a layer was deposited at a site (*ante quem* for the date *before* deposit).

trade silver: Silver objects made by settlers for Amerindian trade.

transverse profile: A section through the shortest axis of a feature.

tundra: A level or undulating, treeless plain with permafrost beneath moist black soil on which flowering, earth-hugging herbs grow in an arctic or subarctic environment.

wampum: Strands of polished shells intended originally by the Mid- to North Atlantic coastal Amerindians as pledges or gifts, but subsequently regarded by European settlers as money.

weir: A fence or enclosure set in a stream to lead fish into a trap.

Architecture / Furnishings

art deco: An architectural style in America from 1925 to 1940 characterized by building facades arranged in a series of setbacks featuring geometric form and hard-edged low relief decoration in the same material as the building, which is often metal or glazed bricks or terra-cotta.

balustrade: A row of balusters (upright supports) with a rail running along the tops.

bay: A compartment of a building, sometimes extending outward from the walls; an embayment or bay window.

belt course: A horizontal course of brick or stone, usually marking the floor of a second or higher story of a building.

Brussels carpet: A carpet of a style popular in the nineteenth century, characterized by colored worsted yarns fixed in a web of strong linen thread and drawn into loops to form the pattern.

bulkhead: An upright partition that separates compartments, or a retaining wall on a waterfront.

chancel: That part of a church above the transept containing the altar and choir seats.

check wall: A wall to retain a mass of material.

Chippendale: A furniture style of the eighteenth century, characterized by the graceful, ornate design of Thomas Chippendale.

cornice: Moulded projection surmounting a frieze, or an architectural crowning element atop a wall.

counterfort: In eighteenth-century parlance, the strong masonry wall containing and supporting the earth revetment protecting a fort.

cribbing: A framework, usually of timber, to support a fill.

cupola: A small, usually rounded structure built on a roof.

Doric: The oldest and simplest of the Greek architectural orders; a capital consisting of a square above a circle.

dormer: A window projecting through a sloping roof; also the sloping roof containing the window.

dry-laid brick: Bricks laid without mortar, characteristically lining a pit to permit water to flow in or out.

English bond: Bricks laid with one or more courses of stretchers alternated with a course of headers.

fanlight: The semicircular window above a door characterized by decorative ribbing bars opening like the ribs of a fan.

Federal: Ca. 1790–1810 neoclassical style in furniture and house embellishment, popular after the establishment of the federal U.S. government.

Flemish bond: Bricks laid with alternate headers and stretchers.

gable: The triangular end of a building, from the eaves to the ridge of the roof.

gambrel: A roof with a ridge in the center and a double slope on each side, with the lower slope steeper than the upper one.

Georgian: An architectural style associated with the first four Georges who reigned in England, characterized by strict symmetry.

Greek revival: An architectural style popular in America from 1820 to 1860, adapting the classic Greek temple front with Doric-, Ionic-, or Corinthian-order capitals on columns with full entablature above and a low-pitch pediment.

header: A brick laid perpendicular to the wall, showing only the end of the brick, which may be glazed.

hipped (hip) roof: A roof with sloping sides and sloping ends.

Italianate: Architectural style popular in America from 1840 to 1880, characterized by rectangular or nearly square two- or three-story houses with wide eaves supported by large brackets; low-pitch hipped roofs, often with a cupola; and tall first-floor windows.

jamb: A projecting column or other piece forming the side of a door or other opening, such as a fireplace.

joist pocket: A recess in masonry walls to receive the end of a joist that supports a floor.

lintel: A flat architectural member spanning an opening and bearing the load above.

mansard roof: A roof with two slopes on all sides, the lower steeper than the upper, often with dormer windows on the lower slope. The slopes can be concave, convex, or straight.

nave: In a church with a cross plan, the long central hall flanked by the cross-member transept.

Palladian: Classic-style revival based on the architecture of Andrea Palladio. Elements of this style became popular in America in the eighteenth century.

pediment: Triangular space that forms the gable end of a low-pitched roof in classical architecture.

peg mortise: A cavity cut into a wooden or masonry member to receive a peg or tenon.

pent eave: An extended projection of the roof beyond the building wall.

piazza: An arcaded and roofed gallery structure, often in back of a house.

pilaster: A column that projects (a third or less of its width) from a wall and is attached to it.

portico: A covered colonnade, often at the entrance of a building.

row house: A house joined at the side or end to another house, or to other houses.

Second Empire: A style promulgated by the Second French Empire between 1860 and 1890 in America, characterized by imposing two- or three-story structures in a square block surmounted by a mansard roof. The windows are arched and pedimented with molded surrounds. Doors are often arched and double. In Philadelphia, City Hall is the most conspicuous example.

stretcher: A brick laid lengthways, parallel to the wall.

transept: In the cross-like plan of a church, the part that crosses at right angles to the nave (or greater length); below the apse or choir heading the cross.

water table: In architecture, a horizontal line of bricks extending half a stretcher from the wall or less, forming a drip line for rainwater running down the wall. In land forms, the level of groundwater that can be reached by a well.

Windsor chair: A spindle-backed wooden chair with a saddle seat and spread legs.

Military / Manufacturing

abatis: A defensive system of spiked sticks used to impede the invader.

arsenal: A storage area for military weapons and supplies.

breach-loading: Loading a gun by inserting the charge and projectile into the open chamber of the breach rather than into the muzzle with a ramrod.

cartridge: A pre-assembled propellant charge and projectile for a gun.

chevaux-de-frise: A defensive obstacle used to close a water passage, usually iron-spiked staves set in rock-filled cribbing so as to damage the hull of a ship.

demilune: A small defensive earthwork, usually attached to or associated with a larger earthwork, characterized by an arc shape (literally, "half moon").

fuze: Same as fuse. A combustible material enclosed in a cord or tube designed to transmit fire to an explosive charge.

magazine: A storage area for explosive military supplies.

ordnance: Heavy artillery, cannon.

palisades: A defensive fence of vertical timbers placed side by side.

percussion caps: See primer.

primer: A cap or tube containing percussion powder, used to ignite an explosive charge in a weapon.

rampart: An earthwork built for defensive purposes.

rolling mill: A factory where wrought iron is flattened into manageable dimensions for manufacturing objects.

shrapnel: Originally a projectile consisting of a case filled with a powder charge and a large number of metal balls, usually lead, designed to explode in flight; now shell, or mine fragments.

spall gunflint: A gunflint made from a fragment of rock rather than a knapped blank shaped for the purpose.

Ceramics

basalt: A black, vitreous stoneware with matte surface, imitative of black volcanic stone; developed by J. Wedgwood.

basket-edged: A simulated basket-weave pattern molded on a plate edge.

bisque: The unglazed body of a ceramic after firing.

bone porcelain: A "soft paste" porcelain, the flux for which in firing is furnished by calcined beef bones, finely ground.

calcining: Heating at high temperature to drive off moisture, but without fusing, as in burning bones for the bodies of porcelain wares.

Canton: Blue-on-white Chinese porcelain regarded by dealers as less select than Nanking, which comes from the same kilns and is the same ware.

creamware: Yellowish-white earthenware of high quality developed in England in the mid-eighteenth century.

delftware: Tin-glazed Dutch earthenware decorated with blue paint under a glaze; predominantly seventeenth-century, copied in England in the eighteenth century.

earthenware: A slightly porous, low-fired, opaque ceramic.

graphite: Soft, black, lustrous carbon used in making crucibles.

ironstone: White, durable earthenware of hard texture developed in England early in the nineteenth century.

kiln: Housing—usually of brick, with a fire box and vent—in which pottery, bricks, or tiles are stacked for firing.

lead-glazed: Glaze produced on pottery by dusting with lead oxide before firing.

Lowestoft: Soft-paste porcelain made at Lowestoft, England, from 1757 to 1802; the name was commonly given to Chinese porcelain decorated with motifs commissioned from England in the latter part of the eighteenth century.

majolica: Like faience and delft, a tin-glazed, enameled earthenware.

mochaware: Coffee-color–tinted earthenware with painted designs, sometimes banded, popular in the first half of the nineteenth century.

Nanking: Porcelain, usually made at Ching ti Chen, but labeled by dealers as a "preferred" quality of blue-and-white–decorated ware.

pearlware: A high-quality earthenware with a yellowish tinge that has been whitened by the addition of a small amount of cobalt blue to a clear glaze. This "blueing" may be perceived in the ridge around the base of plates and wherever else it may gather. Developed by Wedgwood at about 1775, it is characterized by blue-edged and transfer-printed decoration. It was produced in the late eighteenth and early nineteenth century, though it is still made.

polychrome: Decorated with a variety of colors.

porcelain: Hard-fired, translucent pottery originating in China.

queensware: Creamware of fine quality, elegantly decorated; developed, but not invented, by Wedgwood, notably in his 1771 set of 1,000 table pieces commissioned by the Empress of Russia.

redware: Red-bodied earthenware, usually utilitarian.

sagger pot: A box of fired clay with side openings in which ceramic objects are fired, shielding them from discoloring by oxidation.

salt-glazed: Glazed by introducing common salt into the kiln so that it volatilizes; a technique used on stoneware.

scratchware: Wares decorated by scratching the surface of the unfired pot and washing a color into the scratch before glazing, as in scratch-blue white stoneware. The scratch may also make a design through the slip.

Seger cone: A ceramic cone that fuses and droops at a given temperature in a kiln, indicating the appropriate heat for firing; named after German ceramist Herman A. Seger (1839–1894).

shell-edged: Having a scalloped edge (e.g., a plate), thus resembling a shell.

slip-decorated: Decorated with patterns "combed" or otherwise fashioned by making patterns in the slip (see "slipware"), exposing the paste beneath, before glazing and firing.

slipware: Red- or yellow-paste earthenware, usually lead-glazed over a white slip.

Staffordshire: A district in England where several potteries produced a variety of white stoneware and other wares characterized by fancy molded figures and vessels.

stoneware: Hard, high-fired, vitrified, opaque ceramic ware with an "orange peel" surface; usually salt-glazed.

transfer-printed: Decorated by applying a decalcomania to the surface and glazing over the print; a technique used commonly but not exclusively on pearlware.

treading room: A room in which pottery clay is kneaded, or "treaded," preparatory to molding or throwing on a wheel.

trivet: A ceramic tripod on which vessels are placed in a kiln to keep them from adhering to the floor when fired.

waster: A discarded ceramic piece spoiled in the kiln.

Whieldon: Name of a basic creamware by Thomas Whieldon, Little Fenton, Shropshire, who between 1724 and 1770 specialized in elaborate figurines and fanciful shapes in vessels.

Glass

case bottle: A square bottle with flat sides for shipping in a compartmented case.

lead glass: Glass made with lead oxide, with refractive values and a tendency to assume a purplish color in sunlight.

Silesian glass: A clear, potash-lime glass suitable for decorative engraving, produced in the first half of the eighteenth century in the Bohemian-Silesian area of east-central Europe in the upper Oder River valley bordering the Sudeten mountains.

soda glass: Typically clear glass made with anhydrous sodium carbonate.

References Cited

ABEL, LELAND
  1964   "Excavations at Independence Hall, Philadelphia." Report on file at Independence
          National Historical Park, Philadelphia.

ABERNETHY, LLOYD
  1982   "Progressivism, 1905–1919." In *Philadelphia: A 300-Year History,* edited by Russell
          F. Weigley. New York: W. W. Norton.

ALBRECHT, JOSEPHINE F.
  1969   "Caleb Pusey House I: Penn's Mill and Its 'Keeper' at Landing Ford Plantation in
          Upland, Pennsylvania." *Bulletin of the Archaeological Society of Delaware* 7:1–16.
  1972   "Caleb Pusey House III: History Hidden in the Earth." *Bulletin of the Archaeological
          Society of Delaware* 9:2–27.

ALDERFER, GORDON
  1951   *The Montgomery County Story.* Norristown, Pa.: Commissioners of Montgomery
          County.

ALEXANDER, L. T.
  1978   "Clay Tobacco Smoking Pipes from the Caleb Pusey House." Archaeological Society
          of Delaware, paper no. 9.

ANDERSON, BART
  1959   "The Barns-Brinton House, U.S. Route No. 1, Pennsbury Township, Chester County,
          Pennsylvania." Historic American Buildings Survey. Washington, D.C.: Library of
          Congress.

ANGEL, J. LAWRENCE, JENNIFER OLSEN KELLEY, MICHAEL PARRINGTON,
AND STEPHANIE PINTER
  1987   "Life Stresses of the Free Black Community as Represented by the First African
          Baptist Church, 8th and Vine Streets, Philadelphia, 1823–1841." *American Journal
          of Physical Anthropology* 74:213–229.

ANONYMOUS
  1934   "Excavation Work at Pennsbury Is Being Resumed." *Pennsylvania Archaeologist* 4(2):
          14–15.
  1938   "Restoring Pennsbury Manor as Pilgrim's Mecca." *Pennsylvania Archaeologist* 9 (2):
          47–48.

ANTHONY, DAVID W., AND DANIEL G. ROBERTS
  1987   "The Bachman Site (36 NM 80): Prehistoric Occupations in the Middle Delaware
          Valley." Report prepared for the Federal Highway Administration and the Pennsylva-
          nia Department of Transportation. John Milner Associates, West Chester, Pa.

ARMSTRONG, EDWARD, ED.
  1860   "Record of Upland Court: From the 14th of November 1676 to the 14th of June
          1681." In *Memoirs of the Historical Society of Pennsylvania.* Vol. 7. Philadelphia: J. B.
          Lippincott.

ATTICUS (PSEUDONYM)
  1838   *Hints on the Subject of Interments within the City of Philadelphia.* Philadelphia:
          William Brown.

AUBUREY, THOMAS
    1923   *Travels Through the Interior Part of North America.* Boston: Houghton Mifflin.

AUERBACH, KATHRYN ANN, AND JEFFREY L. MARSHALL
    1983   "Snodgrass Farm, Also Known as Vanartsdalen Farm, Lower Southampton Township, Bucks County, Pennsylvania: Report on Physical, Historical, and Archaeological Features." Bucks County Conservancy, Doylestown, Pa.

BAKER, STEVEN
    1972   "A House on Cambridge Hill (Site 38–GN2): An Excavation Report." Research Manuscript Series no. 27. Columbia: South Carolina Institute of Archaeology and Anthropology.

BALTZELL, E. DIGBY
    1979   *Puritan Boston and Quaker Philadelphia: Two Protestant Ethics and the Spirit of Class Authority and Leadership.* New York: Free Press.

BARBER, EDWIN ATLEE
    1909   *The Pottery and Porcelain of the United States.* New York: G. P. Putnam's Sons.

BARNES, CAROL
    1968   "Subsistence and Social Organization of the Delaware Indians: 1600 A.D." *Bulletin of the Philadelphia Anthropological Society* 20 (1): 15–29.

BARNES, FRANK
    1956   "Historic Site Survey, Fort Mifflin, Philadelphia, Pennsylvania." U.S. Department of Interior, National Park Service, Mid-Atlantic Region, Philadelphia, March 23, 1956.

BARON, STANLEY WADE
    1962   *Brewed in America: A History of Beer and Ale in the United States.* Boston: Little, Brown and Co.

BARRATT, NORRIS STANLEY
    1917   *Outline of the History of Old St. Paul's Church, Philadelphia, Pennsylvania.* Philadelphia: Colonial Society of Pennsylvania.

BARRETT, BRENDA, AND VANCE PACKARD
    1973a   "Preliminary Summary Report on Excavations at Camp Schoolhouse." Unpublished manuscript on file at Pennsylvania Historical and Museum Commission, Harrisburg, Pa.
    1973b   "Preliminary Summary Report on Excavations at Commissary," pp. 1–7. Unpublished manuscript on file at Pennsylvania Historical and Museum Commission, Harrisburg, Pa.

BARRETT, DAVID
    1982   "The Use of Socio-Economic Ranking in Two Archaeological Projects in the City of Philadelphia." Paper presented at the Annual Meeting of the Archaeological Institute of America, December 29, 1982.

BASALIK, KENNETH J.
    1980   *The MacIlvane House: An Analysis of Historical Archaeology.* Master's thesis, Temple University.
    1984   Archaeological Testing at Hagy Brothers' Limekilns, Plymouth Meeting, Pa. Report prepared for the Plymouth Meeting Historical Society.

BASALIK, KENNETH J., RONALD BERGE, ALAN TABACHNICK, ORLOFF MILLER, WENDY BACON, AND CHRISTOPHER DORE
    in prep.   "Phase III Data Recovery, Mid-County Expressway, I-476, Section 200, Delaware County, Pennsylvania." Report prepared for the Pennsylvania Department of Transportation. Cultural Heritage Research Services, North Wales, Pa. Forthcoming.

BASALIK, KENNETH J., AND ANN R. BROWN

n.d.   "Phase I Archaeological Survey, Pennsylvania Turnpike Downingtown Interchange Modification and Expansion Project, Uwchlan Township, Chester County, Pennsylvania." Report prepared for Uwchlan Township, Pa. CHRS, Chester, Pa.

BASALIK, KENNETH J., AND JOHN P. MCCARTHY

1982   "Discerning Patterns in an Urban Context: An Example from Philadelphia." In *The Conference on Historic Site Archaeology Papers 1979* 14:20–27.

BASCOM, F., E. T. WHERRY, G. W. STOSE, AND A. I. JONAS

1931   *Geology and Mineral Resources of the Quakertown-Doylestown District, Pennsylvania and New Jersey.* Bulletin 828. Washington, D.C.: Geological Survey, U.S. Department of the Interior.

BATCHELER, PENELOPE H.

1973   "Historic Structures Report, Architectural Data Section, City Tavern." Denver Service Center, National Park Service, Denver, Colo.

1976   "Independence Hall: Its Appearance Restored." Chap. 16 in *Building Early America*, edited by Charles E. Peterson. Radnor, Pa.: Chilton Book Co.

BECKER, MARSHALL J.

1976   "The Okehocking: A Remnant Band of Delaware Indians in Chester County, Pennsylvania during the Colonial Period." *Pennsylvania Archaeologist* 46:25–63.

1977a   "Summary Report on the 1976 Excavations at Governor Printz State Park, Essington, Pennsylvania, (36 DE 3)." Manuscript on file at Pennsylvania Historical and Museum Commission, Harrisburg, Pa.

1977b   "'Swedish' Colonial Yellow Bricks: Notes on Their Uses and Possible Origins in 17th Century America." *Historical Archaeology* 11:112–118.

1978a   "An Eighteenth Century Witch Bottle in Delaware County, Pennsylvania." *Pennsylvania Archaeologist* 48 (1–2): 1–11.

1978b   "Report of the 1978 Excavations at Pennsbury Manor, 36 BU 19." Report on file at the Pennsylvania Historical and Museum Commission, Harrisburg, Pa.

1979   "Éthnohistory and Archaeology in Search of Printzhof: The 17th Century Residence of Swedish Colonial Governor Johan Printz." *Ethnohistory* 26 (1): 15–44.

1980a   "Family Tradition and the Location of William Brinton's Cabin." Manuscript on file at West Chester University, West Chester, Pa.

1980b   "Preliminary Report of the 1980 Excavation Program at the Montgomery Site (36 CH 60) in Chester County, Pennsylvania." Manuscript on file at West Chester University, West Chester, Pa.

1980c   "Wampum: The Development of an Early American Currency." *Bulletin of the Archaeological Society of New Jersey* 36:1–11.

1982   "The Montgomery Site, 36-CH-60: A Late Contact Lenape (Delaware) Site in Chester County, Pennsylvania." Manuscript on file at West Chester University, West Chester, Pa.

1983a   "The Boundary Between the Lenape and Munsee: The Forks of Delaware as a Buffer Zone." *Man in the Northeast* 26:1–20.

1983b   "The Lenape Southern Boundary: Cultural Interaction and Change in the Early Contact Period 1550–1610." Manuscript on file at West Chester University, West Chester, Pa.

1984a   "The Lenape Bands Prior to 1746: The Identification of Boundaries and Processes of Change Leading to the Formation of the 'Delawares.'" In *The Lenape Indian: A Symposium*, edited by Herbert C. Kraft, 19–32. Publication No. 7 of the Archaeological Research Center, Seton Hall University, South Orange, N.J.

1984b   "Lenape Land Sales, Treaties, and Wampum Belts." *Pennsylvania Magazine of History and Biography* 108:351–356.

1984c   "The Swedes and Dutch in the Land of the Lenape." *Pennsylvania Heritage* 10 (1): 20–23.

1985   "Cash Cropping Among the Lenape in the Early Contact Period: An Episode of Pseudo-Agriculture by a Foraging People." Manuscript on file at West Chester University, West Chester, Pa.

1986   "The Okehocking Band of Lenape as an Example of One Mode of Adjustment to Colonial Expansion: Cultural Continuities and Accommodations in Southeastern Pennsylvania." In *Strategies for Survival*, edited by Frank W. Porter III, 43–83. Westport, Conn.: Greenwood Press.

1987a   "The Forks of Delaware, Pennsylvania during the First Half of the Eighteenth Century: The Migration of Some 'Jerseys' into a Former Shared Resource Area North of Lenape Territory and its Implications for Cultural Boundaries and Identities." Abhandlungen der Völkerkundliche Arbeitsgemeinschaft no. 55. Nortorf, West Germany.

1987b   "The Moravian Mission in the Forks of the Delaware: Reconstructing the Migration and Settlement Patterns of the Jersey Lenape during the Eighteenth Century through Documents in the Moravian Archives." *Unitas Fratrum*, special issue: "The American Indians and the Moravians" 21/22:83–172.

1988   "A Summary of Lenape Socio-Political Organization and Settlement Pattern at the Time of European Contact: The Evidence for Collecting Bands." *Journal of Middle Atlantic Archaeology* 4:79–83.

1989   "Lenape Population at the Time of European Contact: Estimating Native Numbers in the Lower Delaware Valley." In *Symposium on the Demographic History of the Philadelphia Region, 1600–1860*, edited by Susan E. Klepp. *Proceedings of the American Philosophical Society* 133 (2): 112–122.

1990a   "The Lenape and Their Migrations in the 17th Century." *The Towanda, Pennsylvania Settler* [Bradford County Historical Society] 28 (1): 1–45.

1990b   "A Wolf's Head Pouch: Lenape Material Culture in the Collections of the Skokloster Museum, Sweden." *Archeomaterials* 4 (1): 77–95.

BEERS, DOROTHY GONDOS
1982   "The Centennial City, 1865–1876." In *Philadelphia: A 300-Year History*, edited by Russell F. Weigley. New York: W. W. Norton.

BERNABO, J. CHRISTOPHER, AND THOMPSON WEBB III
1977   "Changing Patterns in the Holocene Pollen Record of Northeastern North America: A Mapped Summary." *Quaternary Research* 8:64–96.

BERNSTEIN, LEONARD
1950   "The Working People of Ph.   lelphia from Colonial Times to the General Strike of 1835." *Pennsylvania Magazine of History and Biography* 74:322–339.

BESCHERER, KAREN, CONRAD M. GOODWIN, JUDSON KRATZER, AND ANNE YENTSCH
1990   "The Gardens at Grumblethorpe, Germantown, Pennsylvania." Landscape Archaeology Report no. 2, Morven Research Group in Landscape Archaeology, Princeton, N.J.

BEVAN, BRUCE
1984   "Ground-Penetrating Radar for the Search for Redoubt 5." Report prepared for the U.S. Department of the Interior, National Park Service, Mid-Atlantic Region, Philadelphia.

BEVAN, BRUCE, AND JEFFREY KENYON
1975   "Ground-Penetrating Radar for Historical Archaeology." *MASCA Newsletter* 11 (2): 2–7.

BIDDLE, MARTIN, DAPHNE HUDSON, AND CAROLYN HEIGHWAY
1973   *The Future of London's Past.* Worcester, U.K.: Rescue, A Trust for British Archaeology.

BLOMBERG, BELINDA

in prep. a   "Archaeological Data Recovery in the Vicinity of Twelfth and Arch Streets at the Site of the Pennsylvania Convention Center, Philadelphia, Pennsylvania." Report prepared for the Philadelphia Industrial Development Corporation. John Milner Associates, Philadelphia. Forthcoming.

in prep. b   "Archaeological Investigations at the Site of the Bourse Garage/Omni Hotel at Independence Square, Philadelphia, Pennsylvania." Report prepared for Bourse Garage Associates and the Kevin F. Donohoe Company. John Milner Associates, Philadelphia. Forthcoming.

BLUMIN, STUART M.

1973   "Residential Mobility within the Nineteenth-Century City." In *The Peoples of Philadelphia*, edited by Allen F. Davis and Mark H. Haller, 37–51. Philadelphia: Temple University Press.

BOGUCKI, PETER I., AND RICHARD E. CAUFFIEL

1975   "Archaeological Investigations at the Thaddeus Kosciuszko National Memorial, Independence National Historical Park, Philadelphia, Pa." Report on file at Independence National Historical Park, Philadelphia.

BORSTLING, HENRY

1965a   "Resistivity Survey of Graeme Park, Horsham, Pennsylvania." Report on file at the Pennsylvania Historical and Museum Commission, Harrisburg, Pa.

1965b   "Resistivity Survey of Hope Lodge, Whitemarsh, Pennsylvania." Report on file at the Pennsylvania Historical and Museum Commission, Harrisburg, Pa.

BOWER, BETH ANNE

1975   "The Pottery-Making Trade in Colonial Philadelphia: The Growth of an Early Urban Industry." Master's thesis, Brown University.

1985   "The Pottery-making Trade in Colonial Philadelphia: The Growth of an Early Urban Industry." In *Domestic Pottery of the Northeastern United States, 1625–1850*, edited by Sarah Peabody Turnbaugh. New York: Academic Press.

BOWIE, JOHN R., ED.

1990   *Workshop of the World! A Selective Guide to the Industrial Archaeology of Philadelphia.* Philadelphia: Oliver Evans Chapter, Society for Industrial Archaeology.

BRAZER, JOHN

1841   "Burial of the Dead." *The Christian Examiner* (November 1841): 137–163; (January 1842): 281–307.

BRIDENBAUGH, CARL

1938   *Cities in the Wilderness: The First Century of Urban Life in America, 1625–1742.* New York: Ronald Press.

1955   *Cities in Revolt: Urban Life in America, 1743–1776.* New York: Alfred A. Knopf.

BRIDENBAUGH, CARL, AND JESSICA BRIDENBAUGH

1942   *Rebels and Gentlemen: Philadelphia in the Age of Franklin.* New York: Reynal and Hitchcock.

BRONNER, EDWIN B.

1982   "Village into Town, 1701–1746." In *Philadelphia: A 300-Year History*, edited by Russell F. Weigley. New York: W. W. Norton.

BROWN, WILLIAM FINDLAY

1905   *A Digest of Laws and Ordinances Concerning Philadelphia.* Philadelphia: J. L. H. Bayne.

BRUMBAUGH, G. EDWIN

1959   "Fort Mifflin on Historic Mud Island in the Delaware River, Philadelphia. A Report to the Greater Philadelphia Movement. Nov. 19, 1959." Philadelphia Historical Commission, Philadelphia.

BUCKS COUNTY CONSERVANCY
1979 "Preliminary Research Report for Historic Sites Survey of Bucks County." Bucks County Conservancy, Doylestown, Pa.

BUDKA, METCHIE J. E., ED.
1965 *Under Their Vine and Fig Tree: The American Diary of Julian Ursyn Niemcewicz.* Elizabeth, N.J.: J. E. Budka.

BUREAU OF WATER
1902 *Ninety-Ninth Annual Report of the Bureau of Water for the Year Ending December 31, 1901.* City of Philadelphia Bureau of Water.

BURNETT, EDMUND CODY, ED.
1921–1936 *Letters of Members of the Continental Congress.* Washington, D.C.: The Carnegie Institution of Washington.

BURNSTON, SHARON ANN
1975 "Report on the Faunal Analysis of Head House East Archaeological Project, Feature 10." Unpublished manuscript on file at the Pennsylvania Historical and Museum Commission, Harrisburg, Pa.

1976 "Animal Bones and the Social System: Man-Animal Relationships in Colonial Philadelphia." Unpublished manuscript in author's possession.

1978 "Human Infant Remains from an Eighteenth Century Philadelphia Trash Deposit." Master's thesis, Temple University.

1982 "Babies in the Well: An Underground Insight into Deviant Behavior in Eighteenth Century Philadelphia." *Pennsylvania Magazine of History and Biography* 106 (2): 151–186.

BURT, NATHANIEL, AND WALLACE E. DAVIES
1982 "The Iron Age, 1876–1905." In *Philadelphia: A 300-Year History,* edited by Russell F. Weigley. New York: W. W. Norton.

BUTLER, MARY
1947 "Two Lenape Rock Shelters near Philadelphia." *American Antiquity* 12 (4): 246–255.

BUTTERFIELD, L. H., WENDELL H. GARRETT, AND MARJORIE E. SPRAGUE, EDS.
1963 *Adams Family Correspondence.* Cambridge: Belknap Press of Harvard University Press.

CACCHIONE, EDWARD, AND BERNARD MION
1934 "Philadelphia Region When Known as Coaquannock, 'Grove of Tall Pines,' and as First Seen by the White Men, with Indian Villages, Aboriginal Names of Localities, Streams and Islands, and Their Interpretation." Philadelphia City Planning Commission. Map on file at the University Museum of Archaeology and Anthropology, University of Pennsylvania.

CALLENDER, DONALD, CHRISTOPHER DRENNEN, RICHARD GOETZE, LIZ GREEN, STEPHEN JANDRASZAK, AND SEAN MAHONEY
1975 "Ridley Creek State Park Historic Building Survey No. 1 (North of Gradyville Road)." Report on file at Bishop Mill Historical Institute, Ridley Creek State Park, Media, Pa.

CAMPBELL, J. DUNCAN
1956 "Report on Excavation, Washington Square, Philadelphia, Pennsylvania 12–20 November, 1956." Manuscript on file at the Penn Mutual Life Insurance Company, Philadelphia, and the William Penn Memorial Museum, Harrisburg, Pa.

1958 "Archaeological Field Report, Graeme Park." Report on file at the Pennsylvania Historical and Museum Commission, Harrisburg, Pa.

1959 "Archaeological Survey, Fort Mifflin, Philadelphia, Pennsylvania." Report on file at the Pennsylvania Historical and Museum Commission, Harrisburg, Pa.

1962   "Valley Forge Park, Archaeological Investigations, 30 April–1 June 1962: Preliminary Summary Report," pp. 1–2. Report on file at the Pennsylvania Historical and Museum Commission, Harrisburg, Pa.

1966   "Archaeological Tests, Varnum's Brigade Area, 22–24 August 1966," pp. 1–3. Report on file at the Pennsylvania Historical and Museum Commission, Harrisburg, Pa.

CARBONE, VICTOR A.
1976   "Environment and Prehistory in the Shenandoah Valley." Ph.D. diss., The Catholic University of America, Washington. Ann Arbor, Mich.: University Microfilms.

CAREY, MATHEW
1837   *A Plea for the Poor.* Philadelphia: Mathew Carey.

CARLSON, JANICE
1974   "X-ray Fluorescence Analysis of Metal Artifacts from the Caleb Pusey House." *Transactions of the Delaware Academy of Science* 5:317–331.

CARR, KURT W.
1989   "The Shoop Site: Thirty-five Years After." In *New Approaches to Other Pasts,* edited by W. Fred Kinsey III and Roger W. Moeller. Bethlehem, Conn.: Archaeological Services.

CAVALLO, JOHN
1983–84   "Fish, Fires and Foresight: Middle Woodland Economic Adaptations in the Abbott Farm National Landmark." *North American Archaeologist* 5 (2):111–138.

CEE JAY FREDERICK ASSOCIATES AND JOHN MILNER ASSOCIATES
1981   "Resource Protection Plan: A Framework for Decision-Making in Protecting the Cultural Resources of the Pennsylvania/Delaware River Coastal Zone." Report on file at the Pennsylvania Historical and Museum Commission, Harrisburg, Pa.

CHESTON, EMILY READ
1953   *John Bartram, 1699–1777, His Garden and His House: William Bartram, 1739–1823.* Philadelphia: The John Bartram Association.

CLARKE, J. O.
1929   "Report of Park Engineer, Valley Forge State Park, on Explorations along Valley Creek." In *Report of the Valley Forge Park Commission, 30 August 1927 to 1 June 1929,* p. 32. Report on file at the Pennsylvania Historical and Museum Commission, Harrisburg, Pa.

CLAUSSEN, W. E.
1970   *Wyck: The Story of an Historic House 1690–1970.* Philadelphia: M. T. Haines.

CORPS OF ENGINEERS, U.S. ARMY
n.d.   *Fort Mifflin.* Philadelphia: Technological Liaison Branch, Philadelphia District.

COSANS, BETTY J.
1969   "Interim Report: Excavation of the Morton Mortonson House Kitchen Wing." Report on file with John M. Dickey, Architect, Media, Pa.

1975   "Franklin Court Report," 6 vols. Report prepared for Independence National Historical Park, Philadelphia.

1976   "Interim Report: The 8 South Front Street Site." Report on file at the Philadelphia Historical Commission.

1977   "Area F: Historical Report." Report on file at Independence National Historical Park, Philadelphia.

1982   "A Report on an Archaeological Survey at the Site of the Proposed General Services Administration Office Building, Chester, Pennsylvania." Report prepared for Wagner Associates. John Milner Associates, West Chester, Pa.

1984   "A Report on a Phase I Archaeological Investigation at the Site of the Proposed Society Hill Sheraton Hotel, Front and Dock Streets, Philadelphia, Pennsylvania." Report prepared for Rouse and Associates. John Milner Associates, West Chester, Pa.

COSANS-ZEBOOKER, BETTY

1985 "Front Street: A Study of Mobility, Migration, and Multiple Occupancy in Mid-Nineteenth Century Philadelphia." Paper presented at the Annual Meeting of the Society for Historical Archaeology, Boston.

COSANS-ZEBOOKER, BETTY, AND DAVID BARRETT

1985 "Archaeological Investigations in Association with the Center City Commuter Rail Connector: A Study of Nineteenth Century Urban Development in Philadelphia and Spring Garden." Report prepared for the City of Philadelphia, Department of Public Property. John Milner Associates, West Chester, Pa.

COSANS-ZEBOOKER, BETTY, AND RICHARD MEYER

1985a "Philadelphia Convention Center, Civic Center Reconstruction Alternative: Phase I Archaeological and Architectural Investigations." Report prepared for the Philadelphia Industrial Development Corporation. John Milner Associates, West Chester, Pa.

1985b "Philadelphia Convention Center, Franklintown Proposal Alternative: Phase I Archeological and Architectural Investigations." Report prepared for the Philadelphia Industrial Development Corporation. John Milner Associates, West Chester, Pa.

COSANS-ZEBOOKER, BETTY, RICHARD MEYER, AND VIVIAN YOUNG

1985 "Philadelphia Convention Center, Reading Site Alternative: Phase II Archaeological and Architectural Investigations." Report prepared for the Philadelphia Industrial Development Corporation. John Milner Associates, West Chester, Pa.

COSANS-ZEBOOKER, BETTY, AND MICHAEL PARRINGTON

1983 "Preliminary Archaeological Testing in the Forebay and New Mill House, Fairmount Waterworks, Philadelphia, Pennsylvania." Report prepared for the City of Philadelphia Water Department. John Milner Associates, West Chester, Pa.

1984 "I-95 Access Improvement Program: Phase II Archaeological Investigations." Report prepared for The Delta Group and the Pennsylvania Department of Transportation. John Milner Associates, West Chester, Pa.

COTTER, JOHN L.

1958 "Archaeological Excavations at Jamestown, Virginia." Archaeological Research Series No. 4, Washington, D.C.: National Park Service.

1964a "Archaeological Observations in the Basement of the East Wing Building, Independence Hall: Sub-Floor Walls." Report on file at Independence National Historical Park, Philadelphia.

1964b "Archaeological Report on the Investigation of a Brick Vault Catchment, 'Cistern No. 2,' Beneath the Cement Floor, Basement of Old City Hall." Report on file at Independence National Historical Park, Philadelphia.

1965 "Archaeological Notes and Summary: South Wall of Second Bank, Independence National Historical Park." Report on file at Independence National Historical Park, Philadelphia.

1966a "Archaeological Appendix 'C' in Historic Structures Report II on Independence Hall." Proposal by Lee H. Nelson, Architect. On file at Independence National Historical Park, Philadelphia.

1966b "Man Full of Trouble: The Story of Philadelphia's Oldest Inn." Report on file at University Museum, University of Pennsylvania.

1966c "Preliminary Report on Archaeological Investigations at the Pennsylvania Encampment at Valley Forge, July–October 1966," pp. 1–9, Appendix I. On file at Valley Forge National Historical Park, Valley Forge, Pa. and the University Museum, University of Pennsylvania.

1968 "Current Historic Sites Archaeology in Pennsylvania and New Jersey." *Bulletin of the Philadelphia Anthropological Society* 19 (2): 2–4.

1969 "Fort Mifflin Archaeological Feasibility Study." Report on file at the University Museum, University of Pennsylvania.

1972 "Further Observations on the Hut 9 Excavation," pp. 1–3. Report on file at the University Museum, University of Pennsylvania.

1975 "Archaeological Investigation of Waynesborough: A Field Exercise by the Students of the University of Pennsylvania." Report on file at the University Museum, University of Pennsylvania.

1976 "Harriton Archaeological Tests: Summary Report." Report on file at the University Museum, University of Pennsylvania.

1977 "An Archaeological Feasibility Study of Grumblethorpe." Prepared for the Society for the Preservation of Philadelphia Landmarks. Report on file at the University Museum, University of Pennsylvania.

1980 "Excavating Ben Franklin's House." *Early Man* 2 (2): 17–20.

1985 "The Archaeology of Sporting America." *Expedition* 27 (2): 57–61.

COTTER, JOHN L., AND JOSEPH H. HALL IV
1979 "The Wyck Site: An Archaeological Feasibility Study, July–August, 1979." Report on file at the University Museum, University of Pennsylvania.

COTTER, JOHN L., ROGER W. MOSS, JR., BRUCE C. GILL, AND JIYUL KIM
1988 "The Walnut Street Prison Workshop: A Test Study in Historical Archaeology Based on Field Investigations in the Garden Area of the Philadelphia Athenaeum." Philadelphia: The Athenaeum.

COTTER JOHN L., AND LEE H. NELSON
1964 "Summary of Archaeological Cooperative Work at the North and South Entrances, Independence Hall, and in Front of the East Wing Building, Independence Hall." Report on file at Independence National Historical Park, Philadelphia.

COTTER, JOHN L., AND DAVID ORR
1975 "Historical Archaeology of Philadelphia." *Historical Archaeology* 9:1–10.

COTTER, JOHN L., AND STUDENTS
1967 "Physick House Garden Archaeological Tests." Report on file at the University Museum, University of Pennsylvania.

1969 "Philadelphia's Urban Renewal and the Loss of Heritage: The Federal Building Site." Report on file at the University Museum, University of Pennsylvania.

1975 "Ridley Creek State Farm Project: Excavation of the Water Supply System and Sawmill Complex." Report on file at the University Museum, University of Pennsylvania.

1978a "Archaeological Excavations at Grumblethorpe: The Ice House Test by Partial Excavation." Report prepared for the Society for the Preservation of Philadelphia Landmarks. Also on file at the University Museum, University of Pennsylvania.

1978b "An Archaeological Feasibility Study of the Grange in Haverford Township, Pennsylvania." Report prepared for the Friends of the Grange, Haverford, Pa. Also on file at the University Museum, University of Pennsylvania.

COX, J. LEE, JR.
1984 "Underwater Archaeology Project: A Preliminary Survey to Analyze the Potential Presence of Submerged Cultural Resources in the Delaware and Susquehanna Rivers." Report on file at the Pennsylvania Historical and Museum Commission, Harrisburg, Pa.

CRAMP, ARTHUR J.
1921 *Nostrums and Quackery.* Chicago: American Medical Association.

CRANE, BRIAN D.
1986 "The Burial of a British Soldier in Germantown, Pennsylvania." Senior honors thesis. On file at Dept. of Anthropology, University of Pennsylvania.

CRESS, GEORGE, AND JOHN P. MCCARTHY
1985   "Vine Street Expressway, L.R. 67045: A Phase II Archaeological Investigation in the Block Bounded by Vine, Callowhill, Seventh, and Eighth Streets, Philadelphia, Pennsylvania." Report prepared for Michael Baker, Jr., and the Pennsylvania Department of Transportation. John Milner Associates, West Chester, Pa.

CRESS, GEORGE D., MICHAEL PARRINGTON, WILLIAM R. HENRY, JR., TOD L. BENEDICT, AND PHILIP CARSTAIRS
in prep. a   "Archaeological Data Recovery at the Bailey Tenant Site (36 DE 72), Delaware County, Pennsylvania." Report prepared for the Pennsylvania Department of Transportation. John Milner Associates, West Chester, Pa. Forthcoming.

in prep. b   "Archaeological Data Recovery at the Charles Brown Site (36 DE 73), Delaware County, Pennsylvania." Report prepared for the Pennsylvania Department of Transportation. John Milner Associates, West Chester, Pa. Forthcoming.

in prep. c   "Archaeological Data Recovery at the Isaac Free Site (36 DE 71), Delaware County, Pennsylvania." Report prepared for the Pennsylvania Department of Transportation. John Milner Associates, West Chester, Pa. Forthcoming.

in prep. d   "Archaeological Data Recovery at the Rhoads Whetstone Factory Complex (36 DE 76), Delaware County, Pennsylvania." Report prepared for the Pennsylvania Department of Transportation. John Milner Associates, West Chester, Pa. Forthcoming.

in prep. e   "Archaeological Data Recovery at the Sloan Springhouse (36 DE 75), Delaware County, Pennsylvania." Report prepared for the Pennsylvania Department of Transportation. John Milner Associates, West Chester, Pa. Forthcoming.

in prep. f   "Archaeological Data Recovery at the Speakeasy Dump (36 DE 74), Delaware County, Pennsylvania." Report prepared for the Pennsylvania Department of Transportation. John Milner Associates, West Chester, Pa. Forthcoming.

in prep. g   "Archaeological Data Recovery at the Taylor House Outbuildings (36 DE 81), Delaware County, Pennsylvania." Report prepared for the Pennsylvania Department of Transportation. John Milner Associates, West Chester, Pa. Forthcoming.

CROSS, DOROTHY
1956   *Archaeology of New Jersey, Volume II: The Abbott Farm.* Trenton: Archaeological Society of New Jersey and New Jersey State Museum.

CROWL, G. H., AND R. STUCKENRATH
1977   "Geological Setting of the Shawnee Minisink Paleo Indian Site." In *Amerinds and Their Paleoenvironments in Northeastern North America,* edited by W. S. Newman and B. Salwen. *Annals of the New York Academy of Sciences* 288:218–222.

CROZIER, DANIEL G.
1977a   "Archaeological Investigations, Area F, Independence National Historical Park." Report on file at Independence National Historical Park, Philadelphia.

1977b   "Archaeological Survey Report, Area F." Report on file at Independence National Historical Park, Philadelphia.

1978a   "Archaeological Investigations of the Deshler-Morris House, Germantown." Report on file at Independence National Historical Park, Philadelphia.

1978b   "The Archaeological Salvage of the City Tavern Site." Report on file at Independence National Historical Park, Philadelphia.

CUSHMAN, JULIE MARTIN, AND DANIEL G. ROBERTS
1981   "A Preliminary Archaeological Survey in Selected Areas of the Delaware River Coastal Zone, Southeastern Pennsylvania." Report prepared for the Pennsylvania Historical and Museum Commission, Harrisburg, Pa. John Milner Associates, West Chester, Pa.

CUSTER, J. F.
1984   *Delaware Prehistoric Archaeology.* Newark, Del.: University of Delaware Press.

CUSTER, J. F., AND E. B. WALLACE

1982   "Patterns of Resource Distribution and Archaeological Settlement Patterns in the Piedmont Uplands of the Middle Atlantic Region." *North American Archaeologist* 3:139–172.

DANKO, GEORGE M., AND SARA MATTHEWS

1976   "The Lower Rawle Farm: A Pilot Oral History, 1907 to 1965." Report on file at the University Museum, University of Pennsylvania, and Bishop's Mill Historical Institute, Ridley Creek State Park, Media, Pa.

DAVIS, WILLIAM WATTS HART

1876   *History of Bucks County, Pennsylvania from the Discovery of the Delaware to the Present Time.* Doylestown, Pa.: Democrat Book and Job Office Printers.

DECUNZO, LU ANN, KEITH DOMS, AND JOEL T. FRY

1989   "Final Phase II Report: Cultural Resources Survey of the Magdalen Society Site at the Site of the Futures Center, The Franklin Institute Science Museum, 36 PH 33." Report prepared for the Franklin Institute Science Museum. Clio Group, Philadelphia.

DECUNZO, LU ANN, AND DOUGLAS SANFORD

1978   "An Archaeological Feasibility Study of Fallsington, Pennsylvania." Report on file at the University Museum, University of Pennsylvania.

DEETZ, JAMES

1967   *Invitation to Archaeology.* New York: Natural History Press.

1971   *Man's Imprint from the Past.* Boston: Little, Brown and Co.

1988   "American Historical Archaeology: Methods and Results." *Science* 239:362–367.

DEIHL, RICHARD, AND RICHARD FIDLER

1965   "Graeme Park Report, 1965." Manuscript on file at the Pennsylvania Historical and Museum Commission, Harrisburg, Pa.

DEISHER, HENRY K.

1933   "South Mountain Indian Quarries." *Pennsylvania Archaeologist* 16 (2): 1–13.

DENT, JOHN

1962   *The Quest for Nonsuch.* London: Hutchinson and Co.

DERNER, KAY

1968   *Patent Medicine Picture.* Tombstone, Ariz.: The Tombstone Epitaph.

DERRY, T. K., AND T. I. WILLIAMS

1960   *A Short History of Technology.* New York: Oxford University Press.

DESILVER, ROBERT

1828   *DeSilver's Philadelphia Directory and Stranger's Guide for 1828.* Philadelphia: Robert DeSilver.

DIAMONDSTONE, JUDITH M.

1966   "Philadelphia's Municipal Corporation, 1701–1776." *Pennsylvania Magazine of History and Biography* 90:183–201.

DICKEY, JOHN M.

1975   "The Restoration of the Morton Mortonson House." Paper presented at the Annual Meeting of the Society of Architectural Historians, Boston.

DITCHBURN, ROBERT

1966   "Report on Excavations at Valley Forge, August 15–25, 1966," pp. 1–6. Report on file at the Pennsylvania Historical and Museum Commission, Harrisburg, Pa.

DONEHOO, GEORGE P.

1928   *Indian Villages and Place Names in Pennsylvania.* Baltimore: Gateway Press.

DUNN, MARY MAPLES, AND RICHARD S. DUNN
    1982   "The Founding, 1681–1701." In *Philadelphia: A 300-Year History*, edited by Russell F. Weigley. New York: W. W. Norton.

DU PONCEAU, PETER S., AND J. R. TYSEN
    1852   *Memorial of the American Philosophical Society.* Vol. 1, no. 1: *Minutes of the Provincial Council of Pennsylvania.* Philadelphia: Joseph Severns and Company.

EGLOFF, BRIAN, VANCE PACKARD, AND J. M. RAMSAY
    n.d.   "The Excavation of Four Hut Sites at the Outer Defensive Line of Valley Forge," pp. 1–11. Report on file at the Pennsylvania Historical and Museum Commission, Harrisburg, Pa.

ESTHER, LUCIA E.
    1966a   "First Carbon, Graeme Park, 1700–1801." Manuscript on file at the University Museum, University of Pennsylvania.

    1966b   "Preliminary Report, Graeme Park Archaeological Excavation, 1966." Manuscript on file at the Pennsylvania Historical and Museum Commission, Harrisburg, Pa.

    1967   "Preliminary Report, Graeme Park Archaeological Excavation, 1967." Manuscript on file at the Pennsylvania Historical and Museum Commission, Harrisburg, Pa.

EVANS, JIM
    1985   "The Early Bird Gets the Worm." *Old Bottle Magazine*, pp. 8–10.

FAGEN, M. D., ED.
    1975   *A History of Engineering and Science in the Bell System.* New York: Bell Telephone Laboratories.

FAŸ, BERNARD
    1933   *The Two Franklins: Fathers of American Democracy.* Boston: Little, Brown and Company.

FEDERAL WRITERS' PROJECT
    1988   *WPA Guide to Philadelphia.* Prepared for the Commonwealth of Pennsylvania by the Federal Writers' Project of the Works Progress Administration. Philadelphia: University of Pennsylvania Press.

FISHER, BARBARA
    1962   "Maritime History of the Reading." *Pennsylvania Magazine of History and Biography* 82:160–180.

FLADMARK, KNUT R.
    1983   "Times and Places: Environmental Correlates of Mid to Late Wisconsinian Human Population Expansion in North America." In *Early Man in the New World*, edited by Richard Shutler, Jr., 13–42. Beverly Hills, Calif.: Sage Publications, Inc.

FOLEY, VINCENT P.
    1965   "Market Square Archaeological Project: Interim-Completion Report." Manuscript on file at the Philadelphia Historical Commission.

FORKS OF THE DELAWARE CHAPTER
    1980   "The Overpeck Site (36 BU 5)." *Pennsylvania Archaeologist* 50 (3): 1–46.

FRANKLIN, BENJAMIN
    1749   *Proposals Relating to the Education of Youth in Pennsylvania.* Philadelphia: Benjamin Franklin.

FREY, SYLVIA R.
    1981   *The British Soldier in America: A Social History of Military Life in the Revolutionary Period.* Austin: University of Texas Press.

FRY, JOEL T.
    1986   "Flower Pots as Determiners of Status?" Paper presented at the Annual Meeting of the Society for Historical Archaeology, Sacramento, Calif., January 8–12, 1986.

1988 "A Summary Report of Archaeological Work to Date at the Turbine Pump Wet Well, Fairmount Water Works." Report prepared for the Philadelphia Water Department.

in prep. "Archaeology and John Bartram's Garden: Artifact Analysis and the Material Remains of Historic American Gardens." Ph.D. diss., University of Pennsylvania. Forthcoming.

FUTHEY, JOHN S., AND GILBERT COPE

1881 *History of Chester County, Pennsylvania*. Philadelphia: L. H. Everts.

GARVAN, ANTHONY N.B.

1963 "Proprietary Philadelphia as Artifact." In *The Historian and the City*, edited by Oscar Handlin and John Burchard. Cambridge: MIT Press and Harvard University Press.

1972 "Final Report, Highway Salvage Archaeological Program, Delaware Expressway." Report prepared for the Pennsylvania Department of Transportation.

GATTER, CARL W.

1975 Letter in "Our Readers' Views," *The Philadelphia Bulletin*, August 14.

1981 *Documentation Collection on the Slate Roof House*, 9 vols. On file at Independence National Historical Park, Philadelphia.

1982 "Archaeology at the Site of the Slate Roof House Well." Report on file at Independence National Historical Park, Philadelphia.

GEFFEN, ELIZABETH M.

1982 "Industrial Development and Social Crisis, 1841–1854." In *Philadelphia: A 300-Year History*, edited by Russell F. Weigley. New York: W. W. Norton.

GELL, ELIZABETH ANN MORRIS

1968 "Preliminary Report on the Excavation of Two Privies Under Old City Hall, Independence National Historical Park, Philadelphia." *Bulletin of the Philadelphia Anthropological Society* 1 (1): 3–14.

GEORGE, STAUGHTON, BENJAMIN M. NEAD, AND THOMAS MCCAMANT, EDS.

1879 *Charter to William Penn and Laws of the Province of Pennsylvania, Passed between the Years 1682 and 1700*. Harrisburg, Pa.: Lane S. Hart.

GIANNINI, ROBERT L., III

1980 "Ceramics and Glass from Home and Abroad." In *Treasures of Independence: Independence National Historical Park and Its Collections*, edited by John C. Milley. New York: Mayflower Books.

1981 "Anthony Duché, Sr., Potter and Merchant of Philadelphia." *Antiques* 119 (1): 198–203.

1988 "Thaddeus Kosciuszko National Memorial Furnishing Plan." Report on file at Independence National Historical Park, Philadelphia.

GILBERT/COMMONWEALTH ASSOCIATES

1979 "Cultural Resources Overview and Sensitivity Analysis for the Delaware River and Bay." Report prepared for the Philadelphia District, Corps of Engineers.

GILLESPIE, W. M.

1873 *A Manual of the Principles and Practices of Road-Making*. New York: Barnes and Company.

GLENN, MARSHA L.

1978 *The John Bartram House, 59th Street and Elmwood Avenue, Philadelphia, PA*. Philadelphia: John Bartram Association.

GODDARD, IVES

1978 "Delaware." In *Handbook of North American Indians*. Vol. 15, *Northeast*, edited by Bruce G. Trigger, 213–239. Washington, D.C.: Smithsonian Institution.

GODDEN, GEOFFREY A.
1964   *Encyclopedia of British Pottery and Porcelain Marks.* New York: Bonanza Books.
1965   *Illustrated Encyclopedia of British Pottery and Porcelain.* New York: Bonanza Books.

GOGGIN, JOHN M.
1964   *Indian and Spanish Selected Writings.* Hialeah, Fla.: University of Miami Press.

GOODWIN, BRUCE K.
1964   *Guidebook to the Geology of the Philadelphia Area.* Bulletin G41, Pennsylvania Geological Survey, Fourth Series. Harrisburg, Pa.

GOWANS, ALAN
1964   *Images of American Living: Four Centuries of Architecture and Furniture as Cultural Expression.* Philadelphia: J. B. Lippincott.

GREENE, JEROME A.
1974   "Historic Structures Report, Historical Data Section: Area F, Independence National Historical Park, Pennsylvania." Report prepared for the Denver Service Center, National Park Service, Denver, Colo.

GROUP FOR ENVIRONMENTAL EDUCATION
1984   *Philadelphia Architecture: A Guide to the City.* Prepared for the Foundation of Architecture. Cambridge: MIT Press.

HAGNER, CHARLES V.
1869   *Early History of the Falls of Schuylkill, Manayunk, Schuylkill and Lehigh Navigation Companies, Fairmount Waterworks, etc.* Philadelphia: Claxton, Remsen, and Haffelfinger.

HALL, JOSEPH H., IV
1972a   "A Brief Study of the Zooarchaeology of the Pennsylvania and Virginia Line Huts at Valley Forge," pp. 1–5. Report on file at the University Museum, University of Pennsylvania.
1972b   "The Excavation of Hut 9 on Outer Line Drive, Valley Forge, American Civilization 572, University of Pennsylvania, August 11, 1972," pp. 1–3. Report on file at the University Museum, University of Pennsylvania.
1978   "Archaeology at the Highlands: Social Stratification and the Egalitarian Ideal in Whitemarsh, 1795–1850." Ph.D. diss., University of Pennsylvania.

HALL, JOSEPH H., IV, AND HELEN SCHENCK
1979   "Synthesis of Archaeological Data, Independence National Historical Park." Report prepared for the Denver Service Center, National Park Service, Denver, Colo.

HALLY, DAVID J.
1961   "Archaeological Excavations at Graeme Park, Montgomery County, Pennsylvania, 1961." Manuscript on file at the Pennsylvania Historical and Museum Commission, Harrisburg, Pa.
1962   "Archaeological Excavations at Graeme Park, Montgomery County, Pennsylvania, 1962." Manuscript on file at the Pennsylvania Historical and Museum Commission, Harrisburg, Pa.

HANSON, LEE, AND DICK PING HSU
1975   "Casemates and Cannonballs: Archaeological Investigations at Fort Stanwix, Rome, New York." Publications in Archaeology series, no. 14, National Park Service, Washington, D.C.

HARTZOG, SANDRA
1979   "Palynology and Late Pleistocene Environment on the New Jersey Coastal Plain." *Newsletter of the Archaeological Society of New Jersey* 112:14–18.

HAZARD, SAMUEL
[1860] 1976   *Pennsylvania Archives.* Philadelphia: Joseph Severns and Company.

HECKEWELDER, JOHN

1819   *Transactions of the Historical and Literary Committee of the American Philosophical Society.* Vol. 1, *Historical Account of the Indian Nations.* Philadelphia: Abraham Small.

HEITE, EDWARD F.

1982   "Cultural Resources Reconnaissance in Connection with Petty Island Back Channel." Report prepared for the Corps of Engineers, Philadelphia District, Department of the Army.

HENIG, MARTIN, AND KATHARINE MUNBY

1976   "Some Tiles from the Old Cheshire Cheese, London." *Post-Medieval Archaeology* 10:156–159.

HENRY, WILLIAM R., JR., AND DANIEL G. ROBERTS

1986   "Archaeological Monitoring at the Barns-Brinton House, Pennsbury Township, Chester County, Pennsylvania." Report prepared for the Radnor Restoration and Building Company. John Milner Associates, West Chester, Pa.

HERMAN, BERNARD

1976   "Sycamore Mills, An Industrial Village." Report on file at the Bishop's Mill Historical Institute, Ridley Creek State Park, Media, Pa.

HERSHBERG, THEODORE

1976   "The Philadelphia Social History Project: An Introduction." *Historical Methods Newsletter* 9 (2–3).

HERSHBERG, THEODORE, AND ROBERT DOCKHORN

1976   "Occupational Classification." *Historical Methods Newsletter* 9 (2–3).

HERSHEY, WILLIAM D.

1974   "Independence Hall Sidewalk Salvage Project, 1974." Report on file at Independence National Historical Park, Philadelphia.

HEYL, FRANCIS

1917   *The Battle of Germantown in Philadelphia History.* Philadelphia: The City History Society, pp. 43–64.

HIGBEE, HOWARD W.

1965   *Stream Map of Pennsylvania.* University Park, Pa.: Pennsylvania State University, College of Agriculture, The Agricultural Experiment Station.

HOFFMAN, ROBERT F.

1984   "A Phase I Archaeological Survey of a Proposed Parking Lot and Access Road at Pennypacker Mills, Perkiomen Township, Montomery County, Pennsylvania." Report prepared for the Montgomery County Department of Parks and Historic Sites. John Milner Associates, West Chester, Pa.

HOOD, DEBORAH

1971   "Development of the Dock Creek Area, 1682–1784: A Study in the Cultural Use of Natural Space." Report prepared for American Civilization 571, University of Pennsylvania. On file at the University Museum, University of Pennsylvania.

HOOD, GRAHAM

1968   "The Career of Anthony Duché." *Art Quarterly* 31:168–184.

1969   "New Light on Bonnin and Morris." *Antiques,* June: 812–17.

1972   *Bonnin and Morris of Philadelphia: The First American Porcelain Factory, 1770–1772.* Chapel Hill: University of North Carolina Press.

HUEY, PAUL R.

1967   "Sketches of Artifacts Excavated for the Pennsylvania Historical Salvage Council, Philadelphia, 1967." Unpublished manuscript in author's possession.

1968a   "Description and Analysis of Saggers from the Bonnin and Morris China Factory, Southwark, Philadelphia, 1770–1772." Manuscript on file at the University Museum, University of Pennsylvania.

1968b   "The Old China Factory Neighborhood in Southwark, Philadelphia, after 1777." Manuscript on file at the University Museum, University of Pennsylvania.

HUNTER, CHARLES EDWARD
   1979   "The Archaeology of High Ward, Philadelphia." Ph.D. diss., American University.

HUNTER, CHARLES E., AND HERBERT W. LEVY
   1976   "Report on the Archaeological Salvage Excavations on the Northwest Side of Market and Front Streets." Report prepared for the Pennsylvania Department of Transportation.

HUNTER, CHARLES, AND VANCE PACKARD
   1973a   "Preliminary Summary Report on Excavations at Varnum's Headquarters, 1972–1973," pp. 1–21. Report on file at the Pennsylvania Historical and Museum Commission, Harrisburg, Pa.

   1973b   "Preliminary Summary Report on Excavations at Washington's Headquarters, 1973," pp. 1–8, K1–5, unnumbered. Report on file at the Pennsylvania Historical and Museum Commission, Harrisburg, Pa.

HUSEMAN, MARJORIE
   1975   "A Study of British Transfer-Printed Pottery Found in Franklin Court in Philadelphia." Report prepared for American Studies, University of Pennsylvania. On file at the University Museum, University of Pennsylvania.

JACKSON, CHARLES O.
   1980   "Death Shall Have No Dominion: The Passing of the World of the Dead in America." In *Death and Dying: Views from Many Cultures*, edited by Richard A. Kalish, 47–55. Farmingdale, N.Y.: Baywood Publishing Company.

JACKSON, JOSEPH
   1932   *America's Most Historic Highway, Market Street, Philadelphia* (new edition). Philadelphia: John Wanamaker.

JACKSON, KENNETH T.
   1975   "Urban Deconcentration in the Nineteenth Century: A Statistical Inquiry." In *The New Urban History*, edited by Leo F. Schnore, 110–144. Princeton, N.J.: Princeton University Press.

JEHLE, PATRICIA ANNE, AND KURT W. CARR
   1983   "The Southeast Pennsylvania Upland Archaeological Project: Intrasite Analysis of Plowzone Sites." Report submitted to the Pennsylvania Historical and Museum Commission, Harrisburg, Pa., by the Bureau of State Parks.

JELLETT, EDWIN C.
   1904   "Germantown, Old and New: Its Rare and Notable Plants." Philadelphia: Horace F. McCann.

JENNINGS, FRANCIS
   1986   "Brother Miquon: Good Lord!" In *The World of William Penn*, edited by Richard S. Dunn and Mary Maples Dunn. Philadelphia: University of Pennsylvania Press.

JENNINGS, SAMUEL M.
   1852   *The Life of William Penn.* Philadelphia: Hogan, Perkins, and Co.

JOHN MILNER ASSOCIATES
   1979   "Historical and Archaeological Survey of Frankford Arsenal, Philadelphia, Pennsylvania." Report prepared for the Corps of Engineers, Baltimore District, Department of the Army. John Milner Associates, West Chester, Pa.

JOIRÉ, KENNETH M., AND DANIEL G. ROBERTS
    1986   "Archaeological Monitoring in Conjunction with the Replacement of Utility Lines at Morton Homestead, Prospect Park, Delaware County, Pennsylvania." Report prepared for the Redevelopment Authority of the County of Delaware. John Milner Associates, West Chester, Pa.

JORDAN, RICHARD H.
    1978   "Report on the Bryn Mawr College Excavations at the Highlands Society, Fort Washington, Pennsylvania." Report on file at the Pennsylvania Historical and Museum Commission, Harrisburg, Pa.

JORDAN, RICHARD H., AND M. E. COLLEEN LAZENBY
    1983   "Archaeological Investigations at Pennsbury Manor Site West Field (36 BU 172)." Report prepared for Falls Township, Pa.

JORDAN, RICHARD H., AND PAMELA DE TOLEDO
    1976   "A Report on the 1975–76 Archaeological Investigations of the Inner Line Fortifications at Valley Forge State Park, June 1976," pp. 1–17. Report on file at the Pennsylvania Historical and Museum Commission, Harrisburg, Pa.

KARDAS, SUSAN, AND EDWARD M. LARRABEE
    1982   "Archaeological Survey for Two Landfill Sites at the Fairless Works, U.S. Steel, Falls Township, Bucks County, Pennsylvania." Report prepared for The Chester Engineers. Princeton, N.J.: Historic Sites Research.

    1986   "Exploratory Archaeology at Three Historic Sites: Graeme Park, Pennsbury Manor, Moon-Williamson House." Report prepared for the Pennsylvania Historical and Museum Commission. Princeton, N.J.: Historic Sites Research.

KAUFFMAN, BARBARA E., AND RICHARD J. DENT
    1982   "Preliminary and Faunal Recovery and Analysis at the Shawnee-Minisink Site (36 MR 43)." In *Practicing Environmental Archaeology: Methods and Interpretations*, edited by Roger W. Moeller, 7–12. Occasional Paper No. 3. Washington, Conn.: American Indian Archaeological Institute.

KELLEY, JENNIFER OLSEN, AND J. LAWRENCE ANGEL
    1989   "The First African Baptist Church Cemetery: Bioarcheology, Demography, and Acculturation of Early Nineteenth Century Philadelphia Blacks. Volume III, Osteological Analysis." Report prepared for the Redevelopment Authority of the City of Philadelphia. Smithsonian Institution, Washington, D.C.

KENT, BARRY C.
    1980   *Discovering Pennsylvania's Archaeological Heritage.* Harrisburg, Pa.: Pennsylvania Historical and Museum Commission.

KENT, BARRY C., JANET RICE, AND KAKUKO OTA
    1981   "A Map of 18th Century Indian Towns in Pennsylvania." *Pennsylvania Archaeologist* 51 (4): 1–18.

KENT, DONALD H., ED.
    1979   *Pennsylvania and Delaware Treaties, 1629–1737.* Vol. 1, *Early American Indian Documents: Treaties and Laws, 1607–1789.* Washington, D.C.: University Publications of America.

KENYON, JEFFREY L.
    1975   "Preliminary Investigation of the Franklin Square Powder Magazine in Philadelphia." Report on file at the Philadelphia Historical Commission.

    1976   "Summary Report on the Application of Ground Penetrating Radar to the Stenton Mansion Complex." Museum Historic Research Center, University Museum, University of Pennsylvania.

1977a   "Back-Testing for Evaluation of Selected Radar Profiles at the Stenton Mansion Complex." Museum Historic Research Center, University Museum, University of Pennsylvania.

1977b   "The Gorgas Mill Complex Project." Ph.D. diss., University of Pennsylvania.

KENYON, JEFFREY L., AND BRUCE BEVAN
1977   "Ground Penetrating Radar and Its Application to a Historical Archaeological Site." *Historical Archaeology* 11:48–55.

KENYON, JEFFREY L., AND STANLEY M. HUNTER
1974   "Archaeological Feasibility and Basic Research Study of Yellow Springs Tract, Chester County, Pennsylvania." Museum Historic Research Center, University Museum, University of Pennsylvania.

KENYON, JEFFREY L., STANLEY M. HUNTER, AND HELEN SCHENCK
1975   "Basic Historic Research and Archaeological Feasibility Study of Bartram Park." Museum Historic Research Center, University Museum, University of Pennsylvania.

KENYON, JEFFREY L., STANLEY M. HUNTER, HELEN SCHENCK, AND PATRICIA THATCHER
1975   "Stenton Barn Project: Archaeological Evaluation of Stenton Barn for Proposed Restoration." Museum Historic Research Center, University Museum, University of Pennsylvania.

KENYON, JEFFREY L., JACQUELINE THIBAUT, AND HELEN SCHENCK
1977   "Report on the Preliminary Archaeological Excavations Conducted at Yellow Springs, Chester County, Pennsylvania." Museum Historic Research Center, University Museum, University of Pennsylvania.

KERRIGAN, JAMES, AND VANCE PACKARD
1973   "Report on the 1973 Archaeological Excavations at the Site of General Jedidiah Huntington's 1778–9 [*sic*] Quarters, Valley Forge State Park, Montgomery and Chester Counties, Pennsylvania, November 15, 1973," pp. 1–9. Report on file at the Pennsylvania Historical and Museum Commission, Harrisburg, Pa.

KIER, CHARLES F., AND FRED CALVERLY
1957   "The Raccoon Point Site, An Early Hunting and Fishing Station in the Lower Delaware Valley." *Pennsylvania Archaeologist* 27 (2): 61–101.

KIM, JIYUL
1978   "The Applicability of South's Methods as Tested on the Walnut Street Prison Site." *The Conference on Historic Sites Archaeology Papers, 1977,* pp. 107–144.

KIMBALL, DAVID A.
1961   "Furnishing Plan for the Bishop White House, Volume I, Part B, Historical Narrative, Part C, Documented Accounts of Historic Furnishings." Report on file at Independence National Historical Park, Philadelphia.

1989   *Venerable Relic: The Story of the Liberty Bell.* Philadelphia: Eastern National Park and Monuments Association.

KING, ROBERT E., AND MARY HANCOCK
1970   "A Feasibility Study for Possible Future Excavations in Search of Governor Johan Printz's Settlement in Tinicum Island." Report on file at the University Museum, University of Pennsylvania.

KINGSLEY, ROBERT G., JAMES A. ROBERTSON, AND DANIEL G. ROBERTS
in prep.   "The Archaeology of the Lower Schuylkill River Valley in Southeastern Pennsylvania." Report prepared for the Philadelphia Electric Company. John Milner Associates, West Chester, Pa. Forthcoming.

KINSEY, W. FRED, III
1975   "Faucett and Byram Sites: Chronology and Settlement in the Delaware Valley." *Pennsylvania Archaeologist* 45 (1–2): 1–103.

KITTREDGE, SELWYN
1974   "Digging up Viking and Mediaeval Dublin." *Archaeology* 27 (2): 134–136.

KLEIN, H. A.
1963   *Graphic Worlds of Peter Breugel the Elder.* New York: Dover Press.

KNECHT, RICHARD A., AND RICHARD JORDAN
1984   "Archaeological Investigations at Keyser Mill (36 MG 164), Evansburg State Park, Lower Providence Township, Montgomery County, Pennsylvania." Report prepared for the Bureau of State Parks, Pennsylvania Department of Environmental Resources.

KOLB, CHARLES C.
1971   "Excavations at Harriton, 1971: Archaeological Site Report for Harriton, Bryn Mawr, Pennsylvania." Bryn Mawr Occasional Papers in Anthropology, no. 1. Bryn Mawr, Pa.: Bryn Mawr College.

KRAFT, HERBERT C.
1970   *The Miller Field Site, Warren County, New Jersey.* Part 1, *The Archaic and Transitional Stages.* South Orange, N.J.: Seton Hall University Press.
1974   "Indian Prehistory of New Jersey." In *A Delaware Indian Symposium*, edited by H. C. Kraft, 1–56. Anthropological Series, no. 4. Harrisburg, Pa.: Pennsylvania Historical and Museum Commission.
1975   *The Archaeology of the Tocks Island Area.* South Orange, N.J.: Archaeological Research Center, Seton Hall University Museum.
1984   "The Northern Lenape in Prehistoric and Early Colonial Times." In *The Lenape Indian: A Symposium*, edited by Herbert C. Kraft, 1–10. Publication no. 7. South Orange, N.J.: Archaeological Research Center, Seton Hall University.

KRAMER, EMMANUEL M.
1979   "The Archaeology of Local History in Glenside, Pennsylvania." *Old York Road Historical Society Bulletin* 39:27–39.
1982   "The Penn House Site." *Old York Road Historical Society Bulletin* 42:36–50.

KUNKLE, W. MERRILL
1963   *Soil Survey of Chester and Delaware Counties, Pennsylvania.* Washington, D.C.: Soil Conservation Service, U.S. Department of Agriculture.

LAPSANSKY, EMMA, AND BETTY COSANS
1968   "Excavation in the Basement of the Kensington Methodist Episcopal Church, Northeast Corner of Marlborough and Richmond Streets, Philadelphia, Pennsylvania." Report on file at the University Museum, University of Pennsylvania.

LAPSANSKY, EMMA J., AND JAMES R. ZAKAS
1968   "Excavations of July and August, 1968 at the Bonnin and Morris Porcelain Factory Site, 124 Alter Street, Southwark, Philadelphia, Pennsylvania." Report on file at the University Museum, University of Pennsylvania.

LA ROCHEFOUCAULD-LIENCOURT, FRANCOIS A. E., DUC DE
1796   *On the Prisons of Philadelphia, by an European.* Philadelphia: Morcau de St.-Mary.

LASSEN, CORYL
1976   "Preliminary Report: Basement Site at 310 Cypress Street." Report on file at the University Museum, University of Pennsylvania.

LAWRENCE, CHARLES
1905   *History of the Philadelphia Almshouses and Hospitals From the Beginning of the Eighteenth to the Ending of the Nineteenth Centuries.* Philadelphia, Pa.: [privately printed].

LAZENBY, COLLEEN, AND SAMUEL LANDIS
1983 "Report on Archaeological Excavations at the Snodgrass Farm, Lower Southampton Township, Bucks County, Pennsylvania." Bucks County Conservancy, Doylestown, Pa.

LEEDECKER, CHARLES H.
1983 "Managing Archaeological Resources in Fairmount Park." Report prepared for Wallace, Roberts and Todd. Soil Systems Division, Professional Services Industries, Marietta, Ga.

LEVERETT, FRANK
1957 *Glacial Deposits Outside the Wisconsin Terminal Moraine in Pennsylvania.* Pennsylvania Geological Survey, fourth series, bulletin G7. Harrisburg, Pa.

LEVY, HERBERT
1978 "Report on the Archaeological Services (Document Search) for the Center City Commuter Rail Connection." Report prepared for the City of Philadelphia, Department of Public Property.

LEWIS, LYNNE G.
1979 "Archaeological Investigations at Cliveden, Germantown, Pennsylvania, 1978–1979." Report prepared for National Trust for Historic Preservation. Report on file at Cliveden and at National Trust for Historic Preservation, Washington, D.C.

LEWIS, MARY BUTLER
1969 "Morton Mortonson House, Norwood, PA: Archaeologists' Report." Report on file with John M. Dickey, Architect, Media, Pa.

LIGGETT, BARBARA
1967 "Report on the Completion of Hope Lodge Contract." Report on file at the Pennsylvania Historical and Museum Commission, Harrisburg, Pa.
1970a "Archaeological Work at Franklin Court." Manuscript on file at Independence National Historical Park, Philadelphia.
1970b "Completion Report, Franklin Court." Report on file at Independence National Historical Park, Philadelphia.
1970c "The Dock Project, Philadelphia: Artifact Methodology." Report on file at the Pennsylvania Historical and Museum Commission, Harrisburg, Pa.
1970d "Summary Report on Archaeology at Stenton." Report prepared for the National Society of the Colonial Dames of America, Philadelphia.
1971a "The Archaeology of Philadelphia: The Dock and Budd's Row." Paper presented at the Annual Meeting of the Society of Architectural Historians, Chicago.
1971b "Final Report: Archaeology at the Franklin House Site." Report on file at Independence National Historical Park, Philadelphia.
1971c "Final Report, Franklin Court." Report on file at Independence National Historical Park, Philadelphia.
1973 *Archaeology at Franklin's Court.* Harrisburg, Pa.: The McFarland Company.
1975 "Urban Archaeology in Eastern United States." Ph.D. diss., University of Pennsylvania.
1977 "Excavations at Fort Mifflin." Report on file at the Atwater-Kent Museum, Philadelphia.
1978a "Archaeological Excavations at the New Market Site." Unpublished manuscript in author's possession.
1978b "Archaeological Survey, the Manayunk Canal." Report prepared for the City of Philadelphia Water Department.
1978c *Archaeology at New Market: Exhibit Catalogue.* Philadelphia: The Athenaeum.
1978d "Final Report on the Excavations of the North Salient, Fort Mifflin." Report prepared for the Department of Recreation, City of Philadelphia.

1981 *Archaeology at New Market: Excavation Report.* Philadelphia: The Athenaeum.

n.d. "Dock Creek Report." Report on file at the American Philosophical Society, Philadelphia.

LIGGETT, BARBARA, AND SANDRA LAUMARK
1979 "The Counterfort at Fort Mifflin." *Bulletin of the Association for Preservation Technology* 11 (1): 37–74.

LINDESTROM, PETER
[1656] 1925 *Geographiae Americae, With an Account of the Delaware Indians, Based on Surveys and Notes Made in 1654–1656 by Peter Lindestrom.* Translated and edited by Amandus Johnson. Philadelphia: The Swedish Colonial Society.

LLOYD, SANDRA MACKENZIE
1986 "Historic Structures Report on Wyck." Prepared for John M. Dickey, Architect, Media, Pa.

LONG, AMOS, JR.
1963 "Outdoor Privies in the Dutch Country." *Pennsylvania Folklife Magazine* 63 (3): 33–46.

LOPEZ, CLAUDE ANNE
1981 *Benjamin Franklin's Good House.* Handbook 114. Washington, D.C.: Department of the Interior.

LORRAIN, DESSAMAE
1968 "An Archaeologist's Guide to Nineteenth Century American Glass." *Historical Archaeology* 11:35–44.

LOSKIEL, G. H.
1794 *History of the Mission of the United Brethren among the Indians in North America.* Translated by Christian Ignatius LaTrobe. London: The Brethren Society for the Furtherance of the Gospel.

MAASS, JOHN
1973 *The Glorious Enterprise: The Centennial Exposition of 1876 and H. J. Schwarzmann, Architect-in-Chief.* Watkins Glen, N.Y.: American Life Foundation.

MACDONALD, WILLIAM K., AND ALEX H. TOWNSEND
1975 "Barns-Brinton House, Chadds Ford, Pennsylvania: A Report of Archaeological Excavations Undertaken by National Heritage Corporation." Report prepared for the Chadds Ford Historical Society. National Heritage Corporation, West Chester, Pa.

MACKENZIE, SANDRA F.
1979 "What a Beauty There Is in Harmony: The Reuben Haines Family of Wyck." Master's thesis, University of Delaware.

MANT, A. KEITH
1957 "Adipocere: A Review." *Journal of Forensic Medicine* 4:18–35.

MARTIN, JOSEPH PLUMB
1979 *Private Yankee Doodle, Being a Narrative of Some of the Adventures, Dangers, and Sufferings of a Revolutionary Soldier,* edited by George E. Scheer. Philadelphia: Acorn Press.

MARTIN, PAUL S.
1958 "Taiga-Tundra and the Full-Glacial Period in Chester County, Pennsylvania." *American Journal of Science* 256:470–502.

MASON, J. ALDEN
1947 "The Broomall Rock Shelters." *Tredyffrin Easttown History Club Quarterly* 6 (4): 81–88.

MASON, RONALD J.
　　1959　"Indications of PaleoIndian Occupation in the Delaware Valley." *Pennsylvania Archaeologist* 29 (1): 1–17.

MASSEY, JAMES C.
　　1969　*Historical American Buildings Survey, Fort Mifflin.* Washington, D.C.: Library of Congress.

MCCARTHY, JOHN P.
　　1984a　"Archaeological and Architectural Investigations of Selected Outbuildings at the Peter Wentz Farmstead, Worcester Township, Montgomery County, Pennsylvania." Report prepared for Montgomery County Department of Parks and Historic Sites. John Milner Associates, West Chester, Pa.

　　1984b　"Phase II Archaeological Investigations at the Site of the Proposed Society Hill Sheraton Hotel, Front and Dock Streets, Philadelphia, Pennsylvania." Report prepared for Rouse and Associates. John Milner Associates, West Chester, Pa.

　　1984c　"Vine Street Expressway, L.R. 67045: A Phase II Archaeological Investigation in the Block Bounded by Ninth, Tenth, Vine, and Winter Streets, Philadelphia, Pennsylvania." Report prepared for Michael Baker, Jr., and the Pennsylvania Department of Transportation. John Milner Associates, West Chester, Pa.

　　n.d.　"Report on Test Excavations in the Mill Village: Edgemont House No. 109 Test Pit Project." Report on file at Bishop's Mill Historical Institute, Ridley Creek State Park, Media, Pa.

MCCARTHY, JOHN P., BETTY COSANS-ZEBOOKER, AND WILLIAM R. HENRY, JR.
　　1985　"Philadelphia Privies and Their Fills: A Consideration of Their Interpretive Value." Paper presented at the Middle Atlantic Archaeological Conference, Rehoboth Beach, Del.

MCCARTHY, JOHN P., AND STEPHEN H. GRAFF
　　1983　"Archaeological Survey Report, I-476, Task Force Alignment." Report prepared for the Federal Highway Administration and the Pennsylvlania Department of Transportation. Cultural Heritage Research Services, New Castle, Del.

MCCARTHY, JOHN P., AND JAMES MOFFET
　　1980　"Sycamore Mills: A Rural Industrial Village at the Beginning of the 19th Century." Report on file at Bishop's Mill Historical Institute, Ridley Creek State Park, Media, Pa.

MCCARTHY, JOHN P., AND DANIEL G. ROBERTS, EDS.
　　in prep.　"Archeological Data Recovery at the Site of the Society Hill Sheraton Hotel, Front and Dock Streets, Philadelphia, Pennsylvania." Report prepared for Rouse and Associates. John Milner Associates, West Chester, Pa. Forthcoming.

MCCARTHY, JOHN P., EVELYN M. TIDLOW, GEORGE CRESS, AND STEPHANIE PINTER
　　1987　"Vine Street Expressway, L.R. 67045: Archeological Data Recovery in the Block Bounded by Ninth, Tenth, Vine, and Winter Streets, Philadelphia, Pennsylvania." Report prepared for the Pennsylvania Department of Transportation and the Federal Highway Administration. John Milner Associates, Philadelphia.

MCDANNELL, COLLEEN
　　1987　"The Religious Symbolism of Laurel Hill Cemetery." *Pennsylvania Magazine of History and Biography* 111 (3): 275–303.

MCFARLAND, JOSEPH
　　1942　"Rummaging in the Museum II: The Petrified Lady." *Transactions and Studies of the College of Physicians of Philadelphia,* 4th ser., 10 (2): 138–143.

MCGREGOR, MALCOLM, AND JOHN MOLLS
　　1975　*Uniforms of the American Revolution.* New York: Macmillan.

MCHUGH, WILLIAM P.
  1983   "Delaware River Comprehensive Navigation Study (Interim): Cultural Resources Sensitivity Reconnaissance." Report prepared for the Corps of Engineers, Philadelphia District, Department of the Army.

MCNETT, CHARLES W., JR., ED.
  1985   *Shawnee Minisink: A Stratified Paleoindian-Archaic Site in the Upper Delaware Valley of Pennsylvania.* New York: Academic Press.

MCNETT, CHARLES W., JR., B. A. MCMILLAN, AND S. B. MARSHALL
  1977   "The Shawnee-Minisink Site." In *Amerinds and Their Paleoenvironments in Northeastern North America,* edited by W. S. Newman and B. Salwen. *Annals of the New York Academy of Sciences* 288:282–296.

MELVIN, FRANK W.
  1940   "The Romance of the Pennsbury Manor Restoration." *Pennsylvania History* 7:3.

MERCER, HENRY C.
  1923   "An Attempt to Find the Site of the Indian Town of Playwicky." *Bucks County Historical Society Journal* 5:500–508.

MEYER, RICHARD, AND BETTY COSANS-ZEBOOKER
  1984   "I-95 Access Improvement Program: Phase I Archaeological Investigations and Phase I and II Architectural Investigations." Report prepared for The Delta Group and the Pennsylvania Department of Transportation. John Milner Associates, West Chester, Pa.

MEYER, RICHARD, AND MICHAEL PARRINGTON
  1983   "A Preliminary Cultural Resources Survey of the Proposed Philadelphia Convention Center Site Bounded by Race, Market, Eleventh, and Thirteenth Streets, Philadelphia, Pennsylvania." Report prepared for Eastern Real Estate Company. John Milner Associates, West Chester, Pa.

MID-ATLANTIC ARCHAEOLOGICAL RESEARCH (MAAR)
  1977   "A Cultural Resource Survey of the Delcora Sewer Force Main Project." Report prepared for Betz Environmental Engineering, Newark, Del.
  1978   "Archaeological Data Recovery Operations at the Morton Homestead." Report prepared for BCM Environmental Engineers, Newark, Del.

MILLER, GEORGE L.
  1984   "George M. Coates, Pottery Merchant of Philadelphia." *Winterthur Portfolio* 19:37–49.

MILLER, RICHARD G.
  1982   "The Federal City, 1783–1800." In *Philadelphia: A 300-Year History,* edited by Russell F. Weigley. New York: W. W. Norton.

MOORE, JACKSON W.
  1959a   "Archaeological Investigations of the Carriage House." Report on file at Independence National Historical Park, Philadelphia.
  1959b   "Excavation of the Portico Site, Independence National Historical Park, Philadelphia, PA." Report on file at Independence National Historical Park, Philadelphia.
  1960   "Archaeological Data." In "Historic Structures Report, Part II on Dilworth-Todd-Moylan House." Report on file at Independence National Historical Park, Philadelphia.

MORLEY, JOHN
  1971   *Death, Heaven and the Victorians.* Pittsburgh, Pa.: University of Pittsburgh Press.

MORTON, ROBERT
  1877   "The Diary of Robert Morton." *Pennsylvania Magazine of History and Biography* 1 (1): 1–39.

MOWER, D. ROGER, JR.
    1983   *Bartram's Garden.* Philadelphia: John Bartram Association.

MULCAHY, JAMES M.
    1956   "Congress Voting Independence: The Trumbull and Pine-Savage Paintings." *The Pennsylvania Magazine of History and Biography* 80 (1): 74–91.

MYERS, ALBERT COOK
    1937   "Preliminary Report on the Archaeological Research at Pennsbury." In *Sixth Report of the Pennsylvania Historical Commission, 1931–1934,* 42–46. Harrisburg, Pa.: Pennsylvania Historical Commission.

MYERS, SUSAN H.
    1977   "A Survey of Traditional Pottery Manufacture in the Mid-Atlantic and Northeastern United States." *Northeast Historical Archaeology* 6 (1–2): 1–13.

    1980   *Handcraft to Industry: Philadelphia Ceramics in the First Half of the Nineteenth Century.* Washington, D.C.: Smithsonian Institution Press.

NASH, GARY B.
    1986   "The Early Merchants of Philadelphia: The Formation and Disintegration of a Founding Elite." In *The World of William Penn,* edited by Richard S. Dunn and Mary Maples Dunn. Philadelphia: University of Pennsylvania Press.

NASH, GARY, AND BILLY G. SMITH.
    1975   "The Population of Eighteenth-Century Philadelphia." *Pennsylvania Magazine of History and Biography* 99 (3): 362–368.

NATIONAL HERITAGE CORPORATION
    1975   "Master Plan, Peter Wentz Farmstead." Report prepared for the Commissioners of Montgomery County, Pennsylvania. National Heritage Corporation, West Chester, Pa.

NELLIGAN, MURRAY H.
    1969   "Special Report, Fort Mifflin, Pennsylvania: The War for Independence." National Survey of Historic Sites and Buildings, March 12, 1969. National Park Service, U.S. Department of the Interior, Philadelphia.

NELSON, LEE H.
    1976   "Independence Hall: Its Fabric Reinforced." Chap. 15 in *Building Early America,* edited by Charles E. Peterson. Radnor, Pa.: Chilton Book Co.

NELSON, LEE H., AND JOHN L. COTTER
    1964   "East Wing Sidewalk Well Report." Report on file at Independence National Historical Park, Philadelphia.

NELSON, PAUL D.
    1976   "Lee, Gates, Stephen, and Morgan: Revolutionary War Generals of the Lower Shenandoah Valley." *West Virginia Quarterly* 37 (3): 186–194.

NEWCOMB, WILLIAM W., JR.
    1956   *The Culture and Acculturation of the Delaware Indians.* Anthropological Papers, no. 10, Museum of Anthropology, University of Michigan.

NOËL HUME, IVOR
    1970   *A Guide to Artifacts of Colonial America.* New York: Alfred A. Knopf.

OHNO, MARK
    1978   "Hilton Hotel Site Excavations, Philadelphia." Report on file at the University Museum Library, University of Pennsylvania.

OKIE, R. BROGNARD
    1941   "The Recreation of Penn's Manor." *Tredyffrin Easttown History Club Quarterly,* April 1941 and July 1941.

OLSEN, STANLEY J.
1964   "Food Animals of the Continental Army at Valley Forge and Norristown." *American Antiquity* 29 (4): 506–509.

ORR, DAVID G.
1977   "Philadelphia as Industrial Archaeological Artifact: A Case Study." *Historical Archaeology* 11:3–14.

ORR, DAVID G., BROOKE S. BLADES, AND DOUGLAS V. CAMPANA
1985   "Archaeological Survey within the Virginia Brigade Area, Valley Forge National Historical Park." Report on file at Valley Forge National Historical Park, Valley Forge, Pa.

ORR, DAVID, AND HERBERT LEVY
1985   "The Point Breeze Gas Works." Unpublished manuscript on file at Mid-Atlantic Regional Office, National Park Service, Philadelphia.

PACKARD, VANCE
1972   "Salvage Archaeology at Valley Forge." *Pennsylvania Heritage* 5 (4).

1973   "Valley Forge Interim Report," pp. 1–5. Report on file at Pennsylvania Historical and Museum Commission, Harrisburg, Pa.

PALMER, ARLENE M.
1979   "A Philadelphia Glasshouse, 1794–1797." *Journal of Glass Studies* 21:102–114.

PARRINGTON, MICHAEL
1979a   "Archaeology at Area F, Independence National Historical Park, Philadelphia." Report on file at Independence National Historical Park, Philadelphia.

1979b   "Excavations at the 'Seed House' at Bartram's Garden, Philadelphia, 1979." Report prepared by the Museum Institute for Conservation Archaeology, University of Pennsylvania.

1979c   "Geophysical and Aerial Prospecting Techniques at Valley Forge National Historical Park, Pennsylvania." *Journal of Field Archaeology* 6 (2): 193–201.

1979d   "Report on the Excavation of Part of the Virginia Brigade Encampment, Valley Forge, Pennsylvania 1972–1973." Report prepared for the National Park Service by the Museum Applied Science Center for Archaeology, University of Pennsylvania.

1979–80   "Revolutionary War Archaeology at Valley Forge, Pennsylvania." *North American Archaeologist* 1 (2): 161–176.

1980a   "Archaeology at Sansom Street, Area F, Independence National Historical Park, Philadelphia, PA, 1979." Report on file at Independence National Historical Park, Philadelphia.

1980b   "Archaeology at Wyck, Germantown, PA." Report prepared by the Museum Institute for Conservation Archaeology, University of Pennsylvania.

1980c   "Salvage Archaeology at Area F, Independence National Historical Park, Philadelphia." Report on file at Independence National Historical Park, Philadelphia.

1981a   "Medical Archaeology in Philadelphia: A Study of Early Twentieth Century Medicine Bottles Excavated at Bartram's Garden." *Expedition* 23 (3): 34–38.

1981b   "Salvage Archaeology at the State in Schuylkill Fishing Club, Andalusia, Bucks County, PA." Report prepared for the State in Schuylkill Fishing Club, Andalusia, Pa.

1983   "The History and Archaeology of Philadelphia Roads, Streets, and Utility Lines." *Pennsylvania Archaeologist* 53 (3): 19–31.

1984a   "An Archaeological and Historical Investigation of the Burial Ground at Old St. Paul's Church, Philadelphia, Pennsylvania." Report prepared for J. S. Cornell and Sons. John Milner Associates, West Chester, Pa.

1984b   "Frederick Graff: Waterworks Engineer Par Excellence." *American Public Works Association Reporter*, September, 4–5.

1987 "Cemetery Archaeology in the Urban Environment: A Case Study from Philadelphia." In *Living in Cities: Current Research in Urban Archaeology*, 56–64. Special Publication Series, no. 5. Ann Arbor, Mich.: Society for Historical Archaeology.

PARRINGTON, MICHAEL, GEORGE CRESS, AND EVELYN M. TIDLOW
1986 "A Phase II Archaeological Survey of the Block Bounded by Callowhill Street, Seventeenth Street, and Franklintown Boulevard (Parcel 9), Philadelphia, Pennsylvania." Report prepared for Forest City Dillon. John Milner Associates, West Chester, Pa.

PARRINGTON, MICHAEL, AND ROBERT F. HOFFMAN
1984 "A Preliminary Archaeological Survey of Pennypacker Mills, Perkiomen Township, Montgomery County, Pennsylvania." Report prepared for the Montgomery County Department of Parks and Historic Sites. John Milner Associates, West Chester, Pa.

PARRINGTON, MICHAEL, AND KAREN LIND
1985 "A Phase I Archeological Survey of the Site of the Former Philadelphia General Hospital, Philadelphia, Pennsylvania." Report prepared for the Health Center Facilities Committee, University of Pennsylvania. John Milner Associates, Philadelphia, Pa.

PARRINGTON, MICHAEL, STEPHANIE PINTER, AND THOMAS STRUTHERS
1986 "Occupations and Health Amongst Early Nineteenth Century Black Philadelphians." *MASCA Journal* 8 (1): 37–41.

PARRINGTON, MICHAEL, AND DANIEL G. ROBERTS
1984 "The First African Baptist Church Cemetery: An Archaeological Glimpse of Philadelphia's Nineteenth Century Free Black Community." *Archaeology Magazine* 37 (6): 26–32.

1990 "Demographic, Cultural, and Bioanthropological Aspects of a Nineteenth-Century Free Black Population in Philadelphia, Pennsylvania." In *A Life in Science: Papers in Honor of J. Lawrence Angel*, edited by Jane E. Buikstra, pp. 138–170. Scientific Papers of the Center for American Archeology No. 6. Kampsville, Ill.: Center for American Archaeology.

PARRINGTON, MICHAEL, DANIEL G. ROBERTS, STEPHANIE A. PINTER,
AND JANET C. WIDEMAN
1989 "The First African Baptist Church Cemetery: Bioarchaeology, Demography, and Acculturation of Early Nineteenth Century Philadelphia Blacks (Volumes I and II)." Report prepared for the Redevelopment Authority of the City of Philadelphia. John Milner Associates, Philadelphia.

PARRINGTON, MICHAEL, AND HELEN SCHENCK
1979 "Salvage Archaeology and Science at Independence National Historical Park, Philadelphia." *MASCA Journal* 1 (3): 78–79.

1982 "Historical Literature Review and Archaeological Recommendations for Route 291, Chester City, Delaware County, Pennsylvania." Report prepared for Portfolio Associates, Philadelphia, and the Pennsylvania Department of Transportation.

PARRINGTON, MICHAEL, HELEN SCHENCK, AND JACQUELINE THIBAUT
1984 "The Material World of the Revolutionary War Soldier at Valley Forge." In *The Scope of Historical Archaeology*, edited by David G. Orr and Daniel G. Crozier, 125–161. Philadelphia: Temple University Press.

PARRINGTON, MICHAEL, AND JANET WIDEMAN
1986 "The Archeology of a Black Philadelphia Cemetery: Acculturation in an Urban Setting." *Expedition* 28 (1): 59–62.

PATRICK, STEVEN EDWARD
1987 "Deposited in this City: The Archaeological Evidence of Philadelphia, the Capital City, 1790 to 1800." Report on file at Independence National Historical Park, Philadelphia.

PATTERSON, MARY S.
  1962a   *Rescuing Caleb Pusey's House: A 1683 Pennsylvania Gem.* Pamphlet privately pro-
           duced for the Caleb Pusey House, Upland, Pa.

  1962b   "Saving a Seventeenth Century Pennsylvania Home." *The Germantowne Crier* [Ger-
           mantown Historical Society], September 1962.

PEARE, CATHERINE OWENS
  1957   *William Penn, a Biography.* Philadelphia: J. B. Lippincott.

PENN, WILLIAM
  1909   "Letters of William Penn." *Pennsylvania Magazine of History and Biography* 33:
           303–318.

PIERSON, GEORGE WILSON
  1959   *Tocqueville in America,* abridged by Dudley C. Lunt. Garden City, N.Y.: Doubleday.

PLATT, JOHN D. R.
  1969   "Franklin's House—Historic Structures Report, Historical Data Section." Report on
           file at Independence National Historical Park, Philadelphia.

PLATT, JOHN D. R., WILLIAM M. CAMPBELL, DAVID A. KIMBALL, MIRIAM QUINN,
AND MARTIN I. YOELSON
  1962   "Historic Structures Report." Part 2, "Independence Hall." Chap. 2, "Historical
           Data." Report on file at Independence National Historical Park, Philadelphia.

PLATT, JOHN D. R., MARTIN I. YOELSON, PAUL G. SIFTON, PEARL MILLMAN,
AND MIRIAM Q. BLIMM
  1966   "Historic Structures Report on the Pemberton House." Part 2, Chap. 2. Report on file
           at Independence National Historical Park, Philadelphia.

POWELL, B. BRUCE
  1957   "Exploratory Excavations in the Basement of the John Wagner Building." Report on
           file at Independence National Historical Park, Philadelphia.

  1958a   "Archaeological Data." In "Historic Building Report on Bishop White House." Re-
           port on file at Independence National Historical Park, Philadelphia.

  1958b   "Archaeological Data." In "Historic Building Survey on Dilworth-Todd-Moylan
           House in Independence National Historical Park." Report on file at Independence
           National Historical Park, Philadelphia.

  1958c   "Archaeological Excavations of Carpenters Court." Report on file at Independence
           National Historical Park, Philadelphia.

  1959a   "Archaeological Data." In "Historic Grounds Report, Independence Square." Report
           on file at Independence National Historical Park, Philadelphia.

  1959b   "Archaeological Investigations: East Passageway, Second Bank of the United States,
           Independence National Historical Park." Report on file at Independence National
           Historical Park, Philadelphia.

  1962a   "The Archaeology of Franklin Court." Report on file at Independence National His-
           torical Park, Philadelphia.

  1962b   "Report of the Archaeological Excavation in Old City Hall, Independence National
           Historical Park." Report on file at Independence National Historical Park, Phila-
           delphia.

POWELL, JOHN HARVEY
  1949   *Bring Out Your Dead: The Great Plague of Yellow Fever in Philadelphia in 1793.* Phila-
           delphia: University of Pennsylvania Press.

RABER, PAUL A., ED.
  1985   *A Comprehensive State Plan for the Conservation of Archaeological Resources,* vol. 2.
           Historic Preservation Planning Series, no. 1. Harrisburg, Pa.: Pennsylvania Historical
           and Museum Commission.

RALPH, ELIZABETH, AND MICHAEL PARRINGTON
  1979   "Patterns of the Past: Geophysical and Aerial Reconnaissance at Valley Forge." Report prepared for the National Park Service by the Museum Applied Science Center for Archaeology, University Museum, University of Pennsylvania.

REED, JOHN F.
  1965   *Campaign to Valley Forge*. Philadelphia: University of Pennsylvania Press.

REPS, JOHN W.
  1965   *The Making of Urban America: A History of City Planning in the United States*. Princeton, N.J.: Princeton University Press.

RICHARDS, HORACE G.
  1931   "The Subway Tree: A Record of a Pleistocene Cypress Swamp in Philadelphia." *Bartonia* 13:1–6.

  1956   *Geology of the Delaware Valley*. Philadelphia: Mineralogical Society of Pennsylvania.

  1960   "The Dating of the 'Subway Tree' of Philadelphia." *Proceedings of the Pennsylvania Academy of Science* 34:107–108.

RICHARDSON, EDGAR P.
  1982   "The Athens of America, 1800–1825." In *Philadelphia: A 300-Year History*, edited by Russell F. Weigley. New York: W. W. Norton.

RIGHTER, ELIZABETH C.
  1975   "Archaeological Excavations at the Peter Wentz Farmstead, Worcester Township, Montgomery County, Pennsylvania." Report prepared for the Commissioners of Montgomery County, Norristown, Pa.

  1976   "Archeological Investigations of a Cartway and Various Structures at the Peter Wentz Farmstead, a National Register Site, Schulz Road, Worcester Township, Montgomery County, Pennsylvania." Report prepared for the Commissioners of Montgomery County, Norristown, Pa.

  1982   "Final Report on Archaeological Excavations South of the Coach House at the Wyck House, Philadelphia, Pennsylvania." Report prepared for the Wyck Association, Philadelphia.

RIVINUS, WILLIS M.
  1965   *The Red Man in Bucks County*. New Hope, Pa. [privately published].

ROARK, CAROL SHIELS
  1974   "Historic Yellow Springs: The Restoration of an American Spa." *Pennsylvania Folklife* (Autumn): 28–38.

ROBBINS, CAROLINE
  1986   "William Penn, 1689–1702: Eclipse, Frustration, and Achievement." In *The World of William Penn*, edited by Richard S. Dunn and Mary Maples Dunn. Philadelphia: University of Pennsylvania Press.

ROBERTS, DANIEL G.
  1984   "Management and Community Aspects of the Excavation of a Sensitive Urban Archaeological Resource: An Example from Philadelphia." *American Archeology* 4 (3): 235–240.

ROBERTS, DANIEL G., AND DAVID BARRETT
  1984   "Nightsoil Disposal Practices of the Nineteenth Century and the Origin of Artifacts in Plowzone Proveniences." *Historical Archaeology* 18 (1): 108–115.

ROBERTS, DANIEL G., AND BETTY J. COSANS
  1980   "The Archeology of the Nineteenth Century in the Ninth Ward, Philadelphia, Pennsylvania." Report prepared for the Market Street East Development Corporation. John Milner Associates, West Chester, Pa.

ROBERTS, DANIEL G., BETTY J. COSANS, AND DAVID BARRETT
1982 "Archeological Resources Technical Basis Report, Environmental Impact Studies, Vine Street Improvements, Philadelphia." Report prepared for Gannett Fleming and the Pennsylvania Department of Transportation. John Milner Associates, West Chester, Pa.

ROBERTS, DANIEL G., ROBERT F. HOFFMAN, AND RICHARD MEYER
1983 "Exton Bypass (L.R. 10004) Cultural Resources Technical Basis Report, Chester County, Pennsylvania." Report prepared for McCormick, Taylor and Associates and the Pennsylvania Department of Transportation. John Milner Associates, West Chester, Pa.

ROBERTS, DANIEL G., ROBERT F. HOFFMAN, RICHARD MEYER, AND BETTY J. COSANS
1982 "A Phase I and II Cultural Resource Survey of Two Proposed Alignments for Interstate 78, Lehigh County, Pennsylvania." Report prepared for Betz, Converse, Murdoch and the Pennsylvania Department of Transportation. John Milner Associates, West Chester, Pa.

ROBERTS, GEORGE B.
1968 "Dr. Physick and His House." *The Pennsylvania Magazine of History and Biography* 92 (1): 67–86.

ROBERTS, KENNETH, AND ANNA M. ROBERTS, TRANSLATORS AND EDITORS
1947 *Moréau de St. Mery's American Journey 1793–1798.* New York, N.Y.: Doubleday and Company.

ROBICHAUD, BERYL, AND MURRAY F. BUELL
1973 *Vegetation of New Jersey.* New Brunswick, N.J.: Rutgers University Press.

ROENKE, KARL
1978 "Flat Glass: Its Use as a Dating Tool for 19th Century Archaeological Sites in the Pacific Northwest and Elsewhere." Northwest Anthropological Research Notes Memoir no. 4, published as Northwest Anthropological Research Notes, 1 (2) Part 2, Moscow, Idaho.

ROSENBERGER, LYLE L.
1977 "The Wynkoop House Excavation." *Bucks County Historical Society Journal* 2 (2): 43–55.

ROSENTHAL, LEON S.
1963 *A History of Philadelphia's University City.* Philadelphia: The West Philadelphia Corporation.

ROTHMAN, DAVID J.
1971 *The Discovery of the Asylum.* Boston: Little, Brown and Co.

RUPP, I. D.
1965 *Collection of Upwards of Thirty Thousand Names of German, Swiss, Dutch, French, and Other Immigrants in Pennsylvania.* Baltimore: Baltimore Genealogical Co.

RUSSELL, EMILY W. B.
1981 "Vegetation of Northern New Jersey before European Settlement." *The American Midland Naturalist* 105 (1): 1–12.

SCATCHARD, THOMAS, AND JEANNE SCATCHARD
1978 "An Archeological and Social Evaluation of What May Be America's First Industrial Suburb." *Society for Industrial Archeology Occasional Publication* 3:21.

SCHARF, J. THOMAS, AND THOMPSON WESTCOTT
1884 *History of Philadelphia, 1609–1884.* Philadelphia: L. H. Evarts.

SCHENCK, HELEN R.
1978 "Archaeological Prospecting at Valley Forge." *MASCA Journal* 1:16–17.

1984   "The Upper Forge at Valley Forge." Report prepared for Valley Forge National Historic Park by the Museum Applied Science Center for Archaeology, University Museum, University of Pennsylvania.

1988   "Forging Iron at Valley Forge." *Journal of Metals* 40 (8): 44–46.

SCHENCK, HELEN R., AND REED KNOX, JR.

1985   "Wrought Iron Manufacture at Valley Forge." *MASCA Journal* 3 (5): 132–141.

1986   "Valley Forge: The Making of Iron in the Eighteenth Century." *Archaeology* 39 (1): 26–33.

SCHIEK, ALLEN G.

1969   "Caleb Pusey House II: Chemical Analyses of Some Copper Coins from House Excavations." *Bulletin of the Archaeological Society of Delaware* 7:17–26.

1974   "The Caleb Pusey House: Excavation, Structure, and Contents." *Transactions of the Delaware Academy of Science* 5:295–316.

SCHIEK, MARTHA J., AND KEVIN M. BROWN

1985   "A Phase I Archaeological Survey, Bakers Bay Retirement Center, Philadelphia County, Pennsylvania." Report prepared for The Klett Organization. MAAR Associates, Newark, Del.

SCHOOLER, ALICE KENT, JEFFREY C. BOURKE, AND ELIZABETH C. RIGHTER

1983   "Trevose, The Growden Mansion: A Multi-Disciplinary Study of the Origins and Evolution of Trevose, Bensalem Township, Pennsylvania," 2 vols. Report prepared for the Supervisors of Bensalem Township, Pa. John Milner Associates, West Chester, Pa.

SCHOOLER, ALICE KENT, AND DANIEL G. ROBERTS

1979   "Historical and Archeological Study of Market Street East." Report prepared for the Market Street East Development Corporation. John Milner Associates, West Chester, Pa.

SCHRABISCH, MAX

1937   "The Aboriginal Jasper Quarries at Vera Cruz." *Pennsylvania Archaeologist* 7 (3): 52–54.

SCHUMACHER, PAUL J. F.

1955   "Archaeological Field Notes, Archaeological Project Numbers 2 and 3, Independence Square, Grass Plots 1 and 2." Report on file at Independence National Historical Park, Philadelphia.

1956a   "Archaeological Field Notes, Archaeological Project 15, Bishop White House Basement, 309 Walnut Street, Independence National Historical Park." Report on file at Independence National Historical Park, Philadelphia.

1956b   "Archaeological Field Notes, Archaeological Project Number 9—A, B, C, D, E, Independence Square." Report on file at Independence National Historical Park, Philadelphia.

1956c   "Archaeological Field Notes, Bishop White House." Notes on file at Independence National Historical Park, Philadelphia.

1956d   "Archaeological Field Notes, Project 14, New Hall–Carpenters Court." Notes on file at Independence National Historical Park, Philadelphia.

1956e   "Preliminary Exploration of Franklin Court, Archaeological Project 44, May–September 1953." Report on file at Independence National Historical Park, Philadelphia.

SHOEMAKER, ANN A.

n.d.   "The Red Man in Bucks County." Unpublished manuscript on file at the Mercer Museum, Doylestown, Pa.

SHUSTER, RONALD

1975   "Report on the Excavation Conducted behind Maurice Stephens Farmhouse on the Site of Huntington's Quarters, November 17–20, 1975," pp. 1–15. Report on file at the Pennsylvania Historical and Museum Commission, Harrisburg, Pa.

1976   "The Report on the Investigation of the 18th Century Doorway and Doorsill at the Site Known as Lafayette's Quarters, December 31, 1975–January 15, 1976," pp. 1–14. Report on file at Pennsylvania Historical and Museum Commission, Harrisburg, Pa.

SHUTLER, RICHARD, JR.

1983   "The Australian Parallel to the Peopling of the New World." In *Early Man in the New World*, edited by Richard Shutler, Jr., 43–45. Beverly Hills, Calif.: Sage Publications.

SIEBERT, WILLIAM HENRY

1972   *The Loyalists of Pennsylvania.* Boston: Gregg Press.

SIRKIN, LES

1977   "Late Pleistocene Vegetation and Environments in the Middle Atlantic Region." In *Amerinds and Their Paleoenvironments in Northeastern North America*, edited by W. S. Newman and B. Salwen. *Annals of the New York Academy of Sciences* 288: 206–217.

SKIDMORE, REX A.

1948   "Walnut Street Jail." *Pennsylvania Magazine of History* 39:172.

SMITH, GEORGE

1862   *History of Delaware County.* Philadelphia: Henry B. Ashmead.

SMITH, PHILIP CHADWICK FOSTER

1986   *Philadelphia on the River.* Philadelphia: Philadelphia Maritime Museum and University of Pennsylvania Press.

SMITH, R. A.

1852   *Philadelphia as It Is in 1852.* Philadelphia: Lindsay and Blakiston.

SMITH, ROBERT A., JR.

1956   "The Broomall Rock Shelter Sites." *Pennsylvania Archaeologist* 26 (1): 37–42.

SMITH, ROBERT V.

1967   *Soil Survey of Montgomery County, Pennsylvania.* Washington, D.C.: Soil Conservation Service, U.S. Department of Agriculture.

SMITH, HELEN

1974a   "Report on the Coins Found during the Excavation of the Kitchen and Basement Areas of the Colonial Plantation Farm House CP-B and CP-C." Report on file at Bishop's Mill Historical Institute, Ridley Creek State Park, Media, Pa.

1974b   "Report on the Marbles Found during Archaeological Excavations within the Kitchen, CP-A and Basement CP-B and C Areas." Report on file at Bishop's Mill Historical Institute, Ridley Creek State Park, Media, Pa.

1974c   "Report on the Off-Kitchen Area (CP-7), Kitchen Well (CP-9), Carriage Barn, and Springhouse." Report on file at Bishop's Mill Historical Institute, Ridley Creek State Park, Media, Pa.

SMITH, SARAH A. G.

1976   "Dr. George Logan's Barn at 'Stenton.'" *Germantown Crier* 28(2):45–47.

SODERLUND, JEAN R., RICHARD S. DUNN, MARY MAPLES DUNN, RICHARD A. RYERSON, AND SCOTT M. WILDS, EDS.

1983   *William Penn and the Founding of Pennsylvania, 1680–1684: A Documentary History.* Philadelphia: University of Pennsylvania Press.

SOUTH, STANLEY
1977   *Method and Theory in Historical Archaeology.* New York: Academic Press.

SPRINGER, RUTH
1967   *John Morton in Contemporary Records.* Harrisburg, Pa.: Pennsylvania Historical and Museum Commission.

STAGE, SARAH
1979   *Female Complaints.* New York, N.Y.: W. W. Norton and Company.

STEINMETZ, R. C.
1932   "Digging at Pennsbury." *Pennsylvania Archaeologist* 3 (2): 6.

STEWART, FRANK H.
[1924] 1974   *History of the First United States Mint.* Lawrence, Mass.: Quarterman Publications.

STEWART, R. MICHAEL
1982   "The Middle Woodland of the Abbott Farm: Summary and Hypotheses." In *Practicing Environmental Archaeology: Methods and Interpretations,* edited by Roger W. Moeller, 19–28. Washington, Conn.: American Indian Archaeological Institute.

1986a   "Lister Site (28 ME 1-A): Archaeological Data Recovery, I-195, Segment 1-A, 1-E, 10-D." Report prepared for the Federal Highway Administration and the New Jersey Department of Transportation. Louis Berger and Associates, East Orange, N.J.

1986b   "Shady Brook Site (28 ME 20 and 28 ME 99): Archaeological Data Recovery, I-295, Arena Drive Interchange." Report prepared for the Federal Highway Administration and the New Jersey Department of Transportation. Louis Berger and Associates, East Orange, N.J.

1987   "Gropp's Lake Site (28 ME 100G): Archaeological Data Recovery, I-95, Segment 1-A, 1-E, 10-D." Report prepared for the Federal Highway Administration and the New Jersey Department of Transportation. Louis Berger and Associates, East Orange, N.J.

STEWART, R. MICHAEL, C. HUMMER, AND J. CUSTER
1986   "Late Woodland Cultures of the Middle and Lower Delaware River Valley and the Upper Delmarva Peninsula." In *Late Woodland Cultures of the Middle Atlantic Region,* edited by J. F. Custer, 58–89. Newark, Del.: University of Delaware Press.

STODDART, MARY G., AND REED L. ENGLE
1983   "Stenton." *Antiques* 124 (2): 266–271.

STOKES, DERMOT
1978   *Viking Settlement to Medieval Dublin.* Dublin: Curriculum Development Unit, O'Brien Educational.

STONE, GARRY WHEELER
1984   "The Mount Joy Forge on Valley Creek." In *The Scope of Historical Archaeology,* edited by David G. Orr and Daniel G. Crozier, 87–124. Philadelphia: Temple University Press.

STOWE, WALTER HERBERT, ED.
1937   *The Life and Letters of Bishop William White.* New York: Morehouse Publishing Co.

STRASSBURGER, B., AND HINKE, J.
1934   *Pennsylvania German Pioneers.* Morristown, Pa.: Pennsylvania German Society.

STRUTHERS, THOMAS L., AND DANIEL G. ROBERTS
1982   "The Lambertville Site (28-HU-468): An Early-Middle and Late Woodland Site in the Middle Delaware Valley." Report prepared for Glace and Glace and the Lambertville Sewerage Authority. John Milner Associates, West Chester, Pa.

SULLIVAN, JAMES R.
1959   "Historic Grounds Report." Part 1, "State House Yard, Independence National Historical Park." Chap. 2, "Historical Data." Report on file at Independence National Historical Park, Philadelphia.

SULLIVAN, WILLIAM A.
  1950   "A Decade of Labor Strife." *Pennsylvania History* 17:23–28.

SUTHERLAND, JOHN F.
  1973   "Housing the Poor in the City of Homes: Philadelphia at the Turn of the Century." In *The Peoples of Philadelphia*, edited by Allen F. Davis and Mark H. Haller, 175–201. Philadelphia: Temple University Press.

SWINDELL, W.
  1899   *Annals of the Kensington Methodist Church, 1801–1893.* Philadelphia: Kensington Methodist Church.

TANTAQUIDGEON, GLADYS
  1977   *Folk Medicine of the Delaware and Related Algonkian Indians.* Anthropological Series no. 3. Harrisburg, Pa.: Pennsylvania Historical and Museum Commission.

TAYLOR, FRANK H., AND WILFRED H. SCHOFF
  1912   *The Port and City of Philadelphia.* Philadelphia: International Congress of Navigation.

TAYLOR, ROBERTA Z.
  1981   "Seed Analysis in Historic Sites Archaeology." Master's thesis, Temple University.

TEETERS, NEGLEY K.
  1957   *The Prison at Philadelphia, Cherry Hill.* New York: Columbia University Press.

THAYER, THEODORE
  1982   "Town into City, 1746–1765." In *Philadelphia: A 300-Year History*, edited by Russell F. Weigley. New York: W. W. Norton.

THIBAUT, JACQUELINE
  1975   "Deciphering Fort Mifflin." *Military Collector and Historian* 27 (3): 101–112.
  1982   "To Pave the Way to Penitence: Prisoners and Discipline at the Eastern State Penitentiary 1829–1833." *Pennsylvania Magazine of History and Biography* 106(2):187–222.

THOMAS, RONALD A.
  1978   "An Archaeological Reconnaissance of the Transco Energy Company, Delaware County, Pennsylvania Project Area." Report prepared for Arliss D. Ray, Environmental Consultant. Mid-Atlantic Archaeological Research, Wilmington, Del.

THOMAS, RONALD A., AND LAUREN C. ARCHIBALD
  1981   "A Phase I Archaeological Investigation at the Tacony Access Area, Philadelphia County, Pennsylvania." Report prepared for the Pennsylvania Fish Commission. Mid-Atlantic Archaeological Research, Newark, Del.

THOMFORDE, CHARLES
  1986   "William Penn's Estate at Pennsbury and the Plants of Its Kitchen Garden, Part 2: Description of Plants." Master's thesis, University of Delaware. Also on file at Pennsbury Manor, Morrisville, Pa.

TIDLOW, EVELYN M., FREDERICK L. WALTERS, PATRICK W. O'BANNON,
AND KENNETH JACOBS
  1987   "Historic Structures Report for Pennsbury Manor, Morrisville, Pennsylvania." Report prepared for the Pennsbury Society. John Milner Associates, West Chester, Pa.

TINKCOM, HARRY M.
  1982   "The Revolutionary City, 1765–1783." In *Philadelphia: A 300-Year History*, edited by Russell F. Weigley. New York: W. W. Norton.

TINKCOM, MARGARET B.
  1964   "Cliveden: The Building of a Philadelphia Country Seat, 1763–1767." *Pennsylvania Magazine of History and Biography* 88 (1): 3–34.
  1967   "Market Square." *Germantown Crier* 19 (3): 69–75.

1970   "Southwark, a River Community: Its Shape and Substance." *Proceedings of the American Philosophical Society* 114 (4): 327–342.

TOLLES, FREDERICK B.
1948   *Meeting House and Counting House: The Quaker Merchants of Colonial Philadelphia, 1682–1763.* Chapel Hill, N.C.: University of North Carolina Press.

TOCQUEVILLE, ALEXIS DE
[1835] 1949   *Democracy in America.* New York: Newson and Company.

TOULOUSE, JULIAN H.
1970   "High On the Hawg: Or How the Western Miner Lived as Told by Bottles He Left Behind." *Historical Archaeology* 4:59–69.

TOWNSEND, ALEX H.
1976   "Historical and Archeological Determination, 7 Acre Parcel of Land of U.S. Forest Service, King of Prussia, Radnor Township, Delaware County, Pennsylvania." Report prepared for the U.S. Forest Service. National Heritage Corporation, West Chester, Pa.

1979   "The Barns-Brinton House, Chadds Ford, Pennsylvania: A Report of Archeological Excavations Undertaken in 1978." Report prepared for the Chadds Ford Historical Society. John Milner Associates, West Chester, Pa.

1983   "A Phase I Archaeological Survey of Linwood Municipal Park, Lower Chichester Township, Delaware County, Pennsylvania." Report prepared for Catania Engineering Associates, Chester, Pa.

VAN DOREN, CARL
1945   *Benjamin Franklin.* New York: Garden City Press.

1956   *Benjamin Franklin.* New York: Viking Press.

VAUX, TRINA, ED.
1985   *Historic Rittenhouse, a Philadelphia Neighborhood.* Philadelphia: University of Pennsylvania Press.

WAINWRIGHT, NICHOLAS B.
1982   "The Age of Nicholas Biddle, 1825–1841." In *Philadelphia: A 300-Year History,* edited by Russell F. Weigley. New York: W. W. Norton.

WALDBAUER, RICHARD C.
1976   "310 Cypress Street: An Interim Report on History and Privy Pit Artifacts." Report on file at the University Museum, University of Pennsylvania.

WALLACE, DAVID
1958   "Historic Building Report on Bishop White House." Part 1, Chap. 2, "Historical Data." Report on file at Independence National Historical Park, Philadelphia.

WALLACE, PAUL A. W.
1962   "Historic Hope Lodge." *Pennsylvania Magazine of History and Biography* 76 (2): 115–142.

WARD, JEANNE A., AND JOHN P. MCCARTHY
1990   "An Archeological Evaluation of a Portion of the Site of the Former Philadelphia General Hospital, Philadelphia, Pennsylvania." Report prepared for the Department of Facilities Planning, University of Pennsylvania. John Milner Associates, Philadelphia.

WARFEL, STEVEN G.
1985   "Archaeological Testing and Monitoring Report: Graeme Park, 36 MG 167." Report on file at the Pennsylvania Historial and Museum Commission, Harrisburg, Pa.

WARFEL, STEVEN, AND BARRY C. KENT
1975   Reports on "MacIntosh's Brigade Project Area"; "Huntington's Brigade Project Area"; "Varnum's Brigade Project Area"; "Waterman Grave Work Area—Varnum's

Brigade Area"; "Excavations Along Baptist Road." Reports on file at the Pennsylvania Historical and Museum Commission, Harrisburg, Pa.

WARNER, SAM BASS, JR.
1963   "Innovation and the Industrialization of Philadelphia, 1800–1850." In *The Historian and the City*, edited by Oscar Handlin and John Burchard. Cambridge: MIT Press and Harvard University Press.

1987   *The Private City: Philadelphia in Three Periods of Its Growth*, 2d ed. Philadelphia: University of Pennsylvania Press.

WATERMAN, THOMAS TILESTON
1950   *The Dwellings of Colonial America*. Chapel Hill, N.C.: University of North Carolina Press.

WATSON, JOHN FANNING
1909   *Annals of Philadelphia and Pennsylvania in the Olden Time*. 2 Vols. Philadelphia: Leary, Stuart and Co.

WEAVER, WILLIAM W., AND NANCY D. KOLB
1983a   "Okie Speaks for Pennsbury: Part I." *Pennsylvania Heritage* 8 (4): 22–26.

1983b   "Okie Speaks for Pennsbury: Part II." *Pennsylvania Heritage* 9 (1): 22–26.

WEBER, CARMEN A.
1988a   "Interim Report: An Exploration of Philadelphia's Early Waterfront through the Hertz Lot Excavation." Report on file at the Philadelphia Historical Commission.

1988b   "A Phase I Archaeological Investigation of the Site of the Franklin Institute Futures Center." Report prepared for the Franklin Institute, Philadelphia.

WEBSTER, RICHARD J.
1966   "Historical and Archaeological Report of Lafayette Kitchen Excavation, Valley Forge, Pa., August 1965," pp. 1–57. Report on file at the University Museum, University of Pennsylvania.

1976   *Philadelphia Preserved: Catalog of the Historic American Buildings Survey*. Philadelphia: Temple University Press.

WEIGLEY, RUSSELL F.
1982   "The Border City in Civil War, 1854–1865." In *Philadelphia: A 300-Year History*, edited by Russell F. Weigley. New York: W. W. Norton.

WESLAGER, C. A.
1956   "Delaware Indian Villages at Philadelphia." *Pennsylvania Archaeologist* 26 (3–4): 178–180.

1961   *Dutch Explorers, Traders and Settlers in the Delaware Valley, 1609–1664*. Philadelphia: University of Pennsylvania Press.

1985   *Lenape Ethnology from William Penn's Relation of 1683*. Bulletin no. 18. Wilmington: Archaeological Society of Delaware.

WILDES, HARRY E.
1938   *Valley Forge*. New York: Macmillan.

WILKIN, SIMON, ED.
1889   *The Works of Sir Thomas Browne*. Vol. 3. London: George Bell and Sons.

WILSON, BILL, AND BETTY WILSON
1971   "19th Century Medicine in Glass." Amador City, Calif.: 19th Century Hobby and Publishing Co.

WILSON, BUDD
1982   "Phase I Cultural Resource Survey, Newtown Bypass, L.R. 1141, Bucks County, Pennsylvania." Report prepared for Valley Forge Laboratories, Valley Forge, Pa., and the Pennsylvania Department of Transportation.

WILSON, CHARLES I.
    1967   "The Well in the Entrance Hall of Independence Hall, Independence National His-
            torical Park." Report on file at Independence National Historical Park, Philadelphia.

WILSON, ROBERT H.
    1976   *Thaddeus Kosciuszko and His House in Philadelphia.* Philadelphia: Copernicus Soci-
            ety of America.

WISTER, C. J., JR.
    1866   *The Labour of a Long Life: A Memoir of Charles J. Wister.* Germantown, Pa.: Collins
            Printing House.

WITTHOFT, JOHN
    1951a   "The Pemberton Family Cemetery." *Pennsylvania Archaeologist* 21 (1–2): 21–31.
    1951b   "The Chewed Bullet." *Pennsylvania Archaeologist* 21:3–4, 60–61.
    1952   "A Paleo-Indian Site in Eastern Pennsylvania: An Early Hunting Culture." *Proceed-
            ings of the American Philosophical Society* 96 (4): 464–495.
    1964   "Notes on Wood Floors at the Keith House." Manuscript on file at the Pennsylvania
            Historical and Museum Commission, Harrisburg, Pa.

WOKECK, MARIANNE S.
    1986   "Promoters and Passengers: The German Immigrant Trade 1683–1775." In *The
            World of William Penn,* edited by Richard S. Dunn and Mary Maples Dunn. Phila-
            delphia: University of Pennsylvania Press.

WOLF, EDWIN, II
    1975   *Philadelphia, Portrait of an American City.* Harrisburg, Pa.: Stackpole Books.

WOLF, EDWIN, II, AND MAXWELL WHITEMAN
    1975   *The History of the Jews of Philadelphia from Colonial Times to the Age of Jackson.*
            Philadelphia: Jewish Publication Society of America.

WOLF, MARTHA LEIGH, AND DIANE SEKURA SNYDER
    1982   *A History of West Whiteland.* Exton, Pa.: The West Whiteland Historical Com-
            mission.

WOOD, JULIANA
    1870   *Family Sketches.* Philadelphia: [privately published].

YOELSON, MARTIN I.
    1967   "Preliminary Development Plan for the Graff House." Chap. 2, "Historical Data."
            Report on file at Independence National Historical Park, Philadelphia.
    1975   *Thomas Jefferson in 18th Century Philadelphia.* Interpretative Bulletin no. 74. Phila-
            delphia: Independence National Historical Park.

YOUNG, JAMES HARVEY
    1974   *The Toadstool Millionaires: A Social History of Patent Medicines in America before
            Federal Regulation.* Princeton, N.J.: Princeton University Press.

ZIMMT, WERNER S.
    1981   "Notes on the Development of Chemical Industry in the Nineteenth Century through
            University-Industry Interaction as Illustrated by Two Products Made by John Harri-
            son of Philadelphia." Master's thesis, University of Pennsylvania.

Index

Frankford Arsenal, 54, 65, 68, 217, 266–73, 453

Franklin, Benjamin: and Declaration of Independence, 129, 129 n; and fire prevention, 45, 88; at the Grange, 415–16; house, estate, and family of, 86–91, 142–43, 153, 172, 184 (see also Franklin Court); inventions and scientific experiments of, 88–90, 104, 133, 281; and John Bartram, 276; and postal service, 48; rental properties of, 86, 90, 95 n, 144–45, 159, 182–83, 449; role of, in founding Philadelphia institutions, 43, 45, 46, 48; on Sir William Howe, 50, 257, 352; and Sir William Keith and Graeme Park, 383, 386; and sports, 88–89, 456, 457 n; views of, on artisans, 40

Franklin, Deborah Read, 86–88, 93, 94–95, 453

Franklin, Sarah. See Bache, Sarah Franklin

Franklin, William, 153, 386

Franklin Court, 74, 77, 86–96, 133, 142–45, 159, 182, 449, 450, 468

Franklin Farmers' Market, 61, 297

Franklin Field, 458; potter's field at, 201, 293, 294

Franklin Institute, 296, 296 n, 313

Franklin Square, 50, 217, 263–65, 320

Franklin stove, 90, 281

Franklintown, 290, 294–95

Fraser, John, 66, 268

Free African Society, 53

Free Library of Philadelphia, 71

Free Society of Traders, 43, 164, 234, 235

Friends, Society of. See Quakers

Front and Dock Streets, 234–37, 448–50, 453. See also Dock Creek, filling and paving of

Fry, Joel, 281 n, 468

Furness, Frank, 66, 77, 100, 460 n

G

Galloway, Grace Growden, 372, 373

Galloway, Joseph, 98, 372, 373

Gambling, 43, 180, 454–56

Gambrel Roof House, 364, 365, 368 n

Gardens: Benjamin Franklin's, 90; formal, 267, 329, 338, 339, 341, 342, 344, 347, 349, 360, 361–62, 389, 391, 392, 398, 400, 416, 443, 449, 449 n; kitchen, 361, 396, 397, 449. See also Bartram's Garden; Horticulture; Independence Square, landscaping of

Gas lighting, 56, 59, 312–14, 453

Gasworks: Philadelphia's first, 59, 296 n, 312–13; at Point Breeze, 312, 314–17, 453

Gatter, Carl W., 84, 85, 130, 263

Geology of Philadelphia region, 4–5

Georgian architecture. See Architecture, Georgian

German churches, 320, 323, 400

German farmers, 377, 378, 403–4. See also Peter Wentz Farmstead

German immigrants, 39, 60, 301, 320, 322, 323–24, 337, 358; in Montgomery County, 377, 393, 399, 403–4

German Quakers, 36, 322, 323

Germantown: country estates in, 324, 332, 347 (see also Wyck); founding and development of, 39, 61, 69, 322–24, 328, 400; Market Square in, 323, 323 n, 343, 345, 349, 351, 466; summer homes in, 53, 324, 326 n, 337, 338, 343, 345

Germantown, Battle of, 255, 325, 326, 330, 339, 347, 349, 350, 351–53, 378, 386, 394, 434

Gesner, J. Washington, 413

Giannini, Robert, 468

Gibbs, James, 102

Girard, Stephen, 53, 102 n

Glacial activity, 6, 7, 10, 11

Glassware, domestic manufacture of, xxiii, 241, 327, 327 n, 329. See also Dyottville Glass Works

Gloria Dei Church (Old Swedes'), 37, 40, 217, 223

Gloucester City, New Jersey, 32, 464

Godley, Jesse, 237

Gorgas, John, 282

Gorgas, Joseph, 282

Gorgas Mill Complex, 281–83, 454, 467

Government, city, 36–37, 44–45, 51–52, 64, 66. See also Commissions, elected city

Government of colonial Pennsylvania. See Pennsylvania Assembly

Grace Episcopal Church, 297–98

Graeme, Ann, 383, 387

Graeme, Elizabeth. See Ferguson, Elizabeth Graeme

Graeme, Thomas, 383, 385–86, 388, 389

Graeme Park, 383–89, 454

Graff, Frederick, 55, 128, 467 n

Graff, Jacob, Jr., 128, 129

Graff House, 74, 127–30, 193, 378

Grange, 415–18, 448, 450

Gratz, Hyman, 129

Gratz, Simon, 129

Grave robbing, 199, 320

Gréber, Jacques, 71

Greek Revival. See Architecture, Greek Revival

Green Tree Tavern, 327, 327 n

Gristmills, 282, 283, 358, 378, 390, 391–92, 394, 396, 404, 406, 420, 428, 435, 454, 466

Growden, Joseph, 371–73

Growden, Lawrence, 372–74

Growden, Sarah Biles, 374

Grumblethorpe, 337–42, 413, 449

Guarantee Trust Bank, 77, 100

Guernsey, H. N., 298

Guier, Adam, 304, 305

Guier, Adam, Jr., 305

H

Hagner, Peter V., 267

Haines, Caspar Wistar, 327–28, 330

Haines, Jane, 328

Haines, John Smith, 328, 329

Haines, Margaret Wistar, 326, 327

Haines, Reuben, 326, 327

Haines, Reuben, Jr., 328, 329, 339 n, 454

Haines, Robert B., III, 325

Halfline, John, 311, 312, 453

Hall, Joseph, IV, 329, 398, 400, 401, 447

Hamilton, Andrew, 101–2, 114, 274, 293, 384

Hamilton, William, 293

Harper, Thomas, 154

Harper Houses, 154–55, 157, 158, 450

Harrison, James, 79, 360–61

Harrison, John, 469

Harrison, Joseph, Jr., 61

Harrison, Richard, Jr., 379, 380

Harriton, 378, 379–82, 397

Haverford Township, founding and development of, 39, 376–77, 416

Haviland, John, 54, 107, 110, 113, 154, 175, 296 n

Hazard, Erskine, 57

Hazard's Register, 109

Health care. See Medical care and caregivers; Patent medicines

Hertz lot. See West's shipyard site

Hicks, Elias, 365

Hicksite-Orthodox Separation, 365

Highlands, 398–401, 449

High Ward, 222, 239–41, 450

Hill, Henry, 152, 184–85, 450

Hill-Physick-Keith House, 184–90, 450

Hinsdale, Guy, 318, 318 n, 320

Historic Contact period, Lenape of, 17–27

Historic Sites Act of 1935, 75, 77

Hitner, Daniel, 399

Hoffman, Benjamin R., 418

Hoffman, Nicholas, 394

Hog Island, 465

Holme, Thomas, 35, 36, 138, 191, 216, 263, 295

Homeopathic Medical College of Pennsylvania, 298

Hood, Graham, 246, 249–50, 250 n, 251

Hoof, Joseph, 410, 411

Hope, Henry, 389, 391

Hope Lodge, 389–92, 449, 454

Horse racing, 43, 185, 334, 456

Horticulture, 14, 328, 329, 334, 339. See also Bartram's Garden; Gardens

Hospitals. See Medical institutions; Pennsylvania Hospital

Hotels, 62, 63, 71, 164, 167, 294, 297, 308, 364
Houdon, Jean Antoine, 205, 206
Hough, Jessie, 366, 367
Hough House, 367
Howe, Richard, 255
Howe, William, 48, 50, 165, 255, 256–57, 334, 349, 351, 352, 386, 431, 437
Hudson, Henry, 32
Huey, Paul R., 163n, 220, 246, 249, 251
Humphreys, Joshua, shipyard of, 223, 233
Hunt, William, 318, 318n, 320
Hunter, Charles E., 239, 241
Hunter, George, 305

I

Illegitimate births, 161, 455
Import-export trade, 40, 51, 198, 216, 230, 237, 241, 246, 276, 283, 453, 468
Indentured servants, 40, 424
Independence Hall (Pennsylvania State House), 41, 50, 75, 101–13, 129, 191, 328, 433, 434; and Peale Museum, 56, 107, 313. See also Independence Square
Independence National Historical Park: establishment of, 74–78, 343; impact of, 78, 121, 153, 234
Independence Square (State House Yard), 74, 75; archaeological studies and evidence in, 77, 113–18, 145–47, 448, 449, 450, 455; landscaping of, 105–6, 109, 113, 115, 449n; naming of, 110; Philadelphia's purchase of, 109; during Revolutionary War, 50, 105, 115; wall around, 104, 106, 115, 455
Indian Queen Tavern, 163
Industry: archaeological evidence of, 217, 249–51, 283, 367, 391–92, 396, 453–54; in Bucks County, 356, 358, 366; changes in, in twentieth century, 68, 71; in Chester and Delaware counties, 404 (see also Mills); in early Philadelphia, 39, 43, 235, 246–48, 275, 281, 299, 300; in Germantown, 322, 324, 327–28; in Montgomery County, 378, 383–85, 388, 390; in nineteenth century, 56, 57, 58, 59–60, 274–75, 281, 295, 378, 404n; potential archaeological sites of, 283, 466–69. See also Breweries, brewers; Ceramics, local manufacture of; Dyottville Glass Works; Forges; Gasworks; Lime kilns; Mills; Munitions industry; Ropewalks; Shipyards and shipbuilding; Tanneries
Infanticide, 161, 455
Infectious hepatitis, 164n
Inflation, American Revolution and, 49, 50, 120, 153
Insurance companies, 45, 88, 165, 172, 189
Interstate-95, 217–26, 239, 299, 358, 404n, 453

Irish immigrants, 39, 60, 63, 64, 181, 301, 303, 324, 454, 455
Irwin Building, 77
Italianate architecture. See Architecture, Italianate
Italian immigrants, 66, 68, 69, 324
Italian Market, 154n

J

Jails. See Prisons
Jansen, Dirck, 326
Jayne, David, 61, 279, 451, 452
Jayne Building, 61, 77, 452
Jefferson, Thomas, 108, 127, 128–29, 130, 131, 132, 132n, 133, 191, 205, 334, 378, 399, 449
Jews, 42, 50, 66
John Bartram & Son, 106, 278
John Milner Associates, 84, 199, 221, 234, 236, 266, 284, 290, 295, 297, 298, 303, 304, 308, 372, 396, 404n
John Quincy Adams Public School, 309–11, 455
Johnson, Andreas, 410
Johnson, George Clarence, 340
Johnston, William L., 452
Jones, Absalom, 53
Junto Club, 43

K

Kearsley, John, 102
Keith, Ann Newberry Driggs, 383, 385, 387
Keith, Elsie Wister, 187
Keith, William, 383–85, 388, 389
Kelly, Joseph, 367
Kennedy, Samuel, 404
Kensington, 60, 275
Kensington Methodist Church, 284, 287–89
Kenyon, Jeffrey L., 263, 265, 281–82, 283, 336, 337, 404n
King, Thomas, 360–61
Knight, William, 198
Knor, Jacob, 348
Kosciuszko, Thaddeus, 127, 131–33, 135
Kosciuszko House, 75, 78, 127–28, 131–35, 450
Kyn, Jören, 32

L

Ladley, Thomas, 328
Lafayette, Marquis de, 109, 325, 327–29, 416, 434, 435, 439, 454
Laidley, T. T. S., 267
Lamasure, Edwin, 193
Landfill, 217, 222, 226, 227, 229, 230–32, 453, 463–64. See also Dock Creek, filling and paving of
La Rochefoucauld-Liancourt, Francois, 172

Latrobe, Benjamin, 54, 55, 85n, 108, 110, 127, 456, 467n
Laurel Hill Cemetery, 201–2, 448
Lawrence, Joshua, 301
Lawrence, Thomas, 102
Laws of early Pennsylvania, 36, 408, 454, 455
Lawson's boarding house, 131
Lead poisoning, 170
League Island, 224, 463
LeBrun, Napoleon, 62
Lee, Charles, 82, 431
Lee, Thomas, 85
Lehigh Canal, 358
Lehigh Coal and Navigation Company, 57
Leidy, Joseph, 318, 320–21
Lenape, 3, 16, 17–27, 32, 33, 287, 289, 332, 357, 357n, 358, 360, 362, 363, 368, 406–9 passim, 456; documented settlements of, 27–28, 360, 363; place names used by, 28–29; and trade with Europeans, 237, 332, 405, 407, 453
L'Enfant, Pierre Charles, 257, 262
Lennig Building, 167
Letitia House, 80–81, 206
Levittown, 358, 364
Lewis, Edwin O., 74, 75
Lewis, Evan, 424
Lewis, Henry, 415, 416, 418, 419
Lewis, Henry, Jr., 416
Lewis, Henry, III, 416
Lewis, Lynne G., 348–50
Lewis, Margaret, 416
Lewis, Mary Butler. See Butler, Mary
Lewis, Ralph, 424
Liberty Bell, 105, 110, 111
Liberty lands. See Northern Liberties
Library Company of Philadelphia, 43, 77, 99, 277, 334
Liggett, Barbara, 85, 95n, 144, 155, 158, 164n, 235, 258, 262, 281, 334–37, 391–92
Lime kilns, 235, 378, 390, 427n
Lingelbach, William E., 74
Linnaeus, Carolus, 276, 334
Lippincott, Henry, 367
Lit Brothers, 67, 69
Logan, George, 334, 335, 337
Logan, Gustavus, 334
Logan, James, 41, 80, 82, 276, 332, 334, 335, 337, 362, 383, 385, 448
Logan, William, 334, 337
Logan Square, 66–67, 71, 290, 295–96
London Coffee House, 43, 222
Lower Merion Township. See Merion Township
Lower Rawle Farm, 427–28
Loxley, Benjamin, 98, 248
"Lunatic asylum," 294